Our Daily Bread

Exposition of the Readings

of Catholic Mass

James H. Kurt

AuthorHouse™
1663 Liberty Drive
Bloomington, IN 47403
www.authorhouse.com
Phone: 1 (800) 839-8640

Published by AuthorHouse 03/23/2018

ISBN: 978-1-4208-0839-1 (sc)
ISBN: 978-1-4208-0840-7 (e)

Print information available on the last page.

This book is printed on acid-free paper.

Nihil Obstat:
Rev. Anthony Figueiredo
Censor Librorum

Imprimatur:
+ Most Reverend John J. Myers, J.C.D., D.D.
Archbishop of Newark, New Jersey
July 15, 2004

The Nihil Obstat and Imprimatur are official declarations that a book or
pamphlet is free of doctrinal error. No implication is contained therein that
those who have granted the Nihil Obstat and Imprimatur agree with the
contents, opinions, or statements expressed.

Scripture (and commentary) quotes taken from
New St. Joseph Sunday Missal, Catholic Book Publishing, N.J., 1999
and
Vatican II Weekday Missal, Daughters of St. Paul, Boston, Mass., 1975.

All quotes are from the day's readings, unless otherwise noted.
Some liberty has been taken in capitalization,
particularly re the male pronoun for God the Father, Son, and Holy Spirit.

for Daily Communicants
and All Those Who Hunger for the Word of God

"I will inspire you with wisdom
which your adversaries will be unable to resist."

Lk. 21:15

Table of Contents

Author's Notes

Before Beginning:

While reading the Scriptures through three times (before the dawn of each day), I shall mine their message by seeking parallel meaning in the separate passages and pointing up a line from one which epitomizes their complementary significance.

It is from the Scriptures themselves I shall draw water.

Upon Completion:

In the process of composing this work I have discovered a certain harmony inherent in the juxtaposition of any two (or three...) Scripture passages. This is indicative of the fact that sacred Scripture is whole, is, in essence, one Word, and so all its parts are integrally related.

Finally, this exposition is by no means an exhaustive reflection of even my own understanding of the readings of Catholic Mass, for each time I read them something new, or some different emphasis, do I find. Holy Scripture is indeed an inexhaustible ocean of wisdom.

Overall:

I have read the Bible cover to cover five times and written daily about the Scriptures for Mass for the past eight years running – five in a spiritual diary, two on this work, one on chanted verses for each Mass... and currently a sentence a day. (You may go to my website – address on back of book – to review these and other writings.)

May the Light of God's Word shine forth here for you.

Introduction

I find that the general bent of naturalist inquiry into Scripture, so predominant in our modern times, ironically makes it approaching impossible for the well-studied exegetes to see beyond the nose of their collective face. I have found their understanding as deep as a puddle (which serves but to muddy the ground for a time), where Scripture is, as Augustine tells us, a vast ocean which can never be drained. All this skeptical questioning of Holy Scripture is as the cat chasing his tail: it is useless activity; and if the cat should somehow succeed, he would only injure himself.

We should not ask ourselves what the writer is saying but what God is saying to us in these verses – why are they here in this way? Or do we not believe it is an inspired Word written to His desire? I find no point in questioning matters in Scripture unless the literal is clearly absurd. Obviously Jesus is not an actual door; but there is no reason to doubt the hundreds of years men are said to have lived (for instance) as if God, who created us to be immortal in the beginning – and with whom we will live eternally in the end – cannot allow man to continue alive as long as He pleases and decide to curtail his life span at a later time. Nor is He unable to stop the sun in the sky, which He Himself created, or perform any other miracle as spoken in His Word. This, and so much else which is questioned, is clearly within God's power and bears investigation only by those who lack faith. And these will never find answer anyway. (The Word will never change; come as a child to it.)

Even yesterday, at the end of the Pentecost novena, the commentator in my missal writes of John's assurance as to the veracity of his gospel (21:24), "The pronoun 'we' points to others who helped develop this profoundly theological gospel," despite the denial of these "others" by the Douay-Rheims version, proven simply by John's same use of the pronoun "we" in the first chapter (v.14,16) to refer to himself and the Christian community. And the idea that the gospel is somehow "developed" rather than inspired *witness*, as John himself clearly states, cuts to the heart of the blindness of our scholars.

And Christ's words to the Pharisees become relevant again, albeit ironically: "You search the Scriptures, because in them you think that you have life everlasting. And it is they that bear witness to me, yet you are not willing to come to me that you may have life" (Jn.5:39-40). Our scholars' blindness to the Lord's presence in Scripture and before their eyes is the same, though today one wonders if there is any faith that life everlasting is anywhere. And how appropriate the Lord's chastisement: "How can you believe who receive glory from one another, and do not seek the glory that is from the only God?" (Jn.5:44). And as He says, "But I know you have not the love of God in you" (Jn.5:42). So how can they be expected to see...?

Jesus stands before us in His Word. It is sufficient guide for us to find Him, if we read it in His Spirit. The Lord guides through His Church, despite its imperfections, even the selection of texts we find at Mass; for His desire is that we know Him well. Let us see what we have before us: this is true science.

So I set forth in the Spirit on this day of Pentecost by His power and grace to shed light on our daily bread.

> Amen, Lord Jesus, make yourself known.
> In the Father make your home here in these rooms.
> I love you, my Lord and my God.

I. ADVENT

A. First Part of Advent

First Week

Sunday (A)
(Is.2:1-5; Ps.122:1-9; Rm.13:11-14; Mt.24:37-44)

"Come, let us climb the Lord's mountain,
to the house of the God of Jacob,
that He may instruct us in His ways,
and we may walk in His paths."

"Beat [your] swords into plowshares." "Throw off the works of darkness and put on the armor of light." "It is the hour now for you to awake from sleep," and to "stay awake! For you do not know on which day your Lord will come." And even now He calls you to "go up to the house of the Lord" and "pray for the peace of Jerusalem."

Advent has come, and so we are reminded of the Lord's coming and our need to be prepared. He will not come in vain, and will not accept any vanity into His kingdom. His is a kingdom of light into which no darkness enters. His is a place of peace where "rivalry and jealousy" and all "the desires of the flesh" find no provision.

If in the days of Noah they were blind to the time of their visitation, and so "the flood came and carried them away," how can it be the same with us, who have the first coming of Christ in the manger and on the cross to stir us to wakefulness? If we live now as in the days of Sodom, how much greater will be our punishment? If we allow our house to be "broken into" though we have His voice calling to our hearts, what could make us think that He will take us with Him when He comes again?

It is indeed time to wake from the sleep of sin and "stream toward... the Lord's mountain." There we shall rejoice in His grace as His "relatives and friends"; there we shall find the light of His teaching. "For from Zion shall go forth instruction, and the Word of the Lord from Jerusalem," and it shall fill the earth with holiness.

The Lord has been born in our midst. The Word has been made flesh and walked among us. Now we are called to become like Him, to walk in His ways of peace. And so when He returns at the end of time, we will be prepared to "set foot within [the] gates" of His kingdom.

Sunday (B)

(Is.63:16b-17,19b,64:2-7; Ps.80:2-4,15-16,18-19; 1Cor.1:3-9; Mk.13:33-37)

> "Would that you might meet us doing right,
> that we were mindful of you in our ways!"

"O Lord of hosts, look down from heaven, and see." "Rouse your power, and come to save us." Do not "let us wander, O Lord, from your ways, and harden [not] our hearts so that we fear you not." We are your fruitful vine, but "we have all withered like leaves... for you have hidden your face from us and delivered us up to our guilt. Yet, O Lord, you are our Father; we are the clay and you are the potter." "May your help be with the Man of your right hand." May we be formed in His image and so be pleasing to you. May we be ready for His return, and our final meeting with you, our Lord and God.

Brothers and sisters, we must be as the Corinthians, among whom "the testimony of Christ was confirmed," who "are not lacking in any spiritual gift as [they] wait for the revelation of our Lord Jesus Christ." He travels now abroad in the kingdom of His Father, but He will return. And He has indeed left us "each with his work"; all are gifted by God and called to bear fruit in the time that is ours now... "May He not come suddenly and find [us] sleeping." When He "rend[s] the heavens and come[s] down, with the mountains quaking before [Him]," may we not be found quaking as well, having slipped into the slumber of sin, having been covered with this world's darkness. Rather, let Him meet us doing right at whatever hour He may come. Let us constantly serve our God and "He will keep [us] firm to the end, irreproachable on the day of our Lord Jesus Christ."

"What I say to you, I say to all: 'Watch!'" In many ways does He indeed say it: "Be watchful! Be alert!" Keep your eyes open! Stay awake! Be ready! But ever He tells us to remember that we are "called to fellowship with [the] Son, Jesus Christ our Lord." And as "God is faithful" so must we too be faithful to our call, giving witness always to the glory of our Lord.

Now is the time to turn from our sin and be formed in His image. Let the prophet not say over us: "There is none who calls upon [His] name, who rouses himself to cling to [Him]." Let us prepare ourselves for His coming by walking rightly in His ways.

Sunday (C)

(Jer.33:14-16; Ps.25:4-5,8-10,14; 1Thes.3:12-4:2; Lk.21:25-28,34-36)

"You are God my savior,
and for you I wait all the day."

So does David sing of the "just shoot" that will be raised up after him; so does he anticipate the coming of Jesus into our midst. But, though the Messiah has been born, though He has come among us now, yet the Lord will not "fulfill the promise [He] made to the house of Israel and Judah" until Jesus returns on the last day. And so, we too await our Savior.

And how should we wait? Brothers and sisters, you know "how you should conduct yourselves to please God," to be found "blameless in holiness before our God and Father at the coming of our Lord Jesus with all His holy ones." You have been guided in His truth and instructed by the one who "teaches the humble His way." "The friendship of the Lord is with those who fear Him, and His covenant, for their instruction." And you fear Him, and so receive His instruction. Continue to do so. Continue to "increase and abound in love for one another." Let not the sum of your good works diminish in the least, but "strengthen your hearts," and what you have been doing for Him, "do so even more." Until the Day He comes your justice must increase.

And "what is coming upon the world" you know as well. The end of the world is upon us and has been since Christ's crucifixion. All is passing away and shall soon be no more. The nations will look, but they will not see the things they trusted in so vainly. Only "the Son of Man coming in a cloud with power and great glory" will be known; He will be all that is seen. And will you recognize Him? And will He recognize you?

Brothers and sisters, with the Lord's own words I will leave you: "Be vigilant at all times and pray that you have the strength to escape the tribulations that are imminent and to stand before the Son of Man." Wait expectantly.

Monday

(Is.2:1-5 or Is.4:2-6; Ps.122:1-9; Mt.8:5-11
I shall treat of both first readings)

"Pray for the peace of Jerusalem!"

For it shall come. "The mountain of the Lord's house shall be established as the highest mountain.... All nations shall stream toward it," and there the Lord will give judgment. And His judgment will cause the banishment of war, for all shall be one in Him, and to all He shall grant "shelter and protection," by night and by day.

The coming peace and unity all find on the holy mountain of Jerusalem prophesied by Isaiah is signaled in our gospel passage today as the Gentile centurion approaches Jesus with a request made in great faith. His surpassing faith prompts the Lord to reveal the truth of the coming kingdom: "Many will come from the east and the west and will find a place at the banquet in the kingdom of God with Abraham, Isaac, and Jacob." For it is faith that brings us to Him and to His blessings.

Certainly the serving boy for whom the centurion intercedes receives healing from the Lord; and certainly all those who "go up to the house of the Lord" in faith shall themselves be gratefully received. I pray we all remain in Zion, remain in "her place of assembly," and so find refuge from "storm and rain" and from the "heat of day." The New Jerusalem we know is the Catholic Church, is the faith handed down by Jesus through His apostles and blessed by the guidance of the Holy Spirit. We know that within these walls we shall always find peace and protection, and we pray for all to stream toward the truth and the glory found in this House. There all shall find cleansing from their sins; "with a blast of searing judgment," the Lord has created this Virgin Bride. So, "let us walk in the light of the Lord!"

As Jesus remarks to His followers, "I have never found this much faith in Israel," He is calling them to an increase in their faith. He calls us, too, brothers and sisters, to act more readily upon His commands. Let us not fall short in our service to Him, and the peace of Jerusalem shall just as readily be ours.

A. I. 1. Tues.

Tuesday
(Is.11:1-10; Ps.72:1,7-8,12-13,17; Lk.10:21-24)

"The earth shall be filled with knowledge of the Lord,
as water covers the sea."

And so, "There shall be no harm or ruin on all my holy mountain," says the Lord.

The vision is sure: "The wolf shall be the guest of the lamb... the lion shall eat hay like the ox... the child shall lay his hand on the adder's lair," for all shall live as one in the Spirit of the Lord. "Justice shall flower in His days, and profound peace" – such is the vision to which all hearts aspire.

Jesus is the fullness of that peace. And so He says to His disciples, "Blest are the eyes that see what you see," for what "prophets and kings wished to see," what Isaiah prophesies for us today, is present there before them.

5

Advent

And He is present before us. But we can only see and hear Him if we are as "merest children," else His presence will be hidden from our eyes. He wishes to reveal Himself, desires to lead us to the Father whom He alone knows, to whom He alone can lead us – but to find such fullness of vision, to gaze upon the face of God, to be filled with His wisdom and knowledge as is His Son, we must first fear Him, as He does, and seek to abide by the words and the commands that come to us by "the breath of His lips." All must be slain that is wicked in us, and His justice and faithfulness shall be ours.

"May His name be blessed forever; as long as the sun His name shall remain," for He Himself is light, and indeed His dwelling is glorious. With judgment and justice He is endowed, and in the light of His wisdom and grace we stand eternally blessed. But are our eyes open to Him?

Now should we pray for the Lord's light to fill us, for His knowledge to cover us, that our eyes may be open to see Him, that we shall not miss Him as He comes.

O Lord, prepare our hearts to see you,
and the blessing of your presence, your peace,
among us.

A. I. 1. Wed.

Wednesday
(Is.25:6-10; Ps.23:1-6; Mt.15:29-37)

"The hand of the Lord will rest on this mountain."

And He will heal us. And He will lead us. And He will feed us.

Jesus went up onto a mountainside along the Sea of Galilee and sat down to teach and to heal. The sick were laid at His feet. Isaiah says, "On this mountain the Lord of hosts will provide for all peoples." This mountain is the Lord. It is Jesus who reaches out His hand to heal those lying at His feet. It is Jesus who raises the bread for blessing and gives all to eat. And it is He who "will destroy death forever." "This is the Lord for whom we looked."

And it is through His Church Jesus works; through the blessing of the priest who raises the bread and the cup, Jesus gives us His Body and Blood – this is our "feast of rich food and choice wines" envisioned by Isaiah. It is He who forgives our sins, He who removes "the reproach of His people," wiping away "the tears from all faces" in the confessional. He anoints us with the oil of the Spirit in Baptism; He joins us as one in holy Matrimony... He shepherds us with the Word of His teaching, leading us "in right paths," "beside restful waters," to "dwell in the house of the Lord" forever.

"Let us rejoice and be glad that He has saved us!" If "only goodness and kindness" follow us all our days, what have we to do but rejoice? If we have a Lord who looks with such pity upon our hunger, what need we fear? If it is He who "spread[s] the table" before us, even here in this world, "in the sight of [our] foes," where sin besets us... what can we lack? If "cripples, the deformed, the blind, the mute, and many others" were healed of their maladies, what sickness of ours is beyond His redemption?

In this world we "walk in the dark valley." In this world we hunger. Here "the veil that veils all peoples" is upon us. But here, too, He is with us to refresh our souls and feed us with His Body and Blood in the New Jerusalem.

Thursday
(Is.26:1-6; Ps.118:1,8-9,19-21,25-27; Mt.7:21,24-27)

"Trust in the Lord forever!
For the Lord is an eternal rock."

Sand or rock? Upon which do we build our house? If we "take refuge in the Lord" and enter "the gates of justice," we shall find salvation in the Lord's kingdom; if we "trust in man" and "princes," we shall be leveled with the dust – our house shall collapse and we be "completely ruined."

The choice is set before us. "Those in high places" will be humbled to the ground; those who find refuge in the empty things of this world will find no protection on the day of His coming. But for the "nation of firm purpose," which "comes in the name of the Lord," "He sets up walls and ramparts to protect." And they shall "give thanks to the Lord" as they enter the gates of His holy city.

Jesus states clearly, "Only the one who does the will of my Father in heaven" will enter His kingdom: the one "who hears my words and puts them into practice" is he who is wise. And the putting into practice is key. Jesus has come in the flesh, and flesh there must be to our deeds. He is real, and we must be as real as He in our love. Otherwise we deny Him. We deny His coming if we do not live His way. God is not across the ocean or in the sky; He walks upon this earth now and must be *in our lives*. Only this will bring us strength. Only this will enable us to stand when the torrents come and the winds blow and buffet our house – for these have no power over those who are set in the Hand of God, who *do* His bidding.

"Blessed are those who hear the word of God and keep it" (Lk.11:28). We cannot but think of these challenging words from our Lord, referring greatly to the Mother of God – whose service to the Lord we particularly celebrate in these days of preparation – and cannot but hope to abide by

Advent

them and become the handmaiden Mary has shown herself to be, that the eternal blessings of God might be ours as well. In Him let us trust. In Him let our faith be set. And let us do His will.

A. I. 1. Fri.

Friday
(Is.29:17-24; Ps.27:1,4,13-14; Mt.9:27-31)

"The eyes of the blind shall see."

O "that I may gaze on the loveliness of the Lord and contemplate His temple." That out of "gloom and darkness" I might be taken, and come "to dwell in the house of the Lord all the days of my life." That I could feel His hands touch my eyes, that I might have the faith to believe they shall be open to His glory...

Brothers and sisters, we are blind. All of us. All of us lack understanding. All of us falter in faith. For who among us is there that gazes continually upon the Lord's presence? Who among us has entered His glory? Who among us possesses no arrogance and has "nothing to be ashamed of"? If yet we toil upon this earth, groaning as we await the redemption of our bodies, then yet do we continue in a measure blind. Yet do we seek His face. And if yet seeking "to see the bounty of the Lord in the land of the living," then yet have we to find it in its fullness; and so, yet do our eyes lack of the light that is the Lord, our salvation.

But certainly we are not without hope. Most certainly His hand is upon us even now. Most certainly His presence comes to us each and every day. Clearly His light shines in our midst in the Sacrament we receive and in the Word we hear, and so we can with confidence heed the exhortation of the psalm of David: "Wait for the Lord with courage; be stouthearted, and wait for the Lord." For He comes, and we know this. We are catching up to Him, and this is our joy. Yes, today do we know we *shall* see Him, for our eyes do glimpse Him even now.

In the meantime, brothers and sisters, as we wait, as the light that has dawned upon the world rises to our eyes, as He comes to fill our vision, let us strive to avoid speaking any word which "condemns a man." Let us know that indeed we "err in spirit" and need the Lord's light to guide us, and we shall become free of that which blinds us. And we shall be the lowly who are raised to His presence.

8

Saturday
(Is.30:19-21,23-26; Ps.147:1-6,Is.30:18; Mt.9:35-10:1,6-8)

"On the day the Lord binds up the wounds of His people,
He will heal the bruises left by His blows."

"Cure the sick, raise the dead, heal the leprous, expel demons." With these words Jesus sends His disciples forth proclaiming, "The reign of God is at hand!"

The prophecy of Isaiah has been fulfilled. The Savior has come. The Teacher is at our side now speaking into our ears, "This is the way; walk in it." And of all our sins He cleanses us; from all our sickness He heals us. Indeed, "as soon as you call He will answer you," for He is ready to wipe all tears from your eyes.

And what must be our response to a Lord who "heals the brokenhearted and binds up their wounds"? We must be the same as He. We must go forth as He has, teaching, proclaiming "the good news of God's reign," and curing "every sickness and disease." It is our call to make others whole in heart, mind, soul, and body; and so, to whatever need is present – and there are many or the Lord would not ask us to "beg the harvest master to send out laborers to gather His harvest" – we must apply the grace of God. He will do the work that is needed, but He needs us to work through.

To what glory all are called; what a wonderful message we have to bring forth! Isaiah, the great prophet, only touches upon it when he cries out that the Lord "will give rain for the seed that you sow in the ground" (see how He will bless your work!) and when he proclaims: "The light of the moon will be like that of the sun and the light of the sun will be seven times greater." This vision is for all who turn to the Lord for healing.

We have been bruised, brothers and sisters. No doubt, our sins have brought wounds to our souls. But the Lord will bind up all these; in His surpassing pity He will raise us all from death as He "rebuilds Jerusalem." Let us bring this message forth.

Second Week

Sunday (A)
(Is 11:1-10; Ps.72:1-2,7-8,12-13,17; Rm.15:4-9; Mt.3:1-12)

"His dwelling shall be glorious."

Wrought in the justice that has "pity for the lowly and the poor," in His days the Lord "shall rescue the poor man when he cries out, and the afflicted when he has no one to help him." The reign of the Lord "the Gentiles shall seek out" and "all the nations shall proclaim His happiness." For He is just. Though "with the breath of His lips He shall slay the wicked" and "the chaff He will burn in unquenchable fire," indeed, "profound peace" awaits His poor and lowly children: "There shall be no harm or ruin on all [His] holy mountain" – He shall "gather His wheat into His barn."

What encouragement we find in the Scriptures today; what hope is here. Isaiah's vision of peace among creatures, founded in the wisdom and justice of our blessed Lord, is without comparison; and it is confirmed in our beautiful psalm. Paul's words are so true – this "was written for our instruction" that "in harmony with one another" we might "with one voice glorify the God and Father of our Lord Jesus Christ."

And who is called by "the voice of one crying out in the desert"? To whom is the message given to "Repent, for the kingdom of heaven is at hand!" Each of the readings and the psalm make clear that *all* the nations are called, Gentile as well as Jew – His Day is a day for all people. John the Baptist reveals that all are called when he says to the Pharisees, "God can raise up children to Abraham from these stones." Indeed, the stoniest hearts, the most distant from the altar of the living Lord, are called now to enter His holy presence.

None is precluded from the table of our God. But none is presumed accepted. What the Baptist says to the Pharisees, he says to us all: "Produce good fruit as evidence of your repentance." If this greatest of prophets can say in truth, "I am not worthy to carry His sandals," how much must we all guard against the pride of presumption of worthiness for the kingdom. "The ax lies at the root of the trees"; may there be fruit now upon our leaves to be gathered into His glorious reign.

A. I. 2. Sun. (B)

Sunday (B)
(Is.40:1-5,9-11; Ps.85:9-14; 2Pt.3:8-14; Mk.1:1-8)

"Behold, I am sending my messenger ahead of you;
he will prepare your way."

And so, "John the Baptist appeared in the desert proclaiming a baptism of repentance for the forgiveness of sins." And so comes "the voice of one crying out in the desert," in the desert that is our fallen lives: "Prepare the way of the Lord, make straight His paths."

Turn from your sins, brothers and sisters. Repent. It is the Lord's will that "all should come to repentance," that all should be "found without spot or blemish" on the day of His coming, on the day all "the elements will be dissolved with fire." With the fire of the Holy Spirit does the Lord Jesus come now to baptize, that what John has cleansed from our souls might be gone forever – that the new person we become by this baptism of water might be made complete, might become hardened and lasting in the furnace of His love.

God "proclaims peace to His people. Near indeed is His salvation to those who fear Him." Hear what His prophet says, for he cries "out at the top of [his] voice" that indeed all hearts might listen: "Here is your GOD! Here comes with power the Lord GOD, who rules by His strong arm." Yes, "the mouth of the Lord has spoken," and now the WORD is in our midst, walking amongst us as our shepherd and "leading the ewes with care." The "justice [that] shall walk before Him, and prepare the way of His steps," has come, and now the level highway that leads to His kingdom we must tread – there is no denying the road that is set before us.

Christ is coming, brothers and sisters, and Christ has come. The Baptist has prepared His path, and He, the Son of God, has walked it. And now we await His return in glory. And "the Lord does not delay His promise"; His return is sure. Already we see the "glory dwelling in our land." He waits for you to come now to Him. In patience He looks for you to turn. Turn to Him now in earnest; with all your soul cry out His Name. "Jesus Christ the Son of God" dawns on the horizon. Embrace His love; walk His sacred path.

A. I. 2. Sun. (C)

Sunday (C)
(Bar.5:1-9; Ps.126:1-6; Phil.1:4-6,8-11; Lk.3:1-6)

"All flesh shall see the salvation of God."

Yes, at a particular point in time, in the year delineated so precisely by Luke in our gospel, "the word of God came to John the son of Zechariah in the desert." The Holy Spirit whispered in his ear, set his heart on fire, and so called him to cry out the coming of the Lord upon the nation. And "John went throughout the whole region of the Jordan," calling all souls to "a baptism of repentance for the forgiveness of sins"; being thus inspired, what else could he do? The Spirit so powerfully upon him, of what else could he think? The long-awaited Savior is finally near – and the people must be ready.

And so, sinful flesh is made clean in the Jordan River. And so "the rough ways [are] made smooth," "the winding roads... made straight," for nothing crooked shall meet the Messiah. We do not come to Him in sinful garb.

11

O "Jerusalem, take off your robe of mourning and misery; put on the splendor of glory from God forever." Plunge yourself into the waters that make new. Let all of the old man be washed away. "For God will show all the earth your splendor; you will be named by God forever the peace of justice, the glory of God's worship." "See your children gathered from the east and the west at the word of the Holy One, rejoicing that they are remembered by God," joyful that He has come. All the earth shall be blessed through you and the royal tree that grows in your midst.

"When the Lord brought back the captives of Zion, we were like men dreaming." How can it be our salvation has come? And now "God is leading Israel in joy by the light of His glory, with His mercy and justice for company." In His Church this day we dwell; into His presence ever we come. Obedient to the cry of the prophet's voice, we turn from our sins and are made anew. And now our daily bread we consume.

What joy should fill our hearts, brothers and sisters! that the Lord has come to dwell with us. We eat "the fruit of righteousness that comes through Jesus Christ for the glory and praise of God," and the strength we find herein He will "complete" on the day of His coming again. Let our hearts be set on fire as was John's. Let us cry out to all flesh that the salvation of God is nigh.

A. I. 2. Mon.

Monday
(Is.35:1-10; Ps.85:9-14,Is.35:4; Lk.5:17-26)

"A highway will be there, called the holy way."

Jesus is the highway; holy is He! He is the stream that "will burst forth in the desert." It is He who "strengthen[s] the hands that are feeble [and] make[s] firm the knees that are weak," that they might walk along His way. It is He who forgives sins. For "no one unclean may pass over" the safe path He makes in the wilderness of this world, and He wishes to "give His benefits" to all of faith. "Near indeed is His salvation to those who fear Him."

"Then will the lame leap like a stag, then the tongue of the dumb will sing," prophesies Isaiah. And Jesus says to the paralyzed man, "Get up! Take your mat with you and return to your house." And what did the man do? "He picked up the mat he had been lying on and went home praising God." "We have seen incredible things today!" the crowd exclaims in awe, for the great vision of the prophet Isaiah has come to pass before their eyes: before them is being set the path to paradise.

"Hear what the Lord proclaims," brothers and sisters: "Justice shall walk before Him, and salvation, along the way of His steps." Along His holy way "the redeemed will walk. Those whom the Lord has ransomed will return and enter Zion singing, crowned with everlasting joy." All those forgiven their sins will enter their homes praising God. Yes, the "desert and the parched land... will bloom with abundant flowers, and rejoice with joyful song." We once paralyzed in our sin, by His hand, by His word, along His holy way, shall walk once again.

He has come. "Here is your God, He comes with vindication; with divine recompense He comes to save you." In Him "kindness and truth... meet, justice and peace... kiss." In Him we are made whole by the breath of His mouth, by the words from His lips. And now we have "a journey to make." Now there is a way to walk. Let us remain upon this highway. Let us preserve the healing He has brought to our bones. Let us now live in faith with our Lord.

A. I. 2. Tues.

Tuesday
(Is.40:1-11; Ps.96:1-3,10-13,Is.40:10; Mt.18:12-14)

"Like a shepherd He feeds His flock;
in His arms He gathers His lambs."

His is the voice which "speak[s] tenderly to Jerusalem." It is He who "give[s] comfort to [His] people." For "it is no part of [the] heavenly Father's plan that a single one of these little ones shall ever come to grief."

Like a shepherd He leads us. With great concern He watches over His flock, careful that none is led astray. And diligent is He in finding the one who "wanders away." This is indeed "good news." These are indeed "glad tidings," which make even "the trees of the forest exult." For He cares about each one of the many of His creatures, and shall bring all back to Him by the sound of His gentle voice.

And of His sweet voice we must cry out. "Sing to the Lord; bless His name; announce His salvation day after day." For all the earth must know that "He shall rule the world with justice and His peoples with constancy." And so "a voice cries out: In the desert prepare the way of the Lord!" May all hearts be ready to meet Him. When "every valley shall be filled in, every mountain and hill shall be made low... then the glory of the Lord shall be revealed, and all mankind shall see it together." O that that glorious day might come!

"Though the grass withers and the flower wilts, the word of our God stands forever." And so He stands behind us, whispering into our ears of the way we should walk. And so He calls to our hearts, carrying us "in His bosom" with care. And so His eternal presence ever comes to our tired bodies, our fading souls, and gives them life, and brings them back from

13

their straying paths upon this dying earth. And so it is that all "exult before the Lord, for He comes; He comes to rule the earth."

It is only in His eternity that we shall find a home, brothers and sisters. And into these arms He now gathers us. And with His food He now feeds us. Let us partake of His presence in Word and in Sacrament as we await His coming.

A. I. 2. Wed.

Wednesday
(Is.40:25-31; Ps.103:1-4,8,10; Mt.11:28-30)

"My yoke is easy and my burden light."

How we do become "weary and find life burdensome." How we can "faint and grow weary," "stagger and fall" from the burden of sin and our inherent weakness. But O how "He gives strength to the fainting; for the weak He makes vigor abound." For indeed He is the Creator of the universe – "by His great might and the strength of His power" all things come to be – and His Son is the redeemer of our souls. "The Lord is the eternal God" and "they that hope in the Lord will renew their strength; they will soar as with eagles' wings." Trust in Him who "pardons all your iniquities" and "heals all your ills."

What a promise Jesus holds forth for those who come to His "gentle and humble" heart: "Your souls will find rest." We know that the great St. Augustine has told us that only in God do our souls find rest. How we wander aimlessly in trackless wastes seeking comfort for our souls, rest for our weary bodies, taking refuge in the various attractions of the world and the vain promise they hold. How late in life all of us come to the fulfilling promise of Jesus, for any time spent apart from Him is but wasted.

And thank the Lord that He is "merciful and gracious." Thank Him that "not according to our sins does He deal with us." For what hope would we have then? But this great God who has no equal, who holds the world in His hand, "redeems your life from destruction, He crowns you with kindness and compassion" despite your sins, if you but come to Him as He calls.

How patiently Jesus waits for each of us, this only Son of God, this image of the Father and embodiment of His love. How gracious He is toward us poor creatures. Will you not take His "yoke upon your shoulders and learn" from Him? Will you not find refreshment from all your sins and forgiveness of all your crimes? Will you continue to turn your face away from Him who watches over all and weigh yourself down with anxiety? Or will you come to Him, your only hope? Take the light burden of His gracious Word upon your souls and do His will in this world.

Thursday
(Is.41:13-20; Ps.145:1,8-13; Mt.11:11-15)

"I will make you a threshing sledge,
sharp, new, and double-edged."

A "worm" and a "maggot" are we. We are "the afflicted and the needy [who] seek water in vain, [our] tongues… parched with thirst." But holding our right hand, the Lord speaks to us: "Fear not, I will help you." "I will open up rivers on the bare heights… I will turn the desert into a marshland, and the dry ground into springs of water." And has not John the Baptizer come, into the desert, into the wilderness, and there poured the water of God's compassion upon us for the forgiveness of sins?

Lush trees now grow in the desert: we who were once empty are now filled with God's grace. And yes, "the hand of the Lord has done this, the Holy One of Israel has created it." For all these wonders accomplished in our midst are but to "make known to men [His] might and the glorious splendor of [His] kingdom." Indeed, we now "thresh the mountains and crush them, to make the hills like chaff," but all this is done in His power.

And how then do we understand Jesus' words: "From John the Baptizer's time until now the kingdom of God has suffered violence, and the violent take it by force"? We know that John spoke boldly in the name of God; unafraid of his oppressors, he called all to repentance. We should all learn from the power of God he displayed in crying out in the wilderness. We know also that at the time Jesus spoke the above words, John was imprisoned in Herod's dungeon, suffering genuinely the violence of this generation. We know Jesus Himself will be crucified. We know all the apostles (save John) will be martyred for the faith – all His children suffer under the weight of the cross imposed by the violent of this world.

But we know also that this very cross is the means God has chosen to reveal most poignantly His powerful hand at work. For the nails which fix our hands to the wood have no power over us, and so by the humble acceptance of the violence of this age we do most dramatically destroy, crush into dust, the mountains of this world. And we upon whom the greatest violence is inflicted indeed effect the greater violence upon our oppressors, for by this sacrifice wickedness is destroyed and the righteous enter the kingdom of heaven. Let us act with such strength from God, brothers and sisters, for the sake of the kingdom.

Friday

(Is.48:17-19; Ps.1:1-4,6,Jn.8:12; Mt.11:16-19)

"Time will prove where wisdom lies."

No doubt it lies with God. It lies with the Son of Man, come for our salvation.

"I, the Lord, your God, teach you what is for your good, and lead you on the way you should go." Is it not our essential call to obey His Word, to listen for His voice and follow in His way? Are they not happy who hear the Word of God and keep it? Is this not wisdom, to walk in the way of our Creator, with the One who loves us above all? Does not all our misery stem from disobedience to His sacred commandments? Do we not simply lose all love in our hearts in this way of our own making? Does this not bring our death?

If we would but follow the Lord, our "prosperity would be like a river," no doubt. Our "descendants would be like the sand," for "like a tree planted near running water" we would flourish with the wisdom which comes from the font of life which is the Lord, and one would we become with all the children of His eternal kingdom.

We cannot expect the Lord to dance to the tune we pipe or wail to the dirge we sing. It is the height of foolishness for the creature to attempt to impose its will on the Creator. But such is our pride, the source of our wickedness. And so, deaf, blind, and empty are we when we seek to turn the order of the universe back upon our God. For "like chaff which the wind drives away" our own foolish counsels can all but come to naught. The branch cannot grow apart from the vine, nor can the tree bear fruit without the water which gives it life.

"Happy the man who… delights in the law of the Lord and meditates on His law day and night." For then the nourishing waters are upon him; then the light of wisdom fills him – then he shall bear fruit a hundredfold and never taste of death. For the Hand of God will be upon him to lead him to the eternal kingdom, where His wisdom will be proven true.

Saturday

(Sir.48:1-4,9-11; Ps.80:2-4,15-16,18-19; Mt.17:10-13)

"Like a fire there appeared the prophet Elijah
whose words were as a flaming furnace."

Elijah has come, to "restore everything." The word has fallen like fire from heaven to prepare a path for the Lord to tread. The Baptist has cried out as a voice in the wilderness for us to make our hearts ready for the coming of the Lord.

But, sadly, "they did not recognize him and they did as they pleased with him." They rejected the voice crying to them and attempted to cover over the way the word had cleared before them. He who came "to turn back the hearts of fathers toward their sons, and to re-establish the tribes of Jacob," was himself turned back; and they cast him into prison and beheaded the great prophet.

Yet the way remains open to us. He whom the prophet hailed has come into our midst, and His presence cannot be taken away – even to the end of the age (which is upon us). And we must join with our psalmist today in calling upon Him to "come to save us," to "look down from heaven, and see," to "take care of this vine" planted by His right hand. "Give us new life, and we will call upon your name," must be our prayer, especially in this Advent season, for we must awaken and enliven the path to God the Baptist has served to blaze in our hearts. We must know now Him whom he has hailed.

And, yes, with this Elijah and with the Son of Man, we too will suffer at the hands of those who would silence the Word, who would extinguish the fire set upon the earth. But the fire is eternal and its light and power cannot be dimmed, much less extinguished. It will purify those who seek the face of God and destroy those who turn from Him. It cannot be otherwise. Now that the Lord has come, His angels wait in expectation to purge the world. Once more only the prophet Elijah will appear and the flaming furnace his words prepare will be fulfilled in God's eternity by the return of the Son of Man. In absolute glory the Lord will reign.

Third Week

Sunday (A)
(Is.35:1-6,10; Ps.146:6-10,Is.35:4; Jas.5:7-10; Mt.11:2-11)

"Make your hearts firm, because the coming of the Lord is at hand."

Hope. What hope have we. And so we should "be patient, brothers and sisters, until the coming of the Lord." Indeed, we must endure "the early and the late rains" – having been converted to the Lord we shall be purged of all sin on the last day – but, though "hardship" be with us now, our hope should be firm in Him who comes, in Him who "is standing before the gates" even now.

Jesus is the fulfillment of the vision given Isaiah and the salvation sung of by our psalmist. By Him, "the blind regain their sight, the lame walk, lepers are cleansed, the deaf hear, the dead are raised, and the poor have the good news proclaimed to them." Should not He who has power over all maladies, and even death, bring us hope in the kingdom to come? Should not our seeing these wonders wrought by Jesus instill great faith in our hearts? Should we not even rejoice now in our suffering, knowing well that "sorrow and mourning will flee away" when He comes, that the very suffering we experience now will then be no more? Patience. Indeed, patience brings us hope, enables us to endure all, even joyfully.

And does Jesus not seek to encourage greater hope, greater faith in our hearts by His words about John the Baptist? "What did you go out to the desert to see?" He asks the crowds, addressing their longing for truth, their desire for hope, and confirms that the prophet they sought was indeed greater than all "among those born of women." But He does not stop there. How much farther He leads them: "The least in the kingdom of heaven is greater than he." Remarkable. What hope have we, to be greater than the Baptist. For the Baptist is himself a man, who himself suffers and struggles, inquiring if Jesus is "the one who is to come," and must himself be assured by the Lord. But in heaven no question will remain. This desert in which we seek the Lord will come to full bloom "with abundant flowers."

Keep the faith in joy, brothers and sisters. We have every reason for hope; we have firm witness of His grace, at work in us even now.

A. I. 3. Sun. (B)

Sunday (B)

(Is.61:1-2,10-11; Lk.1:46-50,53-54; 1Thes.5:16-24; Jn.1:6-8,19-28)

"A man named John was sent from God."

Here is the one of whom the prophet speaks, and who can rightly proclaim the words inscribed by Isaiah: "The spirit of the Lord God is upon me, because the Lord has anointed me." Here is he who has come "to announce a year of favor from the Lord and a day of vindication by our God." The Spirit is upon him and he speaks of the coming Messiah. He has been sent by God to "testify to the light."

But who heeds his proclamation? Who is able to hear this voice crying and find the joy of the path it would blaze in their hearts? How many are still as the priests and Levites and Pharisees of today's gospel, inquiring so blindly, "Who are you"? How many are as the commentators of the missal I read, who term the prophecy of Isaiah a "poem," and state that the Canticle of Mary is "a song that Luke put into the mouth of Mary"? How many have no sense of prophecy, or the Spirit, or God Himself? How many are deaf to John's cry?

Our brother Paul instructs us: "Do not quench the Spirit. Do not despise prophetic utterances." And yet the greatest of all prophetic utterances are watered down in ankle-deep wisdom. "My soul proclaims the greatness of the Lord," Mary declares. The Spirit wells up in her spirit and she cannot but "rejoice in God [her] Savior." These are not words put into her mouth by any man; her prophecy does not come from the pen of a scribe but from the very Spirit of God!

The Word of God cannot be chained; the voice "crying out in the desert" cannot be tamed by those "not worthy to untie" the mysteries hidden in sacred Scripture. Paul will be put under house arrest; the Baptist Herod will cast into his dungeon; the Christ shall be crucified – but the Word of God will go forth, and nothing shall silence its voice. The testimony to the light must be heard, "so that all might believe through Him"; there will ever be proclaimed "liberty to captives and release to the prisoners" by the power of Jesus Christ, until all hear of the mercy He has "on those who fear Him."

A man named John was sent, not to testify to himself, but to prophesy the grace of God; and his voice will cry out the way to the ends of the earth and to the end of time.

A. I. 3. Sun. (C)

Sunday (C)
(Zep.3:14-18a; Is.12:2-6; Phil.4:4-7; Lk.3:10-18)

"Rejoice in the Lord always.
I shall say it again: Rejoice!"

"Shout for joy, O daughter Zion! Sing joyfully, O Israel! Be glad and exult with all your heart, O daughter Jerusalem!" Zephaniah exclaims. "Shout with exultation, O city of Zion"! Isaiah urges. And Paul is overwhelmed with the spirit of rejoicing. Why such joy? Whence such celebration? "The Lord, your God, is in your midst, a mighty savior," Zephaniah declares. "Great in your midst is the Holy One of Israel!" Isaiah proclaims. And Paul tells us simply: "The Lord is near." What could bring greater joy than such a prospect?

And so we "have no further misfortune to fear." And so we should be "confident and unafraid." And so we should "have no anxiety." For the Lord will "renew [us] in His love." "Our strength and [our] salvation is the Lord," and "the peace of God that surpasses all understanding will guard [our] hearts and minds in Christ Jesus." Why should we not be joyful if He Himself "will rejoice over [us] with gladness," if because of us He sings "as one sings at festivals." Should we not match His joy poured out for our sakes and sing the song of salvation?

And it is John the Baptist who hails most clearly the song of salvation coming into our midst. It is he who "preached good news to the people" with all the power of God, exhorting them to holiness that they might be gathered as "wheat into His barn." By him "the people were filled with expectation"; by him and by his pronouncement of the coming of Him who "will baptize [them] with the Holy Spirit and fire," the song of joy is ignited in their hearts. He calls us all, by the Spirit that filled Isaiah, to "give thanks to the Lord, [and] acclaim His name." It is he who "among the nations make[s] known His deeds, [who] proclaim[s] how exalted is His name." And the souls of even tax collectors and soldiers turn to him in anxious anticipation.

And yes, what about us, brothers and sisters? Is the joy of Christ brimming over in our hearts, despite any situation? Do we hear the voice of the Baptist – and the prophets and the apostles – crying out His way of peace? And do we follow as the voice instructs? Indeed, the Lord is near; He is in our midst. Let us welcome Him with the purest of joy.

A. I. 3. Mon.

Monday
(Nm.24:2-7,15-17; Ps.25:4-9; Mt.21:23-27)

"A star shall advance from Jacob,
and a staff shall rise from Israel."

And the light of that star is reflected in the eyes of Balaam, who, though a pagan, is gifted by God with the clear vision to see the beauty and wonder of "Israel encamped, tribe by tribe," "like gardens beside a stream," "like the cedars planted by the Lord." And as He is seen in the nation of Israel blessed by the Lord, so His glory is reflected in the heart and words and actions of everyone who believes and proclaims in truth that Jesus is that star, that Jesus is the Son of God.

Those who remain close to the teaching of Jesus, and to His ways, "shall have the sea within reach." There shall be an abundance of wisdom at the ready for those who are graced with ears to hear His words. "He teaches the humble His way," yes, and guides us on straight paths which lead directly to the Most High. And "with eyes unveiled" we shall gaze not only on His reflection in the fields of this earthly existence, but on Him Himself as He is in heaven.

The teaching of Jesus is divine and He Himself is divine, above whose authority there is no other. But His light can only be seen, His words can only be understood by those whose hearts are open to truth and willing to walk the path He sets. If the "chief priests and elders of the people" closed themselves off from Him in a political quandary, we must not do so. Instead

20

we must be as His apostles, in whom the tribes of Israel are truly aligned perfectly, and have as ready a response as we know Peter had on the shores of Galilee, as Thomas had when He appeared in their midst: He is our Lord, our God. This we must see. This we must know. And this we must proclaim.

The star has risen in our midst; the Savior has come. Now we await the fulfillment of that light and must bring it to bear in this generation. Now we must follow that star where it leads.

Tuesday
(Zep.3:1-2,9-13; Ps.34:2-3,6-7,17-19,23; Mt.21:28-32)

"I will leave as a remnant in your midst
a people humble and lowly,
who shall take refuge in the name of the Lord."

All have been "rebellious and polluted"; all have been as she who "hears no voice" and "accepts no correction." But the Lord now comes to "change and purify the lips of the peoples, that they may all call upon the name of the Lord, to serve Him with one accord." Who is it who hears the voice of the Lord to "not be ashamed of all [our] deeds, [our] rebellious acts against [Him]"?

"Let me make it clear that tax collectors and prostitutes are entering the kingdom of God before you," Jesus states simply and directly to the chief priests and elders. These lowest of society, these most polluted, have put faith in John's preaching of "a way of holiness," but those most esteemed, the elder son whose words bear the stamp of God but whose actions are far from Him, are held back from entering the kingdom by their pride, perhaps thinking they are already there.

How sad. How can it be that those so steeped in the holy Scriptures do not hear the words of David's psalm: "The Lord is close to the brokenhearted; and those who are crushed in spirit He saves"? Or how are they blind to the vision of the "humble and lowly" the Lord deems to bless? For that matter, how do they hide themselves from the great prophet's declaration that the Lord "will remove from [their] midst the proud braggarts"?

Our words alone will not save us, brothers and sisters. However great the lines of the scribe or the preaching of the priest, it will mean nothing if not lived in flesh and blood. Better to say no to God, as the younger son, and then turn to Him and do His will. Certainly we all stray; and this we must recognize. But just as certain is that all must turn to Him, after regretting our sin, and do as He commands.

Do not be afraid. The Lord will "destroy remembrance of evildoers," but count not yourself as in allegiance with them. Be among those who "speak no lies" and you "shall pasture and couch [your] flocks with none to disturb [you]." The vision of God and His Spirit shall be your own.

Wednesday
(Is.45:6-8,18,21-25; Ps.85:9-14,Is.45:8; Lk.7:18-23)

"There is no just and saving God but me."

Jesus is "He who is to come"; His deeds speak for themselves. "There is no other!"

"Justice shall walk before Him, and salvation, along the way of His steps." How evident this is in Jesus' life, for wherever He goes He teaches wisdom; whomever He touches He heals. God created the world "not to be a waste" but "to be lived in," and so Jesus sets free all captives – the blind, the lame, the deaf... He releases all from sin. Yes, "the Lord Himself will give His benefits; our land shall yield its increase." The justice which descends from the heavens, which falls from His lips "like dew from above," will cause "salvation [to] bud forth."

"Near indeed is His salvation to those who fear Him." We see Him. We hear Him. If our hearts are open to Him, we witness His working every moment of our lives. For He is "the creator of the heavens... the designer and maker of the earth," and His Hand is at work in all things – He cannot be separated from His creation. The light and the darkness are made by Him, and for us who love Him "truth shall spring out of the earth, and justice shall look down from heaven." "For He proclaims peace to His people." For those who love Him, there is only light.

And we know that Light is Jesus. It is to witness to Him the Baptist came; and now he hears of the fulfillment of the way he has prepared. We must find "no stumbling block" in the Lord. We must join in proclaiming His good news, in walking in His way – in letting our deeds speak for themselves as wrought by the Hand of the loving Creator and His redeeming Son.

Be of light, brothers and sisters, of justice, of peace. Let kindness and truth meet in all your words and deeds and you will be sons and daughters of the one "just and saving God" – and you will be blessed forever.

Thursday

(Is.54:1-10; Ps.30:2,4-6,11-13; Lk.7:24-30)

"For a brief moment I abandoned you,
but with great tenderness I will take you back."

We are "the barren one who did not bear," the "wife married in youth and then cast off" by our God. Once "forsaken and grieved in spirit," blushing for the "shame of [our] youth," now the Lord takes us home and promises us His love. "My love shall never leave you nor my covenant of peace be shaken," the Lord in His mercy assures us. Though we be as those in the days of Noah, deserving of His destructive wrath, yet He takes pity on us, not only sparing our lives, but also promising to expand our space, to increase us in His blessed generosity beyond what we could imagine.

"At nightfall, weeping enters in, but with the dawn, rejoicing." Yes, our sin has made us sad; our separation from God has invited His wrath and made us less than what we are. But though the Lord may punish in His justice, yet "His anger lasts but a moment; a lifetime His good will." David sings, "You changed my mourning into dancing," for indeed great is His mercy toward us; tender is His touch upon us as He brings us "up from the nether world" and places us at His side in the kingdom, as His holy bride.

And the Baptist makes the way the redeemed must walk. Necessary is "the baptismal bath he administered" in order to realize God's plan for the salvation of our lives. He is the messenger who goes ahead of the Lord, preparing the path that leads to our being "born into the kingdom of God," where our greatness cannot be measured for it will be in union with Him who is "God of all the earth." Indeed, we must turn from our sins to find our way to this unity; we must repent in tears and turn back to Him. And He will be quick to rescue us, and we will be blessed to rejoice forever, to "break forth in jubilant song" at the graces poured forth upon us by our God in the forgiveness of our sins.

His tender Hand is near us, waiting to touch us. Is it your will to be wed to the Most High God? Then receive the baptism He requires and you will be made fruitful in the kingdom of God.

Friday

(Is.56:1-3,6-8; Ps.67:2-3,5,7-8; Jn.5:33-36)

"My house shall be called a house of prayer
for all peoples."

The Truth has come, and all nations are drawn to Him.

23

Advent

None is excluded in the House of God; His holy Temple is a place where all take refuge, where all find fulfillment, where all find joy. He only asks that we heed His testimony, that we see the works which He performs and act in accordance with His holiness. "Observe what is right, do what is just, for my salvation is about to come, my justice, about to be revealed," the Lord says to us all. Set yourselves on right paths with Him who has come, and you will be readily accepted into His presence.

"Loving the name of the Lord and becoming His servants," this is what brings us into His house. No matter who we are, no matter where we are, no matter when we are, we will be brought "to [His] holy mountain and [made] joyful in [His] house of prayer," if we follow His ways. Exult in the light of the Lord, know that Jesus is the Temple to which your heart is drawn and your "holocausts and sacrifices will be acceptable on [His] altar."

His justice is for all; His love extends to the ends of the earth. David's prayer is answered in Jesus: "May your way be known upon earth, among all nations your salvation." For now does He "rule the peoples in equity"; now "the earth has yielded its fruits." Now the blessing of our God falls upon all whose hearts turn to Him.

"May all the ends of the earth fear Him!" Then will all be drawn into His house of prayer and know His love. This day shall not be long in coming; come now to "the lamp, set aflame and burning bright" for all eternity. Enter into the flesh of Christ.

A. I. 4. Sun. (A)

Fourth Sunday (A)
(Is.7:10-14; Ps.24:1-7,10; Rm.1:1-7; Mt.1:18-24)

"God is with us."

How shall we "ascend the mountain of the Lord"? How shall we scale the heights and come to know Him as He is, He who "founded [the earth] upon the seas and established it upon the rivers"? Only by the Son, who "will save His people from their sins," are we made ready to stand in His presence. "For it is through the Holy Spirit this child has been conceived," and we are made holy by the blessing of His presence among our kind.

He is one like us. Can you believe it? Can you understand it, understand its significance and the grace it is as a gift from God? Joseph struggled, certainly, to believe, to understand, to accept the greatness of this gift to him and to his people. The angel of the Lord had to come to him to convince him to receive such great grace into his life, into his home. But he did. He did believe, and he did fulfill his role in the coming salvation.

And, yes, what of us? We "are called to belong to Jesus Christ... called to be holy." Paul answered the call from God to be His apostle and "bring

24

about the obedience of faith"; again, what of us? Do we answer the call to holiness? Do we reflect that obedience? The time is upon us now. The great sign has been fulfilled in our midst. Jesus has been born and stands with us now to lead us to the purity of the Father – are we prepared to make this Child our own?

What greater truth can be proclaimed than that God is with us? What greater grace can we receive than the forgiveness of our sins, than the preparation of our hearts for heaven? Jesus accomplishes these blessings now for all who desire to enter the presence of God, for He *is* the presence of God among us; He Himself is divine grace. His mercy is upon us.

"Grace to you and peace from God our Father and the Lord Jesus Christ," brothers and sisters. The power of the Lord be upon your souls. May the "Spirit of holiness" establish you with the Son as a child of the Father. Be of "the race that seeks for Him," and you shall find Him present, dwelling in your homes.

A. I. 4. Sun. (B)

Fourth Sunday (B)

(2Sm.7:1-5,8b-12,14a,16; Ps.89:2-5,27,29; Rom.16:25-27; Lk.1:26-28)

"The Lord God will give Him the throne of David His father."

"I have made a covenant with David my chosen one, I have sworn to David my servant: forever will I confirm your posterity and establish your throne for all generations." Here is the promise made to King David. Upon his seeking to build a house for the Lord, "the Lord... reveals to [David] that He will establish a house for [him]." Through the prophet Nathan, the Lord declares to His humble servant: "When your time comes and you rest with your ancestors, I will raise up your heir after you, sprung from your loins, and I will make his kingdom firm." This would seem like all the world to refer to the great King Solomon, but it does not. For, like the earth itself, Solomon and all his gold – and even "the rest from all [his] enemies," the peace the Lord establishes under his reign – will pass away; they cannot "endure forever" and neither can such a kingdom. The prophet speaks of a kingdom established in heaven (where all by nature endures forever), not one of the earth.

And so it is not Solomon of whom the prophet and the psalmist speak, but Jesus, He whose coming is hailed today by the angel's words to the Blessed Virgin: "He will rule over the house of Jacob forever, and of His kingdom there will be no end." For Abraham has died and Jacob has died and David has died and Solomon has died... and their graves are with us to this day. But Jesus, Jesus lives; Jesus lives forever at the right hand of His Father.

It is indeed Jesus who most truly says to the Lord God, "You are my Father, my God, the Rock." It is He who is His only Son: it is He who is God Himself, consubstantial with the Father. This is "the revelation of the mystery kept secret for long ages but now manifested through the prophetic writings"; this is "the command of the eternal God, made known to all nations to bring about the obedience of faith": Jesus is the Christ, the Messiah, the only Son – and we must worship Him.

Come now, brothers and sisters, to this Child Mary bears by the power of the Holy Spirit. In Him your peace shall be established in the Father's kingdom. Come to His holy throne, enter into His eternal reign... and with His humble king, and with His humble Mother, you shall be blessed forever.

A. I. 4. Sun. (C)

Fourth Sunday (C)
(Mi.5:1-4a; Ps.80:2-4,15-16,18-19; Heb.10:5-10; Lk.1:39-45)

"Blessed is the fruit of your womb."

From the womb of Bethlehem-Ephrathah, from the womb of Judah, has come forth "one who is to be ruler in Israel; whose origin is from of old, from ancient times." Now "she who is to give birth has borne"; now has our Savior come. Though He has existed from before time, it is now He is made flesh in the womb of this simple virgin.

"When Christ came into the world, He said; 'Sacrifice and offering you did not desire, but a body you prepared for me.'" And so God comes in His own flesh to take away our sins. Prepared in the womb of the Immaculate Virgin, in this bright cave He is knit with sinews as we... and who could proclaim loudly enough the majesty of this humble event; who could declare in fullness the blessing of this Mother and Child? And their union is one which will save our race, as shown already in the Baptist's leap for joy in his own mother's womb. The Holy Spirit is working fully in the wombs of these mothers and in their children's flesh and blood.

And so the psalmist finds answer for his prayer to God: "Rouse your power, and come to save us." For here comes "He [who] shall stand firm and shepherd His flock by the strength of the Lord, in the majestic name of the Lord, His God"; here is the One whose "greatness shall reach to the ends of the earth." And so shall all who trust in Him be saved.

In body He comes like a Rock upon whom our feet stand firm. In the Spirit has He been formed in His Mother's womb. And, yes, blessed is she "who believed that what was spoken to [her] by the Lord would be fulfilled"; and blessed are all those who have faith in the Son she bears. For all time meets in this moment; all prophecy speaks with one voice of the birth of this Holy One. And so, let us pray to God the Father: "Protect what

26

your right hand has planted, the Son of Man whom you yourself made strong," that we might praise forever the glory of your presence, in the salvation you have made known. May the peace He is be with us always.

A. II. Dec. 17.

B. Second Part of Advent

December 17
(Gn.49:2,8-10; Ps.72:3-4,7-8,17; Mt.1:1-17)

"May He rule from sea to sea,
and from the River to the ends of the earth."

Since "the scepter shall never depart from Judah," the reign of Jesus, His descendant, His fulfillment, is without end – He is King forever. And so, "tribute is brought to Him, and He receives the peoples' homage," which is in itself their salvation.

Who is this Lion of Judah, fulfillment of Jacob's prophetic blessing of his son? What sort of king have we? It is in the words of our psalm we find His kingship revealed: "He shall defend the afflicted among the people, save the children of the poor." For Jesus, though fierce as a lion in His judgment – for there is nothing untrue in Him – reveals primarily the love of God the king must embody. In His reign, "the mountains shall yield peace for the people, and the hills justice." First is the love He brings to this generation; second, its complement, justice.

And of what worth is the "family record of Jesus Christ, son of David, son of Abraham," we find in our gospel today? Be not overly bored by it, my brothers and sisters, for in its mundaneness it holds the key to our salvation. For it reveals how very real Jesus is, that He is part of our human family; and should this not make us rejoice, that the Son of God is also Son of Man? And though the forty-two or so names may not be familiar to our ears, we should know at least that there are all kinds in this family tree of Jesus, from great men and women of faith humble before their God, to wicked kings and a prostitute. There is thus hope for us all.

Jesus is indeed the fulfillment of the promised son of Abraham, and son of David, the king who sits on the throne forever. It was of Mary He was born, and Mary's husband was Joseph. And since husband and wife are one – and though theirs was only a spiritual communion, it is in the spiritual communion unity is truly found – we trace His line through this humble man. And we pray we shall enter into communion with the Lord ourselves and live in the reign of this King in whom "all the tribes of the earth shall be blessed."

Today we praise our brother in the flesh and pray to be made one in His Spirit. May He indeed rule over all.

December 18
(Jer.23:5-8; Ps.72:1,7,12-13,18-19; Mt.1:18-24)

"He will save His people from their sins."

Each of our readings today mentions the salvation of our Lord. The above quote is from our gospel; our psalm states, "The lives of the poor He shall save"; and in our first reading it says, "In His days Judah shall be saved." The very name "Jesus" – as given to Joseph by the angel of the Lord – means "God saves". The great God of the universe, the living God who has brought us all to birth, comes among us, "is with us" ("Emmanuel") to save us, to redeem us, to bring us back to our "own land"... to be again with the Father.

And this "righteous shoot to David," this king who "shall reign and govern wisely," who "shall do what is right and just in the land," is born from above, not below. As the angel also tells Joseph, "It is by the Holy Spirit that [Mary] has conceived this child." The Virgin is with child! Alleluia! A greater sign, a more complete love from the Father we could not imagine. And so we sing with our psalmist: "Blessed forever be His glorious name; may the whole earth be filled with His glory." Indeed, all nations, not only Judah, shall be saved by this Blessed Child.

"The days are coming," brothers and sisters, and are already here. The Lord walks among us. The Child has been born, and is being born in each of us; and as a people He comes to us. Mary "bore a son"; Joseph named Him "Jesus", as instructed, and Jesus He is – His salvation has come forth. You must receive Him into your home with the Mother who bore Him. You must have faith that He is from above. Let Joseph be your model in care for the Savior, and He shall care for you for all eternity. Like Mary, nourish the Lord every day of your life.

His love is growing in us all. His presence is becoming known. The promised of the ages dwells with us with His justice, and His kingdom is being built as we speak. No more will our sins condemn us. No more will we hide our faces from the Lord. We shall be free once more, and this time forever, for the Lord has heard the cry of the poor.

December 19
(Jgs.13:2-7,24-25; Ps.71:3-6,8,16-17; Lk.1:5-25)

"From my mother's womb you are my strength."

How the above line from our psalm is reflected both in Samson and in John, and how parallel are the lives of these two great men. Of John it is said, "He will be filled with the Holy Spirit from his mother's womb"; of Samson, "This boy is to be consecrated to God from the womb" and "The Spirit of the Lord began to be with him." The birth of both is announced by an angel of the Lord. Both will be born of women who were barren. Both will be nazirites, who shall "never drink wine or strong drink," and whose head "no razor shall touch." Both come for the deliverance of the people, though Samson only from "the power of the Philistines" while John comes to "prepare for the Lord a people well-disposed," that we might have eternal salvation.

Of course, Jesus, too, will have His birth announced by the angel of the Lord; He will be born of a woman from whom it seems no child could come – a consecrated virgin – and this of the Holy Spirit, who is with Him even before time. His is a new testament, however, signified by His birth of a woman of youth and not old age. Though hailed by the old, He brings the newness of God into our midst. His birth fulfills all the births and words and wisdom of the prophets and judges and kings of the Old Testament.

But, returning to our psalm and its universal call in the voice of Christ (words which apply to all in their quest for God), we should remember today that for all, God is our "rock of refuge" on whom we "depend from birth." "You have taught me from my youth," the psalmist declares to the Lord, and so it should be true with us all that from the womb "till the present [we] proclaim [His] wondrous deeds." He works in all our lives, brothers and sisters; He has brought us all to birth and is acting now, His Spirit upon us, to see that we are born into His kingdom.

The great figures of the Old Testament, and especially John, are models from whom we can all learn, holy men whom we can certainly admire. But as our Lord has stated clearly, none of those born of woman can compare with those born into the kingdom of heaven. And so, let us take our strength for our journey from His prophets and from His Word; from His Spirit let us receive what we need in this life for our journey to His paradise. As strong as were Samson and John, so much stronger can we now be by His Body and His Blood, our holy food on this earth, and by His Spirit upon us.

29

December 20
(Is.7:10-14; Ps.24:1-7,10; Lk.1:26-38)

"Blessed are you among women."

"The virgin shall be with child and bear a son, and shall name Him Immanuel because 'God is with us.'" "The virgin's name was Mary." And she has given birth to the Savior.

"Who may stand in His holy place?" King David sings in our psalm. "Who can ascend the mountain of the Lord?" Clearly, Jesus is He. But just as clear is that we are all called to be as He, and that she has been, she who is so like Him – she that is indeed His Mother. It is she who "seeks the face of the God of Jacob," she "whose hands are sinless, whose heart is clean, who desires not what is vain…" and so she "receive[s] a blessing from the Lord," the greatest blessing: the Son of God.

Fearful is she in her great humility in the awesome presence of the Lord. Questioning is she in the perfect innocence of her consecrated virginity. But obedient only is she as she hears of the answer to her devout prayer for the pregnancy of her kinswoman, and so assumes the role most native to her, the one she has promised to fulfill: "the maidservant of the Lord."

O glorious Virgin Mary! You who worship so perfectly, so completely, the One who owns "the earth and its fullness, the world and those who dwell in it," and so bring that very fullness to us all, teach us to be like Jesus your Son, whom you imitate so absolutely, so naturally. Teach us to be as He who is flesh of your flesh. Be our Mother as well, that we might be brother and sister and mother to the Lord. Aid us in giving our total consent to the will of God. "O highly favored daughter! The Lord is with you." Pray He be with us now, too.

"With that the angel left." Upon receiving her wholehearted acceptance of her call, his mission is finished, and so he goes. Brothers and sisters, may the angel leave our presence so satisfied that the call of the Lord for our lives will be so well answered. Take heart that "nothing is impossible with God" and that as blessed as she is, so blessed does the Lord call you to be – if you but say "yes" to His word burning in your soul and lay down your life as has the Mother of God. Give the Lord your "yes" this day.

December 21
(Sgs.2:8-14 or Zep.3:14-18; Ps.33:1-3,11-12,20-21; Lk.1:39-45)

"Let me see you, let me hear your voice,
for your voice is sweet, and you are lovely."

"Who am I that the mother of my Lord should come to me?" – she who comes bearing the Christ child, she whose very voice magnifies the presence of the Lord. Listen to the witness of Elizabeth: "The moment your greeting sounded in my ears, the baby stirred in my womb for joy." Mary carries the Son of God not only in her womb, but in her soul; the Spirit working within her serves to inspire him who shall go before the Lord, and so she paves the road the forerunner of Jesus shall tread.

How one are mother and child! Never so evident has it been than in this passage from Holy Scripture. For Mary's voice carries the very presence of Jesus, and Elizabeth's ears convey that presence to her child. Here is that relationship of love depicted in our reading from the Song of Songs exemplified most clearly; here is the oneness of lover and beloved. And the loveliness of the lover becomes the loveliness of the beloved; the blessing of the Child becomes the blessing of the Mother – and in this love the earth brings forth its fruit.

"The fig tree puts forth its figs, and the vines, in bloom, give forth fragrance." "The Lord, your God, is in your midst," and He blesses all with His presence. He calls to your soul to come forth and know His love. "Springing across the mountains, leaping across the hills," He hastens to your side. He visits you. He visits you, speaking to your heart, calling you to arise and join Him. As Mary visits Elizabeth, "proceeding in haste into the hill country," to bring her Son to the son of Elizabeth and so producing joy in this unborn child's heart – so she brings her sweet Jesus to us this day, her voice speaking of His glory to the ears of Mother Church.

And so she becomes our Mother; and so she becomes our lover, for she bears the great lover of all souls to wed Himself to us as He is so perfectly wed to her. His sweetness comes to us through His "beautiful one," causing our hearts to rejoice at the sound of her voice and leading us to sing songs of praise to His holy name. Let us raise the joyful shout to our God!

A. II. Dec. 22.

December 22
(1Sm.1:24-28; 1Sm.2:1,4-8; Lk.1:46-56)

"His mercy is from age to age
on those who fear Him."

The Magnificat of Mary mirrors but, if I may say, far surpasses the Canticle of Hannah in beauty, in wonder, in grace... even as the perfection of the Son she bears far exceeds the blessing of the prophet Samuel. As Jesus brings to fulfillment the greatness of all who came before Him, so Mary's song expresses that perfection in the light of the same divine mercy.

31

Advent

Mercy indeed is infused in each line she utters under the power of the Spirit. Mercy and truth, a love completely open to the blessings of God is hers and is revealed in the words which fall like cleansing rain from her immaculate lips. She is blessed, she knows, and she shall be called blessed; for the truth, the Word of God, cannot be hidden, must be raised to meet the eyes and ears of all who seek His grace. For "the hungry He [gives] every good thing," and the lowly He raises "to high places." She is "His servant in her lowliness" and the joy of such blessing she cannot help but proclaim with all her being.

Hannah brings the child she has conceived in answer to her prayer, through the intercession of Eli – by the grace of God – and dedicates him to the Lord, leaving him at the temple. She, too, "exults in the Lord" for the fact that, in the Lord's will, "the barren wife bears seven sons"; for she who was thought sterile has borne the great man of God, Samuel. Mary, in her grateful appreciation for the blessing upon her, will not need to leave her child at the temple, for He has been conceived entirely of the Holy Spirit and is Himself the Temple of the Lord, wholly dedicated to the will of the Father from before the inception of time.

As the ancient Israelites found the direction and guidance of God through the ministry of Samuel, as by him they were led to serve the Lord their God, so now in this the end of the age we have Jesus, the perfect light of guidance through the grace and mercy of God, to lead us to the total service of the Lord that Mary embodies so well. God is "mighty," brothers and sisters; "holy is His name." Let us rejoice in Him who "has upheld Israel His servant, ever mindful of His mercy," and let us make that same blessed mercy the leaven that lifts us unto heaven. To Him let us sing our song of praise.

A. II. Dec. 23.

December 23
(Mal.3:1-4,23-24; Ps.25:4-5,8-10,14,Lk.21:28; Lk.1:57-66)

"His name is John."

Yes, "the hand of the Lord [was] upon him," whose name signifies the grace of God, who comes at the end of the age to turn men's hearts back to God, who prepares the way we must walk to find the instruction and purgation of the Lord.

We must be purified by "the refiner's fire." We must be purged of all dross "like gold or like silver that [we] may offer due sacrifice to the Lord," that we might be called children of the One God. The Day is coming; the Lord is returning to the temple, and we must be prepared to welcome Him – and so John is born, sent in the spirit of Elijah the prophet to cry out the way

32

in the wilderness of this world. By the Spirit of the Lord, he "shows sinners the way; he guides the humble to justice," leading them to the Son who stands ready in Truth to teach and to save. The people do well to wonder at the birth of this holy child, for well will they do to follow his exhortation, and come to praise of the living God.

This John leads us to something new, as even the originality of his name among his relatives signifies; he assists us in making the turn, the conversion to the New Covenant in the blood of Christ. From the Old and as a prophet of old, he leads us to the dawn of new light in this world. Jesus he comes to proclaim. Without this grace of God to be washed in the river of our sins, how could we stand on "the great and terrible day" of the Lord's coming? How could we bear His light, His fire?

"All the paths of the Lord are kindness and constancy toward those who keep His covenant and His decrees." Praise God we have the instruction of the Lord with us now to guide us to life everlasting; and thank God we have been made ready by "the messenger of the covenant" to stand in the light of that wisdom. The Lord teaches us now, brothers and sisters; the Lord is with us to instruct us in His way and, "like the fuller's lye," to make us white. Let us not make the grace of forgiveness John has wrought by the hand of God among us come to naught – let us listen closely now to the Word of God to which his voice has led us.

P.S. Re the Bible, the Word of God – a quote by St. Hippolytus from today's Office: "Sacred Scripture is God's gift to us and it should be understood in the way He intends: we should not do violence to it by interpreting it according to our own preconceived ideas."

A. II. Dec. 24.

December 24
(2Sm.7:1-5,8-12,14,16; Ps.89:2-5,27,29; Lk.1:67-79)

"Your house and your kingdom will endure forever."

The Lord builds a house for us; He is that House.

"Forever will I confirm your posterity and establish your throne for all generations," the Lord promises David, and accomplishes His word by Himself entering the line of the king. Thus "He has visited and ransomed His people. He has raised a horn of saving strength for us in the house of David His servant" in the Person of Jesus the Christ. And so we shall find "freedom from [our] sins" and "the kindness of our God" shall remain upon us.

"To guide our feet into the way of peace," Jesus has come. To bring "salvation from our enemies and from the hands of all our foes," He stands among us. Zechariah's joy at the birth of John, his son, is really the joy in the coming one, for whom John but "prepare[s] straight paths." The Spirit inspires this old priest to sing primarily of the fulfillment of the promise long held by his people, the promise of Abraham, the promise of David – the promise of finding fulfillment as God's chosen ones, held in His hand, in His temple, in His house, and protected from all harm while worshiping Him in spirit and in truth. This Jesus accomplishes.

And so, "we should serve Him devoutly, and through all our days, be holy in His sight," for no greater gift have we than this opportunity for holiness in the one true Son of God and in the House He establishes. Should not the Church be our home? Has not the Lord provided for the building of its walls? Has He not provided His own flesh and blood to be spread upon its altar? Has He not "fix[ed] a place for [His] people Israel... that they may dwell in their place without further disturbance"? Has He not said, "My kindness is established forever," and "in heaven... confirmed [His] faithfulness"? And should we not enter His house, enter His heaven, and praise His holy Name?

Here we stand, with His Word, with His Body and Blood. Here we have His teaching and His food. What more need we? And this day the Child who is the House of God approaches. Are we ready now for His coming?

II. CHRISTMAS

A. Octave of Christmas

Christmas, Midnight Mass
(Is.9:1-6; Ps.96:1-3,11-13; Ti.2:11-14; Lk.2:1-14)

"Today in the city of David
a savior has been born for you
who is Christ and Lord."

Here is the "infant wrapped in swaddling clothes and lying in a manger"; here is He who saves all from sin, born into our humble humanity.

Yes, "a child is born to us, a son is given us," and "upon His shoulder dominion rests." This little one wrapped in our own flesh is indeed named "Wonder-Counselor, God-Hero, Father-Forever, Prince of Peace. His dominion is vast and forever peaceful," for He rules all the earth with His loving justice. And so what should we do but "announce His salvation, day after day"? What can we who are overwhelmed with the joy of His presence in our midst do but "tell His glory among the nations; among all peoples, His wondrous deeds." For He has come for all nations and all people, to live in their hearts this day.

"Let the heavens be glad and the earth rejoice"; and let all mankind join the angels in their song of praise: "Glory to God in the highest and on earth peace to those on whom His favor rests." The Lord has come "to deliver us from all lawlessness and to cleanse for Himself a people as His own," to bring His surpassing peace to all souls set on His goodness and His glory. So, let us be "eager to do what is good," that we might be as He is, that we might share in His eternal peace.

To Bethlehem the Virgin came at the time of the census. There "the time came for her to have her child," He who is our Bread of Life. For He is enrolled among our number now; God has been made man – and nothing could give life to waiting souls like this miracle of new birth in our midst. And so, let us know the humble shepherd's awe; let us hear the word the angel brings, for he "proclaim[s] to [us] good news of great joy that will be for all people." Jesus our Savior is with us today.

Christmas Day
(Is.52:7-10; Ps.98:1-6; Heb.1:1-6; Jn.1:1-18)

"You are my Son; this day I have begotten you."

The coming of the One prophesied by Isaiah and hailed by John these many days is fulfilled in our midst at this blessed moment in time. And so in our dark world, the light that is God now shines.

"Hark! Your sentinels raise a cry, together they shout for joy, for they see directly, before their eyes, the Lord restoring Zion." To "all the ends of the earth" He makes "His salvation known: in the sight of the nations He has revealed His justice." For the Lord God walks among us now as man; He "who is the refulgence of His glory, the very imprint of His being," is now revealed, is now made flesh; "full of grace and truth," He appears in our midst.

"In the beginning was the Word, and the Word was with God, and the Word was God." And He through whom "all things came to be," who brought life, "the light of the human race," now shines – and now we come to know Him; now we hear the Word spoken to our ears... now we can say, "The Word became flesh and made His dwelling among us." The Word no longer hidden, God no longer speaks "in partial and various ways," but now "through the Son" the fullness of truth, the blessing of peace, is upon us.

"How beautiful upon the mountains are the feet of Him," for He comes "announcing peace... announcing salvation." No longer need we wander in darkness, wondering, *Where is our God?* He is here. He is Jesus. He washes all darkness from our minds, He accomplishes "purification from sins," and He sits "at the right hand of the Majesty on high," giving power to be like Him, "to become children of God, to those who believe in His name, "who were born not by natural generation nor by human choice nor by a man's decision but of God." Come, see and know the transcendent glory standing in our midst.

And so, what have we to do but rejoice? Though "no one has ever seen God," though He has seemed to us beyond understanding, yet "the only Son... has revealed Him." So let us "sing joyfully before the King, the Lord" "with the harp and melodious song." Let us "break into song" and "sing praise." For He whom "all the angels of God worship" has come for our salvation, and our Christmas should be only merry.

God be with you, brothers and sisters. Jesus love you.

C. Oct. Sun. (A)

Holy Family (A)
(Sir.3:2-6,12-14; Ps.128:1-5; Col.3:12-21; Mt.2:13-15,19-23)

"Let the peace of Christ control your hearts,
the peace into which you were also called in one body."

Christmas

A man is a man, a woman is a woman, and children are children – this does not change with time or culture. All are called to be one in the love and sacrifice of Christ; all are one holy family.

Why do we find it necessary to make excuses for Holy Scripture and the "patriarchal family pattern" it reflects and "the subordinationist family ethic of the Biblical culture" (from the commentary of the missal from which I take today's readings)? How is it we have lost the beauty of Paul's words on the complementary nature of the conjugal relationship? How is it the family has become bereft of Christ?

One would think Paul states, "Husbands, beat your wives," instead of "Husbands, love your wives, and avoid any bitterness toward them," by the way his text is avoided like the plague. Why such ignorance of what is actually present in Scripture? And if the Scripture is perverted, why do we not "in all wisdom... teach and admonish one another," instead of casting the wisdom of the Lord from our presence, or rationalizing it away. Is it a sin for a wife to be submissive, to respect her husband; for children to be obedient toward their parents; for the husband and father to lay down his life for his family? Is power to be defined by the dictates of the world, or by the cross? Do we desire to control, or to love?

"Blessed is everyone who fears the Lord, who walks in His ways!" Here is the key to our roles, in the exclamation of our psalmist. "Do everything in the name of the Lord Jesus, giving thanks to God the Father through Him," Paul summarizes his teaching. Hear in his letter the call to "compassion, kindness, humility, gentleness, and patience, bearing with one another and forgiving one another," even as the Lord has done with us. Be led by the Word of the Lord and His instruction and guidance. You, husbands, do you reflect Joseph's obedience to the Word of God brought by the angel? Do you care for your families as God calls? Are you mothers like Mary, moving according to the protective hand upon your hearth, your house? And children, do you honor your father and mother's authority over you as Jesus, who, though the Son of God, humbled Himself to be the child in this Holy Family? Let us all be as Christ – honoring, obeying, humbling ourselves... in a word, loving one another as He has loved us. Then we will be of the family of God.

C. Oct. Sun. (B)

Holy Family (B)
(Gn.15:1-6,21:1-3; Ps.105:1-9; Heb.11:8,11-12,17-19; Lk.2:22-40)

"The child grew and became strong, filled with wisdom,
and the favor of God was upon Him."

What child is this of whom Simeon the prophet, filled with the Holy Spirit, declares to the Lord, "My eyes have seen your salvation, which you prepared in the sight of all peoples," even as he holds Jesus in his arms? This indeed is He who is the "light for revelation to the Gentiles, and glory for [His] people Israel"; this indeed is the fulfillment of the promise made to Abraham, foreshadowed in the birth of Isaac, by whom Abraham's descendants would be "as numerous as the stars in the sky and as countless as the sands on the seashore." "Binding for a thousand generations," forever, was the covenant the Lord "entered into with Abraham and by His oath to Isaac," and now that covenant is brought to perfection in the sight of Simeon and Anna; now "all who were awaiting the redemption of Jerusalem" could rejoice and "give thanks to the Lord," for to the temple had come the Christ of God: here is the Messiah.

"Rejoice, O hearts that seek the Lord!" for in Jesus His Son you shall find Him. Though raised in a humble family in the town of Nazareth, this is He who raises all His chosen unto heaven, who brings salvation to His people. And so rejoice indeed "you descendants of Abraham, His servants, sons of Jacob, His chosen ones!" for even as "there came forth from one man, himself as good as dead," innumerable descendants, even as the Lord fulfilled His promise to Abraham by the birth of Isaac, so the Lord's promise to Simeon "that he should not see death before he had seen the Christ of the Lord" is fulfilled in all our midst even this day. Listen to the prophet's proclamation: the light has come! We are no longer in darkness, no longer in mournful anticipation. And so with Anna we should come forward now and speak "about the child" to all who will listen, to all who long to hear the good news of God.

Brothers and sisters, let the Lord grow in our midst. In this Holy Family that is His Church let Him be nurtured and known. For God's favor rests upon Him alone and by no other child does salvation come. Today He is presented to all waiting hearts.

Holy Family (C)
(1Sm.1:1:20-22,24-28; Ps.84:2-3,5-6,9-10; 1Jn.3:1-2,21-24; Lk.2:41-52)

"Did you not know that I must be in my Father's house?"

If Hannah says of Samuel, "As long as he lives, he shall be dedicated to the Lord" even as she leaves her son with Eli in the temple, should not Jesus be equally dedicated to God, being His true Son? If as John rightfully says of all those who live in God's love and follow His commandments, "We are God's children now," how much greater a child of God is He who serves to make us children? And so, where should He be but the temple of the Lord?

Christmas

But Jesus' parents do not look for Him there, indeed are "astonished" to find Him there – and thus perplexed at His answer to them – because they have no word that He will be like Samuel, that they are to leave Him in "the midst of the teachers." Surely Mary knows of her own kinship with Hannah, for this is indicated clearly in her Magnificat, which mirrors so closely Hannah's own canticle of praise upon conceiving *her* son. But that Jesus should be separated from them at this time, that He should in essence begin His ministry, begin plying the leaders of the people with revelatory questions so that "all who heard Him were astounded at His understanding and His answers," now, at twelve years of age, is not known to them. Thirty is the customary age for the start of one's ministry, is it not? And their Son has not even reached His bar mitzvah yet!

It must be noted that Jesus gives place to the customs of the race. We are told "He went down with [Joseph and Mary] and came to Nazareth, and was obedient to them." Though certainly the Son of God is prepared to teach even as He begins to talk, yet He does not remain in the temple at this time. He is obedient. And obedient particularly to Mary, who shall indeed indicate to Him the start of His ministry, at Cana. And He shall be obedient there to her, too, even though He says then that it is not His time.

The Son must be in the Father's house, for more than any of God's children His "soul yearns and pines for the courts of the Lord. [His] flesh and [His] heart cry out for the living God." His heart is ever "set upon the pilgrimage," for in the temple is His home. But the truly Beloved Child of God remains among us in our mundane lives, taking the cross of earthly existence upon Himself, enduring all for the sake of God's children. And through His Mother's intercession even "Jesus advanced in wisdom and age and favor before God and man." So may we all. So may we all be so obedient, so prepared for the Father's House.

C. Oct. Dec. 26.

St. Stephen
(Acts 6:8-10,7:54-59; Ps.31:3-4,6-8,17,21; Mt.10:17-22)

"They proved no match for the wisdom and spirit
with which he spoke."

The world cannot stand up to the Word of God; even death has no power over those who trust themselves to His Spirit.

A model of faith is Stephen. A perfect trust in the Lord made this martyr shine before the persecution of men. He made the Lord his "rock of refuge" and so the Lord did "lead and guide" him even unto heaven, hidden in "the shelter of [His] promise from the plottings of men."

40

It is this trust Jesus speaks of in our gospel when He warns His apostles beforehand of the persecution which awaits them. He tells them that when they are dragged before rulers to "give witness... on [His] account": "Do not worry about what you will say or how you will say it... the Spirit of your Father will be speaking in you." And it is this trust, even unto death, that Stephen exemplifies so perfectly.

David echoes Jesus' words on the cross in our psalm: "Into your hands I commend my spirit," and Stephen lives them in our first reading. While being stoned to death he prays, "Lord Jesus, receive my spirit" (and proceeds to forgive those who kill him). And so this feast of our first martyr follows our celebration of the birth of our Lord, for it is in this world we are handed over to death, and it is in this world we must suffer in love. Entirely we must trust ourselves to the care of God to find the vision of heaven – "I see an opening in the sky, and the Son of Man standing at God's right hand" – which becomes Stephen's own.

The words we speak, if they are blessed by God, will bring us inevitably to heaven. If it is the Spirit who works in us, what need we fear? For what is more powerful than He? Where is greater truth to be found? And so, to whom else should we turn? "Whoever holds out till the end will escape death," brothers and sisters. Though "hated by all" for our love of Jesus, if we continue ever to love even those who hate us, His Spirit will lift us unto Him and provide all we need, in words and works, to conquer the evil of this world.

May the sweet blood of Jesus cover all His children and bless their witness to Him.

C. Oct. Dec. 27.

St. John
(1Jn.1:1-4; Ps.97:1-2,5-6,11-12; Jn.20:2-8)

"He saw and believed."

And "the eternal life that was present to the Father and became visible to us," which John now proclaims, is Jesus Christ the only Son of God, risen from the dead and present to us now even as He sits with the Father.

John has seen Him. He has believed in Him. His "hands have touched" Him and so he "proclaim[s] the word of life" made so real in his midst. What else could he do but declare that which burns in his heart? What else could be the Evangelist's desire but to share the blessing he has known as "the one Jesus loved"? For brimming with love this apostle is, and only in writing of this joy, only proclaiming it to the world and seeing others enter into such selfsame blessing will make his joy complete. To this he has been called by the Lord.

41

Christmas

"Light dawns for the just," David declares, as if in his psalm to presage the coming of Christ and John's own words on the coming of Light to this earth. And indeed the just shall see Him, and gladness shall be "for the upright of heart." For all the just shall "be glad in the Lord... and give thanks to His holy name," for their souls drink deeply of the salvation in their midst; they know Him whom their hearts love. They see Him, and believe.

And I note the special significance "the piece of cloth which had covered the head" of Jesus – which was "not lying with the wrappings, but rolled up in a place by itself," as John tells us in his gospel – seems to have as a catalyst to belief. John had seen the wrappings before entering the tomb, but not this cloth, and it is when he enters he sees and believes. It is as if the Lord left it neatly rolled up in a place by itself to indicate to them that He had not "been taken from the tomb" by robbers, as Mary Magdalene (another beloved of Christ) seems to fear. Why would a thief take time to do such a thing? And so, Jesus' touch is upon the cloth.

"All peoples see His glory" now, brothers and sisters. By the witness of John and all the apostles, eyes are opened to His presence. Let us see Him with John; let us touch Him... and let us know His touch upon our hearts, and so continue to proclaim His glory.

C. Oct. Dec. 28.

Holy Innocents
(1Jn.1:5-2:2; Ps.124:2-5,7-8; Mt.2:13-18)

"The blood of His Son Jesus cleanses us from all sin."

And as martyrs of the Church, these innocent children slaughtered by Herod participate in the pouring forth of the blood of Christ.

"Out of Egypt I have called my son." What does the prophet mean but that by the only Son all shall be redeemed of their sins – that out of sin all are called, all are drawn by the Lord? "Broken was the snare, and we were freed" when the child was born, when He died upon the cross.

And that death is begun already in the slaughter of the holy innocents, whom indeed we commemorate as martyrs this day. In their sacrifice the cross is already known, though the Child Jesus be but a boy. No greater evil, no greater act of sin could be than Herod's cruel decree to "massacre all the boys two years and under in Bethlehem and its environs." And in the "sobbing and loud lamentation" rising from the town where Jesus was born we hear presaged our own cry, our own beating of our breasts as we gaze upon the crucified body of God's Holy One.

It is sin that brings the slaughter of the innocent children, and it is sin that causes Christ's crucifixion. And we are participants in that sin, brothers

42

and sisters. "If we say, 'We have never sinned,' we make Him a liar and His word finds no place in us." For He has come because of the sin which encompasses mankind, to redeem us from its sentence of death. And the blessed apostle John makes clear that we are indeed all participants in sin, and if we deny this fact we make His sacrifice null for our lives and continue to walk in darkness. We must all bewail our sins and the horrors they have wrought, and from their snare we shall be released – else the "raging waters" will overwhelm us.

The souls of the innocents slaughtered by the evil king have been preserved, for their "help is in the name of the Lord, who made heaven and earth." Our souls, too, shall be redeemed "if we acknowledge our sin," our complicity in evil. For "He who is just can be trusted to forgive our sins and cleanse us from every wrong" if we are but able to see we are not innocent as He, or they.

C. Oct. Dec. 29.

Fifth Day
(1Jn.2:3-11; Ps.96:1-3,5-6,11; Lk.2:22-35)

"The way we can be sure we are in union with Him
is if one who claims to abide in Him
conducts himself just as He did."

"The darkness is over and the real light begins to shine," and we must live in that light.

"My eyes have witnessed your saving deed displayed for all peoples to see," declares Simeon in his prophecy over the Christ child. "In accord with the dictate in the law of the Lord," though He Himself is God, Jesus is dutifully brought to the temple by Mary and Joseph to be "consecrated to the Lord" as every first-born male must. And there the "just and pious" Simeon who so patiently "awaited the consolation of Israel," the coming of "the Anointed of the Lord," takes the child "in his arms" and blesses God for His gift, His mercy.

Learn from these the attitude all must have. In their faithful observance of the commands of God and the inspiration of the Spirit, they fulfill His Word. And so light dawns for us and we know of its presence in our midst. Now we must continue to "announce His salvation, day after day tell His glory among the nations; among all peoples, His wondrous deeds." Our deeds must mirror His deeds; His light, "a revealing light to the Gentiles, the glory of [His] people Israel," we must shine. The sign has come; the new commandment which has been of old must now be realized in each of us. As a sword has pierced the heart of the Blessed Mother, so it shall pierce the heart of everyone who unites himself to the Blessed Child, who follows in the steps of our blessed Lord.

"The thoughts of many hearts [shall] be laid bare." There will be no hiding from this light that has come. If you think you can claim to know Him "without keeping His commandments," without conducting yourself "just as He did," you must know that your lie will be exposed. "The man who continues in the light is the one who loves his brother." Only this will save you, for only love is of light; hatred is only of darkness, and in the Lord there is no darkness.

Let us join with Simeon in proclaiming His salvation. Let us join with David in singing of the "splendor and majesty" of the Lord. "Praise and grandeur are in His sanctuary." And let us do this principally with our very lives, becoming as the temple of God who is presented to us this day.

C. Oct. Dec. 30.

Sixth Day
(1Jn.2:12-17; Ps.96:7-11; Lk.2:36-40)

"The world with its seductions is passing away
but the man who does God's will endures forever."

Upon what is your eye fixed? Do you seek the Lord as has Anna these many years, "constantly in the temple, worshiping day and night in fasting and prayer," or are you seduced by "carnal allurements, enticements for the eye, the life of empty show." Indeed, "all these are from the world" (and what appropriate description of the extreme vanity which grasps the world in this day), and indeed are all passing away into the nothingness from which they spring. And those whose hearts are fixed upon them shall pass away with them, while he whose heart seeks the Lord passes to the eternal life of heaven.

"Give to the Lord the glory due His name!" David exclaims in his psalm today, and, yes, much glory is due Him. "Through His Name [our] sins have been forgiven"; through Him we "have conquered the evil one." Do you know "Him who is from the beginning"? Does "the word of God [remain] in you"? Is it His love you have, or love for the world, wherein His love finds no place to dwell? "The Lord is King," brothers and sisters. He alone is worthy of our worship, worthy of our attention, worthy of our praise. Waste not your breath on the empty illusions of this passing world.

Anna "gave thanks to God and talked about the child to all who looked forward to the deliverance of Jerusalem." Do you look forward to such deliverance? Do you care to hear of the glory of the Lord spoken of by this prophetess? Or have you better things to do? What sporting event, television program, or party takes precedence in your life?

We live in a vain world, brothers and sisters. And that vanity permeates this modern society, presenting itself as an accepted good. It is not easy to conquer the hold such illusions cast upon our waiting eyes – only in Jesus will you find the strength to overcome these seductions. As "the child grew in size and strength, filled with wisdom, and the grace of God… upon Him," so will you learn to make progress as you "tremble before Him"; so will you grow in His will to eternal life, as you turn away from the carnality of this life. Keep your eyes upon His light, rising from the darkness.

Seventh Day
(1Jn.2:18-21; Ps.96:1-2,11-13; Jn.1:1-18)

"The Word became flesh and made His dwelling among us."

And we must dwell with Him, remaining in His light, walking in His way. "Through Him all things came into being," and we who have come into being by Him, "who believe in His name," must "become children of God."

In our first reading, John warns against the antichrists who come in this "final hour" to lead astray all those not founded in truth. Elsewhere he warns against anyone who does not recognize Jesus as the Son of God, as the Christ come among us. Certainly there are more than a few antichrists today, looking to distract believers from "the Holy One." But as John says, "All knowledge is yours": if we believe in Jesus, we have the truth written within us. Yet we must beware of faltering, for "no lie has anything in common with the truth." Remain in His Church.

Our psalm of David encourages us to "exult before the Lord," to "sing to the Lord; bless His name." And well we should this holy day to know of the Christ that has come "to rule the world with justice." The Word has become flesh and left His flesh and His Spirit with the Church He has founded on the apostles – great is the joy of those who find their home there.

And in our gospel we hear John's beautiful and clear explication of the divinity of Jesus, the Word ever in God's presence from the beginning, the Word that is "God." There are pseudo-religions that change the Evangelist's words to say that the Word was "a god"; such is the work of the antichrists spoken of by Paul. For only in the clear recognition of Jesus as "God the only Son," only in the unequivocal proclamation of His divinity – that He is *God* – is salvation found. For this is Truth, Truth brings light, and the light has no discourse with the darkness of lies.

Come to Him who has come unto you, brothers and sisters. Seeing Him you see God and know God. And knowing God you "know the truth" and

Christmas

so exult in the joy of His presence in His Word, in His Sacraments, in His Church… in His love. Praised be the Lord and His dwelling among us.

Oct. Jan. 1. (A,B,C)

Mary, Mother of God
(Octave of Christmas)
(Nm.6:22-27; Ps.67:2-3,5-6,8; Gal.4:4-7; Lk.2:16-21)

"The shepherds returned, glorifying and praising God
for all they had heard and seen,
just as it had been told to them."

The blessing of God, His holy Son, was upon the shepherds, and it is upon us all. For "God sent His Son, born of a woman" that His "way be known upon earth," "that we might receive adoption as sons." And what greater blessing could man know than to fulfill his call as son of the living God?

We are blessed, brothers and sisters, and we should proclaim it as the shepherds. The blessing invoked upon the people by Aaron has been realized in the birth of the Son. Through Him "the Lord let[s] His face shine upon [us]" – this is His grace come. And how else but in haste should we travel to Him? How quickly we should arrive at His side. And how amazed all should be upon hearing the blessings we have known, at the hand of our God.

Mary is she who is truly blessed, and we honor especially today she "who kept all these things, reflecting on them in her heart." For so obedient was she to God's will that He was "conceived in [her] womb" and made flesh in our sight. So, let us thank her today for the blessing she has brought into our midst. As we are now sons of the Father with the Spirit of the Son "crying out, 'Abba, Father!'" in our hearts, so we are sons of Mary, too, for the Lord's divinity cannot be separated from His humanity – the two meet as one in Jesus Christ. This is our great blessing.

From "an infant lying in the manger" shall come the salvation of our race, and the Mother of this renewed race, consecrated to God in Him who is "named Jesus," we commemorate with our hearts and our voices in praise this holy day. May she now be the instrument by which "the Lord bless[es]" and "keep[s]" us; may she pray this day that "His face shine upon us." And may all her children be one in the blessing of Christ, her Son. Amen.

Second Sunday after Christmas...
(when not Epiphany)
(Sir.24:1-2,8-12; Ps.147:12-15,19-20; Eph.1:3-6,15-18; Jn.1:1-18)

"May the eyes of your hearts be enlightened,
that you may know what is the hope that belongs to His call."

The Creator commanded Wisdom: "Among my chosen put down your roots." She dwells in Jerusalem; in Israel she makes her home. And who is of Jerusalem but he who is blessed "in Christ with every spiritual blessing in the heavens," those whom He "chose in Him, before the foundation of the world" – with Wisdom who was created "before all ages, in the beginning" – "to be holy and without blemish before Him." And that "true light, which enlightens everyone," the Lord, the Word of God which shines like Wisdom as "the light of the human race," is now our own. For "those who did accept Him He gave power to become children of God," and so now He yet makes "His dwelling among us... full of grace and truth."

"Glorify the Lord, O Jerusalem; praise your God, O Zion. For He has strengthened the bars of your gates; He has blessed your children within you." So our psalmist does sing of the glory of God made known to Jacob in the gracious command of love He has given them, and now fulfilled in their midst in the Person of Jesus. Here is the Wisdom of God; here is the pure effulgence of His grace. May indeed our hearts be enlightened to know the hope to which we are called.

I pray that "the Father of glory may give you a Spirit of wisdom and revelation resulting in knowledge of Him." May Paul's words invoked upon the Ephesians be your own, and may you be His own children in the light of His grace. Wisdom will lead you home. The Word sown in your souls will bring you to life in Him.

B. From January 2 to Epiphany

January 2
(1Jn.2:22-28; Ps.98:1-4; Jn.1:19-28)

"Remain in the Son and in the Father."

In our gospel John the Baptist tells the priests and Levites sent by the Pharisees, "There is... one who is to come after me – the strap of whose sandal I am not worthy to unfasten." This Messiah has come, "The Lord has

47

made His salvation known: in the sight of the nations He has revealed His justice," David proclaims in our psalm, and continues to invite us to sing praise of Him. It is the anointing that comes from Jesus that John, in our first reading, encourages us to hold on to, for it is true and leads invariably to the Father of all.

We must come to the Father; we must find ourselves in the presence of all truth, in the hands of our Creator, who loves us beyond all telling. And the way to the presence of the Father, in whom we find our true home, is Jesus the Christ. He is the Son and the only one who can lead us to the Father, for He and the Father are inextricably one. We cannot deny the Sonship of Jesus, His oneness with the Father – that He is the Christ, upon whom all true anointing rests – and come to know God. Jesus is the means the Father provides to come to Him; it is through Him alone we find the promise of eternal life. We must "remain in Him," that we may "not retreat in shame at His coming."

Those who do not believe in Jesus, who do not recognize Him as the only Son and so only way to the Father, are not to be persecuted – but they are not to be believed. Jesus is all. Those who know Him know this; they indeed have His anointing in their hearts. This "anointing teaches [us] about all things and is true." It is this knowledge of His salvation, of His glory, which John instructs us to remember: His Word grows in our hearts. But again, this Word is not a weapon for the persecution and destruction of others – it is the means for the manifestation of light.

Remain in Jesus, brothers and sisters, and eternal life with the Father will be assured you.

C. to Epiph. Jan. 3.

January 3
(1Jn.2:29-3:6; Ps.98:1,3-6; Jn.1:29-34)

"Look there!
The Lamb of God who takes away the sin of the world!"

"This is God's chosen One." This is He upon whom "the Spirit descend[s]" – who takes away our sins and makes us pure by His own baptism "with the Holy Spirit." He who walks with Him walks in holiness, for "everyone who acts in holiness has been begotten by Him" – we have become "children of God" because we have now the grace of the only Son.

Listen to the manner in which the Baptist "sing[s] joyfully before the King, the Lord" in our gospel today: "I saw the Spirit descend like a dove from the sky, and it came to rest on Him." How like music, like "the harp and melodious song," is his witness to the Lord Jesus Christ. His exclamation of Jesus as the holy Lamb of God, offered as a sacrifice pure

48

and undefiled, resounds to the ends of the earth more eloquently and with greater power than "the trumpets and the sound of the horn" of which David sings in our psalm. Here is the voice proclaiming the Truth, the message our ears have so longed to hear.

"The very reason [John] came baptizing with water was that [Jesus] might be revealed to Israel," and "the reason [Jesus] revealed Himself was to take away sins" – all this for our salvation. Yes, brothers and sisters, "in Him there is nothing sinful." And we must be like Him. Insofar as we sin, we have "not seen Him or known Him." Insofar as a man "keeps himself pure, as He is pure," he is His child, knowing Him most intimately, and may exclaim in wonder with John the evangelist: "What love the Father has bestowed on us in letting us be called children of God!"

All sin and struggle with sin all the while they are on earth. There are many times when we must admit that we do not see Him or know Him in order for Him to be revealed in our lives, in order for us to find His blessed purity. We must confess our sins that we might sing His praise. But all the while the Son is with us, the Lamb intercedes to remove our sins. And always we must look to Him whom the Baptist proclaimed to be "what we are," to become "like Him" when His light comes to its fullness and His Spirit is all we know.

January 4
(1Jn.3:7-10; Ps.98:1,3,7-9; Jn.1:35-42)

"When Jesus turned around and noticed them following Him,
He asked them, 'What are you looking for?'"

Brothers and sisters, what Jesus asks the first two disciples He asks each of us who follow in their wake. What do we seek? Why are we following Him? What is it we hope to find at the place where He stays?

David makes clear in our psalm that the Son of God, "His holy arm," has been revealed in our midst – in "wondrous deeds" He "comes to rule the earth." "The world and those who dwell in it" should resound with joy. Him whom John the Baptist points out in no uncertainty is with us now. There is no other whom we should follow. And so we do. And so we come to Him each day, to receive our daily bread. Seeing where He lodges, we come to stay with Him.

But what does the Lord see when He looks upon us? Does He stay with us? When Andrew brought his brother Simon to Jesus, He "looked at him and said, 'You are Simon, son of John; your name shall be Cephas (which is rendered Peter).'" Jesus upon looking at Peter sees the Rock on which He will build His Church. Peter's holiness, the strength he has in God and for

49

God, is evident to the Lord. Jesus knows what Peter seeks, and both have found what they are looking for. Is it upon our hearts as well to find the holiness of heaven, to become one with the Son of God?

"The man who acts in holiness is holy indeed, even as the Son is holy," but "the man who sins belongs to the devil." Holiness or sin? Jesus or the devil? The choice is clear, and must be evident in our lives. "No one begotten of God acts sinfully" and "no one whose actions are unholy belongs to God." The first letter of John, our first reading, could not more simply state our call in the Lord: to be holy, not to sin... to love our brothers and sisters well – to be as Jesus, the Son most holy.

Jesus will turn and see us; His eyes are upon us now. What does He see as He looks upon your heart? What is your answer to His question, "What are you looking for?" Let His dwelling be all you seek.

C. to Epiph. Jan. 5.

January 5
(1Jn.3:11-21; Ps.100:1-5; Jn.1:43-51)

"We should love one another."

In our gospel, "first [Jesus] came upon Philip" – whose name means "love" – and invited him to follow Him. Love brought with him one in whom "there is no guile," and he (Nathanael) declared openly to the Lord: "You are the Son of God; you are the king of Israel." And so we must all be of love, and be without deceit. We must all "know that the Lord is God; He made us, His we are; His people, the flock He tends." The Lord must find us all at peace "under the fig tree" with consciences that have "nothing to charge us with." And great things wrought by the hand of God we shall see before our eyes.

"The Lord is good," and we must be like Him. The Lord is of love, and loving as He does we pass "from death to life": "The way we came to understand love was that He laid down His life for us; we too must lay down our lives for our brothers." In our first reading today, how well John speaks of the love all need. Here is the voice of a man, an apostle in the Spirit of Christ, who loves "in deed and in truth," and since he does "not merely talk about it," but lives it, his words are alive with that truth. Love. This is "the message [we] heard from the beginning." This laying down our lives is our guiding light leading us to the eternal life of heaven.

And so we should "serve the Lord with gladness." We should "come before Him with joyful song." We should declare openly that He is God, as our love leads us to do. His "kindness endures forever"; yes, His love is for eternity, and we must come to share in that great gift of love. "The man who does not love is among the living dead," but he who loves lives forever.

The world will hate us because it is not of love; but all the more we should be encouraged to love, to die to the hatred the world brings and find our place in peace under our fig tree with the Lord who is love itself.

Let us love and be of love, brothers and sisters, and we shall live forever with our Lord and the angels of heaven.

January 6
(1Jn.5:5-13; Ps.147:12-15,19-20; Mk.1:7-11)

"God gave us eternal life,
and this life is in His Son."

How reassuring John is to us who believe – "I have written this to you to make you realize that you possess eternal life" – for how easily we can forget the grace that is ours "in the name of the Son of God." How sure he is. How clear in his explanation. How loving. One has little reason to wonder why he was beloved of the Lord, for this love bleeds in all his words and leads us to that love of Christ that is eternal life.

The Father's witness has been given clearly, "You are my beloved Son. On you my favor rests." Mark, too, makes certain that Jesus is the Son of God. How can we forget the words of the Father? And how can we forget the blood He has shed on our behalf, and the water that flows like baptism from His side? "It is the Spirit who testifies to this, and the Spirit is truth." If you have the Spirit dwelling in you, you know this – it sets your heart on fire, and is indeed as the breath of life. How can we know anything but eternal life when baptized in the Holy Spirit by the Lord?

"He has granted you peace in your borders," our psalmist proclaims; and in the Spirit we have only peace – nothing lacking rest can enter there. And now "with the best of wheat He fills [us]," now that we receive His body in the Eucharist. What bread indeed we eat! Here is the bread of life. We have His Word born in the Spirit spoken to our ears, and on His very presence we sup. Such witnesses! What more need we to believe?

"Jesus is the Son of God," brothers and sisters. This alone you need remember. When all else fails and darkness pervades, know that Jesus is with you and bringing you to life.

January 7
(1Jn.5:14-21; Ps.149:1-6,9; Jn.2:1-12)

"He hears us whenever we ask for anything according to His will."

In our gospel, the waiters come to Mary; their misfortune is witnessed by her compassionate heart: "They have no more wine," she tells her Son. She knows what she is saying, she knows what she is asking... and Jesus knows, too. And though He seems not prepared to answer her concern (you see, our concern is her concern, and she makes it His), yet she says to the servants standing by the words which perhaps best exemplify the Mother's relationship to the Son – "Do whatever He tells you."

Has Jesus a choice now? Can He rebuff her request to "reveal His glory"? It is a miracle she asks for the benefit of those in need, and the Lord cannot turn her down. Do you see this? Do you understand the significance of this scene, here at the very inception of Jesus' ministry, especially those who doubt our Blessed Mother's intercessory power with her Lord, her Son? And do you think the power for finding answer to prayer with her beloved Jesus, the Son of God, is somehow shortened in ensuing days? Does death conquer it? Is she no longer the blessed of all generations? Has this blessed generation come to an end?

"We know that He hears us whenever we ask" and that "what we have asked Him for is ours." This is our confidence in God's compassion and love. And we know too that the Blessed Mother stands beside our Lord and prepares the prayers we would offer Him, putting them into the words, the Spirit, we cannot express. If we give them all to her, they will all be made effective, and we will taste of "the choice wine" which has been kept in store for us until these latter days.

Through this miracle at Cana "His disciples believed in Him." Here He offers them a sign of His divinity – here they find "discernment to recognize the One who is true... the true God and eternal life." And so the wedding feast truly begins. And so we "praise His name in the festive dance" and "sing praise to Him with timbrel and harp." "The children of Zion rejoice in their king," for He has answered their deepest prayer: here in our midst is the Son of God.

C. Epiphany. (A,B,C)

C. Epiphany to Baptism of the Lord

Epiphany of the Lord
(Is.60:1-6; Ps.72:1-2,7-8,10-13; Eph.3:2-3a,5-6; Mt.2:1-12)

"They were overjoyed at seeing the star,
and on entering the house
they saw the child with Mary His Mother."

And so our prophecy of Isaiah and our psalm of David come to pass: "Raise your eyes and look about; they all gather and come to you... the riches of the sea shall be emptied out before you, the wealth of nations shall be brought to you." And "the kings of Tarshish and the Isles shall offer gifts; the kings of Arabia and Seba shall bring tribute. All kings shall pay Him homage, all nations shall serve Him." And so we have the revelation made known to the Apostle Paul and all His holy ones: "The Gentiles are now coheirs, members of the same body, and copartners in the promise in Christ Jesus through the gospel."

Yes, the Light of Jerusalem has come, and it draws the ends of the earth by its radiance. Here is the star which rises in our midst; here is the true light which shines upon all men. And all men are drawn to it – none can deny its brightness before us, its truth and its glory. And who is this king but the One of "justice" and "profound peace"? Who is He but the One who "shall have pity for the lowly and the poor; the lives of the poor He shall save." And so all must make themselves poor before Him, laying their gifts at His blessed feet.

Today we celebrate the coming of Light to the nations, the manifestation of Jesus Christ to this world covered in darkness. And we find our hope and our joy in Him as did the magi two thousand years ago. For He continues to reveal Himself to our hearts. He continues to show His peace and justice to all who look for His coming. Let our eyes be raised to the heavens and our hearts be diligent in seeking Him, and we will be led to His crib. There the Mother holds Him in her arms; there before such beauty we should empty our souls in adoration of His blessed presence, like these magi who "prostrated themselves and did Him homage." Then we shall rise fulfilled.

C. to Bapt. Mon.

Monday
(1Jn.3:22-4:6; Ps.2:7-8,10-11; Mt.4:12-17,23-25)

"Every spirit that acknowledges Jesus Christ come in the flesh belongs to God."

And for every spirit that acknowledges Him, He answers all prayers: "Whatever we ask we shall receive at God's hands." "Ask of me and I will give you the nations for an inheritance..." And so, when "they carried to [Jesus] all those afflicted with various diseases and racked with pain," He heard this prayer made in faith, made in the belief that He could do this, and as Matthew so simply and wonderfully states, "He cured them all." They had listened to His preaching: "Reform your lives! The kingdom of heaven is at hand." They accepted it, humbly, taking no offense at His words and His actions – but believing in Him. And so He could perform such wonders for them, He whose spirit is true; and so "on those who inhabit a land overshadowed by death light has arisen."

And now we should "give heed" and "take warning"; now we should "put the spirits to the test to see if they belong to God." Now we must clearly acknowledge Jesus as the Christ and know what John tells us, "There is in you One greater than there is in the world," and follow that Spirit within us. Are we "keeping His commandments and doing what is pleasing in His sight"? Do we "remain in Him"? He is never far away and He will hear all of our prayers and cure us of all ills, if we but believe in Him, if we but heed His teaching – if we reform our lives. We show our belief in Him when we follow His commandments, and we follow His commandments when we reform our lives. Thus we prove that we speak His language; in our love we reveal His Spirit in us.

"The Lord said to me, 'You are my son, this day I have begotten you.'" Even in our psalm are spoken the words of the Father to Jesus; and they are spoken to us, if we believe that He is the Christ. This is the salvation the Father offers; it is for us to accept it and live it. For a greater gift we cannot expect, more love He could not show – this is His Son, this is God... believe in Him. There is nothing else you need seek.

C. to Bapt. Tues.

Tuesday
(1Jn.4:7-10, Ps.72:1-4,7-8,11; Mk.6:34-44)

"Justice shall flower in His days, and profound peace,
till the moon be no more."

Our psalm (of Solomon, the king of peace and wisdom) relates the infinite justice of God, He who "defend[s] the afflicted among the people" and "save[s] the children of the poor." Such is the judgment of our God, who "rule[s] from sea to sea, and from the River to the ends of the earth": His perfect justice He showers upon all.

And how is this justice effected? It is already evident from what we have said, from what our psalmist has sung of His Name, and our letter from John leaves no question – "God is love." His ultimate justice and love have been "revealed in our midst in this way: He sent His only Son to the world that we might have life through Him." In sending Jesus "as an offering for our sins," His perfect love and perfect justice meet and kiss and become one. He bleeds for us, and so our sins are forgiven.

And what clearer proof that we all "have life through Him" is shown in our gospel, in which Jesus feeds the masses. First He teaches them with the Word "at great length." Having pity on them, He feeds their souls with Truth. But His pity does not end there – His concern extends to the physical

54

as well as the spiritual... for He knows all our weakness, and He feeds the peoples' bodies as well as their souls.

What a beautiful picture this is: the people "neatly arranged like flower beds," Jesus raising the bread to heaven and pronouncing the blessing, the disciples distributing it, and Jesus Himself dividing the fish among them. All eat and all are satisfied. Here is a picture of the Lord's justice and love. And this scene we enact each day at Mass, listening to His Word, His teaching, and then eating the bread of life He distributes among us. May the Lord be praised!

And what have we to do to receive this bread of life but heed the words John offers and "love one another." For "love is of God; everyone who loves is begotten of God and has knowledge of God." And this knowledge we find in our love is that His justice is true and endures forever in the perfect peace His presence brings. Let us have faith forever.

C. to Bapt. Wed.

Wednesday
(1Jn.4:11-18; Ps.72:1-2,10,12-13; Mk.6:45-52)

"If we love one another, God dwells in us,
and His love is brought to perfection in us."

Jesus has just fed the five thousand men with the five loaves and two fish. He has performed a great miracle before the eyes of His disciples and through their hands. Yet "their minds were completely closed to the meaning of the events," and when He comes walking toward them on the water in the middle of the night as their boat is tossed about by a storm, they are "terrified." They are afraid because they are not yet perfect. John tells us in his first letter, a letter of love: "Love is not yet perfect in one who is afraid" and "perfect love casts out all fear." The disciples will not be perfect, will remain afraid, until after the death and resurrection of the Lord, and, really, until Pentecost, when the Spirit falls upon them. As John states, "The way we know we remain in Him and He in us is that He has given us of His Spirit."

His Spirit is the Spirit of love and He, our Lord Jesus, is Himself love. John follows both the clauses, "If we love one another" and "When anyone acknowledges that Jesus is the Son of God," with the statement that God dwells in us. Jesus and love are equated as the Spirit and love are equated above. Why? Because "God is love" and both Jesus and the Spirit are God, and so are love.

Brothers and sisters, our love must be brought to perfection, and it is "brought to perfection in this: that we should have confidence on the day of judgment" – that we should have no fear of the punishment we deserve, that we know fully of His love. Jesus takes a step to preparing the disciples against the judgment, against fear and for love, by walking toward them on the water. He means to teach them that they should not be afraid of the wind and the waves which rock our boat in this world, nor should they be afraid of His miraculous, overwhelmingly loving presence. Let us learn what Jesus would teach the disciples: "Do not be afraid!" "For He shall rescue the poor man when he cries out." He is love and He will save us. Let our minds open to His presence as we love one another, and let that love be brought to absolute perfection in us. May His Spirit be with you.

C. to Bapt. Thurs.

Thursday
(1Jn.4:19-5:4; Ps.72:1-2,11,14-15,17; Lk.4:14-22)

"Today this Scripture passage is fulfilled in your hearing."

Today the Son has come into our midst. Today He has "unrolled the scroll" of the Word of God and read aloud the words written of Him for all to hear. Today the WORD is brought to life. As "appealing" as is the discourse which flows forth from His gracious lips, so much greater is the Spirit that is upon Him. For by that Spirit and in His sacred flesh He shall "bring glad tidings to the poor... proclaim liberty to captives, recovery of sight to the blind, and release to prisoners." In word and deed He "announce[s] a year of favor from the Lord." In Him all time comes together. In Him it is all one moment. And this moment reveals the love of God.

And by the Son we are begotten, by His love: "Everyone who believes that Jesus is the Christ has been begotten of God." And so, children we become with the one Child most blessed. And if we are all one child born of the love of God and His Word, what can we do but love one another? Does one not love his own flesh and bone? And so, "whoever loves God must also love his brother," for his brother is of him as he is of God and both are His children in love, born of the flesh of the one Christ.

"In Him shall all the tribes of the earth be blessed." It is not for the few He has come, but for all. For God is the Father of all and the Son possesses and reveals all that is of the Father. "All nations shall proclaim His happiness," for all peoples shall find their happiness in Him alone, who is love and which love is itself our happiness and our hope.

Speak to us, Lord Jesus. Work through us, dear God. Let your Commandment of love be fulfilled in us. Let our love be fixed on God and let us love our brother. May we hear the words you speak in our midst today. May your Spirit make us children of the Father.

Friday
(1Jn.5:5-13; Ps.147:12-15,19-20; Lk.5:12-16)

"Whoever possesses the Son possesses life."

What does our psalmist mean when he sings: "He has granted peace in your borders; with the best of wheat He fills you," but that we are in Christ? What are those "borders" but the flesh of Christ? What is this wheat but the manna, the Sacrament of His Body He gives us to feed upon during our earthly journey? And this word which "runs swiftly," what is it but the Spirit which enlivens the Body of Christ, which brings the flesh of Christ to life? And why should we not "glorify the Lord," the God of life, who provides His Son and His Spirit, who makes the world and all that is in it, who calls us to believe, as the human beings we are, in the name of the Son, that we might find all three who testify to truth and "are of one accord"?

It is through the Son we come to the Father by the power of the Holy Spirit. If we believe in God the Father, we believe "the testimony He has given on His own Son's behalf," and we find the eternal life that is thus ours through the Son. May the Spirit run quickly to us and teach us and guide us along the way of God.

In our gospel Jesus heals a leper. He reaches out His hand "to touch him" and so draws him into Himself, into the borders of His holy flesh, and he is made whole. He wills it so, that the bars of all our gates be strengthened, that all enter into Him – that we be healed, whole in Him, and that our children, the fruit of our own bodies be blessed by their truly being begotten therefore of Him. If we are in Him, so will our children be, so will all the works we perform. But we must come as the leper, "bowed down to the ground." We, too, must see Jesus and be moved to humble ourselves before His loving glory. In faith we, too, must desire His touch upon our flesh, to be released from all sin, to be made whole again. And we must do as He instructs us through the power of the Spirit; then we shall find life with the Father in heaven.

If it is remarkable that the Son of God would draw the leprous man into His sacred flesh and make him His own, it is perhaps more remarkable that He would do the same for us poor sinners – that being possessed by Him, we possess Him, and so we enter life by the flesh of Christ.

Saturday
(1Jn.5:14-21; Ps.149:1-6,9; Jn.3:22-30)

"The Son of God has come and has given us discernment
to recognize the One who is true."

John's disciples had difficulty recognizing "the One who is true." They saw everyone "flocking to Him" and away from their master, so they came to their master questioning. But John was forthright: "I am not the Messiah," he said, "I am sent before Him." And now that He has come, the Baptist's joy is complete.

Brothers and sisters, "we know that we belong to God, while the whole world is under the evil one." "We are in the One who is true." Jesus has brought us to such knowledge. And this knowledge, this reality of the eternal life of God, should make us rejoice with our psalmist. It should make our lives ones of thanksgiving in which we "praise His name in the festive dance" and "with timbrel and harp." For, yes, "the Lord loves His people" and we are His faithful who "exult in glory." Let us "be glad in [our] maker."

The world is under sin, and there is deadly sin, which destroys the soul, lurking in the world. The devil is real as well, and will not simply go away. And though only God can cast him away ultimately, we can pray against much of his work in this world, "petition[ing] God," interceding for our brothers who falter in sin that is not deadly... and finding their release through the grace of God. With this "confidence in God: that He hears us whenever we ask for anything according to His will," we have a great gift and a great strength in this dark world – we can bring light to it, the light of the only Son. But we must always be as "the body" He adorns "with victory." We must have the same attitude as the Lord's "best man," and say with the Baptist, "He must increase while I must decrease." We must find our joy in Him and not in our works or in our pride. He is all and He is true, and He leads us to the kingdom in His baptism in water and the Spirit. Brothers and sisters, we must see the grace we have in our midst. Jesus is ours.

Baptism of the Lord (A)
(Is.42:1-4,6-7; Ps.29:1-4,9-11; Acts 10:34-38; Mt.3:13-17)

"God anointed Jesus of Nazareth with the Holy Spirit and power."

And so He anoints us all in the baptism our Savior has wrought. As Jesus humbled Himself to be baptized by John, so must we bow our heads before Jesus and receive holy baptism at His hands. As He has laid down His life for us, so must we lay down our lives for one another. As "He went about doing good and healing all those oppressed by the devil," so God is with us to do the same.

"The Spirit of God descend[ed] like a dove and [came] upon Him. And a voice came from the heavens, saying, 'This is my beloved Son, with whom I am well pleased.'" So Matthew recounts the Baptism of our Lord. And how similar is the beginning of our reading from Isaiah: "Here is my servant whom I uphold, my chosen one with whom I am well pleased, upon whom I have put my spirit." The chosen one of the ages now walks amongst us, the Spirit of God upon Him. His justice now extends to the ends of the earth, calling all into His blessed confines. None who come to Him does He reject. The "eyes of the blind" He opens, the prisoners He brings "from confinement" in the sin and darkness of the dungeon that is this world to the heavenly light of His presence walking among us in sacred flesh. "In every nation whoever fears Him and acts uprightly is acceptable to Him," for He loves all.

And so should we not sing out in praise of the glory of the Lord to which we are all called as did David at the completion of the tabernacle of God? For here stands the true Tabernacle, here stands its fulfillment... before us is God who calls us not only to look upon but to enter into His doors and dwell within Him in His heart, in His bosom – one with His sacred flesh and blood. The law is now written on our hearts, not only pages of a book; now the Spirit speaks to those who remain close to Him. Now we hear the "mighty" and "majestic" "voice of the Lord... over the waters": "the God of glory thunders." "In His temple all say, 'Glory!'" And should we not "give to the Lord the glory due His Name"? Does not our cup overflow as Peter's to declare the salvation that comes at the hand of our God?

Jesus has come. The Spirit is with us. Go now in the Spirit and power of God.

Baptism of the Lord (B)
(Is.55:1-11; Is.12:1-6; 1Jn.5:1-9; Mk.1:7-11)

"A voice came from the heavens,
'You are my beloved Son; with you I am well pleased.'"

Brothers and sisters, God "has testified on behalf of His Son." With His own voice and by "the Spirit, the water, and the blood," He has borne witness that Jesus is the Christ. And should we not believe and so conquer the world?

To the waters Jesus comes, and by His baptism makes them holy, that we in turn might be made holy by our baptism in them. Upon Him the Spirit descends like a dove, that new life might be breathed into our souls. And for our sake He will be crucified, that in His blood we may be redeemed. All speaks of our salvation! The water, the Spirit, and the blood – and all He is and does – give credence to the declaration from the mouth of the Father that this is His Son, and that we shall find life in Him alone. The Baptist has been sent to prepare the way before Him, proclaiming, "One mightier than I is coming after me." Let us "listen, that [we] may have life."

Do your souls not desire the food from heaven? Are you not "thirsty," are you not hungry for the bread of Truth? Listen to the Lord, "Heed me, and you shall eat well, you shall delight in rich fare." For though high are His "ways above your ways" and His "thoughts above your thoughts," though this food is well beyond your grasp, yet as "from the heavens rain and snow come down" and nourish the earth, so does the Spirit descend upon us, so do the waters of baptism nourish our faith – so does the blood of His sacrifice become our spiritual drink and His body our spiritual food. And so we become "confident and unafraid." And so by our faith we do conquer the world.

Brothers and sisters, "the one who believes that Jesus is the Son of God" "is begotten of God," for he becomes a son even as He is. And what power has the earth over Him who created it? And so what can stand before such faith? And nourished by this faith what can we do but love, as our God who is but love? To believe in Him is to love Him and to love Him means to love others; for faith in God who has always been brings love of those who are with us now, and so hope for heaven which is to come. This is the will of God for our souls this day. This is the life into which He would baptize our race. So, let us "sing praise to God for His glorious achievement" as we cleanse ourselves in the water His Son makes pure.

C. Baptism. (C)

Baptism of the Lord (C)

(Is.40:1-5,9-11; Ps.104:1-4,24-25,27-30; Ti.2:11-14,3:4-7; Lk.3:15-16,21-22)

"Heaven was opened
and the Holy Spirit descended upon Him
in bodily form like a dove."

"Beloved: The grace of God has appeared." Here we see its clear evidence in the Baptism of our Lord. Here He who "baptize[s] [us] with the Holy Spirit and fire" has the Spirit descend upon Himself. In our stead He places Himself (as He shall on the cross), and by the Spirit's presence upon Him, we ourselves are made clean. This Jesus, this Son of God, shall "save us through the bath of rebirth and renewal by the Holy Spirit," the Spirit which is united with His own, which *is* His own.

And so does He who "rules with a strong arm" enter our midst. And what does He say? "Speak tenderly to Jerusalem, and proclaim to her that her service is at an end, her guilt is expiated." He who is "clothed with majesty and glory," who has "constructed [His] palace on the waters" and made "the clouds [His] chariot"; He who "travel[s] on the wings of the wind" and "make[s] the winds [His] messengers, and flaming fire [His] ministers"... He comes begging the prophet: "Give comfort to my people." O brothers and sisters, "the kindness and generous love of our God [has] appeared" and our souls have been "justified by His grace." And now we are "heirs in hope of eternal life," life that is in His gentle hands alone.

O Lord, "when you send forth your Spirit, [we] are created and you renew the face of the earth." And so this day you send your Spirit forth; upon your Son your Spirit rests, and remains. His prayer – which is no other than our own – you answer, and witness to us that He is the Chosen One. Upon us, too, let your Spirit rest. As "in [your] arms" you gather "the lambs," so let us be gathered with your Holy Lamb and know the Spirit's power upon us, that to us, too, heaven will be opened, and we may enter there in the wake of our Lord. Let the waters of heaven pour upon us. Alleluia!

III. ORDINARY TIME

A. Sundays

1. Year A

Second Week

(Is.49:3,5-6; Ps.40:2,4,7-10; 1Cor.1:1-3; Jn.1:29-34)

"I am made glorious in the sight of the Lord,
and my God is now my strength!"

John the Baptist testifies that Jesus is "the Son of God," the One upon whom he has seen "the Spirit come down and remain." And we are all His servants, made holy only in Him. John declares his own servitude, speaking of "the one who sent [him] to baptize with water," and stating, "A man is coming after me who ranks ahead of me because He existed before me." His witness to Jesus and the strength he takes from Him is clear, as is the case with St. Paul, who declares himself "called to be an apostle of Christ Jesus by the will of God," and goes on to say that, indeed, all the Church is "called to be holy" in Jesus Christ. This call from the Lord to be His servant, and that it is through His servants the Lord shows His glory, is prophesied in strength by Isaiah in our first reading, showing that even before Christ came to be born among us He indeed existed and through Him the Father called His servants, His children, to Himself. For Isaiah speaks for God, saying, "I will make you a light to the nations, that my salvation may reach to the ends of the earth." Here he speaks of Jesus; here he knows even in his time of the salvation the Lord brings.

And David in our psalm echoes the same theme of the servitude of Christ and the servitude in Christ to which all are called, and which acts as a light to this world. "Ears open to obedience you gave me," proclaims the great and humble king, and sings as if in the voice of Christ: "In the written scroll it is prescribed for me, to do your will, O God, is my delight, and your law is within my heart!" What great blessing it indeed is to share in the servitude of Jesus, to have His song placed in our mouths, to make our lives "a hymn to our God." He makes us His own and we share in the blood that flows through His veins when we place ourselves in the service of the Lord.

The Lord calls. He is among us now and has made His salvation known. Through the prophets, through the Baptist, through His apostles and martyrs and saints – through "all those everywhere who call upon the name of our Lord Jesus Christ" He reveals His glory day to day. It is His desire that we be strong in Him as we join to Him and are baptized by Him with the Holy Spirit. His grace and peace He would leave with us, His glory He would reveal through us, if His servants we would make ourselves this day.

Find your strength in Him, brothers and sisters. He stoops toward you and hears your cry, and will instill His song of praise in your hearts, to be declared to all the world.

Third Week

(Is.8:23-9:3; Ps.27:1,4,13-14; 1Cor.1:10-13,17; Mt.4:12-23)

"Light has arisen."

"Anguish has taken wing, dispelled is darkness: for there is no gloom where but now there was distress." Yes, "a light has shone"; Jesus has come. No longer do we walk in darkness. So we should proclaim with David: "The Lord is my light and my salvation"; we should long to dwell in the Temple He has built, "gaz[ing] on the loveliness of the Lord." Here in His House we "see the bounty of the Lord in the land of the living." Here in His Church we come to the paradise He has come to establish in this land of darkness.

The light dawns as Jesus calls His disciples to His side. Here are the beginnings of His Church, the coming of light to this earth. The Lord calls Peter and Andrew, and James and John, and they respond, and they follow the light. And the light goes forth as He goes "around all of Galilee, teaching in their synagogues, proclaiming the gospel of the kingdom, and curing every disease and illness among the people." Do you see how the light grows? Do you know the light reflected in the disciples' eyes, which shall take root and become known to all the world? Here indeed is the Church begun, the holy House of God – the New Jerusalem. And nothing shall disturb its growth; nothing shall dim or block the light that has come.

Yet what division is upon the Church Christ has founded here on the shores of Galilee. How has it come to be that we are so disobedient to Paul's instruction "that there be no divisions among [us], but that [we] be united in the same mind and in the same purpose"? How many more rivalries have we than the Corinthians. Not only do those separated from the Church declare their peculiar allegiance to various people or nations, saying, "I belong to Luther," or "I belong to Calvin," or "I belong to England" – and now there are some 360 different denominations, one for every day of the year, it seems – but within the Catholic Church deep divisions arise between "liberal" or "conservative" theologians, thus bringing darkness upon God's people. The Church remains, and nothing shall overcome it, but what a poor sign it is to the world as the devil has his day in its division.

The Lord has come bringing "abundant joy and great rejoicing" for those who remain in His light. The unbroken flame rises up from these first apostles Jesus called on this one morning by the Sea of Galilee. The net extends from their hands and draws in all who truly seek to dwell in the presence of God.

Fourth Week
(Zep.2:3,3:12-13; Ps.146:6-10,Mt.5:3; 1Cor.1:26-31; Mt.5:1-12a)

"God chose the lowly and despised of the world,
those who count for nothing."

Who are the children of God? Who are those who inherit the kingdom of heaven upon the death of Christ, His only Son? Those who make peace, those who are meek – those who seek His righteousness and suffer for it, dying as the Son has... those the Lord blesses. For how can one enter a man's house and be called his child if he does not reflect the character of that man? And so, if the Lord "gives food to the hungry" and "sight to the blind," sustaining "the fatherless and the widow," must we not do the same to be of Him? If "the Lord raises up those who were bowed down," must we not be on our knees before Him, seeking His grace and serving His will, if we hope to be seated at His side? And so, let us heed the prophecy of Zephaniah: "Seek justice, seek humility; perhaps you may be sheltered in the day of the Lord's anger."

The Lord's anger will come. Justice must be done. Those who are insulted and persecuted falsely for the sake of the Son will find the reward of their patient endurance; and those proud souls who have shown no mercy to His little ones but have spoken with "a deceitful tongue" the boasts of their own greatness while consuming in their avarice the poor of the earth cannot but find their reward as well, for "the way of the wicked He thwarts." (Could He be a God of love and justice if He did otherwise?) "God chose the weak of the world to shame the strong," and His love and His justice shall be known in His judgment of each of them on the Day He comes.

"I will leave as a remnant in your midst a people humble and lowly, who shall take refuge in the name of the Lord." Brothers and sisters, we must be this lowly people; we must be those who trust in Him, who suffer with Him, who love as He has loved, and die as He has died. What other refuge have we? Where else can we make our home? It is Jesus "who became for us wisdom from God, as well as righteousness, sanctification, and redemption." Let us boast only in Him and in His sacrifice. Knowing the poorness of His Spirit and the mercy which bleeds in His heart, living it with our lives, we cannot help but find the kingdom of God. It is those bowed down in the dust of this world whom the Lord chooses as His own.

Fifth Week

(Is.58:7-10; Ps.112:4-9; 1Cor.2:1-5; Mt.5:13-16)

"Your light must shine before others,
that they may see your good deeds and glorify your heavenly Father."

And how shall "your light break forth like the dawn" except that you "share your bread with the hungry, shelter the oppressed and the homeless; clothe the naked when you see them, and do not turn your back on your own." Indeed, you must "remove from your midst oppression, false accusation, and malicious speech," for only "the man who is gracious and lends, who conducts his affairs with justice," only for him "light shines through the darkness" – as he is thus light being brought to this world of darkness and sin – only "he shall not fear," for "his heart is firm, trusting in the Lord." And he shall stand on the last day, when the light comes to its fullness.

This emptying oneself of all that is evil and finding oneself in all that is just by "lavishly [giving] to the poor," by feeding all those in need, is as Paul comes to the Thessalonians: "I came to you in weakness and fear and much trembling." "I resolved to know nothing while I was with you except Jesus Christ, and Him crucified." "Not with persuasive words of wisdom" does he come "but with a demonstration of Spirit and power." Embracing the cross he empties himself entirely of all selfishness, of all that is not of God, and thus the light that shines through him is entirely of the Lord, and serves as genuine food to the hungry soul.

Brothers and sisters, to whom is the Lord speaking in our gospel but to us? Who is "the light of the world," what is the "city set on a mountain" but the Church? If we are not "the salt of the earth," bringing out the flavor of justice and love from the flesh of the Body, who shall be? And what shall become of us and the world, therefore, but "to be thrown out and trampled underfoot"? Sometimes we look to others – to government, to business, to science – to lead the way. But all that need be is that *we* light the lamp that is in our grasp by the cross of our Lord Jesus Christ, and the house shall be illumined; we shall no longer fear or worry for the fate of those in need, for we shall be present to serve them. But if "under a bushel basket" we place the light that is ours, what can the world be but dark; and what can the people do but suffer? Brothers and sisters, we are called to shine the love of God. The time has come to do so.

67

Sixth Week

(Sir.15:15-20; Ps.119:1-2,4-5,17-18,33-34; 1Cor.2:6-10; Mt.5:17-37)

"Oh, that I might be firm in the ways
of keeping your statutes!"

The clear theme of today's readings is the need to "exactly observe" the commands of the Lord, to keep His law "with all [our] heart." It is this walking "in the law of the Lord" that makes us blessed in His sight.

It is popular to believe that Jesus' coming somehow nullifies the law and makes it unnecessary for our lives. The Lord makes it quite clear the opposite is true: "I have not come to abolish but to fulfill." In fact, He could not make the point more certain than His saying, "Until heaven and earth pass away, not the smallest letter or the smallest part of a letter will pass from the law." Indeed, He does not say only that killing subjects one to judgment, but even anger at one's brother. Not only is committing adultery wrong, but "everyone who looks at a woman with lust has already committed adultery with her in his heart."

Simply because forgiveness is greater in the presence of Jesus does not mean punishment is less; it is in fact greater as well, and more than greater – eternal. Now "the Spirit scrutinizes everything." Now even the smallest of sins is exposed to the all-encompassing light of Christ and to the "all-seeing... eyes of God." The sins being more greatly exposed, of course the forgiveness is greater, for there is that much more for the all-compassionate God to forgive. But by the same token, for those who do not come to Jesus to receive His grace and mercy, for those who choose death over life... the punishment is certainly all the greater; for more they see upon their souls about which to gnash their teeth. And now the choice that is made by the will of man is no longer temporal: it is made eternal by the Son of Man. There is no release from Gehenna, and Jesus comes to usher us into Heaven or see our souls cast into Hell. And further warning is found in the saints, who have said that most must pay "the last penny" in the fires of Purgatory before entering the heavenly gates.

The Lord gives no one "license to sin." All shall be responsible for their actions against Him and against His wisdom and love. All are commanded to act justly before Him, if we hope to come into His kingdom. "Yes" is "yes" with the Lord, and "no" is "no": no deception will stand before Him. We must pray each day for the wisdom to follow Him, and so find His everlasting grace upon our souls even as we journey through this world.

Seventh Week

(Lv.19:1-2,17-18; Ps.103:1-4,8,10,12-13; 1Cor.3:16-23; Mt.5:38-48)

"Be holy, for I, the Lord, your God, am holy."

In the Book of Leviticus God says, "You shall love your neighbor as yourself," and this is good. But in the gospel Jesus adds, "Love your enemies" – and this is better. In the old law we are commanded, "Take no revenge and cherish no grudge against any of your people"; but in the new we hear, "Offer no resistance to anyone who is evil," and even, "Pray for those who persecute you." For now it is revealed that all are God's children, and so all must be loved as brothers.

"Is this wise?" you say, to love our enemies. "Is this not foolishness?" Indeed the wisdom of the world would call it so, but we are called to "become a fool, so as to become wise" in the eyes of God. For what the Lord calls us to in this is no less than to be like Him, to become the very "temple of God" where "the Spirit of God dwells." "Merciful and gracious is the Lord," and so are we called to be. "Not according to our sins does He deal with us," and so we should not deal with others according to theirs. Our "Father has compassion on His children," and we must have the same for all.

Has any of you put the words of the Lord into practice? Has anyone sought to discover such love? If you have then you know the glory it holds, the glory of a love which surpasses all. And though justice is not wanting for those who reject it, His love cannot but be poured upon all.

O the happiness of the soul that receives such grace! O the joy of him who knows the blessing of such utter sacrifice! What greater blessing can there be than to "be perfect, just as [our] heavenly Father is perfect"? With David the soul alight with God's love sings: "Bless the Lord, O my soul; and all my being, bless His holy name." With Mary the Mother of God our soul proclaims His greatness as we come to know "all His benefits" in the service of His love. And our transgressions are put far from us; and the Lord's grace abounds within us – and like His Son do we become, who upon the cross forgave even those who nailed Him to this tree.

Brothers and sisters, no greater love will we ever find. It is this gift of holiness our Lord calls us to this day. Let us love as He.

Eighth Week

(Is.49:14-15; Ps.62:2-3,6-9; 1Cor.4:1-5; Mt.6:24-34)

"Seek first the kingdom of God and His righteousness,
and all these things will be given you besides."

Today's gospel is the Lord's beautiful exhortation not to be anxious about the things of this world: God takes care. "Do not worry about your life, what you will eat or drink, or about your body, what you will wear," Jesus instructs us. And how true it is that "the birds of the sky," who "do not sow or reap," are fed in abundance, and that there is nothing more splendidly clothed than the flowers of the field. And do we indeed think the Father will not care just so for our lives? Yet all we do is worry about these passing things, even as our soul calls us to peace.

"Only in God is my soul at rest; from Him comes my salvation," David so poignantly and appropriately sings. And with this trust in his rock of refuge he knows he "shall not be disturbed at all." Similarly, St. Augustine has declared, from his own experience of pursuing worldly cares, that only in God do our souls find rest. Are these witnesses not enough to trust in the salvation that comes from God alone? Then hear of the undying love God holds for His creatures in the prophecy of Isaiah: to those who fret, "The Lord has forsaken me; my Lord has forgotten me," he asks the simple yet profound question, "Can a mother forget her infant, be without tenderness for the child of her womb?" Yet greater than a mother's love is the Lord God's care for us, for "even should she forget" (as seems to happen all too often in this age of abortion), the Lord states with certainty and full assurance, "I will never forget you."

And much like this inclination to anxiety about the cares of life, and coming from the same faithless source, is our proclivity to judge others. How many of us heed St. Paul's warning not to "make any judgment before the appointed time, until the Lord comes"? How many cannot trust that "He will bring to light what is hidden," that all things He sees – that we need not do His job for Him. "The one who judges me is the Lord," Paul states. Really, who else can do so? As by no other hand does our food come, so by no other tongue shall all be judged.

"Trust in Him at all times, O my people! Pour out your hearts before Him." Try it, and you will see – He alone provides all things. Set your hearts on Him and He will take care.

Ninth Week

(Dt.11:18,26-28,32; Ps.31:1-4,17,25; Rom.3:21-25,28; Mt.7:21-27)

"Take these words of mine into your heart and soul."

Our first reading and gospel are virtually identical today. 'In one, Moses tells the Israelites: "I set before you here, this day, a blessing and a curse"; in the other, Jesus tells His disciples a parable of the same blessing and curse. Moses speaks of the "blessing for obeying the commandments of the Lord" and the "curse if [the Israelites] do not obey the commandments of the Lord"; and Jesus states clearly, "Everyone who listens to these words of mine and acts on them will be like a wise man who built his house on rock... and everyone who listens to these words of mine but does not act on them will be like a fool who built his house on sand." The blessing and the curse – following the Word of God and not following the Word of God.

And we must note that there are two parts to be fulfilled to obtain the blessing of the Lord. In Jesus' words, we must both "listen" and "act." And though it seems Moses stresses acting in his call for obedience, it is his words that are quoted above – and what is it to take words into our heart and soul but to listen? The Lord must first dwell in us. As St. Paul conveys so beautifully, we "are justified freely by [the Lord's] grace through the redemption in Christ Jesus, whom God sent forth as an expiation, through faith, by His blood," and therefore we must *listen* to this grace and open ourselves always to this grace at work in our hearts. And then we must act upon it. We must hear God speaking to us *and* do His will. It does no good only to sit and listen, for then our faith will soon die. Nor does it do any good to act without listening to God, for then we are as an empty gong. The faith we profess must be realized in the works of the Lord; without either faith or works we have nothing at all, and find but the Lord's curse.

Brothers and sisters, today let us call out to God with our brother David: "Be my rock of refuge, a stronghold to give me safety." Let us "take courage and be stouthearted, all you who hope in the Lord." For if we take His words to heart and if we do the will of God, we will be "set solidly on rock." Indeed it shall be said one day, "The rains fell, the floods came, and the winds blew and buffeted the house." All houses shall be touched thus by the hand of God. Let it be said of our house that it "did not collapse," but – taking our strength in the Lord, dwelling in His Word – like a "fortress" stood ever in the blessing of His light.

Tenth Week

(Hos.6:3-6; Ps.50:1,8,12-15,23; Rom.4:18-25; Mt.9:9-13)

"Go and learn the meaning of the words,
'I desire mercy, not sacrifice.'"

How important it is to learn the meaning of these words, for they hold
the essence of Jesus' Person and mission, but how often they are
misunderstood.   Many there are who hold to their sins and offer as
justification the forgiveness of Jesus – as many as pat themselves on the
back for their piety.   So unclear is the mind of man, and prone to false
interpretation. Later in our same psalm today the Lord chastises His people,
"When you see thieves, you befriend them; with adulterers you throw in
your lot."   Yet I have heard the badly misled (and not a few there are)
cherish their lies and their adulterous eyes, quoting Jesus' words: "I did not
come to call the righteous but sinners." They condemn the churchgoers as
hypocrites and think continuance in sin will bring them to heaven.

What confusion reigns! How can it be that Abraham's faith is "credited
to him as righteousness" in our second reading and our psalm declares: "To
the upright I will show the saving power of God," when our gospel states
Jesus hasn't come to call the righteous? It is not difficult to understand,
nothing is difficult to understand, if one but takes a minute to think, to ask
the Lord. It should be obvious to all that Jesus does not call us *to be* sinners.
He does not come saying, "Increase your sin in my sight and you shall be
saved." Rather, when He comes – and at the heart of His ministry – He calls
all to "repent, for the kingdom of heaven is at hand." What the Lord calls
sinners to is to *turn away* from their sins: the physician comes to heal us of
just such sickness as sin brings. What does He tell the adulterous woman
but "Go and sin no more," not, "Your sins are fine."

The point is, Jesus by His very nature has come to redeem us from our
sins: "He was handed over for our transgressions and was raised for our
justification." He is our Savior who "come[s] to us like rain, like spring rain
that waters the earth," and He cannot cleanse us from sin if we do not
recognize that we *do* sin. Thus when He says, "I did not come to call the
righteous," He is speaking of those, like the Pharisees, who *see* themselves
as righteous, as perfect, as needing no physician to heal them – for how can
the Lord heal those who see themselves as well? And this is what we who
seek to be close to the Lord, we who attend Mass each day and say our
prayers, must avoid. For it is a grave trap to think that such "sacrifices"
themselves will save us. God's works are certainly necessary and will
follow those who believe, but we must remember that, truly, we do *nothing*
– all good is the Lord's doing – and it is mercy that the Lord desires. And

He cannot share this love of God with those who presume perfection in His sight. Every day we must recognize our sin before Him to be saved.

Brothers and sisters, let it not be that our "piety is like a morning cloud, like the dew that early passes away." Let our faith not be but skin deep. If the love of God does not pierce our hearts, what are we worth? Let all be as Abraham who "was strengthened by faith and gave glory to God." Let all "offer to God praise as [our] sacrifice and fulfill [our] vows to the Most High." Let we who always sin turn ever further from our sin and to the merciful arms of Jesus.

O. 11. Sun. (A)

Eleventh Week

(Ex.19:2-6a; Ps.100:1-3,5; Rom.5:6-11; Mt.9:36-10:8)

"I bore you up on eagle wings,
and brought you here to myself."

As the Lord rescued the Israelites from slavery to the Egyptians and brought them into His presence in the desert of Sinai, so in the same way, in a full manner, "God proves His love for us in that while we were still sinners Christ died for us." God loves us and draws us to Himself. He is "moved with pity" when He sees us "like sheep without a shepherd." And so He sends the Good Shepherd in Jesus His Son; and so Jesus sends out His apostles to us, so that by their hands we might be freed from sin and the grasp of the devil and be reconciled with God through Christ.

And once "we have... received reconciliation," the Lord promises us, "If you hearken to my voice and keep my covenant, you shall be my special possession, dearer to me than all other people, though all the earth is mine." These words He speaks to His chosen ones are the same Paul declares to the Romans when he says, "If, while we were enemies, we were reconciled to God through the death of His Son, how much more, once reconciled, will we be saved by His life." For saved by the crucifixion of Jesus, "justified by His blood" poured upon us, His life is now with us; and remaining in the way He has set before us, obedient to His command of love... laying down our lives as He has, we indeed become "a kingdom of priests, a holy nation." And this Jesus Himself confirms when He instructs His apostles, "Without cost you have received" – He has saved us through no merit of our own... "without cost you are to give" – all our lives are to be sacrificed for Him and for His holy people.

Brothers and sisters, we are "His people, the flock He tends." The Lord first called the sons of Jacob, and so Jesus first sends His apostles to "the lost sheep of the house of Israel," to know the fulfillment of the promise made to them in ancient times. And now the Catholic Church is become the

Ordinary Time

New Jerusalem, the new house in which the Lord does dwell, and all are called by God's love into its secure confines. As He revealed His love when He "gave [the apostles] authority over unclean spirits to drive them out and to cure every disease and every illness," so now the power of God rests upon His Church to draw all men unto the Father by the ministry of His anointed ones.

The Lord saves us from all sin; let us come now to be with Him.

O. 12. Sun. (A)

Twelfth Week
(Jer.20:10-13; Ps.69:8-10,14,17,33-35; Rom.5:12-15; Mt.10:26-33)

> "For your sake I bear insult,
> and shame covers my face."

Jeremiah "hear[s] the whisperings of many" who seek to "denounce him"; those who "watch for any misstep" plot his destruction: "Perhaps he will be trapped, then we can prevail, and take our revenge on him." Like David he has "become an outcast to [his] brothers, a stranger to [his] mother's children." And for what does he suffer such persecution but for speaking the truth of God's word to his fellow Israelites? As David declares to the Lord, "The insults of those who blaspheme you fall upon me"; both the prophet and the king endure persecution for righteousness' sake.

But both prophet and king declare victory in their struggle: "The Lord is with me, like a mighty champion; my persecutors will stumble, they will not triumph." Through the power of God it is they who "will be put to utter shame, to lasting, unforgettable confusion." The Lord hears their pleas for help, their prayers come before Him, "for the Lord hears the poor, and His own who are in bonds He spurns not." And so both king and prophet end in joy, in utter hope, as David proclaims, "Let the heavens and the earth praise Him, the seas and whatever moves in them"; and Jeremiah likewise calls all to honor our unfailing God: "Sing to the Lord, praise the Lord, for He has rescued the life of the poor from the power of the wicked."

And, brothers and sisters, in what greater way is this salvation from the grasp of evil better known, more fully realized, than in our Lord Jesus Christ? Paul tells us, "Through one man sin entered the world, and through sin, death, and this death came to all men." What greater persecutor have we than death itself? But now "the grace of God and the gracious gift of the one man Jesus Christ overflow for the many" – now all are saved by Him who has died, and has risen. Its clutches no longer hold dominion.

So Jesus exhorts the Twelve, and all who would conquer death and all sin, to "fear no one": "Do not be afraid of those who kill the body but cannot kill the soul." What power has the prince of this world over our immortal

74

souls now that Jesus has come? He can't touch us by his persecutions; and so now we are called to "proclaim on the housetops" what we "hear whispered" by the Lord in our hearts. Now with Jeremiah and David we must fearlessly "speak in the light," for the Lord has made us a promise, and His Word is true – "Everyone who acknowledges me before others I will acknowledge before my heavenly Father." But if we deny Him, He will deny us. Therefore, let us be heedless of the shame and the pain we share with our Savior and never fear to declare His truth in love to all. Nothing is greater than the power of His Word.

Thirteenth Week
(2Kgs.4:8-11,14-16a; Ps.89:2-3,16-19; Rom.6:3-4,8-11; Mt.10:37-42)

"Whoever loses his life for my sake will find it."

The Lord encourages us today to "take up [our] cross and follow [Him]," to place Him first in our lives to find the reward He holds. And in our second reading Paul says the same, reminding us that "we were indeed buried with Christ through baptism into death," that we have "died with Christ... to sin once and for all" – this is our cross – and that laying down our lives before the Lord we now find ourselves "living for God in Christ Jesus"; we now find ourselves "raised from the dead by the glory of the Father [that] we too might live in newness of life" with Him who is Life itself.

And Jesus sends us forth as His disciples, saying, "Whoever receives you receives me, and whoever receives me receives the one who sent me." Thus, by our lives we call others to die with Christ that they too might live with Him in eternity, that they too might be blessed as we. Others should see in us the Lord and be prompted to give of themselves as we do, as He does – that in Him all might rejoice.

In our first reading we find a woman who has proven the truth of Christ's statement, "Whoever receives a prophet because he is a prophet will receive a prophet's reward." Quite literally does she give her "cup of cold water" to the great prophet Elisha, feeding him "whenever he passed by" and even making a place for him to stay in her home. She has recognized "that he is a holy man of God" and is drawn to him, desiring to have his godliness near her life. And by sharing her food and her home, she is laying down her life; by serving this "righteous man" she is serving God, and so she will know the blessing of God.

"This time next year you will be fondling a baby son," is the holy man's promise to the woman; and no greater blessing could she hope for. Here is life to her. Here is that "newness of life" of which Jesus speaks so well exemplified in our sight. And we should know that the same will be our own. "In the light of [His] countenance" we shall "know the joyful shout." "At [His] name [we] rejoice all the day." "The praises of the Lord [we] will sing forever," for His Son has been born in our midst; our life has come to us, has suffered and died, and now sits with the Father on high. And to Him do we come with all we are. Before Him do we lay down our lives... and all we give freely He blesses.

O. 14. Sun. (A)

Fourteenth Week
(Zec.9:9-10; Ps.145:1-2,8-11,13-14; Rom.8:9,11-13; Mt.11:25-30)

"Come to me, all you who labor and are burdened,
and I will give you rest."

A remarkable confluence of Scripture today, extolling the "great kindness" of our King, who comes to us "meek, and riding on an ass, on a colt, the foal of an ass," and inviting us to take refuge in Him and in His blessed humility.

Yes, upon a beast of burden, upon the young offspring of a beast of burden comes He who bears the burden of all our sins. Not on horse or in chariot does He come, for horse and chariot He casts into the sea: by Him "the warrior's bow shall be banished, and He shall proclaim peace to the nations." It is not the rich and powerful of this world He dies for, it is not their stead in which He stands, for the Lord has "hidden these things from the wise and the learned" of this world and "revealed them to little ones." This we see in the "little one" His Son has become. This we find when we imitate His sacrifice.

David's psalm echoes the Lord's own words – "The Lord lifts up all who are falling, and raises up all who are bowed down" – and Paul says the same when he declares, "The one who raised Christ from the dead will give life to your mortal bodies also, through His Spirit that dwells in you." For what is it to "put to death the deeds of the body," that by the Spirit we may live, but to humble ourselves in the sight of God, to bow down before God and men and bear His light burden? For though we be crushed by the weight of labor and persecution in Jesus' name, yet we live eternally in "His dominion [which] shall be from sea to sea, and from the River to the ends of the earth."

The Lord Jesus states clearly, "I am meek and humble of heart," and like Him, and like His Father, we are called to be. And for the grace of Him who is "compassionate toward all His works" we should "rejoice heartily" with our Savior, who exclaims today, "I give praise to you, Father, Lord of heaven and earth"; for all His works "give [Him] thanks" and "[His] faithful ones bless [Him]" for His faithfulness. "A just savior is He," and "the glory of [His] kingdom" and His "might" are known in His mercy, are felt in the comforting hand He stretches forth to lift up the humblest of our kind. "Praise [His] name forever and ever."

Fifteenth Week
(Is.55:10-11; Ps.65:10-14,Lk.8:8; Rom.8:18-23; Mt.13:1-23)

"The seed sown on rich soil
is the one who hears the word and understands it,
who indeed bears fruit."

Comes the Word of God. To our eyes, to our ears. A seed sown within our hearts. May it find rich soil in which to grow, that we might know "the redemption of our bodies."

"The rain and the snow come down and do not return there till they have watered the earth... so shall [God's] word be that goes forth from [His] mouth." For indeed it makes the earth "fertile and fruitful, giving seed to the one who sows and bread to the one who eats": it nourishes the expectant soul and provides seed for its increased growth. All is given life by the Word of God.

What Isaiah prophesies, David sings – "You prepared the land: drenching its furrows, breaking up its clods, softening it with showers, blessing its yield." And by this grace which falls from heaven, consuming the manna which is its fruit, His children know the "bounty" of the Lord; for His "paths overflow with a rich harvest." Hardly can we contain the blessings of "the valleys blanketed with grain."

Jesus has come. The Lord has "visited the land and watered it." The grace of God is in our midst in heavenly flesh and blood. And we are left dumb; for the Word of God indeed silences our tongue. What can we say as we see His fields coming to life? How can we speak of the beauty of a land bathed in light? Deeply into our souls His words do fall, and we awaken, we arise as His children of light, beginning now to understand the blessing at our fingertips, the redemption we do find in the Body and Blood of Christ. And though we "groan within ourselves," we know these are the "labor pains" of growth. For in this cleansing rain purging our hearts we come to be "set free from slavery to corruption and share in the glorious freedom of the children of God."

What a wonderful word we have from our Lord: "Blessed are your eyes, because they see, and your ears, because they hear." What a promise He makes to those who gaze upon that which the prophets longed to possess: "To anyone who has, more will be given and he will grow rich." And so, what confidence we who are granted "knowledge of the mysteries of the kingdom of heaven" should have in His grace-filled Spirit; and what fruit we should thus bear, even to life everlasting.

Sixteenth Week
(Ws.12:13,16-19; Ps.86:5-6,9-10,15-16; Rom.8:26-27; Mt.13:24-43)

"First collect the weeds and tie them in bundles for burning;
but gather the wheat into my barn."

Such are the Lord's instructions to the harvesters, His angels that come "at the end of the age," when "just as weeds are collected and burned up with fire," so will "all who cause others to sin and all evildoers" be thrown "into the fiery furnace, where there will be wailing and grinding of teeth. Then the righteous will shine like the sun in the kingdom of their Father."

"Whoever has ears ought to hear." Though the Lord is a God "merciful and gracious, slow to anger, abounding in kindness and fidelity"; though He is "good and forgiving... attend[ing] to the sound of [our] pleading" and "permit[ting] repentance for our sins" – though while the grass grows He is patient and waits for the weeds which have been sown to turn to Him, yet the time of harvest shall come: the time to judge the living and the dead. And so it is that the One who is "lenient toward all" shall reveal to all that indeed He does "show [His] might when the perfection of [His] power is disbelieved." The obstinate of heart shall not remain forever; sin must be burnt with fire, and so those who cling to it and its sower, the evil one.

There is time. There is time and He who has "the cure of all" reveals indeed that "the just must be kind." But the end presses on; it is upon us. And the time and lenience granted those who toil vainly for the evil one will but serve to prove their deserving of the Lord's inevitable justice. They will but harden themselves further, to their own perfection of sin, meriting in the end the undeniable punishment of the loving and just One.

And the same is true of the just themselves. The time given by our gracious God, though it seem troublesome for the weeds of sin that prick our hearts, is but a means of proving, is but a refinement of the perfection of our God's love within us. And so we must be patient as the tree does grow, acceptant of the pains it brings. And so we must but watch as the leaven rises, and we with it come to Christ. Yes, "the one who searches hearts knows what is the intention of the Spirit." Take confidence in this. Just as the Lord knows the path to perdition the wicked sow within their souls, so He knows clearly the hope we have for heaven. And all shall reach their perfection in Him.

Seventeenth Week

(1Kgs.3:5,7-12; Ps.119:57,72,76-77,97,127-130; Rm.8:28-30; Mt.13:44-52)

"The revelation of your words sheds light,
giving understanding to the simple."

Wisdom. The "pearl of great price." How precious the ability "to distinguish right from wrong" by the grace of God, and to choose the right way at all times. For finding the pearl is one thing, a gift from the Lord, but wisdom is revealed in him who "goes and sells all that he has and buys it," knowing there is no treasure greater than the heavenly light shining from the face of God.

It is heaven we must desire. What else is of any worth, my friend? And in His justice, in His truth, in the wisdom and understanding that come from the touch of His hand and the words from His mouth alone will we find what is the desire of all the righteous souls.

Solomon demonstrates that he "love[s] [the Lord's] commands more than gold," and this pleases the God who seeks to rule His heart. He shows that he is the son of his father David by coming humbly before the Lord, recognizing that he is "a mere youth, not knowing at all how to act." And such utter dependence on the Lord's grace He cannot but bless, declaring to His servant: "I give you a heart so wise and understanding that there has never been anyone like you up to now, and after you there will come no one to equal you." Because the young king has made the desire to "know what is right" his request of his God, he receives this, and so much more.

All knowledge, all wisdom is given to Solomon, and shall not be taken away. But perhaps we should note that what he is given here in such abundance, he shall not heed throughout his life – for he shall not always sell all else to follow in the light of the Lord's decrees. Perhaps none but Jesus Himself can do this wholeheartedly; but none should also make the riches of the earth, which contradict the heavenly treasure, his abiding desire, as the older king shall do. All must strive to remain in His light, to be as "the scribe who has been instructed in the kingdom of heaven... who brings from his storeroom both the new and the old," who serves as the angels that "separate the wicked from the righteous" – even on this earth distinguishing evil from good.

"Brothers and sisters, we know that all things work for good for those who love God, who are called according to His purpose." Paul's words reflect the wisdom of God. For truly His elect are known to Him from before time; truly He calls us "to be conformed to the image of His Son." And truly we know that by the justification of our souls under the cross of Christ we shall come to the glorious presence of the Father in heaven. And

79

this is all that matters. "Do you understand all these things?" Then place all in His hands.

Eighteenth Week
(Is.55:1-3; Ps.145:8-9,15-18; Rm.8:35,37-39; Mt.14:13-21)

"The eyes of all look hopefully to you,
and you give them their food in due season."

And the song of David, and the prophecy of Isaiah, are fulfilled in Jesus and the heavenly banquet He sets before us this day. For the Lord "open[s] His hand and satisf[ies] the desire of every living thing"; "without paying and without cost" all come to His table to eat.

"You who have no money, come, receive grain and eat." The "rich fare" the Lord provides cannot be bought with money, for the earthly food "fails to satisfy." Only that paid for by the blood of the Son gives life; in His sacrifice we find "the everlasting covenant," the union with God and with His love which all our souls desire. And we know, as Paul testifies, that nothing "will be able to separate us from the love of God in Christ Jesus our Lord."

Does Jesus not give witness to the love of God today? Does He not show that "the Lord is good to all and compassionate toward all His works"? For though "He withdrew in a boat to a deserted place by Himself," though He sought to be alone with His Father in prayer, when followed by the crowds He took pity and "cured their sick." And though He had been with them all the day and evening drew on, when the disciples urge Him to "dismiss the crowds so that they can go to the villages and buy food for themselves," Jesus responds: "There is no need for them to go away; give them food yourselves." And He feeds them, without cost and without discriminating between one and the next. All sit at His table today; and we are told that "all ate and were satisfied." And why not? For the bounty of the Lord is indeed the richest fare.

Do we follow Jesus as diligently as these in the wilderness, brothers and sisters? We know the food He provides us now every day. And we have been shown clearly that "the Lord is near to all who call upon Him, to all who call upon Him in truth." Let us partake well of this feast set before us, which gives us now a foretaste of heaven. Freely let us come to Him, and be fed by His holy hand. And our expectant souls shall be forever satisfied, for His hand is always open.

Nineteenth Week

(1Kgs.19:9a,11-13a; Ps.85:8-14; Rm.9:1-5; Mt.14:22-33)

"When he heard this, Elijah hid his face in his cloak
and went and stood at the entrance to the cave."

For the Lord was in the "tiny whispering sound."

God speaks in silence. His Word sinks deeply into our souls, piercing the spirit within us, and so what can we be but afraid? His still, small voice brings us into His awesome presence.

Brothers and sisters, it is the same NAME of God revealed to Moses the lawgiver that is spoken to Elijah the prophet here on the same "mountain of God, Horeb." This WORD, this NAME (YHWH), invokes fear, for it silences the tongue, stilling all distraction we might make, and so allows the purity of God to pass into us. What but fear, what but holy wonder, can penetrate our very bones when we become thus surrounded by His presence, when He penetrates the core of our being? "The Lord will be passing by" is the promise made to Elijah; and in the silent WORD the Lord's promise is kept.

And is it not this same WORD in which Jesus rested when "He went up on the mountain by Himself to pray"? Is it not this same WORD the Lord brought to Peter and the apostles when He "came toward them walking on the sea" as their boat "was being tossed about by the waves"? As He stepped into the boat with His blessed Rock, is it not so that "the wind died down"? My brothers and sisters, Jesus is this WORD spoken to Elijah, this NAME given Moses, made flesh in our midst. And in His presence "the strong and heavy wind," "the earthquake," and "the fire" become as nothing, as all distractions cease and we find ourselves at the feet of "the Son of God."

Upon coming from this mountain Moses led his people out of Egypt. Upon coming from this mountain Elijah will anoint two kings, and a prophet to succeed himself. Upon coming from the silence of the mountain, Jesus – as He did before in calling His twelve apostles – comes to confirm the call upon Peter and his brothers even as He sees that His mission must increase with the death of John the Baptist. From the silent WORD all is spoken. It is His NAME for which we must listen, that we might "speak the truth in Christ."

"Near indeed is His salvation to those who fear Him, glory dwelling in our land." And so, let us "hear what God proclaims; the Lord – for He proclaims peace," and in His peace alone will we discover our true and lasting home. (Fear not the troubling of your soul; He breathes a light calm upon the waters.)

Twentieth Week

(Is.56:1,6-7; Ps.67:2-3,5-6,8; Rom.11:13-15,29-32; Mt.15:21-28)

"God delivered all to disobedience,
that He might have mercy upon all."

(In love let me speak, O Lord.)

Brothers and sisters, the Lord has said, "My house shall be called a house of prayer for all peoples." Yet our scholars and leaders make it a den of unbelief. Like the scribes and Pharisees of Jesus' day, they are deaf and blind to the light of God. We must not follow in their steps, but speak the truth of the presence of Christ that all might enter the portals of the Lord.

I ask you: How shall the Lord's "way be known upon earth; among all nations, [His] salvation," if His Truth is blunted, if His Word is watered down into an alphabet soup? The commentary of the missal I read states of our gospel: "Matthew took this story from Mark... He molded it to bring out a message for the Church of his day." And so again, and continuously, those who presume to speak for the Church know nothing of God's Word. In their excessive analyzing, in their presumption and fabrication, they themselves attempt to mold the divine Scriptures to fit the vision of their blinded eyes, unable to see the Lord who stands before them. It is remarkable how ignorant these "intelligent" beings are to the simple fact that "prophecy has never been put forth by man's willing it," that "men impelled by the Holy Spirit have spoken under God's influence" (2Pt.1:21). And so they seek to make the Bible as any other sacred text, and the Church no different than the next.

Why? So that there will be "an open-minded respect for all who seriously follow their religious convictions, provided of course that they fulfill their obligation to find the truth." But what they do not see is that the very condemnation of people they seek so anxiously to avoid, they are themselves effecting, in an eternal fashion. For they do not open the loving arms of the Catholic Church and speak of the acceptance of all into its grace and favors. They themselves do not "fulfill their obligation" to the truth for they know not what truth is: that Jesus is *the way, the truth, and the life* is not heard by those who thirst for it most of all.

And they do not see the absolute beauty of the woman's cry, "Please, Lord, even the dogs eat the scraps that fall from the table of their masters." (Or Jesus' wonderful exclamation, "O woman, great is your faith!") They do not see the way is not easy for any to come to salvation – be it the Gentile to whom the gates had seemed to be shuttered (though even throughout the Old Testament the Lord makes it very clear that "foreigners who join themselves to the Lord... them [He] will bring to [His] holy mountain") or the Jew who must repent of the hardness of his heart. They do not witness that all must come crawling on their knees to Jesus, and so how can they preach it? Their eyes are not open to see that the daughter who is healed is more than just the woman's blood offspring, but all the Gentile race; and they do not call all these to the light of His face. May the Lord have mercy on their disobedience. "May God bless us, and may all the ends of the earth fear Him."

Twenty-First Week
(Is.22:19-23; Ps.138:1-3,6,8; Rom.11:33-36; Mt.16:13-20)

"I will give you the keys to the kingdom of heaven.
Whatever you bind on earth shall be bound in heaven;
and whatever you loose on earth shall be loosed in heaven."

Thus the Lord grants principal authority in His Church to His rock, Peter. Thus He prophesies what He has promised: the power and teaching given those who sit on Moses' seat shall pass to this new leader He appoints to guide the flock of the New Jerusalem. And is this designation, or redesignation, of power not remarkably foreshadowed in our first reading: "I will place the key of the House of David on Eliakim's shoulder; when he opens, no one shall shut; when he shuts, no one shall open"? For the Lord has said to "Shebna, master of the palace: 'I will thrust you from your office and pull you down from your station... and give over to [Eliakim] your authority.'" The same declaration Jesus has made to the chief priests and leaders of the people, and here He indicates its fulfillment.

"He shall be a father to the inhabitants of Jerusalem, and to the house of Judah." Is this not the case with our Papa, our Pope, whom the Lord has assigned in His "inscrutable" judgment to feed His sheep? "Oh, the depth of the riches and wisdom and knowledge of God!" whose mind no man has known. For see the authority He gives to man, He who has all power to give. Even unto heaven does the reign of the apostles now extend, with Peter in the fore. And "the gates of the nether world shall not prevail against it," for it is granted by "the Christ, the Son of the living God" through the revelation of His "heavenly Father." "I will fix Him like a peg in a sure spot," the Lord states of Eliakim; and now no surer peg is there than Peter, through whose care all "worship at [the Lord's] holy temple."

"Your kindness, O Lord, endures forever." Your love for your sons on earth reaches unto heaven. And so you grant us blessings beyond our imagining; you strengthen us beyond our weak frame. And as to the apostles you deliver authority, so one in your grace all become. How shall we repay you for your kindness toward us? How shall we care for the gift you give? How shall we maintain your presence among us, except that in your love you remain? Bless this House and all its leaders; may "in the presence of the angels [we] sing your praise."

Twenty-Second Week
(Jer.20:7-9; Ps.63:2-6,8-9; Rom.12:1-2; Mt.16:21-27)

"Offer your bodies as a living sacrifice,
holy and pleasing to God, your spiritual worship."

Paul says the same as Jesus when the Lord calls us to "take up [our] cross," to lose our lives for His sake. And as Paul instructs the Romans: "Do not conform yourselves to this age but be transformed by the renewal of your mind," so Jesus teaches Peter, and all His apostles and disciples, when He insists he think as God and not as man.

Why? Why is the Lord so harsh with this Rock of the Church (and, as I say, with us all)? The answer is spoken clearly in our reading from Jeremiah. In it the prophet declares in near desperation: "The Word of the Lord has brought me derision and reproach all the day." He goes so far as to say the Lord has "duped" him, making evident that he had not expected to become "an object of laughter" upon taking on the mantle of prophecy. "Everyone mocks me," he cries; and yet he "must cry out" still the way of the Lord. Yet he must call the people from their sins and warn them of the "violence and outrage" that is near them. He cannot remain silent, though he would greatly wish to, because the Word of the Lord is "like fire burning in [his] heart, imprisoned in [his] bones," and he can do nothing but shout it from the rooftops, though it bring him scorn.

And what has this to do with Peter? Peter has just declared that Jesus is the Son of God, the Messiah, and it is his voice above all that will cry out this truth to the ends of the earth; thus he and his fellow apostles must know clearly that to which they are called. As the Lord "must go to Jerusalem and suffer greatly... and be killed," so must they walk the same path of persecution. This they must see. The contradiction of the cross they must realize, even as they preach it in this hostile world. For to it they must give themselves completely.

How? How can it be that the Christian take up such foolishness in the eyes of the world? How can it be that we die so freely, that we suffer such mockery, such persecution at the hands of sinners? Is it not that our "flesh pines and [our] soul thirsts like the earth, parched, lifeless, and without water" for the living God? And is it not because we know that "as with the riches of a banquet shall [our] soul be satisfied"? The key is in this gospel quote: "The Son of Man will come with His angels in His Father's glory."

84

The key is believing on the third day He was raised. If we have this faith it becomes easy to deny the pleasures of the flesh, for even in this we find the eternal life of the Spirit. Because our "soul clings fast" to God and to the hope that is only in Him, we are able to cling fast to His cross and so "discern what is the will of God, what is good and pleasing and perfect." And so we die with Him to live.

O. 23. Sun. (A)

Twenty-Third Week
(Ez.33:7-9; Ps.95:1-2,6-9; Rom.13:8-10; Mt.18:15-20)

"O wicked one, you shall surely die."

The Lord declares to the prophet Ezekiel: "You, son of man, I have appointed watchman for the house of Israel." He is to "speak out to dissuade the wicked from his way," that the sinner might not "die for his guilt" and that the prophet himself might not be "responsible for his death" by his silence.

As the Lord calls Ezekiel, so He requires all the Church to "warn the wicked, trying to turn him from his way." We must be diligent with all those in our care, all those we find in need, not in order to deliver condemnation upon souls but to invite all to "bow down in worship" and "kneel before the Lord who made us." How can someone know this great glory if there is sin upon his soul? And how will he know to turn from his sin if those the Lord gives words to speak hold their tongues as the sheep goes astray? And what shall become of this soul who has not offered the word of loving wisdom, but rather determined in himself that there is no hope for the sinner he sees?

Brothers and sisters, when we are called to declare: "'You shall not commit adultery; you shall not kill; you shall not steal; you shall not covet,' and whatever other commandment there may be," it is out of love for the soul we see straying that we speak. For love is "the fulfillment of the law"; it sums up all its precepts, and so all its precepts are expressed in love. Do not think the law is opposed to love – love and justice are one in God; and the Lord does not call us to ignorance or acceptance of sin, but to truth and salvation.

"Jesus said to His disciples, 'If your brother sins against you, go and tell him his fault'"; do not pretend the fault does not exist, but confront him, for his sake and your own. For "if he listens to you, you have won over your brother" – you will have brought him back to the fold. However, "if he doesn't listen," the Lord calls us further: "Take one or two others along with you." Bring objective witness to sway your loved one from evil. And "if he refuses to listen to them, tell the Church." Ah, the Church! The keeper of the Spirit of Truth and the flame of wisdom which no man can deny. What teaching the Lord has left with Her! And what power: "Whatever you bind on earth shall be bound in heaven, and whatever you loose on earth shall be loosed in heaven." For here are those "gathered together in [Jesus'] name," and He indeed is "in the midst of them." And if the soul "refuses to listen even to the Church," what hope has it of finding salvation? But at least you have done all you can.

All must be done in justice and in love to save the soul straying in this land. This is why the Lord has left us the Church; this is why He has left His Spirit – and we are called to speak His Truth, that salvation might come to all.

O. 24. Sun. (A)

Twenty-Fourth Week
(Sir.27:30-28:9; Ps.103:1-4,8-12; Rom.14:7-9; Mt.18:21-35)

"Should you not have had pity on your fellow servant,
as I had pity on you?"

How like the Lord's own wisdom is that of Sirach; how like His teaching. For have we not heard the Master say, "Forgive your neighbor's injustice; then when you pray, your own sins will be forgiven," in His instruction to His disciples on how to pray? And does He not impart this same lesson by parable today?

"Wrath and anger are hateful things, yet the sinner hugs them tight." O the woe of the unforgiving heart! "Could anyone nourish anger against another and expect healing from the Lord?" How can we "refuse mercy to another" and "seek pardon for [our] own sins"? Do we not know that anger is itself a deadly sin, mortally wounding our anxious souls? Do we who sit in judgment think in our hearts that we are without sin, that we are perfect as He who is Most High? If indeed "we are the Lord's" then we will act as the Lord and look with "kindness and compassion" upon others. Instead of condemnation we would practice divine forgiveness, for indeed mercy is the Father's defining trait in His relationship with His children.

But no, rather than putting "wrath" and "enmity" and "hate" as far from our hearts as the Lord has "put our transgressions from us," we cherish these abominations, setting them as trophies in our corrupted souls. Again, what woe there is for the unforgiving soul! For the same torture we would inflict upon others for their sins against us shall be the torture we ourselves shall face – then we will know what justice is! Then we will know the wrath of God! Then He who alone has power and wisdom and love to judge rightly shall inflict *His* punishment on all His wicked servants.

My brothers and sisters, fellow servants of the Lord in both life and in death, the Lord cannot emphasize enough to us the need for forgiveness. We must first and always recognize and remember the sinners we have been and the grace we have received at our Lord's hands. And with this ever in mind and heart we *must* come to others with that same mercy. It is this He desires of us, and He will accept nothing less.

O. 25. Sun. (A)

Twenty-Fifth Week
(Is.55:6-9; Ps.145:2-3,8-9,17-18; Phil.1:20-24,27; Mt.20:1-16)

"You too go into my vineyard, and I will give you what is just."

Our readings today reveal that the Lord is near, merciful, and just, and that these three qualities are one in God. For the Lord's justice is shown in His mercy, and His mercy in His nearness to us. And so we should "praise [His] name forever."

Isaiah conveys to us that the Lord's thoughts and ways are "as high as the heavens are above the earth" with respect to our own thoughts and our own ways. As David proclaims, "His greatness is unsearchable." But the prophet also encourages the faithful to "seek the Lord while He may be found, [to] call Him while He is near"; and the king declares, "The Lord is near to all who call upon Him, to all who call upon Him in truth." And is not the closeness of our great God – made most evident in the presence of Jesus among us – illustrated in the Lord's parable? Does not the landowner go out at all times of day to draw laborers into his vineyard? Even to the final hour He invites us into His kingdom, coming to us always with the hope of making us fruitful workers upon His land.

And why does the Lord remain so near? Why does He call to us so incessantly? Is it not because He is so "generous and merciful," because He is "good to all and compassionate toward all His works"? Is it not that we should turn from our idleness and the wickedness of our thoughts and ways that He ventures into the marketplace to find us? Does Jesus not come to redeem us from this world of sin? And should we not therefore "turn to the Lord for mercy, to our God who is generous in forgiving," whose calling us to work in His vineyard is more that He should be able to give us all we need than that we might labor for Him?

And is His mercy not proven by His form of justice? For does He not give all a full day's pay, even those with Him but an hour? Do not all who come to His kingdom know the blessings He pours forth? This is His way, this is His justice – the way of mercy and love. And it is by this love He remains so near us who may now proclaim with Paul: "Christ will be magnified in my body, whether by life or by death," for His love is

87

inseparable from us who believe, who have entered into His vineyard and share in His blood.

And should we not be merciful as He? Should His justice not become our own? We should not be as those servants who "grumbled against the landowner" for His generosity, courting envy in our hearts, but allow the Lord to be "free to do as [He] wish[es] with [His] own money." Should we not wish the same joy upon all souls as we ourselves have been blessed to know? Though we may have had to bear "the day's burden and the heat," should this limit our generosity to others who have come late? We should rather with our Lord desire all to enter His vineyard, to be close to us, that all might receive the benefit of His merciful justice. We should thank Him that His ways are not our own, for then never would He have come near to us, and empty and idle we would be standing still.

O. 26. Sun. (A)

Twenty-Sixth Week
(Ez.18:25-28; Ps.25:4-9; Phil.2:1-11; Mt.21:28-32)

"Tax collectors and prostitutes
are entering the kingdom of God before you."

Why? How can it be that such sinners gain such privilege, such grace? Is it for their sins? Shall we all become as they? We *should* be like them, but not in sin – in repentance. For it is because they have "turned away from all [the] sins that [they] committed" that they are saved; it is because they are "tax collectors and prostitutes" no more. And so we are all called to turn away from the sin which each of us surely has.

David sings beautifully of this in our psalm: "The sins of my youth and my frailty remember not," as he begs the Lord for His kindness. For all that we have done in our ignorance and our weakness we should seek the Lord's mercy, for He assures us throughout our readings that "He shows sinners the way" when they come humbly before Him.

When the first son in Jesus' parable responds to his father's request for him to work in the vineyard, "I will not," what does this son do but sin against his father? – just as each of us sins against our heavenly Father when we turn from His will to blindly follow our own. But what did the son show when he "afterwards changed his mind and went" but his contrition and repentance at his insubordination, thus illustrating the manner in which our consciences should lead *us* from our own disobedience? And as Jesus makes clear, it was this son who "did his father's will" and so will be blessed by him.

Our reading from Ezekiel makes this theme of turning from sin and finding blessing even clearer. It states in certain terms of the wicked man that "if he turns from the wickedness he has committed, and does what is right and just, he shall preserve his life." With such assurance, why should we delay our own conversion, which must be effected day to day?

St. Paul presents the attitude we must have before others and God in order to find the Lord's grace. He states: "Humbly regard others as more important than yourselves," and then gives the clear example of the most humble of all, the Lord Jesus Christ, who "emptied Himself, taking the form of a slave, coming in human likeness." He so "humbled Himself" that He became "obedient even unto death, death on a cross." And so should we be proud? Should we harden ourselves in our sin, or rather turn and empty ourselves of all that is not of Him? The salvation repentance finds is indicated also in the fact that, because of Jesus' humility, "God exalted Him and bestowed on Him the name which is above every other name." So let us not hesitate to join the tax collectors and prostitutes among us who bend the knee before Him; let our "tongue confess that Jesus Christ is Lord," and we shall know His reward.

Twenty-Seventh Week
(Is.5:1-7; Ps.80:9,12-16,19-20,Is.5:7; Phil.4:6-9; Mt.21:33-43)

"The kingdom of God will be taken away from you
and given to a people that will produce its fruit."

"Let me now sing of my friend, my friend's song concerning his vineyard. My friend had a vineyard on a fertile hillside; he spaded it, cleared it of stones, and planted the choicest vines; within it he built a watchtower, and hewed out a wine press. Then he looked for the crop of grapes, but what it yielded was wild grapes." Of course, this "vineyard of the Lord is the house of Israel, and the people of Judah are His cherished plant; He looked for judgment, but see, bloodshed! for justice, but hark, the outcry!" And so the Lord promises to "take away its hedge, give it to grazing, break through its wall, let it be trampled! Yes, [He] will make it a ruin."

Jesus' parable in our gospel today echoes precisely Isaiah's "song": "There was a landowner who planted a vineyard, put a hedge around it, dug a wine press in it, and built a tower." But now the prophecy is brought to fulfillment; now the rotten grapes come to maturity, and so the ruin of the vineyard will be complete. For in their rejection of the Son the hope of Israel is lost: none further has the Father to send them; herein they utterly spurn His love. How shall they be turned to producing good fruit if He who is the source of all goodness they destroy in their souls? There is nothing left but to remove the vineyard from them.

89

Ordinary Time

"A vine from Egypt [the Lord] transplanted; [He] drove away the nations and planted it." But for its unfaithfulness He has "broken down its walls." Indeed, in a scant few years after the crucifixion of the Messiah the temple in Jerusalem will be utterly destroyed – the worship upon which the faith of the Lord's people is founded will be no more. And it shall not return. But even as this temple built by hands the Lord lays waste, He yet answers our psalmist's plea to Him: "Look down from heaven, and see; take care of this vine, and protect what your right hand has planted." For as He destroys, so He builds; as Christ is killed, so His Church is planted. And it shall grow unto eternity.

The fulfillment of all prophecy, the New Jerusalem, is in our midst now. In the Catholic faith the worship at Jerusalem comes to maturity. And though many would see it removed – and perhaps by man's reason one might say for its sins it should be – though many come in their presumption to build anew... there is no call from the Lord for any of this, and these man-made structures will also fall to ruin. What God builds now He builds on a foundation which lasts forever, against which even the gates of hell shall not prevail. Only on the day of judgment, only when the kingdom has come, will this House be needed no more – for then all that will be will be His Church.

So, "brothers and sisters, have no anxiety at all, but in everything, by prayer and petition, make your requests known to God." Truly does the Lord's "face shine upon us" in this holy Temple, and it shall not be moved. See that you not remove yourselves from it but "keep on doing what you have learned and received and heard and seen" in its confines. Listen to His Word spoken to your hearts, and receive well the broken Bread of this holy sacrifice and the Blood of this heavenly vine. And bear fruit in His name.

O. 28. Sun. (A)

Twenty-Eighth Week
(Is.25:6-10; Ps.23:1-6; Phil.4:12-14,19-20; Mt.22:1-14)

"On this mountain the Lord of hosts
will provide for all peoples
a feast of rich food and choice wines."

"The kingdom of heaven may be likened to a king who gave a wedding feast for his son." It may be equated with "juicy, rich food and pure, choice wines," with "calves and fatted cattle ready to be eaten." A great banquet is the kingdom of heaven!

But, of course, though we speak here of food and eating, we know that it is not this we should thus seek on this earth, for these things are but of the earth and are only used to help us understand the heavenly fruits which are

90

ours in the kingdom of God. Paul makes this clear in his attitude toward food and the provisions that are of this world: "In every circumstance and in all things I have learned the secret of being well fed and of going hungry, of living in abundance and of being in need," and it truly matters not to him whether he is rich or poor in material things; all that matters is that we "can do all things in Him who strengthens" us – all that matter are the "glorious riches in Jesus Christ." Food and feasting are but metaphors for the things that in this world are unseen.

However, it is so that "the feast is ready" even here on this earth. It is true that the Lord "spread[s] the table before" us even in this world, even "in the sight of [our] foes." He does not leave us poor humans alone without real food to strengthen us for our journey. But this food is spiritual fare; His Body and Blood are not juicy and rich to our taste, to our bellies, but to our souls. This food nourishes the Spirit He has planted within us, and helps it ever to grow. Though real as our own flesh and our own blood, yet it truly is of heaven, and lends the glory of God to this bone of His bone.

"God will fully supply whatever you need," brothers and sisters; have no fear of being in want and no anxiety to build up abundance on this earth. He indeed is beside you always, giving your soul blessed "repose." Make it your aim to "dwell in the house of the Lord." Then "on that day" He reveals His kingdom, you will "rejoice and be glad," saying, "Behold, our God, to whom we looked to save us!" Then you will enter His presence forever. Prepare your soul for the wedding feast of heaven.

O. 29. Sun. (A)

Twenty-Ninth Week
(Is.45:1,4-6; Ps.96:1,3-5,7-10; 1Thes.1:1-5b; Mt.22:15-21)

"I am the Lord and there is no other,
there is no God besides me."

O brothers and sisters, how clear our Scripture today makes it that "great is the Lord and highly to be praised; awesome is He beyond all gods." Indeed there is no other God. It is He who grasped the "right hand" of even the pagan king, Cyrus, "subduing nations before him, and making kings run in his service." The heart of this king and all kings and all lands are in His hands – He alone rules all nations! Do you see this? Do you understand that if He calls this foreigner by "name, giving [him] a title," that there is none that is beyond His reach, that is not under His eye? By the Lord's power this pagan has conquered the nations of the world. And why? Why does He arm him who knows Him not? "So that toward the rising and the setting of the sun people may know that there is none beside [Him]."

Our psalmist sings so well of the singular power of the Lord God: "All the gods of the nations are things of naught, but the Lord made the heavens." Again I ask, do you see this? All nations recognize Him who made the heavens and the earth; even these "tremble before Him." And so all are called to "tell His glory among the nations, among all peoples, His wondrous deeds." For all must be encouraged to "give the Lord the glory due His name"; all must be offered the honor of knowing the greatness of our God.

One of these peoples who have come to knowledge of the one God we hear of in our second reading. Paul calls the Thessalonians "brothers and sisters loved by God" for their "work of faith and labor of love and endurance in hope of our Lord Jesus Christ." He gives thanks to God the Father that this Gentile people has come to faith in Him "with much conviction." What has been proclaimed so long now bears fruit. For even the millennium before, our psalmist had called the "families of nations" to "bring gifts, and enter His courts," to "worship the Lord in holy attire." None has ever been barred from adoring Him who is the One God and Father of all. But now the Gospel comes not "in word alone, but also in power and in the Holy Spirit." Now the word is anointed by Jesus' blood. So now all nations indeed come before Him, giving "the Lord glory and praise."

And when Jesus says, "Repay to Caesar what belongs to Caesar and to God what belongs to God," He does not remove anything from under God's domain. For even the things of Caesar are in God's hands (as is the coin between Jesus' fingers today), as the Son makes clear in His words before Pilate: "You would have no power over me if it had not been given to you from above" (Jn.19:11). And, "the Lord is King" and King is His Son, and "He governs the peoples with equity." Let all declare the glory of Him besides whom "there is no other."

O. 30. Sun. (A)

Thirtieth Week
(Ex.22:20-26; Ps.18:2-4,47,51; 1Thes.1:5-10; Mt.22:34-40)

"If ever you wrong them, and they cry out to me,
I will surely hear their cry."

In this simple statement by the Lord is revealed the essential nature of our God in His relation with His people. It demonstrates certainly what He says of Himself, "I am compassionate," for what is He telling us but that He has an ardent care for the poorest among us and the injustice they suffer? But it also demonstrates the justice of God itself, for what does He mean when He says He will "hear their cry" but that He will punish the wicked for

92

their heartless crimes? He states clearly, if any should "wrong any widow or orphan... [His] wrath will flare up, and [He] will kill [him] with the sword."

Now in the Church today we find an arbitrary and utterly deceptive and false separation of members into "liberal" or "conservative" camps, as if the Lord and His Church could be limited by either assignation. The liberal hears "love God and neighbor" and ignorantly excuses himself from keeping the law; and the conservative grasps the law so tightly he squeezes the very life, the very love, out of it. The Lord is neither liberal nor conservative, but may be said to be both – and that to the extreme in both cases. First of all, He has come to liberate us from our sin, to free us from the sentence of death all justly deserved as much as the adulteress or the thief on the cross He forgave. No one could be more liberal in His free giving of Himself and His love. What compares to the shedding of His blood, and the free gifts we gain thereby? Yet it must not be forgotten that the Lord Jesus is absolutely conservative in His teachings and in His ways; at all costs He preserves the truth. For though He says that "the whole law and the prophets depend on these two commandments" of love of God and neighbor, He does not thereby do away with the whole law. Indeed, He strengthens it. Does He not say not a single letter, nor even part of a letter, will pass away until all the law is fulfilled? Does He not tell us now that even to look at a woman lustfully is adultery and to be angry with another is as murder (see Mt.5:17-30)? And will He not come at the end of the age and judge all hearts, separating the evil from the good and casting them into eternal darkness and eternal flames? Though He "delivers us from the coming wrath" if we love Him, failing that, we cannot but be thrown into hell.

The Lord has two hands and either taken alone is ineffective, is, in fact, wicked, for either alone falls short of love and truth. The Lord is absolutely kind and absolutely just: these two meet and kiss in Him. And so they must in each of us. We must be "model[s] for all the believers." Let it be said that from us "the word of the Lord has sounded forth," that "in every place [our] faith in God has gone forth" – that we have carried both His love and His truth to every heart we touch. Then we shall rightly call the Lord our "rock" and our "deliverer"; then we shall exclaim, "Praised be the Lord" and be "safe from [our] enemies." Then He will hear our cry and save us, and all who truly love Him, for then we will be His disciples.

O. 31. Sun. (A)

Thirty-First Week
(Mal.1:14b-2:2b,8-10; Ps.131:1-3; 1Thes.2:7b-9,13; Mt.23:1-12)

"Have we not all the one Father?
Has not the one God created us?"

93

And should not those who serve in His stead, bringing the word of God to waiting hearts, be as He is, loving all as He does and thus giving "glory to [His] name"?

"I have stilled and quieted my soul like a weaned child. Like a weaned child on its mother's lap, so is my soul within me," King David declares, thus revealing the blessed relationship of the faithful, humble disciple and His Lord. We are indeed as little children before God, and He loves us as a tender Father, as the One who has made us with great care. And so we should take our peace upon His lap.

And when the sheep of the flock come to the shepherds the Lord has appointed to teach in His Name, they should find a reflection of the Father's presence – in these one should discover His love. Yes, they must instruct according to the Word placed upon their souls by their ordination, but they should not merit the words Jesus speaks of the Pharisees: "They preach but they do not practice." For if "all their works are performed to be seen," if they teach and preach without love, without living the word of God themselves, soon the flock will be led astray by their vanity and turn from the word they speak itself. Malachi prophesies to the priests of his day: "You have turned aside from the way, and have caused many to falter by your instruction." If these leaders show no reverence of God themselves, who will be led to reverence by their instruction?

Yes, still our duty is to God Himself and our worship is of Him alone – and so Jesus teaches the people, "Do and observe whatsoever [the scribes and Pharisees] tell you, but do not follow their example" – but He also demands of His followers that they not possess the vanity of these proud leaders. O if all approached the service of Paul, how blessed our Church would be! Listen to his words to the Thessalonians: "Brothers and sisters: we were gentle among you, as a nursing mother cares for her children," for he and his fellow workers "were determined to share with [them] not only the Gospel of God, but [their] very selves as well," so much did they love their flock with the love of God.

And this is as all pastors are called to be, "working night and day" for the little ones in their care. "Feed my sheep," the Lord commanded His Rock; and all our priests are called to feed the members of the Church not only with the Word of God, but also with His love, that they might learn to take refuge in Him who is Father of all. I ask you, has the Lord not become incarnate in our midst? And should that Incarnation not be known in all our flesh and in all our bone? Then let us serve one another in love.

Thirty-Second Week
(Wis.6:12-16; Ps.63:2-8; 1Thes.4:13-18; Mt.25:1-13)

"Stay awake, for you know neither the day nor the hour."

O Lord, "through the night-watches I will meditate on you: you are my help, and in the shadow of your wings I shout for joy." "As with the riches of a banquet shall my soul be satisfied, and with exultant lips my mouth shall praise you"; for though "my soul thirsts like the earth, parched, lifeless and without water" for you, O Living God, I have "gazed toward you in the sanctuary to see your power and your glory," and you have met me with your "kindness." Your Wisdom "graciously appears to [me] in the ways, and meets [me] with all solicitude."

"Resplendent and unfading is Wisdom, and she is readily perceived by those who love her, and found by those who seek her. She hastens to make herself known in anticipation of their desire; whoever watches for her at dawn shall not be disappointed, for he shall find her sitting by his gate. For taking thought of Wisdom is the perfection of prudence, and whoever for her sake keeps vigil shall quickly be free from care."

I could not say it any better, or any differently, than the sacred author. Do not these words perfectly illustrate the Lord's message in our gospel today – Stay awake! Keep your lamps burning! Seek Wisdom! Be ready, and she will come to you; and you will be gathered into the marriage feast. Foolishly sit in darkness, unconcerned for your fate, and these ominous words shall resound in your barren soul: "Then the door was locked." And then there shall be no entering.

I must again remark on the astounding lack of wisdom in the commentary of the missal I read. It states, "Paul is under the misconception that our Lord will return during his lifetime," ignorantly assuming that when he says, "We who are alive, who are left until the coming of the Lord," he is referring to himself and his companions. O my! Where do they derive the oil for their lamps? He is no more referring directly to himself in this instance than he is when he says, "If we believe that Jesus died and rose" – it is of the whole Church, of whatever time or place, he is speaking! How can our "scholars" not see this; and how can they be so ready to utter blasphemy against Holy Scripture and the Lord's Apostle, suggesting that he purports some greater knowledge of the Lord's return than the Lord Himself? Do they think he is as ignorant, or proud, as they?

Brothers and sisters, we indeed have great hope of resurrection. When "the Lord Himself, with a word of command, with the voice of an archangel and with the trumpet of God, will come down from heaven," we will be caught up with Him "in the air," in His heavenly presence. But we must have His light within ourselves and keep watch for His Hour, waiting through the night for the dawn of His Day.

Thirty-Third Week
(Prv.31:10-13,19-20,30-31;   Ps.128:1-5;   1Thes.5:1-6;   Mt.25:14-30)

> "When one finds a worthy wife,
> her value is far beyond pearls."

And so the Lord is pleased to bless His "good and faithful servant[s]"; for His Church is as His Bride and Her faithful members He invites to share His joy.

With more than the talents of "a man going on a journey" are we entrusted by the Lord. To us He is more like the husband "entrusting his heart" to his wife. All He gives over to us, even His very life, His absolute love – His blood itself He pours out for us. And are we as the good wife who "works with loving hands," who "puts her hands to the distaff and [whose] fingers ply the spindle"? Do we work diligently with all the gifts the Lord imparts to us and thus increase their yield? Are we as she who "brings [her husband] good, and not evil, all the days of her life," delivering unto the Lord the honor due His Name? If so, then as the worthy wife receives "a reward for her labors" and as "her works praise her at the city gates," so shall the Lord richly bless our labors, and the angels at the gates of heaven welcome us with song.

Brothers and sisters, "You are children of the light and children of the day. We are not of the night or of darkness. Therefore, let us not sleep as the rest do, but let us stay alert and sober," doing the Lord's will in all things. Let us not be as the "useless servant" who "dug a hole in the ground and buried his master's money." The graces the Lord gives us are not meant for such darkness, but indeed to be brought into the light of day that they might spread "like a fruitful vine" throughout the face of the earth. This is the call of His Church, and we must be faithful in the work with which we have been entrusted: His love must reach to the ends of the world.

And each "shall eat the fruit of [his] handiwork" when the day of the Lord comes upon us. The soul which has courted darkness in its distrust and laziness shall find the spouse that awaits her; but "blessed shall [she] be, and favored," "who walk[s] in [the Lord's] ways!" She shall indeed not fear the "sudden disaster" that comes upon the wicked, but shall celebrate "the prosperity of Jerusalem" in her Master's house "all the days of [her] life." For in none does the Lord take greater delight than she who returns an increase of His invaluable love.

Last Week: Christ the King
(Ez.34:11-12,15-17; Ps.23:1-6; 1Cor.15:20-26,28; Mt.25:31-46)

"Whatever you did for one of the least brothers of mine,
you did for me."

Jesus is King. It is He to whom the Father has "subjected everything" and who "must reign until He has put all His enemies under His feet," until He has "destroyed every sovereignty and every authority and power"; and it is He who then "hands over the kingdom to His God and Father... that God may be all in all." Yes, "when the Son of Man comes in His glory, and all the angels with Him, He will sit upon His glorious throne, and all the nations will assemble before Him." And He who is the Good Shepherd will separate the sheep beneath His rule "one from another": it is He who will say to the righteous, "Come, you who are blessed by my Father. Inherit the kingdom prepared for you from the foundation of the world"; and to the unrighteous, "Depart from me, you accursed, into the eternal fire prepared for the devil and his angels." He will judge all souls, for all souls are in His hands. Yes, He is King.

And yet this King is with His subjects; this Shepherd is hidden in His sheep – He is the Shepherd who "finds Himself among His scattered sheep." Indeed, in His power He promises to "pasture [His] sheep": "The lost I will seek out, the strayed I will bring back, the injured I will bind up, the sick I will heal"... but more than this, more than this is our King to us. For He is a King who not only serves the poor and broken, but who *is* the poor and broken Himself. Though all power and glory and honor are with Him who is exalted as Head over all, He travels with the least of His children; He makes Himself one with the least of all creatures. Does He not say, "I was hungry and you gave me food, I was thirsty and you gave me drink, a stranger and you welcomed me, naked and you clothed me, ill and you cared for me, in prison and you visited me"? O how He unites Himself with our humanity! His love is beyond our comprehension.

And, brothers and sisters, it should be obvious what we are now called to do; if we wish to be "brought to life... each one in proper order," following "Christ the firstfruits," we must walk in His way. If we wish to sing with David His humble king, "You anoint my head with oil; my cup overflows" – if indeed we desire to share in His eternal kingship, we must on the dust of this earth serve Him in the least among us... we ourselves must be the least, as He is. Alleluia to our exalted King!

2. Year B

Second Week

(1Sm.3:3b-10,19; Ps.40:2,4,7-10; 1Cor.6:13c-15a,17-20; Jn.1:35-42)

"The Lord came and revealed His presence,
calling out as before, 'Samuel, Samuel!'"

The call of Samuel, the call of Peter and his brother(s), and the call of us all to "glorify God in [our] body." As "Samuel was sleeping in the temple of the Lord" when the Lord called to him, so we must all have the Holy Spirit within ourselves, we must each "know that our body is a temple of the Holy Spirit," if we are to hear and answer the call of God. As the disciples were so set upon finding the Christ, so our hearts, too, must be set upon Him, if we are to hear the words: "We have found the Messiah." He lives, brothers and sisters, and in His Temple He dwells. And each of us He would make His temple; each of us He calls to be His disciple this day. Listen for His voice, and go as you are led.

Samuel was but a boy when he was called, and with the pure obedience of a child he responded to God's voice. Blessed was he to live with the high priest in the Lord's temple, a forerunner of Christ in his living with the Lord from his youth, in his dedication to God and His will. But now the Temple that is Jesus has come into the world, and makes His home with any so inclined, any who would take their rest at this holy Tabernacle of God. He comes indeed now to make His home with us, even in the Sacrament He offers each day. And do we respond as the boy Samuel?

"John was standing with two of his disciples, and as he watched Jesus walk by, he said, 'Behold, the Lamb of God'"; and so the two disciples find themselves called, and so they follow the Lord: "they went and saw where Jesus was staying, and they stayed with Him that day." And one called his brother first to the Lord; and so Peter, the rock of the Church, comes to Christ... and so are all gathered unto the Lord. And John still points to Jesus to this day, and Peter is still the rock of His teaching and the minister of His Body – and we are all now joined to them.

"Do you not know that your bodies are members of Christ?" brothers and sisters. Do you not understand that you are called to a holiness that equals His own? This you should know, this you should understand – His call you should hear ringing in your ear. And "with ears open to obedience" you should answer, "Here I am," and become one with the Blessed Lamb, pure as the flesh of His sacrifice.

Third Week

(Jon.3:1-5,10; Ps.25:4-9; 1Cor.7:29-31; Mk.1:14-20)

"Jonah made ready and went to Nineveh,
according to the Lord's bidding."

And so the reluctant prophet set out on his journey to the profligate pagan city of Nineveh to "announce to it the message" the Lord imparts, to call it to repentance of sin. Finally Jonah is faithful to the Lord's command, and his work bears fruit.

And as Jonah went walking through the city, "announcing 'Forty days more and Nineveh shall be destroyed'" here among his nation's enemies, so "Jesus came to Galilee proclaiming the gospel of God: 'This is the time of fulfillment,'" calling His own people to repentance, that they might enter the City in which He dwells. And in the same steps as our Savior, those whom He calls walk. Today we see Simon and Andrew and James and John follow Him. Soon the other apostles will fall in line... and so all the disciples of the Lord walk in the way He has trod. And you, brother, do your feet walk the same path of apostleship; do you heed His call to repentance and reflect the kingdom of God with all your life? Let the earth beneath your feet be the same earth that Jesus walked.

May all come to repentance: this is our Savior's will. This is the purpose for which He and all His prophets and apostles are sent – that men might turn from their sin and join Him in heaven. "Thus He shows sinners the way." Thus "He teaches the humble His way." Thus all who are humble and recognize their sin before Him He blesses, leading them on right paths to Him. "When God saw by [the Ninevites'] actions how they turned from their evil way," He also turned from His punishment of them. And thus Jonah's call is heeded; and thus the Lord's will is done.

All He will likewise save, if they turn from their sins; if we do not set our hearts on this passing world, we shall be free of its condemnation. Whether "weeping" or "rejoicing" here should make no difference if our lives are lived for the world which never passes from us, which stays with us even as the Lord Jesus who has come into our midst. Let us all cry out with our psalmist David:

"Your ways, O Lord, make known to me;
    teach me your paths,
    guide me in your truth and teach me,
    for you are God my Savior."

And the Lord's will shall be done in all of us.

99

Fourth Week
(Dt.18:15-20; Ps.95:1-2,6-9; 1Cor.7:32-35; Mk.1:21-28)

"A prophet like me will the Lord, your God,
raise up for you from among your own kin."

Thus does Moses speak to the people as he prepares to leave them, and they prepare to enter the Promised Land. He prophesies most immediately the anointing of Joshua, who will take his place as leader of the Israelite nation and guide them into the holy land, as well as all the prophets who shall follow... but most especially, of course, he hereby prophesies the coming of the only Son of God, the Lord Jesus Christ, who will be raised up from among us, a man as we are, to be God in our midst. No greater fulfillment of this promise could there be: no more real could God make His presence known to us. Here on this earth He stands, and speaks.

Our reading from Deuteronomy makes clear the nature and role of the prophet; in this passage we see the inception of this gift, of this power God gives to man. When the people begged Moses, "Let us not again hear the voice of the Lord, our God, nor see this great fire anymore," for fear of death after having witnessed the Lord's most powerful theophany at Mount Horeb, the Most High answered them and promised instead, "I will raise up for them a prophet like you from among their kin, and will put my words into his mouth; he shall tell them all that I command him." Here is the very definition of a prophet: one who speaks for God. Out of a prophet's mouth come the words of the Lord, not his own.

And what a Prophet is Jesus! And, of course, so much more than a prophet – the only Son. "For He taught them as one having authority"; His words of rebuke: "Quiet! Come out of him!" cast out all unclean spirits... His power is immeasurable as God's power is immeasurable – all is in His hands and at the command of His voice. For His words are not His own (though intimately His own); they are His Father's. He does only the Father's will and so is the Father's Son. In them together the Spirit moves! Upon all regions of the earth His Word goes forth.

"Oh, that today you would hear His voice," brothers and sisters, and "bow down in worship before Him," knowing who is here before you now and consecrating yourself entirely to Him. Then you would but "sing joyfully" and be filled with "thanksgiving" as, free from sin, from all darkness – from all that is unclean – you come to full union with the promised One of all the ages and make your home in His heart, obedient to His blessed, protective commands, and so find yourself "free of anxieties" as you think only of "how [you] may please the Lord." Alleluia! He has come.

Fifth Week

(Jb.7:1-4,6-7; Ps.147:1-6; 1Cor.9:16-19,22-23; Mk.1:29-39)

"He heals the brokenhearted
and binds up their wounds."

In our first reading, Job is about as brokenhearted as a man could be, beset entirely by the devil's trials as he is. "Swifter than a weaver's shuttle" his complete loss of goods and family and his own health has come upon him. And so he seems to see his days "come to an end without hope." More miserable a creature there could not be.

In our gospel we are told that "Simon's mother-in-law lay sick with a fever" and that the people of the town in which Jesus found Himself "brought to Him all who were ill or possessed by demons." Surrounded is He with the afflictions man suffers, the weakness to which our fallen race is so prone. It seems that all are indeed "brokenhearted" and wounded; as Simon Peter says upon finding the Lord praying in a deserted place the next morning: "Everyone is looking for you." All need so greatly the healing only He brings.

And He does heal all who come to Him. As even before His birth into this world He served to set Job free from the clutches of Satan and grant him a new life which was beyond his hope; as Simon's mother-in-law "He approached, grasped her hand, and helped her up," the fever fleeing His touch; as "He cured many who were sick with various diseases, and He drove out many demons" from those gathered at the door of the house where He stayed... so He continues "preaching and driving out demons," not only throughout Galilee and all of Judea and all of Israel, but to this day to the ends of the earth through His holy Church.

Our Lord has become "a slave to all so as to win over as many as possible." Our weakness He has taken upon Himself to remove our weakness from us. Our diseases, our darkness, our sin... our "months of misery" He has borne that He might heal us of all infirmities – that He might bind up our broken hearts. Our salvation comes at the touch of His hand, at the breath of His mouth. Let us rise and walk with Him, for the Dawn has come and His grace-filled blood is upon us.

Sixth Week

(Lv.13:1-2,44-46; Ps.32:1-2,5,7,11; 1Cor.10:31-11:1; Mk.1:40-45)

"I said, 'I confess my faults to the Lord,'
and you took away the guilt of my sin."

101

The leper in our gospel confesses his faults to the Lord when he says, "If you wish, you can make me clean," for by these words he recognizes that "he is in fact unclean" – that he is a sick man in need of a physician. And Jesus takes away the guilt of his sin when He responds, "I do will it. Be made clean." For by a mere word from His mouth we are purged.

That the sinner should cry out his guilt is evident even in the ancient Book of Leviticus; it gives specific instructions for the actions of the leper, whose sin has made him unclean: "The one who bears the sore of leprosy shall keep his garments rent and his head bare, and shall muffle his beard; he shall cry out, 'Unclean, unclean!' As long as the sore is on him he shall declare himself unclean." Here is a graphic representation of the way we sinners should present ourselves to the Lord. Like the leper who cries to Jesus on his knees, we should never hide our sin from the Lord; our "guilt [should be] covered not." For the Lord indeed sees all things – nothing is hidden from Him – so we fool only ourselves if we attempt to hide; and He can't heal us of our affliction if we do not come into His light. We must come before Him in all humility for the poison upon our souls, and He will save us from our sin.

How sincere is the leper's contrition to move the Lord to such immediate pity! How pitiable indeed he is, as to a final hope for cleansing waters he comes with head bowed to the earth, his years of suffering evident in his shaking voice. Whimpering like a dog he humbles himself before the Lord... and a tear we find in Jesus' eye – inevitably He reflects our penitence in His grace. Let your heart break before Him! Bleed before the Lord who bleeds for you! Expose your sores to His eyes and His light shall cure them all.

Finally, brothers and sisters, let us indeed "be imitators" of Paul, "not seeking [our] own benefit but that of the many, that they may be saved," that people will keep "coming to [Jesus] from everywhere" to find the healing of their "sore of leprosy," to discover salvation from their sins. For He does "will it" for everyone – the redemption of all He holds in His arms of sacrifice. Let all souls show themselves to His priests; let all confess their sins openly, that reconciliation with God and one another all may know. O Lord, take away the sin from my soul! (Thank you for the sacrament you leave with us.)

O. 7. Sun. (B)

Seventh Week
(Is.43:18-19,21-22,24b-25; Ps.41:2-5,13-14; 2Cor.1:18-22; Mk.2:1-12)

"It is I, I, who wipe out, for my own sake, your offenses;
your sins I remember no more."

What a wonderful promise the Lord makes to us today, and proves His word true in Jesus His Son.

Yes, the Lord "has regard for the lowly and the poor," and so He looks with pity on the paralytic lowered through the roof for healing. Jesus "help[s] him on his sickbed" and "take[s] away all his ailment," both spiritual and physical, first granting him forgiveness of sins, then calling him to "rise, pick up [his] mat, and go home." And so indeed his sins are gone, remembered no more, and so he is made whole... and so the home to which he returns is more than the one with walls and a roof – he returns to his eternal home in the arms of the Lord.

How the Lord indeed reveals that He is "doing something new!" For do not all the people exclaim, "We have never seen anything like this" at the healing of the paralytic? And is it not right that they should glorify God in such a manner? What could be more remarkable than the teaching and healing and forgiving presence of Jesus in our midst? How could God fulfill His promises in a greater way? It could not be. "God is faithful," indeed, and "the Son of God, Jesus Christ" is He who is the Father's "yes" to all His promises. What can we do but rejoice in such grace?

"O Lord, have pity on me; heal me, though I have sinned against you." "In the desert [you] make a way, in the wasteland, rivers"; to the desert and wasteland of my sinful soul bring your cleansing waters. As you took pity on the paralytic, as you called him to rise from the unyielding pull of his mat, so call me to lift myself up from the mire of sin into which I have fallen. Let your promise be fulfilled in me: wipe out my offenses and remember my sins no more, that I might walk resolutely to my home in heaven and there "stand before you forever." I give you my "yes" of faith this day.

Eighth Week
(Hos.2:16b-17b,21-22; Ps.103:1-4,8,10,12-13; 2Cor.3:1b-6; Mk.2:18-22)

"The letter brings death, but the spirit gives life."

If we went by the letter of the law alone, all would be dead: none would know the salvation of the Lord. For none could keep the law in total; all fall short in sin. And any measure of sin merits condemnation.

But we have a God who "pardons all [our] iniquities," who "redeems us from destruction." "Not according to our sins does He deal with us," not according to the law alone. For Jesus has come bringing "a new covenant, not of letter but of spirit," and by its grace all sinful souls are made new. Here is the Word "written not in ink but by the Spirit of the living God, not on tablets of stone but on tablets that are hearts of flesh." And for this we should be eternally grateful to the Lord, that He has brought His living, forgiving presence amongst us.

"I will espouse you to me forever," says the Lord to the straying soul burdened by the edicts of the law which convict it of its sin. "In right and in justice, in love and in mercy," I will come to you, and set you free from the bonds of your infidelity, is the promise our "gracious" God makes. And in Jesus Christ this espousal is fulfilled by the power of the Holy Spirit, through whom the Lord purges us of all sin and prepares our hearts to receive Him. Yes, we are wed to the Father, wed to the glory of God, though once we had been far from Him.

And, "can the wedding guests fast while the bridegroom is with them?" If "as far as the east is from the west, so far has He put our transgressions from us," what can we do but rejoice in His presence? For now indeed we are renewed; now indeed we wear new skins – now indeed we are brought to life!

The power of the Spirit is upon all those redeemed by the blood of Christ, and with the Father in heaven these blessed souls become one. Death has been overcome, sin cast out, and into us now the Spirit breathes eternal life. So should "all [our] being bless His holy name"; so with the Word of God "written on our hearts" we should declare the Savior of all ages.

O. 9. Sun. (B)

Ninth Week
(Dt.5:12-15; Ps.81:2-8,10-11; 2Cor.4:6-11; Mk.2:23-3:6)

"I relieved his shoulder from the burden."

Yes, the Lord has "led [us] forth from the land of Egypt." As Israel "came forth from the land of Egypt," as he was released from the bondage of slavery, so we are released from the bondage of sin. It is this freedom we celebrate on the Lord's Day.

"Take care to keep holy the sabbath day as the Lord, your God, commanded you." This commandment is from of old, and it is made new in the blood of Christ poured out for our refreshment on His altar this day. And should this not be cause of rejoicing for all holy souls? Should we not "take up a melody and sound the timbrel" at His command that we "should rest" in Him and in His grace? For though we were once wearied by sin and starved for mercy, now we find that even as David and his men "ate the bread of offering that only the priests could lawfully eat," so we are given the Bread of angels to restore us in our need. The Lord but calls us to "stretch out [our] hand" to receive His food, to receive His healing; and would we grieve Him by a "hardness of heart" that would keep us from His presence this day? The Lord has indeed released us from slavery; He has indeed made us whole. And He desires that we accept His grace in Word and Sacrament each Lord's Day.

In uniting ourselves with our Savior we discover that we are "always carrying about in the body the dying of Jesus." But this burden is not like the burden we once knew in the land of Egypt. For though we are now "afflicted" and "persecuted," we are "not constrained" or "driven to despair." For the burden of the cross is made light by Him who carries it for us, and we carry it ourselves that "the life of Jesus may also be manifested in our body." So we have exchanged the debilitating burden of sin for the redeeming burden of Christ, and are thereby led to new life.

"Brothers and sisters: God who said, *Let light shine out of darkness*, has shone in our hearts to bring to light the knowledge of the glory of God in the face of Jesus Christ." And so on the day of the sun we gather as one to celebrate the light of the Son shining in us. "Observe the sabbath day," brothers and sisters, and make its glory known every day of your lives.

O. 10. Sun. (B)

Tenth Week
(Gn.3:9-15; Ps.130:1-8; 2Cor.4:13-5:1; Mk.3:20-35)

"With the Lord is kindness
and with Him is plenteous redemption."

We hear today recounted in our first reading our first parents' tragic fall from the grace of God into the boundaries of hell – for now they tend to hide themselves from His glorious face. O such disobedience that has caused such painful separation of the crown of creation from the Creator's hand! And what greater punishment than this can we know: not to be eternally in His presence as was His intent? And for such sin inflicted upon our race our psalmist is caused to plea: "Out of the depths I cry to you, O Lord; Lord, hear my voice!" For release from the "iniquities" upon his soul he begs the Lord... and so is proclaimed the cry of us all.

And does the Lord hear? He cannot help but hear, for "with [Him] is forgiveness, that [He] may be revered." He draws His children back to His paradise by the cords that are the blood of Christ, "that the grace bestowed on more and more people may cause the thanksgiving to overflow for the glory of God." "Knowing that the one who raised the Lord Jesus will raise us also... we are not discouraged... For we know that if our earthly dwelling, a tent, should be destroyed, we have a building from God, a dwelling not made with hands, eternal in heaven." Sin may well be at work within us, causing the body to die, causing us to give up our lives – forcing us to put no stock in the passing things of this life; but through this sacrifice the Lord is at work building our home in heaven. Paul sums up this redemptive process so beautifully when he says, "This momentary light affliction is producing for us an eternal weight of glory beyond comparison." For the affliction indeed passes with these passing things, but His house is eternal.

And in our gospel we see well that Jesus has come and "plunder[ed] the house" of Satan. "He drives out demons" from this decaying house in which we dwell, dividing it against itself and breaking the hold Satan has on souls by the corrupted influence of the flesh. Anointing fallen man with the purity of the Holy Spirit, as by fire sin is consumed. What devil can stand in this light? What influence has sin upon our souls with Jesus as our God? And so we poor fallen creatures become as His own, as His "brother and sister and mother," for by the grace that comes only from the Son, again we become one with the Father – in joy we stand before His loving gaze. "More than sentinels wait for the dawn, let Israel wait for the Lord," for now has our redemption come.

O. 11. Sun. (B)

Eleventh Week
(Ez.17:22-24; Ps.92:2-3,13-16; 2Cor.5:6-10; Mk.4:26-34)

"They that are planted in the house of the Lord
shall flourish in the courts of our God."

The imagery today is of trees and plants and the growth and strength of the kingdom of God. "The just one shall flourish like a palm tree, like a cedar of Lebanon shall he grow," our psalmist rejoices, and adds, "They shall bear fruit even in old age; vigorous and sturdy shall they be." In our gospel Jesus tells us that the kingdom of God is like the seed that grows gradually, imperceptibly into ripe grain ready for the harvest, and compares it also to the mustard seed, "the smallest of all the seeds on the earth," which "springs up and becomes the largest of plants and puts forth large branches, so that the birds of the sky can dwell in its shade."

God is the seed from which all is sprung. Jesus is the "tender shoot" spoken of by Ezekiel. Taken from "the crest of the cedar," the humble bloom of the house of Israel, He is "planted on a high and lofty mountain" – raised up to the right hand of the Father – and by the power of the Holy Spirit, thence He "put[s] forth branches and bear[s] fruit, and become[s] a majestic cedar": His apostles and prophets go forth and plant the Word of God in all hearts; and as it grows unto heaven and blossoms forth in the works of every Christian, the Church is made to stand fast in the sight of the Lord. "Birds of every kind shall dwell beneath it"; everyone who seeks refuge from the heat of the sun that is this world of sin beating down upon

106

the human soul shall find in His Church a place of peace and comfort, a house in which he is nourished and sent on his flight, carrying the love of our God across the heavens to all lands.

Brothers and sisters, let us be "courageous," as indeed Paul declares we are. Let us be strong and sturdy lowly trees growing by the grace of God to heavenly heights in all our deeds on earth. Though "we would rather leave the body and go home to the Lord," though we would today see the kingdom of heaven fulfilled before our eyes, yet as long as we have the flesh of this tree enrobing our souls, let us always "aspire to please Him," to please our God, to grow closer each day to where He sits on His throne in the kingdom, that when we "all appear before the judgment seat of Christ" we "each may receive recompense" and together "sing praise to... [the] Most High."

Twelfth Week
(Jb.38:1,8-11; Ps.107:23-26,28-31; 2Cor.5:14-17; Mk.4:35-41)

"Who then is this whom even wind and sea obey?"

Need you ask? If you must, I will tell you: this is He who "shut within the doors the sea, when it burst forth from the womb"; He who "set limits for it and fastened the bars of its door" – He who speaks to Job: "Here shall your proud waves be stilled!" This is the Lord, the great I AM!

When the Lord "raised up a storm wind" against those "trading on the deep waters... which tossed its waves on high... their hearts melted away in their plight." But "they cried to the Lord in their distress [and] from their straits He rescued them." Is not He who "hushed the storm to a gentle breeze, and the billows of the sea were stilled," the same God who in our gospel when the disciples cry out, "We are perishing," because "a violent squall came up and waves were breaking over the boat" – is this not the same God who "rebuked the wind, and said to the sea, 'Quiet! Be still!'" by whose hand "the wind ceased and there was great calm"? The power is the same and the God is the same. Jesus is Lord!

And is it not this same God, this same Christ, who stills the waves of your own pride when its waters begin to fill your boat with sin, when it seems you shall sink into the deep and never return? Do you not know your sin? Do you not know His power? Is it not the Lord's great power and the peace we find by its great grace of which Paul, too, speaks when he says, "The old things have passed away; behold, new things have come"? Is it not the same salvation he refers to when he declares, "Whoever is in Christ is a new creation"?

Brothers and sisters, "Let us cross to the other side." Let us allow the Lord to bring us "to [our] desired haven." Through the tribulation of this life let us pass, impelled by "the love of Christ," knowing He holds power over all the proud waves of the sinful sea in His redeeming Hand. Let Him but speak a word to our impenitent hearts to break the waves we raise up and make us whole.

"Do you not yet have faith?" Then indeed be dead in Christ and live "no longer for [yourselves] but for Him who for [our] sake died and was raised." This is the Lord our God. Silence your tongue before Him.

O. 13. Sun. (B)

Thirteenth Week
(Ws.1:13-15,2:23-24; Ps.30:2,4-6,11-13; 2Cor.8:7,9,13-15; Mk.5:21-43)

"God formed man to be imperishable;
the image of His own nature He made him."

"God did not make death, nor does He rejoice in the destruction of the living." "By the envy of the devil death entered the world, and they who belong to his company experience it," but God has nothing to do with death: He is but Life, and would have us be with Him where He is.

It is the Lord's will that all live, that all are rescued from death and destruction; and so Jesus "became poor, so that by His poverty [we] might become rich," and so He died that we might live... and so He comes healing us of our disease and raising us from the dead. David witnesses to His power in our psalm today – "You brought me up from the nether world, you preserved me from among those going down into the pit" – and in our gospel Jesus heals the woman of her flow of blood and wakes Jairus' daughter from her sleep.

"Little girl, I say to you, arise!" the Lord whispers to the child of twelve as He holds her by the hand, and "she [arises] immediately and walk[s] around." Despite the commotion and the ridicule of the crowd outside, the Lord enters her room and calls quite clearly to her heart... Do you hear Him? Do you hear Him speaking? Does He not call to all our hearts to rise from the dead, from the death of sin or complacency, or whatever disease has gripped our lives? What He speaks to the little girl He says to all: "Rise from your slumber, O sleeper!"

It is not death to which we are called, but life. This Jesus clearly shows in His ministry upon the earth. And though this life can only be fully known having entered the gates of heaven, and though each day we are called to lay down our lives, to die as the Lord has shown us – though this indeed be a world of suffering for the Christian soul who always carries his cross, we know the Mighty One, the Creator of the universe, holds us each in His loving hand, and He will turn our "mourning into dancing" as He breathes life upon us again. "At nightfall weeping enters in, but with the dawn rejoicing," as we see that never really do we die, as we discover in His presence among us our eternal life... as we sense even now our blessed immortality. Remain with Him forever.

Fourteenth Week
(Ez.2:2-5; Ps.123:1-4; 2Cor.12:7-10; Mk.6:1-6)

"My grace is sufficient for you,
for power is made perfect in weakness."

And so Ezekiel, though he is being sent to those "who have rebelled against [God]," to those who are "hard of face" and "obstinate of heart," yet must declare, "Thus says the Lord," yet must call to their rebellious hearts "whether they heed or resist." Likely they will resist him; likely they will persecute him, as they have all the prophets, but still he must "lift up [his] eyes" to Him who is "enthroned in heaven" – despite his weakness before these lions, he must stand strong with God.

And "so are our eyes on the Lord, our God"; so do we look to Him constantly for His mercy and protection. "We are more than sated with contempt: our souls are more than sated with the mockery of the arrogant, with the contempt of the proud." The believing Christian cannot but be persecuted by the wickedness of the world, pervasive in all men's hearts, for he stands in constant opposition to the lust and greed and violence with which fallen man seeks to fill his soul. What can we be but weak in the face of such a hardened enemy? And yet we must make that enemy our friend; yet we must say with Paul: "I am content with weaknesses, insults, hardships, persecutions, and constraints, for the sake of Christ." For we know that the power of God is with us despite our humiliation; we know that He acts just the same to thwart the wicked.

On the cross they mocked the Lord; they spurned His goodness and looked with contempt on His love, a love which died for them who beat Him. And today we see that Jesus "came to His native place... to teach in the synagogue," despite the fact that they would "[take] offense at Him." They cannot believe this humble carpenter's son could teach with such wisdom: "Where did this man get all this?" they ask in doubt of His origin. The Lord's weak appearance belies the mighty Spirit which is upon Him; and those who are blind to truth and so slow of heart to believe cannot but mock and stone Him who alone would give them strength.

Brothers and sisters, to whatever people you go let them know "that a prophet has been among them"; show them all that Christ has risen from the dead. There may be some who will turn from their sin, and even if rebuked, you will maintain the power of the grace of God within. Always remember, it is not you who speak but the Lord.

Fifteenth Week
(Amos 7:12-15; Ps.85:8-14; Eph.1:3-14; Mk.6:7-13)

"Justice shall walk before Him,
and prepare the way of His steps."

And so when the disciples are sent out, the Lord "instruct[s] them to take nothing for the journey but a walking stick." The walking stick signifies that the carrier is on an itinerant mission, and the walking stick serves to support the traveler along his way. The walking stick is the cross of Christ, which does both these things and brings all the grace and guidance we need on our journey through life. The walking stick is prepared in justice, the justice of the blood of Christ, and so it brings all who take it up to the kingdom of God.

The Father "has blessed us in Christ with every spiritual blessing in the heavens," and so, what more do we need than His cross, since in it "we have redemption by His blood"? And now we are "sealed with the promised Holy Spirit, which is the first installment of our inheritance toward redemption as God's possession," and thereby ready to walk the path He sets before us this day. The cross of contradiction going before us, we join the apostles who "went off and preached repentance." Amos, too, heeded this call to chastise the people for their sins. And for this he, too, suffered the cross, being commanded by the power of the world: "Off with you, visionary, flee to the land of Judah!" But still he continues to preach repentance, still he is faithful to the Lord's instruction to "prophesy to [His] people Israel." And so must all His apostles be.

We need not fear the persecution upon us for "near indeed is [the Lord's] salvation to those who fear Him." To those who are faithful to His call, "the Lord Himself will give all His benefits." We have all we need "in accord with the riches of His grace that He lavished upon us," and we must only be "holy and without blemish before Him" – as is His desire – to find every blessing we require. And He will give us "authority over unclean spirits"; He will enable us to cast all evil from His sight. And so "to the praise of His glory" there will be "glory dwelling in our land." His justice walks now before us; let us go in the way of His steps. His cross is all we need for the journey.

Sixteenth Week
(Jer.23:1-6; Ps.23:1-6; Eph.2:13-18; Mk.6:30-34)

"I myself will gather the remnant of my flock
from all the lands to which I have driven them
and bring them back to their meadow."

"The Lord is my shepherd; I shall not want. In verdant pastures He gives me repose." How true to Isaiah's prophecy are King David's words; and how true is Jesus as the "righteous shoot to David" who "shall reign and govern wisely," who shepherds the people of God. And how blessed "the house of the Lord" in which we dwell "for years to come."

Brothers and sisters, is not that shore onto which Jesus disembarks in our gospel today the place where He "refreshes [our] soul"? Does He not make these "restful waters" for all who are "like sheep without a shepherd"? For is He Himself not the ocean in which we are cleansed and so find our peace; does His teaching not shepherd our wayward hearts into secure pastures?

"He came and preached peace to you who were far off and peace to those who were near." Is Paul not true in his preaching when he claims that through Jesus all "have access in one Spirit to the Father"? Though before there may have been Gentile and Jew and a "dividing wall of enmity" between the two, though still division may persist in the nations of man, yet the Son has come "that He might create in Himself one new person," that He "might reconcile both with God." And so all are one in His peace which He offers "through the cross."

"This is the name they give Him: 'The Lord our justice,'" for He does "what is just and right in the land." To this land He has come; upon this earth He has disembarked. And now "moved with pity" He teaches us truth; "He guides [us] in right paths for His name's sake." And faithful is He in His promise to "appoint shepherds" to lead us in His grace. Already in our gospel we see the apostles rejoice in "all they have done and taught" by His authority. And so, peace we should find now in the walls of His Church, our daily bread offered at His pulpit and upon His altar.

Thank you, Lord, for fulfilling your promise in our midst each day.
Thank you for shepherding us to eternal glory.

Seventeenth Week
(2Kgs.4:42-44; Ps.145:10-11,15-18; Eph.4:1-6; Jn.6:1-15)

"They shall eat and there shall be some left over."

Ordinary Time

O Lord, "the eyes of all look hopefully to you, and you give them their food in due season; you open your hand and satisfy the desire of every living thing." You are He who is "just in all His ways and holy in all His works," and eating the food you offer, we become holy as well.

Brothers and sisters, if we "live in a manner worthy of the call [we] have received, with all humility and gentleness, with patience, bearing with one another through love, striving to preserve the unity of spirit through the bond of peace," what shall not be ours? Will the cup upon our table not overflow? For then we shall be holy as He is holy. And what does it mean to be holy but to be perfect, to be complete? Did not those reclining on the grass eat as much bread "and also as much fish as they wanted"? Is it not true that they "had their fill"? And will those who come to the table of the Lord today, to partake of the sacrifice offered on His altar, be found wanting? No, certainly not. For as far as Jesus' miracle of feeding the five thousand with five loaves surpasses Elisha's feeding the hundred with twenty loaves, thus far and more does Jesus' feeding our bodies and souls with His Bread and Wine surpass the miracle we hear of today in our gospel. For now billions eat. Now all who come are fed. Without limit souls are satisfied, and satisfied unto heaven.

Two notes I would make regarding our readings today. The first is that when Jesus performed this miracle of feeding the five thousand, "the Jewish feast of the Passover was near." The Evangelist does not state this in vain: it is on the feast of the Passover Jesus shall offer Himself as the new Lamb of whose flesh all must partake – it is this day He shall institute the Eucharist. And note, too, Elisha's immediate words upon being offered the twenty barley loaves as a gift: "Give it to the people to eat." What is given him he offers to all, and so prefigures our Lord's generous sacrifice of Himself – and so exemplifies the attitude we all must have to whatever the Lord provides. For then it is we show faith in our God's providential hand; and it is then we participate in the abundant outpouring of His gifts upon all who await His blessing. "One body and one Spirit" are we all, and to this oneness there is no limit.

O. 18. Sun. (B)

Eighteenth Week
(Ex.16:2-4,12-15; Ps.78:3-4,23-25,54; Eph.4:17,20-24; Jn.6:24-35)

"Do not work for food that perishes
but for food that endures for eternal life,
which the Son of Man will give you."

Their bellies rumbling in the desert, "the whole Israelite community grumbled against Moses and Aaron," calling out for food to satiate their

112

hunger. How they long to be beside their "flesh pots" in Egypt, where they "ate [their] fill of bread" – even if they should die there. Their great concern is for the food which perishes.

And in our gospel, too, Jesus upbraids the crowd who follow Him, saying, "You are looking for me not because you saw signs but because you ate the loaves and were filled," the Lord having just fed the five thousand. They, too, seek the satiation of their physical hunger while remaining blind to the spiritual food Jesus is.

This lack of comprehension of the life in the Spirit the Lord would impart is exemplified in the name the Israelites give the bread from heaven God has provided for their pilgrimage. "Manna" they call it, after the question they "asked one another, 'What is this?' for they did not know what it was." And how little do those who question Jesus understand of "the bread of God... which comes down from heaven and gives life to the world." Even as they say, "Sir, give us this bread always," they do not see that He stands before them, and that they have already partaken of the bread He is. And so, most will turn away, their hearts more set upon the belly than the spirit. And so, with the belly many will perish.

Brothers and sisters, "You should put away the old self of your former way of life, corrupted through deceitful desires, and be renewed in the spirit of your minds, and put on the new self, created in God's way of righteousness and holiness of truth." Listen to your brother Paul, for he speaks of Jesus and the new life He brings. Here on our altar is "the bread of angels"; and would you turn to eating rotting flesh? The Lord calls you into the heavenly kingdom; and would you choose slavery in the land of sin instead? "Abundance" of food in "His holy land" is now set before us by the Son of Man – partake of this bread of everlasting life, the flesh and blood of Christ.

O. 19. Sun. (B)

Nineteenth Week
(1Kgs.19:4-8; Ps.34:2-9; Eph.4:30-5:2; Jn.6:41-51)

"Strengthened by that food, he walked forty days and forty nights
to the mountain of God, Horeb."

As the forty days and forty nights Noah found himself protected from the rains by the Lord; as the forty years the Israelites were guided through the desert; as the forty days Jesus found strength in the Word of God while fasting in the wilderness... as Elijah is fed for his journey, so we for the fullness of our days feed upon "the bread of life" as we travel to the heavenly kingdom of our Lord. Here is our ark; here is our manna – here is all the strength and protection we need. He is our food.

113

"His praise shall be ever in my mouth," for His food is ever on our altar, and this Sacrament fills us with nothing but joy. If we had not this food, indeed "bitterness, fury, anger, shouting, and reviling" would come from our mouths so poisoned by the fruit of the world. But as it is "Christ loved us and handed Himself over for us as a sacrificial offering to God for a fragrant aroma," and thus we "taste and see how good the Lord is" and cannot but "glorify the Lord" and "extol His name."

That "the angel of the Lord encamps around those who fear Him and delivers them" is illustrated clearly in the trials of Elijah. Overwhelmed by "all [his] fears," the "afflicted" prophet "prayed for death, saying, 'This is enough, O Lord! Take my life.'" But "from all his distress [God] saved him," for an "angel of the Lord... touched him, and ordered, 'Get up and eat, else the journey will be too long for you!'" And Elijah "got up, ate, and drank" the food and water the Lord provided, and made it safely to the mountain where the Lord God would speak to him.

"This is the bread that comes down from heaven so that one may eat it and not die." All strength and blessing come from the Lord through His only Son. And being drawn to Him and so discovering the Father of all, what can our faces be but "radiant with joy," the joy of His eternal, loving presence? Let us come this day to the holy mountain of God, our Lord Jesus Christ.

O. 20. Sun. (B)

Twentieth Week
(Prv.9:1-6; Ps.34:2-7; Eph.5:15-20; Jn.6:51-58)

"Amen, amen, I say to you,
unless you eat the flesh of the Son of Man and drink of His blood,
you do not have life within you."

Wisdom "has spread her table"; "she has dressed her meat, mixed her wine." And now she sends out "her maidens," calling "from the heights out over the city... 'Come, eat of my food, and drink of the wine I have mixed!'" Let the simple hearts, those who seek understanding and refreshment, "turn in here." Here is bread that He gives "for the life of the world." Yes, His "flesh is true food, and [His] blood is true drink." Jesus, the only Son, has come "down from heaven" and now spreads the table before us, in fulfillment of the Scriptures, in answer to all prayers.

Are not our priests His maidens calling souls forth to the altar where we feed? Is the Church not His city where His voice resounds, where His blood is outpoured? And so we should heed the instruction of Paul today and "watch carefully how [we] live, not as foolish persons but as wise," seeking the precious bread that opens all eyes. "Do not get drunk on wine, in which

114

lies debauchery"; rather, "be filled with the Spirit" that comes to you in this wine made holy, in His sacred blood.

Brothers and sisters, let us "address one another in psalms and hymns and spiritual songs, singing and playing to the Lord in [our] hearts, giving thanks always and for everything in the name of our Lord Jesus Christ to God the Father." For what greater joy could there be than to partake of this Blessed Sacrament? And so, "glorify the Lord with me, let us together extol His name," that we may indeed be "radiant with joy, and [our] faces may not blush with shame." For the wise come to this table and eat, and so have life everlasting. For the Lord is here in our midst, in flesh and blood. Here is the house with "seven columns" in which His children ever dwell. The foolish may fall by the wayside, but the wise receive eternal life.

O. 21. Sun. (B)

Twenty-First Week
(Jos.24:1-2a,15-17,18b; Ps.34:2-3,9,16-21; Eph.5:21-32; Jn.6:60-69)

"Do you also want to leave?"

How like the questions pertaining to the marriage vows is our Lord's inquiry of the Twelve, and Joshua's statement to the Israelites he has just brought out of the wilderness into the Promised Land. "If it does not please you to serve the Lord, decide today whom you will serve," Joshua says, "as for me and my household we will serve the Lord." And Jesus seeks to find from His apostles if they will be like "many of His disciples [who] returned to their former way of life and no longer accompanied Him" after His teaching on the Bread of Life.

Do you take Jesus to be your husband? To honor and obey, to love... to "become one flesh" with Him who is "the Holy One of God"? You are free to leave, or you are free to come unto Him. Though He knows your heart and your choice, yet you are free to make it as you please. How shall you answer the Lord?

Paul renders a beautiful account of the love of husband and wife, relating it well "to Christ and the Church." "Husbands should love their wives as their own bodies... no one hates his own flesh but rather nourishes and cherishes it, even as Christ does the Church." And what can the good wife do when loved "as Christ loved the Church and handed Himself over for her," bleeding and dying on the cross to wash away all our sins – what can she do when confronted with such utter sacrifice for her sake alone but revere her husband and respect his every wish? In loving such a man she finds her joy. (How the wife of Joshua must have beamed to hear her husband's public declaration that he and his household would follow the Lord! Who could argue with such blessed authority?)

And now, what of you and I, brothers and sisters, we who have the most faithful husband of all? Do we "bless the Lord at all times"? Does our "soul glory in the Lord" as King David's today? Do we realize how He "watches over all [our] bones" and makes them pure as His own? Or will we be fool enough to leave His loving embrace? The words must come from your mouths as well, and mean them: "We also will serve the Lord, for He is our God."

O. 22. Sun. (B)

Twenty-Second Week
(Dt.4:1-2,6-8; Ps.15:1-5; Jas.1:17-18,21b-22,27; Mk.7:1-8,14-15,21-23)

"Humbly welcome the word that has been planted in you
and is able to save your souls."

Welcome it, yes, and "be doers of the word and not hearers only." For how else shall you show that the word of God is planted in you except that you bear fruit? All that is planted well indeed grows and bears fruit in the light of God.

Brothers and sisters, God "willed to give us birth by the word of truth that we may be a kind of firstfruits." "What great nation has statutes and decrees that are as just as this whole law?" Indeed the Law of God is whole, the Law of God is perfect – the Law of God gives life. For this reason Moses instructs the people: "You shall not add to what I command you nor subtract from it," for the Law is holy as He, and keeping it we prove ourselves to be so holy; keeping it we cannot but "give evidence of [our] wisdom and intelligence to the nations." Yes, with the Lord "there is no alteration or shadow caused by change." His light is perfect, and His light is eternal, and we must be children of His holy light.

But what of those for whom the washing of hands has become more important than keeping the commandments of God? What about those over whom Isaiah prophesies: "This people honors me with their lips, but their hearts are far from me"? Woe to these, for they have not the word of truth planted in them and so only evil things "come out from within," and thereby they are defiled. O may the Lord never pronounce over our souls: "In vain do they worship me"! O let us never be producers of the evils of this world!

"Every perfect gift is from above, coming down from the Father of lights," and he "who thinks the truth in his heart and slanders not with his tongue" knows the gifts of the Creator and walks in His holy light. No "great nation is there that has gods so close to it as the Lord, our God, is to us whenever we call upon Him." For His truth is indeed within us and this word comes straight to His ear. The beat of our hearts is known to our God as we worship in spirit and in truth. The only food that saves souls is laid upon our table. The Word of God we consume and so are made His children, caring for "orphans and widows in their affliction" and keeping ourselves "unstained by the world."

Twenty-Third Week
(Is.35:4-7a; Ps.146:2,6-10; Jas.2:1-5; Mk.7:31-37)

"He makes the deaf hear and the mute speak."

The Lord makes all whole. He "sets captives free" from all their afflictions as He redeems us from all our sin. "Here is your God, He comes with vindication; with divine recompense He comes to save you." This is He who "has done all things well"; this is the Lord Jesus Christ.

"And immediately the man's ears were opened, his speech impediment was removed, and he spoke plainly." By a word: "'Ephphatha!' – that is, 'Be opened!'" the deaf mute is healed by Jesus, causing all to be "exceedingly astonished." And in their astonishment their eyes are opened, for "the Lord gives sight to the blind." And so He who sustains "the fatherless and the widow" and "gives food to the hungry" stands before the eyes of all now; and so indeed is fulfilled the prophecy of Isaiah: "Then will the eyes of the blind be opened, the ears of the deaf be cleared... Then the tongue of the dumb will sing." And so streams "burst forth in the desert" and "the lame leap like a stag," for He comes – He comes to heal all nations.

Brothers and sisters, God chose "those who are poor in the world to be rich in faith and heirs of the kingdom that He promised to those who love Him." He chose the blind; He chose the lame; He chose the deaf and the mute – He chose the hungry and oppressed. He chose you and me in all our sin, in all our weakness before Him, and came to release us from all fear. Making no distinction except to favor the soul who thirsts for Him, He came bringing "springs of water." And these waters heal. And these waters set us free. And these waters remove our "shabby clothes" and don us "with gold rings and fine clothes" spun by the hand of God.

Brothers and sisters, "adhere to the faith in our glorious Lord Jesus Christ." For He is glorious indeed, and coming into His assembly with all your imperfections purged from your soul, you shall know such glory and not be able to withhold yourself from proclaiming such glory. Yes, you shall be one with "the Lord [who] shall reign forever." He shall be "your God, O Zion, through all generations," and with tongue loosened and renewed you shall sing "Alleluia" to the Lord forevermore. Know now His power upon you.

117

Twenty-Fourth Week
(Is.50:5-9a; Ps.116:1-6,8-9;   Jas.2:14-18;   Mk.8:27-35)

"I shall walk before the Lord in the land of the living."

A simple enough statement made by our psalmist today, or so it seems. For what does it mean to walk with Jesus along the way of the Almighty God? What does such travel entail? Is it but to impart a word of peace and blessing to those in need, and continue merrily along? Is it but to say, "I have faith in God"? Words alone will not get us where we expect to be; we must *walk* in the way of the Lord, and to walk means to work.

And what is this work with which faith cannot dispense; what does it entail? It could not be more succinctly stated than it is by Jesus to the crowds and His disciples in today's gospel: "Whoever wishes to come after me must deny himself, take up his cross, and follow me." It is in the Lord's steps we must walk, and, yes, those steps lead inevitably to crucifixion. This cannot be avoided. Do you not hear the Lord's rebuke of Peter? Then how can you begin to explicate a life in Christ without His cross fixed firmly upon your shoulder? How can you think that "the land of the living" may be found by easy means? It cannot.

Listen to the words of the Servant spoken through the prophet Isaiah: "I gave my back to those who beat me, my cheeks to those who plucked my beard." This and more the Lord did willingly to reveal the way you must walk – this all the children of Israel, all God's holy ones, take upon themselves all for the sake of the Gospel.

But lest you lose heart in the face of all you must undergo, all the suffering you must accept to gain the kingdom, let me tell you something else. All those who take up the cross say also with the Servant, "He is near who upholds my right." Do you hear what He says? "The Lord God is my help"! Do you understand its significance? We are with Christ and Christ is with God and so none of the blows of this world can hurt us. Indeed, they do not touch us, for it is Jesus who suffers all these blows for our sake. Though the cords may lacerate our skin, they cannot approach our soul, for the Lord indeed takes from us all "distress and sorrow" and saves our very lives. Thus the psalmist sings, "He has freed my soul from death, my eyes from tears, my feet from stumbling." For He in whose sight we live our lives has already endured all evil, and now preserves us from its clutches. And so in this cross which seems so dark and foreboding, there is ultimate joy.

Twenty-Fifth Week

(Ws.2:12,17-20; Ps.54:3-8; Jas.3:16-4:3; Mk.9:30-37)

"Where jealousy and selfish ambition exist,
    there is disorder and every foul practice."

And can there be any greater foul practice come from jealousy and selfish ambition than that of which we hear in our first reading from the Book of Wisdom, for here the wicked plot the death of the Son of God – here the horrible persecutions which the Messiah and all His followers undergo at the hands of the proud souls are spoken of: "With revilement and torture let us put the just one to the test that we may have proof of His gentleness and try His patience." And so the Lamb of God shall endure His "shameful death," according to the dark threats they breathe.

"The haughty have risen up against me, the ruthless seek my life; they set not God before their eyes," David cries unto the Lord. He too knows those who "kill and envy," who "fight and wage war" against the righteous one because he puts them to shame, because he "reproaches [them] for transgressions of the law," his justice and truth ever a sign of contradiction against "the passions that make war in [their] members," from which they refuse to be released.

But it is indeed so, as even their own words condemn the wicked, that "God will take care of [the just one]," that "God will defend him and deliver him from the hand of his foes." "Behold, God is my helper; the Lord sustains my life," David exclaims in the midst of his trial – for indeed the help of the Lord is ever with us; He shall always "defend [our] cause." And the wicked shall ever be put to death for their sins against Him.

And what of the disciples today? It is true that "they had been discussing among themselves on the way who was the greatest." At this point in the journey they still are "arguing about" petty matters which lead but to condemnation, even as Jesus speaks of His imminent death. But their vain pride shall not last the day. For even in the Lord's placing a child in their midst there is a kind of turning point; ashamed they can only be now, and soon, so soon, they will follow their blessed Lord to their own cross of crucifixion.

Set yourselves on the right path, brothers and sisters. Be not afraid to ask the Lord of His way and of the help you need to follow. But do not ask in vain or your evil desires will destroy you, and you shall not know His kingdom. Let no jealousy rule your hearts, but order your lives according to the Lord's pure wisdom, and be "full of mercy and good fruits," as even our "gentle" and "compliant" Lord. Keep this Child ever before your eyes.

119

Twenty-Sixth Week

(Nm.11:25-29; Ps.19:8-10,12-14; Jas.5:1-6; Mk.9:38-43,45,47-48)

"Would that all the people to the Lord were prophets!
Would that the Lord might bestow His Spirit on them all!"

There is of course a striking similarity between our first reading and our gospel today. In one, Joshua, "who from his youth ha[s] been Moses' aide," zealously proclaims to his master (after being informed that two men who had not gone to the tent of meeting to receive God's Spirit as instructed were "prophesying in the camp"): "Moses, my lord, stop them." And in the other, John, the Lord's beloved disciple, conveys *his* message to Jesus: "Teacher, we saw someone driving out demons in your name, and we tried to prevent him because he does not follow us," he, too, attempting to thwart the Spirit of God which does not go forth in channels that seem proper. But Moses' answer above could not be more strongly stated, and Jesus says plainly to His disciples, "Do not prevent them. There is no one who performs a mighty deed in my name who can at the same time speak ill of me." And so, let goodness go forth, unto the ends of the earth.

Indeed, Moses' cry is the Lord's will, and it is this will Jesus has come to realize – that all may embrace what is right and true and so come to the kingdom of heaven. However, inherent in Moses' exclamation is also the unfortunate fact that most do not have the Spirit of God; most are *not* walking in His name. More often than not the "wanton sin" which James so graphically presents to our eyes and ears is the state of man; and so the horrible miseries he even more graphically represents become their fate. And so, to accomplish His work of salvation upon the face of the earth, the Christ must necessarily be severe in His speech, in His warning and His instruction: "If your hand causes you to sin, cut it off... If your foot causes you to sin, cut it off... If your eye causes you to sin, pluck it out" – better these measures than the fires of Gehenna... better any pain on this plane than the eternal punishments of the hell wrought by the sins so much a part of all our lives.

With great wisdom David speaks of the precepts of the Lord. First he recognizes that "the law of the Lord is perfect, refreshing the soul" and "fear of the Lord is pure, enduring forever"; then, seeking to endure forever with the Lord of all, he declares to God of His laws: "Though your servant is careful of them, very diligent in keeping them, yet who can detect failings?" And even wiser is he to cry out, "Cleanse me from my unknown faults!" for he knows only this thorough cleansing will make him any prophet of God; only if he be "blameless and innocent" will he maintain the Lord's Spirit

120

within himself. And so the same is true for all the Lord would gather into His arms, all who seek His eternal reward.

Twenty-Seventh Week
(Gn.2:18-24; Ps.128:1-6; Heb.2:9-11; Mk.10:2-16)

"This one, at last, is bone of my bones
and flesh of my flesh."

The beauty and blessing of marriage, the marvel it is, and how it reaches unto heaven.

"It is not good for the man to be alone. I will make a suitable partner for him." This is the loving thought of our Lord God while looking upon the man He has created. And so from the body of the man God creates woman. How indelibly one are these two, in origin, in destiny, and in the eyes of their Creator. Inseparable should they be: "one flesh."

And if it were so, if these lived as He intended, the blessings sung of by our psalmist today would be upon all: "Your wife shall be like a fruitful vine in the recesses of your home; your children like olive plants around your table." Then would we reflect the glory of God and His love for His Church and its children. Then would we "see the prosperity of Jerusalem all the days of [our] life."

The love of man and woman, of husband and wife, is truly as the love of God for His bride, the Church. Hear what St. Paul says of the Christ, who has come to bring "many children to glory": "He who consecrates and those who are being consecrated all have one origin." Does he not say Jesus has become as our brother, made perfect through suffering – "flesh of [our] flesh"? Does the Lord not thus wed Himself to us by the incarnation and death of His only Son? And look at Jesus in our gospel, surrounded by children waist deep. He has just spoken of the sanctity of marriage and now He clearly conveys its blessed fruits, both for husband and wife on earth, and for Him and His Church. He declares of the children He has called to Himself, "The kingdom of God belongs to such as these," and then "He embrace[s] them and bless[es] them," wedding them unto His heart.

As woman is born out of the side of man, as she is flesh of his flesh, so the Church is born out of the pierced side of the Lord, from the blood and water that flow from there, becoming one with His blessed Body. And let all men and women know, every husband and wife understand, that their marriage is blessed alone by God and finds its life in Him. It is He to whom they are truly wed, and their offenses against one another offend only Him. If you seek to separate from one another, you work to separate yourself from God; for as He is love, so He is every marriage, and to Him you are

121

beholden to bear fruit in His name. Great will be the blessing upon your home if you cherish your oneness in Him – great as the blessings upon His Church, which in His love He does now form. Make all your love one with Him.

Twenty-Eighth Week
(Wis.7:7-11; Ps.90:12-17; Heb.4:12-13; Mk.10:17-30)

"The word of God is living and effective,
sharper than any two-edged sword."

"Penetrating even between soul and spirit, joints and marrow, and able to discern reflections and thoughts of the heart... everything is naked and exposed to the eyes of Him to whom we must render an account." Here is His Spirit of Wisdom, whose "splendor... never yields to sleep," who has "countless riches at her hands." It is this penetrating Wisdom we must pray to be with us, if we are to save our immortal souls. Without her nothing has any worth at all.

How shall we "number our days aright" and "gain wisdom of heart"? How shall we walk the road the Lord leads us upon and find His "gracious care" to "prosper the work of our hands"? How shall we avoid the emptiness the riches of this world inevitably bring and acquire the conviction needed to follow the Lord? The allure of gold, of mammon, is so great, is so easy to set our hearts upon – how shall we hear what the Lord says in love to the man who falls on his knees before Him: "Go, sell what you have, and give to the poor and you will have treasure in heaven"? How shall we give up house and family and lands all "for [His] sake and for the sake of the Gospel" to find "a hundred times more" these things, "with persecutions, and eternal life in heaven"? Only by the Wisdom that comes from God, never by the thoughts of our own heart.

Clearly the disciples do not yet understand this or they would not ask with such amazement, "Then who can be saved?" when told of the difficulties riches bring. For still, though not for long, their hearts are set on the things of this earth, and still they judge with a worldly eye. The vision that comes of the pure light of Wisdom will not be theirs until the flame of the Holy Spirit burns in their souls. Then their own spirits will be one with the Lord and they will be able to discern that "all gold, in view of her, is a little sand." Then the length and breadth and depth of their mission they will comprehend.

Let the word of God be heard by all, spoken by all His prophets and priests. Let it pierce many hearts, that some may be saved by the grace that enters where it bleeds. Here is the only way to life.

Twenty-Ninth Week
(Is.53:10-11; Ps.33:4-5,18-20,22; Heb.4:14-16; Mk.10:35-45)

"We have a great high priest who has passed through the heavens,
Jesus, the Son of God."

And this is He who is both priest and victim, for "He gives His life as an offering for sin" – He Himself is our sacrifice. Here is one who is able "to sympathize with our weaknesses... one who has similarly been tested in every way, yet without sin." Here is He who has suffered the affliction of our fallen state but to raise us up with Himself from the mire, from the lowly condition we have come to know as our own. Here is He who "give[s] His life as a ransom for many."

But why? Why is the Lord "pleased to crush Him in His infirmity"? Why is our high priest so humbled in the sight of all? Why is there such suffering in the world...? Why need you ask? Why need you question the will of God? Do you not believe that "upright is the word of the Lord, and all His works are trustworthy"? Do you not realize that the Lord looks with kindness upon all "those who fear Him... to deliver them from death and preserve them in spite of famine"? Do you trust your own eyes more than the vision of God?

But if you must know, the Lord God tells you, "Through His suffering, my servant shall justify many, and their guilt He shall bear." If you must inquire, hear that it is for your sin there is suffering in the world and the Lord and His followers must carry the cross. You need look no further than the blood on your hands... But seeing this, do not fear – rejoice. Rejoice, for now we may "confidently approach the throne of grace to receive mercy and to find grace for timely help." Now the Savior does "lord it over" us by His sacrifice. Now this "slave of all" has "authority over [us]" by the suffering He has undergone. And now we must join Him on this cross.

"The cup that I drink, you will drink, and with the baptism with which I am baptized, you will be baptized" – His words to James and John are spoken to us all. Glorious is the sacrifice to which we are called. For He who is both priest and victim would now lift us with Himself through the veil of pain to the holy heavens, that knowing the fruit of "His affliction," with Him all might "see the light in fullness of days."

"Our soul waits for the Lord"; it suffers with Him. And it is not disappointed by the sacrifice it shares.

123

Thirtieth Week
(Jer.31:7-9; Ps.126:1-6; Heb.5:1-6; Mk.10:46-52)

"They departed in tears,
but I will console them and guide them."

Through Jeremiah the Lord prophesies that His people Israel "shall return as an immense throng," that He will "gather them from the ends of the world, with the blind and the lame in their midst." And in our gospel we see Jesus "leaving Jericho with His disciples and a sizable crowd," picking up the blind Bartimaeus along the way. How the Lord fulfills the ancient prophecies. And now Jesus stands as our high priest in heaven, "offer[ing] gifts and sacrifices for sins," bringing all by His cross to the kingdom of God.

"Those that sow in tears shall reap rejoicing." Brothers and sisters, we are all like the blind Bartimaeus, sitting "by the roadside begging," calling out to the Lord for forgiveness and guidance, saying to Him as He calls us before Himself, "Master, I want to see." How blind we all are, how deaf and how lame. How we need our vision renewed by the Lord of all, that indeed we might see as He sees, with a purity beyond the scope of our race, to penetrate the mysteries which shroud us like the blind man's cloak in this life. We must throw off the darkness, cast aside the shroud of death that weighs upon our shoulders by our sins and take upon ourselves the cross of Christ and walk with Him "on the way," on the road to the New Jerusalem. How shall we know the "brooks of water" which satiate our thirst, "the torrents in the southern desert" that cleanse our arid souls and bring them to life once more, except by the tears we cry, except with hearts reaching out and voices reaching up to Him who is so far above *our* ways? In His way alone we will find the "level road" on which "none shall stumble." Only by this cry will we know the graces our high priest offers all our lives.

"Although [we] go forth weeping, carrying the seed to be sown, [we] shall come back rejoicing, carrying [our] sheaves." For the Lord shall not forget us; He will not pass us by and leave us in our tears alone. But through our tears we shall see His holy light descend like a dove of peace upon our souls. Yes, we shall see; our eyes will be opened and our path will be set. And He shall guide us every step of our way. And "our mouth [will be] filled with laughter, and our tongue with rejoicing" on that holy Day. Praise our merciful God!

Thirty-First Week

(Dt.6:2-6; Ps.18:2-4,47,51; Heb.7:23-28; Mk.12:28-34)

"You are not far from the kingdom of God."

If you "fear the Lord, your God, and keep, throughout the days of your lives, all His statutes and commandments," you will have "long life"; the Lord will "give you a land flowing with milk and honey." The promise spoken by Moses to the people stands true, and truer, today. If we "take to heart these words which [both Moses and Jesus] enjoin on [us] today," the kingdom shall indeed be not far from us. For these words are life-giving, they are the heart of the law, the heart of God's love, and so breathe the breath of life upon the obedient soul: "Hear, O Israel! The Lord our God is Lord alone! You shall love the Lord your God with all your heart, with all your soul, with all your mind, and with all your strength." (And the seconding of the Commandment is like it: "You shall love your neighbor as yourself.") This Command, this word of Truth and Life, the ancient Israelites inscribed upon their doorposts and lintels, and wore upon their person, never to forget what wisdom had been imparted unto them.

And now we, where shall we wear this essential Command, which silences even the hardest skeptics...? It should be inscribed upon our hearts. It should pour forth as praise from the mouth of all, all the faithful exclaiming with David in song, "I love you, O Lord, my strength." "The Lord lives! And blessed be my rock!" Our hearts indeed should overflow with love of God, who is so near us.

O brothers and sisters, do you not know how near He is to you now? Do you not know that Jesus "is always able to save those who approach God through Him, since He lives forever to make intercession for [us]"? Do you not know that you have a high priest who is "holy, innocent, undefiled, separated from sinners, higher than the heavens," and that He draws you unto the Heaven where He dwells? No longer do we turn to weak men, as even Moses was, but to "a Son, who has been made perfect forever." And His Sonship we share even this day when we love as He has loved.

Love God, brothers and sisters. Love Him with heart and soul, mind and body. Let the four corners of the universe declare His praise and honor His Name in unending love of all. It is Jesus' blood, Jesus' love, which courses through our veins now. How much closer can we come than this Bread of Life? Heaven has come to earth in flesh of love, and raises these earthen vessels we are unto the gates of the kingdom. On the doorstep you stand; only enter in.

Ordinary Time

Thirty-Second Week
(1Kgs.17:10-16; Ps.146:1,7-10; Heb.9:24-28; Mk.12:38-44)

"She, from her poverty, has contributed all she had,
her whole livelihood."

Jesus sits in the temple and watches as "the crowd put[s] money into the
treasury." When He sees "a poor widow... put in two small coins worth a
few cents," He calls His disciples over, and speaks the truth to them:
"Amen, I say to you, this poor widow put in more than all the other
contributors to the treasury." Whatever wealth anyone else might have
stuffed into the box cannot begin to compare to her whole sacrifice – it
mimics His own.

And in our first reading we find another poor widow sacrificing her
livelihood to the Lord and His prophet. It is the time of a great famine upon
the land (called down from heaven by Elijah himself) and the widow has
nothing left to eat but "a handful of flour in [her] jar and a little oil in [her]
jug." She tells us her situation: "Just now I was collecting a couple of
sticks, to go in and prepare something for myself and my son; when we have
eaten it, we shall die." A last supper. Straits most of us can only imagine.
Yet when the prophet Elijah asks her, "First make me a little cake and bring
it to me," invoking the name of the God of Israel and promising His
blessings, this woman who is not even of the house of Israel does not
hesitate to give first to this stranger of the only sustenance she has for
herself and her son. Another sacrifice mimicking Christ's own.

Both widows' sacrifices shall be blessed by the Lord; we can be assured
of this. For "the widow He sustains"; it is He who "gives food to the
hungry" and "protects strangers"... and any offering made in His name can
only be multiplied. Indeed, Elijah proves himself not to be as the Pharisees
who "devour the houses of widows," for by his presence with his benefactor
"she was able to eat for a year, and he and her son as well," the flour and the
oil remaining until the rains returned. "The Lord keeps faith forever."

Brothers and sisters, Christ "has appeared at the end of the age to take
away sins by His sacrifice." He does this "once for all," and so does not
"offer Himself repeatedly." But we, brothers and sisters, we must join with
that sacrifice – it is for us to offer ourselves as He has, as these widows
have, if we are to partake of its graces. As it is manifested on our altar each
day, we renew our commitment to be sharers in the blood He shed. As we
drink from His cup let us remember always that it is our very lives that we
are giving up. And the Lord will bless us as His own. And with these
widows we shall sit at His table in heaven.

126

Thirty-Third Week
(Dn.12:1-3; Ps.16:5,8-11; Heb.10:11-14,18; Mk.13:24-32)

"He will send out the angels
and gather His elect from the four winds,
from the end of the earth to the end of the sky."

On that Day "the sun will be darkened, and the moon will not give its light, and the stars will be falling from the sky." On that Day we "will see 'the Son of Man coming in the clouds' with great power and glory." "It shall be a time unsurpassed in distress," but "everyone who is found written in the book" of Life "shall escape"; all His chosen He shall rescue. For He will not "suffer [His] faithful one to undergo corruption," but "show [him] the path to life" and give him "fullness of joys in [His] presence."

Brothers and sisters, the Lord has taken "His seat forever at the right hand of God; now He waits until His enemies are made His footstool." Though "He has made perfect forever those who are being consecrated" and "there is no longer offering for sin," the time is yet to be fulfilled for all His chosen to partake of His "one sacrifice for sins" – He who is our "allotted portion and [our] cup" must be drunk to the full by all His elect, must be made perfect as He by joining in His sacrifice. And though "He is near, at the gates," ready to break in upon our world in His time and according to His ways, yet "this generation will not pass away until all these things have taken place": all the tribulations must come upon this earth, and all His children must be made ready for His Day.

Brothers and sisters, He "hold[s] fast [our] lot" and "with Him at [our] right hand [we] shall not be disturbed." "Heaven and earth will pass away, but [His] words will not pass away," and it is in His word we trust. So let your heart and soul rejoice and your body abide "in confidence," for "the wise shall shine brightly like the splendor of the firmament" on the Day of the Lord's return. We shall not join those who "shall be an everlasting horror and disgrace" but "shall live forever" in the light of His face. Hear the word the Lord speaks to your heart; see the signs before your eyes. Join yourself to His holy sacrifice, and you shall know "the delights at [His] right hand forever" in heaven where He now reigns.

Last Week: Christ the King
(Dn.7:13-14; Ps.93:1-2,5; Rv.1:5-8; Jn.18:33b-37)

"My kingdom does not belong to this world."

"The Lord is King, in splendor robed," our psalmist cries. "King" is our word for our great Lord; it is the best our imperfect thoughts and pale vocabulary can utter. But much more than king is our Lord Jesus Christ, for kings do come and go but "His kingship shall not be destroyed"; His "throne stands firm from of old" – it is "from everlasting" to everlasting. More than a king... He is God.

"'I am the Alpha and the Omega,' says the Lord God, 'the one who is and who was and who is to come, the almighty.'" He has no beginning or end but is Himself the beginning and end of all things. He "came into the world to testify to the truth," and now His truth is spoken, and His kingdom is coming. "Behold, He is coming amid the clouds, and every eye will see Him, even those who pierced Him. All the people of the earth will lament Him. Yes. Amen." None shall be able to hide from the Truth, from the King of "all peoples, nations, and languages." And the same vision as John has Daniel had so many centuries before: "I saw one like a Son of man coming, on the clouds of heaven," He whom the Ancient One gives "dominion, glory, and kingship." And the testimony of two witnesses holds true, cannot be broken. He is coming, and all are called to "serve Him."

Brothers and sisters, He "loves us and has freed us from our sins by His blood," which He offers without a fight before Pilate this day. By His sacrifice He "has made us into a kingdom, priests for His God and Father." And the kingdom we are is not of this earth, is "not here"; and the sacrifice we offer now is heavenly – it comes down to us from above... this miraculous blood we drink and shed ourselves in His Name.

Here our King stands before us, standing in the hearts of all His holy ones. He who lives forever now draws us into the kingdom where He ever remains. Not of this world, we come before His radiant majesty. "To Him be glory and power forever and ever. Amen."

3. Year C

Second Week
(Is.62:1-5; Ps.96:1-3,7-10; 1Cor.12:4-11; Jn.2:1-11)

"As a bridegroom rejoices in his bride
so shall your God rejoice in you."

"There was a wedding at Cana in Galilee, and the mother of Jesus was there. Jesus and His disciples were also invited to the wedding." And it is here Jesus "revealed His glory"; here the beginning of His signs would take place in His changing water into wine.

But why? Why here at a wedding? And why this transformation as His first miracle? He would have begun His ministry some twenty years prior, in the temple at Jerusalem at the age of twelve. Would this not have been a more appropriate place, and a more marvelous age? But His Blessed Mother drew Him from there then, and He was obedient to the wisdom she offered by gift from her Spouse, the Spirit. She would teach Him of our human condition, and lead Him to bear His own patiently, that our high priest might be able to sympathize with our nature. Indeed, to all He seemed an ordinary man.

And now it is she who leads Him to accept His station as the Son of Man. Here at that most blessed, most cherished of human events – one which St. Paul tells us mirrors Christ's own union with the Church, one spoken of repeatedly by the prophets of old (as does Isaiah today) to demonstrate the Lord's great love for His people, and one which at the end of time (a time so marvelously depicted by John in the Book of Revelation) will be fulfilled in our midst in the descent of the New Jerusalem, the Bride, the Holy Church, from Heaven to earth... here at this feast so human and yet so divine, He simply changes water into wine. As Eve the wife of Adam once offered her husband the apple he would consume to produce our fall, so here the "Woman," Mary, the Mother of the Lord and Spouse of the Spirit, offers Jesus His ministry, which will lead to the death that redeems us all.

And the water becoming wine indicates the transformation we all undergo, baptized in the Spirit of the Lord, wed unto heaven. And this transformation produces in the Church the "spiritual gifts," the outpouring of knowledge and prophecy and healing St. Paul speaks of today: our marriage to God cannot help but produce blessed fruit in us, even as God's espousal of Mary has produced the only Son.

129

And, of course, each day we drink the spiritual wine, the wine become blood, poured forth upon our table, upon the altar of the Church. And this primarily feeds our spirits, sustains us human beings with food from heaven, not of earth. One with the Lord do we become by the consumption of this sacred fruit; in this Sacrament our Bridegroom rejoices in us His Bride and calls us to rejoice in Him, to "sing to the Lord a new song" of the purest love as we "worship [Him] in holy attire," in the finest, the purest of wedding garments – in His flesh and blood. Sing alleluia to our God!

O. 3. Sun. (C)

Third Week
(Neh.8:2-4a,5-6,8-10; Ps.19:8-10,15; 1Cor.12:12-30; Lk.1:1-4,4:14-21)

"He opened the scroll so that all the people might see it."

These words are spoken of Ezra the scribe who "brought the law before the assembly" of all Israel as he stood above them preparing to read the word of God, but it surely more distinctly refers to Jesus the Christ, the Incarnate Word of God, who reveals Himself to the souls in the Nazareth synagogue today. As "Ezra read plainly from the book of the law of God, interpreting it so that all might understand," so the Word is perfectly read and interpreted for us in the Person of Jesus Christ.

Jesus came "into the synagogue on the sabbath day. He stood up to read and was handed a scroll of the prophet Isaiah. He unrolled the scroll and found the passage" in Isaiah which speaks of Him: "The Spirit of the Lord is upon me, because He has anointed me..." Thus is "fulfilled in [the people's] hearing" the salvation promised from all time; the presence of the Word is with us in flesh and bone.

Brothers and sisters, the eyes of all are filled with vision of His light, of His glorious being in our midst; all ears are filled with the sound of His voice, like gently rolling thunder soothing our hearts. And so we see. And so we hear. And so His Church has eyes and ears of the Lord, for we become "Christ's body and individually parts of it." Our feet now walk with Christ and our hands serve Him, and all for the blessing and honor and upbuilding of the whole. If I write this to you now and you hear, do I write for myself alone? Is it even I who write at all? Are not all things in the Body in the Lord, taking strength from Him and nourishing in turn all its parts? What are we apart from the Body – we could not stand alone! Does the Lord not reveal these things to us in the opening of Scripture before our eyes? Is He not whole and one with all?

In our first reading *all* wept at the words come from the mouth of Ezra, and *all* celebrated together this day of feasting. All stood as one when the book was raised, and all were prostrate as the name of the Lord was praised.

The Body is one, as St. Paul tells us, and none go off on their own: "If one part suffers, all the parts suffer with it; if one part is honored, all the parts share its joy."

Brothers and sisters, "the ordinances of the Lord are true, and all of them just." Let us live as one in the WORD of the Lord, "the words of [our] mouth and the thoughts of [our] heart find[ing] favor before" our God, that the world might see the truth and the light of Christ alive in His Body.

Fourth Week
(Jer.1:4-5,17-19; Ps.71:1-6,15,17; 1Cor.12:31-13:13; Lk.4:21-30)

"I am with you to deliver you, says the Lord."

When God calls Jeremiah to prophesy "against Judah's kings and princes, against its priests and people," He tells him to "gird [his] loins" and commands: "Be not crushed on their account." For though his people "will fight against" him, they shall "not prevail over" him. The Lord makes Jeremiah "a fortified city, a pillar of iron, a wall of brass" able to stand against attacks of any in "the whole land"; He preserves His prophet's life despite any danger or threat.

In our gospel Jesus is likewise protected by God from any harm *His* people would inflict upon Him. Here in the synagogue of Nazareth, Jesus is called to prophesy against the faithlessness of the people; and though before He spoke His harsh word of truth they had "all spoke[n] highly of Him," now "filled with fury" they drive Him "out of the town, and lead Him to the brow of the hill... to hurl Him down headlong." But the deliverance promised Jeremiah and sung of so beautifully by our psalmist is with the Lord's only Son as it had been with His prophet, and "Jesus passed through the midst of them and went away." Though they would not accept the deliverance He brings, He is delivered from them.

"O my God, [you] rescue me from the hand of the wicked"; you indeed are "my rock of refuge, a stronghold to give me safety." O Lord, "let me never be put to shame," but "in your justice rescue me, and deliver me." For you are "my rock and my fortress," "my hope" who never fails to save. May I walk through all the difficulties of this world, all the darkness of sin and temptation and suffering, with you at my side, therefore with nothing to fear. Make me strong as your prophet, as your Son, for my life is in your Hand.

Brothers and sisters, soon all persecution will pass away with all the imperfect trappings of this desolate earth, and only God's love will remain. Let us be as He who "endures all things"; let us be of love. And nothing of

131

this world shall touch us as we pass through its midst, shielded by the Word of God, guarded by His eminent love.

Fifth Week
(Is.6:1-2a,3-8; Ps.138:1-5,7-8; 1Cor.15:1-11; Lk.5:1-11)

"Put out into deep water and lower your nets for a catch."

"Whom shall I send? Who will go for us?" "the voice of the Lord" asks in the presence of the angels and Isaiah. "Here I am… send me!" is the prophet's response. And so this "man of unclean lips" having been purged of his uncleanness by an ember from the altar of God is ready to speak for "the King, the Lord of hosts!" Grace come through the seraphim prepares his soul to do the will of the Lord.

"By the grace of God I am what I am," Paul, "the least of the apostles," declares, having been saved from his persecution of the Church of God and made the great Apostle to the nations, he knows, only by the favor of the Lord Most High. And now the Gospel he preaches with a mouth anointed by the blood of Christ, the word of God which he speaks, brings salvation to all who "hold fast" to it.

And Peter, too, the first of apostles, we find coming to faith and power in the Lord by His grace-filled call. A catch of fish is what touches *his* soul and makes him fall to his knees, "a sinful man." And as He has deemed to stoop to the level of Isaiah and Paul, so the Lord reaches out his hand to Peter, lifting him to his feet and speaking to his ear his call of "catching men." And so the Rock of the Church is born.

King David sings in truth when he says: "All the kings of the earth shall give thanks to you, O Lord, when they hear the words of your mouth." And having heard these words speak clearly to their hearts, so are our prophet and apostles set to proclaim with David "the glory of the Lord" to all who likewise hear. And certainly the grace given them "has not been ineffective," for even now a multitude is drawn into "the presence of the angels," where they "worship at [the Lord's] holy temple and give thanks to [His] name."

Alleluia! Join His call. Let your nets to the depths descend, to draw up souls redeemed by the Gospel of God, that many might sing "Holy, holy, holy" to our heavenly King.

Sixth Week

(Jer.17:5-8; Ps.1:1-4,6,40:5; 1Cor.15:12,16-20; Lk.6:17,20-26)

"If for this life only we have hoped in Christ,
we are the most pitiable people of all."

For His reward is in heaven; His kingdom is not of the earth. And our faith is in His resurrection.

It is not to this world we come, not in the things of the earth we make our boast, for he "who seeks his strength in flesh" is he "whose heart turns away from the Lord" and His holy kingdom... but we are among those "whose hope is the Lord." The contrast could not be clearer than it is today in our readings: on the one hand is he who "delights in the law of the Lord" and so follows His ways; and on the other, he who "walks in the way of sinners," finding his delight in the world. And the blessing and the curse each respectively finds is also made obvious for us – one path leads to resurrection and life, the other to a miserable death. And which shall we choose, the kingdom of God or the prison of man... the blessing or the curse?

"Woe to you who are rich... to you who are filled now... to you who laugh," for a fate worse than death awaits you – the pleasures you take in your insolence will soon turn to the most despicable bitterness. You stand "in a lava waste, a salt and empty earth," and in it you shall sink if you do not soon look to the light of Christ. The poor and hungry souls who weep and mourn for your salvation, who suffer persecution by your haughty tongue will soon "rejoice and leap for joy" – on the day of resurrection you can count. And what will become of your own soul when you stand, or cringe, before the otherworldly light of your Creator? What shall you then say?

The time is short. The rewards of heaven are near. Let us take strength in the Lord's resurrection. Let us bear joyfully His cross. Though drought be upon the land, and though it show itself in His Church, we must be one with Him who "still bears fruit," planted eternally beside the nourishing streams of our Christ. Him they stripped of even His clothing; His skin they scourged at the devil's command. His flesh they nailed to the dying tree – a worm and no man. But He lives, be assured of this; His Spirit never fails. And body and soul He looks out from heaven, waiting for us to join Him there...

133

Seventh Week

(1Sm.26:2,7-9,12-13,22-23; Ps.103:1-4,8,10,12-13; 1Cor.15:45-49; Lk.6:27-38)

"Who can lay hands on the Lord's anointed
and remain unpunished?"

This does David say of Saul the king of Israel – of him who has come into the desert to hunt David down and kill him – even as he stands beside a sleeping Saul, well able to "nail him to the ground with one thrust of the spear." But even though it seems that "God has delivered [his] enemy into [David's] grasp," he foregoes the opportunity, humbly respecting him whom God has ordained. Thus does he presage Christ's own teaching to "love your enemies."

It is so in the heavenly teaching of the Lord that we who are to be like "the second man, from heaven," and not like "the first [who] was from earth, earthly"; it is so that if we are to hear His words and be like Christ Himself – and who else is there to be like? – we must treat all men as David treats Saul, as if God's anointing is upon them. All must be respected as blessed by God; all must be loved as His children. Even if they hunt us down and kill us, even if they take all things from us, yet we must pray for their souls... for still God's blessing is upon them, and we must bless them with Him.

Brothers and sisters, "He Himself is kind to the ungrateful and the wicked." Do you see this? Though in the end He will judge (and not we), yet nothing cuts short the love of God; no act of man keeps him from the Lord's abundant grace. And we must "be merciful, just as [our] Father is merciful," if we hope to come into His kingdom and look upon His face. For only those who are of Him enter there. If you love as a sinner loves, if you love like an earthly man, with an earthly mind and an earthly heart, expecting something in return, how can you hope to be where He is, He who does not measure His love in earthly terms? Unending is His love, surpassing all and overwhelming all in its infinite greatness... and will you count the pennies that you offer? You need only look upon the cross, upon the corpus fixed firmly there, to see the love to which you are called: you must "bear the image of the heavenly" man.

And you need only look clearly at what the Lord has done in your own life, He who "pardons all your iniquities, [who] heals all your ills," to understand His call. "As far as the east is from the west, so far has He put our transgressions from us." And should we not do the same for others who have sinned against us, who have nailed us to the tree? Or would you fall short of His love? "Merciful and gracious is the Lord," and if He does not "requite us according to our crimes" but treats us "as a father [who] has

134

compassion on his children," so all men should be as the Lord's blessed children in our eyes.

Eighth Week
(Sir.27:4-7; Ps.92:2-3,13-16; 1Cor.15:54-58; Lk.6:39-45)

"Be firm, steadfast,
always fully devoted to the work of the Lord."

Brothers and sisters, "in the Lord your labor is not in vain," for "the just one shall flourish like the palm tree, like a cedar of Lebanon shall he grow." If you are "planted in the house of the Lord," "vigorous and sturdy" shall you ever be, "bear[ing] fruit even in old age." You shall remove "the wooden beam" that plagues your eye and thus find the vision to remove the splinter from the eye of your brother. You will be like your teacher, like the Lord, sharing in the power only He possesses.

"When fully trained, every disciple will be like his teacher." And we must be trained, we must be tested in tribulation, molded in the furnace of the Lord's chastising Word. We must know that "a good tree does not bear rotten fruit, nor does a rotten tree bear good fruit," and so if there is rottenness come from us, we must cast it in the fire. For only goodness should be born from the store of our heart, and that in abundance, else how shall we be called disciples of Jesus... how shall we be like Him in every way? Falling short of His perfection will not get us where we want to be: we must see that "this which is corruptible clothes itself with incorruptibility."

Our readings today equate work with speech, the quintessential human activity, one which indeed shows "the bent of one's mind." And so when the Lord says, "From the fullness of the heart the mouth speaks," He indicates not only the words passing our lips but all the actions that follow in their wake. By these fruits, as by our words, shall we be tested and judged. Thus must our hearts and our words and all our actions be founded in Jesus, the tree of life.

"The fruit of a tree shows the care it has had." Only by a man's fruit shall you know him. And what does your fruit speak of you? What does your speech reveal? Do you "sing praise to [the Lord's] name" in all you do; do you declare the glory of the "Most High" with every word? Brothers and sisters, only what is hard and true is lasting; only what is rooted in Him can stand the test of holy fire. Perform all your labor according to the mold Christ prepares, and your fruit shall reach unto heaven.

Ninth Week

(1Kgs.8:41-43; Ps.117:1-2; Gal.1:1-2,6-10; Lk.7:1-10)

"When he comes and prays toward this temple,
listen from your heavenly dwelling."

Here Solomon prays for "the foreigner, who is not of [God's] people Israel, but comes from a distant land to honor" Him. He begs the Lord: "Do all that foreigner asks of you, that all peoples of the earth may know your name, may fear you as do your people Israel." Be clear about the king's prayer, brothers and sisters. It is not that "we should be open-minded in our dealings with people who seek God honestly but in a different way," as the commentator in my missal puts it, but that there is but one way, one God, and that peoples of all nations should worship Him, and so find His grace and mercy.

We should not be as the duplicitous, brothers and sisters (who also would tell us the above prayer was "figuratively put into the mouth of King Solomon"). We should not patronize others with a deceptive tongue of unbelief. Certainly one should never be violent in word or deed toward those of other faiths, of any faith (or of no faith); as Christians we are called to respect all souls, for all souls are made in the image of God. But such an attitude of untruth delivers only disrespect and serves to keep those needing the light of Christ very much in the dark.

We must look to the Apostle Paul for our model in teaching, for it is "not from human beings nor through a human being" that he receives his call to preach, but from God. And so he is not interested in "currying favor with humans," with tickling their ears by telling them what they want to hear – he is interested only in the truth. Listen to his words: "Even if we or an angel from heaven should preach to you a Gospel other than the one we preached to you, let that one be accursed!" And so what of those who would water down the inviolable Gospel of the Lord Jesus Christ, who would teach that there is some other way to heaven other than Him?

What of the Roman centurion, you ask? This man receives answer to his prayer because of his ardent faith in God and in His Son. The Jews witness to him: "He loves our nation and built the synagogue for us." So humbled is this soul before the Lord and Christ that he asks Him not to "enter under [his] roof." "Such faith" does he have in Jesus that he knows He needs but to "say the word and let [his] servant be healed." This man's heart is on no strange god. He is indeed a true Israelite!

"This temple... is dedicated to [God's] honor." "Praise the Lord, all you nations; glorify Him all you peoples!" It is to the Lord and the Lord alone that all souls may come to find salvation. And Jesus is the way there.

Tenth Week

(1Kgs.17:17-24; Ps.30:2,4-6,11-12; Gal.1:11-19; Lk.7:11-17)

"O Lord, you brought me up from the nether world."

"You preserved me from among those going down into the pit." For I was dead, but now I live. These should be the words of us all, for the Lord indeed is our salvation – our life breath comes from Him, and He will preserve us from all death. No longer in sin, we rise to new life.

The resurrecting power of God is clearly evident in our readings today. We see both Jesus and Elijah raising the dead. And perhaps the rising of Paul from the blind pit into which he'd fallen, which led him even to persecute and attempt to destroy the Church, is the most remarkable resurrection.

What we should take from today's readings is the sure knowledge that God is life and that life has no origin other than Him. Paul proclaims the Word he preaches comes only from God through the revelation of Jesus Christ – emphasizing that no man taught him the Word which burns in his soul (a Word which gives life to all who hear it) – and in both the gospel and the first reading those who witness the raising of the dead attribute rightly its source to the Lord. In one they proclaim, "God has visited His people," and in the other the widow of Sidon states of Elijah: "The word of the Lord comes truly from your mouth." This is the character of the Word, this is the quality of God – He gives life. And so we know Him.

And we indeed are all as the widows in today's readings; we are all bereft of our only sons, of the light of our eyes and our very life. We mourn for the loss of our souls which is imminent because of our sin. And we, too, weep. Who shall save us? Who shall speak a word to us to revive us, to return our life breath, to restore our souls? Jesus comes to us. He visits our city, He comes to our door. His Word approaches our hearts and calls to us to arise – He breathes upon us the breath of new life. His apostles go forth from the foundation set in Peter, and this true Gospel is that which shall save the world, which shall bring it from its mourning to joy.

But do we mourn the loss of our souls? Do we bewail that which is taken from us by sin? Do we see the death upon us? We must come as widows calling upon the Lord to find His Word at work in our hearts, bringing us to life. And we must share that Word with others. Once raised from the dead, we must proclaim what the Word has done for us. We must recognize His power at work in the world.

May the Word go forth to the ends of the earth, speaking of the saving power of God. May it raise all from death.

Eleventh Week

(2Sm.12:7-10,13; Ps.32:1-2,5,7,11; Gal.2:16,19-21; Lk.7:36-8:3)

"I said, 'I confess my faults to the Lord,'
and you took away the guilt of my sin."

"Who is this who even forgives sins?" It is Christ the Lord, the promised One, the Messiah – the Savior of the human race. But the Pharisee and the others at table "nullify the grace of God." Simon does not welcome Jesus as a prophet, a brother, or even a respected traveler; instead, he sits back in judgment of the Son of Man: "If this man were a prophet..." he speculates to himself, all the while blind to the tears of the woman, ever remaining cold to her repentance. And even when Jesus speaks to him by name and confronts him with his own guilt, even after he reveals to him the coldness of his welcome to Him whom he should be glorifying, he is not repentant. He cannot be forgiven even a little, for he has no love in his heart.

How different David's reaction (in our first reading) to the exposure of his great sin to the light. He does not hide from the truth. He does not pretend all is well. He falls to his knees in tears and confesses his guilt at the feet of the prophet of God. And so he finds forgiveness. David recognizes the chastising hand of the Lord and the great grace that is found by it. The woman, too, sees the truth of her sins in the face of Christ and longs to find the grace of forgiveness. The Pharisee hardens his heart.

"A person is not justified by works of the law but through faith in Jesus Christ," Paul proclaims in our second reading. It is not that the law is bad or that it should be abandoned, as Christ Himself confirms; it is simply that the law alone will not bring us to justification, it does not serve to make us one with God – the death of Christ and faith in Him is necessary for this. If the Pharisee had truly kept the law well, he would have recognized and celebrated Jesus' coming, for, indeed, He and His love are the very heart of the law – to which Christ has also witnessed. The greatest commandment is recognized by the whole nation of Israel as love of God and neighbor. But the Pharisee fails even to exhibit basic hospitality, an essential work of the law, to the Lord. He knows not Jesus because his adherence to the law is false, is but a pretense. If he followed the law rightly it would lead him to the justification found in Jesus; but love, the heart of the law, is far from his sight.

Let us, brothers and sisters, not be blind as the Pharisee. Let us not take refuge in our own works and ignore the Lord who walks amongst us. If we do not recognize our sins against Him, we shall never come to the light of salvation, we shall never know His surpassing love. Let us be as David and

138

as the woman: let us "bathe His feet" with our tears of repentance. He is waiting to forgive.

Twelfth Week
(Zec.12:10-11,13:1; Ps.63:2-6,8-9; Gal.3:26-29; Lk.9:18-24)

"They shall look on Him whom they have pierced."

Jesus is the Christ of God. It is He who suffers, He who has been pierced for our sins, and He whose blood cleanses us as we look upon Him, as we cry out in tears for the pain we have caused Him and resolve to follow Him now in His way of the cross. What is the "fountain to purify from sin" but the blood poured forth in His sacrifice, and what is it we thirst for but to drink in full the grace contained therein? And it is our great grace to suffer with Him, to take up our cross daily and share in His sacrifice, denying ourselves to find Him and His life. This is what makes us one, with Him and so with one another: this is the baptism that redeems us and makes us whole.

Do we live out our baptismal vows? Do we follow Him in the way of the cross? Are we truly longing for the Lord, pining for Him, gazing upon Him – what is the banquet we seek to satisfy our souls? Are we one in His Spirit, loving Him above all others? Or do we set our souls on the empty pleasures of this life? These we must lose to find Him. Here in solitude the Lord tells the disciples quietly and sincerely, knowing the vanity and thirst for power the devil would plant in their souls – "The Son of Man must suffer greatly." How He desires them to hear His teaching. How He longs to keep them from the evil one and see that their hearts are not fixed on this life. He knows only this will save them. He knows only repentance brings the life of God, and so He approaches them in the silence of God that His words might sink deeply into them.

And they will listen. And they, too, will all die. They will understand the sacrifice that leads to life. And what of us? The Lord speaks to us, too, today. His words are here written down and proclaimed for our ears to treasure. Do we turn to this fountain of forgiveness, mourning for our sins "as one mourns for an only son"? And does our mourning lead us to lay down our lives?

Nothing of this world will suffice. His Body and Blood alone are our food and drink here in this life. They make us one and make us strong, and by them He will uphold us, if our hearts are set on losing this life to find Him.

Thirteenth Week

(1Kgs.19:16b,19-21;   Ps.16:1-2,5,7-11;   Gal.5:1,13-18;   Lk.9:51-62)

"No one who sets a hand to the plow and looks to what was left behind
is fit for the kingdom of God."

We must follow Jesus. And the path He walks leads to the cross.

Our gospel tells us, "When the days for Jesus' being taken up were
fulfilled, He resolutely determined to journey to Jerusalem." Jesus knows
what awaits Him in Jerusalem. He knows how He will weep over the city
for its lack of faith, and He knows their lack of faith will bring His
crucifixion. Yet into the waiting arms of death He travels, undeterred. And
how many there are who proclaim their desire to walk with Him; how many
volunteer to follow in His way. But how little they know of the difficulty
found on that road: "The Son of Man has nowhere to rest His head" – we
must give up our homes. "Let the dead bury the dead" – we must leave
behind our family. Yes, we must never look "to what was left behind,"
namely, "the desire of the flesh" of which Paul speaks. We are now "guided
by the Spirit"; the flesh no longer holds sway over us. That which is
opposed to the Spirit we must give no thought to anymore.

Look at Elisha, the powerful prophet, in our first reading. He is called
by the master, Elijah. Yes, he fails to follow immediately, but look at what
he does in saying good-bye to his family. He takes what has been his
livelihood to this day and sacrifices it utterly: he slaughters the oxen and
even uses "the plowing equipment for fuel to boil their flesh," giving the
meat as food for his people. Nothing remains to call him back; he effects a
total departure from his old self.

Brothers and sisters, we must take such complete refuge in the Lord.
We must say with David, "O Lord, my allotted portion and cup, you it is
who hold fast my lot." All must be given over to Him and entrusted to His
care. It does us no good to hesitate on our journey with Him or take up
things which will weigh us down along the way.

"Do not submit again to the yoke of slavery," Paul exhorts us. Leave all
the desires of this world behind to find the freedom known only in heaven.
Then we will proclaim with David: "I set the Lord before me; with Him at
my right hand I shall not be disturbed." We will know His mantle of
strength and protection in our call to walk with Him; the yoke of slavery to
sin will be broken from our shoulders. We are truly free, brothers and
sisters, only insofar as we follow Him, submitting ourselves to the cross.

O Lord, take all that keeps us back from following in your way, that in
such death to self we may draw nigh to your kingdom. Your cross is the
path to life.

Fourteenth Week

(Is.66:10-14c; Ps.66:1-7,16,20; Gal.6:14-18; Lk.10:1-12,17-20)

"The Lord's power shall be known to His servants."

Paul states: "May I never boast except in the cross of our Lord Jesus Christ." Jesus instructs: "Rejoice because your names are written in heaven." The bottom line is that "the laborer deserves his payment."

The prosperity of Jerusalem shall flow "like a river" over those who work as laborers in the field of the Word of God: "peace and mercy" shall be to the "Israel of God." All "who were mourning over her," all who have suffered the indignity of the cross in this exile of ours, shall indeed rejoice as they "suck fully of the milk of her comfort" in the heavenly kingdom which the Lord brings to us this day. Indeed, "let us rejoice in Him. He rules by His might forever." And we share in His reign who serve Him now beneath the shadow of the cross.

Satan falls now "like lightning from the sky"; we "tread upon serpents and scorpions," crushing them underfoot by the power the Lord gives us as we tread this earth in His Name. Sent forth with nothing, we have everything, for He who provides from the throne of heaven is with us. "As nurslings" we are carried in the arms of the New Jerusalem "and fondled in her lap." "As a mother comforts her child, so will I comfort you," the Lord assures us; and indeed in the cross we bear, "the marks of Jesus" on our bodies, we find the open gate that leads to the house of peace: the wounds themselves are the doorway.

"The kingdom of God is at hand for you," my brothers and sisters. I proclaim it in your hearing this day. "Peace" and the "grace of our Lord Jesus Christ be with your spirit, brothers and sisters." Peace be to your house. You shall know His peace and find His healing as you accept His sweet cross upon your backs. "When you see this, your heart shall rejoice and your bodies flourish like the grass"; for in that day you shall be a "new creation." You will say with Paul, "The world has been crucified to me, and I to the world," and you will make your abode in heaven. That day is upon you now, brothers and sisters. Heed the Lord's call to go forth as lambs in the midst of wolves, and you shall find His incomparable blessing of the peace which passes all understanding – you shall come into His kingdom.

"Hear now, all you who fear God, while I declare what He has done for me." For me "He has changed the sea into dry land" and by the blood of His cross cleansed these feet to which the dust did once cling, that I might enter heaven. Walk now in His power, I beg you, children of the Lord. "The harvest is abundant." Let us go forth laboring and eating of this Bread.

141

Fifteenth Week

(Dt.30:10-14; Ps.69:14,17,30-31,33-34,36-37 or 19:8-11; Col.1:15-20; Lk.10:25-37)

"He lifted him up on his own animal, took him to an inn,
and cared for him."

This "Samaritan traveler... was moved with compassion" upon seeing the poor victim on the road. And so he "poured oil and wine over his wounds" and provided for his healing. Such is the love to which we are called.

In our first reading, Moses exhorts us: "Heed the voice of the Lord, your God, and keep His commandments... Return to the Lord, your God, with all your heart and all your soul." We are told this commandment of love is not far from us, but in our very hearts and on our very tongues – "You have only to carry it out."

In our second reading, Paul tells of Jesus' presence in all creation: "In Him were created all things in heaven and on earth... He is before all things, and in Him all things hold together." He tells us, too, that it is by "the blood of His cross" that all things are reconciled, that peace comes. And in our gospel, the commandment to love God and neighbor is clearly presented, both in the words of the law, and in a parable of its employment.

The commandment we have is indeed to love, brothers and sisters, to love God and to love neighbor. This word burns in our hearts. We *must* "carry it out." It does little good simply to know the law; it must be put into practice to have merit. And who are we called to love? Jesus makes it quite clear that we are called to love all who are in need; we are called to respond with compassion at the sight or the cry of any of His "lowly ones," His "victim[s]." Remember that Paul has told us that Jesus lives in and through *all* creation: He is not in some and not in others. So, mustn't we help our Lord when He is in need? Has He not told us, "What you do to the least of my brothers, you do to me"? Is not every soul in His blessed Hand?

And we must be His blessed hands here on this earth. We must indeed be like Him. Let us look at David's psalm. In it we hear the cry of those "afflicted and in pain" calling on the favor of the Lord: "In your great kindness answer me with your constant help." Here we see that in "great mercy" the Lord turns toward those who seek Him. Brothers and sisters, "the Lord hears the poor" and we must be as He is. We must cry out to Him ourselves in our own need, yes, but we are also called as His disciples to serve in His place, to share His love – to pour His blood upon the wounds of those in need.

Let us pray to the Lord that we will turn away from selfishness and judgment and, turning toward Him, open our hearts and our hands in love to all, for all are in need of His refuge and His love.

Sixteenth Week

(Gn.18:1-10a; Ps.15:1-5; Col.1:24-28; Lk.10:38-42)

"There is need of only one thing."

Whether we teach or whether we serve, all must be done in the Name of the Lord. If it is not sitting at His feet that we do all things, if all is not a prayer offered in His Name, to His glory, it is all quite worthless.

How "anxious and concerned about many things" we often are. How like Martha we often struggle under the burden of our duties without a proper heart for service. And so how often, in the words of our psalm, we are like one who "takes up a reproach against his neighbor." How like Martha we fail to be as one who "honors those who fear the Lord," even if that holy one is our sister. Jesus is at work there in her midst, in the words of Paul, "teaching everyone with all wisdom," but Martha cannot stop to hear His words, and would take the word from her sister's heart. And so the Lord must be put to work, performing the other task Paul outlines, that of "admonishing everyone." Can she really think that the passing needs of the body take precedence over the eternal need of the soul?

Brothers and sisters, we are no less ignorant of the presence of Christ in our midst; we are no less ignorant of His Word speaking to our souls when we rush through our daily tasks – be they to teach or to serve – as if we are on some nonstop treadmill which is beyond our control. Each day and at every moment, the Lord calls to us, and each day and at every moment we must listen. With His Name written clearly upon our hearts we should act, and not otherwise. We must think and say with Paul, "I am a minister in accordance with God's stewardship given to me to bring to completion for you the word of God," whether we bring forth that Word by word or by action. Again, if we do not listen to His voice, if it is not this that moves us, that animates our work, all our afflictions are useless, for they are not united to the cross of Christ.

Let us take Abraham as our example. He greets the Lord as He comes to him. He rushes about to prepare Him a meal and care for His needs. Indeed, "he waited on them under the tree while they ate." But he did all of this with a prayer in his heart; he performed all his diligent service out of love for Him whom he served. He could see clearly it was God he waited upon, and so all his frantic work was no burden; he found only joy to be in the presence of His God. So must be our attitude in all we do, brothers and

143

sisters. It cannot be otherwise. All we do must be done for Him; we must ever keep His presence in our hearts, and with this one needful thing fixed firmly within us, all of our lives will be blessed. And we, too, will be holy. We, too, will be made whole by the power of His Word at work within us.

Seventeenth Week
(Gn.18:20-32; Ps.138:1-3,6-8; Col.2:12-14; Lk.11:1-13)

"Ask and you will receive; seek and you will find;
knock and the door will be opened to you."

Prayer. Our wonderful gift from God. Our sharing in His will.

The Lord ordains that Abraham should speak with Him, and so He stops and waits to hear the prayer of His favored one. And so in this mystical scene from our first reading, we are given a holy model for our own petitions of the Lord. Indeed, first we see that the Lord waits upon us to approach Him – His ears are ever open to our pleas. (As we read elsewhere, He knows what we need before we ask.) Second, Abraham prefaces his prayer with acknowledgment of the justice of God, thus revealing the confidence we must have that the Lord will answer any righteous request. Third, Abraham shows the manner in which we must come before our God. Though we must be persistent, thus manifesting our genuine concern for the prayer we offer, we must realize to whom we speak and come before Him in deep humility: "See how I am presuming to speak to my Lord, though I am but dust and ashes!" says Abraham, and it is with words such as these that he precedes each of his persistent requests. And because of his faith and humility, his prayer is answered and Lot is spared from the destruction of Sodom.

And, of course, our greatest model of prayer is found in our gospel. When Jesus finishes praying, the disciples beg Him to teach them to pray. First He shares with them the Lord's Prayer, wherein we give ourselves to the providential hand of God and reflect His grace and forgiveness. He then relates a parable on the necessity and blessings of perseverance in prayer – we must never be discouraged in our prayer. Finally, the words which drip like honey from His mouth: "Ask and you will receive..." and His blessed assurance that the Father will "give the Holy Spirit to those who ask Him."

The Lord loves us and wishes to share all of Himself with us. We must but come as children before Him and we will know the kindness of which David sings, and we will sing with him: "I will give thanks to you, O Lord, with all my heart, for you have heard the words of my mouth." Indeed, "the lowly He sees"; His "right hand saves" them. Forsaking not the work of His hands, He rather justifies them, giving them life even by the recognition of their voices before Him. Thus we are "raised with Him through faith in the power of God." "Having forgiven us all our transgressions" through the cross of Christ, the Father now brings the humble to life through the Spirit of His Son. It is in His hearing our prayer that this grace is best known, for therein our spirits become one with His own.

O Lord, hear and answer us as we call upon you each day in all faith and humility. Make us your own sons and daughters in the Spirit of Christ.

Eighteenth Week
(Ec.1:2,2:21-23; Ps.90:3-6,12-14,17,95:7-8; Col.3:1-5,9-11; Lk.12:13-21)

"If you were raised with Christ, seek what is above,
where Christ is seated at the right hand of God."

Yes, "all things are vanity!" without God. All is empty, for "like the changing grass" our life "wilts and fades"; we are turned "back to dust," and so what becomes of the earthly desires we pursue? Where do "immorality, impurity, passion, evil desire, and the greed that is idolatry" lead us but to the grave – and what do they do for us here but keep our hearts from what truly matters?

See the difference between the man in our first reading who "labors under the sun" in "toil and anxiety of heart" and those in our psalm who "shout for joy and gladness" all their days, for the latter say to the Lord, "Prosper the work of our hands," putting all things into the care of Him who indeed holds all things in His loving embrace. One's heart is set on "what is on earth," and so he is blinded by the flesh into which he puts all his hopes. Like both the man in the crowd and the one in the parable of our gospel, his sights are set on his possessions and the feeding of his belly – both of which shall rot away. The other's heart, however, is set on "what is above." He is rich in "what matters to God" because he has died to the vain things of this earth, dying with Christ to their illusion and, so, rising with Christ to the life and glory of heaven. As one sinks into hell, the other rises to newness of life "in the image of [his] Creator."

In what image is our own life made? What do we pursue with heart and soul as we tread this earth? Are we consumed by the mud at our feet, miring ourselves in selfishness and sin; or do we indeed rise above the greed which tempts our hearts to "eat, drink, be merry"? If we are truly raised with Christ as we proclaim as Christians, we would be seated at God's right hand with Him, knowing that He is our only refuge, our only God. But so many are distracted by the idolatrous images that surround us in this world. So many desire to be rich and famous, to satiate their appetites in gluttony and drunkenness, to do what pleases their flesh in sexual immorality. And what shall become of these but that the worm shall consume them and they will cry out with Qoheleth, "Vanity of vanities! All things are vanity!"

Brothers and sisters, with Jesus and with Paul I encourage you to find the treasure that is meaningful in life. Set aside the earthly passions that drown the soul, and seek what is alive with Christ. We have a great call in this world to bring the Lord's light and life forward, to make Him present in our own flesh, in all our work. With Him in our hearts, nothing is done in vain, for such "bountiful harvest" as this is stored up for heaven, which shall never pass away. Let us make His resurrection our own; even as we die to the empty desires of this earth, let us rise unto God as a holy sacrifice.

O. 19. Sun. (C)

Nineteenth Week
(Ws.18:6-9; Ps.33:1,12.18-20,22; Heb.11:1-2,8-19; Lk.12:32-48)

"You also must be prepared, for at an hour
you do not expect, the Son of Man will come."

"Our soul waits for the Lord." Though we do not know the day or the hour of His return, we must always be ready for His coming. As the ancients, the Hebrew fathers and especially Abraham the father of faith himself, we must ever be seeking our heavenly homeland. By faith the ancients, who saw the promise only from afar, "awaited the salvation of the just"; by faith Abraham "sojourned in the promised land as in a foreign country." As he dwelled in tents, nonetheless, "he was looking forward to the city with foundations, whose architect and maker is God." With the incarnation of Christ, and in His death and resurrection, what greater assurance have we of that which we hope for. We now have Jesus speaking to our hearts: "Do not be afraid any longer, little flock, for your Father is pleased to give you the kingdom." How much more are we called to follow His way in faith; how much more we should now be prepared for the coming of the Son of Man.

"Gird your loins and light your lamps and be like servants who await their master's return from a wedding, ready to open immediately when He comes and knocks." If the Lord finds us "vigilant on His arrival," how blessed will we be. If we have distributed well the food He has put in our charge here, if His work we have accomplished according to His word, we shall ourselves sup at the table the Lord prepares for us in the heavenly homeland. But all we are given here, all the graces and blessings which are ours through Jesus and through His Church, we are responsible for; by them we must bear fruit in patience and in faith, Peter first, as the first of servants, and all of us beneath his charge in proportion to "the food allowance" placed in our hands for distribution at the proper time. (This refers primarily to our priests, but we all do share in the priesthood of Christ, and all are graced with a measure of the flesh of Christ to share with the world.)

"Exult, you just, in the Lord," for what was held "in secret" by "the holy children" of times past has now come to light in the presence of our Lord Jesus Christ. Now we await the second coming of Christ with a "sure knowledge" far surpassing the one granted our fathers. We are "the people He has chosen for His own inheritance," and a promise so sure should spur us on to a readiness that is meet to such a wonderful gift. The Lord is coming to sit us at table at the place He now prepares; let us "make preparations" of our own, remaining ever the servants of Christ, that we shall not be taken unawares when it is time to fold up our tents in this world and join the Lord in glory. Hear Him knocking even now at the door of your hearts.

Twentieth Week
(Jer.38:4-6,8-10; Ps.40:2-4,14,18; Heb.12:1-4; Lk.12:49-53)

"Though I am afflicted and poor,
yet the Lord thinks of me."

Persecution is necessarily a part of every Christian's life. Not many of us will struggle "to the point of shedding blood" as has Jesus, as has Paul, as have all the apostles (but John); and not many of us will be thrown into muddy cisterns as is Jeremiah... but all will remain "afflicted and poor" in their striving against sin and have to endure "opposition from sinners" as they grow in holiness before their Lord and God. Jesus is anguished at the baptism He must endure in carrying the cross of division set in opposition to the forces of sin in this world, and so all who call themselves Christian take this same cross upon their shoulders. If we do not suffer for the faith, we must question whether we have become lukewarm and worthless, but to be spit from the mouth of God.

Division must necessarily come as we follow in the steps of Jesus, "the leader and perfecter of faith." As the princes of the people were set against Jeremiah for his prophesying in truth against the nation, spelling out the danger it faced for its sin, so opposition will come to us even from friends and family as we seek to draw closer to Jesus; for the world is set in opposition to the cross, and any who yet cling to the world and its sin will inevitably be insulted by our resistance to its ways. And so persecution comes to those who remain faithful to the ways of Christ.

But your hearts should not be troubled, brothers and sisters, for though the world of sin encompasses us now and often closes in, we indeed have a "great cloud of witnesses" surrounding us with their protection. As

147

Ordinary Time

Jeremiah had Ebed-melech to intercede with the king to draw him from the muddy mire, so we have Jesus now to intercede with the Father for us to lift us out of the dark cistern that is the world. And not only Him do we have at our side, but all those who have suffered with Him – all the saints and all the martyrs, all the apostles and prophets – who stand at His side in the heavenly kingdom and with Him reach down to assist us.

So fear not, little ones, remember Jesus: "For the sake of the joy that lay before Him, He endured the cross, despising its shame." He "has taken His seat at the right of the throne of God" and we shall soon join Him there with all His angels and saints if we but endure the persecution with Him now a little while. The Lord thinks of those who are afflicted and poor. He blesses their sacrifice and makes it fruitful (by which we may draw even sinners unto Him). Continue ever to run the race of faith.

O. 21. Sun. (C)

Twenty-First Week
(Is.66:18-21; Ps.117:1-2,Mk.16:15; Heb.12:5-7,11-13; Lk.13:22-30)

"People will come from the east and the west
and from the north and the south
and will recline at table in the kingdom of God."

"I come to gather nations of every language; they shall come and see my glory," even those of "distant coastlands that have never heard of my fame, or seen my glory," says the Lord. The Word goes forth. The Word goes forth to the ends of the earth and it will open the eyes and ears of all peoples. But who shall be ready for its coming?

Indeed, Isaiah's prophecy and the verses of our psalm are in harmony with the Lord's own words: all the nations shall come, all shall "praise the Lord," and all shall find a place in His kingdom. The light that goes forth, the glory of the Lord, knows no boundaries, is not limited by constructs of time and place – there are no walls in its way. All nations. All tongues. All peoples at all times and in all places are called forth by the all-encompassing love of our God and our Savior. You are welcome at His table, my brother, my sister, whomever you are, wherever you are. It is the Lord's will that all come to Him who is the Father of all nations and of all creation. But do you know the way?

The way of the Lord is not easy; it is narrow and rough – it is one wrought with chastisement, with discipline. "For what 'son' is there whom his father does not discipline?" And how can you expect to come into His paradise if the soil of this world still clings to your soul? The cross is the way to the kingdom; only the scourging discipline of the Lord will enable us to sit with Him.

148

And this discipline, this cross, is of love. Do you see this? Do you see how much the Father loves you in His reproof of your sin? "At the time, all discipline seems a cause not for joy but for pain, yet later it brings the peaceful fruit of righteousness to those who are trained by it." If you have not learned this basic lesson of the working of the Lord's love, you "will not be strong enough" to enter His gate. You must "not be disjointed but healed" as the Lord takes from you all that is unfit for His presence. Your suffering the loss of this life is all that will bring you to heaven.

We note that even the above words of the Lord are as chastisement to the Israelite people who walk with Him, for He is telling them they are not alone in the call to God; other nations shall indeed enter before they. And as this pride in their heritage must be wrested from them before they are prepared for the kingdom, so all that limits the love of the Lord from working in our lives must be taken from us before we may enter in. Fear not the pain this brings. The "wailing and grinding of teeth" outside His gates is more painful by far – and for this suffering there is no healing anymore.

O. 22. Sun. (C)

Twenty-Second Week
(Sir.3:17-18,20,28-29; Ps.68:4-7,10-11; Heb.12:18-19,22-24a; Lk.14:1,7-14)

"Humble yourself the more, the greater you are,
and you will find favor with God."

Is this not the message of Jesus' parable in today's gospel, and indeed of all our readings – and indeed the essence of our Christian lives? "Take the lowest place." Exalt not yourself in the sight of God, who sits at table with you, whose presence is everywhere, and is a guest far greater than you. Give your place to the poor, provide for them out of your means, as He has done, and then you will know the glorious vision of heaven where He dwells.

The Pharisees are blind to the presence of Jesus; because of their pride and desire for esteem, they cannot see the guest of honor in their midst. They observe Him carefully, ready to judge Him, but it is He who sees them and seeks to instruct them in their ignorance. The Lord is most out of place here among the proud. He looks around for lowly ones, but finds none. The poor have not been invited to this feast; the blind here do not recognize their need for Him... and so this banquet is not like that of heaven. And so, who of these will partake of His Body and Blood and come to "the heavenly Jerusalem"?

"God gives a home to the forsaken," David declares in our psalm, and we are called to be like God. Jesus makes this quite evident in His instruction to the host of the banquet: "Invite the poor, the crippled, the

Ordinary Time

lame, the blind," who are unable to repay such kindness, and then "you will be repaid at the resurrection of the righteous." This attitude of self-giving we must make our own, knowing our own lowliness in the sight of God, and the vision of heaven of which our second reading speaks will be ours as well. Then we will come with the "countless angels in festal gathering" and "the assembly of the firstborn" into the presence of Jesus and the holy blood of His sacrifice. "The just rejoice and exult before God," and with them we too shall rejoice, if we make ourselves humble before Him.

It is no mystery that "everyone who exalts himself will be humbled, but the one who humbles himself will be exalted." No, the teaching is clear, and only by living it will we find its fruit, brothers and sisters. "My child, conduct your affairs with humility, and you will be loved more than a giver of gifts," Sirach instructs us; for how can you find favor with God (or with anyone) if you have no respect for Him? And if you do not see the greatness of the God before you, how shall you enter His kingdom?

Our place before God is with faces to the ground. This is just. This is right. By this He will be pleased and so lift our heads to gaze upon His countenance.

O. 23. Sun. (C)

Twenty-Third Week
(Wis.9:13-18b; Ps.90:1,3-6,12-14,17; Phlm.1:9-10,12-17; Lk.14:25-33)

"Whoever does not carry his own cross and come after me
cannot be my disciple."

The wisdom of the cross, that blessed necessity for every Christian's life. What does it teach us? How does it call us to act? Its wisdom is not of this earth, for the "corruptible body burdens the soul," but the counsel of the "Holy Spirit from on high" brings the freedom to be sons of God. This wisdom can only be found by knowing we are but dust and renouncing all things of dust to serve the living and true God.

"Who can know God's counsel, or who can conceive what the Lord intends?" our first reading from the Book of Wisdom inquires of us. Indeed, things before our eyes, things of this earth, "we find with difficulty," so who can understand things of heaven? How shall we attain the vision of God, of whom our psalm states, "A thousand years in your sight, are as yesterday, now that it is passed, or as a watch in the night"? How can we who wilt and fade "like the changing grass" come to the surpassing knowledge our Lord possesses?

Jesus answers the question. He turns to the crowds who follow Him, who are excited by His presence but unaware of the demands made upon every Christian's life, and He teaches them this wisdom that is of God. It is

150

His essential lesson: Be prepared to give up all things for the sake of the kingdom. Put nothing before your worship of God. Renounce all your possessions and be ready to die for Him – only then can you approach the glory He brings to this earth. Only by the wisdom of His cross will you find the kingdom of God. For indeed "the earthen shelter" and all its concerns weigh down the mind, weigh down the spirit, and keep it from attaining to God; they must therefore be left behind to find the freedom of sons of the Most High.

The Lord comes to "teach us to number our days aright, that we may gain wisdom of heart." It is this teaching Paul seeks to impart to Philemon as he asks him to forgive the slave that has wronged him and accept him back "forever, no longer as a slave but more than a slave, a brother." This same forgiveness, which is divine not earthly, is that which is asked of us all by the Lord. For so we have been forgiven by Him, so we who were sinful slaves have been made His brother... and so we must do the same for others. It is no longer the mind of man by which we judge but the mind of God, and the grace of this wisdom we gain only by carrying our cross. It is this which shapes us in His image, which imparts to us His wisdom – and by this the work of our hands shall prosper.

O. 24. Sun. (C)

Twenty-Fourth Week
(Ex.32:7-11,13-14; Ps.51:3-4,12-13,17,19,Lk.15:18; 1Tm.1:12-17; Lk.15:1-32)

"The Lord relented in the punishment
He had threatened to inflict on His people."

Redemption is ours, brothers and sisters. Though we are great sinners, the Lord has mercy on us when we turn to Him; for, as Moses interceded for the Israelites in the desert, so Christ Jesus intercedes for us now before the throne of His Father. Indeed, He "came into the world to save sinners," sinners like you and me.

What examples of sinners we have throughout our readings today – what examples of great sinners and the greatness, the abundance of God's grace. Where shall we begin? In our first reading the people of Israel had fallen into the depths of depravity as they passed through the desert. While Moses was on the mountain receiving the Ten Commandments, they were far below, "making for themselves a molten calf and worshiping it." To it they sacrificed, and in drunken revelry proclaimed it God. Yet because of Moses' intercession the Lord held back His blazing wrath against them. He did not destroy them.

In our second reading we find "the foremost" of sinners, the apostle Paul, recognizing his own great guilt as arrogant persecutor of the Church and, in the same breath, witnessing to the manner in which he was "mercifully treated" by the Lord, that he might indeed be "an example for those who would come to believe in [Jesus] for everlasting life." If the Lord can turn him who was the primary persecutor of Himself and His people into a leading apostle of His Word, how might He not convert our own hearts, or the hearts of any, to Him and to His will?

And, of course, in our gospel we have the parable of the prodigal son, he who "squandered his inheritance on a life of dissipation" yet when he came to his senses and returned home was openly received into the waiting arms of the same father whose property he swallowed up. The Lord makes so clear in His parable today the great desire God has to take the sinner in His arms, to place him on His shoulders; indeed, "there will be more joy in heaven over one sinner who repents than over ninety-nine righteous people who have no need of repentance." Brothers and sisters, we all have need of repentance, and the Lord welcomes us all.

After all this, perhaps our most poignant witness to God's forgiveness and grace comes in King David, who has been adulterous and murderous but who cries out to the Lord in our psalm, "Thoroughly wash me from my guilt and of my sin cleanse me." His "contrite spirit," his humble begging is heard by the Lord, as is the repentance of us all. Through the blood of Jesus, all ignorant sinners may be saved.

O. 25. Sun. (C)

Twenty-Fifth Week
(Amos 8:4-7; Ps.113:1-2,4-8; 1Tm.2:1-8; Lk.16:1-13)

"If you are not trustworthy with what belongs to another,
who will give you what is yours?"

This world and the things of it are not our own; we are children of heaven. Yet we are here amongst these things which are foreign to us. And so, what should we do? With all the Lord puts in our hands as we pass through this generation we must honor God. Though in the world of mammon, we must use it to serve our God in heaven. Thus we shall prove ourselves worthy to enter into that kingdom which is above, which is our true home. This call is stated simply in the Lord's Prayer when we say, "On earth as it is in heaven" – we must bring the kingdom of God to bear in this place we find ourselves.

In our first reading, Amos makes clear what our attitude should *not* be with regard to the riches or power we may find at our disposal. We must never "trample upon the needy and destroy the poor of the land." We must never reflect the greed of these merchants who cannot wait for the sabbath,

152

the Lord's Day, to end, that they might satiate their thirst for wealth, and this by dishonest means. The Lord will condemn such pride and avarice.

In our second reading, Paul gives a clearer idea the manner in which power should be employed in his exhortation to prayer for those in position of authority. God "wills everyone to be saved and to come to knowledge of the truth," and if our kings seek to maintain peace in the world, they will save not only themselves, but provide ground for others to come to God. Again, all that is given us, be it riches, power, wisdom or strength, must be given over to service of the Lord. We must be as He "who gave Himself as ransom for all" in His teaching, in His healing, indeed, in the laying down of His very life. And so, if we ourselves are teachers, we must be as Paul and do so "in faith and truth," without any deceit. And when we offer prayers, we must always lift up "holy hands, without anger or argument." In our prayer should always be forgiveness of others.

In our gospel parable Jesus illustrates and commends not deceitful dealings with others' wealth, but to be wise in what is given us, to turn the riches of this world against the prince of this world (Satan), and use them for the good of the kingdom. Even in these things which are the devil's we must work to serve our Master in heaven. And so we feed the hungry, we clothe the naked, we pray for those in power, that the Lord who is "high above all nations" and whose glory is "above the heavens" might stoop down to us and through us fulfill the mission of Christ; for "He raises the lowly from the dust, from the dunghill He lifts the poor." And we must do the same to find our place with Him in heaven.

O. 26. Sun. (C)

Twenty-Sixth Week
(Amos 6:1,4-7; Ps.146:2,5-10; 1Tm.6:11-16; Lk.16:19-31)

"Keep the commandment without stain or reproach
until the appearance of our Lord Jesus Christ."

The Lord is coming. First of all, know this. "The King of kings and Lord of lords, who alone has immortality, who dwells in unapproachable light, and whom no human being has seen or can see" will reveal Himself "at the proper time." Shall come the end of this world and the birth of the new in the presence of our all-holy God. Do not doubt this. Do not question it in your hearts. But believe.

Second, know the nature of our God. This our psalm makes abundantly clear: "The Lord gives sight to the blind" and "protects strangers... The fatherless and the widow He sustains, but the way of the wicked He thwarts." And since "the Lord raises up those who were bowed down," we must bow down and serve Him, bringing His love to this world; keeping

Ordinary Time

"faith forever" we must give "food to the hungry," showing His unending compassion to all those in need.

Third, know the fate which awaits those who fail to adhere to His command of love, those who stain themselves with comfort and riches in a vain existence and have no heart for those who suffer now by their lack. As He prepares a place of refuge in Abraham's bosom for those who "pursue[d] righteousness, devotion, faith, love, patience, and gentleness," so a place is set for those "who dressed in purple garments and fine linen and dined sumptuously each day" but who were "not made ill by the collapse of Joseph," who had no regard for the destruction of God's people – who stepped over and upon the poor lying at their doors as they pursued the fatting of their bellies. "A great chasm is established" between the redeemed and the condemned; as Lazarus had no way to enter the door of the house of the rich man, so the rich man cannot pass now into the arms of God... only now that darkness without is eternal – his torment shall not end.

It is popular to believe that Jesus somehow did away with punishment, that in His all-embracing love there is no longer need for justice, and so hell is no longer a factor. The "God of the Old Testament" is presented as the one of punishment with Him of the New conversely being of love. Brothers and sisters, they are one and the same God. And as in the time before Christ, the Lord forever showed compassion for the humble of the earth, so now Jesus shows condemnation to the wicked who refuse to turn from their ways. Only now the love and justice, which are also one, are made eternal by the coming of the end of the age in the Person of Jesus Christ. Continue to keep yourselves pure and serve the Lord – His Day is at hand.

O. 27. Sun. (C)

Twenty-Seventh Week
(Hb.1:2-3,2:2-4; Ps.95:1-2,6-9; 2Tm.1:6-8,13-14; Lk.17:5-10)

"The vision still has its time,
presses on to fulfillment, and will not disappoint."

And we are servants of this Gospel.

And so, with faith and in patience we must accomplish "what we [are] obliged to do." We must serve the Word of God. Never hardening our hearts against the voice we hear, rather, we should "stir into flame the gift of God" we are blessed with as Christians, as Catholics; "the Holy Spirit that dwells within us" should be our refuge and our guide – it should be our stronghold despite any "destruction and violence" we witness before us. For we know that if we endure till the end, till the fulfillment of the vision of the Gospel, though we deserve it not, the Lord will call to us when we "come in from plowing or tending sheep in the field and say, 'Come here immediately

154

and take your place at table.'" Indeed, He has promised in His mercy and His glorious benevolence to put on His apron and serve us, His "unprofitable servants," at table in the eternal kingdom. But have we the faith to believe? Have we the patience to endure? Listen to His assuring words: "Wait for it, it will surely come, it will not be late." His Word is certainly true and the vision written "clearly upon the tablets" of our hearts, if we believe.

And we show our faith when we "sing joyfully to the Lord," when we "bow down in worship" before Him in spite of any "clamorous discord" that surrounds us in this world. In such praise in the face of the darkness of evil we bear "hardship for the Gospel with the strength that comes from God." Yes, He alone is our strength; it is from Him alone that we find the faith and patience to endure and produce fruit upon this earth. So, "let us kneel before the Lord who made us. For He is our God, and we are the people He shepherds." Though we cry out, "How long, O Lord?" with the prophet Habbakuk, we know that if we listen to the instructions of the Apostle Paul to "take as [our] norm the sound words [we] heard from [him]," "in the faith and love that are in Christ Jesus" we shall endure, and we shall find answer to our prayer.

The vision is coming to fulfillment. The Lord of all is with us now. Let us "not be ashamed of [our] testimony to our Lord," but proclaim with courage the word the Spirit prompts in our hearts – *Jesus is Lord!* Let us say it. Let us not be afraid of it or its consequences. Let the truth of God cross our lips even as it stirs the faith within us. Jesus is Lord, and His Kingdom comes. Do not delay your service of Him.

O. 28. Sun. (C)

Twenty-Eighth Week
(2Kgs.5:14-17; Ps.98:1-4; 2Tm.2:8-13; Lk.17:11-19)

"All the ends of the earth have seen
the salvation by our God."

"The word of God is not chained." It cannot be imprisoned. It is free. And it cannot be limited by national boundaries; it is for everyone. The universal call of salvation is made most clear in our readings today: in our first reading, Naaman the Syrian is healed of his leprosy, and in our gospel a Samaritan is healed of the same. Both are foreigners and essentially enemies to Israel, but it is these two we hear of today to make clear that the Word of God and His power are unbounded.

And when these foreigners are healed, they return praising God; they make clear their faith in the Holy One, much to the shame of those who are native to His House, who may often lack such recognition of the Lord and

155

His work in their lives. This is perhaps the greatest message of today's readings, that we must be as the Samaritan who, "realizing he had been healed, returned, glorifying God in a loud voice, and... fell at the feet of Jesus and thanked Him." For this is what the Lord desires of us, thanksgiving, a sacrifice of praise. How clearly this is shown in Naaman as well, whose offerings of gifts are repelled by Elisha, the man of God, "despite Naaman's urging," but who will not leave without earth from the land of Israel, declaring, "I will no longer offer holocaust or sacrifice to any other god except the Lord." The Lord desires of us our praise and worship of Him only, and when we come bearing this gift of ourselves, He says to us, "Stand up and go; your faith has saved you."

And it is unto the end we must remain faithful, praising God for the graces He gives, if we hope to "obtain the salvation that is in Christ Jesus, together with eternal glory." We should hear in Paul's teaching in our second reading of the means to salvation and the means to condemnation. The Lord "remains faithful, for He cannot deny Himself." He is God; He holds salvation and glory. If we persevere with Him, dying with Him, giving all our selves always to His service, "we shall also reign with Him." It cannot be otherwise because the Lord indeed blesses those who come to Him. But "if we deny Him, He will deny us," and this cannot but be, too, for He cannot dwell with untruth.

The Lord's Truth extends to the ends of the earth now; His Word goes forth to all, and in all salvation may be known through Jesus Christ. But who will trust in Him and fall at His feet in praise of Him as they find healing for their sin? Let it be so with us all.

O. 29. Sun. (C)

Twenty-Ninth Week
(Ex.17:8-13; Ps.121:1-8; 2Tm.3:14-4:2; Lk.18:1-8)

"Call out to Him day and night."

How faithful is the Lord. How true is He. As our psalmist so well states, "He neither slumbers nor sleeps." Indeed, "He is beside [us] at [our] right hand"; always "the Lord will guard [us] from all evil" – "The Lord will guard your coming and your going, both now and forever." But are we so faithful to Him, turning to Him for His eternal help?

"Pray always without becoming weary." This is our instruction today. This is the "wisdom for salvation" sacred Scripture brings us. Do we receive the "correction" and "training for righteousness" it would impart? Do as Jesus asks: "Pay attention to what the dishonest judge says." Though he "neither fear[s] God nor respect[s] any human being," yet because of the widow's persistence, he renders a just decision for her. And do you think

God will not hear us when we call out to Him? Do you think He is so "slow to answer"? Rather, "He will see to it that justice is done... speedily." For ever He waits for us to turn to Him; always He longs to do justice for us – it is His great joy to answer our prayers.

Learn from our reading from the Book of Exodus. It informs us, "As long as Moses kept his hands raised up, Israel had the better of the fight, but when he let his hands rest, Amalek had the better of the fight." And it was not until Aaron and Hur supported him and "his hands remained steady till sunset" that "Joshua mowed down Amalek and his people with the edge of the sword." And so the sword of the Spirit shall not truly be our own, we will not truly be victorious in the battle against sin, until we remain always in the presence of the Lord, until we, like Him, no longer slumber or sleep.

Brothers and sisters, "proclaim the Word; be persistent whether it is convenient or inconvenient," as Paul exhorts us. In sacred Scripture and the power of the Spirit we find our source for right living; by these we become "equipped for every good work." And consistently good works are found by us only if our prayer is consistent and good. Only if we remain steady and persistent in our calling out to Him at all times will He "not suffer [our] foot to slip." Let us "lift up [our] eyes toward the mountains," seeing always whence our help comes. The Lord prays for us always; let us join Him in prayer.

Thirtieth Week
(Sir.35:12-14,16-18; Ps.34:2-3,7,17-19,23; 2Tm.4:6-8,16-18; Lk.18:9-14)

"O God, be merciful to me a sinner."

"The one who humbles himself will be exalted," for it is the lowly the LORD hears. And in no greater way, and for no greater benefit, do we humble ourselves than to recognize our sinfulness before God. It is then we prove ourselves His own, for it is then Truth is with us.

We must guard ourselves ever from the sin of pride, brothers and sisters; it is just such presumption that breaks down the spiritual life, for it separates us from our proper place before our Lord and God. "The Lord is close to the brokenhearted"; "He hears the cry of the oppressed." He does not come to heal those who are well, nor does He respond to the prayer of the oppressor; and our life on this earth is one of continual healing, and whenever we judge another we condemn our souls.

"May it not be held against them!" is Paul's prayer for his unjust accusers and those who have deserted him. (How like Christ's prayer from the cross it is!) He is crushed before the courts of this world and yet does not judge, and yet does not condemn. For he is the servant of the Lord and shows himself faithful to such a call. Even as he is "poured out like a libation," he remains faithful, unwavering in his hope of standing before and being redeemed by "the just judge." He knows fully that "the Lord redeems the lives of His servants" and that "He who serves God willingly is heard," and so he humbles himself when accused, trusting that "the Lord will rescue [him] from every evil threat and will bring [him] safe to His heavenly kingdom."

Yes, "the prayer of the lowly pierces the clouds." How blessed are they who know their humble place before the Lord, for He hears them and comes quickly to rescue them when they cry out to Him in all their humility. And of course our greatest rescue must be from sin, that which has made us base before His eyes. To its recognition and for its overcoming by the Lord's grace we must dedicate ourselves every day of our lives. And so we cry out for forgiveness. And so we return to our homes justified.

O. 31. Sun. (C)

Thirty-First Week
(Wis.11:22-12:2; Ps.145:1-2,8-11,13-14; 2Thes.1:11-2:2; Lk.19:1-10)

"The Son of Man has come to seek and to save what was lost."

How beautifully the readings speak today of our "Lord and lover of souls" whose "imperishable spirit is in all things" and who is "good to all and compassionate to all His works." It is indeed "in accord with the grace of our God and Lord Jesus Christ" that we be glorified in Him and He in us, and so we praise Him: "Every day I will bless you, and I will praise your name forever and ever."

The Lord "love[s] all things that are"; all is made by Him, so how could He not but love all. Though to Him "the whole universe is as... a drop of morning dew come down upon the earth," He loves it all with a most personal affection, shown in the grace-filled coming of His Son among us. And why has this Son come but to forgive? Why has He walked the earth but to call men back to their place in the loving heart of the Father? Why has He come but to show the Father's loving mercy?

And appropriate is Paul's warning "not to be shaken out of your minds suddenly" in fear of the Lord's imminent return in judgment. Here is remedy against all the false prophets predicting the sudden end of this universe God has created, as if they could move His hand, as if they could know His mind. Whence does this come but the same grumbling of the people when Jesus moved to go in to sup with Zacchaeus, the famous sinner? Whence does this come but a failure to understand the Lord's wisdom and love and manner of working in the world, a failure to see that what the Lord does is "rebuke sinners little by little, warn[ing] them and

158

remind[ing] them of the sins they are committing, that they may abandon their wickedness and believe in [Him]"?

It is evident that the majority in the crowd would have preferred, in fact, rejoiced in seeing, Zacchaeus' utter destruction. They expected the Lord's punishment on this sinner, and desired it to come immediately. Why? Again, they knew not God's love or the Lord's purpose. Why? Even more to the point: they were sinners themselves who failed to recognize their sin and realize their own need for mercy – and so had neither the Lord's patience, nor His love.

How well that loving forgiveness is illustrated in our gospel; how like the parable of the Prodigal Son. As the son returns to the father, Zacchaeus goes ahead and climbs the tree. As the father sees the son from far off and goes to him, so Jesus spies Zacchaeus in the tree and calls to him. As the father's generous love sparks the son's complete repentance, so Jesus' acceptance of Zacchaeus brings salvation to his house, shown in his generous penance. I pray we all seek the Lord who seeks for us and act as Zacchaeus, who "came down quickly and received Him with joy," as the Lord freely offers His love and forgiveness to our souls. Praise Him for His kindness!

Thirty-Second Week
(2Mac.7:1-2,9-14; Ps.17:1,5-6,8,15; 2Thes.2:16-3:5; Lk.20:27-38)

"On waking I shall be content in your presence."

Our hope is in the resurrection, brothers and sisters. It is this which gives us strength, and it is our endurance which brings us to His presence.

Brothers and sisters, indeed, as Paul wishes us, we have "everlasting encouragement and good hope" through the grace of our Lord. He strengthens our hearts "in every good deed and word" and guards us "from the evil one." Thus our hearts should be directed "to the love of God and to the endurance of Christ."

We have as our example today these seven brothers spoken of in the Second Book of Maccabees, who showed the endurance of Christ and their faith in the resurrection to life despite the severity of their torture at the hands of the wicked of this world – and all this before the coming of Christ into the world and the great graces He has since imparted to His Church. If they could die so for the law alone, to what deeds should we not be able to attain? If in the presence of their torturers they could state with such confidence, "The King of the world will raise us up to live again forever," what should we not be able to declare in the name of Him who has now been raised from the dead and ascended to glory? If they were so well able

159

to regard their suffering "as nothing," how much easier should be our own sacrifice, we who stand "in the shadow" of His cross and have His wounds in which to take refuge? Indeed, such greater reason have we to hold to "the hope God gives of being raised up by Him."

"That the dead will rise" there should be no doubt in our hearts. The fact that "to Him all are alive" should be firmly fixed as a peg in the deepest recesses of our souls. Certainly, this is who we are, children of the resurrection, with the calling to come to Christ, He who has been raised to life. I pray we shall all be "deemed worthy to attain to the coming age and to the resurrection of the dead." Children of God, may we be like angels in His presence when we rise. May our minds not be darkened by the night upon this earth, but let our hope be fixed on the coming morning and our faith strengthen us to endure until we stand with Him on that new day.

O. 33. Sun. (C)

Thirty-Third Week
(Mal.3:19-20; Ps.98:5-9; 2Thes.3:7-12; Lk.21:5-19)

"For you who fear my name,
there will arise the sun of justice with its healing rays."

The end comes. The end of the Church year approaches, and the end of time is always upon us. What shall it mean for us, the fact that "there will not be left a stone upon another stone"? That day comes "blazing like an oven" for all evildoers, but for the just the healing rays of the Son of God shine down – will we be burned with the proud like stubble, or made whole in the presence of God?

Yes, "He comes to rule the earth; He will rule the world with justice and the peoples with equity." He is just and so He cannot but judge with justice. How shall we prepare for His coming? What do we do as we wait? Paul gives us wise instruction, simple instruction, which should be simply heeded: "Work quietly." It is not for us to be anxious or afraid; it is not for us to fall into disorder or become lazy... it is but for us to remain occupied with the work of God, however simple, however wonderful, that working be. We may be as St. Theresa and her little way, giving ourselves to the Lord in the simple tasks we perform day to day; or we may be as the missionaries for whom she prayed, going out to the ends of the earth, handed over to "synagogues and to prisons," being "led before kings and governors" to give witness to the name of Christ – "and they will put some of you to death" – but to whatever we are called, always it must be the Lord and His Spirit which are at work in us, helping us to persevere to the end. Not all shall die in the cause, but all must remain faithful to His voice.

Brothers and sisters, sometimes it is the hardest thing simply to go on day to day. Regardless of our situation, we can become distracted and, failing to find the wisdom of Christ, seek to "prepare [our] defense beforehand," to put the words of the Lord into our own mouths – to decide for ourselves what the Lord would have us do. It is the simplest thing to accept His will, to bask in the rays of His glory... and yet so anxious do we become in our waiting that we cannot hear His still, small voice speaking to our hearts. We must persevere. We must go on. We must listen. He is coming, and if we fear His holy Name, we shall have nothing else to fear: we shall be made whole.

O. 34. Sun. (C)

Last Week: Christ the King
(2Sm.5:1-3; Ps.122:1-5; Col.1:12-20; Lk.23:35-43)

"This is the King of the Jews."

On earth, our King rules from a cross; in Paradise, upon a glorious throne. O Lord Jesus, "here we are, your bone and your flesh." May we die with you that we might reign with you in your holy kingdom.

"All the tribes of Israel came to David" and anointed him king of Israel. He had been called by the Lord as shepherd and commander of Israel, and now he would finally receive his kingship. And he would make Jerusalem the city of the king, and make it holy when he brought the ark of the covenant within its walls. And so, here on earth David reigned, as God's anointed. And so Jerusalem becomes the place of worship, within whose gates all rejoice to set foot. And there "are set up judgment seats, seats for the house of David."

And so Jesus is called the Son of David, for He inherits this earthly kingdom blessed by God, anointed anew to reign from Jerusalem. But, of course, His kingdom is more than that of the flesh, for it is His own flesh that makes it holy – He is the Temple not made by human hands, through whom all things blessed of the earth and of heaven came to find their being: "In Him were created all things in heaven and on earth." He indeed is the beginning of all things and the fullness, or the end, of all things; nothing, and in particular the Church, exists apart from Him.

And to what heavenly rule are we all thus called by His "making peace by the blood of His cross." By His sacrifice we shall indeed be saved; He will remember us when He comes into His Kingdom. And there shall be true rejoicing, for there the cross shall be borne no more. Having consumed all our sins and the darkness and death of this life, it shall be transformed into the throne of glory.

Even now the Lord calls to us from the cross; even now His suffering beckons us. Even now we must turn to Him, our King, in our sin and let Him take our corrupted flesh and bone upon Himself to find the blessed reconciliation of our souls in the hand of God. As His forgiveness pours upon us in His blood, we come to the fullness of His heavenly kingdom and "share in the inheritance of the holy ones in light." Long live our King, who dies upon a cross.

B. Weekdays

1. Year I

First Week

Monday
(Heb.1:1-6; Ps.97:1-2,6-7,9; Mk.1:14-20)

"This is the time of fulfillment."

Brothers and sisters, no longer does God speak to us "in fragmentary and varied ways"; this is "the final age," in which "He has spoken to us through His Son, whom He has made heir of all things and through whom He first created the universe." With full voice does He make Himself known now, for "this Son is the reflection of the Father's being, and He sustains all things by His powerful word." Jesus is the Christ, and in Him the will of God is fulfilled.

And is it any wonder the disciples "immediately abandoned their nets and became His followers," that at once they joined Him in "proclaiming the good news of God"? For here is the One they have been waiting for, the voice they have been longing to hear, and what can they do but heed His call to join in speaking the very Word of God? James and John even "abandoned their father Zebedee," a good man, for the greatest of men, the Son of Man, God Himself, had come to them: their hearts could not resist for here indeed was the pure reflection of their Father in heaven, whom even Zebedee desired above all. (With his blessing we can presume they go, the "nets in order" they leave behind.)

O brothers and sisters, do you know who this is has come into your midst? Do you realize who has joined your race? This Jesus whom the Father deems His Son sits at "the right hand of the Majesty in heaven," "far superior to the angels," far superior to all creation, for indeed all creation has come to be through Him, who is one in being with the Father. Here is the heart of our creed, this Jesus, this Christ, who is God Himself, and yet also Man with us. Of His Son the Father says, "Let all the angels of God worship Him," and indeed "all gods are prostrate before Him." He is "the Most High over all the earth, exalted far above all gods," who are no gods at all, unable to stand before the glory of His majesty.

And so should *we* not bow down to Him? Should *we* not follow when He calls, "Come after me"? Do we not wish to join with Him who is our salvation, who has "cleansed us from our sins," on the way that leads to "the

164

reign of God"? Yes, the kingdom of God has come to us in the Person of Jesus the Son; there is nothing more to wait upon. The time has come. Let us now follow Him.

Tuesday
(Heb.2:5-12; Ps.8:2,5-9; Mk.1:21-28)

"A completely new teaching in a spirit of authority!"

Thus do the people exclaim at the power of the word which issues forth from the mouth of Christ, into whose hands "all things" have been subjected. The devils see Him and shriek: "I know who you are – the holy one of God!" They know Him and they fear Him, for He has indeed "come to destroy" them and whatever authority they seem to have. He it is who has come to return man to his rightful "rule over the works of [God's] hands." God has "crowned [man] with glory and honor, and put all things under his feet"; and though "at present we do not see all things thus subjected" because of man's sin, because he has subjected himself to the works of the devil, yet Jesus has come to bring "many sons to glory," to reveal in His own person the power of God present in all mankind.

And how does the Lord Jesus Christ destroy the devils? How does He redeem man from their clutches, from their possession? By suffering. By dying. Yes, even now we "see Jesus crowned with glory and honor" – the glory and honor to which we are all called – "because He suffered death." By suffering death He conquered death, and thus any power the devil wielded by its weight upon our souls. And we are free! The devils are cast from us because He has walked among us; He has come into the synagogue and "taught with authority." And so the pride of the devil is broken, and we see the angels' place as servants to man as we see the dignity to which men are called in this Son of Man.

And the Lord "is not ashamed to call [us] brothers." Though by our weakness, by our sinfulness, our disobedience, certainly we merit shame – and so, rightly does David cry to God, "What is man that you should be mindful of him, or the son of man that you should care for him?" – yet He does care for us, He is mindful of us... He suffers and dies for us, taking our shame upon Himself in His only Son. And what the Lord has earned we should not spurn, but treasure the grace that is ours through our Brother's sacrifice. Let us put ourselves under His authority that His authority might be our own, and the devil shall be gone.

Wednesday
(Heb.2:14-18; Ps.105:1-4,6-9; Mk.1:29-39)

"Since He Himself was tested through what He suffered,
He is able to help those who are tempted."

And help them He does. Die for us He must. Each healing is a move of love which takes His life as sacrifice for our sins.

Jesus died on the cross for us, yes. He opened His arms and let His healing blood pour forth for all "the children of Abraham," all those of faith. But His whole life, and especially His ministry of preaching and healing, is a dying, is a robbing of "the devil, the prince of death, of his power." We see clearly in our gospel today how Jesus "free[s] those who through fear of death had been slaves their whole life long," how He lays down His life for "the whole town [which] was gathered outside the door" of "the house of Simon and Andrew." After healing Simon Peter's mother-in-law of a debilitating fever, He cures all who press upon Him, all "who were variously afflicted"; from them "the demons He expelled."

And in these cures, in these expulsions of demons, do we not see our "merciful and faithful high priest" who has come "to expiate the sins of the people" at work in "blood and flesh," dying for the nation's salvation? Has the Lord not equated such healing with salvation, declaring there is no difference between forgiving sins and saying "be well" to the troubled soul (see Mk.2:9)? And do not these demons desire to cry out that He is the Christ even as He gouges the life from them as He Himself dies? Does their rule not escape them now with every word of the Spirit He speaks? But He does "not permit the demons to speak," for they would reveal who He is only that He might be tempted to become ruler on earth of these people who would certainly seek to crown Him king. But the salvation He brings rises beyond this dying life, and the Son of God has no relations with the prince of darkness and his lying rule.

And so our Lord "went into [the] synagogues preaching the good news and expelling demons throughout the whole of Galilee." So He went forth robbing the devil of His reign, suffering and dying all the while, all the way to the cross, where His ministry is accomplished. And we, brothers and sisters, do we not continue His ministry to this day? Has the Lord not left the dying to us now – a cross upon each of His disciples' backs to fill up what is yet lacking in His sacrifice? Is this not the great gift He gives us? And in His steps, by the apostles' instruction, in union with His Church, do you walk through the suffering and darkness of this world to the Lord's eternal light? For your sake has He died. So "seek to serve Him constantly" as He does you.

Thursday
(Heb.3:7-14; Ps.95:6-11; Mk.1:40-45)

"Today, if you should hear His voice,
harden not your hearts."

Today we see Jesus continuing His healing ministry, and we see how it becomes "no longer possible for [Him] to enter a town openly" because of the public proclamation of His wondrous and powerful works. We see also how, though "He stayed in desert places… people kept coming to Him from all sides," for His work must be accomplished. But we see most particularly the way we must come to Him to find our own healing.

"Come, let us bow down in worship; let us kneel before the Lord who made us," David sings, calling all to their proper place before God. And this the leper in our gospel does today, indicating indeed to all the attitude we must have toward Jesus, the place we must find at His feet. With soft hearts we must come before our Lord in tears for the sin upon our souls. Not like those in the Egyptian desert can we be, those who "saw [His] works for forty years" yet "tested and tried" Him constantly. This generation indeed He "loathed" in His anger, calling them "a people of erring heart" who "know not [His] ways." On the contrary, our hearts must burn with a tender love of God and one another as we approach the Lord in the desert where He waits to save us from our sin. He will match any tenderness of our own. "Moved with pity" we shall find Him, ready to gather our broken spirits into His arms.

"Take care, my brothers, lest any of you have an evil and unfaithful spirit and fall away from the living God." See that your hearts are never "hardened by the deceit of sin." It is always "today" and the Lord is always calling to your soul, always requiring your life from you – always offering His love to you. Offer your own in return, that you shall not be cast from His presence, that you shall not be ostracized like this leper from the community, but remain ever in His holy fold as "the flock He guides" with His gentle hand… and finally that you might "enter into His rest." He calls you to healing at His hand; hear and answer on your knees.

Friday
(Heb.4:1-5,11; Ps.78:3-4,6-8; Mk.2:1-12)

"The promise of entrance into His rest still holds."

But only those with faith in Him shall be made whole.

Paul says of the Israelites in the desert, "The word which they heard did not profit them, for they did not receive it in faith." Though they had seen "the glorious deeds of the Lord and His strength and the wonders that He wrought," they yet became "wayward and rebellious, a generation that kept not its heart steadfast nor its spirit faithful to God." Yet they disobeyed and disbelieved. And so they entered not into His rest; they received not the grace of union with the Lord in His peaceful kingdom, but rather died in the desert in their sin. Thus does Paul warn us not to "fall in imitation of Israel's unbelief," but ever to "strive to enter into that rest" God holds for all His faithful.

And the faith necessary to enter God's rest is illustrated clearly in our gospel today, as is the woe of unbelief. It is "when Jesus saw [the] faith" of those who lowered the paralytic through the ceiling to Him that He said to this poor soul, "My son, your sins are forgiven"; and it is upon hearing these grace-filled words from the Savior's mouth that some of the scribes, those faithless souls so much the descendants of their faithless fathers, grumbled against Him and accused Him of "blasphemy." And as the Lord here makes clear the equation of forgiveness and healing ("Which is easier, to say to the paralytic, 'Your sins are forgiven,' or to say, 'Stand up, pick up your mat, and walk again'?"), commanding indeed the paralyzed man: "Stand up! Pick up your mat and go home," so does this healed soul, washed clean of all his sin, with his companions and all those of faith who stand "awestruck" as they look on... so do these enter God's rest – even as the scribes gnash their teeth.

Brothers and sisters, "God rested from all His work on the seventh day," and that rest awaits all at their completion of the Lord's work in this world. This truth Jesus reveals in our midst even this day. And so we "should put [our] hope in God, and not forget the deeds of God but keep His commands"; for "it is we, who have believed, who enter into that rest," so long as we keep faith in Him.

O. 1. Sat. (I)

Saturday
(Heb.4:12-16; Ps.19:8-10,15,Jn.6:63; Mk.2:13-17)

"Nothing is concealed from Him."

In God's eyes all men are sinners; this is what His penetrating vision cannot help but see. Yet it is just such sinners as we He has come to call, to call away from our sin. The Pharisees cannot bear this sword of truth to pierce their soul, and so they take up the sword of anger against those who are being redeemed, and He who is redeeming them. Let us not be as these hardened hearts, brothers and sisters, but expose our sin to the Lord's sharp gaze, that He might heal us by His grace.

That Jesus Himself sees all that is in a man is indicated by His "overhearing the remark" of the complaining Pharisees today, and more clearly elsewhere in His reading their and His disciples' thoughts without a word being spoken (e.g. Mt.17:25). As nothing is concealed from the Father, so nothing is concealed from the Son: "The reflections and thoughts of the heart" are open to Him. And He knows the troubles that affect each of us. And these, even of the Pharisees, He would heal, even as a wise physician – but we indeed must come with our souls exposed and prepared for surgery.

And though this process can be painful, and though we might say to ourselves, "We are not deserving" – though the questions of the Pharisees might be our own – yet we must witness Jesus' attitude toward Levi and his fellow tax collectors/sinners. Yet we must see how He defends these from attack, not bringing their shame before them as the Pharisees would, but with a heart set only on forgiveness. For indeed "we have a great high priest," one who takes our sins upon Himself, one who suffers with us our weakness in order to save us from its consequences. And so with Levi and his friends we should "confidently approach the throne of grace to receive mercy and favor," both in the confessional and at the Eucharistic table, for our need He has come to fill with His love.

"The law of the Lord is perfect, refreshing the soul"; Jesus is this law made flesh. "The command of the Lord is clear, enlightening the eye"; to remove the darkness of our vision, the all-seeing God has come. "The fear of the Lord is pure, enduring forever," and as long as we come before Him, trembling for our sin, we shall live on in His love.

> Shine your light upon our souls, O Lord,
> and remove all darkness from them.
> In your grace you make us whole;
> with you let us be holy.

Second Week

Monday
(Heb.5:1-10; Ps.110:1-4; Mk.2:18-22)

"You are a priest forever,
according to the order of Melchizedek."

Without beginning or end is the holy priesthood of our Lord; high above all sacrifices reigns His own.

"Taken from among men" is Jesus our high priest "and made [our] representative before God." Like others He is in this respect; yet the "gifts and sacrifices" He offers are infinitely greater than any that have ever been, for it is Himself He lifts up for our sins. "He is Himself beset by weakness," though not His own; He is Himself pierced for transgression, though not of His making – and in the cross of our condition He bears "in the flesh," in the crucifixion He suffers at our hands, does the high priest become the victim whose blood covers the earth with redemption. Yes, "Son though He was, He learned obedience from what He suffered; and when perfected, He became the source of eternal salvation for all who obey Him." What other high priest can boast as much?

And yet the people would limit the grace that pours forth in the blood of His sacrifice, in the sweet-smelling flesh He offers, to a dying law which has been corrupted by the hands of man. They fail to see that the old is subsumed by the new... and so the Lord seeks to teach them to receive the "new wine" He would pour into their hearts with minds open to the light of God. They do not yet know the joy His disciples experience just being in the presence of the Messiah, the bridegroom of all faithful souls; as yet their hearts have not been circumcised by the nails of the sacrifice He makes in their name. But soon their time will come, we pray. When He is lifted up, perhaps they shall see.

And in our psalm we have David's verse of Jesus: "The Lord said to my Lord: 'Sit at my right hand till I make your enemies your footstool.'" Jesus is David's Lord even then, for Jesus our Savior has always been. Beautifully does David speak of this as well, in the voice of God: "Before the daystar, like the dew, I have begotten you." As the dew covers the earth unseen before the sun rises, so before the Father pronounced the words "Let there be light" – first bringing the universe into being by the power of His Word – Jesus was eternally present, even as the water the Spirit moved upon.

And so He has "princely power," seated at the right hand of God. And so He "rule[s] in the midst of His enemies," His sacrifice destroying the death which seemed to take hold of Him. And so, like the order of Melchizedek, which came well before the institution of the Israelite's priestly line, from all eternity His salvific priesthood is – and shall last until the end of time.

Tuesday
(Heb.6:10-20; Ps.111:1-2,4-5,9-10; Mk.2:23-28)

"I will indeed bless you, and multiply you."

God promised to bless Abraham, to make his descendants numerous as the stars; and "He swore by Himself," "by oath," to carry out His promise, thus giving an unshakable, "unchangeable" "firmness to [the] promise." The Lord does not go back on His word. And so, "after patient waiting, Abraham obtained what God had promised"; He became the father of many nations, of all those of faith.

Now if God is so faithful, should we who are "heirs of His promise," who are children of Abraham in the faith and so the sharers of the same blessings promised to him, should not "we who have taken refuge in [God]... be strongly encouraged to seize the hope which is placed before us"? For we, "through faith and patience, are inheriting the promises"; and greater promises than Abraham do we receive at the hand of our Lord now, for our "hope extends beyond the veil through which Jesus, our forerunner, has entered on our behalf." As David "entered God's house... and ate the holy bread which only the priests were permitted to eat," and "even gave it to his men," so Jesus enters His Father's house, passing through the gates of heaven into the sanctuary, into the holy of holies, and there partakes of bread at His Father's hand... and indeed shares it with us, His brothers.

O brothers and sisters, each day we partake of the bread of the angels from the hand of the Lord; it surrounds us like the "standing grain" around the disciples. And does it not prove to us that "great are the works of the Lord, exquisite in all their delights"? Does it not reveal to our souls that our hope in Him is "a sure and firm anchor," that His love for us is strong and all His promises are fulfilled in our midst, before our eyes? "God is not unjust." No, "gracious and merciful is the Lord." "Holy and awesome is His name," and He shares the glory of His presence with all His children: "He has given food to those who fear Him." So, let us "not grow lazy" in faith but take strength in this food He supplies. "He will not forget [our] work and the love [we] have shown Him by [our] service." But let us continue to serve Him in our brothers; let us "show the same zeal till the end," that all His promises we may taste. Indeed, the more we eat His bread, the more we accomplish His work, the more His blessings are multiplied, in us and in the world!

"The sabbath was made for man, not man for the sabbath." The gift of God's rest is ours, releasing us from slavery. Freedom we find in His name, blessing we find in His promise – His rest is upon us as we remain in Him.

171

Ordinary Time

And "He will forever be mindful of His covenant": His blessings shall ever increase in our souls.

O. 2. Wed. (I)

Wednesday
(Heb.7:1-3,15-17; Ps.110:1-4; Mk.3:1-6)

"Without father, mother, or ancestry,
without beginning of days or end of life,
like the Son of God he remains a priest forever."

We hear today more specifically about "Melchizedek, king of Salem and priest of the Most High God," whose name means "king of justice" and also "king of peace," who is therefore so like our King Jesus; it is in his line the Lord takes His place.

"Yours is princely power in the day of your birth, in holy splendor," King David declares of his Lord and our Lord. Indeed before the dawn of light upon earth, Jesus is King: He is the only-begotten Son of God whose rule is from everlasting to everlasting; and His priesthood, like that of Melchizedek, is "in virtue of the power of a life which cannot be destroyed" – not by physical descent but by spiritual ascension. From God Himself He receives His kingship and His priestly anointing.

In contrast to the eternal priesthood and princely headship of our Lord and Savior, we see in our gospel those whose power comes only by "virtue of a law expressed in a commandment concerning physical descent," and which is, therefore, passing away. Indeed, before their eyes it passes this day as Jesus stands before the Pharisees at the front of the synagogue and calls them to acceptance of the greater glory now in their midst. But they "closed their minds against Him" as they refused to realize the limitations of their own calling as leaders of the people, choosing to cling to a dying law and a power which is being taken from them even as a greater is offered, rather than stretching forth their hands to the Lord, in whom the law takes life and finds fulfillment, through whom all power comes...

Yes, the Lord "stretch[es] forth" "the scepter of [His] power" even as the man stretches forth his "shriveled hand" here at the front of the synagogue, before all the people and their teachers on a sabbath day, and finds it "perfectly restored." The same He would do for each of them and for all of us, if we but recognized His transcendent power and glory, if we but realized He is the Son of God.

Thursday

(Heb.7:25-8:6; Ps.40:7-10,17; Mk.3:7-12)

"Jesus is always able to save those who approach God through Him,
since He forever lives to make intercession for them."

O how the people approach Him today, seeking healing, seeking grace: "a great crowd followed Him from Galilee, and an equally great multitude came to Him from Judea, Jerusalem, Idumea, Transjordan, and the neighborhood of Tyre and Sidon" – from all around they came to press upon Him, to press upon Him... "All who had afflictions kept pushing toward Him to touch Him. Unclean spirits would catch sight of Him, fling themselves down at His feet, and shout, "'You are the Son of God!'" So great were their numbers He needed to take refuge in a fishing boat. O "the press of the crowd against Him," the press of the crowd. They could not resist drawing toward Him who stood at the center of the universe, Him who stood in the place of God, Him who was God. Greater than the pull of gravity was the pull of their hearts toward salvation.

And do you think He has left you, brother? Do you say, "Where is He now that I need healing, that I may press upon Him myself?" He has not left you alone; He has multiplied His presence and increased His grace through the ministry of His apostles. They now go out to those who would press upon Him, and through these priests they find the high priest, He who is "holy, innocent, undefiled, separated from sinners, higher than the heavens." Indeed, He is not on earth anymore and His ministry is not earthly – yet He is ever present to all who stretch forth their hands to Him. Do you not know the immense mercy available to you in the Sacrament of Confession? Do you not realize the heavenly food you eat in Holy Communion? Press upon Him this day; approach the priests who, despite their imperfections, hold the power He has left in our midst, and to your loving God you will come.

"Jesus has obtained a more excellent ministry now," and "He is mediator of a better covenant," an eternal covenant. Brothers and sisters, "we have such a high priest, who has taken His seat at the right hand of the throne of Majesty in heaven, minister of the sanctuary and of that true tabernacle set up not by man but by the Lord." What greater gift could we ask for? How much more exalted could we be called to be than to receive mercy from Him who dwells in the heart of the Father, than to take food from the hands of Him who holds the hand of God?

O Lord, "may all who seek you
exult and be glad in you,

173

And may those who love your salvation
say ever, 'The Lord be glorified.'"

Friday

(Heb.8:6-13; Ps.85:8,10-14; Mk.3:13-19)

"I will be their God
and they shall be my people."

"Near indeed is His salvation to those who fear Him, glory dwelling in our land"; for absolute oneness do we find with our Lord and God through the ministry of His only Son. For the Lord has said of His new covenant, "All shall know me, from least to greatest," promising: "I will place my laws in their minds and I will write them upon their hearts." There shall be no separation from His presence for those who believe; His "kindness and truth shall meet" in us as they have in Jesus. Alleluia!

But yet does the time move toward perfection. Though the new covenant be fulfilled in Jesus, it is still being fulfilled in the world and among those who dwell in the world. We know this because the Lord says of the covenant to come, through His prophet Jeremiah: "They shall not teach their fellow citizens or their brothers, saying, 'Know the Lord'" – there being no need any longer to teach the perfected – and also, "Their sins I will remember no more," meaning that sin will no longer exist. But Jesus upon commissioning the twelve apostles sends them out "to preach the good news" and "to have authority to expel demons," and to this day there is need, and great need, for instruction in the Word of God and healing by the expulsion of sin in Holy Confession. This ministry still in place, we know we have yet to reach perfection; we know we have yet to find absolute oneness with Christ and His sacrifice... and so, perfect union with the Father yet awaits us.

"He appointed the twelve as follows: Simon to whom He gave the name Peter; James, son of Zebedee; and John, the brother of James (He gave these two the name Boanerges, or 'sons of thunder'); Andrew, Philip, Bartholomew, Matthew, Thomas, James son of Alphaeus; Thaddeus, Simon of the Zealot party, and Judas Iscariot, who betrayed Him." Upon these the new covenant is founded. By their ministry it shall grow, taking root in the world and bearing much fruit. And though Matthias must take the place of the traitorous Judas, there is no breaking the line that comes from these foundation stones: all of the coming kingdom is traced to them and from them, for they are anointed by the Son and by them God will make all His children.

Brothers and sisters, "the Lord Himself will give His benefits; our land shall yield its increase." In His Church as in His arms make your home, for His blessings are upon us and shall be fulfilled.

Saturday
(Heb.9:2-3,11-14; Ps.47:2-3,6-9; Mk.3:20-21)

"Behind the second veil was the tabernacle called the holy of holies."

To this holy of holies in the temple of Jerusalem only the high priest could come, and only once a year. So holy was it deemed. This tabernacle contained the ark of the Lord with the two tablets upon which the commandments of God were written, and some manna from the Israelites' travels through the desert. This was truly sacred ground for God's chosen people, a place they held in awe.

In our gospel the people press upon Jesus; they gather in great numbers at the door of the house where He is staying, sensing that this place is a holy of holies, that there is something inside that makes it sacred. But from this holy tabernacle they are not excluded for its sanctity, but welcomed by Him who is inside, who makes it holy. So much does He welcome those who come to His door that He does not take time even to eat. Better He should feed those who come to Him with His sacred presence than that He should feed Himself, for He will not see any turned away.

My brothers and sisters, Jesus has "entered once for all into the sanctuary, passing through the greater and more perfect tabernacle not made by hands, that is, not belonging to this creation," and He Himself has become the "holy of holies": He Himself is the sacred sanctuary in which God reposes. And He is with us. To this day He is in our presence. Do you not know that He rests in every tabernacle of every one of our churches on this earth? Do you realize the holy of holies that is in our midst? And when He is exposed upon our altar for all to adore, do you realize that here "God sits upon His holy throne"? And do you come to Him? More than a mere image or reflection of the glory of heaven, truly that transcendent glory is present in this bread the angels consume, and which is offered us here.

And so, should we not "shout to God with cries of gladness" or prostrate ourselves in absolute reverence at this the presence of "the Lord, the Most High, the awesome... the great King over all the earth" here in our midst? Should we not receive Him worthily, realizing that here is the holiest of holies whom we cannot reverence too greatly, whom we cannot worship enough? "God mounts His throne amid shouts of joy; the Lord, amid trumpet blasts," and we should join in this celebration and "sing praise to our King" before the throne upon which He sits, before the Tabernacle in which He rests.

Come to Him in sacred wonder. In this Sacrament He waits. May "the blood of Christ... cleanse our consciences from dead works to worship the living God!"

Third Week

Monday
(Heb.9:15,24-28; Ps.98:1-6; Mk.3:22-30)

"His death has taken place for deliverance from transgressions."

By his death Jesus has disarmed the devil; the Lord has destroyed Satan's power by His holy sacrifice. Because of Jesus' innocent blood, "Satan has suffered mutiny in his ranks and is torn by dissension," for none of his adversarial accusations can stand before such pure love. "He cannot endure, he is finished"... and with him, sin also dies, for there is no longer anyone to accuse us of our sin. It is as if Jesus says, "Kill me if you will," and once having done so, Satan has nothing left in his arsenal. Once taking all our sins out of his bag and piercing the Savior through with their cumulative strength, what more power has he to effect death? Death has its day, and life – the life that is the love of the Son – has triumphed over it: our sins' effects have come full force against our Lord and Maker, and "His right hand has won victory" over them.

And so this great promise the Lord can make, this astounding statement He brings to our ears: "I give you my word, every sin will be forgiven mankind and all the blasphemies men utter." Though the sin against the Spirit will not be forgiven – for how can he who calls salvation condemnation find the grace of God; how can lies find discourse with Truth? – yet all the sins man has committed in his ignorance and lust will be washed clean in Jesus' blood when any soul comes humbly to Him. And in consequence of this blessed mercy, "those who are called may receive the promised eternal inheritance," for our Savior has "entered heaven itself that He might appear before God now on our behalf." Yes, He serves as mediator now, interceding before the Father against our transgressions, that He might prepare for us a path to His kingdom. His cross and His sacrifice stand as our ladder unto heaven.

"The Lord has made His salvation known" by the offering of His Son, and to "all the ends of the earth" "His holy arm" is revealed. He has appeared once in weakness to take away our sins, but "He will appear a second time not to take away sin but to bring salvation to those who eagerly

176

await Him." And so, as we are washed clean of sin in His blood, we must stand ready for His final coming, for our promised reward, "sing[ing] praise to the Lord."

Tuesday
(Heb.10:1-10; Ps.40:2,4,7-11; Mk.3:31-35)

"I have come to do your will, O God."

But what is this will of God? How do we know it? How shall we live it? The will of God is known through the obedience of the Son, in His sacrifice for our sins; and all who seek to do the will of God must follow in His way, offering themselves freely, innocently, to the Lord for the sake of the Body of Christ.

"Who are my mother and my brothers?" Jesus asks the crowd. Who enter into His fold, becoming children of God the Father? "Whoever does the will of God." Whoever does the will of God is the only answer He could make. Whoever is as His mother and says, "Behold the handmaiden of the Lord; be it done unto me according to your word"; whoever is as His brother apostles and suffers martyrdom for the faith, unafraid to speak out in His name; whoever is like the simple sheep surrounding Him in the gospel today, listening so obediently to the heavenly words He utters... these are "brother and sister and mother" to Him. O what a glorious family to be among!

Brothers and sisters, we no longer have "only a shadow of the good things to come" but rather a "real image of them" in the flesh and blood of the only Son. The salvation of our God is abstract and fleeting no more, for the Lord has come in a body to make ever so real for us the glory of God. Our hearts should leap up at His presence; our ears should be "open to obedience" to hear and heed His voice. Our mouths agape, we should wonder at His presence among us and desire only to become one with Him who holds our very lives in His sacred heart, in the Spirit upon the flesh He is.

O have we not "waited, waited for the Lord"? And how should we not act now that He has "stooped toward" us, now that He has humbled Himself to become man? A spirit of exultation should fill us, for by His presence with us He "put[s] a new song into [our] mouth, a hymn to our God." Our hearts are set on fire with the anointing of the Holy Spirit and we can no longer "restrain [our] lips," but must declare even with our precious Lord: "I have come to do your will," to join in your blessed sacrifice – to know the glory of kinship with you, my God, by whom we are all called.

177

O Lord, "I have made no secret of your kindness and your truth in the vast assembly." I declare it on these pages. Please gather me this day into your holy family.

Wednesday
(Heb.10:11-18; Ps.110:1-4; Mk.4:1-20)

"I will put my laws in their hearts
and I will write them on their minds."

He will plant His seed firmly upon "good soil," and it shall yield fruit abundantly. Let us be open to receive His word each day.

Today we hear Jesus' well-known parable of seed sown in four places: "on the path," "on rocky ground," "among thorns," and "on good soil"; and the Lord makes clear that only in the last place will the seed bear a profitable yield. And, of course, the Lord hereby calls each of us to consider what place we make for the seed with our lives. Clearly, "what the sower is sowing is the word," and just as clearly, our hearts are the ground into which that word is sown. Therefore, the question is: What kind of hearts have we for the word of God, for His love? The seed does not change; in every place it is sown the same. It is only the soil which changes, and thus determines its fruitfulness. Are our hearts barren of the Spirit, or wrought with stones or choking thorns... or do we make a welcome place for the love of God to take root in our lives and grow? Though our tree shall be known by its fruit, we must know where our heart stands with God, and so this question Jesus would bring to our minds, not to condemn us for our emptiness or hardness of heart but that we might turn to Him and bear fruit in His light, that He might take away the "sins and... transgressions" that keep us void of life.

Do you know the Spirit at work in your hearts, brothers and sisters, at work in your souls? Is His word taking root in you and being nourished by the waters of the Lord? "To you the mystery of the reign of God has been confided," and so, what a pity it would be to turn from His instruction, or fall short at all in preparing a place for the Lord to reside. The Spirit burning in our hearts, the blessing of His pure light, is all we should thirst for in our lives. "Like the dew" before the dawn He comes; each morning you should find yourself wet with that dew and set to do good works in His name.

Yes, brothers and sisters, upon the heart of each of His children, the Lord God writes His name, places His law, His love, by the blood of His only Son. He thus makes us one with His infinite presence, ever giving growth to our tree. With His word piercing our souls, our soil is prepared to receive His seed. Let us therefore open our hearts to His light touch – His finger, His breath, His word, inscribing His NAME at the center of our being – and we shall grow in Him even unto the kingdom.

Thursday
(Heb.10:19-25; Ps.24:1-6; Mk.4:21-25)

"Since we have a great high priest who is over the house of God,
  let us draw near in utter sincerity and absolute confidence."

Let us shine our light without fear, for it is the light of the Lord and cannot be removed. "Let us hold unswervingly to our profession which gives us hope, for He who made the promise deserves our trust." Do you think He will fail you in your commitment to Him? No, His love is always first to come; you need but follow.

And let us "encourage one another," brothers and sisters, even as Jesus does us all in our gospel today. Let us "rouse each other to love and good deeds," calling one another to shine our light, the light that is in each of our hearts by the grace of our Savior. "Our hearts sprinkled clean from the evil which lay on our conscience and our bodies washed in pure water," ready we are to do His will in this world; "the blood of Jesus assures our entrance into the sanctuary," and so, with our place in heaven set firm, we hesitate not to put our love "on a stand" and let it pierce the darkness all around.

"We should not absent ourselves from the assembly," brothers and sisters. We should not think we need not gather together in His name. For we cannot take strength alone to fight our battles in this world; apart from one another we will be worn down by sin, by pride. Our light is not our own but is meant to be shared; indeed, it belongs to the whole community for it belongs only to the Lord. And it can only grow and increase when given in measure to others; otherwise it will be taken from us.

So let us draw near our Lord as we draw near each other in the sharing of our gifts. Let us be as "he whose hands are sinless, whose heart is clean, who desires not what is vain," and our gifts will be acceptable one to another, and our lives will be acceptable to God. And we shall "ascend the mountain of the Lord" and "stand in His holy place" – the place He makes for us by His sacrifice... "We shall receive a blessing from the Lord, a reward from God our Savior," if we seek His face alone.

Do not be afraid. Hide not your light. Enter His presence, do His will, accepting the grace He imparts to our lives. He calls you to join in His sacrifice.

Friday

(Heb.10:32-39; Ps.37:3-6,23-24,39-40; Mk.4:26-34)

"You need patience to do God's will
and receive what He has promised."

Brothers and sisters, "we are not among those who draw back and perish, but among those who have faith and live." Whatever "great contest[s] of suffering" may be before us or behind us or upon us even now, we do not "surrender [our] confidence" in the Lord but stand strong, enduring all by our "trust in Him" and so coming by these means to the kingdom of God.

My friends, we know we have "better and more permanent possessions" in heaven, and so "the confiscation of [our] goods" upon this earth, the "insult and trial" we have to endure, and even the prison into which we may be thrown, hold no sway over our souls and do not deter our resolve to follow the way of Christ – in fact, they but increase our firmness in the Lord. For seeing how "He delivers [us] from the wicked and saves" us when we "take refuge in Him" reveals to our souls the firmness of His hand upon us and the passing nature of any vain temptation or torture. We comprehend hereby that we need but "commit to the Lord [our] way… and He will act"; He is the one who preserves us from all harm and sees that fruit is born in our lives.

And so, day by day we come to Him; night after passing night we approach His presence. We grow in His sight even as "the soil produces of itself first the blade, then the ear, [and] finally the ripe wheat in the ear." Even unto the day of judgment we shall grow so gradually, so blessedly, steadily producing fruit in His glorious light, and thus avoid any condemnation. For He has taken possession of our souls; His hand is upon us now, and from such marvelous grace we cannot turn our faces away.

"A brief moment, and He who is to come will come; He will not delay," says the Lord; and so, brothers and sisters, let us "live by faith" as the Lord's "just man," knowing full well that "He will make justice dawn for [us] like the light," that on His Day we shall be drawn into the kingdom of God. "Bright as the noonday shall be [our] vindication," so let us endure all patiently and bravely in this world, ever bearing fruit in His name.

Saturday

(Heb.11:1-2,8-19; Lk.1:68-75; Mk.4:35-41)

"Why are you so terrified?
Why are you lacking in faith?"

"Faith is confident assurance concerning what we hope for, and conviction about things we do not see," our brother Paul would have us know, and realize. We all hope for something; there is ever something we all long to see. The eyes are set in the front of the human head and always he is looking at what is before him, straining to see what is ahead. And what is it we hope to see further along this road we tread? What is our hope for the future – what is set indelibly in our hearts, calling us forward to tomorrow? Are we as Abraham, who was "looking forward to the city with foundations," to the city of God, and so was able to uproot himself from his city here on earth, "not knowing where he was going," and dwell in tents? Have we the same hope as he?

If we have his hope, we should have his faith as well, and more. For what upon this earth is worthy of greater assurance than the coming of the kingdom of God? Is there any firmer promise in which to believe? And if Abraham and all the "men of old" were able to live by faith and so find God's approval and His blessing, how much more should we be ready, how much greater confidence should we have, we upon whom the light which they only "saluted... from afar" has dawned? To our eyes has been brought what they were kept from seeing; and so our faith should go beyond hope – it should be most real, utterly unshakable by the vicissitudes of this world. For He is here, He who was "promised through the mouths of His holy ones, the prophets of ancient times."

Brothers and sisters, it is time to "cross over to the farther shore" with our Lord. What Moses could only view from afar is now present to us in the flesh of Christ: heaven is in our midst, and nothing should we fear... no room for doubt should we make. In the words of our gospel we witness the disciples coming gradually to see Him who has entered their boat, who has power over all. And their fear shall leave them soon, even as awe overtakes them. And we must be the same, and more. For upon us the Spirit has already come, completing the Trinity's presence among us. Nothing more is there to look forward to than our life in heaven, and nothing for our crossing do we lack. Sure indeed should we now be. And so, "rid of fear and delivered from the enemy" by Him who is all-powerful, "we should serve Him devoutly, and through all our days, be holy in His sight." Let faith find its fulfillment now in the lives we lead in His name. Cast all fear away, and love.

Fourth Week

Monday
(Heb.11:32-40; Ps.31:20-25; Mk.5:1-20)

"They broke the jaws of lions, put out raging fires,
escaped the devouring sword…"

In each of these descriptions of the powerful deeds of the men of old, what is conquered is an instrument of death, and so what is indicated is the power of God – from whom these men derive their strength – to destroy death itself. This is made more obvious in the fact that "women received back their dead through resurrection" by their faith in God, and is apparent even in those who "were tortured and did not receive deliverance"; for they suffered all "in order to obtain a better resurrection," one not simply of the earth and the body, but one which is absolute, one which pertains to spirit and body in heaven… and we can be assured they received such reward.

Brothers and sisters, death is the devil's instrument, but life is of God; and the Lord of life holds power over all death and banishes it by His word. That death is the devil's tool, so ready at his hand, is made evident after Jesus "gave the word, and with it the unclean spirits came out and entered the swine": immediately "the herd of about two thousand went rushing down the bluff into the lake, where they began to drown." As the demons had driven the man of Gerasene into the tombs upon taking possession of him, so they drive these swine to their demise. Death is the devil's will; he would see the destruction of all life.

And what of those men of old who seem so much like our possessed man today; what about those who "dwelt in caves and in holes of the earth" and "went about garbed in the skins of sheep or goats, needy, afflicted, tormented"? How do these differ from the poor soul of Gerasene? Does the devil not have power over them, too? The answer is no – the two are clearly different. The power the devil had over the ancient prophets, which is witnessed most fully in Christ Himself as well as all His followers, is a power only over the body, over the physical circumstances of life. As with Christ and His followers, the spirit, the soul of these ancients, remained untouched by the devil's claw. The same is not so for the poor soul among the tombs: of him the devil had taken possession body and soul. And, you might say, Is the strength exhibited by the demoniac not like that of Samson when he broke the chains of the Philistines? What of this similarity? My friends, the chains upon the demoniac were meant to help preserve his life, and when he "pulled the chains apart and smashed the fetters" by the strength of the devil, it was only that he could continue "gash[ing] himself

182

with stones"; whereas Samson broke his fetters by the power of God in order to preserve his life from the clutches of the Philistines. (One must always use right judgment and discern well, especially the things of the spirit, avoiding preoccupation with the superficiality of circumstances and jumping to quick conclusions.)

"Love the Lord, all you His faithful ones!" Keep "constant" in faith and "from the plottings of men" and "the strife of tongues" He will "shelter" you. Whether overcoming or being overcome by death in this life, the life of heaven awaits you and is with you.

Tuesday
(Heb.12:1-4; Ps.22:26-28,30-32; Mk.5:21-43)

"Let us keep our eyes fixed on Jesus,
who inspires and perfects our faith."

Like the woman in our gospel who saw Him in the crowd and with great confidence made her way toward Him but to reach out and "touch His clothing," knowing in her heart that by this she "shall get well"; like the official of the synagogue who draws near and falls at His feet begging healing for his daughter, who even after being told, "Your daughter is dead," does "not grow despondent or abandon the struggle" but takes refuge in the Lord's encouragement to trust; like all the "cloud of witnesses" that have sought Him, that have believed in Him, that have never taken their eyes off Him or His love – let us be saints who "lay aside every encumbrance of sin which clings to us and persevere in running the race which lies ahead," and we shall receive our reward even as those who have gone before us have done. By endurance in faith we shall find Jesus.

Sin it is, of course, that is the greatest obstacle to sanctity in the Lord, to achieving our goal of eternal life in heaven; death and disease are merely the fruits of this poisonous tree. And so the "fight against sin" is truly our greatest struggle, for once sin is set aside, peace comes to our souls and we are no longer anxious or fearful, despite any workings of the devil – despite the destruction in his hands. The woman's "flow of blood" (for as many years as Jairus' daughter, "a child of twelve," has been alive) is but symptomatic for us of the greater affliction of transgression against God. And even the young girl's death is nothing really, for it is so that "she is [only] asleep," as the Lord says, and not dead at all... and so death and disease mean nothing unless they are accompanied by sin. It is *this* plague which must be overcome.

And for this healing we come to Him. For this grace we must press upon Him, like the crowds who surround Him this day. And like the raised child's parents our "astonishment [will be] complete," for we shall be clean: we shall be alive in the Lord. "To Him alone shall bow down all who sleep in the earth"; by Him alone all shall be raised. So let us keep our eyes and our hearts fixed upon Him, knowing "they who seek the Lord shall praise Him" – in Him our faith is complete. "To Him alone [our] soul shall live"; therefore, let us bleed with Him this day.

O. 4. Wed. (I)

Wednesday

(Heb.12:4-7,11-15; Ps.103:1-2,13-14,17-18; Mk.6:1-6)

"Whom the Lord loves, He disciplines;
He scourges every son He receives."

Like His only Son we must be. For without discipline where would we be? Apart from the Lord's chastising hand, into what state would we fall? Without the cross, how could we find the kingdom?

If the Lord did not scourge us, we would be blind as His countrymen in our gospel today, who question even what their ears behold and their eyes see – dead to His presence we would remain. Only the dust of His flesh would we look upon, thinking He is no more than our sinful selves; far short of His divinity would we fall. And so a word of chastisement He brings to our hearts, as He does those of "His native place," of "His own house," condemning our failure to honor God in His prophets and in His Son, calling us beyond our eyes of flesh to the breath of the Spirit.

O how our "lack of faith distress[es] Him"! O how He would stir within us "that holiness without which no one can see the Lord"! For "the kindness of the Lord is from eternity to eternity toward those who fear Him," and His kindness He would have all know. But failing of a reverent awe for the Most High Lord, what do we do but grovel in the dust? Our hearts cannot know Him if they are not humble; our souls cannot bless Him if they are not holy... and so we lose "all His benefits" by a stubborn pride. This is not the will of God.

Brothers and sisters, the Lord "knows how we are formed; He remembers that we are dust." But from the dust He calls us to join Him on high, to rise above our earthen state. In His compassion the Father would have us be even as He is; and so He sends His only Son to suffer for our sins, to show us the path to holiness we must walk. "So strengthen your drooping hands and your weak knees"; fear not the cross of Jesus. For by it you will be made strong, you will be made whole; through it "the grace of God" will pour, and make you as His own.

Peace soon follows every cord of scourging; the nails in our hands open our souls to the Spirit's movement, to the Lord's love, as by this bleeding our sins are purged. And in His light we shall soon stand, "all [our] being bless[ing] His holy name." Then we shall no longer question His wisdom but in His mercy make our home.

Thursday
(Heb.12:18-19,21-24; Ps.48:2-4,9-11; Mk.6:7-13)

"You have drawn near to Mount Zion
and the city of the living God,
the heavenly Jerusalem..."

"...to the assembly of the first-born enrolled in heaven, to God the judge of all, to the spirits of just men made perfect, to Jesus, the mediator of a new covenant, and to the sprinkled blood which speaks more eloquently than that of Abel." Alleluia! "Great is the Lord and wholly to be praised in the city of our God." And great is our call to dwell in His blessed City with all His holy ones, and with our Lord. Could there be a greater cause for joy? For "His holy mountain, fairest of heights, is the joy of all the earth," and the joy of heaven.

To the New Jerusalem we are drawn, brothers and sisters, to the fairest heights. Holiness in the Lord is our call – to dwell with our Lord forever. But what is the road that leads to such a blessed mountain? How do we who tread the dust of this earth find our way to heaven? Evident the Lord makes the path today in the summoning of His apostles. In their call we find our own.

"Do not bring a second tunic," Jesus says to the Twelve as He sends them forth to preach and to heal. For they are to make no provision, to put no stock in the things of the earth... "to take nothing on the journey." Their trust must be entirely in Him and the word with which He anoints them: the power He gives, the grace He provides, is sufficient not only to cast out demons, but to find all we need for our day-to-day lives. The Lord teaches us as He teaches them that our faith must be complete, our spirits wholly set on His will, if we are to make our way across the dust of this earth to His kingdom. Nothing short of the sacrifice He Himself offers first will bring us there. His sprinkled blood must be upon us, and work through us.

"O God, we ponder your kindness in your temple"; we marvel at your grace. For no longer by "fearful... spectacle" of "blazing fire" and "gloomy darkness" do you make yourself known to us. No longer are you "untouchable," Lord. But present in our midst, sandals upon your feet, you, O unapproachable glory, draw near to us, and so enable us to draw near to you, to touch you, O wounded Savior. And your sandals you place upon our feet and invite us to walk in the way you have shown. May we do so, Lord, as humbly as thou; and so to our eyes and our hearts make your kingdom known.

All the saints in heaven, pray for us. All His holy angels, watch over our way. May our feet stand forever upon the Lord's holy mountain. In His heavenly City let us make our home. (In His Church, in His Mass, He is with us.)

O. 4. Fri. (I)

Friday
(Heb.13:1-8; Ps.27:1,3,5,8-9; Mk.6:14-29)

"I will never desert you, nor will I forsake you."

A series of parallels we have today between our first reading and our gospel. Paul instructs us in his letter to the Hebrews not to "neglect to show hospitality" to our "fellow Christians," since we may be "entertain[ing] angels" thereby; but it is not angels Herod entertains at his birthday banquet, and a false sense of hospitality leads him to grave sin, as when Herodias' daughter requests the Baptist's head on a platter, "because of his oath and the presence of his guests," he "dispatch[es] an executioner."

Paul also tells us to "be mindful of prisoners as if [we] were sharing their imprisonment"; and it seems almost against himself Herod indeed sympathizes with John. We are told, "When he heard him speak he was very much disturbed; yet he felt the attraction of his words." He knows John is the angel he should better entertain, but denies the voice speaking to his heart. And so Paul's warning, "You may yet suffer as they do," proves true with Herod, who is clearly imprisoned by his own fear that John has been raised from the dead to haunt his soul.

Of course, the central cause of all Herod's problems is his breaking the command Paul expresses succinctly: "Let marriage be honored in every way and the marriage bed be kept undefiled," for it is "on account of Herodias, the wife of his brother Philip, whom he had married," that John chastises Herod, that the king has the prophet imprisoned, and that he is cornered into murdering him. And so now he knows very deeply the extent to which "God will judge fornicators and adulterers." Indeed, his adulterous relationship and his niece/daughter's dance of lust stand as examples comparable to the profligate lands of Sodom and Gomorrah for their immorality, for their opposition to the Father's love.

It is the Father's love and our trust therein which rises above the immorality and violence so present in our gospel. At the heart of Paul's letter is his paraphrase of today's psalm: "The Lord is my helper, I will not be afraid; what can man do to me?" Indeed the faith in God David sings of so confidently – "Though an army encamp against me... though war be

186

waged upon me, even then will I trust" – is what the Baptist holds in his own spirit, even as he extends his neck for the executioner's blade. He knows well that the Lord "will hide [him] in His abode in the day of trouble," and so no trouble does his death cause him: the Lord will certainly "set [him] high upon a rock," keeping him untouched by the lust and destruction which surround him in Herod's dank prison. It is Herod upon whom darkness shall fall.

"Your presence, O Lord, I seek. Hide not your face from me." Through all things let me remain in your light. And as John's life ended, this greatest of "leaders who spoke the word of God" to us, so let my own, in faith in you, O Lord, who are with us forever.

Saturday
(Heb.13:15-17,20-21; Ps.23:1-6; Mk.6:30-34)

"The Lord is my shepherd;
I shall not want."

All things are cared for by the Lord; our work and our rest are in His hands. Nothing need we fear. No good desire goes unfulfilled – His sheep He loves.

Brothers and sisters, "through Christ may [the God of peace] carry out in you all that is pleasing to Him." Let Him guide you "in right paths" for the accomplishment of His will. In "good deeds and generosity," in obedience to superiors, in every intention of the heart, "continually offer God a sacrifice of praise, that is, the fruit of lips which acknowledge His name," for this thanksgiving He desires before all deeds and in all deeds; such praise will ensure His blessing, and lead to greater praise, and so greater blessing! Have every confidence that the Lord "will furnish you with all that is good, that you may do His will," and rejoice always in all you accomplish by His grace.

See in our gospel that when "the apostles returned to Jesus and reported to Him all that they had done and what they had taught," "He said to them, 'Come by yourselves to an out-of-the-way place and rest a little.'" They have done His work faithfully, and now He would give them rest; now He would refresh and renew their souls. "Beside restful waters He leads me": in a "boat by themselves" He takes them. "In verdant pastures He gives me repose": "to a deserted place" the boat goes. And though upon arrival at their destination the people wait "like sheep without a shepherd" and so their work must resume, this does not distract from the promised rest which awaits the finishing of our work in this world, and indeed but emphasizes that our rest shall be complete only in heaven.

For now the Lord watches over. Now He cares for us like needful sheep. Now He takes upon Himself all our fears and burdens, and calls us to do the same for all. What should we want? What do we need when we do the Lord's will? In this laying down of our lives all is provided; in our work we take our rest, we eat our bread. For He is with us with His "goodness and kindness"; He remains at our side even in darkness... We become one with our Shepherd, and no further grace we desire.

O. 5. Mon. (I)

Fifth Week

Monday
(Gn.1:1-19; Ps.104:1-2,5-6,10,12,24,31,35; Mk.6:53-56)

"How manifold are your works, O Lord!
In wisdom you have wrought them all."

It is the Lord who "fixed the earth upon its foundation not to be moved forever," and "with the ocean, as with a garment [He] covered it" – "the earth is full of His creatures." By the Word of His mouth all comes into being, and is sustained, sustained in the goodness of God.

Here as we read the beginning of sacred Scripture, we might do well to quote St. Bonaventure from the day's Office of Readings. In speaking of knowledge of Christ as "the main source of a firm understanding of the truth of all sacred Scripture," He states: "It is impossible, therefore, for anyone to achieve this understanding unless he first receives the gift of faith in Christ. This faith is the foundation of the whole Bible, a lamp and a key to its understanding." But how many read God's Word as though in a dark room.

The prevailing lack of faith and so blindness to the truth of Scripture is evident again today in the commentary of my missal, which says of the Creation prophecy in Genesis, "The story is divided artificially," giving as example the fact that "the sun is created after light." How indeed we grope in darkness without the light of the Spirit; without childlike faith we shall never understand God's Word, never enter His kingdom. Is the light of God dependent upon the sun or the stars? When our psalmist sings of the Lord "robed in light as with a cloak," is it sunlight of which he speaks? Does the light of the Lord not necessarily precede the limited light of the sun – which the Lord has but made "to govern the day" for a time – even as it shall be all by which we see when the sun and the moon and the stars pass away? Where is your faith, where is your understanding... why is the Lord's light not in you, my brother?

Brothers and sisters, as the people of Gennesaret upon seeing Jesus "immediately recognized Him" and "scurried about" to bring all their sick to

188

Him, so we must be drawn by the light of God to the Truth that is Christ the Lord. He is in every page of Scripture. He is at work with the Father in Creation. He is the all-powerful Word which brings all into being by its eminent wisdom made flesh before our eyes; and we shall never know the wonder of God's works and the wonders He has wrought in our own soul unless we come to faith in Him. In Jesus are all God's works revealed. He is the light of the universe. (And though His radiance extends beyond our sight to infinite galaxies, it is here in this dome between clouds and sea we dwell, the earth from which we have been formed solidly beneath our feet.)

Tuesday
(Gn.1:20-2:4; Ps.8:2,4-9; Mk.7:1-13)

"God created man in His image;
in the divine image He created him."

At God's word "the water teem[s] with an abundance of living creatures... birds fly beneath the dome of the sky," and "the earth bring[s] forth all kinds of living creatures," too. And "God saw how good it was." Then God conceived the crown of His creation and said, "Let us make man in our image, after our likeness." And so, "little less than the angels He made him" and gave him "dominion over the fish of the sea, the birds of the air, and all the living things that move on the earth." And all this was "very good" in God's eyes. Alleluia!

But what does man do with this ultimate blessing from His Creator: he takes the freedom and power placed in his hands and makes himself a slave to "cups and jugs and kettles," forever trying to wash his hands clean of the sin upon them. God gives man "rule over the works of [His] hands, putting all things under his feet," and all man can do is trample upon them as he forgets the God who made him.

"How accurately Isaiah prophesied about [us] hypocrites when he wrote... 'Empty is the reverence they do me because they teach as dogmas mere human precepts.'" Placing our traditions and practices above God's commandments we lose sight of the glory upon us, of the majesty of God's works around us, as we lock ourselves in a dark and empty room of our own making. And all the creatures God has placed in our unclean hands suffer too, as our hearts turn from their stewardship to our selfish plottings. And so, though we are crowned by God "with glory and honor," we crown Him with thorns.

O Lord, "what is man that you should be mindful of him, or the son of man that you should care for him?" Lord, come and restore us to our former glory. Father, let us give you true honor. May your Word be made fruitful in our lives and we become as your Son. Let all be blessed and made holy again in your sight. In Jesus' blood please wash our hands, that we might help you build your peaceful kingdom.

Wednesday
(Gn.2:4-9,15-17; Ps.104:1-2,27-30; Mk.7:14-23)

"The Lord God formed man out of the clay of the ground
and blew into his nostrils the breath of life,
and so man became a living being."

In addition, "out of the ground the Lord God made various trees grow that were delightful to look at and good for food." These would feed the body of the man. But only spirit feeds the soul.

Body and soul. They meet in man and become one, yet one is the cause of life while the other passes. When God formed man out of the clay of the ground, what He held in His hands was the body, and at the time it was dead. Not until He breathed into him did man become alive: in this breath he found his soul. And the time shall come when this form does rot, but not the soul. Only in heaven will we have bodies that live eternally with our spirits (though certain saints – as did our Blessed Mother – may know this holy union even here on earth}.

And so does Jesus tell us "that nothing that enters a man from outside can make him impure," and, to make this point graphically clear, adds, "It does not penetrate his being, but enters his stomach only and passes into the latrine." What is of the body is just so passing, and therefore of no consequence. It is "what emerges from within a man" that "makes him impure." For sins such as "acts of fornication, theft, murder," etc. are not the result of the food we eat, but of the thoughts in "the deep recesses of the heart." These are what make a man impure – or, by contrast, which will make him pure. It is the soul that is capable of good or evil, not the body. And even though it is eating of the fruit of "the tree of the knowledge of good and bad" that causes man's downfall, this is not the result of the fruit itself, but of the covetousness and pride of man's disobedience. It is the 'eating,' the desire of the eye and the heart and the act which follows, which constitutes the sin, and not the fruit eaten.

Our psalmist speaks of the body and soul as well. It is so that by the Lord we are "filled with good things," that He gives us "food in due time," food we need for our survival; but as the psalmist says of the soul, "If you take away their breath, they perish and return to the dust." How quickly we would die, in a moment or two, without the breath of God in our nostrils, without His Word to give us life. And what great care we should take of the spirit that enters our beings. May our souls ever be set upon our God and His teaching. May our every thought and word and action be of Him, that we shall never be disobedient. O Lord, "when you send forth your Spirit, [we] are created, and you renew the face of the earth." Give us your divine breath of life in our nostrils this day.

(Note re the "second" Creation in Genesis: the account in today's reading does *not* contradict that of the previous two days. The "time" spoken of here is the one Day of Creation (note "the earth *and* the heavens"), not any one day of the seven. And though "no grass of the field had sprouted" before God made man, yet it is alive, "brought forth" in the earth and minded by the stream "welling up"... much like an unborn child in the womb.)

Thursday
(Gn.2:18-25; Ps.128:1-5; Mk.7:24-30)

"A man leaves his father and mother and clings to his wife,
and the two of them become one body."

And Jesus leaves His Father's side and His mother's care, and takes to wife His chosen people. From His side indeed we are born, and become His holy family.

To the "sons of the household" Jesus comes; among the Israelites He walks, calling them to His table to eat the food of eternal life, of eternal union with Him and His Father. Those who were conceived by God, who were taken as a rib from His own side and formed as His special bride, Jesus seeks to bring to full nuptial blessing in Him. For this He would even die (as any man should for his wife). But one "approached Him and crouched at His feet" who was not among those called to the "table first," who was not of the family of the Chosen. Unfazed by His rebuff she continues begging, not for "the food of the children" but just for their "leavings," their crumbs, knowing even this will be enough to join her to His banquet, believing only a word from His mouth will save her own daughter from the devil's clutches and bring her to His sacred presence.

And moved is He by her who is unmoved by His rebuke. And so, "when she got home, she found the child lying in bed and the demon gone." And so she finds herself and her family wed to Jesus the Christ. Why? Because she is one who does indeed "fear the Lord," who does in fact "walk in His ways"; crawling on her knees before Him, she finds herself "happy" and "favored," eating "the fruit of [her] handiwork." She knows she is not one of the "wild animals" or of the "birds of the air": she is made in God's image, a human being, and is inextricably drawn to His side, the side from

191

which she has been born… and thus she finds her life and becomes with her daughter (with all us Gentile people) one of the "olive plants around [His] table," grafted onto His "fruitful vine."

Let man love woman as his own flesh, and let all men love one another as fellow children, for our Father in heaven loves us all much more greatly and draws us all to be wed to Him through our Bridegroom, His only Son. As His side is opened by the lance and so we His Church are born in His blood, washed clean by His holy water, so let husbands give themselves for their wives, knowing they are "taken from" their own sides. Yes, let us all die for one another that the love of God might extend to "the recesses of [His] home," from which no soul is excluded. In His blessed marriage feast let us all shout for joy!

O. 5. Fri. (I)

Friday

(Gn.3:1-8;   Ps.32:1-2,5-7;   Mk.7:31-37)

"The eyes of both of them were opened,
and they realized that they were naked."

How different this opening of the eyes of Adam and Eve is from the opening of the deaf man's ears in our gospel; for our first parents' eyes were opened unto blindness, but the deaf mute's ears and tongue only to light.

Why this difference? Why such contrast in the freeing of the senses to receive their signals? Why is one evil and the other good? The opening of the eyes of the man and the woman brings their downfall because they are not prepared for what they see. They seek to be "like gods who know what is good and what is bad," but they have not the skins to hold such wine of wisdom. And so they burst. And so they died before the glorious light suddenly before them… and so "the man and his wife hid themselves from the Lord God among the trees of the garden," for they could not show their faces of dust before His Face of Majesty. (Indeed, the woman first erred when she "answered the serpent," when she responded to his enticement, not realizing she was no match for his "cunning"… much as she failed to understand she is no match for God's wisdom.)

On the other hand, the opening of the deaf man's ears and the loosing of his tongue is prepared by Jesus Christ, He in whose presence we are able to see light itself, He who provides the new wineskins for our becoming like God, enabling us to stand before the wonder of His Holy Face. Notice how "Jesus took him off by himself away from the crowd" before healing the deaf mute; see how this contrasts with Adam and Eve's hiding from God. Where they would avoid the glance of the Lord, Jesus brings the man closer to Him by drawing him away from the crowds; and there, more perfectly in

192

His presence, He heals him. And the man is healed, of course, because he himself does not hide: he is brought openly by his friends to Jesus. In this way he "acknowledged [his] sin" before God; his "guilt [he] covered not" (as the man and woman covered their nakedness with fig leaves). No, in his "spirit there is no guile," and so his "fault is taken away"; and so, paradoxically, he who "confess[es] his sin to the Lord," as the humble King David, finds that by the Lord his "sin is covered" – he is forgiven.

Brothers and sisters, let us learn to open our tattered souls to our Lord and God, never to hide; for to hide is hell and the Lord calls us to Him in the light of heaven. And He will prepare our eyes to see, and He will make our ears ready to hear, and our tongues shall be loosed to praise His name and exclaim our amazement at His grace... for we shall be released from the blindness of sin and be as His Son, who alone can answer the devil.

O. 5. Sat. (I)

Saturday
(Gn.3:9-24; Ps.90:1-6,12-13; Mk.8:1-10)

"You are dirt,
and to dirt you shall return."

Because of the fall we come face-to-face with this truth: our own mortality, our own humility, that we are but a creature made from the dust of the earth. And this truth we must understand. Because we have "eaten from the tree of which [God] had forbidden [us] to eat," "thorns and thistles" the earth brings forth for us and "by the sweat of [our] face shall [we] get bread to eat," until we learn our place – for our own sakes – before our Creator, or "until we return to the ground, from which we were taken."

"Cursed be the ground because of you!" the Lord God exclaims to the man. The womb of the woman, like the earth for man, shall bring her pain in bearing children, in bearing her fruit... and the serpent shall eat dust "all the days of [his] life." If now we should eat of the tree of life, to what state would we be condemned! How shall we be saved from such a fate, wherein our own flesh brings upon us such pangs – how shall we escape ourselves? And how shall we look upon God again?

"Teach us to number our days aright," our psalmist cries, "that we may gain wisdom of heart." And what is he asking but that we realize, as God would teach us, that though He is "from everlasting to everlasting," that though for Him "a thousand years are as... a watch of the night," we are "like the changing grass, which at dawn springs up anew, but by evening wilts and fades." So passing is our life. This indeed we must comprehend, for this is truth, and failing to understand it we shall not find answer to our prayer: "Return, O Lord! How long? Have pity on your servants!" But

193

knowing our limitations before our God, He comes quickly to remedy our weakness.

See how Jesus looks upon those who "were without anything to eat," those whose bodies fainted before His eyes. Listen to the thought of His heart: "My heart is moved with pity for the crowd. By now they have been with me three days and have nothing to eat. If I send them home hungry, they will collapse on the way. Some of them have come a great distance." O how the Lord has pity on us! O how He knows our plight – that we are but fading grass, having been far removed from His sight! And how He wills to feed us, to nourish those who come to Him, who share the "three days" of His trial. For though they toiled not, "the people in the crowd ate their fill" in the most peaceful of fields. The Lord had come to save them! And now eternal life is upon them.

Brothers and sisters, we need no longer fear our dying flesh, for the Lord feeds us with Bread that does not fail, that brings life eternal to the lowly body that eats it. And so, no longer are we dust alone, though to dust our body may return. But we become immortal souls in the hand of our Savior, eating from the tree of life He is. In all humility let us receive His gift, His saving presence among us. And to God we shall return, and now forever.

O. 6. Mon. (I)

Sixth Week

Monday
(Gn.4:1-15,25; Ps.50:1,8,14,16-17,20-21; Mk.8:11-13)

"Sin is a demon lurking at the door:
his urge is toward you, yet you can be his master."

Thus does the Lord encourage Cain not to hang his head at his failures in worship but to learn from his errors and be strong. Here already in Scripture we see how redemption is possible, how God gives us power to conquer sin. But Cain does not fight off the demon at his door but instead attacks his brother Abel, killing him who has overcome sin. The jealous demons write their name in Abel's blood, by the hand of Cain his brother.

And the Pharisees are the same as Cain. It is they of whom our psalmist sings, they who "recite [the Lord's] statutes, and profess [His] covenant with [their] mouth," but whose hearts are far from Him and who "hate discipline and cast [His] words behind" themselves. It is they who "sit speaking against [their] brother," for indeed they come to "argue with Jesus," to "test" Him who is most especially their brother, who is their Messiah. And it is they who will shed their brother's blood, who will conspire to kill their own

194

"mother's Son." And though Jesus Himself "correct[s] [them] by drawing [their sin] up before [their] eyes," yet, like Cain, they refuse to see the evil taking hold of them, and so will be unable to turn from it. And their punishment shall be greater than that of Cain, for so much greater is their sin. As Cain is banished from the soil which had been his own, so the covenant which the Lord had given into the Chosen people's possession shall be taken from their leaders' hands, and they shall be left empty – except for the hope of turning to Him and cleansing themselves in Jesus' blood.

The sign the Pharisees seek is essentially one they would make with their own hands, one which they would find at their command. But "no such sign will be given" them, for then truly would they be condemned. They must come to the sign Jesus is and accept it as the Lord God offers – their attempts to control the Father's will are perhaps the most tragic of transgressions. They say, as does Cain, that God must accept matters their way and are not humble to His Son's teaching. And so, sadly for them, "He left them" there on the shore alone, burning in their jealousy.

Fight the demons, brothers and sisters. Ward off sin in all its forms. The Lord promises we shall have the strength, if we are willing to turn from our sins and accept His chastising word... and wash ourselves in His cleansing blood. But if we remain "resentful" and so "deaf" to the Lord's correction, what shall save our souls? And with Cain we will wander restlessly the earth, avoiding the glorious presence of the Lord.

O. 6. Tues. (I)

Tuesday
(Gn.6:5-8,7:1-5,10; Ps.29:1-4,9-11; Mk.8:14-21)

"The voice of the Lord is over the waters,
the Lord, over vast waters."

"Mighty" indeed is the voice of God, but who can hear it? Who listens to its "majestic" ringing in their ears?

In the time of Noah the Lord's "heart was grieved," for He "saw how great was man's wickedness on earth, and how no desire that his heart conceived was ever anything but evil." So great was the Lord's grief over man's disobedience that He uttered the saddest words we could hear: "I am sorry I made them," and resolved to "wipe [them] out from the earth." If we have not pleased our Father, what hope have we of life? If we have not listened to His voice, what can we hear but a sentence of condemnation?

It seems Jesus' heart is grieved, too, today at His disciples' ignorance of His instruction. Here in a boat upon the waters His voice chastises their slowness to comprehend His call to wakefulness in the Spirit: "Are your

195

minds completely blinded? Have you eyes but no sight? Ears but no hearing?" and finally, "Do you still not understand?" And though He seems eminently frustrated by the fact that their vision is still trained so stubbornly on the bread of earth rather than the Bread of heaven, though they so quickly forget the miracles He has worked and the power He has revealed, yet He shall not remove them from His sight, but continue in patience with their schooling.

For just as "Noah found favor with the Lord" and thus served to salvage our race from utter destruction, so the Lord's apostles have found favor with Him. And Jesus knows that as "Noah did just as the Lord had commanded him," putting complete faith in God's word, so these disciples will also in strength and in faith carry out His mission after His own death and resurrection, after His ascension into heaven... and with the Holy Spirit's power upon them. As in Noah's ark God keeps man's "issue alive over all the earth," preserving them from the flood, so now in the barque of Peter "all the [Lord's] household" takes refuge from the fiery destruction that is coming upon the world in these the last days.

Like the "one loaf" the disciples hold in their hands is the Church of the Lord – it is all that is needed for food in this world. And so as we sail along to the farther shore, let us listen to God's mighty voice speaking through Her. As the end approaches, be sure to heed the Lord's instruction: "Keep your eyes open!" Beware the hypocrisy and pride of the powers that be.

O. 6. Wed. (I)

Wednesday
(Gn.8:6-13,20-22; Ps.116:12-15,17-19; Mk.8:22-26)

"Noah then removed the covering of the ark
and saw that the surface of the ground was drying up."

A return to earth, the flood waters having ceased. A new day dawns in this "the first month, on the first day of the month." The world is made anew, and it shall last, and man shall last upon it, until the last day comes. Here is the second Creation, the first re-creation... the new generation extending from Noah. After the cleansing rain, a soft white glow is upon the earth, a radiance of God's presence.

Gradually it comes to us, this vision of new life that is the Lord Himself. Three times Noah sent the dove forth from the ark before the blessed moment came when "it did not come back," when all could rejoice that the waters had subsided. And twice the Lord touched the blind man's eyes before "his sight was restored and he could see everything clearly." Just as first the dove came back quickly, then with a "plucked-off olive leaf" in its bill (showing that the tops of trees were visible), before finding a place to make a home; so first the man sees people "like walking trees" before the Lord touches Him again and perfect vision becomes his own. It is only gradually – day by day, week by week, year by year – that we come to full awareness of the Lord and with Him make our home.

And once out of the ark, "Noah built an altar to the Lord." And how pleased the Lord is with the "sweet odor" of the sacrifice he offers. Here is the beginning of the sacrifices at the heart of Jewish worship which shall find their place in the temple at Jerusalem, "in the courts of the house of the Lord," and know their fulfillment in the eternal sacrifice of the only Son. Of course, it is not the odor alone which pleases the Lord, but what it signifies: Noah thinks first of Him who always thinks first of us, and so engages God in a marvelous mutual love. Here our second human father reveals to the Lord that the goodness He has planted in us is not gone, that it is not necessarily so that "the desires of man's heart are evil from the start," that he is capable of love... though this truth shall not be known in full until the redemptive offering of Christ on the cross.

"As long as the earth lasts, seedtime and harvest, cold and heat, summer and winter, and day and night shall not cease," and mankind shall not be struck again from the land. "How shall [we] make a return to the Lord" for this special blessing? And how shall we repay Him for "the cup of salvation" we now "take up," the cup which holds the blood of the Son? For Noah's sacrifice is indeed made complete in our midst, before our eyes, and the waters that once threatened to overwhelm us now recede as we discover our home in the heavenly kingdom. We must show that the fullness of God's love exists in us and join our lives to our Savior's holy sacrifice.

Thursday
(Gn.9:1-13; Ps.102:16-23,29; Mk.8:27-33)

"The children of your servants shall abide,
and their posterity shall continue in your presence."

In our first reading from Genesis, God remakes the world. As once He sent forth Adam and Eve upon their creation, so now He blesses Noah and his sons with the same words: "Be fertile and multiply and fill the earth." Here we are reminded that "in the image of God has man been made," and once again God calls man to "abound on the earth and subdue it," giving him power over all its living creatures. And now a promise is added, a covenant is made "between [God] and the earth," sealed with the sign of the rainbow – "never again shall all bodily creatures be destroyed by the waters of a flood; there shall not be another flood to devastate the earth"... We shall endure on the land He has made for us.

197

And the Lord works to remake His people in our gospel as well, as "on the way He ask[s] His disciples... 'Who do you say that I am?'" He is the new Creation, He is "the Messiah," and in Him all children shall be remade in the image of God, shall become as His only Son. And these truly shall endure, their posterity shall continue forever in the presence of Him who never dies. Even after the final destruction of this earth and those who cling to it by the fire of God, even beyond the covenant made with Noah, which shall so soon pass with the dust from which we were made... eternally we shall remain in the new heavens and the new earth, the ones which themselves will never pass away. For God's promise to Noah is only for as long as the earth endures, but the earth is indeed passing away: only the covenant Jesus is bringing to His disciples and their posterity is one which is lasting as Heaven.

But to achieve this covenant, to found it firmly in the soul of Peter and his brothers and all us children of these servants, death must come to the only Son, and so surely to us all. The paradox seems difficult to comprehend, but with the vision of God, who "look[s] down from His holy height," it is easy to see: as long as the earth endures and we upon it, so long shall sin also endure. (This is what the Lord sees when "from heaven He [beholds] the earth.") Thus the only way to "release those doomed to die" by their imprisonment to sin is for the corrupted vessel in which we dwell to pass from the Lord's sight. Thus does Jesus Christ die. This must He do in the place of evil man and all his abominations that the world now in the hands of Satan might be destroyed, and the Spirit of God come to life. And so His sacrifice brings our salvation, brings us new life in the New Jerusalem, where the servants of the Lord increase and multiply. In the domain He has prepared by His blood, let us ever remain.

O. 6. Fri. (I)

Friday
(Gn.11:1-9; Ps.33:10-15; Mk.8:34-9:1)

"What profit does a man show who gains the whole world
and destroys himself in the process?"

Listen to what the men of old said among themselves at a time when "the whole world spoke the same language, using the same words." As they were migrating, they stopped in a valley and declared: "Come, let us build ourselves a city and a tower with its top in the sky, and so make a name for ourselves; otherwise we shall be scattered all over the earth." Hear how their desires reflect the Lord's warning, "Whoever would save his life will lose it." For the Lord will thwart their plans made in a vain pride quite apart from Him and see that what they fear shall indeed come to pass – from this point they shall be forced to continue their migration, being scattered to the four corners of the earth. Like David when he sought to number the people in his kingdom rather than allowing their increase in the sight of God, they do not put trust in the Lord but in the work of their own hands to make themselves a name. And such work, such plans, cannot but come to ruin.

"The Lord brings to naught the plans of nations; He foils the designs of peoples"; only "the plan of the Lord stands forever, the design of His heart, through all generations." And we must thank God that this is so. For left to our own devices, we would go on "doing whatever [we] presume to do." Thus does God save us from doing as we please because "He who fashioned the heart of each, He who knows all their works," knows well how inclined the human heart is to evil; He has witnessed the destruction that ensues when we are left to ourselves, and from this fate He would rescue our souls. And so does He "confuse their language" at the Tower of Babel; so from there "He scattered them all over the earth" – to keep them from the sinful plots they would concoct.

Of course, our tongues are united again after Pentecost; we become one people under one God once more. And indeed, "happy [is] the nation whose God is the Lord." But those who are set apart from Him, who do not lose their lives "for [His] sake and the Gospel's," do better in separation, where their sin is not as able to thrive. And so, until that day "when He comes with the holy angels in His Father's glory," until the time of fulfillment of the coming oneness of all the children of God, only those who dedicate themselves entirely to Jesus and His cross will "see the reign of God established in power" here on this earth – even as "this faithless and corrupt age" courts its inevitable destruction in its unyielding pride.

O. 6. Sat. (I)

Saturday
(Heb.11:1-7; Ps.145:2-5,10-11; Mk.9:2-13)

"Rabbi, how good it is for us to be here."

In yesterday's gospel Jesus promised, "Among those standing here there are some who will not taste death until they see the reign of God established in power." And today we witness the keeping of that promise, as upon "a high mountain" Jesus is transfigured before the eyes of Peter, James, and John. In all His glory does the Christ appear, with Elijah and Moses standing near and the voice of God the Father speaking of the blessing of His only Son. Indeed, how good it is for these apostles to be here!

But what these favored apostles see is not for their eyes alone; through them all shall come to believe and so find vision of our glorious Lord. Through them and their witness, faith is strengthened in all our hearts, faith

199

which enables us to "perceive that the worlds were created by the word of God, and that what is visible came into being through the invisible." Yes, the invisible is made known to all our eyes by the power of God, and all the Lord's disciples join Peter, James, and John on Mount Tabor, basking in the vision of the glorified Son.

Know first though, brothers and sisters, that "anyone who comes to God must believe that He exists, and that He rewards those who seek Him." Indeed, first one must have faith, or to one's eyes nothing will be revealed. Have faith and know that God is a loving God, that He desires greatly to share His glory with all His children of faith; even as He has with Peter, James, and John; even as He has with Abel, Enoch, and Noah; even as He has with Moses and Elijah. But it is only "because of faith the men of old were approved by God," only because of faith His apostles were able to see His Light shining – and only by your faith that you too will come into His presence. Have you their "confident assurance" burning in your souls? It is not far from you.

O Lord, "let all your faithful ones bless you. Let them discourse of the glory of your kingdom and speak of your might." Let all proclaim the favor with which you have deigned to grace our lives. Now that you have "risen from the dead," now that our cause for faith is made complete, now that its firm foundation is set... open our mouths to declare your glory. We know that you had to "suffer much and be despised" and that with Elijah, with the Baptist, "they did entirely as they pleased," but we do not fear the persecution which must come – only let us be where you are.

O. 7. Mon. (I)

Seventh Week

Monday
(Sir.1:1-10; Ps.93:1-2,5; Mk.9:14-29)

"There is but one, wise and truly awe-inspiring,
seated upon His throne: It is the Lord."

"The Lord is King, in splendor robed," and He alone knows "wisdom's root" and all "her subtleties"; for it is He who created her and "poured her forth upon all His works." And so He alone, whose "throne stands firm from of old," He alone understands all things, and can answer any question. And should we not be awestruck by His presence?

That the Lord is robed in splendor as King over all we have seen only recently. Even today He descends from the mountain on which He was transfigured; and though His face no longer shines more brightly than the sun, yet "immediately on catching sight of Jesus, the whole crowd was

200

overcome with awe" and rushed up to Him, for still His glorious presence overwhelms. At the base of the mountain the crowd and the disciples are engaged with the scribes "in a lively discussion" about the condition and fate of a poor child horribly possessed by a demon. Their words are empty wind, but the one with all answers approaches. And with a measure of faith from the boy's father and those surrounding, He casts out the devil which even the disciples could not command, and which the scribes could not comprehend.

"What an unbelieving lot [we] are! How long must [the Lord] remain with [us]? How long can [He] endure" our lack of wisdom and grace? Brothers and sisters, why do we so lack faith? Why do we say to the Lord, "If you can"? Do we not know that "everything is possible to a man who trusts"? Do we think the Lord's power is somehow cut short? Yes, we are weak and pitiable creatures, blind to the glory which surrounds us, but He is not! He *is* that glory, and that glory He shines for us. We need but come to Him with the awe the crowd shows today, and He will do all things for us.

"All wisdom comes from the Lord and with Him it remains forever"; and for us "fear of the Lord is glory and splendor," for by fear of the Lord are we graced with His wisdom. And then what shall we lack of His power? Indeed, we shall by holy fear come to know the "holiness [that] befits [His] house" and so dwell with Him who is "from everlasting." Do you believe this, my brother, my sister? Come to the One who is seated far above us, and you shall do His work here on earth with the wisdom His Blessed Mother imparts to all her blessed children.

O. 7. Tues. (I)

Tuesday
(Sir.2:1-11; Ps.37:3-5,18-19,27-28,39-40; Mk.9:30-37)

"My son, when you come to serve the Lord,
prepare yourself for trials."

Is Jesus not "teaching His disciples in this vein" when He speaks of His imminent death, a death they shall share, and calls them to "remain the least one of all and the servant of all," even as He is? Their arguing about importance reveals that they have not understood who they are, and so He would remind them that "in fire gold is tested, and worthy men in the crucible of humiliation."

A kind of humiliation is upon the Lord's disciples today as they fall silent in shame for "arguing about who was the most important," as Jesus stands a humble, silent child "in their midst" and calls them to embrace him, even as He has. They must make themselves lower than even this "little child," they must be even more "sincere of heart and steadfast," if they are

201

to find the reward which awaits them. Yes, they must "cling to Him" even as He clings to them – even as He clings to this child – and "thus will [their] future be great"; thus will they come through the Son to the Father in heaven.

"Crushing misfortune" awaits the Lord's disciples, for soon He shall be taken from them, and they will understand what His death means. But as long as they continue to "fear the Lord... [their] reward will not be lost"; for "three days after His death He will rise," and those who give their lives as He has done, even as the least of all, shall also know what His resurrection means.

O brothers and sisters, "the Lord watches over the lives of the wholehearted; their inheritance lasts forever," and we must be counted among their number. The Lord "forsakes not His faithful ones"; there is no one who has "hoped in the Lord and been disappointed." So let our hope be in Him and our service be for Him, and He will help us to endure "whatever befalls" us. If He is our "refuge in time of distress," we shall know our salvation, for whoever stands with Him in times of trial will also stand with Him in glory. Let us but remain humble before Him, as a child; let us but accept the children He would place in our arms... and the birth pangs we find will but lead us to our home in heaven.

To His house the Lord leads us, even in this life. Let us listen to His teaching.

O. 7. Wed. (I)

Wednesday
(Sir.4:11-19; Ps.119:165,168,171-172,174-175; Mk.9:38-40)

"Those who serve her serve the Holy One;
those who love her the Lord loves."

Such is wisdom, she who "instructs her children and admonishes those who seek her," she under whose counsel we become the children of God.

And I cannot help but think as I contemplate this personification of wisdom, how well and how appropriately she is embodied by our Blessed Mother, she who was immaculately conceived, she under whose mantle even Jesus our Savior "advanced in wisdom and age and favor before God and man" (Lk.2:52). "To Jesus through Mary" is the motto of the fortunate souls who have consecrated themselves to the Virgin (even as St. Louis De Montfort most wisely instructs), and it is through her intercession that we find God's graces and favors lovingly bestowed upon us. She is our dear Mother, and instructs us as she has her Son.

Indeed it is His beloved disciple John whom the Lord must admonish today, teaching him that those who do the Lord's work serve Him, and these

202

He blesses; and, of course, it is this same disciple to whom Jesus will entrust His Blessed Mother – and she to him – even while dying on the cross: "He said to His mother, 'Woman, behold your son.' Then He said to the disciple, 'Behold, your mother.' And from that hour the disciple took her into his home" (Jn.19:26-27). And now as she has taught Him, so she shall teach His beloved, shall teach all His Church, how to follow the Holy One. And certainly the home into which John gathered the Virgin Mary was more than an earthly domicile: even "from that hour" he took her into his heart.

And she is with us still; she is with him who remains (see Jn.21:20-23), with the Church here on earth, serving as our Mother, guiding us in all wisdom. And, my brother, my sister, do not be discouraged if "at first she puts [you] to the test... and tries [you] with her discipline," for she only seeks to learn that your "heart is fully with her," and so, fully with her Son; she only longs to teach you wisdom. She will come back "to bring [you] happiness and reveal her secrets" to you. And as long as you remain with her, she will hold you in her loving arms as no other mother, and form you in the divine image of her blessed Son.

O Lord, "those who love your law have great peace," for in your wisdom all question and doubt flee. Discipline me by your Word and form me in the womb of your Blessed Mother. "Let my soul live to praise you," for I would be in your company forever. May your wisdom and grace keep me from "the hands of despoilers."

O. 7. Thurs. (I)

Thursday

(Sir.5:1-8; Ps.1:1-4,6,40:50; Mk.9:41-50)

"Mercy and anger are alike with Him;
upon the wicked alights His wrath."

"The way of the wicked vanishes." It must vanish. It cannot but vanish, for there is no place for wickedness in the kingdom of God. And so, what is wicked must "be thrown into Gehenna": what is to "enter life" must be purified. Thus does the Lord command – Cut off your hand! Cut off your foot! Tear out your eye! Remove even with violence whatever causes you to sin to preserve your life unto heaven. For it is indeed better that you "enter life maimed" or "crippled" or "with one eye," than to have your whole body cast into the fires of hell.

Do you fear being "plunged into the sea with a great millstone fastened around [your] neck"? Does this seem a terrible fate? The fires of hell are infinitely worse, and those of purgatory approach them. Know that "everyone will be salted with fire"; everyone must be purified of sin. And you can refuse this truth and so find yourself in the place "the worm does

203

not die and the fire is never extinguished," you can delay your purgation and suffer a measure of these flames in the state of purification after death – or you can remove the sin from your soul by the grace of God now, while there is yet time and His mercy is yet abundant.

"Great is His mercy; my many sins He will forgive," you say, and you are not wrong. But do you know how the mercy of God affects the sinful soul? Do you think it a pleasant experience to be cleansed, to be refined as by fire? Do you not understand that the Lord's love and justice, His mercy and anger, are one for the wicked. Yes, "the Lord will exact the punishment" that brings refreshment and renewal. He must. How else shall you be purged and purified for heaven? All the sins upon your blackened soul are removed only by the chastising flames of His love.

So, "delay not your conversion to the Lord, put it not off from day to day." Be not a fool "adding sin upon sin," for every transgression must be accounted for. But the Lord's blood will wash me clean, you may say, if you have some sense of His redemptive sacrifice. Yes, but it is still *your* soul that must be cleansed, and you shall own the purgatorial fires. And so, hasten this day to the confessional; turn resolutely from your sin. Then pray for the Lord's indulgence, and you may be spared even temporal punishment for your transgressions (and even serve in the Lord's stead to release others from the pain of purgatorial flames).

O. 7. Fri. (I)

Friday
(Sir.6:5-17; Ps.119:12,16,18,27,34-35; Mk.10:1-12)

"They are no longer two but one flesh."

How much more clearly could the Lord speak of the unity found in marriage and so the respect due this sacrament? How better could He get His point across to you that marriage is indissoluble, that it is not to be played with, that you commit adultery as you consider divorcing your spouse? "At the beginning of creation God made them male and female." And by this Jesus does not mean that two separate creatures were made – He means that every one of God's human beings is both male and female, and that in marriage one finds his wholeness in the sight of God.

When Adam was formed of the dust of the earth, Eve was already present within him, in his very body. She was not created apart from him, but taken from him, "from man" – which is the meaning of "woman." Adam when he was first made held both male and female in himself, and when woman was taken from him, built of his rib, the two did not cease to be one. Thus does he recognize Eve as flesh of his flesh and bone of his bone. Thus the two are inseparable. In marriage this inherent unity returns, is fulfilled. "Therefore, let no man separate what God has joined."

And if "a faithful friend is a sturdy shelter; [and] he who finds one finds a treasure," how much more of a shelter is a spouse in whose body one makes his home – how much more valuable a treasure? A friend and more is made by the marriage vow, for truly the spouses become one with one another, and one with the Lord. And so, "when you gain a friend, first test him, and be not too ready to trust him." Know that you are joining yourself to this spouse body and soul, and such commitment is not to be taken lightly or falsely, with an eye toward leaving "when sorrow comes." Beware, lest you find "a friend who becomes an enemy," or that you yourself are not a trustworthy mate. For once joined you cannot be separated, try in vain as you will. One might as well cut off a healthy limb as seek divorce, so grotesque is the proposal. Worse than this, it is as cutting out one's heart, for how can one divide blood that is commingled?

But you who are faithful of heart, know what blessing awaits you, for "a faithful friend is a life-saving remedy, such as he who fears God finds." And if you seek "discernment, that [you] may observe [God's] law and keep it with all [your] heart," your spouse shall serve as savior to you, who are united with her to Christ. In her you will find your life, even as the two become one.

Saturday
(Sir.17:1-15; Ps.103:13-18; Mk.10:13-16)

"Let the children come to me
and do not hinder them."

O how the Lord "looks with favor upon [our] hearts, and shows [us] His glorious works"! And because "His majestic glory their eyes beheld, His glorious voice their ears heard," so the "people were bringing their little children to Jesus to have Him touch them," so they were offering their precious loved ones into the arms of the Savior. And should we not all come to Him, should we not all run into His arms... are we not all His children?

Brothers and sisters, "the Lord from the earth created man, and in His own image He made him." Do you hear that? *In His own image* we are made, as His sons and daughters. "He endows [us] with a strength of His own... He forms our tongues and eyes and ears, and imparts to [us] an understanding heart." He makes us as Himself, and then fills us with His presence! And should we not come to Him, should we not come to His only Son, our own dear brother, the perfection of our race, that all disfigurement might be taken from us and we might radiate the light of God, that we might be remade in His image?

The Lord is only love and "His eyes are ever upon [our] ways" to guide us to His love. He is "as a father [who] has compassion on his children." Yes, "the kindness of the Lord is from eternity to eternity toward those who fear Him," and those who fear Him are His children. But this fear, this overwhelming awe at the love the Maker of the universe has toward His simple creatures, is not one which makes us run from Him, but which moves us to leap into the arms of our Redeemer, into the arms of Him whose arms are always open to receive us, always open to embrace His children.

We know our blessed brother John has told us with holy affection that "we are God's children now" (1Jn.3:2). Of this grace at the hands of our Lord he has spoken most eloquently, most simply – most lovingly. And it is so for all who love Him. And so we should not hinder our hearts from coming to Him, from embracing Him as He embraces us... from giving ourselves to Jesus (particularly in the Sacrament), that we might be formed in His image. Come to Him who is one with the Father, and one with the Father you shall become.

Eighth Week

Monday
(Sir.17:19-27; Ps.32:1-2,5-7,11; Mk.10:17-27)

"Jesus fixed His gaze on them and said,
'For man it is impossible but not for God.'"

With these incisive words and particularly with this intent look, Jesus "encourages those who are losing hope." His disciples are "completely overwhelmed" at His statement: "It is easier for a camel to pass through a needle's eye than for a rich man to enter the kingdom of God," and to keep them from falling into despair at the impossibility of such a proposition, He seeks to teach them that "with God all things are possible." For truly none can be saved but by the grace of God.

"As Jesus was setting out on a journey a man came running up, knelt down before Him and asked, 'Good Teacher, what must I do to share in everlasting life?'" How like "the penitent [for whom] He provides a way back" is this man on his knees before the Lord today. And even after the Lord seems to rebuff his advance, how he persists, begging further word from the Master with the reply to Jesus' listing of certain commandments, "Teacher, I have kept all these since my childhood." Please tell me more, he seems to cry out. And so "Jesus looked at him with love," a love that is

206

beyond the bounds of this world and beyond the bounds of the law – a love that makes all things possible, even the attainment of the kingdom of God, even for us wretched sinners. "How great the mercy of the Lord, His forgiveness of those who return to Him!" "Happy is he whose fault is taken away, whose sin is covered"; for among the dead we would be if not for His divine mercy.

But O "how hard it is to enter the kingdom of God." Though wrought with the Lord's grace, how difficult it is to accompany Christ on His journey. For our hearts are not on His love but on the things we must give up, and so, how readily we turn away in sadness. It is indeed out of love Jesus calls the rich man from his possessions to His side; this is indeed an immeasurable grace pouring forth from the heart of God... but who among us can accept it? Who among us truly seeks everlasting life?

"God watches over the host of highest heaven, while all men are dust and ashes." While "the thoughts of flesh and blood" are obscure, as the wise man tells us, and his possessions of even less consequence; while the sun itself "can be eclipsed" and all things of the earth are passing... yet the kingdom of the Lord endures and holds promise of shelter for the contrite spirit of a humble man. For dust may pass easily through the eye of any needle, and we can be united with the vision of God; for us too all things are made possible, if we humble ourselves in the ashes – if we fall sincerely at the feet of the Lord, and accept His word.

Tuesday
(Sir.35:1-12; Ps.50:5-8,14,23; Mk.10:28-31)

"The just man's sacrifice is most pleasing,
nor will it ever be forgotten."

Peter is moved today to voice his fear that all that he and his fellow apostles have offered, even their very lives, will not be enough to secure the kingdom of God. But Jesus reassures all who serve Him: "I give you my word, there is no one who has given up home, brothers or sisters, mother or father, children or property, for me and for the Gospel who will not receive in this present age a hundred times as many... and persecution besides – and in the age to come, everlasting life." None should fear that their sacrifice will be wasted, "for the Lord is one who always repays," and repays in full, multiplying whatever gifts we offer beyond our expectations.

"But offer no bribes, these He does not accept!" You will never be able to extort graces from the Lord, and so should always come without expectation of return. Make all your sacrifices as "freewill gifts," for only that which is given "generously" and "in a spirit of joy" does He smile upon.

Bring your gifts to the altar expecting nothing but the cross, in this find your return, and the glory of the resurrection shall indeed be yours. You must learn from those whom the Lord rebukes, though their "holocausts are before [Him] always" – only "he that offers praise as a sacrifice glorifies" the Lord, and so you must find joy in your cross.

O how "the just man's offering enriches the altar and rises as a sweet odor before the Most High." "He who observes the commandments" and "gives alms," he who performs "works of charity," who "refrain[s] from evil" and "avoid[s] injustice"... O how this man "pleases the Lord"! For his life is as a "sacrifice of praise," an offering of peace and an atonement for sin, which cannot but reach to the throne of God. Yes, "to him that goes the right way [the Lord] will show the salvation of God." Of this you can be assured.

O. 8. Wed. (I)

Wednesday
(Sir.36:1,5-6,10-17; Ps.79:8-9,11,13; Mk.10:32-35)

"Take pity on your holy city,
Jerusalem, your dwelling place."

The prayer of the wise man is good, but I see that the same answer the Lord gave James and John when they asked to sit "one at [His] right hand and the other at [His] left" in His glory, could be given to Sirach: "You do not know what you are asking." For neither knows the implication of their request – neither can see that it will only be fulfilled in a painful death.

In our gospel Jesus is leading the disciples "on the road going up to Jerusalem," a crowd following behind. There He will "fulfill the prophecies spoken in [His] name." There He will "fill Zion with His majesty, [His] temple with [His] glory." But the keepers of the keys of the temple "will condemn Him to death"; they will thereby destroy the Temple itself. In this way only will the "prophets be proved true." In this way only He will "deliver us and pardon our sins." In this way only will He "with [His] great power free those doomed to death." For the prophets have said that the Servant must suffer. The prophets have said that the Son must die. There is no other way that "three days later He will rise." There is no other way for Him to redeem those condemned to die.

This must sink into our hearts; this we must understand, we who run so freely from the cross, who think it is a facile thing to "inherit the land." The Lord will indeed have pity on our souls; He will indeed answer "the prisoners' sighing" and forget "the iniquities of the past." But Heaven is attained only by those who drink from His cup; the glory of God is known only by those who share in Jesus' "bath of pain." No other way will we be

208

cleansed of our sins. No other way will we be made ready. The cross is the path to the New Jerusalem, and we must walk it with our Lord.

And so, be not lazy about the work He has set before you; fail not to "serve the needs of all." If you think of yourself and some vain reward, you will never find the blessing which awaits "those for whom it has been reserved." His "compassion come[s] quickly to us" if we but share in His blood.

Thursday
(Sir.42:15-25; Ps.33:2-9; Mk.10:46-52)

"As the rising sun is clear to all,
so the glory of the Lord fills all His works."

"How beautiful are all His works! even to the spark and the fleeting vision!" "Can one ever see enough of their splendor?" Yet how blind is man to their glory! How much we need to receive the Lord's vision.

"By the word of the Lord the heavens were made; by the breath of His mouth their host"; "at God's word were His works brought into being." And so, bathed in His grace what can heaven and earth be but a wonder to behold? Then why is it we see only darkness? Why are our eyes so blind to His presence in all the creatures He has made only for good? Is it not that we say "I see"? Is it not that we tell ourselves, "There. Now I have God in my hands. Now His ways I understand"?

My poor friends, you can never plumb the depths of God's works, for "even God's holy ones must fail in recounting the wonders of the Lord." It is He alone who "plumbs the depths and penetrates the heart; [your] innermost being He understands." And He sees as He looks into your soul that you are blind, that you do not see Him as He is... and He longs to call you up closer to Himself. "The Most High possesses all knowledge": He remembers the past, He sees the future – the moment is in His hand. And you yourself He would hold in His hand and move according to His will, if only you would let Him.

Come to the Lord like the blind man you are; do not let the scolding of the world hinder your plea to His compassionate heart. "You have nothing whatever to fear from Him!" for He eternally asks, "What do you want me to do for you?" seeking always to grant you sight. Then when you feel His touch upon your eyes, be as Bartimaeus and "immediately... follow Him up the road." For on that road your vision will ever be increased. On that road you will learn to "pluck the strings skillfully, with shouts of gladness"; you will share in His wisdom and wonder as you "sing to Him [your] new song."

On the road our Savior trod you will find "the strength to stand firm before His glory."

Rise and walk with Him in faith this day. "He gathers the waters of the sea in a flask"; "not a single thing escapes Him" – and so He is certainly not blind to your needs. To His glory He calls you: shine with Him now more brightly than the sun.

Friday
(Sir.44:1,9-13; Ps.149:1-6,9; Mk.11:11-26)

"They are as though they had not lived,
they and their children after them."

This line from Sirach could refer well to the Jewish nation symbolized by the fig tree "withered to its roots." For "never again shall anyone eat of [its] fruits"; its temple now destroyed shall never be rebuilt. And yet Sirach speaks not of those who have perished in sin, and so are never to be known again in the sight of God, but of "godly men" of Jewish ancestry who, though "there is no memory" of the particulars of their actions in time – as there is with the great patriarchs and prophets of old – yet are of the race of those "whose virtues have not been forgotten": the memory of their goodness lives on in the heart of God, and "through God's covenant with them their family endures."

The covenant is removed from the hands of the Jewish people. This is indicated clearly in our gospel today not only in the withered fig tree, but in Jesus' driving out those who had made their station in His Father's temple. These shall be replaced by the Lord's appointed servants, and the Church shall be built where the temple once stood. But this does not mean that the godly deeds of the godly men under the covenant of old are forgotten now that the New Covenant has been instituted; nor does it mean those in His Church are beyond reproach.

Let us look more closely at the Lord's interaction with the fig tree, for it can teach us much. First, Jesus "felt hungry" – He desires our souls. Then He saw "a fig tree some distance off" – far removed are we from His sacred presence. He is attracted by its "foliage" – it has the appearance of fruit and life. But "when He reached it He found it had nothing but leaves..." There is no fruit upon it to satisfy His hunger; and so for its uselessness He curses it to dust. As He has done with the faithless Jews, so will He do with the faithless among us.

But "it was not the time for figs," you say, as if to justify your emptiness. My brothers, in the Lord's kingdom it is *always* time for figs – we in His Church are ever called to bear fruit in His name, in season and out of season: our souls are required of us this very day. And if we satisfy not God's hunger for our fruits of prayer and charity, if we too have polluted His house with acts of "buying and selling" instead of the worship demanded of us... if we have gilded the temple to attract the eye but are utterly barren within, what shall He say when He enters our temple area? What action shall He take against those who serve as thieves of His love? They shall indeed be blotted from His Book of Life.

But those who "put [their] trust in God," those who serve Him in spirit and in truth, shall not be forgotten by the Lord, whether their names are known in this world or not. "For the Lord loves His people, and He adorns the lowly with victory." It is not the "acclamations from the crowd" in which Jesus puts His heart, but in doing the will of God. And so all who are like Him shall secure with Him their place in heaven. "Let the children of Zion rejoice in their King," for none "in the assembly of the faithful" is forgotten.

Saturday
(Sir.51:12-20; Ps.19:8-11; Mk.11:27-33)

"When I was young and innocent, I sought wisdom.
She came to me in her beauty,
and until the end I will cultivate her."

O how Sirach speaks of his love, of the wisdom that is the light of his life! He is "resolutely devoted to her" and does "never weary of extolling her." To his teacher he gives "grateful praise," for he treasures her sweetness above all things.

"I will ask you a question. If you give me an answer, I will tell you on what authority I do the things I do." So does wisdom speak. So does the Lord inquire as to what is in the hearts of the scribes and Pharisees and priests. But there He does not find wisdom's radiant beauty; there He finds nothing, for these leaders are so empty, so pitifully vain. Rightly do they say, "We do not know," for there is no light in them – only the dark connivings of the world's greed and pride.

And can wisdom answer him who has no ears? Can she speak to those who do not listen to her voice whispering in their souls? She does not engage in useless activity and cannot wed herself to those whose spirits are impure, whose hearts are not set on her fruits. "In cleanness I attained to her," Sirach happily declares, for he "purified even the soles of [his] feet" to find her. But these men who weary so easily of her "great instruction," who would so readily look upon the riches of this world, how can they taste her sweetness? How can they gaze upon her infinite beauty...?

211

And so the Lord turns away from them. He cannot tell them "on what authority [He] do[es] the things" they see displayed so powerfully before their eyes, for their eyes are blind and their hearts are turned against Him. They do not wish to know the answer to their question; they do not truly seek wisdom. And she does not come to those who do not desire "her secrets."

"The decree of the Lord is trustworthy, giving wisdom to the simple." In silence, in obedience, in humility and purity you will hear the Lord speaking. And He will guide you to all His grace; and His name alone you will bless and praise. What great profit you shall find if from your innocence you cultivate wisdom until the end of time.

Ninth Week

Monday
(Tb.1:1-2,2:1-9; Ps.112:1-6; Mk.12:1-12)

"The stone rejected by the builders
has become the keystone of the structure."

First, Tobit is not a parable; it is not a "story". A parable begins, as does Jesus' own in our gospel, with a statement such as, "A man planted a vineyard..." It is always "a man", a generic man, never a particular man in a particular place at a particular time, as is the case with Tobit. For parables deal expressly with the universal. Though one may derive universal significance from the life of Tobit, it is his life itself which is related to us and not that of an "Everyman". (How this simple fact is overlooked I can only attribute again to a lack of faith which blinds reason.)

This aside, today we see the persecution and mockery "a sincere worshiper of God" suffers before the face of the world. It is evident in Tobit's being "hunted down for execution" for performing the corporal work of mercy of burying the dead, as well as in the wagging of his neighbors' tongues; and it is, of course, fulfilled in the crucifixion of Christ, which the Lord speaks of today to the elders of the people in a thinly-veiled parable of their persecution of all the prophets.

What a good man Tobit is, desiring to share his feast with the poor and rising even from table to do the work of God, always ready to serve Him. And how he weeps for the oppression of his people. Jesus is just the same, coming from the majesty of the Father's table in heaven to call us to His wedding feast, and weeping over those who, like Jerusalem, fail to hear His voice.

Our lot in this world is one of suffering and persecution, but it is not without hope. For we know that as Job found greater wealth in his latter days and Tobit shall be rewarded for his patient endurance, so the Lord is resurrected from the grave. It is our psalm which reminds us of this promise despite any darkness around us: "The Lord dawns through the darkness, a light for the upright... the just man shall be in everlasting remembrance."

So let us not lose heart on the hard road we tread, but endure all patiently with Jesus, for we shall find our place in His joyful kingdom; we shall drink the wine of His vineyard.

Tuesday
(Tb.2:9-14; Ps.112:1-2,7-9; Mk.12:13-17)

"His heart is firm, trusting in the Lord"

Today in our reading and gospel we find just men put to trial and testing. Our Lord is steadfast before the devious inquiry of the Pharisees and Herodians, answering them with a wisdom greater than Solomon's; for what can Jesus, who is Himself the Word made flesh, do but take refuge in the Father with whom He is one. And so wisdom is His to answer His foes, and He is unmoved, indeed moving with "amazement" those who would trap Him.

The heart of Tobit does not remain as secure. We see in his anger that his trust in the Lord has been shaken. He has always been just, generously giving to those in need, taking the plight of his people to heart. Indeed, it is after performing a good work – "fatigued from burying the dead [I] went to sleep next to the wall of my courtyard" – that his trial comes upon him. Here is a man who has done all he could to help his fellow Jewish exiles suffering persecution at the hands of the Ninevites, and now he is stricken with blindness.

But the Lord does not leave him alone; He does not cast him out. For two years his needs are cared for by Ahiqar, and then his wife is able to work to meet their expenses. And successful she is over and above expectations. Yet he is prodded into anger by her good reward. His response (in the words of St. Dorotheus, from today's Office of Readings) "breaks the cover on the passionate anger within him," an anger, an unease, he has likely been harboring for some time. It is an anger, we can surmise, that comes from the helplessness his blindness has brought upon him. He is no longer in control of his fate, but must depend on others for survival. And though the Lord provides, he finds it too difficult to trust in this provision. (He may indeed be particularly resentful that it is now his wife who provides for him, taking the role he believes in his heart he should play.)

We can certainly understand Tobit's frustration over his condition. Few but Jesus would stand up well to such trial. But Jesus is our ideal. It is to be like Him that we are called. We shall always need to do battle against the sins that are ever with us, but as St. Dorotheus says of the Christian, "The more perfect he grows, the less these temptations will affect him. For the more the soul advances, the stronger and more powerful it becomes in bearing the difficulties that it meets."

Let us set ourselves to trust in the Lord and so ever find security in Him. We must place all in His hands, even unto death, and then we shall be free.

> Let not the things of Caesar weigh upon you;
> you belong to God and not the world.

O. 9. Wed. (I)

Wednesday
(Tb.3:1-11,16-17; Ps.25:1-9; Mk.12:18-27)

"He is the God of the living, not of the dead."

Rich readings. First of all, we see the striking similarity between the story woven by the Sadducees to thwart the wisdom of the Lord and the situation in which Sarah finds herself. In both cases, seven – the number representing fullness – husbands have died. In one the wife has also died; in the other, she wishes for death. And in both there have been no children, no fruit, no new life. Death in its fullness is throughout today's readings, as even Tobit begs to die.

In addition to death, our readings are also clearly about prayer. In our first, Tobit and Sarah pour out their hearts in tears before the Lord whom they so love. Our psalm is the lifting up of the soul in prayer to God by the humble. And the Sadducees questioning of Jesus is also a kind of prayer, though one which comes from a hardness of heart, inauthentic and insincere.

And what has the Lord to say of death; what is the answer to these prayers? We know that God always answers our prayers, though often in ways we do not expect. Such is the case here. Neither Tobit nor Sarah will get the death they seem to seek; instead, Raphael – the angel whose name means "to heal" – "was sent to heal them both." And the Sadducees, "who hold there is no resurrection," will not find confirmation for their creed which clings to death as the end of all. Yet all will be answered according to the disposition of their hearts, and in this sense all receive exactly what they seek, for the Lord looks upon the heart. The prayer of Tobit and Sarah is not really to die but "to be delivered from such anguish" – it is healing they seek, and this they shall find. And the Sadducees, who do not really seek an answer of the Lord regarding resurrection, whose hearts are closed

214

to the life-giving power of God, will likely not hear the words of Christ... and so by their ignorance come to adhere more firmly to their creed of death.

We do get what we ask for. As our psalm tells us, the Lord "teaches the humble His way." The compassion and kindness which are synonymous with God are known to those who trust in Him; but "those shall be put to shame who heedlessly break faith," for the compassion of our Lord finds no place in them. For them there is no hope, no life, no resurrection from the dead... and they shall not know how God answers prayer.

Brothers and sisters, let us pour out our hearts before our Lord and God, and know His healing grace, and find His everlasting life.

Thursday
(Tb.6:11,7:1,9-14,8:4-7; Ps.128:1-5; Mk.12:28-34)

"Love the Lord your God"
and
"Love your neighbor as yourself."

On these two great commandments rest all the Law and the Prophets. By them we shall be "not far from the reign of God." In them the Lord leads us into His bridal chamber, where we shall be made one with Him in glory forever.

Here on earth we dimly mirror the love of the Lord for His Church in our marriage of husband and wife; in this, love of neighbor is known in its most intimate and complete way. But always love of God must precede love of any creature, for it is "those who fear the Lord" who are happy, who "eat the fruit of [their] handiwork" and see their children prosper.

Tobiah has such love. Such strength of love does he have in his heart for Sarah that he hesitates not at all even in the face of death. Seven have died before him, but he gives fear of this not a thought. And it is not in his lust that he takes such great strength; he is not led foolishly by his eyes and his loins. It is indeed his fear of the Lord, the love for his God and his desire to keep His commands, in which he finds unwavering hope. Even from his marriage bed does he rise to invoke the name of God, demonstrating his "noble purpose." He recognizes that God first must be praised, and that it is He who gave Adam his Eve.

Jesus loves us just so, brothers and sisters, and even greater than this is His love for His bride. He heeds fully the command of God regarding His Church: "Take her and bring her back safely to your father." He comes to us, as it were, on a long journey, the angels of the Lord blessing His steps, and seeks without fear His rightful wife, who has languished so long

215

surrounded by death. This death He takes upon Himself, facing it with faith
and prayer alone to show us the love God has for us, and that we must have
for one another. And wedding us unto Himself, He redeems us from the
death we have known and makes us so fruitful in His Name. Yes, brothers
and sisters, we must love the God who has loved us so, and love one another
the same.

     May God bless all marriages;
     may they witness to the love the Lord has for His Church.
     Amen.

Friday
(Tb.11:5-15; Ps.146:2,7-10; Mk.12:35-37)

"The Lord gives sight to the blind."

Now in His teaching Jesus truly begins to open the eyes of the people.
We have witnessed this week His fielding their questions regarding theology
and the law, but He now takes a step further, revealing to them and to us the
Truth itself – that He Himself is the Son of God. "The majority of the
crowd heard this with delight." Many eyes begin to open, many hearts
begin to see... but will they remain so joyful when Jesus reveals Himself to
them completely (on the cross)?

And of course, our first reading speaks principally about the opening of
Tobit's eyes, as he who has been blind these four years is healed by the fish
gall acquired through the intercession of the angel Raphael. But the reading
is really about more than this: it shows the love of his parents in their
longing for Tobiah's return. Notice that as his eyes are opened, Tobit
exclaims, "I can see you, son, the light of my eyes!" as he weeps with his
arms around him. And at the very beginning of the reading we find Anna,
his mother, "watching the road," looking desperately – she has been there
for weeks – for Tobiah to return from his journey. When she sees him, she,
too, throws her arms around him, and says, "Now that I have seen you
again, son, I am ready to die!" as she sobs aloud... It is not so much the fish
gall that has cured Tobit's blindness, for the light of his eyes, that which
causes them to see, he himself ascribes to Tobiah his son. And it is not so
much seeing Tobiah that brings such absolute joy to his mother, as it is
being with him again, knowing that he is alive – for she had seriously feared
him dead.

Brothers and sisters, are we like Anna and Tobit? Do we watch
vigilantly for the return of the only Son of God? We proclaim that our eyes
have been opened to know Him as our Savior, but is He truly the light of our
eyes? Even today do we make seeing Him and knowing Him the life that

brings breath to our souls and makes our hearts beat? Are we the "oppressed," the "hungry," the "captives" – those who are "bowed down" of whom our psalm speaks – who will thus know His "justice," His "food," His "freedom"... His "resurrection"?

We must love dearly our Holy Catholic Church, for it is essential here on this earth, where it is the keeper of the Father's vineyard; but we must remember Jesus goes beyond religion, beyond theology and laws. For He is more than these. He is what sets us apart from any other religion, for He is a person, the second Person of the Trinity – God. Let us open our eyes and our hearts and follow Him with our lives, knowing He is our only Son, our hope, the light of our eyes. For He who is the Son of Man is also the Son of God.

Saturday
(Tb.12:1,5-15,20; Tb.13:1-2,6; Mk.12:38-44)

"Almsgiving saves one from death."

We must give alms, yes; and the greatest of alms is the gift of ourselves to God.

In our gospel we hear of perhaps the most famous example of almsgiving: the poor widow who gave her two copper coins to the temple treasury; and in our first reading we complete the Book of Tobit, he who is himself a great biblical model of almsgiving, and who is here instructed by the angel Raphael on the merit of giving alms. Yes, the widow gives generously all her money, without hesitation and without a thought. Unlike those who give from their surplus, "she gave from her want, all that she had to live on." She holds back nothing. And at the prompting of Tobit, Tobiah offers half of all the many riches gained from his journey to his guide, Raphael (not realizing he is an angel with no need of these things).

As Raphael reveals himself to Tobit and his son, he extols the great merit of almsgiving, which he states is better even than prayer and fasting. He wishes to tell them of the value of almsgiving, it is true, but he wants Tobit to know that his generosity has been witnessed by God and that it has saved him from the death he had asked for. Raphael lets Tobit know, too, that he has been tested by God (in being stricken with blindness) to prove that his generosity is genuine. It must be shown that his virtue is not vain as the scribes', who "recite long prayers for appearance' sake" to cover the fact that they "devour the savings of widows." Does he have the heart of the poor widow in his generosity, or does he just like to parade around in the robes of such virtue?

217

The key to the merit of all our almsgiving is found in Raphael's initial response to Tobiah's offer: "Thank God! Give Him the praise and the glory." All our good works must be done for the praise of God as witnesses to His glory. "Before all men, honor and proclaim God's deeds, and do not be slack in praising Him," the angel exhorts us all. And it is this praise of God we must give first before any treasure of the world. This praise of God and telling of His Name is the greatest of almsgiving. Do you think it is the two coins which save the widow, or can you see the heart for God from which they are offered? Do you think the widow is giving her coins for show, or is it obvious to you that it is her love of God which drives her to this act? We can easily surmise that this woman's life is one of prayer to God, a genuine prayer unlike the vanity of the scribes, and it is this which most pleases God and saves her very soul; for she is empty of all else but Him. And of all the many acts of kindness Tobit has performed, all the dead he has buried and offerings he has given, perhaps none is above his obedience to the angel's final command: "Write down all these things that have happened to you." For by his laying down of his life and the Lord's marvelous grace working in it, more than two thousand years later, we still receive the spiritual gifts contained therein; his praise of God with "full voice" still comes to our ears and gives us hope that we too might be raised up from any vanity in our own generosity and see the face of God.

Let us praise the Lord with all our lives and give all our selves to Him.

Let us live to praise the Lord.

O. 10. Mon. (I)

Tenth Week

Monday
(2Cor.1:1-7; Ps.34:2-9; Mt.5:1-12)

"Blessed are those persecuted for holiness' sake;
the reign of God is theirs."

Here is the core teaching of our faith. Here are the beatitudes, the call to sweet humility which flows like blessed honey from the lips of our Savior. And that teaching is that the humbled shall be exalted, that those who mourn and sorrow for the lack of love we find in this tainted world and who strive to bring that love to the hard heart of man shall be blessed, are blessed, for they share in the sufferings of Christ, who wept for the sins of His people, who, looking out upon them from the cross cried: "My God, why have you forsaken me?" Why has this world made in the image of Christ turned so against Him, and when shall it return to the love of God? And we who cry with Christ, even for our enemies, even for the most despicable criminal, we shall know the joy He finds – like the repentant thief, we shall be this day with Him in paradise.

"Just as you share in the sufferings, so you will share in the consolation," St. Paul so concisely states. One can hear him brimming with joy as he speaks of the comfort we find in the Lord in all our afflictions, and the grace of sharing that consolation with others. This is our great possession. This is the kingdom of God within us: to see through all trouble and affliction, to conquer it in Jesus' Name – to find such strength even while here on earth to overcome all evil and come to heaven. "Blest are you when they insult you and persecute you... Be glad and rejoice." How marvelously the Lord exhorts us to come to the glory of heaven, to overcome the dark with light. For light it is where we dwell, and this light is unconquerable.

Let us make room for Him in our hearts, brothers and sisters; let us give place to Him in our lives. Let us even in the simplest ways show heaven's glory here on earth. If we are lowly and we are true, our light cannot help but shine. And for those who seek it our lamps will shine, and we shall illumine one another. Let sweet humility be your treasure and the Lord's peace your goal in life.

The angel of the Lord is around us to save us. Nothing of this earth shall touch us. Let us lay down our lives to destroy death's bonds.

Tuesday
(2Cor.1:18-22; Ps.119:129-133,135; Mt.5:13-16)

"God is the one who firmly establishes us."

"Light of the world" and "salt of the earth" – this is what we are by the power of God. It is by Him we are "set on a hill" to give "light to all in the house"; it is we who preserve the integrity of creation. It is a holy call and a demanding one, and we should not waver in our resolve to follow the Lord and fulfill His work and His will; for it is indeed His will that we show His goodness before the eyes of men, and so "He who anointed us and sealed us" will always strengthen us for our task – by Him who holds the entire world in His palm, our own work will be made light.

But heed the words of our readings: we must always give our "yes" to God. Having put our hand to the plow, we cannot turn back. In fact, we should say with the psalmist, "I gasp with open mouth in my yearning for your commands"; so great should be our love for God and for His life-giving words that ever do we thirst more greatly for the love and the light He brings us through our walking in them. His discipline is redeeming and freeing; and as we drink in its light, as we find ourselves becoming one with

Him and with His Son who has shown us clearly and completely the way of perfection, we become the light He is. And we cannot but shine that same light to others, directing them to Him who establishes all holy souls in His blessed kingdom.

What joy should be ours as we find ourselves becoming one with God as His children of light. What absolute exhilaration is evident in Paul's preaching to the Corinthians, as well as in our psalm. The source of such excitement is his firmness in faith; the Spirit is speaking in his heart and he is not afraid. Indeed, he takes his very life, his daily bread, in proclaiming it.

Have we such faith in our hearts, or have we somehow gone flat? Can we proclaim our unwavering trust in the Lord, or is our light still shaded by doubts and fears? If our love for God is true and our love for one another is real, we shall be firmly established – our light shall go forth.

Let us pray to Him that from the light of His words we shall not be distracted. The light of His presence is all that matters. Shine forth His light to the world.

O. 10. Wed. (I)

Wednesday
(2Cor.3:4-11; Ps.99:5-9; Mt.5:17-19)

"Not the smallest letter of the law,
not the smallest part of a letter,
shall be done away with until it all comes true."

Jesus comes to fulfill the law and the prophets. The law watches over us while we are here in this world. It guards us and puts to death the sin that is inherent in our earthly nature. There is great glory in this blessed protection, as is witnessed in our psalm today – "Holy is the Lord, our God" – because it acquaints us with God's justice and, as said, watches vigilantly over us to maintain our standing in the presence of God. But the law does not bring us to the fullness of God's love; it does not bring us into the heavenly kingdom and "the glory that endures." Moses brings the Israelites to the banks of the Jordan, but he does not cross over with them. He looks out over the Promised Land from his place on the mountaintop, but does not enter therein. It is Joshua who leads the people into the land promised through Moses (as even he does in today's Office of Readings). And so it is Jesus who brings us to the heavenly kingdom by His law of love.

In speaking elsewhere of the glory of love (1Cor.13:8), Paul tells us that prophecy shall fail and tongues shall cease but love is eternal, favored well beyond any other gift. Prophecies speak of earthly matters and the law is for our earthly nature, but love speaks of God and heaven. We must be very

220

careful to heed the words of Christ and realize that as long as we are in this world and subject to the sin that our flesh brings, the law has a prominent place in our lives and cannot be jettisoned prematurely – as many advocate by their lack of diligence to its precepts, presuming heaven before its time – yet we must always remember that it is the glory of heaven and not of earth to which Jesus calls us, and that there the law will be fulfilled; there we shall be made perfect in the light of God.

The law is "destined to pass away" only insofar as it is fulfilled, and therefore it never really passes away but is subsumed by a greater law. Let us continue to glory in the chastising hand of God and in the service of purification the law provides us. Let us come by its means to the flesh of Christ, and by the grace of God enter fully into Him.

Jesus is our Promised Land, brothers and sisters; with the law as our guide, but above all with faith in our hearts, let us come into His holy, eternal, loving presence. We have the manna of the Eucharist to share this day; tomorrow we shall feast in fullness on the Bread of Life that is Jesus Christ.

O. 10. Thurs. (I)

Thursday
(2Cor.3:15-4:1,3-6; Ps.85:9-14; Mt.5:20-26)

"See the splendor of the gospel showing forth the glory of Christ."

Today the gospel is preached: Jesus, the image of God, has come among us, "glory dwelling in our land," and removed the veil from our understanding so that now we "are being transformed from glory to glory into His very image by the Lord who is the Spirit." The words of life are spoken by the Lord; the Holy Spirit comes amongst us as light to illumine our minds and lead us beyond the bounds of the law to the kingdom of God itself. And we must live in that light, we must make it our own, becoming children of the light of the Spirit of God, "that we in turn might make known the glory of God shining on the face of Christ." He has indeed come amongst us, salvation is at hand, and we must become perfect as the Father is perfect, as Jesus who is the pure reflection of the Father is perfect – we must allow the Spirit to remove any taint of darkness from our souls.

Jesus tells us, "Unless your holiness surpasses that of the scribes and Pharisees you shall not enter the kingdom of God." Here He means that the law may lead us out of Egypt, it may serve to release us from the bonds of this world of sin, but this guard we have while treading this earth is not enough to bring us into the promised land, into the heavenly kingdom to which we are called. And as long as we concern ourselves only with fulfilling the minimal requirements of the law (not to murder, not to commit adultery...), we will continue to suffer; we will remain unfulfilled. Jesus calls us to greater than that: He calls us into His very light of perfection in the presence of the Father. This call is implanted upon the soul of each one of us, and as long as we ignore it, as long as we veil our minds to the depth and the breadth of this call to perfection with Christ... as long as we say, "Well, I haven't killed anyone," and stop there... so long we will remain unsatisfied, so long will the fires burn – so long will we be in prison paying the last penny.

Jesus is calling you now, brothers and sisters; Paul and all the true preachers of Holy Church are calling you now to remove the veil from your eyes, to come into the Lord's light – to cease to make excuses for your sins, however small they may seem – to seek perfection in Christ... to find the kingdom of God. The Spirit will aid you in your journey; He will be with you every step of your walk on the way of perfection, be assured of this. The Lord does not call us to Himself and then leave us alone to struggle vainly. He is with us through all our trials. But we must come to Him and live in His light of purity, and shine that light for others to see.

O. 10. Fri. (I)

Friday
(2Cor.4:7-15; Ps.116:10-11,15-18; Mt.5:27-32)

"While we live we are constantly being delivered to death for Jesus' sake, so that the life of Jesus may be revealed in our mortal flesh."

In our gospel we continue to see how the grace of Jesus supersedes the Law of Moses. Yesterday we were told not only must we not murder, but that we must not even be angry with or speak ill of another. Today Jesus tells us the commandment against adultery applies even to our eyes, to our thoughts, and that God allows no divorce... And of what does Jesus speak but that which Paul tells us as well – that our bodies, our sinful flesh, must die in order for the glory of God contained therein to shine. Jesus makes this graphically apparent when He speaks of gouging out our eye and cutting off our hand: the body must provide no hindrance to entering the reign of God, and so it must die; sin must indeed be rooted out of us.

"In earthen vessels" we are, weak and mortal, subject to the afflictions of time. The trials of this world therefore do not escape us and indeed are necessary for us to overcome, to purify, our mortal flesh. We must be chastised. We must suffer. But we do not suffer in vain. "We are persecuted but never abandoned; we are struck down but never destroyed." The trials of this earth have no ultimate hold over us; in fact, they do not lead to death but to life. Why? Solely because it is "the dying of Jesus" we carry in our bodies; entirely because we unite our suffering to Christ's, it becomes redemptive and not destructive. "We have that Spirit of faith," and that Spirit of faith is life to us even in our greatest afflictions; and that Spirit of faith turns the deaths we undergo to new life. How? By our overcoming of these deaths and thereby giving death to sin.

A man is addicted to alcohol – this is a temptation and an affliction for him. By the power of Christ and faith in His Name, he puts down the bottle. Who can measure the grace at work in him? Who can capture the life he now knows? And we all have our addictions, be they anger or lust or greed or whatever, and they all must be overcome. And as we overcome them, what freedom do we find. For in this we thwart the devil's plan to bring us to destruction by the weakness of the flesh. He does not like to see our faith in Jesus spawning such resurrections. And neither does the world like to see a man make progress in God. So the afflictions will be doubled; the world and the devil will attack our weak human vessels all the more. But "precious in the eyes of the Lord is the death of His faithful ones"; and the more we set aside the sins of the flesh, the more He will bless us – the greater He will preserve us from evil.

He that is in us is far greater than he that is in the world, brothers and sisters. And the more the devil tempts us, the stronger only do we become, because the God of life holds even this purveyor of death in His all-powerful hand. We must but have faith and we will find life; through all our afflictions we will rejoice.

O. 10. Sat. (I)

Saturday
(2Cor.5:14-21; Ps.103:1-4,8-9,11-12; Mt.5:33-37)

"The love of Christ impels us who have reached the conviction
that since one died for all, all died."

How strong is Paul's "yes" for the Lord. With what ardor does he cry out: "The old order is passed away; now all is new!" How purely he is led in the Spirit to call to our very souls, "In Christ's name: be reconciled to God!" He has no need to swear by earth or heaven of his conviction that Jesus died for our salvation. He is indeed a new creation and can but speak of that which he knows to the depths of his soul; driven by the miracle of his own reconciliation to God, he desires naturally – by the supernatural grace at work within him – to draw others to "become the very holiness of God."

Paul sings out with our psalmist: "Bless the Lord, O my soul; and all my being bless His holy name." He cries out with David: "He pardons all your iniquities, He heals all your ills." This is the truth which impels him, which he cannot but preach – that our sins are forgiven in Christ the Lord and we need but to come to Him to be raised up to new life. This is his ministry of reconciliation; this is the message entrusted to him... and he must appeal for God's holy will to be accomplished in us.

Let me join in his shout, let me state so unequivocally – let us all be convicted with Paul of the love God has for us, of the death He has died for us... of the new life we have in Him. Yes, let us indeed shout it from the rooftops, let us cry it out for all to hear. Many are on the path to destruction, many are dying in their transgressions; *all* are inclined to the condemnation the devil has wrought in our lives, and all must be encouraged, all must hear the exhortation to turn from their sins. May we give our "yes" firmly to God and our "no" firmly to the devil, that others might know in our very lives of the holiness of God and the glory to which He calls us.

"Merciful and gracious is the Lord": this the world must know. "As far as the east is from the west, so far has He put our transgressions from us": this the sinful heart wallowing in the darkness of doubt must hear. The blood of Christ must be shown to all. Let us not hesitate to speak the great truth of God's salvation through Christ the Son. Let us not fail to live His new life every day of our lives.

The Lord calls. The sound of His voice is unmistakable. All our sin is dead in Him; through Him we are raised to life. May this Word go forth to the ends of the earth, and may we help carry it there.

O. 11. Mon. (I)

Eleventh Week

Monday
(2Cor.6:1-10; Ps.98:1-4; Mt.5:38-42)

"When a person strikes you on the right cheek,
turn and offer him the other."

"Now is the acceptable time! Now is the day of salvation!" Alleluia! And how do we know the salvation of the Lord except by the cross. This is our joy. These "difficulties, distresses, beatings, imprisonments, and riots"; the "hard work, sleepless nights, and fastings" – these crosses bring us immeasurable joy, for through them we share in the suffering of Christ and so also in His resurrection glory. Thus the Lord can encourage us not to seek to avoid such suffering; thus He instructs us to be prepared to suffer over and above that which comes to us – for He knows that as we give of ourselves in this ready way, as we lay down our lives without hesitation, we shall find ourselves in the hand of God, we shall come quickly to join Him in heaven. With Paul, we must "present ourselves as ministers of God, acting with patient endurance amid trials," and His salvation will be made known in us. And we will rejoice with Paul in all our sorrows. And we will be able to exclaim with him, "We seem to have nothing, yet everything is ours!" For the fullness of Christ will reside with us.

Give. Give, and do not count the cost. How hard it is for us to freely give of our possessions, much less of our very lives. Are we ready to "give to the man who begs" from us? Are we prepared to care for others' needs? Or do we hold tightly to our possessions, calling them our own? And what of the possession of our pride and the protection of ourselves from injury? What of our judgment of others? Are we ready to give these up so completely? Can we turn the other cheek to those who do us wrong, offering the pain to God and finding great comfort there, or do we need to strike back against the offending party, exacting the retribution due us according to the law? Do we indeed live by the law, or have we transcended the law: do we now live by the Law of love? Are we a new creation in Christ?

It is not easy to lay down our lives in such a way as Christ calls us. The world ever mocks the absurdity of this sacrifice. But we who are in Jesus should know the absolute truth of Paul's words and Jesus' instruction. If we are to be Christians, we must know the joy and freedom that come from suffering all with Him who is our salvation. *He is all that matters.* If we have Him, we have all things. Come to this truth, brothers and sisters; leave behind the fears wrought by attachment to the things of this world. This world is of sin anyway. As we lose our possessions for Him, He gives us all the more. As the body dies, the spirit comes to life. What the devil would take from us, let us give him, for he cannot touch the life that is Christ: our souls are in the hand of God. And, as with Job, all will be restored to us, and more, in the day of the Lord. So, "wielding the weapons of righteousness with right hand and left," let us learn always to turn the other cheek to our persecutors.

Tuesday
(2Cor.8:1-9; Ps.146:2,5-9; Mt.5:43-48)

"Love your enemies, pray for your persecutors."

Our psalm today begins with praise of God and the proclamation of the happiness of those "whose hope is in the Lord," for it is He who "gives food to the hungry" and "raises up those that were bowed down." Freeing captives, giving sight to the blind, protecting strangers... such is our God and Father. And in our gospel Jesus tells us, "You are sons of your heavenly Father," and "you must be made perfect as your heavenly Father is perfect." We must be His image, doing the things He does.

Paul presents Jesus, the only Son of the Father, as our model in generosity. In his gentle reminder he states: "For your sake He made Himself poor though He was rich, so that you might become rich by His poverty." He also presents to us the Macedonians, whose "overflowing joy and deep poverty have produced an abundant generosity." And Jesus makes clear that our generosity, our "sharing in the service" of God, must extend beyond our friends. The Father makes no distinction – "His sun rises on the bad and the good, He rains on the just and the unjust" – and so we are challenged "to know the grace of God" completely by giving our love to all, even as Christ's arms are open to everyone as He hangs on the cross.

How is it that poverty produces such generosity? And how can we share in both with our God? The poverty of which the Apostle speaks and which Jesus exemplifies and calls us to follow is the emptying of self of all which is our own, and in the very act of emptying, of giving, is generosity itself. Whether it be a man of riches handing over his money or a man of great love performing acts of kindness, he who has is divesting himself of that which he has to enrich another. We remember that when the woman touched the hem of His garment, Jesus perceived power had gone forth from Him (Mk.5:30). Here is that emptying of love to heal the other. And on the cross, of course, Jesus emptied Himself completely… and so He died.

Should we be afraid, brothers and sisters, of sharing so completely in Jesus' love? Do we think that if we give to others, we will have nothing remaining for ourselves? Is Jesus hanging on the cross the end of the story? No, brothers and sisters, we should not be afraid. We must see, indeed, that the more we give, whether of money or of love, the more we are bound to receive. Do you think that God does not see your generosity? Do you not realize that He rewards those who are His children? Do you think Christ still hangs on the cross?

Come to the holiness of God, brothers and sisters; there is no greater grace on earth. Give of yourselves entirely, love even your enemies, and you shall know in ineffable wonder the surpassing love of God for all. Such is our call and our joy.

O. 11. Wed. (I)

Wednesday
(2Cor.9:6-11; Ps.112:1-4,9; Mt.6:1-6,16-18)

"Keep your deeds of mercy secret,
and your Father who sees in secret will repay you."

In the ground, hidden and secret, the seed is planted. From the womb of the earth it sprouts, and gives its yield. We plant the seed; God provides the seed. And it is through His power that anything which we plant grows and increases. So it is with our generous acts, as well as our prayer and fasting.

"Happy the man who fears the Lord... His generosity shall endure forever." For "He who supplies seed for the sower and bread for the eater will provide in abundance; He will multiply the seed you sow and increase your generous yield." Trusting in Him, we shall know His blessings; and greater blessings than these shall we know and shall others know, who praise God for the gifts He provides. Wonderful it is to behold God's ever-increasing generosity; more wonderful yet to participate in it. It is a fountain welling up to eternal life, in which we are cleansed and made of light.

But let us take to heart the warning of the Lord this day: "Be on guard against performing religious acts for others to see." The world does not see God, it cannot know God. Thus God is termed "hidden" and "secret." And though we are to make God known to the world, we cannot do so unless we exist where He is. In the recesses of our heart, in the quiet, we shall find Him. In the center of our being we must place Him. Closing the doors of our rooms, entering the stillness of our souls... kneeling there we shall find Him. And He shall hear us, and He shall reward us with the blessing of answered prayer, of fruitful yield in His Name. If we do not remain with Him there in secret – even in the midst of the city, even among the distractions of this world – all our actions will be in vain. It does us no good to gain the whole world and lose our souls; and all our good deeds are empty show without Him who is goodness at their core.

"He who sows bountifully will reap bountifully." Let us know the blessing of bearing fruit in God. Let us give generously, knowing that for all the good we do, the Lord will provide yet more seed for us to sow, and we shall reap in abundance His heavenly blessings. If we do all without fanfare, but quietly, humbly, secretly trusting all to His care – the blessing of His presence we shall keep with us, and we shall see our works and our prayers bear fruit in the kingdom of God.

> May God bless all humble souls with His bounty.
> May He reveal Himself to their hearts.

Thursday
(2Cor.11:1-11; Ps.111:1-4,7-8; Mt.6:7-15)

"Your Father knows what you need before you ask Him."

And what we need is to be holy as He is holy. And it is this we ask for in the Lord's Prayer. We simply seek to be like Him, and that all obstacles

227

to holiness be removed from us. And like a loving father He meets our needs.

And Paul is a father to the community at Corinth; he loves them "with the jealousy of God Himself." He has given them in marriage to Christ and is solicitous that the wedding chamber not be corrupted by false doctrine. "Super apostles" have come among them who "win a hearing by the sheer multiplication of words," rattling on like empty wind and taking money from Paul's children for the sound and the fury they bring. But they signify nothing by all their skill; they are but ravenous wolves amidst the flock.

Paul says of himself, "I may be unskilled in speech but I know that I am not lacking in knowledge"; and how his words echo Christ's own, that we should not get lost in mere words. And how like a father knowing and caring for the needs of his children is Paul. In our psalm, too, is reflected the Father's "gracious and merciful" nature which Paul shows to the Corinthians: "Sure are all His precepts… wrought in truth and equity." This knowledge of God is what must be conveyed, and it is this Paul offers the people.

And like a caring father who provides sacrificially for his children, Paul refuses to take return from them for his work: his work among them is a labor of love for which he seeks no recompense. By this they must learn how freely God gives to those who seek Him and be purged of their notion that it is those whom they pay, and greatly, who care for them. Indeed, the Father knows always what we need, and gives it freely to those who simply come as repentant children. He exacts no cost and requires no dramatics to receive His presence and His love.

Forgive my folly here, but why do you turn to the icons and idols of this glamorous age to find the peace you seek, when in His Church the Father waits to answer all your needs? Do not be led astray by the powerful-seeming images which surround us in this day; come to the Lord of all, and before Him in silence kneel and pray:

> "Our Father in heaven,
> hallowed be your name,
> your kingdom come,
> your will be done
> on earth as it is in heaven.
> Give us today our daily bread,
> and forgive us the wrong we have done
> as we forgive those who wrong us.
> Subject us not to the trial
> but deliver us from the evil one."
> Amen.

Friday
(2Cor.11:18,21-30; Ps.34:2-7,18; Mt.6:19-23)

"Store up heavenly treasure, which neither moths nor rust corrode
nor thieves break in and steal."

It is clear where Paul's treasure lies, and where it does not lie. In the litany of the sufferings and afflictions he has endured as a "minister of Christ," we understand without question his utter lack of concern for the things of this world. How could it be otherwise with one who sacrifices himself so completely, readily bearing "labors" and "beatings" at every turn? He gives not only all his possessions, but his very body for the cause of the Gospel. This is where his treasure lies – in Jesus and in His word – and he lays down all of this earth to see that blessed Word planted in the souls of all and grow to eternal life. Beatings and stoning and hunger are as nothing to him; it is "anxiety for all the churches" which causes him the greatest pain.

And now, though the moths and rust of this world could not touch him and he remained untroubled by the thieves who waylay ships at sea, there is another kind of thief who is attempting to break in and steal, to steal that about which he is concerned the most. False prophets have come along to influence his flock, and this corruption of the Word he cannot bear; so in this emotional diatribe he in effect calls on the Lord to open the eyes of the churches.

And it is not only those at Corinth who need to be roused from their stupor of nodding approval to the voices of all who come speaking high-sounding words in God's Name: we today and everywhere must heed the call to be on guard against the thieves who would break into our souls. How strong and knowledgeable must we be in our faith, now with a history of Church teaching behind us – but how weak we often are.

Paul's words were as caustic salve healing the wounds of his people. I pray they may be so now in calling us to right Church teaching. Each day we hear from those preaching the comfort to be taken in earthly treasure as they bow toward the god of this world – let us stand with eyes of holy light and speak of the unfading glory of heaven. On this may our hearts be set, and on the word of Jesus, that all our afflictions will be as so much dust blown away by the wind, by the Spirit of Truth. In Him let us take our refuge.

Saturday

(2Cor.12:1-10; Ps.34:8-13; Mt.6:24-34)

"Seek first His kingship over you, His way of holiness,
and all these things will be given you besides."

The call to treasure in heaven continues.

What care we for the things of this earth? What is money, what are food and clothing to us? Indeed, they must not be our concern. And what matter to us is our bereavement of these things and other like afflictions which the world may inflict upon us. We are called to be like Paul and be "content with weakness, with mistreatment, with distress," yes, even to boast about such weaknesses in the flesh, because we know that when the world attacks us, Jesus comes to save us. "In weakness power reaches perfection," for when we are afflicted we share in the very "power of Christ," which is all we can depend on in such times, and which comes to us without fail. Thus even our persecutions become cause for rejoicing and proclaiming with David, "Taste and see the goodness of the Lord."

There is a weakness we should avoid, however. The beatings which come to us from outside us are indeed an opportunity for celebration; but the weakness of being distracted by the cares of the flesh and its pleasures is not to be ours. The Lord speaks lovingly to such weakness in us in our gospel today, gently calling us away from such preoccupation, for He knows, and states quite clearly, that such distractions will keep us from the gates of heaven. "You cannot give yourself to God and money." We cannot be divided in this way. Our hearts must be set on the holiness of God, trusting even the needs of the flesh to *His* care, in order to come to vision of heaven – in order to know Christ the Lord and the Father to whom He leads us. Jesus is not concerned for these things and neither should we be. Whether we have or not and in what measure should not matter. We must find the vision of the Lord which rejoices even in our utter bereavement of all things of the earth. Indeed, we cannot come to heaven until we die. "Running after these things" will only kill the life of Christ in us; it is death to such concern which will bring us the true life of heaven.

All that we need will be given us, brothers and sisters, if we set our hearts on Christ. The Lord is not blind to our needs. He sees all and is ever near to assist us in all our troubles. "The angel of the Lord encamps around those who fear Him, and delivers them." We shall "want for no good thing" if we but seek His face. Readiness for heaven must now be with us.

Twelfth Week

Monday
(Gn.12:1-9; Ps.33:12-13,18-20,22; Mt.7:1-5)

"The eyes of the Lord are upon those who fear Him."

There is a plank in our own eye; there is but a speck in our brother's. This is what the Lord sees. And this is what we see if we fear the Lord. If we fear the Lord, we remain humble before Him. If we fear the Lord, we will be released from judgment. If we fear the Lord, we indeed will be as Abram, following His blessed commands.

"Abram went as the Lord directed him," our first reading tells us so aptly today. He left his father's house at a word from God and followed wherever God led, his path illumined only by faith. He walked not by his eyes but only by his faith in the Lord's promise to him; the Lord became his eyes and he trusted himself and all his family and all his possessions to these eyes which watched over him. In darkness and in quiet he sets out, the Lord as his only light and His voice as his only guide. Such faith, such blessed faith and humility.

Such faith must we all have, brothers and sisters, for it cannot be otherwise but that the Lord calls each one of us to such faith, to such trust; He calls each of us from our "father's house" to walk with Him alone and find our way in His presence. Do we fear Him? Do we love Him? Are we humble before Him? If so, we will know the path upon which the Lord leads us; we will hear His voice speaking quietly in our ears and in our hearts. And we will follow Him. And He will bless us and fulfill His own call for our lives. He will remove the plank from our eyes and grace us with the ability to remove the speck from others'. He will be our wisdom in teaching, our strength in serving. We will not go forth vainly in our own power, but will know His hand guiding us in all we do, for all will be done in His Name. Then great things will be accomplished in us. Then we become sharers in the promise of Abraham.

The Lord is our God. He watches over. He judges. He leads. All healing and all grace and blessing come from His hand and not our own. Our eyes see only what is before us; His illumine the universe. But we may share in His vision, we may partake of His presence, if we have faith, if we humble ourselves before Him and go as He directs.

And as He blesses us so with His guidance, as we find ourselves coming into His kingdom, let us not fail to build an altar to His Name, let us remember to praise Him for His grace. And we shall find our path sure; and in time we shall come "by stages" to eternal life.

231

Tuesday

(Gn.13:2,5-18; Ps.15:1-5; Mt.7:6,12-14;)

"How narrow is the gate that leads to life, how rough the road,
and how few there are who find it!"

In our first reading today, the way Abram walks with God is contrasted with the path Lot chooses for himself. Though the road seems wide and clear, this gate leads to damnation, and indeed, as our gospel states, is one which is chosen by the traveler himself; whereas the narrow path is one which is found in God.

Lot and Abram could no longer dwell together; their possessions were too great and the tensions were too high among their servants. Taking "no reproach against his neighbor," acting as the just soul spoken of in our psalm, "Abram said to Lot: 'Let there be no strife between you and me,'" and put the whole land at his disposal, offering to take what remained. So "Lot looked about," Scripture tells us, to see what pleased his eyes, and then "chose for himself," again the words of Scripture, that broad expanse of land which he thought would be fruitful for his needs. And where does this decision he takes by the sight of his own eyes lead him? To the depraved, to the reprobate, to the dogs and swine – to the infamous land of Sodom, whose people "were very wicked in the sins they committed against the Lord." To such we are led by our senses.

Once Lot is gone, how is Abram led to his destination – are his feet led by his own eyes as well? No, the Lord comes to Him as guide. It is He who tells him to "set forth and walk about in the land." It is again God and his faith which serve as his light. And what promise there is by way of this path! But what difficulties one must face to attain it.

When Abram arrived at his destination, "he built an altar to the Lord." (In what contrast is this altar to the unholy sacrifices offered at Sodom.) The altar of Abram signifies both the faith of this just man and the sacrifice necessary to walk with God and find the life to which He leads us. We know that Abram's path will be particularly rough, as will be that of his descendants. There will be slavery and wandering in the desert, and once come into the land of promise, it shall not remain with them. Indeed, it is only we now in the Spirit following the coming of Christ for whom that promise is fulfilled. And yet do *we* struggle. And yet every day must we examine our conscience and reform our lives to prepare ourselves to enter that gate which is so narrow. No sin will it accept. No foolish pride can exist in our hearts if we hope to enter life.

The way is rough, but what blessed protection the Lord gives by His guidance; and we "shall never be disturbed" by the trials of this world but come thereby to the sure promise of heaven.

Wednesday
(Gn.15:1-12,17-18; Ps.105:1-4,6-9; Mt.7:15-20)

"Abram put his faith in the Lord,
who credited it to him as an act of righteousness."

In our gospel today, Jesus teaches us, "You can tell a tree by its fruit." And what can we tell of Abram but that he is a bountiful tree, faithful and strong. Indeed, in his faith is his goodness, and in his children, who reach down even unto this day, his blessed fruit is known.

What holy, gentle conversation the Lord has with Abram, coming to him in visions to speak to his soul, to thus nourish this tree which He has planted upon the earth. And how faithful Abram is, patiently awaiting the growth which comes from God. Here, my friends, is the Lord's relationship with man exemplified. This is how we should be with our God... seeking the Lord, asking Him the questions which are upon our hearts, believing Him as He speaks to us – as He surely does. For such is our God to us: coming to us in our fears, reassuring our souls, remaining ever faithful to us as He brings to maturity the fruit He has planted in our spirit. No doubt we should have of His blessing. His promise is sure.

And so with our psalmist we should celebrate; we should "glory in His holy name." For we are "descendants of Abraham," partakers of the faith brought to fulfillment in Jesus, fruit of the tree of life. And the Lord "remembers forever His covenant." This grace we have been given shall never leave us; the life within us shall remain. And in our days, through our time, as we partake of our daily bread, the Lord continually speaks to us and blesses us, bringing our fruit to maturity as we progress and grow in His Name. And we shall look upon our children's children. Our own trees shall indeed bear fruit in His light. We must but remain faithful to Him; we must but keep diligent as Abram who, though "birds of prey swooped down on the carcasses," stayed by his holy sacrifice.

We shall see the false prophets of our age come to naught; we shall see these trees "cut down and thrown into the fire." And we will see and know the rebirth of true doctrine: our Church we will witness in all its heavenly glory. "Fear not!" the Lord says to Abram, and so He speaks to us. Our descendants shall be numerous as the stars. With all the children of God we shall rejoice. Keep faith in your hearts.

Thursday
(Gn.16:1-12,15-16; Ps.106:1-5; Mt.7:21-29)

"Anyone who hears my words but does not put them into practice
is like the foolish man who built his house on sandy ground."

The Lord hears our words and answers our cries, but He is not so interested in these as in our listening to *His* voice and remaining obedient to Him. His desire is that we always strive to do His will; the recounting of our own deeds rings empty in His ears.

It is ten years since the Lord's call and promise to Abram. Abram and Sarai grow old and the word of the Lord has not been fulfilled. Sarai thinks to resolve the problem, taking matters in her own hands, and Abram, faltering in his faith and failing to turn to the Lord for guidance, instead "heeded Sarai's request" to take Hagar as his concubine. And O what shaky ground Abram would stand upon now! O what turmoil would be wrought by his failure to withstand the torrents that come with time! For now the lashing of the winds would only increase; now his sin would bear a son who would be "a wild ass of a man, his hand against everyone," indeed in continual war with his kinsmen. And when the son of the promise does finally come, his children will be subject to the yoke of the descendants of the son of this "Egyptian maid-servant." Four hundred years they themselves will become slaves to her offspring. And persecution shall follow them through the desert and even into the Promised Land. Though yet blessed, they will not come to the fulfillment of the peace of God; only in the New Jerusalem founded in Jesus' blood will the law given as their guide and the promise of the ages be fulfilled in God's sight.

How empty our psalm rings today, for we are reminded by Abram's fault that we do not "do always what is just"; we remember our own failures to patiently wait on the word of the Lord – we have now in mind our own lack of obedience in hearing and following His command. We see the tangled web we weave when we take matters of our life into our own soiled hands.

But this it is necessary to remember: by our own wills nothing is accomplished. We can do nothing except by God. And let us expect no recompense for that which has its beginning and end in the Lord. Our house will be founded firmly only by silent obedience to the authoritative teaching of Christ.

Jesus, forgive us all our wanderings in the thoughts of our own hearts. Redeem all of mankind in your blood; conform us to the will of God. Hear our cry. Make us silent before you. We are your unworthy servants.

Friday
(Gn.17:1,9-10,15-22; Ps.128:1-5; Mt.8:1-4)

"Can Sarah give birth at ninety?"

Abraham laughs to himself as he asks the question; and indeed many scoff at the idea today, or simply choose to reason the possibility away. And can a leper be made clean in an instant, just by a touch of Jesus' hand and the words "Be cured"? Is the arm of God, who created the universe, somehow shortened to such miracles? Why do we think it so? Wherefore our lack of faith?

God appears to this ninety-nine-year-old man and tells him whose wife is barren, in the words of our psalm: "Your wife shall be like a fruitful vine in the recesses of your home; your children like olive plants around your table." And Abraham laughs. (As will Sarah, too, upon hearing such news – thus the name of their child Isaac: "he laughs".) It's an understandable reaction. Who would not find the thought humorous? But Abraham does something more than laugh: he also "prostrates himself" before the Lord, face to the floor. How many of our modern scoffers would do such as this? It *is* human to question, to doubt; but it is godly to humble oneself in faith. There is a world of difference between a laugh of wonder and the scoffing of the skeptic. The latter shall remain barren, never finding the living water that would make him fertile and fruitful; the former by his fear of the Lord opens himself to His favor, to His blessing – and such life-giving breath of blessing will make him bear fruit abundantly.

This humble faith is perfectly evident in the leper as well, and is indeed the catalyst of his healing. We are told the leper "came forward and did Him homage" – falling on his face like Abraham – and said to the Lord, "If you will to do so, you can cure me." First he shows humility, he shows fear of the Lord; then he expresses his faith. Simply put, he believes in the power of God. And so he is healed. He is made whole, more whole indeed than the Pharisees and priests who stand by calculating how this can be.

God does not come to the proud. He does not show Himself to the self-righteous. He cannot. They refuse Him at every turn. To the humble of heart, to the poor in spirit, the Lord is present – and His blessings they receive. And miraculous are they beyond what the eye can see. Amen.

Saturday
(Gn.18:1-15; Lk.1:46-50,53-55; Mt.8:5-17)

"Is anything too marvelous for the Lord to do?"

Our theme again is faith. Do we believe as Abraham, as Mary, as the centurion? Only such trust will save us.

In our first reading the Lord appears to Abraham. We have here the marvelous scene of faith being born, being conceived. Abraham sits patiently, waiting, praying – expectant of the Lord's return to confirm His word to him. Then, "looking up, he saw three men nearby." There is the Lord before him. His reaction is one we all must learn to follow: he does not hesitate an instant. He runs to them, bows before them (even to the ground), and begs them to stay with him that he might serve them. With haste he has food prepared for them, "and he wait[s] on them under the tree while they [eat]"; his eyes "like the eyes of a servant on the hand of his master" (Ps.123:2), he watches their every move to be certain they are well pleased. (In addition to this quote from Psalms, one cannot help but think of Jesus' words to the church at Laodicea in the Book of Revelation (3:20): "Behold, I stand at the door and knock. If anyone hears my voice and opens the door, I will enter his house and dine with him, and he with me.")

As Abraham sits there gazing at the Lord, He speaks to His servant: "Where is your wife, Sarah?" Here comes that which Abraham has been longing to hear. His heart leaps up, and the Lord states His promise in no uncertain terms. Now Sarah laughs. But Abraham is no longer laughing. The Lord tests him with the question, "Why did Sarah laugh?" to show to Abraham that he no longer thinks the promise too marvelous for the Lord to fulfill. The Lord repeats the promise. Abraham believes to the depths of his soul; He knows the word spoken to him is of truth. And he shall take his wife in fruitful embrace.

How appropriate to hear Mary's Magnificat in our daily bread, she who is the handmaiden of the Lord, who believed the words of the angel and so found the greatest blessing of the Lord and the fulfillment of the promise to Abraham. How like Mary, the model of all the faithful, has her father Abraham come to be.

And, of course, our gospel finds Jesus marveling at the faith of the Roman centurion, greater than any He has found in Israel. It bodes well that all of faith shall be found at table in the kingdom of God, but we must heed Jesus' warning that "the natural heirs will be driven out." For we are the heirs of the Israelites. As Catholics we now hold the covenant. We have the apostolic succession, the sacraments, the teaching – all the gifts are ours. But have we the faith necessary to gain entrance into His kingdom; are we prepared to come to His table and dine with Him who feeds us with the food of everlasting life? Do we believe? This question the Lord puts on all our souls. How shall we answer?

Thirteenth Week

Monday
(Gn.18:16-33; Ps.103:1-4,8-11; Mt.8:18-22)

"While the two men walked on farther toward Sodom,
the Lord remained standing before Abraham."

"Then Abraham drew nearer to Him..."

A marvelous scene. First, as Abraham walks along with the Lord, we hear the Lord's thoughts. The Lord wishes to share His plans with him, not to act apart from His blessed one. He tells Abraham of the imminent destruction of Sodom, knowing he will be concerned for his kinsman, Lot. The Lord then stops and stands still, granting Abraham opportunity to speak. In great humility, but with the strength provided by God, he petitions the Lord. And the Lord is pleased to hear him. He is pleased that Abraham recognizes the justice of God, and He is satisfied with his fear in approaching Him: "I am but dust and ashes!" exclaims Abraham, and comes to each question with trepidation, pausing in silence before each to hear in that silence the Lord calling him to ask further. The Lord hears and answers his prayer to spare Lot.

Evident in this scene is the psalmist's words: "Merciful and gracious is the Lord." How patient and kind and forbearing. How He desires that we draw near to Him and share in His will. And how forgiving is He: "He pardons all your iniquities... He redeems your life from destruction." For Lot He shall spare from that evil land; indeed, to all who repent He shows His favor. His promise is sure.

But we must come to Him in the humility of Abraham. We must not approach Him as does the scribe in our gospel, proclaiming so boldly and so foolishly his willingness to follow Jesus, yet knowing nothing of the glory of God and what following Him entails. Nor must we come so shakily as the disciple who makes excuses. Upon hearing of the difficulties, he attempts to put off following Christ for a time... There is but one time with God, and it is present, and it is now. We must come to Him in humility and find the strength His grace provides as He draws us to Himself.

There is a time to speak, brothers and sisters – a time to speak and a manner of speaking. It is not right to speak until the Lord stops to listen. We must wait on Him and His grace. One does not burst into the court of a king unannounced proclaiming his loyalty to Him who sits on the throne. One waits until called and then pours out one's heart, trusting in the compassion of the Lord.

237

It is His desire to share with us all His works. It is His pleasure to hear our good prayers. But let us realize to whom we speak and come in true faith and humility; and He will hear and answer all our petitions, and we will become sharers in His promised glory.

Tuesday
(Gn.19:15-29; Ps.26:2-3,9-12; Mt.8:23-27)

"Even the winds and the sea obey Him."

"The Lord rained down sulphurous fire upon Sodom and Gomorrah," and "without warning a violent storm came up on the lake, and the boat began to be swamped by the waves." The Lord saved Lot from the destruction of Sodom, and Jesus calmed the winds and the sea, saving the disciples; but how little faith either showed in His power.

Lot seems oblivious to the annihilation about to be wrought by God, hesitating to flee even at the urging of angels. Indeed, he is brought from that place only by force and "by the Lord's mercy," by all appearances deserving to be swept away with the others in their sin. Then upon being carried the greater part of the way, he is too tired to complete the salvation the Lord has begun. And as for the apostles, they quickly dissemble at the threat of the elements, forgetting entirely in whose hands all these forces rest. Indeed, where Lot fails in proper fear for his own protection, the disciples are filled too greatly with concern for their mortal lives. Neither has the holiness or faith necessary for eternal glory.

"Gather not my soul with those of sinners," we should all cry out to the Lord, for indeed we all fall short of the glory of God; and if it were not for His mercy and protection, all would die in their sins. But He has the power to save us, and the kindness besides. Only let us not presume upon His mercy, nor fail to stand strong in His grace and faith. We have one greater than Abraham watching over us and interceding for us with God; let us no longer question His will for us or wonder who it is that controls the wind and the sea, the earth and the fire. Now we should know clearly that these obey Him, and that we must do the same.

Brothers and sisters, can we say to the Lord with David: "Test my soul and try my heart"? Are we prepared to expose ourselves to His refining fire? Would we "walk in integrity" with this son of Jesse, crying out to the Lord, "Redeem me, and have pity on me." If we come to Him and lay our lives before Him, He will certainly enter in and preserve us from all distress. His voice shall resound about us and within us, calming the wind and the waves contending in our hearts. Remember that He has the power.

Remember that He, only He, is alive. And by His grace He will save our lives.

Wednesday
(Gn.21:5,8-20; Ps.34:7-8,10-13; Mt.8:28-34)

"When the afflicted man called out, the Lord heard,
and from all his distress He saved him."

Ishmael is the model of the afflicted man calling out to the Lord and being heard in all his distress. His very name means "he whom God hears" and indeed we see clearly today how, though "it is through Isaac that descendants shall bear [Abraham's] name," nonetheless, the Lord has pity on Ishmael and his plight – his rejection by the mother of the promised child and his wandering in a trackless waste – and declares that of him a "great nation" shall come. Indeed he is left to die by his mother, so desperate had their situation become; but upon the child's crying out, the Lord hears and sends His angel to assist them and assure them of the boy's future greatness.

Ishmael is a son of Abraham; though born of a slave woman, yet "he too is [Abraham's] offspring," and so for this the Lord takes special care to watch over him. For God has chosen Abraham to be the father of many nations and does not wish to see His blessed patriarch distressed. We have already seen how God has heard the prayer of Abraham for Lot; now we see the same regarding Abraham's concern for Ishmael.

We must, brothers and sisters, understand whence our own blessing comes. We are spiritual sons of Abraham, of Moses, of David... but most particularly we are children of Jesus and His apostles, the Church. A far greater intercessor have we in the Son of God Himself, so let us not be afraid to cry out to Him in our need. For if God heard the prayers of Abraham, how much more will He hear the prayers of His Son? And if God watched over the kin and offspring of the blessed patriarch, how much more concern does He have for the children of light born of the blood of Jesus Christ?

Our confidence must be sure in Him, for He cannot help but hear our prayer. Indeed, our gospel tells us that when "the demons kept appealing to Him," even them He heard and granted their plea. If the Lord hears such as these, how can we even begin to doubt His presence to us? Now let us not be afraid to come to Him. Let us not be like the inhabitants of that Gadarene territory who found the Lord too much to bear and "begged Him to leave their neighborhood." Let us not think in our hearts coming to Him we will die, that His light is simply too bright. No. He calls us as children to take refuge in Him.

239

It is His desire to bless our days. Turn not away from Him, for as David sings for us, "Those who seek the Lord want for no good thing"; He hears and answers all our cries.

Thursday
(Gn.22:1-19; Ps.115:1-6,8-9; Mt.9:1-8)

"God put Abraham to the test."

And so is his faith in the living God made known. And so we see to what faith and obedience we are called. All that we hold back from the Lord, all that is due our God – and our neighbor – we must give without hesitation at the voice of His command.

In Leviticus 5, a ram is prescribed as the sacrifice for those who have withheld their tithe, who have shorted the Lord of His due offering. And the same is prescribed for those who cheat their neighbor of what is justly theirs. It is a ram Abraham finally offers "in place of his son," to satisfy the sacrifice called for by the Lord. And what the Lord teaches us in this passage is that, really, what is due to Him is beyond our ability to pay. Not only are our children in His hands (and any other blessings), but our very lives as well are His – all comes to us only as a gift of His love. And His greatest gift shall be His only Son, whom He shall offer without reservation, not withholding Him from such sacrifice on the cross, that what is due Him may be fulfilled by Him, since it is beyond our ability to do so.

Isaac carried the wood of his own sacrifice to "the place of which God had told [Abraham]" to travel. He is as the unknowing sheep led to his own slaughter and is a sign of the Christ who will carry the wood of His own cross, without a word, to His own crucifixion. How can we understand all this? What a test it puts us to! Abraham prepares to slaughter the son of the promise; by the Father's will Jesus is nailed to a cross like the worst of criminals... How can the mind of man fathom the workings and will of God? The question seems overwhelming but the answer is simple – and it is but that we trust in Him and in His love.

In our gospel, "when Jesus saw [the] faith" of the people in "His own town," He was moved to forgive the sins of the paralytic; and in the same breath, by the same power, to heal him. The scribes were indignant at His presumption to forgive sins. "Why do you harbor evil thoughts?" Jesus asks, putting them to the test before revealing to them the authority given Him. And are not their thoughts like our own? Are not their doubts and questions and, indeed, presumptions not like our own hesitation and refusal to come to faith in God and trust in His will and His love? Are not their fears like our own in coming to the foot of the cross and partaking of His blood?

Our psalm makes clear that our God is a loving God, not one of wood or metal, and it is life He desires for His children. Jesus makes clear God's desire for us to be healed, to be whole in His sight – and His beneficence in "giving such authority to men" to effect this desire (particularly in the Sacrament of Confession); we must not think He is otherwise, and we must be prepared to give Him our very lives. For how else shall we come to life but by giving all to Him who holds all in His loving hands? Have faith and trust in Him, brothers and sisters, and obey His command. It brings only life.

Friday
(Gn.23:1-4,19,24:1-8,62-67; Ps.106:1-5; Mt.9:9-13)

"In his love for [Rebekah] Isaac found solace
after the death of his mother Sarah."

And of this love Jacob shall be born; and from him shall come the twelve tribes of Israel, who shall people the earth as the fulfillment of the promise to Abraham.

Sarah had died and "Abraham had now reached a ripe old age." Now conscious of his mortality, Abraham sets his sights firmly on his son and his coming progeny. Now with great resolve he sets to seek a wife for Isaac, telling his servant as he sends him to his people: the Lord "will send His messenger before you, and you will obtain a wife for my son there." And Abraham's faith in God's promise is rewarded, as the servant is led directly to Rebekah. And how inspired is the meeting of Isaac and Rebekah. We are told they are both looking about for one another, and seem to recognize each other immediately, even from a great distance. Indeed, they are brought together by God to fulfill His promise to Abraham.

Notice in our gospel that Jesus seems to be looking around as well: "As Jesus moved about, He saw a man named Matthew at his post where taxes are collected." Like Abraham, Jesus, too, is concerned for His progeny, for those who will follow Him – those who will bring His promise of salvation forth when He has returned to the Father. And He chooses Matthew as an apostle to follow Him. And notice Matthew's response to Jesus' call: "Matthew got up and followed Him." It seems here, too, the love is mutual, that Matthew, too, has been looking about for the Lord, and that the two are drawn together by the Father to ensure the fulfillment of the covenant with His Son. And Jesus, who has just come from public forgiveness of sin, seems not so much to be speaking to the Pharisees' complaining of His eating with sinners, as to Matthew, whom He's calling to carry out His mission of teaching and healing, when He says: "I have come to call, not the self-righteous, but sinners."

The word goes forth. The promise is sure. It comes to us even this day. The Lord provides for its care and will see it through to its fulfillment. In each one of us His salvation is at work even now. Brothers and sisters, mourn not so much for the sin which troubles your heart as you accept the Lord's solace and rejoice in His mercy. With the psalmist, say to the Lord: "Visit me with your saving help, that I may see the prosperity of your chosen ones." Amen.

O. 13. Sat. (I)

Saturday
(Gn.27:1-5,15-29; Ps.135:1-6; Mt.9:14-17)

"Pour new wine into new wineskins,
and in that way both are preserved."

"Jacob." The name means "the supplanter". Here he supplants his twin brother, Esau, whose name means "red earth". Though born second, Jacob receives the blessing of the firstborn. Of what significance is this supplanting, is this blessing of Jacob, who is to be "Israel", and from whom the twelve tribes shall proceed? Far more than some sibling rivalry, it shows the coming of the New Covenant of the spirit which shall supplant the Old of the flesh.

It is not the will of Isaac to bless Jacob; his love is for Esau – who before this time has forfeited his birthright to Jacob in order to feed his hungry belly. But Isaac is blind. He is blind because he, too, is a natural man, a man of the flesh seeking to feed *his* belly. And so the Lord inspires Rebekah to intercede, to see that His will is accomplished. Notice please the words of Isaac when Jacob comes to him dressed in the hairy skin of a beast and the clothes of Esau: "Although the voice is Jacob's, the hands are Esau's." Indeed, the voice is of the spirit; the skin he feels is of the flesh. And the Word must go to the word, the Spirit to the spirit; and so it is Jacob who must receive the blessing, despite the will of Isaac.

And how is Isaac brought to do the Father's will? He is deceived by his own preoccupation with the flesh, with the old wineskin. Upon eating his fill, and drinking his fill of the old wine, he is blinded further. And smelling the clothes of Esau he is inspired to pronounce his blessing. But what Esau possesses in his clothes, Jacob holds in his spirit – this fragrance is that which rises to the nostrils of the Lord. And it is *His* will which must be done. He chooses the spiritual man.

242

And in our gospel, too, we see the blindness of the natural man in his preoccupation with the flesh. John's disciples, like the Pharisees – whose stomachs growl from fasts in which they find no blessing – looked jealously upon the disciples of Jesus, who do not have to endure the penance which is so tedious to these men removed from the Spirit. But in Jesus is the blessing of the Spirit, reflected in God's choosing of Jacob, here fulfilled in the sight of men whose eyes need yet to be opened to its grace.

The new wine is of the Spirit of God, brothers and sisters; we drink it each day in the blood of Christ. Let it not be poured into skins that yet look upon the world with eyes of flesh; rather, be made new as it calls you to be, and preserve your soul unto heaven. It is the Spirit which gives life; the flesh is of no avail.

Fourteenth Week

Monday
(Gn.28:10-22; Ps.91:1-4,14-15; Mt.9:18-26)

"Know that I am with you;
I will protect you wherever you go."

What the Lord says here to Jacob, He says indeed to all of us: He will protect us on our journey; let us but take refuge in Him. Our dearest Jesus is the abode of God, and in Him our souls are safe.

As Jacob sets forth alone from the land of Canaan, he fears that he shall not return to this place of His promised inheritance. But the Lord comes to him in a dream to stand "beside him" and assure him that the promise is firm: "I will never leave you until I have done what I promised you." With these words of encouragement and the vision of heaven's ladder still in his mind, Jacob cries out in "solemn wonder" of that place in which the Lord revealed Himself to His servant. He sets up a memorial stone, thereby to mark "God's abode."

Our psalm today sings of the Lord's protection upon those who trust in Him. He answers our call in distress, rescues us from "the snare of the fowler," and gives us refuge. Thus we "dwell in the shelter of the Most High," abiding in His shadow, covered by His wings of blessed protection. "Because he clings to me, I will deliver him," says our psalmist in the voice of the Lord; and indeed we know that trusting in Him is our salvation.

And in our gospel we discover where such refuge lies; we find Him who is the true house of God, and we are shown the faith which is necessary to make our home there. What Jesus says to the woman, He says to His whole Church: "Courage, daughter! Your faith has restored you to health." Her great faith told her she needed but to "touch his cloak," but to press up against the walls of the temple that is Christ to find healing. And the synagogue leader states simply and clearly *his* faith in the Lord: "My daughter has just died. Please come and lay your hand on her and she will come back to life." Yes, indeed the protection of the Lord, the refuge and strength He is to us in our faith, reaches beyond the grave.

Our own journeys can be arduous, brothers and sisters. At times it can seem as if the Lord is leaving us, as if He is far away. Faith. Faith, brothers and sisters, will see us through all difficulties, even death. We are destined to rise with Him on the last day; we are blessed here now along the way. Jesus is the ladder which leads to heaven; He Himself is the House of God. With faith in Him and in His protection, let us climb with the angels to His abode.

Today in our hearts let us set up for Him a memorial stone, that we might remember His sacred presence. For now we do more than touch the tassel of His cloak; He enters us and we enter Him whole.

O. 14. Tues. (I)

Tuesday
(Gn.32:23-33; Ps.17:1-3,6-8,15; Mt.9:32-38)

"You test my heart, searching it in the night."

"You have contended with divine and human beings," the angel says of Jacob; and so he receives his new name, Israel: "he strives with God". Such striving with the Lord in this night which has set upon the earth is our lot in life. May we prevail upon Him as has Jacob.

As he is about to reenter the Promised Land after fourteen years away, fearful for what awaits – particularly in the face of the potential anger of his brother Esau, whose birthright and blessing he has assumed – Jacob sets himself apart from all things and alone prepares to confront the Lord. We are told he wrestles all the night with a "man," for indeed as such does God appear to him through His messenger. In contending with the Lord, Jacob remains strong and earns the blessing of his new name. He is a worthy combatant in the struggle to know God in this life, and so, "on waking" the next morning, as he goes forth at dawn, he is "content" in God's presence; he is prepared for any danger which lies before him. And reconciliation with Esau he shall find. And the father of the Israelites he has become.

How much easier it is for us to behold the face of God, to come to know Him whom our souls long to see, now that Christ has come. And yet the struggle goes on; it is not over, but rather finds a certain intensification through clarification in the shadow of the cross. We see in our gospel how Jesus Himself struggles. His children are "like sheep without a shepherd,"

244

"lying prostrate from exhaustion," and He must become exhausted as they, as He tours their towns, constantly teaching and preaching and healing all their infirmities – and all this while being accused of doing the work of "the prince of demons" by those in the role of leaders. The struggle Jesus undergoes is most evident in His entreaty to His disciples: "Beg the harvest master to send out laborers to gather His harvest." Jesus desperately needs assistance.

The Lord shall find assistance in His apostles; they, too, shall carry the cross of Christ, laying down their lives for the building up of the Church. But all of us are indeed called under the cross; all of us are beckoned into the struggle for souls, the divine and human drama that is our lot in this world. But first we must be tested, as will be Peter and the apostles; for we must be tried in His holy fire to be purified of any "malice" and "deceit" which clings to us, and so be prepared to enter the struggle, to labor in the fields – to meet our destiny which lies in the heart of our Lord.

There we shall find comfort, but here the dark night is upon us as we strive with God to be made perfect in His sight. May the dawn break upon us and we go forth at His side.

O. 14. Wed. (I)

Wednesday
(Gn.41:55-57,42:5-7,17-24; Ps.33:2-3,10-11,18-19,22; Mt.10:1-7)

"The eyes of the Lord are upon those who fear Him."

In our gospel, Jesus commissions the twelve apostles to go forth after "the lost sheep of the house of Israel" in order "to expel unclean spirits and cure sickness and disease of every kind" and bring His people into "the reign of God." In our first reading, we see that "famine had gripped the whole world," and the lost and hungry sheep of Israel, the sons of Jacob themselves come to Egypt and their forsaken brother Joseph to find food, to find healing for their ills. They have sinned terribly against Joseph, and against God, by selling their younger brother into slavery because of their jealousy of him. Now that God has favored him who was so forsaken, he stands above them with their very lives in his hands, holding not only their food as procurator of Egypt, but also with the power to cast them into prison, or to release them.

Do we see the similarity between Joseph and Jesus? Jesus is the Son of David, the Son of Man, the Savior of the nation of Israel and, in the flesh, one of their own – their favored Son. And He who will be forsaken and sold to the Romans for crucifixion, He whose elder brothers will betray Him into the power of this world, is He who holds their, and our, very lives in His hands. It is when He opens His hands that they are fed; when He says the word, they, and we, are cast into prison – or released. By His word all demons are expelled and all infirmities healed. He indeed has every right to cast our souls into everlasting prison and torment; but, like Joseph, He takes pity on those who have wounded Him: like Joseph, we know that "He wept."

But His weeping does not come automatically. Just as with Joseph, it is prompted by the repentance of His brothers, who have so despised him but now recognize their sin and bewail it to the Lord. His forgiveness and His healing – His salvation – come to those who in like manner "fear Him." Upon these the Lord looks with pity. With these Jesus Himself cries. For these the Lord sends forth His apostles, to heal them and call them into the reign of God. As for the repentant, He will indeed "deliver them from death and preserve them in spite of famine." These lost sheep He will save.

And "the plan of the Lord stands forever": it reaches to us this day. It is eternal, for all who fear Him, in whatever time or place. His word extends now to the ends of the earth, to the twelve tribes of Israel and beyond. Founded firmly in the Twelve (apostles), it now comes to the ears of all mankind. Let us repent even this day, brothers and sisters, be healed, and be fed by the hand of God.

Thursday
(Gn.44:18-21,23-29,45:1-5; Ps.105:5,16-21; Mt.10:7-15)

"It was really for the sake of saving lives
that God sent me here ahead of you."

Remarkable words from the mouth of Joseph as the brothers who sold him into slavery in Egypt stand dumbfounded before him, fearing indeed for their own lives. And indeed Joseph may have been justified to command the ending of their lives to avenge his treatment at their hands. But the Lord has looked with favor upon him who had been "bound with chains," raising him up to be lord of Pharaoh's house and "ruler of all his possessions," and Joseph rightfully attributes such blessing to God and sees His hand at work in all this matter. Here is the great example of trust in God's providential care. And Joseph has but a deep love for his brothers, and will now care for their lives and that of his father.

The same trust in God's providence is asked of the disciples in our gospel. Jesus sends them forth with "no traveling bag, no change of shirt, no sandals, no walking staff," telling them, "Provide yourselves with neither gold nor silver nor copper in your belts": "the workman, after all, is worth his keep," and God will always provide for those who serve Him.

Certainly a great lesson is in this for all of us. Do we have such trust in God? Joseph says that it is God who has, in effect, sold him into slavery that he might later be made a leader in Egypt and save his family from famine, this despite the fact that his own brothers have treated him with such disdain. Do we have such a blessed view of the trials which come our way? Can we see them as the hand of God working, and working for the good? Can we forgive so beautifully those by whom the trials come? Have we such vision that sees the hand of God at work in all things? "All things work for good for those who love God, who are called according to His purpose," Paul tells us elsewhere (Rm.8:28). Can we give all things which happen to us to God and trust that His will shall be done, is done, in them all?

Where is our trust? Is it in money and the things of this world? Do we think that these things will provide for us, will make us happy, will keep us satisfied – are these our gods? Or do we seek and accept the reign of God which the Lord tells us is at hand? Do we receive well His message of peace, His blessing of God's love and care, or do we expel Him from our homes? And do we share His free gift with others?

There is great "famine on the land," a famine of the hearing of God's word and trusting in His hand. Let us come to the Son who has accepted scourging in the will of His Father and find all we need from Him who now sits on His throne. Believe that He does provide, and all will indeed be yours. And your trials will be turned to joy.

O. 14. Fri. (I)

Friday
(Gn.46:1-7,28-30; Ps.37:3-4,18-19,27-28,39-40; Mt.10:16-23)

> "Do not be afraid to go down to Egypt,
> for there I will make you a great nation."

We are as exiles in this world. Indeed, the Lord sends us forth "like sheep among wolves." In Egypt must we dwell for a time, until we are prepared for the coming of Christ.

But here He meets us. Here He weeps over us and so enables us to face the death which is upon us, which indeed surrounds us in this foreign land. Even in our trials, in all our persecutions, He is there: He suffers with us, and we with Him. And His Spirit is very present to lead us; it burns in our hearts to guide us, giving us the words we must speak, assuring us that Jesus is with us in all we do.

As Israel sets forth for Egypt, he is fearful. But he calls upon the Lord in his sacrifices, and in vision once again God comes to him, providing His assurance, His continued blessing. David's psalm speaks so well of the protection and blessing which is ours in this land of exile: "The Lord watches over the lives of the wholehearted; their inheritance lasts forever. The salvation of the just is from the Lord; He is their refuge in time of distress." Yes, He is our refuge in this land where we walk as exiles, in this world which would persecute the Word of God, pursuing it to kill it, to destroy it. But it is even in Egypt that a great nation shall be made of Israel; here, even under slavery, the people of God shall multiply and prosper. And so it is with us who follow Jesus: here in this world of persecution we are refined and made whole, as individuals and as a people; here under the threat of death we come to life, for His gentle yoke is upon us, and in Him we find refuge and even joy in all our sufferings. By undergoing persecution in His Name, we draw so very close to Him; and laying down our lives we find the great love which is without end.

Jesus speaks to us; the Spirit is here with us. There is no need to fear. "Trust in the Lord and do good, that you may dwell in the land and enjoy security." Have faith in the word He speaks to your hearts and be assured that He watches over you here in this land of exile, not only protecting you from the wolves that surround you, but even increasing your blessings all the while. Your home in heaven is assured; see that Jesus is alive now and dwelling with you and you shall be able to close your eyes in peace, knowing all your brothers and sisters, mothers and fathers, sons and daughters, you will see again when the Lord brings you to the land of promise.

Saturday
(Gn.49:29-32,50:15-24; Ps.105:1-4,6-7,33; Mt.10:24-33)

"Whoever acknowledges me before men
I will acknowledge before my Father in heaven."

Joseph does well in acknowledging God before his brothers, as, refusing to take revenge on them, he states of his suffering that "God meant it for good." He thus proves himself a servant of the Lord; realizing that "no pupil outranks his teacher, no slave his master," he asks, "Can I take the place of God?" and so simultaneously accepts the scourgings that come with being a servant of his "father's God." Indeed, further applying the Lord's words to the apostles in our gospel to Joseph, we know that it has been his proclaiming before the world, before Pharaoh himself, the dreams the Lord has spoken to him in the secret of his room that has brought Joseph to this position of eminence wherein he can so dutifully and kindly provide for "the survival of many people." And so, as he prepares to die, as this sparrow falls – even as his father before him "drew his feet into the bed, breathed his last, and was taken to his kindred" – his life ends with confidence that the Lord will acknowledge him before the Father of all, as well as with the faith that his children shall be blessed and come into the land promised them by Him who holds both body and soul in His all-powerful hands.

And what of our own witness? Have we the forgiveness of Joseph, which is the forgiveness of God? Do we "seek to serve Him constantly" and "proclaim all His wondrous deeds," as our psalmist encourages us today? Are we true pupils of this great teacher, faithful to our call to live and to die in His light? Or are we afraid for the body and judging by the dictates of this earthly life?

These are questions we must ask ourselves each day, for each day and at every moment our souls are required of us, lest we die for want of the Bread which comes to us by His holy hands. The Lord holds our life's breath in His hand and "every hair of [our] head has been counted" by Him, so indeed we should fear Him. But that fear is born and finds recompense in love; the fear that comes from the world and its power brings only death to our bodies and souls. Let us simply recognize the truth of His presence and His power to all we meet, to all for whom we are responsible, and our salvation and the blessing of our progeny will be assured. And so with confidence, with faith of the Holy Spirit, we shall die and come to life, this day, and in eternity.

> Lord, make us true servants of your love;
> and gather us into the bosom of Abraham
> and into your sacred heart.

Fifteenth Week

Monday
(Ex.1:8-14,22; Ps.124:1-8; Mt.10:34-11:1)

"The more they were oppressed, the more they multiplied and spread."

The Israelites lived and worked side by side with the Egyptians for some four hundred years; they had virtually become members of the same household. But jealousy overcame a "new king" of Egypt, who determined "to oppress them with forced labor," hoping to break their will as well as their backs. But they only grew stronger because, as our psalm tells us so vividly, the Lord was with them: "Had not the Lord been with us... when men rose up against us, then would they have swallowed us alive." And, quite literally, "then would the waters have overwhelmed" them, for it was commanded that their newborn males be thrown into the river. But the Lord *was* with them, and through all this oppression they only grew stronger.

The Israelites stand as an example for our own faith and its struggle with the world today. Jesus tells us in our gospel that peace shall not be found with the earth, and even those of our own flesh, by following His call. Indeed, He has come, "in short, to make a man's enemies those of His own household." How true this was for the first Christians, all of whom were Jews, and all of whom would find resistance and even persecution for following this way in which Jesus calls us. Division among the family must have been common. But it is no less true today that a man who truly seeks to follow the way of the Lord will meet with the same resistance, even from those who profess to be Catholic and Christian (even from within himself), because the same jealousy the Egyptians had toward the Israelites exists now, and always will, and the same fears the Jews had of Christ also will not easily pass away. The world is ever in opposition to the cross, yet knowing this, Jesus emphasizes that "he who will not take up his cross and come after [Him] is not worthy of [Him]." We are eternally called to turn from the world, in all its forms, and lay down our lives and our wills.

But we are not alone in this mission to overcome the sins of the world. As the Lord was with the Israelites, He is certainly with us. Following Him so closely, it cannot but be that He is near at our sides. And not only He and His Spirit but His people as well are present to us in this struggle we undertake. We do have brothers and sisters in the struggle; there are many who give us "a cup of cold water" along the way. Still the Lord is ever here to help us; still when the world seems to overwhelm us, we are "rescued like a bird from the fowler's snare." Still we grow stronger through all the oppression we endure. Let us praise the Lord for His saving power upon us. Let us continually recommit our lives to His mission on earth, placing Him even before family and friends, and in the losing of our lives we shall come to life and ever grow in His eternal light.

> Strengthen us, O Lord,
>> under the burden of work we endure for you;
>> help us to carry our cross.
> And may we multiply and spread in your Name.

Tuesday
(Ex.2:1-15; Ps.69:3,14,30-31,33-34; Mt.11:20-24)

"I drew him out of the water."

Moses was drawn from "the watery depths" by Pharaoh's daughter and nursed by his own mother. Into the river all male Hebrew children were ordered cast, but by the providential hand of God, this "Moses" is saved.

250

And it is through him his people shall be drawn out from amongst the Egyptians and the slavery put upon them; and it is by the Law spoken through him that those who believe are kept from "the abysmal swamp where there is no foothold," that one finds release from the bonds of sin.

But now Moses' zealous concern for his people has caused him to slay an Egyptian, so he must flee from the face of Pharaoh who seeks to kill him for his offense. And what irony is there that having fought one day for a Hebrew oppressed by an Egyptian, the next day he finds two Hebrews fighting! And what apparent lack of appreciation for his concern for their plight – he who has no fear of being enslaved, living in Pharaoh's palace as he does – do the Hebrews show. How similar is this lack of appreciation to the cities which Jesus reproaches for "their failure to reform" at His preaching and at the miracles He has worked among them. Here is an even greater than Moses, the very Son of God, coming to heal them of all their ills and bring them eternal salvation, but they refuse to turn from their sins that they might find such blessing. What hope is there for them? If the power of God cannot convince them, then indeed the flood shall overwhelm them and they "shall go down to the realm of death," for they refuse to be drawn up out of their sins.

O that this not be said of us, brothers and sisters! We indeed have been drawn out of the water. Baptized by the Spirit who moves upon the waters and nourished at the breast of holy Mother Church, eating the Lord's own Body and Blood and ever finding forgiveness for our sins by his priests' commission, we have been graced with all we need to be led from the darkness of this world, from the abysmal swamp where there is no foothold. We must be ever mindful not to slip back into the watery mire of sin to which this world would draw us and lose the blessing the Lord has provided us to maintain us for the day of judgment. Great miracles the Lord has worked in us; great miracles He works for us this day. Let us never fail to reform our lives and conform ourselves to His grace. Our own death sentence has been removed, washed from us by the blood of Christ; let us not fall again into the swamp of sin, but ever rise to the glory of God.

O. 15. Wed. (I)

Wednesday

(Ex.3:1-6,9-12; Ps.103:1-4,6-8; Mt.11:25-27)

"An angel of the Lord appeared to him
in fire flaming out of a bush."

The Lord appears to Moses. "The God of Abraham, the God of Isaac, the God of Jacob," reveals Himself on Horeb, the mountain of God. He comes to him who, as we are told elsewhere, is the humblest of men, calling

251

him – much as He will later call Peter, James, and John from their nets to be fishers of men – from "leading the flock across the desert" to lead His people out of slavery, out of Egypt, through the desert and to the Promised Land.

In our gospel, Jesus tells us that the Father reveals Himself "to the merest children," not to "the learned and the clever." And so He has come here to Moses, a man whose speech is weak but whose heart is indeed humble as a child, to call him to be the greatest, most godly of men, and to this great task set before him. Like John the Baptist after him – who will be the greatest of men born of woman – he is entirely deferential to the Lord. Here he hides his face, "afraid to look at God," and questions sincerely: "Who am I that I should go to Pharaoh and lead the Israelites out of Egypt?" Such as these the Lord calls; to such as these He reveals Himself. These are they "to whom the Son wishes to reveal" the Father.

"Merest children." Only to these does the Lord reveal Himself. Only to those whose hearts are pure, who take no pride in themselves. In a word, "humble" must we be. "He has made known His ways to Moses, and His deeds to the children of Israel." To them He will show that "the Lord secures justice and the rights of all the oppressed." And as their lives are redeemed from destruction, they will "bless His holy name." Of the kindness of the Lord the earth is filled, but only those who come as children before Him will know "all His benefits." Only those who humble themselves before Him will be raised up to see His glory and live in the light of His presence.

O Jesus, we pray that you will reveal the Father to us. We pray that our hearts will be circumcised and that we will ever bow before the glory that is God. Bring the fire of the Holy Spirit upon us to purge all our iniquity and prepare us to hear your voice, O Word of God. Call us forth to do your will and lead us ever to your holy mountain, that always we might be in your presence, that forever we might worship you in spirit and in truth, as merest children, as sons and daughters of your eternal light. May we never be consumed by sin or the vestiges of our pride, but be brought to life by the grace and power of God. Show us your face and let us indeed live in the light of its holy fire.

O. 15. Thurs. (I)

Thursday
(Ex.3:11-20; Ps.105:1,5,8-9,24-27; Mt.11:28-30)

"My yoke is easy and my burden light."

I AM has come and led His people "up out of the misery of Egypt," up out of slavery. The heavy yoke of sin He breaks from our necks, and in its place we find His gentle presence.

How this world can make us weary! How the Israelites suffered under the iron hand of the Pharaoh. But the Lord says to them, "I am concerned about you and about the way you are being treated in Egypt." And He says to us the same: "Come to me, all you who are weary and find life burdensome, and I will refresh you." To Moses as proof of His presence He even gives His NAME, the silent WORD – "YHWH" – which speaks volumes of His being here and everywhere always: "I AM WHO AM." That gentle, all-present Spirit, that WORD that is Life, is made known to us now in Jesus, the WORD made flesh, He who is "gentle and humble of heart." And so salvation is fulfilled: release from slavery ultimately comes in the gentle yoke of the Son of God. Let us place it upon our shoulders.

I repeat, this world can be burdensome. As it works its way into our hearts and souls, it brings terrible chains which bind us. As the culture of death which surrounds us in this land of exile finds inroads into our homes and penetrates our minds, it can bring a slavish weight to bear. But though the prince of this world and his subjects might harden their hearts against the emancipating Word of God, though they might refuse to allow us to worship our God freely and with all our beings and belongings... yet the Lord "remembers forever His covenant"; from age to age His word is true. And He shall not be lacking for "wondrous deeds," "portents," and "judgments" to assure His people's freedom, to assure their coming gently and wholly into His sacred presence.

"I will stretch out my hand," the Lord tells us. He will stretch forth His hand and break the yoke from our backs with a word from His mouth. And rest shall be ours. Eternal rest in His sacred presence, in the light of His holy face, is inevitably ours as we follow in His humble ways.

Come, brothers and sisters. Fear not Pharaoh. The evil upon us is passing away; only what is real, only what is of His Word – only I AM shall remain. Take His yoke upon you, and be led gently forth.

O. 15. Fri. (I)

Friday
(Ex.11:10-12:14; Ps.116:12-13,15-18; Mt.12:1-8)

"The Son of Man is indeed the Lord of the sabbath."

"There is something greater than the temple here," greater than the Passover and all the feasts of the Lord, greater than the Law... for Jesus and His mercy subsume all these by His holy sacrifice, by His very presence amongst us. And now on the new sabbath day, the words of the psalmist are

253

Ordinary Time

fulfilled: "The cup of salvation I will take up, and I will call upon the name of the Lord," as we offer now even daily the "sacrifice of thanksgiving" – the Holy Eucharist – as each day becomes a "memorial feast" for us. Here we remember and partake of the Lamb "without blemish"; here the blood of the firstborn Son slaughtered for our sakes is applied to the temples our bodies become by its anointing, by our raising of the cup. And heeding Christ's words to be on watch, we are made ever ready for flight from this world of sin and into the arms of our God.

It is an ominous night, that first Passover. The darkness upon the land, the cries of mothers for their firstborn sons foreshadows the horror of the crucifixion of the Lord Jesus Christ, the only Son of God, and the piercing of our consciences which comes thereby. By His sacrifice we cry for our sins; but by this death are we released from bondage to that same sin. By it His mercy is poured upon us from age to age until the end of all time. For now the Passover is made complete; now the sacrifice is truly whole. And all of the old is made new as it is brought to fulfillment in the only Son.

"You have loosed my bonds," O Lord. Each day you prepare my soul for flight from this world by the cup of thanksgiving, the sharing in your sacrifice, you offer to us each day at the hands of your priests. As it is raised and as we "call upon the name of the Lord," you come to us with your merciful anointing, and all guilt we may have incurred is cleansed thereby. O Lord of the Sabbath, O Son of the Most High, O Temple of God and perfection of the Law, see the Lamb we eat at your Command; see the blood which marks our houses, and pass over us in the Day of Judgment – bring us freely into the celebration of your eternal feast in heaven.

As we come to the altar today, brothers and sisters, let us remember the merciful sacrifice the Lord has made for our blessed protection and fulfillment of the hunger we have for His presence. Freely let us partake now of His Body and Blood and so become one with Him who is Lord of all and master of our souls. And let us share His merciful love with the waiting world. Let us enter now the eternal Sabbath.

O. 15. Sat. (I)

Saturday
(Ex.12:37-42; Ps.136:1,10-15,23-24; Mt.12:14-21)

"All the Israelites must keep a vigil for the Lord
throughout their generations."

After four hundred and thirty years, as one man the Israelites left the land of Egypt. More than a million people all told were "rushed out of Egypt and had no opportunity even to prepare food for the journey." And so the exodus from sin we all must make is here prefigured. And in thanks for

254

such grace from the Lord, whose "mercy endures forever," who "freed us from our foes," we keep constant vigil. Knowing the manner of our first release from slavery, we watch now for His return.

"Many people followed Him and He cured them all." All those who walk in the wake of the Lord know His saving power. For He is endowed with the Spirit of God; of Jesus, the prophet writes: "Here is my servant whom I have chosen, my loved one in whom I delight." And so those who approach Him know the "mighty hand" and "outstretched arm" of God in the healing of all their ills. Yet mighty as is His work, so gentle is its coming forth. For it is not in great fanfare but rather great humility that Jesus has come into our midst to save us. Though His works are great, His person is meek. Much as the silent NAME shared with Moses, much as the "still, small voice" which spoke to Elijah, so is this WORD of God made flesh. "He will not contend or cry out, nor will His voice be heard in the streets." For His is a voice which does not pass away with the dimming of its sound; His voice is not a clanging gong, empty of substance, but is filled to bursting with love and mercy, and goes forth in the silence of a pure heart. It is for this silence we listen. It is for His love we keep vigil.

"He sternly ordered them not to make public what He had done." We must join Him in silence. In telling no one, all will know. It is by faith all is done. Indeed, our light shines forth from this quiet heart. Shshsh... (listen for the voice of God).

The Israelites moved at once from the land of bondage. The Lord has set us free from our sins, brothers and sisters, and one day He will come again – He is knocking at the door even now – and take us to the presence of God. Are we watching for His coming? Are we ready to leave all behind? Do we follow Him with such abandon even this day? If we do, the word shall go forth from our lives. If we do, we make Him known, and so we can be sure, "In His Name, the Gentiles will find hope." As we keep vigil for the Lord, His Word goes forth to the ends of the earth and shall lead all souls out of slavery to the mountain of God. Watch, and listen. The time is nigh.

O. 16. Mon. (I)

Sixteenth Week

Monday
(Ex.14:5-18; Ex.15:1-6; Mt.12:38-42)

"The Lord Himself will fight for you;
you have only to keep still."

But the scribes and the Pharisees cannot keep still, cannot hold faith firmly in their hearts, but are anxious for a sign. But it is "an evil and unfaithful age" that is "eager for a sign," and so no sign will bring it salvation. Jesus indeed will die and rise again, but it will be of no avail to those whose hearts are closed, to those who blindly fight by their own power. Indeed, a sign was not needed by either the queen of the South or by Nineveh; the wisdom and the preaching that come from the Lord were enough for them to bend the knee and to repent. These pagans, these foreigners, had hearts open and seeking the word of the Lord – and so shall be saved thereby. But these scribes and Pharisees who hear the wisdom and truth pouring forth from the lips of Christ are deaf to its significance, and so shall be condemned.

The Lord indeed it must be who fights for us, and not we ourselves. We must sing with Moses, "My strength and my courage is the Lord, and He has been my savior." Knowing we can do nothing by our own power, let us shout to our God, "Your right hand, O Lord, has shattered the enemy." Is it Moses' staff and "hand outstretched" which part the Red Sea, or is it indeed the Lord's power? Is it we who save ourselves from the pursuit of sin marching like Pharaoh's army against us, or is it God who hurls "Pharaoh's chariots and army… into the sea"?

"Fear not! Stand your ground, and you will see the victory the Lord will win for you today," brothers and sisters. As He saved the Israelites from the relentless pursuit of the Egyptians, so He will save your soul from the onslaught of sin. You must but trust in Him. Take not refuge in signs and wonders, which you might forget upon their passing, but be still and wait for the Lord, listening for His voice, remaining steady in the faith He instills in your heart, and you will not be shaken by the temptations and distractions and fears brought by the world and its blinded mind. "They sank into the depths of the sea like a stone," Scripture tells us: so it will be with your sins and the temptations which surround you. "These Egyptians whom you see today you will never see again." Have but faith in your hearts.

> Jesus, may we simply know that you are with us
> and follow in your footsteps each day.
> Fight for us, O Lord,
> for the battle is always yours.

Tuesday

(Ex.14:21-15:1; Ex.15:1,8-10,12,17; Mt.12:46-50)

"Thus the Lord saved Israel on that day
from the power of the Egyptians."

The Lord fought for the Israelites, His people. Working great wonders, He brought them forth from the land of Egypt. Indeed, "the Israelites marched into the midst of the sea on dry land, with the water like a wall to their right and to their left." So great was His love for His chosen ones that He saved them in this miraculous fashion, casting their enemies into the sea. Them "the earth swallowed," but His people crossed unharmed.

Here is the prefigurement of the Lord's saving us from sin by His death and resurrection; through the waters of Baptism we now come to "the mountain of [the Lord's] inheritance," our enemies dying in that same water which saves us. In the dark of night, in the death of Christ, we enter the realm of the sea; at dawn we see our enemies lying dead on the shore. But it is no longer those who are related to the Lord by flesh and blood who are brought through the waters to His sanctuary. The chosen ones are no longer of a particular race. "Whoever does the will of my heavenly Father is brother and sister and mother to me." It is a spiritual kingdom to which we are now called, and it is in the Spirit His children are now born.

Shocking this word must have been to the ears of those so used to judging the blessings of the Lord by bloodline. Here is the beginning of Christ's teaching that any and all are called to the table of the Lord. How shocked even Peter was when directed to go to the Gentile people, when instructed to eat, as it were, of the unclean food (Acts 10:13-14). But the Lord makes all clean by His blood. His death and resurrection open the gates of heaven to all who would enter there. To anyone who would follow in His footsteps, the Lord leads on dry land to the promised glory. But do not think, as I so often hear, that there are no casualties in this new exodus. Do not hold so foolishly to the idea that the God of the Old Testament was harsh in His destruction of the Egyptian army but the God of the New effects no such punishment. See that the casualties in this battle suffer a fate worse than drowning in the sea: eternal condemnation awaits those who now harden their hearts against the word of Christ. The warfare is now spiritual rather than physical, and the judgment Jesus passes on the evil generation is now far worse than any before His time had come. As He Himself has said elsewhere, "It would be better for him if a millstone were put around his neck and he be thrown into the sea, than for him to cause one of these little ones to sin" (Lk.17:2).

Ordinary Time

We are brothers and sisters of the Lord, my friends, and so He saves us from the day of judgment. As long as we do His will, His blessing shall be ours. Let us rejoice this day in the justice of God, that He cares for all those who love Him, even as He casts their enemies into the sea.

O. 16. Wed. (I)

Wednesday
(Ex.16:1-5,9-15; Ps.78:18-19,23-28; Mt.13:1-9)

"I will now rain down bread from heaven for you."

He gives us bread to eat; He gives us wine to drink. All our food comes from His hand. He provides for our every need. It is not by our own strength we are fed. It is not by our own strength we produce fruit to feed others. All our grain is from His hand and grows only with His blessing.

The Israelites find themselves in a barren desert and begin to fear for their empty bellies. "Can God spread a table in the desert?" they ask in doubt, and begin to dissemble before the Lord. But it is God's will to teach them a lesson, to show them from whom their sustenance comes, for even when in Egypt their "fleshpots" were provided by Him. But they are a blind and ignorant race, and so He must show them the power of His grace, of His providence. He thus gives them a food they have never seen before, whose very name, "manna", reveals its mystery. And so they partake of this food of the angels; "even a surfeit of provisions He sent them," though their flesh shall not be long satisfied with this heavenly food.

And we, do we realize all our food comes from the Lord? Do we see His hand at work in all things? Or do we go blindly along through this desert as well, listening too carefully to our grumbling stomachs while ignoring His Word in our hearts and presence in our midst? Do we, too, forget all He has done for us? Or do we turn faithfully to Him for His heavenly provisions and find ourselves satisfied with the food from His hands? And thus, do we ourselves yield grain from the good soil He sets us on, increasing "a hundred- or sixty- or thirty-fold" His word in our hearts, that others might be fed too by our God? Jesus sits before us today and calls us to such fruitfulness in His name. Let us not be choked by the cares of this world or fail to have depth of faith within our souls, but let us take the blessed food He provides in His Word and in His Body and His Blood and so be nourished well to provide for others.

The desert in which we find ourselves, by which the Lord tests our faith, can seem to overwhelm us at times. May it never cause us to act as the Israelites, who "tempted God in their hearts by demanding the food they craved." Let us remember that only the "heavenly bread" rained upon us by

258

Him will save us from the temptations and emptiness of this life. I pray He fill you with His bread of eternal life.

Thursday
(Ex.19:1-2,9-11,16-20;   Dn.3:52-56;   Mt.13:10-17)

"Blest are your eyes because they see
and blest are your ears because they hear."

Jesus tells us today, "Many a prophet and many a saint longed to see what you see but did not see it, to hear what you hear but did not hear it." How blessed are we, for the light of His face now shines upon us, for His teaching is now in our ears.

With fear and trembling the Israelites came to Mount Sinai to witness the presence of God. They wished not to be there as He revealed Himself in mighty signs: "There were peals of thunder and lightning, and a heavy cloud over the mountain, and a very loud trumpet blast, so that all the people in the camp trembled." What an astounding scene! For "the whole mountain trembled" and "the trumpet blast grew louder and louder, while Moses was speaking and God answering Him with thunder." Here is the revelation of God in all His majesty as He communicates Himself to His people. Our psalm, too, sings of the glory of the Lord and the praise due Him: "Blessed are you in the temple of your holy glory," "on the throne of your kingdom," "in the firmament of heaven." The Lord is indeed "exalted above all for all ages."

But overwhelming as the Lord is and difficult as it may be to find Him, we must never close our hearts to His presence. Yes, there must always be proper fear for the awesome glory of God, but our eyes must yet be open to see Him and our ears open to hear Him. He comes now to us not in thunder, not in earthquakes – but in a still, small voice... in the gentle presence of our Lord, Jesus Christ. And though this pregnant silence radiating the Word of God may be just as fearful to the heart darkened by the cares of the world, though the refining fire it is may bring a greater pain to the soul being cleansed of its sin, we must not turn away as did the ancient Israelites, as did many of Jesus' time: we must not allow our hearts to be "sluggish" to understand.

He stands before us now, present here at Mass and in all His holy sacraments. Indeed, He comes to us speaking through the people and all the things around us. He is ever calling to our hearts, ever shining His light upon our minds. Do we open ourselves to Him? Do we seek to grow in the Spirit each day, every day...? Blessed are we now that Jesus has come and on the third day been raised from the dead. The Lord instructed Moses: "On

259

the third day the Lord will come down on Mount Sinai before the eyes of all the people." That day is now fulfilled in our sight; let us cleanse our hearts, that we might be prepared to see Him.

Friday
(Ex.20:1-17; Ps.19:8-11,Jn.6:69; Mt.13:18-23)

"What was sown on good soil
is the man who hears the message and takes it in."

"The law of the Lord is perfect, refreshing the soul... The command of the Lord is clear, enlightening the eye... More precious than gold" and "sweeter also than syrup or honey from the comb" is the word of God. How beautifully our psalm speaks of the words of everlasting life which issue forth from the mouth of God, the Law of the Lord embodied in Christ Jesus. And those who follow the command of God shall bear a mighty yield, for "the fear of the Lord is pure, enduring forever."

In our first reading we find the great Law written on stone, our Ten Commandments – the blessed guide of man's walk through this world of sin. They give light to our steps, teaching us ever the way we should go. But great as these words are and necessary as they may be to keep our steps from faltering, to prevent our eye from entering darkness, so much greater is He who sums them up and brings them to completion in His flesh and blood. The love of God and neighbor commanded so clearly to Moses on Mount Sinai here shines in a light beyond our human comprehension. Indeed, to hear its call, to become good soil, we must be made as He is, walking in the grace of divine perfection. Only then will the Word which stirs our souls – in whose light we long to cleanse our hearts and by which we hope to enter God's reign – only through the intercession of Jesus the Son of God, the eternal Word of the Father, will we come to know the realization of the call of God to His children, rendered in His commands.

Thirst for the Word, brothers and sisters. Our souls must indeed have a deep hunger for His presence, for the light that comes only by following Him. Our worship must not be in vain, and we must not be distracted by the allure of this world. Standing fast through any suffering, we must take in deeply the Word spoken to our hearts, ever making greater place for Jesus in our lives. We must put flesh to the words of everlasting life, we must be as the Law walking the face of the earth – we must be as our Savior, Jesus Christ. Then it is we shall know His blessing; then we shall labor with Him and yield a great harvest. Then we shall share in the sweetness of the glory of Him who commands us to walk rightly by His side.

Today let us rejoice in the Lord and in His Law; let us find the light it brings and become children of that light. With Jesus and all His saints in heaven let us hear the Word whispered deeply in our spirits and become doers of that word of God. Then we shall bear fruit unto eternal life.

Saturday
(Ex.24:3-8; Ps.50:1-2,5-6,14-15; Mt.13:24-30)

"All that the Lord has said, we will heed and do."

But will they? Who among them will remain faithful to the covenant they make with God? All the Israelites vow as one to follow "the words and ordinances of the Lord," yet only two men shall come from the desert and enter the Promised Land. Their children shall exhibit greater fidelity, but these, too, shall falter – throughout the history of the chosen people there shall be weeds, sometimes in abundance, sown among the good seed.

And in our psalm, God declares: "Gather my faithful ones before me, those who have made a covenant with me by sacrifice." For "God Himself is the judge," and He will tell how well the "twelve pillars" "erected at the foot of the mountain" stand before Him. He will make known how efficacious has been our sacrifice. Jesus teaches us of God's justice in His parable: "At harvest time I will order the harvesters, first collect the weeds and bundle them up to burn, then gather the wheat into my barn." Indeed, the weeds shall be separated out into everlasting fire, while the wheat which has been true to His Word enters heaven. If we have been faithful to our covenant with the Lord, if we have been hearers and doers of His Word, we have nothing to fear. Love overcomes all fear, and the Lord assures us of His grace: "Call upon me in time of distress; I will rescue you." But if our vows have been in vain, we have much to fear at the hand of the harvest master.

All shall be brought before Him – "The Lord has spoken and summoned the earth, from the rising of the sun to its setting." From east to west they shall be gathered before His judgment seat, and on that last day Jesus shall speak the sentence which awaits us all. The weeds may seem to grow and thrive in this day, but be assured that this day is passing away; His Day shall last for eternity. The enemy shall be cast from His presence forever.

In the desert the people of God were excited to pledge allegiance to the Lord. But what is promised must be done or the pledge is worthless. We, too, profess our faith in God, and indeed His blood is sprinkled upon us daily as we raise the cup of blessing in His Name. This New Covenant far surpasses the Old and thus puts the onus upon us to a far greater degree to heed the words of the psalmist: "Fulfill your vows to the Most High." Let

261

us therefore truly heed and do all that the Lord calls us to. Let us not hesitate to come into the Lord's presence offering Him a sacrifice of praise, but let us not forget the promise inherent in our worship of Him; each day let us grow as wheat before the master of the harvest, His Word providing nourishment for our souls.

O. 17. Mon. (I)

Seventeenth Week

Monday
(Ex.32:15-24,30-34; Ps.106:1,19-23; Mt.13:31-35)

"Eventually the whole mass of dough began to rise."

The kingdom of God comes gradually, grows imperceptibly; from the smallest of seeds it becomes "the largest of plants," and "the birds of the sky come and build their nests in its branches." Indeed, this yeast is kneaded into our hearts, and by its grace we rise gradually unto the form heaven would make us – and so the glory of God becomes ours, and with others we share His grace within us.

See that it is the people's impatience which has led them into sin: "Make us a god to be our leader," they say to Aaron, "as for the man Moses who brought us out of the land of Egypt, we do not know what happened to him." Moses is gone to the mountain forty days to receive the commands of God upon the tablets of stone, but this time is too long for the Israelites to wait, and so when he returns with the "tablets that were made by God, having inscriptions on them that were engraved by God Himself," he finds that they have "exchanged their glory," present so really, so physically, in the Law he carries in his hands, "for the image of a grass-eating bullock."

They could not wait. The God they sought in vain image was coming to them in truth with His Law written in stone, but they did not perceive His approach; and so, taking matters into their own hands, they crafted their condemnation. For now it is but chastisement that awaits them; this, too, comes gradually, and is unavoidable. As the Lord says to Moses, "When it is time for me to punish, I will punish them for their sin."

"So grave a sin" the Israelites commit. It is only because "Moses, His chosen, withstood Him in the breach, to turn back His destructive wrath," that the people were not struck out of the book the Lord has written. Indeed, though they shall all die in their sin in the desert, their generation shall maintain the promise. But it shall not be until Christ Jesus stands in the breach for all, that we who are so prone to evil shall be saved entirely. Only He makes the absolute atonement for the sin of the people, which Moses prefigures in our first reading today.

262

And now that the Son has come, now the seed is planted in our hearts, now the yeast begins to rise in our souls – now the kingdom of God is nigh. From the desert we are thus led, the angel of God going before us. We have but to listen to the word He speaks to us in His blessed parables and apply its truth to our lives, and thus staying the path set before us we will come in time to the kingdom that awaits us. We shall yet see the Lord descend from on high, not carrying tablets in His arms, but carrying us and our salvation in full bloom. And on that holy day we shall eat of the bread He has caused to rise in our hearts and in our lives.

Tuesday
(Ex.33:7-11,34:5-9,28; Ps.103:6-13; Mt.13:36-43)

"The angels will hurl them into the fiery furnace
where they will wail and grind their teeth."

It is the justice of God which is our theme today. And though it is absolutely certain that the mercy of God far surpasses our merit and He does not "requite us according to our crimes," yet it is equally so – and Jesus could not make it more explicit than He does in His explanation in our gospel today – that God's will is not for "declaring the guilty guiltless," and that "the followers of the evil one" shall be punished. It is this invariable necessity of God's justice I highlight today because of its general ignorance in this age.

"Merciful and gracious is the Lord, slow to anger and abounding in kindness," David declares in our psalm. "The Lord has compassion on those who fear Him." Yes, "surpassing is His kindness toward those who fear Him." But what if we should not fear Him? What if we should *not* give Him the love and honor and respect which is rightfully His? It cannot but be that we pervert His kindness and compassion and, by our own will, turn it into the flaming punishment it thus becomes. This is the justice of God: it reaches down "for a thousand generations"; it covers the earth with its forgiveness. But turning from it we inevitably cast ourselves into hell, for there is no place to hide our hardened hearts from His merciful love. Thus our refusal to accept His surpassing kindness is that which provides the kindling for the everlasting flames. And if we deny the existence of hell, we deny the presence of God's love, and our own free will in choosing it or not.

In our first reading there is quite a jump, better than a chapter, in the scene. In the first half Moses is in the tent of meeting where he would serve as judge for the people; in the second half he is on Mount Sinai, where God has led him to receive the Ten Commandments (a second time). The Lord

263

has also promised to reveal His back to Moses – no one can see His face and live – and it is this scene that is spoken of in our gospel. Moses speaks the Lord's silent NAME, "YHWH", and God comes in power, crying to him of His infinite mercy and absolute justice. As the Lord passes by in this way, Moses is overwhelmed and begs God to remain with him and the people, recognizing that they will not be able to take a step without Him. And in His great kindness, but not without appropriate punishment, the Lord will remain with Moses and the Israelites through their desert journey.

"The saints will shine like the sun in their Father's kingdom." The angels shall gather the good seed unto their just reward. And there shall be great rejoicing as the mercy of God thus comes to fulfillment. But none of this can be until "all who draw others to apostasy and all evildoers" are cast out from His presence. Just as the faithless were not permitted to enter the Promised Land but died in the desert, so only those whose hearts burn with the love of God will shine in His kingdom. For the rest only the fires of torment await.

O. 17. Wed. (I)

Wednesday
(Ex.34:29-35; Ps.99:5-7,9; Mt.13:44-46)

"The skin of his face had become radiant
while he conversed with the Lord."

His face shining like the pearl of great price, with whom he speaks, Moses comes down from the mountain carrying the Ten Commandments. Here is a great treasure in His hands, which he has given up all to find. But, of course, the greater treasure is the Word of God from which it takes its meaning and of which Moses converses with the Lord; and the greatest treasure is certainly God Himself, who makes us shine as stars in the night that is this world. "Holy is the Lord, our God."

And so, of course, the greatest treasure we can find here on earth, hidden in this ground from which our bodies are formed, is our Lord Jesus Christ, for He is the very image of God, God Himself, the WORD made flesh in our presence. And thus as the Israelites had the Ten Commandments as the heart of their covenant, so we have a surpassing covenant founded in the Body and Blood of our Lord, in which His presence truly abides. Still we have His words of Truth, still they illumine our faces. But now they are spoken by the incarnate mouth of God; now the veil has been removed from the face of the One who inspires all souls, and our hearts burn with the pure light of His wisdom – and now we have at our fingertips and upon our lips that flesh and blood which make the words so real ... and so, one we become with His holiness.

264

Radiant is the splendor of God. He alone is worthy of our praise. It is He alone we should strive to possess in this life. He is buried here in our hearts; He is waiting deep within our souls for us to uncover our faces, to uncover our minds from the veil which conceals His light. Indeed, He is waiting for us to shine as the pearl of great price, to give light to the world as He does, that all might come to converse with Him with unveiled faces. But we must give up all else to find such grace: this pearl must remain unmixed with baser matter. As Moses was on the mountain forty days and forty nights, neither eating nor drinking, so we must come to Him so utterly, leaving all of this world behind, to find the riches which await us in the heavenly kingdom.

Jesus is the way to that kingdom. In his Word, His Body and His Blood, we find the pearl of great price. And so shall our faces shine radiantly white as we converse with the Lord in His presence for all eternity. Praise Him, brothers and sisters, for His grace at work in your life.

O. 17. Thurs. (I)

Thursday
(Ex.40:16-21,34-38; Ps.84:2-6,8,11; Mt.13:47-53)

"The cloud covered the meeting tent,
and the glory of the Lord filled the Dwelling."

The Dwelling is the Tabernacle of God, the place in which the ark of the covenant holding the Ten Commandments was housed; and so it was God's dwelling-place. And when this cloud lifted from the Tabernacle, the Israelites would set forth; and when the cloud stopped, so would they. In this we see clearly that the Israelites were led by God and by His Law. "In the daytime the cloud of the Lord was seen over the Dwelling; whereas at night, fire was seen in the cloud by the whole house of Israel in all stages of their journey."

Our psalm extols the glory of God and His place of dwelling. It is for Him and to be in His house we yearn. "Happy they who dwell in your house!" the psalmist exclaims. So far surpassing is the glory of the Lord that "I had rather lie at the threshold of the house of my God than dwell in the tents of the wicked." For "even the sparrow finds a home" at the altar of God, and so, how blessed shall we be in His presence.

And in our gospel Jesus completes His parables on "the reign of God," the kingdom of heaven – the House in which we long to dwell eternally. And, of course, here before us stands the new ark of the covenant in the Person of Jesus. Here the new and fulfilling Law of love is housed, by which we are now led. The Spirit descended upon Him as a dove, thus anointing Him with God's glory, and it is this "cloud," this Spirit of Truth,

265

which descends upon us now and by which we walk with God. The Old Covenant and Law are certainly not to be discarded, for "every scribe who is learned in the reign of God is like the head of the household who can bring from his storeroom both the new and the old"; but the Old is indeed subsumed by the New, for the Person of God – Word made flesh, God made man – far exceeds and truly completes the first dwelling, which was but made by human hands. Now the Law has found a new and lasting home.

It is well we understand all that the Lord would teach us. It is necessary that that teaching be complete, or we shall fall short of what our "heart" and "flesh cry out for." "The living God" awaits us; His glory He would give us. Let us be covered by His cloud and be led forth in His Word of Truth to His eternal reign. From "strength to strength" let us go, until we dwell with Him forever, His Word written on our hearts. Amen.

O. 17. Fri. (I)

Friday
(Lv.23:1,4-11,15-16,27,34-37; Ps.81:2-6,10-11; Mt.13:54-58)

"Offer as an oblation to the Lord holocausts and cereal offerings,
sacrifices and libations, as prescribed for each day."

Our first reading and our psalm speak and sing of the honor due our God. The Lord outlines for Moses "the festivals of the Lord" which must be celebrated "at the proper time with a sacred assembly," and our psalmist exhorts us to "blow the trumpet at the new moon, at the full moon, on our solemn feast" in honor of the one true God. We should worship no god but Him and "hold a sacred assembly and do no sort of work" on His sabbaths and on the days He sets aside for celebrating His Name. Due honor and praise must be given our God.

But when Jesus comes into the midst of His people, due honor is withheld. Though they cannot deny His teaching, the wisdom and grace He imparts, yet they are blind to His presence before them. They do not know whence He comes. They cannot see that He is of God. And so because of their limited vision, their "lack of faith," He cannot touch them or heal them as He passes by. Here He stands in their synagogues, but the shout of joy does not go up from their midst because their hearts are shut tight to the divine presence of the Lord. The due praise they are moved to is thus denied, and they break the Law of God.

It is sad when justice is not done to our God. We are the ones who would benefit most from offering due sacrifice and oblation – He has no need of our holocausts – yet we commit this kind of suicide by reserving the honor due Him, resisting thus truly entering His marvelous presence and becoming one with the One who created us and saved us. He invites us to

266

the feast, to the glorious celebration, but we turn down His invitation to join Him at the table of His Body and His Blood. Each day it is prescribed for us to give our souls to Him; in every place the cup of salvation is raised unto the glory of God: here the festival of the Lord is fulfilled in our midst. But how many say they see but bread and wine, they hear but empty phrases. Their hearts are not set on His coming.

We are Jesus' brothers and sisters; we are His mother. We are those who recognize His presence and give glory to His Name. The world cannot see Him; the world does not know Him. But we know Him. Let us "take up a melody, and sound the timbrel, the pleasant harp and the lyre," and with all the music our lives can produce give Him glory in our celebration... with all the work we do and all the rest we take each day in Him. Now is the acceptable time. Today is the day of salvation. Here the feast begins. Let us come into His presence singing for joy.

O. 17. Sat. (I)

Saturday
(Lv.25:1,8-17; Ps.67:2-5,7-8; Mt.14:1-12)

"It is really the number of crops he sells you."

The earth is the Lord's; it is not our own. And it is only by His grace that we share the fruits of the land. "The earth has yielded its fruits; God, our God, has blessed us," our psalm declares. These fruits may be bought and sold, but the land is God's own.

"In this year of jubilee, then, every one of you shall return to his own property." "This fiftieth year you shall make sacred by proclaiming liberty in the land for all its inhabitants." The jubilee year delineated in our first reading makes clear that we are God's and not our own or anyone else's. While we tread this earth, in the forty-nine years leading to the jubilee, land is bought and sold, even slaves are made and taken. But come the jubilee the trumpet is blown and all return whence they came: in this moment we go back to our homes and find the truth – that we are God's alone. All that is bought and sold is only temporary; these crops are consumed and pass away. The land from which they come is in God's hands and does not pass away. To it we must return. For He is our portion and cup.

"May all the ends of the earth fear Him!" Indeed, we should fear Him who holds the earth and all its peoples in His creating hand. We should not presume upon God's mercy and "deal unfairly" as we buy and sell in this world with all that He provides. In our gospel Herod is gripped by fear because he knows he abuses the power given him; he is struck to the heart by John's preaching because his sin is exposed to the light. But instead of proclaiming liberty, instead of returning to the Lord, he hardens his heart

267

against Truth, presumes license and not liberty, and has "John arrested, put in chains, and imprisoned." But, of course, the Word of God cannot be chained; and Herod is not entirely wrong when he claims John has been "raised from the dead" in the person of Jesus, for the same Spirit which worked in this most fruitful of men comes forth fully in the Son of God. Good reason has Herod to fear.

And it must be noted that the beheading of John does not bring his end, but his beginning. It returns him to the land whence he has come. It is as his jubilee, his time to "return to his own property" – to enter the kingdom of God. For his body buried by his disciples is but as the crops bought and sold (and a more fair and abundant dealer in the fruits of this earth the world has not known); it is, of course, his immortal soul which finds liberty now in the land of the Lord.

This world cannot hinder the fruits that are of the Lord. In faith let us remain in Him, producing an abundant yield in His Name, that the way of the Lord "be known upon earth," and that we may come to His salvation at the time of Jubilee. (We shall hear the trumpets resound through the halls of heaven.)

O. 18. Mon. (I – A)

Eighteenth Week

Monday (A)
(Nm.11:4-15; Ps.81:2,12-17; Mt.14:22-36)

"How little faith you have!"

It is the Lord's exclamation to His holy apostles, to the foundation of His Church – to His Rock. And certainly it applies to all of us as it does, too, to the Israelites in the desert. All need greater faith to come upon the new shore of paradise and find healing for all our ills.

As the Israelites tramp through the desert, they grow tired of heavenly food and desire something earthen. Their faith in God is shaken by the lusts of their belly, and their outcry against the Lord grieves His servant Moses. He finds himself unable to carry this stiff-necked people "like a foster father carrying an infant." He breaks under the burden of "all the people" even as Peter – who shall have to carry the whole Church upon his shoulders – trembles at the wind upon the sea. Moses asks for death to find relief, and Peter cries as he begins to sink... and the Lord will "at once stretch out His hand" and catch them both, His ears ever open to the prayers of His holy ones. But greater faith will they both need to have to lead God's people forward. Peter will find it after Pentecost (though not before denying Him three times), and the stubbornness of the Israelites, "the hardness of their hearts," will keep Moses from the earthly Promised Land; only in the next world will he discover paradise.

The faith we need to make it through the desert that is this world and come into the heavenly kingdom of our Lord and God is spoken by those trembling in the storm-tossed boat: "Undoubtedly you are the Son of God," and exhibited by the men of Gennesaret. For they "brought Him all the afflicted, with the plea that He let them do no more than touch the tassel of His cloak." Thus, the same faith the woman in the crowd with the open wound for years had shown Jesus on His way to raise the little child is shown here by these poor sinners, for "as many as touched it were fully restored to health."

A word from His mouth. A drop of His blood. The touch of His hand. The hem of His garment. A crust of bread from His table... This is all we need. If we have faith, in a moment we will be restored to life; we will be redeemed from all our ills, from all our sins – from all the temptations of our bellies and this desert. The sea may rage and contend with the wind, but we will remain calm and patient in His presence: we will walk on water, we will find "honey from the rock," if we have but faith. It is not far away, and that the size of a mustard seed is all we need. Find relief from all your distress by calling upon the Savior.

Monday (B,C)
(Nm.11:4-15; Ps.81:2,12-17; Mt.14:13-21)

"Israel I would feed with the best of wheat."

But the best of wheat they despise, and seek to satiate their appetite with meat. The blessed food from heaven, come from the hand of God, the Israelites soon grow tired of as they travel through the desert. Their stomachs cry out for earthly flesh. As our psalm tells us, the people "heard not" the voice of God but preferred "their own counsels," so He "gave them up to the hardness of their hearts." He will give them the meat they desire, and it will bring plague upon them for their lusts against God.

Yet the Lord ever continues to call His people, and in the presence of Jesus that call is fulfilled. In our gospel we see Jesus taking it upon Himself to feed the hungry masses, caring for their needs, and though some will seek to follow Him just to feed their bellies, others will recognize in His feeding of the five thousand the blessing of God's providence and His loving care for His children; and their hearts will be open to partake of the spiritual food, the Body and Blood of Christ, which shall be offered forth at the table of the Lord after His death and resurrection. The sacrificial love of Jesus Christ will thus become their own as they unite with Him in flesh and blood,

269

in word and deed – in partaking of the best of wheat. He is the food that sustains us.

The fragments left us in the twelve baskets come down to us this day through His twelve apostles and the Church founded by them in His Name. The fragments we find upon our altar today as our priest prays the blessing over them. And we are fed. And we have life. And we are kept from grumbling against the Lord for all that is not ours in this world, and all the vain things our hearts would otherwise desire... and we endure any suffering that comes to us on our pilgrimage to His Promised Land by the grace of the food offered forth through His holy sacrifice. And we thus become like Him.

If there were no food upon our table, if this sacrifice upon our altars were not the Body and Blood of Christ – if His presence were *not* real in this best of wheat, this holy manna – we would faint in the desert of this world and be consumed by our own lusts. But as it is the Lord provides the nourishment we need, and body and soul are kept alive even unto paradise.

Eat His Body and drink His Blood, brothers and sisters,
and you shall live in His paradise.

O. 18. Tues. (I – A)

Tuesday (A)
(Nm.12:1-13; Ps.51:3-7,12-13; Mt.15:1-2,10-14)

"If one blind man leads another, both will end in a pit."

Aaron and Miriam would lead the people, they would presume the place of Moses; but they are blind, they cannot see who it is the Lord calls, who is His chosen. And so the Pharisees, too, are blind guides, deaf and blind to the presence of Jesus, who is God's Chosen One. Considering their own gifts and talents but not recognizing from whom they come and what their limits are, their blindness leads both forth into sin against the Lord and against His anointed. And it will only be by crying out to the Lord, as does David in his psalm, that the sin shall be cleansed from them and a "clean heart" will be created within them.

Aaron does cry out, begging Moses to intercede with the Lord for their sister's leprosy, and so cleansing shall come for her; but we have a fear for the Pharisees, for the Lord says of them, "Let them go their way." Their way leads to destruction; their blindness shall lead them into a pit. If they continue to turn from the Lord standing before them, they shall multiply rather than find forgiveness for their sins. O that their hearts would not be hardened! O that they would cleanse their souls and not their hands! O that they would see what is first with the Lord, and how He must be followed!

"Against you only have I sinned and done what is evil in your sight," with David let them cry out to you, Lord, that they might be washed clean of the guilt into which we are all born, that the leprosy might be taken from their spirits.

We all are in danger of blindness, brothers and sisters, and the affliction which comes from its snares. We must never presume upon the Lord or His chosen leaders, or cast from His presence will we be. It is true that all have sinned. It is so that we all fall short. But we have a greater than Moses in our dear Jesus, who cries out for His wounded Church: "Please, not this! Pray, heal her!" when He sees the afflictions upon us. What are the thoughts of our hearts? What comes out of our mouths? Is it a desire to love Him and a cry for assistance, or do we harden our hearts against His truth?

Let us not follow and become blind guides. There was one man chosen to lead the multitude out of slavery and through the desert, and there is one Man now to lead us to the Father's presence. He has left His Spirit upon His Church, upon His apostles and those who follow His teaching – and most particularly upon His one chosen servant, the rock that is Peter. Let us walk in light, being led along the path He marks out for us by His chosen guide.

Tuesday (B,C)
(Nm.12:1-13; Ps.51:3-7,12-13; Mt.14:22-36)

"The presence of the Lord he beholds."

Throughout the history of salvation, the Lord chooses one man to lead His people. In the Old Testament times, this was Moses; in the New Testament times, it is Peter. Though it is always the Lord Himself who guides and teaches, He ever puts His Spirit upon one particular man to act in His stead. Those who do not follow the Lord and the way He sets forth, who act in presumption against His will and His chosen, are cast from His presence, are stricken by His hand as is Miriam.

"Throughout my house he bears my trust," the Lord says of Moses His servant, "the meekest man on the face of the earth." "Face to face I speak to him," the Lord assures us; and is it not so with Peter as well? It is Peter alone who steps forward to walk upon the storm-tossed sea to the Lord; it is Peter that Jesus will instruct to "feed [His] sheep." He is given the keys to the kingdom. He is the peg set firmly in place. And is it not dissension against the place given this first of the apostles that causes so much disturbance in the Church? Is it not the presumption of Aaron and Miriam, gifted in themselves but not as Moses, which remains with us today and creates the division which ails the people of God? We should cry out for mercy from the Lord for our sins against Him, for it is against Him we sin when we do not follow His appointed ones. We should beg with David, "Cast me not out from your presence, and your Holy Spirit take not from me."

I beg you to notice, my brothers and sisters, especially those separated from the Church and its hierarchy, to whom Aaron, the first of priests, makes his plea for forgiveness and healing. Hear his words: "Ah my lord!" he said to Moses, "please do not charge us with the sin that we have foolishly committed!" And Moses intercedes with the Lord, and Miriam finds healing. And yet do you deny that God gives man authority on earth to intercede with Him for the forgiveness of sins? And yet do you doubt that the Lord places His Spirit on a man and calls him to serve as Moses? All may be priests but not all are chosen to lead; the Lord's is a church of order and not presumption. One there is who beholds His presence, and through Him we know the Lord.

May the Lord catch us and lead us into His boat, for we do falter in our faith and find great difficulty fighting the winds which beset the barque of Peter... O Lord, be with us! Hold not our sins against us! "A steadfast spirit renew within me," may we all cry, and so find forgiveness for our offenses against you, Lord, and against your holy ones. May we all enter your presence and serve you.

O. 18. Wed. (I)

Wednesday

(Nm.13:1-2,25-14:1,26-29,34-35; Ps.106:4,6-7,13-14,21-23; Mt.15:21-28)

"They forgot the God who had saved them."

But He did not forget them. Though He curses them in our first reading for their lack of faith, and though they shall indeed all – except for Joshua and Caleb – die in the desert over forty years, their children shall enter and take the Promised Land from the five tribes which inhabit it; and despite their repeated faltering in following His word, He shall come to redeem them from their exile once again, and in a full way, in the Person of Jesus Christ.

The Israelites grumbled against Moses and against God in the desert. Fearful at the report of the "giants" in the land they were called to seize as their own, they failed to remember the Giant who fought for them, "who had done great deeds in Egypt." "They waited not for His counsel," nor trusted in His protection, and so they dissembled at what their eyes saw and their ears heard, having not the heart of faith, remembering not the word of the Lord. The people of the land may have been giants, but the Lord towers over all the earth. We must always remember His surpassing power.

And in our gospel we find one of the descendants of those who had made the Israelites so fearful to enter the Promised Land groveling at the feet of the Lord, this Son of David, indeed as a dog before its master. How fortunes have changed. Jesus says to this Canaanite woman, "My mission is only to the lost sheep of the house of Israel." See God's love for His people. See how He has kept the word of His covenant not to forget them. See how He yet chooses them from among the nations, sending His Son in the flesh as one of them. And yet, shall they recognize the grace that walks amongst them? Will their hearts be open to accept Him now, or hardened to His call and blind to His presence will they remain?

This question is asked of each one of us, brothers and sisters, for we are the spiritual descendants of the Israelite people. Will we remember Him and His Word amongst us? Do we recall all He has done for us? This Canaanite woman who begs crumbs from the Lord's table is greatly blessed. She has the faith required for the kingdom of heaven. Again in Scripture it is a Gentile, a foreigner, who exhibits the faith the "sons and daughters" should have. The Lord uses such as these to shame His chosen ones and show them how far His love does spread, how great His grace truly is – that it can capture even these giants in its net. And so, should it not capture the Jew? And so, should we not be taken in it as well? Now that His salvation has extended to the ends of the earth, shall His chosen be forgotten? Will they continue to forget their place in His land? I pray it shall not be so for you and I, brothers and sisters, but that we will always remember His Name.

O. 18. Thurs. (I)

Thursday
(Nm.20:1-13; Ps.95:1-2,6-9; Mt.16:13-23)

"'You are the Messiah,' Simon Peter answered,
'the Son of the Living God!'"

With this response, because of this faith come from the "heavenly Father," Jesus declares to Peter, "You are 'Rock', and on this rock I will build my Church." He entrusts to him the keys of the kingdom of heaven, with power to bind and loose. As from the rock Moses struck, "water gushed out in abundance for the community... to drink," so through Peter and the Church Christ has founded we are nourished by the sacraments and true teaching. So the Son of the Living God is with us.

"Let us acclaim the Rock of our Salvation... Come, let us bow down in worship; let us kneel before the Lord who made us. For He is our God, and we are the people He shepherds, the flock He guides." By the hand of Peter the Lord guides the Church born of His blood. Indeed, as Moses led the Israelites through the desert, so Peter leads us now to the gates of heaven.

Let us declare our faith with him; let us echo his words to the Lord, giving Him due praise and "joyfully sing[ing] psalms to Him." He is our God, He is our Savior, and in this Rock we take refuge.

But let us remember, too, not to judge "by man's standards but by God's." His ways are not our ways, as both great leaders had to learn. It seems to our human minds unfair that Moses should be deemed unfit to lead the Israelites to the Promised Land; it is they, after all, who continually tempted him with their grumbling, plotting even to take his life. And why is the Lord so harsh toward Peter, even calling him a "satan"? He is only concerned for Jesus' life, is he not? The Lord does not judge as we judge. He wishes to teach Moses to deepen his love and concern for the people, that anger is never justified in the care of those in one's charge – the Lord does not act in the rashness of anger and anxiety, and neither should we. And to Peter He must show the necessity of the sacrifice of this life, that we must be "put to death" to be "raised up on the third day" – it is the laying down of this life which brings glory.

Really, in both cases the Lord is calling His leaders to lay down their lives for the people, to do as He does and take the people's sins upon themselves. And this is, of course, the call of us all – to be like Him, to join with our Savior, the Son of the Living God, in His sacrifice. What is more against the standards of man than the cross of Christ, as Paul has told us elsewhere, "a stumbling block to Jews and foolishness to Gentiles" (1Cor.1:23) – and yet the source of our salvation. For to come to the Living God we proclaim as our own, this world and its passions must be left behind. The Father dwells in highest heaven and His ways must become our own. Take refuge now in the Rock of Christ and in His Church; this shall lead you to His presence.

O. 18. Fri. (I)

Friday
(Dt.4:32-40; Ps.77:12-16,21; Mt.16:24-28)

"The Son of Man will come with His Father's glory
accompanied by His angels."

The Lord God came to "take a nation for Himself from the midst of another, by testings, by signs and wonders, by war, with His strong hand and outstretched arm, and by great terrors." As He came with power to rescue the Israelites from the bonds of Egypt, so He will come at the end of time, and is come now, to save us from this world of sin. Indeed, the Son of Man shall come fully into His Kingship on the last day and "repay each man according to his conduct."

274

How shall we secure a place in His kingdom? Moses tells the Israelites, in his final address to them before they enter the Promised Land, "You must now know, and fix in your heart, that the Lord is God in the heavens above and on earth below," and that they "must keep His statutes and commandments." Then they will be blessed and prosper. Jesus tells us in our gospel, "If a man wishes to come after me, he must deny his very self, take up his cross, and begin to follow in my footsteps." As it was then, it is now, only the road is more straitened for the goal is more blessed: now it is even unto death we must be obedient to His ways; but now we find not only life on the land, but glory everlasting.

"Among the people you have made known your power," proclaims our psalm today, and indeed our first reading recounts the "wonders of old" the Lord wrought in the midst of His people: with their eyes they saw His "great fire," and with their ears they "heard Him speaking out of the fire." It is, of course, the presence of Jesus we see before us now and hear speaking in our hearts by the fire of the Holy Spirit. He makes His power known to us now in a far surpassing way. And if we wish to know the glory of God burning in our midst and leading us to the eternal kingdom of light, we must be made holy by its power. "O God, your way is holy," our psalm states, and if we wish to follow in His way, we must be holy as He.

The Lord is coming with His holy angels. He shall soon be here in all His glory. Now He has left us a blessed cross to place upon our shoulders; it is this most wonderful of signs by whose testings we are led in power to the eternal reign of our Savior. As intimately as you know His humble cross, as closely as you follow His sacrificial path, so well will you know His Father's glory.

Saturday
(Dt.6:4-13; Ps.18:2-4,47,51; Mt.17:14-20)

"Praised be the Lord, I exclaim,
and I am safe from my enemies."

In our first reading we hear the Shema, the great Commandment of the Mosaic Law – the Lord is God and we must love Him with all our being. Moses exhorts the people "not to forget to the Lord," who brought them out of slavery in the land of Egypt and is about to bless them abundantly in the Promised Land. Quite graphic is he, and are their practices, in encouraging remembrance of the Lord's command. His words are to be drilled into the children, bound at wrists and on foreheads, and written "on the doorposts of... houses and on... gates." And David's psalm mightily extols the love we should have for our Lord: "My God, my rock of refuge, my shield, the horn of my salvation, my stronghold!" the great king of the Israelites exclaims in his overflowing praise for his saving Lord, in whom he finds his strength. Indeed, the Lord is great and greatly to be praised; He is our life and our salvation.

And it is the faith at the heart of our praise of God which saves us from our enemies, which redeems us from our sins. Jesus demonstrates this clearly in our gospel today. "What an unbelieving and perverse lot you are!" the Lord declares in chastisement of His disciples and all those who would seek His graces, His healing, for they have not the faith to rescue the possessed boy from the grip of the devil. Where is their praise of the Lord's Name? Where is their surpassing love of Him? How is it their belief in the Lord's power to deliver from the bonds of slavery has been so easily shaken? Is it not "the Lord alone" who is God? "If you had faith the size of a mustard seed, you would be able to say to this mountain, 'Move from here to there,' and it would move. Nothing would be impossible for you." Let these words be inscribed upon our hearts, that we will never forget the abundant glory of God which we possess by our faith in Him.

Glorious are you, O Lord, beyond all creatures, beyond all existence! Far above us do you sit, and yet how close to our hearts do you remain. There is none who compares with you; there is nothing in the heavens or on earth greater than you, for you have created all that is. Strengthen our failing love, let it match the glory of your presence, that we might be delivered from all sin and conquer all evil in your divine Name. Give us faith and trust in you, and we will praise you forever. Safe from our enemies, we will glory always in your everlasting love.

O. 19. Mon. (I)

Nineteenth Week

Monday
(Dt.10:12-22; Ps.147:12-15,19-20; Mt.17:22-27)

"In His love for your fathers the Lord was so attached to them
as to choose you, their descendants, in preference to all other peoples."

The Israelites are the chosen race, and Jesus the Chosen One of that race. Upon them the blessing rests, and in the Son it is fulfilled.

Our first reading tells us that the Lord is a great God, "who has no favorites, accepts no bribes; who executes justice for the orphan and the widow, and befriends the alien, feeding and clothing him." And the Israelites are called to be made in the image of their Father, showing His might in this way of compassion and truth. "And now, Israel, what does the Lord, your God, ask of you but to fear the Lord, your God, and follow His ways exactly," declares Moses. And so he enjoins upon the people the Lord's word, "His statutes and ordinances," which "He has not made known" to other nations, and which serve as their guide to maintaining His light in their lives. "He has strengthened the bars of your gates... He has granted peace in your borders," our psalm confirms: by the grace of God's law their children are blessed and become "numerous as the stars of the sky."

And in our gospel we see again the fulfillment of the Father's blessing and of His law in the Person of Jesus and the sacrifice He, and we, are called to make. First Jesus makes clear that He is the Son of God exempt from the temple tax – how can the temple pay tax unto itself, or, better yet, how can the temple be paid tax by Him who made it? Jesus is the Chosen One, the chosen of the chosen sons. And His new Law, His new way – which again is but the fulfillment of the law laid out by Moses – is the cross. Moses tells us of the compassion and justice of the Father, who cares for widows and orphans and aliens, and Jesus embodies that love and truth by being "delivered into the hands of men who will put Him to death" for our sin and to show the love God has for us in such utter sacrifice.

Brothers and sisters, allow me to note here that there is no distinction between the love and the justice of God: they are inseparable, the one ever complementing the other. It is out of both love and a sense of justice that the Lord defends the widows and orphans, saving them from their oppressors and gathering them into His arms. His love breeds justice and His justice love. This is the way of God; and this must be our way as His children.

Yes, God loves the world and so He sends His Son to make atonement for our sin. We have sinned and atonement must be made; it cannot be otherwise. And it cannot be otherwise but that God makes that atonement by His love. Let us join to Him as sons in His holy sacrifice. This is our special, blessed call.

O. 19. Tues. (I)

Tuesday
(Dt.31:1-8; Dt.32:3-4,7-9,12; Mt.18:1-5,10,12-14)

"It is the Lord who marches before you;
He will be with you and never fail or forsake you."

"Do not fear or be dismayed," little ones, the Lord is with us and watches over us. Just as it was He who led the Israelites into the Promised Land, so it is He who leads us now into His "heavenly reign."

In our first reading the Israelites stand poised to attain that which they have been so long promised. Centuries after God's call to Abraham and at the end of forty years wandering in the desert, the time has come for them to enter in and take possession of the land the Lord has set aside for them. As they look toward their heritage on the other side of the Jordan River, Moses encourages them: "It is the Lord, your God, who will cross before you." "The Lord alone was their leader," brothers and sisters; and now it is Jesus alone who shepherds us into the kingdom we look upon with bated breath, for which we patiently prepare ourselves. It is He who has crossed before us in His death and resurrection and now faithfully guides us into His Father's reign.

And just as Moses commissions Joshua to lead the Israelites: "You must bring this people into the land which the Lord swore to their fathers He would give them," encouraging him to be brave and trust in God... so Jesus commissions His disciples to lead His sheep, and especially those who are lost or straying, into the kingdom of God – encouraging them to remain humble always, to make themselves lowly like a little child. And His commission extends, of course, to us today; in these readings we hear His voice.

As for "these little ones" of whom Jesus tells us, "I assure you their angels in heaven constantly behold my Father's face," are we not they of whom He speaks? Are we not His innocent doves in need of the Church's wisdom and guidance to find our place in the Lord's kingdom? And certainly even those who lead the flock are members of the flock themselves, for ultimately it is always the Lord who leads, and all must come unto His presence. Let us be assured, little flock, let us take blessed comfort in the Lord's care for His people. "It is no part of your heavenly Father's plan that a single one of these little ones shall ever come to grief." So let us be as children before Him, beholding the face of God. This is His will for all our souls; let us walk confidently with Him, knowing His love and His blood will never fail us. The kingdom awaits our coming.

O. 19. Wed. (I)

Wednesday
(Dt.34:1-12; Ps.66:1-3,5,8,16-17,20; Mt.18:15-20)

"This is the land which I swore to Abraham, Isaac, and Jacob
that I would give to their descendants."

The promise is coming to fulfillment; Moses looks out on the land the Lord so long ago vowed to give the great patriarchs. And though he shall not enter in and dwell there with the people, yet he has confidence that the promise shall be fulfilled. And though after forty years of struggle he will die here at the border, we know he has a greater reward stored up for him in heaven.

278

What is this Promised Land now? Where do we find it today but in the Church founded by Jesus upon his apostles and living in the hearts and lives of all His disciples? This is the Promised Land, the heavenly Jerusalem at work in the world even now. Notice that Joshua "was filled with the Spirit of wisdom, since Moses had laid his hands on him." And "the Israelites gave him their obedience, thus carrying out the Lord's command." In the same way the power of the Holy Spirit coming from Peter and the apostles is passed down to this day in the Lord's Church: the power is indeed from Jesus and His Spirit, but their power works invariably through the deeds of men so ordained. And by that power Joshua will lead the Israelites to the Promised Land even as Peter and his successors lead the Church to our heavenly homeland, insofar as we give obedience to them at the Lord's command.

Jesus in our gospel outlines the special place the Church holds both in judging offenses and offering prayers. He repeats the Church's power to bind and loose from fault, a power that begins with Peter but extends to all His disciples so ordained, and reminds them also of the great strength they take when together they call upon His name: "If two of you join your voices on earth to pray for anything whatever, it shall be granted you by my Father in heaven." The Lord does not work in a vacuum but accomplishes great and wondrous things through those He lays His hands upon.

What great works were accomplished by Moses: "He had no equal in all the signs and wonders the Lord sent him to perform." O "the might and terrifying power that Moses exhibited in the sight of all Israel." Do you think this power dies with Moses? Do you think it has come to an end? No. For his successor Joshua parts the Jordan River by the same power; and now in Jesus and through His Church that power comes to fulfillment. Tremendous are the Lord's "deeds among men." If we but "appealed to Him in words," what wonders would we know. Wars would cease and this world would look much more like the heavenly kingdom He has promised us all. Let us pray with one voice, as one Church, in His Name.

Thursday
(Jos.3:7-11,13-17; Ps.114:1-6; Mt.18:21-19:1)

"My heavenly Father will treat you in exactly the same way
unless each of you forgives his brother from his heart."

The forgiveness of sins and the crossing of the Jordan into the Promised Land is our theme today. Both are very much one and the same.

In our gospel Jesus tells the parable of the merciless servant in order to teach Peter and the apostles of the office of forgiveness which is theirs

279

through His intercession. When one of a king's officials is unable to pay his debt, he "prostrates himself" before the king and begs for time. "Moved with pity," the master lets the official go and writes off the debt. (In just the same way the apostles are to forgive those who repent of their sins.) But the same servant who is forgiven then demonstrates no forgiveness to a fellow servant, demanding from him all that is owed and throwing him in jail. When the king gets wind of the servant's lack of mercy, he removes the forgiveness of his debt and seeks to extract every penny from him. The parable illustrates Jesus' central teaching: we must forgive to be forgiven. And it indicates the power of forgiveness Jesus, the King, gives to His apostles, the officials, the servants – evident in its being prompted by Peter's question regarding forgiveness. The Lord reminds them (and us) of the forgiveness they have received from Him, and that they should carry this gift to others.

A metaphor of this power is presented in our first reading. Joshua, Moses' successor, leads the people across the Jordan River into the Promised Land at the instruction of the Lord. Notice what causes the waters of the Jordan to "halt in a solid bank," allowing the people to pass over on dry land (much as the previous generation had done at the Red Sea). The waters cease flowing "when the soles of the feet of the priests carrying the ark of the Lord... touch the water of the Jordan." Much as Christ and His apostles stand in the breach interceding for the forgiveness of our sins and thus drawing us into the heavenly kingdom, so "the priests carrying the ark of the covenant of the Lord remained motionless on dry ground in the bed of the Jordan until the whole nation had completed the passage." Of old the priests led by Joshua found their power of intercession in the ark of the covenant which held the Ten Commandments; today our priests, led by Peter, find their power of forgiveness in the cross of Christ.

Brothers and sisters, let us all forgive one another from the heart. Let us flee in fear like the "Jordan turned back" on its course the danger of holding a grudge or failing to share the blessings we have received from Jesus. Let us cross the Jordan to the Promised Land ourselves and serve to draw others into the heavenly kingdom. Let us not disappoint our Father and so know His wrath; let us shine His loving mercy forth till all have crossed on dry land.

Friday

(Jos.24:1-13; Ps.136:1-3,16-18,21-22,24; Mt.19:3-12)

"I gave you a land which you had not tilled
and cities which you had not built, to dwell in."

All of our lives come to us by the grace of God, "for His mercy endures forever." It is never by our own hands that anything good is accomplished. As the Lord says to the Israelites, "It was not your sword or your bow," by which they conquered the nations – emphasizing that it was He who destroyed them – so we must know, too, that it is the Lord who goes before us and brings us to the land He has prepared for us; and it is by His hand that all our enemies, all obstacles, are conquered.

Our first reading and our psalm speak particularly of the Lord's finally bringing the Israelites safely into the Promised Land. Joshua, who has by God's grace accomplished the work commissioned upon him through Moses, now seeks to remind the people of the blessings God has bestowed upon them in giving them this fruitful land, that they might not forget their God and the praise due Him. As Moses prepared the people with his speech before they entered the Promised Land, so Joshua exhorts them now that they have attained their goal; and the focus of both addresses is that they not forget their God who provides them with all things.

In our gospel Jesus teaches us of the blessing of chastity, of the sanctity of marriage and the godly call to celibate life. Of what does He speak but of the Promised Land become quite real in the inhabitants of the New Jerusalem. We are told throughout the letters of especially St. Paul that our bodies are temples of the Holy Spirit, and that sins against their purity and integrity are the gravest of offenses, for in these the sin is so real, so present, even to our flesh. In these temples we dwell. These temples we must keep holy, we must keep pure. "It is so difficult," you might say. Then remember the Lord's words to the Israelites; remember that it is He who "slew powerful kings" before them, that it is by His power they conquered, and you will be able to say with them that it is the Lord who "freed us from our foes."

Jesus says of celibacy, perhaps the greatest gift of God and the closest to Him we can come, "Not everyone can accept this teaching, only those to whom it is given to do so," and this is our key to attaining its grace, and indeed the grace of any form of chastity: we must know it is He who works in us and we must seek His blessing "for the sake of God's reign"; and then He will make us steady and strong in the fields of His Promised Land as we call upon and praise His Name.

Saturday

(Jos.24:14-29; Ps.16:1-2,5,7-8,11; Mt.19:13-15)

"We will serve the Lord, our God, and obey His voice."

Like children we must come before the Lord and extol His holy Name. "Completely and sincerely" we must serve Him and He will place His hands upon our heads and bless us. And we will sing with David of the "fullness of joys in [His] presence, the delights at [His] right hand forever." We indeed will be as children, and He will be our God. Listen to the words of Jesus: "Let the children come to me... The kingdom of God belongs to such as these." O to know the blessing of being in the Lord's presence forever!

"My Lord are you. Apart from you I have no good," cries David to his God. Indeed, how our psalm sings the praises of the Lord and the blessing of our refuge in Him. How well it illustrates the fruit of the covenant the people enter into with God at Shechem under Joshua's leadership. The Promise having been fulfilled, Joshua calls the Israelites to renew their commitment to the Lord. And though their fidelity to Him will only be for a short time and the stone set up shall soon be a witness against them, yet their vows are those we must all make in sincerity and in truth. Obeying His voice is indeed our salvation. As David sings, "I bless the Lord who counsels me; even in the night my heart exhorts me." The Lord is ever there for those who trust in Him, who give their lives to Him, who serve Him – who come to Him as a humble child in innocence and love. What greater blessing can we know than to love the Lord who is "a holy God" and so become one with Him? This is our "allotted portion," this is our "cup" – this is the reign of God upon us to which we are called.

"I set the Lord before me," our psalm states, "with Him at my right hand I shall not be disturbed." If we but set our hearts on Him, brothers and sisters, there can be nothing that will move us. If we but take our vows in the Spirit of Truth, He will be ever with us. Let us not be afraid. Let us not be afraid that we will fall, that He will leave us. Let us pursue Him with heart and soul; let us give our lives over to Him.

To serve Him and to love Him is our blessed joy. Let us be as children before Him and reap this joy unto life eternal. Let our covenant with Him be written upon our hearts and evident in all our lives, and we shall stand in His presence forever. Set aside all false gods; listen to His voice. Alleluia!

Twentieth Week

Monday
(Jgs.2:11-19; Ps.106:4,34-37,39-40,43-44; Mt.19:16-22)

"They were quick to stray from the way their fathers had taken,
and did not follow their example of obedience
to the commandments of the Lord."

It is not long before the Israelites break their vows to the Lord, mingling with other nations and worshiping their idols. As soon as the generation which has known Joshua dies out, their children begin to stray. And though the Lord "raised up judges to deliver them from the power of their despoilers," to save them from their enemies when He heard their cry of affliction, repeatedly "when the judge died, they would relapse and do worse." Thus it shall also be with the interminable series of good and evil kings which shall lead to their exile, and thus the necessity of the eternal King, Jesus Christ, under whose reign there is no faltering backward – for He lives forever to intercede.

So evil had the Israelites become that they "sacrificed their sons and their daughters to demons." And one must ask, should the Lord God not punish such deeds? Does He not hold justice in His right hand? Should such action be allowed to transpire? Although the Lord holds compassion in His left hand and always has regard for our affliction when we cry out to Him, He does not, He cannot, allow sin to go unpunished. If He did so it would but grow more grave and the peril to the soul would be greater, and thus He would fail in compassion not only to the victims of oppression but to the soul of the oppressor.

How difficult this is to hear in the materialistic age in which we dwell, where the body is king and possessions take the place of the spirit. How like the young man in our gospel many are when they hear the call to perfection, when they are challenged to give up their possessions, for our souls have become one with our material wealth, and to lose it we think spells death. But it is not death but life to which Jesus calls us, life in the Spirit, which is life itself. And whether we own things or not we must not own them; we must know that all belongs to God, or we shall not belong to God but to the false idols of the nations around us and the death and defilement their evil practices bring. For do we not today sacrifice our children on the altar of abortion in the name of ease and luxury?

"There is One who is good. If you wish to enter life, keep His commandments." If you wish for death, continue to stray.

283

Tuesday
(Jgs.6:11-24; Ps.85:9,11-14; Mt.19:23-30)

"Go with the strength you have and save Israel
from the power of Midian. It is I who send you."

The world is at enmity with God. The kingdom of heaven is not as the kingdom of this earth, thus Jesus tells us that "the last shall come first." For though we pray the Lord's kingdom come now to this earth, it shall not be fulfilled until "the new age when the Son of Man takes His seat upon a throne befitting His glory." We must therefore not judge with the mind of the world but continually struggle against it and its power.

In our gospel Jesus calls the apostles to give up all things for the sake of the kingdom. As He instructs them of the danger of the riches of this world, they are "completely overwhelmed." Judging with an earthly mind, they think riches should be of assistance; but the Lord wishes to teach them of the mind of God, upon which the world is set in opposition. The apostles indeed "have put everything aside to follow" Jesus, and for this they shall receive their reward. But their only reward on this earth will be persecution; it is in heaven their glory shall come.

Yes, the Lord "proclaims peace to His people" and "justice shall walk before Him, and salvation, along the way of His steps"; and though the Lord blesses and guides us in our fight against evil now – imparting to us a share of His Spirit – yet we know "His benefits" shall only be fulfilled in heaven; this is the land which "shall yield its increase." As in our first reading the meat and cakes of Gideon are laid upon a rock, not consumed by the mouth for the sake of the belly but consumed by the fire of the Lord to feed his faith, so it is that the Lord and His angels and all those who follow Him are of the Spirit and not the flesh. And so it is that the Lord chooses those who are least in the eyes of the world, as is Gideon ("My family is the meanest in Manasseh, and I am the most insignificant in my father's house...") and places His power upon them, to show us not only that "for God all things are possible," but more so to instruct us not to put faith in the passing things of this world but in the eternal "justice and peace" of His heavenly kingdom.

We must indeed struggle continually against this world and its power with the strength God gives us, brothers and sisters. In the riches of this life we must never take our ease. For these are set in opposition to God in enmity. God is Spirit and we must be as He is, taking our places in His heavenly glory with the apostles who have laid down their lives and so now judge in righteousness with Jesus the king. Go forth now in His Name.

284

Wednesday
(Jgs.9:6-15; Ps.21:2-7; Mt.20:1-16)

"The last shall be first and the first shall be last."

Jesus, the Son of God and true King, who is first, has made Himself last, and so for His humility will be exalted forever; Abimalech, rebellious son of Gideon, who is least of all his brothers, has made himself first, and so will be humbled for his vain pride.

In our first reading Jotham curses his brother Abimalech from the mountaintop as this least of the trees is anointed king after having murdered all other of his brothers. (There were seventy sons of the judge Gideon – who himself refused kingship.) The people of Shechem have fallen by pride in this son of their own city and so they, too, are cursed for taking refuge in his dark shadow. Abimalech's thorns shall pierce them and shall prove a bitter medicine of purgation for these wayward Israelites. They shall indeed be the death of one another.

In contrast to this false king, in David's psalm we hear of the blessings the true king receives from God, in whom he rejoices and to whom he gives all glory for victory: "O Lord, in your strength the king is glad." It is not by his own will that this king reigns, but by the will of the Father, and so his place is assured and he is exalted and made "a blessing forever." David, too, was the least of his brothers, but unlike Abimalech, who took matters into his own jealous and bloody hands, he trusted always in the Lord and humbled himself before the God of all, and so, "great is his glory in [the Lord's] victory."

And, of course, we know that it is the Son of David, the Son of God, Jesus Christ, who is the King of kings and the Lord of lords: in Him is the blessed kingship of God fulfilled. And, of course, it is His great humility which has made Him so exalted. Did He not take the crown of thorns upon His head? Was He not pierced by the pride of man's rebellion? Did He not accept the bitter wine as He died upon the cross? And so should not all trees bow down to this sanctifying tree, this true vine? Is it not by the fruit of *this* buckthorn that we are purged from our sins against Him who is Most High? He who has been raised on the cross is indeed King of us all, and all others mere pretenders.

Brothers and sisters, it is only in Christ and in the shadow of the tree that is the cross that we shall find blessing, that we shall find glory, that we shall be exalted and receive "a crown of pure gold." Follow no other, for false gods abound and their fall is great. Toil only in the vineyard of the Lord and regardless of the length or breadth of your labor you shall receive your recompense, which is oneness with Him who is eternal and whose generous reign knows no bounds. And be not envious of others' entering in if it is you who must toil long – your service of God should be your joy and a source of great humility.

Thursday
(Jgs.11:29-39; Ps.40:5,7-10; Mt.22:1-14)

"You have made a vow to the Lord.
Do with me as you have vowed."

As with the Blessed Virgin Mary, who is blessed not so much for giving birth to Jesus – or consecrating herself to God as a virgin – as for hearing and doing the word of God, being the handmaiden of the Lord extraordinaire... so the Lord delights not in "sacrifice and oblation," per se, but in "ears open to obedience." In accepting the sacrifice of her fertility (the greatest sacrifice a woman could make, though it may be difficult to realize in these days of abortion and contraception), Jephthah's daughter demonstrates the obedience required of all the redeemed.

"Happy the man who makes the Lord his trust; who turns not to idolatry or to those who stray after falsehood," David proclaims in our psalm today. "The spirit of the Lord" upon him, Jephthah defeats severely the Ammonites, a nation which practiced the sacrifice of their children to their god, Molech. The Lord thus shows disdain for them and their ways. Thus also it should be evident that Jephthah would not do in the spirit of the Lord that which is directly opposed to His will. The sacrifice of Jephthah's daughter is of her fertility – it is her virginity she mourns and not her death. And Jephthah maintains his vow by consecrating her wholly to God, knowing that his generation will cease, since he has no other sons or daughters to bear his name, and thus making a great sacrifice himself. If it were her life itself he offers God, he would be no better than those he destroyed and certainly no son of Abraham, who was taught the truth against such sacrifice so many years before.

This aside, we turn to our gospel. It is clear that Jesus is telling the chief priests and elders of the people that they do not have the obedience required of the redeemed. "In the written scroll it is prescribed" that all must do the will of God, but these who know the Scriptures so well, know nothing of them at all... and so the Word goes out to draw the whole world into the kingdom prepared by God. But to these, too, Jesus has a warning: "The invited are many, the elect are few." If we are "not properly dressed for a wedding feast," if we have not aligned our lives with the will of God, we too shall be thrown "out into the night" with the man who had to "wail and grind his teeth." And this wailing shall not come as holy sacrifice unto the ears of God; it shall not demonstrate our obedience to Him, but rather be the inflicting of judgment upon our souls.

Let us be obedient to the will of God in all things, brothers and sisters. Let us hear His voice alone and follow where it leads.

Friday
(Ruth 1:1,3-6,14-16,22; Ps.146:2,5-10; Mt.22:34-40)

"Wherever you go I will go, wherever you lodge I will lodge,
   your people shall be my people, and your God my God."

How well our readings harmonize this day. Jesus speaks plainly to the keepers of the law the greatest commandments – total love of God and neighbor – and Ruth puts them into practice for our witness. And our psalm sings the praises of our great God of love, whose care for "the hungry" and "the strangers," "the fatherless and the widow," we are called to imitate. Alleluia, indeed.

Ruth is a foreigner, from a land which follows other gods; yet she is willing to leave "her people and her god" to follow Naomi and the living and true God unreservedly. O how this mirrors all our call to leave all of this world behind and follow the Lord and His way. O that we had the courage and faith of this Moabite woman who will become the great-grandmother of King David. How well this illustrates God's call and blessing to any and all who seek Him, who long to walk in His steps. And how well His way of compassion and love is shown in His care for this widow Naomi, who came to Moab hungry and leaves now to return to Israel with this blessed daughter-in-law to be with her and serve her without restraint.

The words of the Lord are so true: "Love the Lord your God with your whole heart, with your whole soul, and with all your mind," and "love your neighbor as yourself." They silence even the hardest of hearts with their radiance. We know that God is love, that through His help we find blessing – that His concern for all those in need extends "through all generations" – and we know that we should be like Him... but how often we fail to practice Ruth's resolve.

This day let us cast off our reservations, brothers and sisters, and cast ourselves upon the love and grace of the Lord. Let us resolve never to "abandon or forsake" Him. Knowing clearly the love of God which comes from the lips of our own Lord of love and our blessed psalmist, and which is embodied by Ruth's profession of faith and commitment to love, let us vow in this spirit to return the Lord's boundless love, for in loving we become like Him whom we love and so stand with Him who "shall reign forever" in the eternal kingdom of light and love. Again I say, now is the acceptable time; today is the day of salvation. Follow Him unreservedly.

Saturday
(Ruth 2:1-3,8-11,4:13-17; Ps.128:1-5; Mt.23:1-12)

"The greatest among you will be the one who serves the rest."

Today we can contrast the faith of Ruth with the Pharisees' of Jesus' time. In our first reading, Ruth says to her mother-in-law Naomi, "Let me go and glean ears of grain in the field of anyone who will allow me that favor." She puts herself at ready service in all humility, despite the potential dangers that come with being a foreign woman working in a place dominated by men who may not have the greatest of respect for women in general and especially for her. In contrast, in our gospel Jesus says of the Pharisees, "They bind up heavy loads, hard to carry, to lay on other men's shoulders, while they themselves will not lift a finger to budge them." These Pharisees have no heart for service; they are sooner the oppressors of the poor and vulnerable, and are rather concerned for "places of honor at banquets" and "marks of respect in public" than the needs of others. How stark the contrast is between she who serves and those who are inflated with pride.

And how true are Jesus' words: "Whoever exalts himself shall be humbled, but whoever humbles himself shall be exalted." Indeed, God's providential hand watches over Ruth as she gleans in the field that "happened to be the section belonging to Boaz of the clan of Elimalech," her father-in-law, and so a close kinsman. Not only does Boaz make provision for her safe and fruitful gleaning of his fields – instructing his young men to do her "no harm" and indeed to leave food behind that it will be easy for her to gather – but he seeks diligently to take her to wife... and through their union she (and Naomi) is blessed with a son who will be grandfather to King David. But what of these Pharisees and their vanity? From them Jesus will take the keys of the kingdom, the teaching authority on earth which they so misuse for their own gain, and give it to others as He builds His Church on Peter and the apostles. And so today we hold up Ruth as a model of faith, while these dead men's bones which walked the earth in whitewashed tombs now find their home rotting in the grave.

"You shall eat the fruit of your handiwork," our psalm proclaims. Those like Ruth who "fear the Lord, who walk in His ways... shall be like a fruitful vine" and their "children like olive plants around" their table. However, those inflated with pride, serving no one but themselves, shall come to naught. Let us heed our Lord's warning today not to exalt ourselves in any work we do, but rather set our hearts on serving others. Then we shall truly be fruitful, for then we shall know the fruits of heaven.

Twenty-First Week

Monday
(1Thes.1:2-5,8-10; Ps.149:1-6,9; Mt.23:13-22)

"You turned to God from idols,
to serve Him who is the living and true God."

Contrast is at the heart of today's readings again. The faith of the Thessalonians and the inspired preaching of Paul are in distinct opposition to the empty ways and words of the scribes and Pharisees.

In our first reading Paul praises the Thessalonians, who are "laboring in love, and showing constancy in hope in our Lord Jesus Christ," telling them: "Throughout every region your faith in God is celebrated." In our gospel Jesus condemns the scribes and Pharisees for their blindness to the presence of God. In contrast to the Thessalonians, they have turned from worship of the true God to idols; their vision set on the gold therein, they are unable to see the temple and how sacred it is – their hearts set on things of this earth and the laws they have contrived, they are blind to the Son of God, who sits upon the throne of heaven, as He stands before them. And not only are their vain beliefs in contrast to the true faith of the Thessalonians, but their failures in carrying the Word of God forth stand also in sharp contrast to Paul's fruitful preaching. Paul's preaching was "one of power; it was carried on in the Holy Spirit and out of complete conviction," and so led to the conversion of many nations. On the other hand, Christ says to the scribes and Pharisees: "You shut the doors of the kingdom of God in men's faces... You travel over sea and land to make a single convert, but once he is converted you make a devil of him twice as wicked as yourselves."

We must be the fruit of the Apostle's preaching, brothers and sisters, and not the vain teaching of those who set their souls on the gold of this world. For as the faithful "sing to the Lord a new song of praise," as they "rejoice in their king" and "praise His name in the festive dance," even so the voice of the wicked will be silenced: they shall choke to death on all their pride. So let us be those who "await from heaven the Son [God] raised from the dead – Jesus, who delivers us from the wrath to come." With the Thessalonians let us prove our faith in our labor of love, working ever for the coming of the kingdom. And "the high praises of God [will] be in [our] throats" and the "glory of all His faithful" will be ours. Turning from all the idols of this blind generation, let us be born now of the Spirit of God.

289

Tuesday

(1Thes.2:1-8; Ps.139:1-6; Mt.23:23-26)

"First cleanse the inside of the cup
so that its outside may be clean."

The Lord rails against the Pharisees again today, calling them from false practice to genuine faith; and in Paul we again see the paragon of true ministry in the Lord's Name.

In our gospel the Lord calls the Pharisees "frauds," for they have the appearance of holiness in clothing and posture and minor actions, but inside are "filled with loot and lust." In our first reading, it is quite evident that the preaching of Paul "does not spring from deceit or impure motives or any sort of trickery," as does the work of the Pharisees. He is not at all guilty of "flattering words or greed under any pretext," seeking the glory of God rather than "glory from men." This, of course, is the central question: do we perform our acts for others to see, from selfish motives of pride and greed and the accolades we might gain from man; or are we laying down our lives for God, giving no thought to our own importance or the opposition we may face? Does our work and our life spring from truth, or does it spring from lie?

"O Lord, you have probed me and you know me," David sings in our psalm today. Truly the Lord is "the tester of hearts." He is familiar with all our ways and the motives whence they come. Indeed, "even before a word is on [our] tongue, behold, [He] know[s] the whole of it." Inside and out He sees us, He scrutinizes us, that He may enter into us and renew us. It is by His grace that the inside of the cup might be made clean and so our work be fruitful in His Name.

And so, what of us, brothers and sisters? What does the Lord see when He peers within our hearts, when His penetrating gaze pierces our soul? Do we meet "the test imposed on us by God" as Paul does and live in "justice and mercy and good faith," or is there but corruption within us which will not allow the Lord's light to enter, thus making us blind to His grace?

The Lord surrounds us so, that we call out with David, "Such knowledge is too wonderful for me; too lofty for me to attain." Indeed, the Lord is far above and beyond our comprehension and His holiness can seem beyond our ability to attain; but if we have hearts that are open and trusting and loving of His Word, we find that He is "gentle as any nursing mother fondling her little ones," that He, in fact, shares with us His very life, and so makes us as His own. The Lord will cleanse the inside of the cup. Let Him act upon your soul.

Wednesday

(1Thes.2:9-13; Ps.139:1,7-12; Mt.23:27-32)

"Make your lives worthy of the God
who calls you to His kingship and glory."

God is our Father, and those who preach "God's good tidings" love us "as a father does his children," for their message is "not as the word of men" but truly "the word of God at work within [those] who believe." Come to the Lord's table. Eat of His Body, drink of His Blood. Become as He is by His holy Word.

Children of light we are called to be, and what is that light but the one which shines in all places at all times and which is inescapable. "Where can I go from your spirit?" David wonders in our psalm. Whether we fly to the heavens or "sink to the nether world," He is there. For Him "darkness itself is not dark, and night shines as the day" because He Himself is light, and where He is, light shines – and He is everywhere.

How can we become children of such an awesome God? How can we enter "His kingship and glory" as Paul exhorts us in our first reading? The only way is by Jesus and the only way is to follow those who bring Jesus to us, whose conduct is "upright, just, and irreproachable" as is Paul's – our means of salvation is the Church, its prophets and martyrs, its teaching and sacraments... its grace which comes to us through Jesus Christ to lead us to the Father of all. On the apostles and their message of the Gospel our faith is set.

In our gospel Jesus again chastises the Pharisees, those who have not been loving and faithful fathers for the people, those from whom care of the kingdom will be taken for the "hypocrisy and evil" within them. For though they present "a holy exterior," it is but the bones of the saints they hold within their whitewashed tombs and not their blessed spirit. Indeed, they shall show themselves murderous as their forefathers, who shed the prophet's blood – and whom they ascribe to themselves by name – in their giving up the fulfillment of the prophets to crucifixion. "Full of filth" inside and lovers of the tomb's darkness, they are not worthy to be called fathers of the Lord's children. And Jesus proves that God's light shines in even the darkest places by exposing their corruption in our gospel today.

Brothers and sisters, beware of following false leaders whose motives are not pure, who do not lay down their lives for the flock. Remain within the walls of the Church, where the Spirit dwells and where the Father nourishes His people on their way to His kingdom and glory.

Thursday
(1Thes.3:7-13; Ps.90:3-4,12-14,17; Mt.24:42-51)

"Stay awake, therefore!
You cannot know the day your Lord is coming."

And what is it to stay awake, to be ready, but to do as Paul exhorts the Thessalonians in our first reading: to continue to grow in holiness until that day we meet with the Lord. This is our essential call.

Here we are, having been converted to the Lord, having found faith in God as our foundation and been appointed servants by Christ until He should return. We are that "faithful, farsighted servant whom the master has put in charge of his household to dispense food at need." Certainly our priests dispense the most necessary food of the Word and the Bread of Life, but all Christians the Lord gifts with His store of nourishment for the people; all of us are called to provide spiritual as well as physical nourishment to our brothers and sisters. We cannot do other than this or we are not Christians, and we will be far from the Lord at His second coming – when He calls to account all His servants.

And each day we must indeed know the Lord's increase and "overflow with love for one another and for all"; we must always grow in the gifts the Lord gives us, not becoming impatient for the time which passes, but ever taking it as opportunity to strengthen our salvation in Christ. We must in this way have the vision of God: "A thousand years in your sight are as yesterday, now that it is past, or as a watch in the night," our psalm declares (expressing the patience Moses and the Israelites needed in their forty years wandering through the desert); and so short should our wait seem if lived in the presence of our God.

And so now as we wait and watch, now as we make ourselves ready for the Lord by the service we perform in His Name, let us entreat the Lord to "fill us at daybreak with [His] kindness," let us pray for Him to "prosper the work of our hands." For all in our hands is our gift from Him to accomplish in His Name and by His grace, and by so numbering "our days aright" in His presence, we shall "gain wisdom of heart" and be awake and ready for His coming.

My prayer for you, brothers and sisters, is Paul's own: "May he strengthen your hearts, making them blameless and holy before our God and Father at the coming of our Lord Jesus with all His holy ones." I pray we shall meet on that happy day.

292

Friday

(1Thes.4:1-8; Ps.97:1-2,5-6,10-12; Mt.25:1-13)

"God has not called us to immorality but to holiness."

And so, "keep your eyes open" and "make still greater progress" in the path that leads to His kingdom. Your lights shining brightly as you await His return, be ready to enter His marriage feast.

"It is God's will that you grow in holiness," Paul instructs us in our first reading. "Conduct yourselves in a way pleasing to God" is his message. For there is a day coming on which the Lord will judge us and all we do; therefore, we must have nothing to do with "immorality" or "passionate desire" or "cheating" – "for the Lord is an avenger of all such things" – and these will find us barred from His kingdom. Rather, we must stay the path we are on, guarding ourselves "in sanctity and honor" and securing even greater gifts and graces from God that we might keep in store against His judgment, against His wrath to come. For if "the mountains melt like wax before the Lord," how strong must we be to stand on that day of His return?

But for those who do stand strong, for those who do acquire "flasks of oil" to keep their torches burning for whatever hour the Lord might come – for them there shall be great rejoicing. This is the fate of the just. "Light dawns for the just; and gladness, for the upright of heart," for their light is like His own and so He weds them unto Himself; to rejoice with the king of all the earth is their portion and cup.

Yes, "the ones who were ready went in to the wedding with Him," but those unprepared were locked outside the doors. And so we must ask ourselves, does Jesus know us? Are we ready for the day of His coming? Do we avoid all stain of sin which detracts from the purity we must maintain as bridesmaids of the Lord? Or is there yet that which keeps us from standing ready at His gates? He will come. He will come again to judge our souls, this Son of God most just, and so we must heed the instruction of the Holy Spirit now to prepare ourselves against that day, ever making progress in His Name.

Let holiness be our treasured possession, brothers and sisters. Let it be a flaming torch growing ever higher by the breath of the Spirit upon our souls, until it reaches unto Him and His kingdom. The Lord's "delay" in coming serves but to weed the evil from the good. Take this time to increase in faith and in knowledge of God. Be as His own.

Saturday
(1Thes.4:9-12; Ps.98:1,7-9; Mt.25:14-30)

"Those who have, will get more until they grow rich,
while those who have not, will lose even the little they have."

Again, brothers and sisters, we must always grow in the gifts and graces of the Lord, never looking down upon what He gives us as too little (or too much), but ever putting such talents to use that they might produce an abundant yield and bring us to the joys of heaven.

"Well done! You are an industrious and reliable servant... Come, share your master's joy!" Do we not wish to hear these words from our gospel today spoken to us on the last day? Do we not wish to be put in charge of greater matters as we enter the joy of the eternal kingdom? Are these not the riches we seek? Then, indeed we must be industrious while here; we must put the Lord's gifts to good use. We must heed Paul's exhortation "to remain at peace and attend to [our] own affairs." In this way of working quietly for the Lord we will certainly make "even greater progress," until we find the victory proclaimed in our psalm. On that day when "the rivers clap their hands" and "the mountains shout with them for joy," the Lord "will rule the world with justice and the peoples with equity"; He will surely give those deserving their reward, while they who have been "worthless, lazy lout(s)," those who have not served Him out of a holy fear, out of love, but have held a judgmental disposition toward Him and withheld a generous attitude toward others, shall be cast into "the darkness outside" where they will ever "wail and grind [their] teeth."

Take hold of what the Lord gives you today: the breath in your nostrils and the beat of your heart are in His hands, and He calls you to employ your mind and body at His affair of bringing the kingdom of heaven and His love to this earth. Whatever work He puts in your hands to accomplish, be not slack in its fulfillment. Go forward with faith and a desire to please Him, and He will ever bless and multiply all you have a mind to do; and this work will keep you from the empty darkness of hell and bring you to the rich fruits of heaven.

Twenty-Second Week

Monday
(1Thes.4:13-18; Ps.96:1,3-5,11-13; Lk.4:16-30)

"He comes to rule the earth."

He is coming, and has come. He set us free from the prison of sin when first He came, and will set us free from death when He comes again and "we shall be with the Lord unceasingly."

In our gospel we read of His first coming "to bring glad tidings to the poor, to proclaim liberty to captives..." Fulfilling the words of the prophets, He brought "a year of favor from the Lord," to heal all those who waited for His coming, who trusted in His word. And though even as His hometown of Nazareth rejected Him and His truth and led Him to "the brow of the hill" to be cast down, so all would turn their backs on Him and deliver Him up for crucifixion; yet His death was not the end and His life was not fruitless. In His walking the earth He brought light into the darkness and in His bleeding on the cross provided means for its fulfillment.

And on the day when He comes again, death shall indeed be banished, darkness will be no more, for "God will bring forth with Him from the dead those who have fallen asleep believing in Him" and "we, the living, the survivors, will be caught up with them in the clouds to meet the Lord in the air." This the apostle Paul makes quite clear. As Jesus "died and rose," so will all who believe in Him do the same: what was brought to us in His first coming – the light to the nations – will be made complete in His second coming in a year of favor that has no end.

And of both of these comings our psalm does sing, for both are gloriously triumphant: "Let the heavens be glad and the earth rejoice, let the sea and what fills it resound..." All creation glories in the coming of God; in His holy presence it finds its fulfillment. Forever it has longed to be joined with Him, and when first He came as man, it rejoiced to see Him; and when He comes "from heaven at the word of command, at the sound of the archangel's voice and God's trumpet" as the Son of God in all His glory, its joy and its song will know no bounds. For then "He shall rule the world with justice and the peoples with His constancy": the world shall never again be moved from His way of truth and light, and neither shall we. Rejoice at His coming, brothers and sisters, and live in His light.

O. 22. Tues. (I)

Tuesday
(1Thes.5:1-6,9-11; Ps.27:1,4,13-14; Lk.4:31-37)

"Wait for the Lord with courage;
be stouthearted, and wait for the Lord."

The Word of the Lord has all "authority and power." The Word of the Lord casts out demons. The Word of the Lord brings light to the soul who seeks Him. In Him we have no fear.

He comes, brothers and sisters; yes, He comes... As He entered the synagogue in Galilee and cast out the evil spirit from the man and from the place, so He will come at the end of the age and cast all evil from the face of the earth. No longer shall the devil have a place here; all darkness will be banished. This hope should bring us but joy. We who are of light should long for the day when the Lord who is "our light and [our] salvation" comes to cleanse the world of evil; if we seek "to dwell in the house of the Lord" we must know that only His authority and power, only His sharp voice speaking truth and shaking the powers of this earth will bring "the loveliness of the Lord" our hearts desire to contemplate forever. As He came to cast out the devil from the man in the synagogue, as He has come to cast all evil from the temple of our bodies, so He must come at the end of the age to cast all sin into hell, that His light and all His children of light might shine in unadulterated glory.

Do not fear. Do not fear the coming of His kingdom, the power of His Word. Though we may be "struck with astonishment" and wonder at "His speech," though the teaching of the Lord leave us "spellbound," yet we should welcome it and seek to increase its presence in our lives and in this world. It is His teaching, it is the power of His Word we are called as children of His light to bring into this world. For, indeed, the world is a dark place, and many there are who fear as the demon the destruction of the darkness in which they have taken what has seemed to them secure refuge. It must be known that in darkness there is no "security," in sin there is no "peace"... Only in Him is true peace and security.

Let us not be anguished at the passing of the darkness which comes by the just wrath of God. Let us not slumber into its clutches and so find refuge there. We must remain vigilant, seeking with eyes of light the coming of Jesus the Christ. We are destined for salvation in Him. In Him let us take comfort and upbuild one another, spreading "His renown" in our hearts and "through the surrounding country."

O. 22. Wed. (I)

Wednesday
(Col.1:1-8; Ps.52:10-11; Lk.4:38-44)

"And He continued to preach in the synagogues of Judea."

The Word goes forth, bringing healing to the hearts of the faithful. The Word goes forth, ever growing among the people. As "the message of truth, the Gospel... has come to [the Colossians], has borne fruit, and has continued to grow," so "it has everywhere in the world." As Jesus has set out "into the open country" to bring "the good news of the reign of God" to all to whom He was sent; as Paul, as Timothy, as Epaphrus – as all the apostles have gone out bringing the Word forth and planting it in the hearts of all who have ears open to the healing touch of God and making them "like a green olive tree in the house of God," so that same Word goes forth today through the apostles the Lord has ordained to carry His message of truth; and so we hear of it in our readings of daily Mass, in our daily bread.

Our "love in the Spirit" must ever grow, brothers and sisters; it must ever move forward. For the Word of God ever moves forward to the ends of the earth bringing the love of God to all, and we must move with it. There is no stopping and staying long in any place along this path we tread with the Lord. As He moved on from town to town doing the will of the Father, so our work must ever travel with Him, until it is accomplished in Him. Here there is no place to stay, no place to lay our heads; here there is only moving forward in the Lord.

And, yes, we are moved "by the hope held in store for [us] in heaven." This is the place to which we travel in all our movements, in all our work and prayer. We know now and it has been openly stated, plainly revealed, that Jesus is the Son of God, and that He makes a place for us in His kingdom. And by our "faith in Christ Jesus and the love [we] bear all the saints," we, too, come into that kingdom, into His presence; with Paul, with the Colossians, with all the faithful who "trust in the kindness of God forever and ever," we find that kingdom being revealed in our very hearts and in our very actions... and so heaven passes through our midst and makes us sons of the Most High.

Let us be healed of all that keeps us from growing to Him, from growing with Him, from moving forward in service of our Lord Jesus Christ. With our words and in our actions let us preach of the glory of God and so move closer to His kingdom.

Thursday
(Col.1:9-14; Ps.98:2-6; Lk.5:1-11)

"You will multiply good works of every sort
and grow in the knowledge of God."

As Simon Peter and the others "caught such a great number of fish that their nets were at the breaking point," so shall it be with any Christian who devotes himself to the work and the will of God. But as the apostles "brought their boats to land, left everything, and became His followers," so we must dedicate our lives entirely to Him if we are to "attain full knowledge of His will through perfect wisdom and spiritual insight." We must leave all else aside and we will become "worthy to share the lot of the saints in light," becoming ever more fruitful as fishers of men and bringers of that light into the world.

"The Lord has made His salvation known," and notice from where He chooses "to teach the crowds." Looking for a mooring, a place from which to preach, "He got into one of the boats, the one belonging to Peter." Yes, it is in the barque of Peter and through the barque of Peter that Jesus manifests Himself, that He brings His teaching forth. In this boat He sits and teaches the nations. It is this boat He encourages to "put out into deep water and lower [its] nets for a catch." For His blessing is upon this boat and him who steers it, as well as the partners he calls "to come and help," that is, James and John and all the other apostles – the bishops and priests and all the holy people beckoned by the Lord through the office of Peter to fill His boats to bursting.

"He rescued us from the power of darkness and brought us into the kingdom of His beloved Son," Paul, another blessed fisher of men, tells us. And the forgiveness of the Lord necessary for one to be called to "a life worthy of the Lord" is evident in the repentance of our leader, our first of apostles, Simon Peter, as he "fell at the knees of Jesus saying, 'Leave me, Lord, I am a sinful man,'" in awe at the presence of God before him. Only by such humility are we drawn from the darkness of sin, only by recognizing our weakness are we made strong – only by bowing down before the Lord and serving others in His name are we made worthy of the kingdom of light. Only then with our psalmist will we "with trumpets and the sound of the horn sing joyfully before the King, the Lord." Rooted in His Church and its service let us ever grow in knowledge and joy before our God.

O. 22. Fri. (I)

Friday
(Col.1:15-20; Ps.100:1-5; Lk.5:33-39)

"New wine should be poured into fresh skins."

"The blood of His cross" is poured forth for us; it becomes the new wine we drink this day, that which makes us new men by its grace. The scribes and Pharisees refuse this new wine, saying, "I find the old wine better," so they cannot see "the image of the invisible God, the firstborn of all creatures," standing before them this day. Do we see Him? Do we hear His teaching? Do we allow His Word and His presence to be poured into us? Do we make ourselves "fresh skins" to receive the wine that is the Lord? Or do we, too, prefer the old? The old man under the burden of sin and death must be put away before the new man of grace and life can enter in.

"In Him everything in heaven and on earth was created, things visible and invisible." Paul tells us Jesus fills all the universe with His presence, for "all were created through Him and for Him. He is before all else that is," and "in Him everything continues in being." He is the source of life and life itself. And He is "head of the body, the Church." "Firstborn of the dead," primacy indeed is His "in everything." First to be born, first to die, He is also the first to be raised to new life... and by His power we are all raised to the new life we now find through His sacrifice. The blood which fills the universe must now fill our beings; we must be filled with His presence, for only by Him does grace come. Only by Him is the Law fulfilled, the Word made real, and the life of heaven become our own.

And those who are present to Him, those who are present with Him – those who are filled with His Spirit cannot help but rejoice. The disciples could not fast while Jesus was with them, while the bridegroom to whom they wed themselves was in their midst, and likewise those who come into the presence of the Lord cannot come but with joy. "Enter His gates with thanksgiving," our psalm declares. "Know that the Lord is God; He made us, His we are." And as we enter into the blessed Body and Blood of Christ, as we come to know the bridegroom of our soul... as His Spirit fills us what can we do but rejoice in the Lord, "whose kindness endures forever," who makes us as His own – who redeems our very souls. Make room for Him in your hearts. There let His blood flow, that you might have new life.

Saturday
(Col.1:21-23; Ps.54:3-4,6,8; Lk.6:1-5)

"Hold fast to faith, be firmly grounded and steadfast in it."

"The Son of Man is Lord," Lord of the universe, Lord "even of the sabbath." He is the Word through whom all things have come and it is He who has "achieved reconciliation" for all with God, the Father. We must be presented to God "holy, free of reproach and blame." We must bow before His Majesty, trust all things to Him, and He will defend our cause. But if we continue to nourish hostility in our hearts against the Lord of all, if we refuse to recognize Him as our God and Savior, if we remain stubborn in our blindness and our sins against His glorious presence... what hope have we? We can only then be shaken in our weakness.

Such is the case so often with the Pharisees, who repeatedly harden their hearts against the Word of God and His presence amongst them. Repeatedly He tries to teach them of truth and the necessity of holding to it, that their rules alone will not sustain them; but continually their hearts are closed. They cannot seem to understand because they cannot seem to bow before

299

Him; and so they see only with their eyes and not with the wisdom that comes through fear of God. And the bedrock foundation, the cornerstone of the Church, they cast aside as they concern themselves with its ornaments.

But we must hold to the faith, to the heart's core of existence itself and the life that is God: Jesus Christ and His holy Gospel must be that which speaks in the depths of our soul. Then we will know and sing with David, "The Lord sustains my life," as we praise His name "for its goodness." Then we will be "unshaken in the hope promised... by the Gospel," for the Gospel will be as the blood coursing through our veins and the food we eat; from it and from the Lord we will draw our life as a man draws water from a fountain.

Such light let us pray we maintain in our lives. Such wisdom and strength which comes only in truth let us make our own. He is happy to give us this life – for this He has died. Let us not turn in blindness from His face but ground ourselves in Him who is the foundation of eternal life.

Twenty-Third Week

Monday
(Col.1:24-2:3; Ps.62:6-7,9; Lk.6:6-11)

"We admonish all men and teach them in the full measure of wisdom, hoping to make every man complete in Christ."

It is Paul's desire to see the nations "enriched with full assurance by their knowledge of the mystery of God – namely Christ – in whom every treasure of wisdom and knowledge is hidden." It is his desire for us all to be filled with this wisdom that is Christ, for it is his call from Christ to bring His Gospel forth to the eyes and ears of the whole world, to "fill up what is lacking in the sufferings of Christ for the sake of His body, the Church." And it is our call to join Him in such sufferings in Jesus' name, that indeed His Word might come to its fullness, that indeed in such suffering we might find with Paul the joy of knowing "the mystery hidden from ages and generations past but now revealed to His holy ones." This "glory beyond price" is ours as we listen to His Word, as we follow in His ways.

Jesus shows Himself to be the model teacher, the teacher of teachers, the Word itself, in our gospel today. "On a sabbath Jesus came to teach in a synagogue where there was a man whose right hand was withered." For Jesus the synagogue was hostile territory, for the scribes and Pharisees "were on the watch" to "find a charge against Him," to catch Him in His teaching. Jesus does not turn away from the danger before Him but confronts them with the limitations of their interpretation of the teaching perhaps most dear to them – the command to keep the sabbath holy. He would teach them the full meaning of this command; He would fulfill this wisdom before them, showing them that God does not preclude the doing of good for others on the sabbath, that this day made for rest is thus truly a day made for healing and that this day is therefore the best to come to Him for healing – for what does He wish for us but our healing, our salvation? But being blind to the love of God and His desire for good and the good of all, they do not perceive His lesson, and make it instead a cause to "destroy" the Son of God.

It is difficult to understand how these leaders of the people could become "frenzied" at the healing of one of their flock – how can this be evil to do on the sabbath? But we must remember that blindness to the will of God is not the sole possession of these scribes and Pharisees. It is a foolishness which is part of us all in our all-too-human thoughts and actions. It is this blindness which the Lord calls us from; it is this wisdom known in Christ to which Paul would direct us all. Let us join with him, with Jesus, in the "work and struggle" to bring God's healing word forth to the hands and hearts of all. "God is our refuge." Let us firmly "trust in Him" and in His wisdom, and we shall be made whole.

O. 23. Tues. (I)

Tuesday
(Col.2:6-15; Ps.145:1-2,8-11; Lk.6:12-19)

"Coming down from the mountain with them,
He stopped at a level stretch where there were many of His disciples."

In our gospel, the Lord has gone "to the mountain to pray, spending the night in communion with God." Then at daybreak He chose His twelve apostles. On His way back down the mountain He comes upon those who have been waiting for Him, and He takes pity on this "large crowd of people" and reaches out His hand to heal them.

Yes, He in whom "the fullness of deity resides in bodily form," as Paul tells us in our first reading, has come down from on high, from His union with the Father, to walk amongst us, to dwell with us – to "pardon all our sins." He "who is head of every principality and power" has bent down to the level of the humble creature dead in sin and circumcised him with the circumcision "which strips off the carnal body completely." He has accomplished this by taking the claim against us, our debt for our sins, and "nailing it to the cross." And baptized into Him and His cross we are "not only buried with Him but also raised to life with Him." The grace that comes from this sacrifice, the healing we find in the touch of His hand and by the power of His word and His blood, we must now treasure. And so Paul tells us we must "be rooted in Him and built up in Him, growing ever stronger in faith," lest we make His sacrifice void.

"The Lord is good to all and compassionate toward all His works," sings David in our psalm today; and how can this be greater shown than in His coming down from heaven to teach us and to heal us, and to fulfill this teaching and healing in dying on the cross? What more could He do for us than to die for us to save us? What greater love could our God impart?

Do not be deceived, brothers and sisters, by "any empty, seductive philosophy... based on cosmic powers rather than on Christ." Avoid any teaching that does not recognize Jesus as the Son of God, as God Himself "in bodily form." Without Jesus there is no salvation, and failing to recognize "the fullness of deity" in Him, we cannot "share of this fullness" to which we are called. Rather, let us sing with David, "Every day will I bless you, and I will praise your name forever and ever." Always in the Lord Jesus let us take our refuge, and in His love; let us ever wait for His coming down from the mountain to touch and heal our hearts. Alleluia.

O. 23. Wed. (I)

Wednesday
(Col.3:1-11; Ps.145:2-3,9-13; Lk.6:20-26)

"Set your heart on what pertains to higher realms
where Christ is seated at God's right hand."

Is this not the central message of the Lord's beatitudes: "Be intent on things above rather than on things of earth." For how could we be blest in poverty, hunger, and weeping if our hearts are set on this earth? And how could riches and fullness and laughter be curses except that they do not find their origin in heaven? Paul makes it explicit: "You have died!" he declares, and leaves no question but that our "life is hidden now with Christ in God." There must our hearts be.

"Put to death whatever in your nature is rooted in earth," the Apostle continues. Lust and anger and deceit have no place in the life of a follower of Christ, for these indeed are sins of this earth which stand in contradiction to the grace of heaven. Therefore, we must set them all aside to become "a new man, one who grows in knowledge as he is formed anew in the image of his Creator." It cannot be that the Lord's children have discourse with evil conduct; those who are called to heaven must "discourse of the glory of [His] kingdom," their souls must "speak of [His] might" and their lives must be lived in His light.

And so the Lord "raised His eyes to His disciples." And so He spoke to them of heaven. And so the blessing of persecution in this world was made

302

known to them, that their hearts might begin to understand. God's world is not this world; His kingdom is not of darkness but of light. And if in the darkness we take our refuge, and if our hearts are not grieved by its injustice... if we fat ourselves on things of the flesh and turn our eyes from the demands of the Spirit... how shall we ever find justice and light? How shall we ever come into the Lord's glorious presence? What will we do then but weep in our emptiness?

The Lord's kingdom is coming, brothers and sisters. Be assured. What this world holds – its passion and death – is passing quickly, like a cloud in the night. The rays of morning are not far from us, for the Lord is even now at our side. And to His side in heaven we shall yet come, if we but accept His blessing. So let us say with David, "Your kingdom is a kingdom for all ages, and your dominion endures through all generations"; and let us enter now into His eternal presence.

Thursday
(Col.3:12-17; Ps.150:1-6; Lk.6:27-38)

"Whatever you do, whether in speech or in action,
do it in the name of the Lord Jesus."

"Sing gratefully to God from your hearts in psalms, hymns, and inspired songs." Such is our speech and action when dedicated to God. Our lives indeed become a symphony of His grace when we "let the word of Christ, rich as it is, dwell in [us]." The "blast of the trumpet... with lyre and harp... with timbrel and dance... with strings and pipe... with sounding of cymbals," which our psalm exhorts in praise of God, are the litany of virtues we are called in both our first reading and our gospel to practice with our Christian lives.

Paul instructs us to "clothe [our]selves with heartfelt mercy, with kindness, humility, meekness, and patience." He invokes "Christ's peace," "thankfulness," and "wisdom made perfect" upon us, and states: "Over all these virtues put on love, which binds the rest together and makes them perfect," making love the key to this hymn we sing and play with our lives, the note to which we continually return and which is ever present at the heart of our melody. And what a perfectly marvelous, heavenly song this is when sung in sincerity and truth.

The sincerity and truth to which we are called is made unmistakable in the Lord's teaching in our gospel. Here we have the greatest challenge to our virtue of love, and its greatest moment. Here the magnum opus is sounded. Jesus has for us a litany of virtues Himself: "Be compassionate... do not judge... do not condemn... pardon... give," and assures us that "good measure, pressed down, shaken together, running over" will be ours if we live by His word. But the love which is the sum of all virtues is most poignantly accentuated in the command which sets the Lord and His grace apart from all others and their teachings, which makes Him so clearly the Son of God. "To you who hear me, I say: Love your enemies," He proclaims to His disciples, and then makes explicit the call to a Christian life: "Do good to those who hate you; bless those who curse you, and pray for those who maltreat you." And more specifically, "When someone slaps you on the cheek, turn and give him the other; when someone takes your coat, let him have your shirt as well." Who can hear these words? Who can heed these commands? Who can live them in speech and action, as has our Lord upon the cross? It is this sacrifice of love to which we are called, and only this will raise our song unto heaven. We must act always out of love.

O. 23. Fri. (I)

Friday
(1Tm.1:1-2,12-14; Ps.16:1-2,5,7-8,11; Lk.6:39-42)

"Remove the plank from your own eye first;
then you will see clearly enough
to remove the speck from your brother's eye."

The answer to Jesus' question to His disciples: "Can a blind man act as guide to a blind man?" is obvious. No. It must be a man of sight, of vision, who leads those who are blind, who are without understanding. Paul has become a prime example of one who is well able to lead others. In our first reading he speaks to Timothy, his "true child in faith," whom he has taught and led and who now stands as a bishop of the early Church. But how did Paul come to be such a profitable apostle? We see in our reading that he has taken the instruction of the Lord, his teacher, to heart, and first recognized and then removed the plank which once rested firmly in his own eye: "I was once a blasphemer, a persecutor, a man filled with arrogance." Indeed, this great Apostle of the Lord was once an egregious persecutor of the Church; and indeed we all have or have had great sins in our lives which have set us in opposition to God – but Paul has faced his sin, found "the grace of our Lord... in overflowing measure," and served to remove innumerable specks from others' eyes. What of us? Do we see our sins? Have we removed them? Do we see clearly enough to "remove the speck from [our] brother's eye?"

"Every student when he has finished his studies will be on a par with his teacher." Paul has humbled himself before Jesus and absorbed the lessons the Lord imparts by the Spirit. Timothy has proven himself a true student and son of Paul. Who is *our* teacher? Where do we get *our* knowledge?

Whom do we imitate? And whom do we lead? Are we falling into ditches following blind men's leads? Are we leading others astray with any false philosophy? Or is it the Lord who "counsels" us as He does David in our psalm? Do we say with him, "O Lord, my allotted portion and cup, you it is who hold fast my lot," and, "I set the Lord ever before me"? Is it His "grace, mercy, and peace" we seek always; or in arrogance do we set about doing the business we think fit?

The teaching of the Lord would lead us to set aside any sin within ourselves, to cleanse our hearts and purify our souls in order to have clear vision. For it is by this holy vision His Church is led forth, and we must be part of this procession.

O. 23. Sat. (I)

Saturday
(1Tm.1:15-17; Ps.113:1-7; Lk.6:43-49)

"Any man who desires to come to me
will hear my words and put them into practice."

Our psalm today declares that God is "enthroned on high" – "High above all the nations is the Lord; above the heavens is His glory." And why is the Lord so glorious, so worthy of our praise...? Because "He raises the lowly from the dust; from the dunghill He lifts up the poor." And Paul tells us the same: he glorifies God as "King of the ages, the immortal, the invisible, the only God" – and why? Because though he is "the worst" of sinners, the Lord has dealt mercifully with him and made him an example of His great love.

The Lord indeed is great and worthy of all praise. Though seated far above us, He reaches down to lift us up to Him. In a word: "Jesus Christ came into the world to save sinners." Humbling Himself to walk and die among us, He calls us to eternal life. But we must answer that call, we must follow His way. We cannot simply call Him "Lord, Lord"; we must indeed "put into practice" His words. If we do not, we cannot find the fruit of His sacrifice for us. Mere words, simple verbal assent, is not sufficient to bring us to the blood of Christ and the redemption it holds. It is by our actions we are judged and not our words. Jesus makes this very clear: "Each tree is known by its yield." If we do not produce good fruit, how can we claim to be a good tree? And doesn't the Lord cut down every tree that fails to bear fruit in His name?

All shall hear His words, all shall know of the glory He offers forth. But shall all be as the apostle Paul and put His words into practice, suffering for the faith He proclaimed? Will all make real the teaching of Christ in their lives? Those who do will find themselves set on a firm foundation –

Ordinary Time

His word will be in their flesh and blood. They will receive Him into their very beings and find Him at the center of all they think and do. Without His presence so firmly fixed within themselves by their living it in their actions, salvation will be far away, and their houses shall crumble. Brothers and sisters, let us not fail to realize the salvation He offers us sinners. In His goodness, let us produce good from our hearts.

Twenty-Fourth Week

Monday
(1Tm.2:1-8; Ps.28:2,6-9; Lk.7:1-10)

"Offer prayers with blameless hands held aloft."

We must pray. We must petition the Lord for the good of the world, that the good of our souls, the Lord Jesus Christ, might be known to all. If we do not intercede, if we do not seek the healing of a people sick with sin, who shall do so? The Lord desires "all men to be saved and come to know the truth." It is our responsibility, it is our call, to bring the love and forgiveness and healing of our Lord forth.

"Hear the sound of my pleading, when I cry to you, lifting up my hands to your holy shrine." Our eyes and our hands must be continually lifted up to the temple of the Lord and to His holy presence. The Lord listens to our prayers, brothers and sisters. The world depends upon our prayers. Those for whom the Lord is "strength" and "the saving refuge" are near to Him, and He waits to hear from them. He longs to hear the petitions of their hearts and is eternally prepared to respond to their pleas. Should not we who are blessed to be within the walls of the Church, who partake of His Word and His sacraments, who have His teaching upon our hearts and His presence in our midst, be concerned for the good of all; should we not long to see the Lord's will done on this earth? Then pray.

And our gospel teaches us that those who disparage the faithful for depending on the intercessions of others, those who think they must always come directly to Jesus to find answer to their petition – those who fail to see the family of God and our connection here on earth with the saints who have preceded us to heaven – are in danger of a vain pride. Learn from the centurion, who says to the Lord, "I did not presume to come to you myself." And why? "For I am not worthy to have you enter my house." And so, first "he sent some Jewish elders to him" (are these not so much like our beloved saints?), and then "sent friends" to deliver the above message of humility. And for his humility, and for his faith in the intercession of others... and for his realization that the Lord hears petitions offered for others and that He

Himself has ministering angels who perform His work at His Word – the Lord holds this centurion in "amazement" and raises him up as a model of faith.

Do we believe? Do we truly believe in the Lord and in His angels and His saints? Do we believe His heavenly kingdom is near to us, and His will is for our good? Then we should not hesitate to lift our hearts and our hands to the Lord in faithful prayer.

Blessed Mother, intercede for us before your Son, Jesus, that we who are not worthy to receive Him into our mortal bodies may be made immortal by His presence within us. May He bring peace to the world.

Tuesday
(1Tm.3:1-13; Ps.101:1-3,5-6; Lk.7:11-17)

"He who walks in the way of integrity
shall be in my service."

"God has visited His people." What the people said when Jesus raised the widow's son from the dead should be said of us all as we pass through this world. That same love that moved Jesus to pity upon seeing the tears of this poor mother should move us all. To all we should say, "Do not cry." To all we should step forward with the love of Christ fixed firmly in our hearts and bring the same grace and healing.

In our first reading Paul outlines the qualities necessary to be a servant of the Lord. At whatever level we find ourselves, to whatever role we are called, we must walk in integrity of heart. All "must be serious"; all "should be temperate"; all should be of peace and never of greed; and all must keep their homes in order. "The man of haughty eyes and puffed-up heart I will not endure," the Lord warns us in David's psalm. And we must heed that warning and walk humbly with our God, seeking to serve Him and our neighbor well, that we might ever be built up in "faith in Christ Jesus."

His servants are blessed. "My eyes are upon the faithful of the land, that they may dwell with me," of the Lord's kindness and judgment David sings. Indeed, those who follow in His ways will do things as great as He – even to the raising of the dead – and shall find themselves raised up on the last day. But as we go through this world we cannot have cold hearts for our neighbors: we cannot allow the faith to die within ourselves. That which has been nurtured within us must be shared with others; then we will "gain a worthy place" at the Lord's side.

All are called to their stations in life; all have a part in the Body of Christ. Let us not set before our eyes "any base thing" but look always to fulfill that call in a trustworthy manner, holding "fast to the divinely revealed faith with a clear conscience." If our conscience becomes clouded, we will be unable to serve Him, and our reward will be placed in jeopardy. Therefore, let us ever maintain His goodness within us and let our actions always reflect the great love of God. The Lord wishes us to be forever in His service.

Wednesday
(1Tm.3:14-16; Ps.111:1-6; Lk.7:31-35)

"God's wisdom is vindicated by all who accept it."

"The Church of the living God" is the "pillar and bulwark of truth," as Paul tells us. And it is those who live the faith, "professing it" with all their beings, who prove its truth. "Wonderful, indeed, is the mystery of our faith"; no greater grace or wisdom could we hope to attain.

"He was manifested in the flesh, vindicated in the Spirit, seen by angels, preached among the Gentiles, believed in throughout the world, taken up into glory..." "Great are the works of the Lord, exquisite in all their delights..." How our first reading and psalm sing of the glory of our God! And how blessed are we to know "the power of His works," to be recipients of His gift of "majesty and glory," to be the children of so great a God. We should indeed praise Him unceasingly for being "mindful of His covenant" with us, for shedding His blood for our salvation, for drawing us into the Father's presence. "He has given food to those who fear Him," and we partake of His glorious meal each day in the Holy Eucharist.

Forget not the blessings the Lord imparts to us, brothers and sisters. "Know what kind of conduct befits a member of God's household." We must not be as the men of Jesus' day who like spoiled children sought to form the Lord in the image they desired of Him, refusing to accept Him and His wisdom as it came to them, as it stood before them in the flesh. How can we presume upon the will of our God and His wisdom? How can we fail to accept the light and grace of the Gospel? What folly it is to judge Him who judges the universe. We must be open to His Word, open to His grace, open to His teaching and the marvelous works known only in adherence to His covenant of absolute truth and love. He is the foundation upon which the Church is set, and a Church living His wisdom and grace is the vindication, the proof, of its eternal efficacy for the good of all.

Rejoice in the Lord always, brothers and sisters, that He has blessed you with knowledge of His glory and fed you with His own body and blood. Eat and drink this food He gives, do all He commands in His eternal wisdom, and with the angels you will behold His face as children of the Most High God.

Thursday

(1Tm.4:12-16; Ps.111:2,7-10; Lk.7:36-50)

"Fear of the Lord is the beginning of wisdom;
prudent are all who live by it."

If "the works of His hands are faithful and just," as His children living
in His Word and as His image, we must "be a continuing example of love,
faith, and purity." If we do not attend to this duty, "so that everyone may
see [our] progress," how shall we "bring to salvation [ourselves] and all who
hear [us]"? Our love of Him must shine forth in all we do.

And what is the fear of the Lord spoken of in our psalm but the love
shown by the woman in our gospel? As she stands behind Jesus, what is she
but fearful, what is she but filled with love? This passage teaches us what
fear of the Lord truly is, and what it isn't. Certainly she is struck to the
heart. Certainly in the presence of such purity she is convicted of her lust;
certainly in the presence of such faith she is convicted of her lack thereof.
But if she were fearful as the world understands the word, would she
presume to touch Him? If she thought He might strike her to the ground,
would she wipe His feet "with her hair, kissing them and perfuming them
with oil"? No, she would die where she stands. But as it is her tears are
sweet, for she knows the forgiveness He holds for her in His sacred hands.

This is the fear of the Lord we all must have; it is this which is the
beginning of wisdom. We must be convicted of our sins, yes; but at the
same moment we must be filled with the overwhelming love of our God.
The two go hand in hand, and it is the practice of this fear of God in love of
Him and neighbor that is the fulfillment of our duty before Him, that will
keep us as a holy example of His presence in the world. The Pharisee in our
gospel lacks this holy fear. First of all, he does not see his sin, and so he is
not moved to love. Failing to view himself in the light of the One present
before him, he fails to find the grace that is the knowledge of our sins – and
so he is not moved to love, and so he does not find forgiveness.

Let us not love little, brothers and sisters, for this would not be wise.
Failing to live in holy fear of the Lord, we shorten His hand's working in
our lives. May we ever, by His grace, be convicted of our sins, and so turn
to Him in love to find forgiveness. We will do this only if we remain ever
in His presence, bowed at His sacred feet. Amen.

Friday

(1Tm.6:2-12; Ps.49:6-10,17-20,Mt.5:3; Lk.8:1-3)

"Those who want to be rich are falling into temptation, and a trap."

Today we hear Paul's famous words: "The love of money is the root of all evil." They are oft-quoted, but how well are they understood and practiced in the avoidance of excessive possessions and inflated bank accounts. Paul tells us, verifiably so, that men "have come to grief amid great pain" because of their passion for money. And the pain is so much the greater if they had been men of faith, which stands so much in opposition to the things of this world.

One must be "content with a sufficiency," Paul teaches us. "If we have food and clothing we have all that we need." But how many are satisfied, grateful to God, for having their needs met? And how many rather thirst for ever-increasing wealth, in which they foolishly believe they shall find peace and comfort? Indeed, it is as an addiction, and blinds us to the providential hand of God and the humility we should have in His presence. Our psalm speaks pointedly and graphically of the vanity of those for whom "the abundance of their riches is their boast," but who, when they die, "shall take none of it": "He shall join the circle of his forebears, who shall never more see light." Indeed, such trust in wealth leads invariably to hell.

Then what should we do? you may well ask. Let us turn to our gospel. It is brief and seemingly of little significance, but gives a concise picture of the life of the Lord and those who followed him. In it we hear that Jesus and the Twelve did what Paul exhorts his disciple Timothy to do (in his letter): "Preaching and proclaiming the good news of the Kingdom of God." This must be our concern. This must be our desire – to fulfill the will and the word of God in our lives. We must "fight the good fight of faith," setting aside all preoccupation with the riches of this earth. And we shall be cared for even as the women who accompanied Jesus and His apostles "were assisting them out of their means." They saw that the Lord and His disciples were clothed and fed. They cared out of love for their basic needs. And God will provide such as these to care for the needs of all who devote themselves to His work.

Let us never fall into the devil's trap and temptation, as he attempts to distract us from the spiritual necessities God demands. Such a fall is mighty indeed. Trust in God's hand and be satisfied with His call.

Saturday
(1Tm.6:13-16; Ps.100:2-5; Lk.8:4-15)

"Keep God's command without blame or reproach
until our Lord Jesus shall appear."

The Lord's "kindness endures forever, and His faithfulness, to all generations," and we must endure with Him, ever showing forth His kindness and faithfulness to the world, until we come to dwell with Him eternally "in inapproachable light."

When God brings His appearance "to pass at His chosen time" will we stand ready? Will we persevere in service of truth until that day of which we know not? Brothers and sisters, "Let everyone who has ears attend to what he has heard." Let us not "fall away in time of temptation." Let us not have our progress "stifled by the cares and riches and pleasures of life." Let us mature. Let us remain faithful in all adversity. Let us always grow in His Word. Let us "hear the word in a spirit of openness, retain it, and bear fruit through perseverance." Then we shall "yield grain a hundredfold"; then we shall know the "joyful song" that reverberates eternally in His "everlasting rule."

Patience. We must have patience. And wisdom. We must know and remember that "the Lord is God; He made us, His we are, His people, the flock He tends." Always we must take refuge in Him, living the "noble profession" to which He calls us as His blessed children to whom "the mysteries of the reign of God have been confided." And knowing this, knowing Him, how can we turn to anything else? What can distract or destroy the heart set on God? It is not possible that anything can overcome us if we stand fast as seed planted by the hand of God and allow His Spirit to perpetually nourish our growth. We must be as plants which bend ever to His light; the cleansing water of His Word must be cherished and preserved by holy souls. And we shall grow.

"Enter His gates with thanksgiving, His courts with praise." This is our destiny; and this is the blessing we find even now as we make continual progress in His Name and rejoice at the gifts and graces He bears us as we struggle ever to bear witness to His glory working in our lives. Stand fast, brothers and sisters, and persevere till the end. May His Word remain in you, His Bread nourish you daily, and you will be kept beyond reproach.

311

Twenty-Fifth Week

Monday
(Ezra 1:1-6; Ps.126:1-6; Lk.8:16-18)

"Those that sow in tears shall reap rejoicing."

The Israelites toiled in tears for four hundred years under the yoke of the Egyptians, then rejoiced to finally enter the Promised Land (after wandering forty years in the desert). For seventy years Judah had been exiled to Babylon, but rejoiced when, remarkably, the king of Persia called them to return to Jerusalem and, with his blessing, to rebuild the temple of the Lord. And now we wait in exile for our Lord to return. But sadness should not overwhelm us in this land of exile. Indeed our lights must shine; for in the shining of these lamps of holiness is the coming of our Lord to this earth. And the more we shine forth His light to this earth, the more we grow in that light, and so the closer the Lord comes to both us and the world.

Tears do tend to be our lot here in this world; such is the way of the cross. We cannot help but mourn the lack of His love and the failure of hearts to come to His peace. Here where hatred and violence so often enter in by the ignorance of man's soul to the Word of God and His presence in our midst, what can we do but cry? But we are not without hope; and it is this hope our readings speak of this day. For if the Gentiles could return the chosen people to their land of promise with such rich and generous gifts, how can we not take hope that the Lord shall "restore our fortunes" as well? And so as we ascend the steps to the temple of our Lord in the highest heaven, may the nations say of us, too, "The Lord has done great things for them," as they look upon our wisdom and grace even in this land where darkness reigns.

"There is nothing hidden that will not be exposed, nothing concealed that will not be known and brought to light." And so we take promise in the fact that that which we cherish now in our souls, the Word and the Bread of the Lord which nourishes us on this journey, shall come to their fulfillment in the joy of the kingdom of heaven. But do not hide that light growing within you, brothers and sisters; shine it forth unashamedly for all to see, and the tears you sow in hope for the salvation of the world shall serve to cleanse your vision to behold the Lord in all His glory.

312

Tuesday
(Ezra 6:7-8,12,14-20; Ps.122:1-5; Lk.8:19-21)

"The elders of the Jews continued to make progress in the building,
supported by the message of the prophets."

And so, returning from exile and with the permission and indeed the financial support of the Gentile king, Darius, the Jews completed the rebuilding of the temple at Jerusalem. And so, the prophecy of the return to the Lord from their sins is in a measure fulfilled here in this act and in the worship which once again transpires in "that house of God." But we know that this is not the fulfillment of the new covenant; this is not the realization of God's promise through Isaiah to write His Name upon the hearts of His people and to be with them forever. Though a sign of its coming, we know that such blessing cannot be fulfilled in buildings and on an earth so corrupted by sin – it can only be realized in heaven.

And so in our gospel His mother and kinsmen come to the Lord, who is the new Temple, the New Jerusalem Himself. They come but do not find easy access for the crowd that has gathered to Jesus to worship at His feet. And this is to show that it is not in our bloodline that we find salvation, but by faith in Him who is the ultimate sacrifice. Indeed, all may come now to this holy sacrifice, all may enter the gates of this Temple... all may rejoice as they set foot within the gates of this New Jerusalem, if all but follow the Word of Truth which issues from His lips. Returning to Jerusalem and having rebuilt the temple, the Levites offered sacrifice "for the rest of the exiles, for their brethren the priests, and for themselves"; but Jesus' one sacrifice is offered daily now for all who would come to the altar, to all who would sup at His table.

"I rejoiced because they said to me, 'We will go up to the house of the Lord.'" How blessed are these words to the ears of the Jew returning from exile, and how blessed now to the peoples of every nation are their fulfillment in our hearing. Brothers and sisters of the Lord, let us hasten our steps toward His presence. Let us long to worship before Him. And let us continue to make progress in the upbuilding of the Church, His Temple, by our daily labor for the God who blesses all our endeavors with His providential care. May His Word be fulfilled in us and in all His people.

Wednesday
(Ezra 9:5-9; Tb.13:1-4,6-8; Lk.9:1-6)

"Turn back, you sinners! do the right before Him:
perhaps He may look with favor upon you, and show you mercy."

As the Word of the Lord comes to our villages and enters our houses, we must treasure it and heed its warning to turn from our sins. If we harden our hearts against its grace and mercy, if we fail to recognize our sin in the blessed light it brings, the Word shall leave, shaking the dust from its feet, and we shall be left alone in despair. But if we turn toward the light it brings and away from our sins, we shall be saved – we shall be healed of all our afflictions.

How wonderfully Ezra humbles himself before the Lord our God, pouring out his soul and the sins of the people of Israel: "Our wicked deeds are heaped up above our heads and our guilt reaches up to heaven." For so often have the people sinned, so often have they turned from Him who chose them as His own... and even here, now that they have been returned from exile by the miraculous grace of God working through Persian kings, now that the Lord has given them "new life to raise again the house of [their] God and restore its ruins," even now they have sinned again.

It is only the love of Jesus, brothers and sisters, and the grace that pours forth through His apostles, which will bring us to the "reign of God." Only He can heal our souls and only He can lift us from the mire of this world – only in His kingdom will we find perfection with God our Father. This alone must we seek. This certainly we must accept with open arms when it comes to us by the grace of our Lord. For, indeed, we know that though we have fallen into "the great abyss," though He may have cast us "down to the depths of the nether world" for our sins, "He has shown [us] His greatness" and lifted our heads up to look upon His face – He has redeemed our race.

So let us rejoice this day "in the King of heaven" and "speak of His majesty," for in our guilt the Lord visits us, He sends forth His Word to heal us. He has given the Twelve and their successors "power and authority to overcome all demons and to cure diseases," so let us welcome their touch and turn from our sins to receive the favor upon us, to find His mercy at work in our midst.

Thursday
(Hg.1:1-8; Ps.149:1-6,9; Lk.9:7-9)

"He who earned wages earned them for a bag with holes in it."

"Bring timber, and build the house that I may take pleasure in it and receive my glory." Rebuild the house of God, the temple of the Holy Spirit you are. Shore up the breaches in its walls and solidify its foundation, that you might "sing to the Lord a new song of praise in the assembly of the faithful," that you might be as those who are "glad in their maker... For the Lord loves His people, and He adorns the lowly with victory." Humble yourself before Him, take care to observe the words of His mouth – turn from your selfish ways and your blindness to His presence, and you shall again sing with delight in a house of blessings.

Are you, too, like Herod, perplexed at the identity of Jesus? Do you, too, question: "Who is this man about whom I hear all these reports?" Be more than "curious to see Him," my brothers and sisters; lay down your lives before Him and His teaching and His redemptive sacrifice, and you shall come to know that He is the Son of God – you shall find Him who is the salvation of your soul, which wanders now far from the safety of the walls of His temple. In His flesh alone will you find your home. Your vain curiosity is not enough to bring you there. Your doubts about His glory must be faced and seen for the emptiness they hold – or you risk beheading yourself in the refusal to bow to Him who is Truth and holds all that matters in His redeeming hands.

"Let the high praises of God be in their throats," our psalmist sings. To such blessing of fulfillment he exhorts our souls. This indeed is "the glory of all His faithful"; for to have our souls filled to overflowing with the praises of our Lord and our God, who loves us to overflowing and desires only for us to know His love in its being lived out in all our days and with all our being... in this we find our home in His blessed hands.

All else but God is vain, and its emptiness will rise to your eyes in a time you do not anticipate. See now that you repair the holes in your very soul, that you might become a temple of His Spirit and find the grace to praise His Name worthily in the assembly of all His chosen ones.

Friday
(Hg.1:15-2:9; Ps.43:1-5; Lk.9:18-22)

"Greater will be the future glory of this house
than the former, says the Lord of hosts."

"Take courage... and work! For I am with you," the Lord says through the prophet Haggai to the remnant of the people returned from exile as they prepare to rebuild the temple. "My spirit continues in your midst; do not fear!" Of course, we know these words of encouragement are eternal, even as we know that "the future glory" of the temple prophesied by Haggai refers ultimately to the Kingdom Christ now builds for us with His Father in heaven, and in whose construction we participate to this day. For Jesus is the Temple not made by human hands, and we are His Body here on earth, raising the walls of this holy place.

"And in this place I will give peace, says the Lord of hosts!" In the former temple, that which relied upon human hands for its construction and could thus be destroyed also by human hands, the peace was necessarily passing. Though the Lord remained present to His people, the temple in which they dwelt, in which they worshiped, was only temporary. The future Temple which holds the glory of God come to fulfillment in the Lord Jesus Christ, to which He leads us and which is, in fact, the Lord Himself – to this Temple there is no end, and its peace is everlasting. There we shall worship eternally.

And this Temple is present to us now; Jesus is in our midst this day, in His Church, in His Sacraments, with His Spirit, in the Word. And we learn from the Lord in our gospel today the way that leads to its realization. Yes, the apostles, in the person of Peter, recognize that Jesus is "the Messiah of God"; but not yet is it to be declared. There are first "many sufferings" He must endure. Indeed, He must "be put to death" before being "raised up on the third day." In the same manner we have much to endure in this world, filling up what is lacking of His suffering, before we come into the eternal glory of His resurrection. We shall "go in to the altar of God" and give Him "thanks upon the harp." He shall receive our song of joy, as in measure He does this day. In fullness we shall know Him. And so, here as we travel toward Him, as we pass through our time of mourning, let us pray with our psalmist:

"Send forth your light and your fidelity;
they shall lead me on
And bring me to your holy mountain,
to your dwelling place..."
(where His glory shall be great).

Saturday
(Zec.2:5-9,14-15; Jer.31:10-13; Lk.9:43-45)

"They shall come streaming to the Lord's blessings."

The Kingdom is being prepared. And as bleak as things may seem upon this earth, the glory of the Lord awaits us all. This is the message of Jeremiah in our psalm and the message given Zechariah by the angel in our first reading. "I will turn their mourning into joy, I will console and gladden them after their sorrows," is the word which sustains us.

Zechariah prophesies at the time the Israelites have returned from exile few in number to a rather desolate, broken-down Jerusalem. But in his vision presented today he sees an angel measuring the great city of peace, apparently for its restoration. And to this prophet at this difficult time in which hope is hard to hold on to is delivered this reassurance: "People will live in Jerusalem as though in an open country, because of the multitude of men and beasts in her midst." The Lord promises to be "the glory in her midst" and an "encircling wall of fire": "Many nations shall join themselves to the Lord on that day."

Jeremiah's message is the same. "He who scattered Israel now gathers them together, He guards them as a shepherd His flock." Yes, even in the darkest moments of our exile here on this fallen earth, there is hope. For ultimately the Lord's love will conquer all; in the end we shall "mount the heights of Zion" – our salvation will be fulfilled.

Jesus tries to convey to the apostles the same message. By telling them, "The Son of Man must be delivered into the hands of men," He seeks to have them understand – even "in the midst of the disciples' amazement at all that Jesus was doing" in teaching and healing the people – that when the time of mourning is brought to bear in their lives, when they see Him offered up for crucifixion... when darkness falls upon the land, then they should be assured that the glorious works they find wrought in their midst by the glorious hand of God shall not be dead at all, but only coming to fulfillment.

Our solace is in our sorrow. Happy are we who mourn. For the passing things we are robbed of here, we know will become eternal blessings in heaven. Taste the pain, my brothers and sisters, the blood at the corners of your mouth, and lift your head to see the nations come streaming to His eternal kingdom.

O. 26. Mon. (I)

Twenty-Sixth Week

Monday
(Zec.8:1-8; Ps.102:16-23,29; Lk.9:46-50)

"The city shall be filled with boys and girls playing in her streets."

"Even if this should seem impossible in the eyes of the remnant of this people, shall it in those days be impossible in my eyes also, says the Lord of hosts." Sometimes we lose sight of the kingdom of heaven. Sometimes our faith fails because of the difficult circumstances in which we find ourselves. Or sometimes our pride can be the obstruction, blinding our eyes to the presence of the Lord in our midst, speaking to us in the children who play all around us, who sit at His side... whose angels behold His face always. Sometimes we lose hope and the promise of eternal life escapes us.

But why? Do we not know that the Lord "has regarded the prayer of the destitute, and not despised their prayer"? Have we not experienced His redeeming grace many times in our lives? Do we not believe Him when He tells His chosen ones: "They shall be my people, and I will be their God, with faithfulness and justice"? Why are we so forgetful of His love for us and distracted by our situation? For the Lord does "hear the groaning of the prisoners"; He does "release those doomed to die"; He does look down "from His holy height" and hear the prayers of His lowly ones, if we but call out to Him.

"I will rescue my people from the land of the rising sun, and from the land of the setting sun." At the center of the universe shall we dwell, "within Jerusalem," with the Lord. This is our promise. And this is our call – to bring others within those gates, to invite all His children to enter His holy presence. Not to look past them in blind ambition, but to set our hearts on serving Him by striving always and only to build up His kingdom even here on earth.

Jesus knows our thoughts, brothers and sisters. He knows how vain we can be in our ways. And so He sets a child before us. He shows us the lowliness we must know to enter the kingdom of heaven. And He presents us with a challenge to gather His children there. Indeed, heaven shall be filled with the laughter of children, but will we hear it – and will we find true reward by increasing it always in His Name? Let your heart not fail or despair of any circumstances, for "the children of [His] servants shall abide, and their posterity continue in [His] presence." Ever maintain hope for the glory of Zion and see it rising in your midst.

O. 26. Tues. (I)

Tuesday
(Zec.8:20-23; Ps.87:1-7,Zec.8:23; Lk.9:51-56)

"Let us go with you, for we have heard that God is with you."

God is with us, brothers and sisters. And though all upon earth turn their faces from Him now, though in ignorance they reject Him and our preaching of His Word – there shall come a day when all nations find their home in Him. In that day the Lord shall reign.

As Jesus sets His face toward Jerusalem and His coming death at the hands of His own people, He passes through many towns and sends harbingers of His drawing nigh. In today's gospel we read of the Samaritans', the dreaded "half-breed" of Israelites, rejection of His presence among them: "The Samaritans would not welcome Him because He was on the way to Jerusalem." And for this should they not be destroyed like Sodom and Gomorrah? request the sons of thunder, James and John. But it is "only to reprimand them" that Jesus makes answer to such an idea. Indeed, they reject the Son of God, but in this moment they certainly know not what they do. Should they be any different than the Jews who will offer Him up for crucifixion or the apostles who will abandon Him?

From the gospel we must take solace, brothers and sisters, when our words fall on deaf ears, when the Word of God seems not to take root in souls. We are only emissaries of His Word, and that Word will bear fruit only in His time. But, of course, at the same moment we mourn rejection, we must be buoyed by the vision delivered by Zechariah in our first reading and confirmed so wonderfully in our psalm, for in it is the Truth of the resurrection that follows the Lord's crucifixion. We are told that "the inhabitants of one city shall approach those of another and say, "Come! Let us go to implore the favor of the Lord," and that "in those days ten men of every nationality, speaking different tongues, shall take hold, yes, take hold of every Jew by the edge of his garment and say, 'Let us go with you, for we have heard that God is with you.'" Not only will they hear the Word of God, they will beg its presence in their lives! For the Lord shall draw them inextricably to His mountain. "And of Zion they shall say: 'One and all were born in her; and He who has established her is the Most High God.'"

Brothers and sisters, we dwell now in Zion; Holy Church is the New Jerusalem. And hearts shall turn to her with longing – she shall find her treasured place here at the end of the age. We need not fear or be anxious, for the day of the Lord shall come, when "all shall sing, in their festive dance: 'My home is within you.'" Continue on to every town, bearing His love.

Wednesday
(Neh.2:1-8; Ps.137:1-6; Lk.9:57-62)

"How could we sing a song of the Lord in a foreign land?"

Our home is in heaven. "The foxes have lairs, the birds of the sky have nests, but the Son of Man has nowhere to lay His head," the Lord tells the soul who would follow His way in our gospel today. Our home is in heaven, and only there do we find joy. And only finding our place there should possess our hearts.

We have a sign of the devotion we must have for the Lord and His Kingdom in our psalm and first reading. Even as the psalmist hangs up his harp and weeps "by the streams of Babylon" for his exile from Jerusalem – "May my tongue cleave to my palate if I remember you not, if I place not

Jerusalem ahead of my joy" – so, too, Nehemiah is most "sad at heart" for his separation from and the ruination of "the city where [his] ancestors are buried." And as the king takes pity on his servant and sends Nehemiah to help rebuild Jerusalem, so, too, does the Lord look upon those who seek in ardent desire their true home with Him in heaven. He knows we are sad at our separation from the kingdom of God; He knows only there we shall find peace in our hearts, and so He calls us along the way He walks.

But also He warns that all else must be set aside if we are to discover that which our hearts desire. "Whoever puts his hand to the plow but keeps looking back is unfit for the reign of God." Does love for the New Jerusalem truly possess us as did love of the old for these exiles in Babylon? Do we, too, recognize our own exile, our own homelessness, and seek with all our souls only the song that is sung in the kingdom of God? Are we prepared to leave this land of exile, this foreign land in which we find ourselves, to come to Him to build with the wood He provides the new walls which will be our shelter and our place of worship even in this life? Or do we look back to this world of sin and find ourselves drawn into its sad state?

The Lord awaits the turning of all toward Him and His kingdom. He desires greatly our returning to His side. The thought of our heart to give up all for Him He confirms with His blessing and love. But we must be clear that this commitment is total, that nowhere else we shall find our joy but at His side in heaven.

O. 26. Thurs. (I)

Thursday
(Neh.8:1-12; Ps.19:8-11; Lk.10:1-12)

"They understood the words that had been expounded to them."

What a blessed day we hear of in our first reading. And what a blessed reception the Word of God finds in the hearing of the people! For "the whole people gathered as one man" and "listened attentively to the book of the law" of Moses as "Ezra the scribe stood on a wooden platform that had been made for the occasion" and "read out of the book from daybreak until midday." And we know that all the people indeed understood the wonder of what was read to their humble, obedient hearts, "for all the people were weeping as they heard the words of the law." They wept for the truth of these words, and for the fact that they as a people were so long without their instruction. The truth of God's Word brought repentance to their hearts, as it should to all.

But ultimately the Word of God caused them, as all, "to celebrate with great joy." Certainly this is its ultimate goal. For as David sings so well of in our psalm today: "The law of the Lord is perfect, refreshing the soul; the

320

decree of the Lord is trustworthy, giving wisdom to the simple." And the rightness of this wisdom brings "rejoicing [to] the heart." For as rich as the food and sweet the drinks the people were encouraged to consume that day as celebration of the glory of God, none could compare with the commands of the Lord, which "are more precious than gold, than a heap of purest gold; sweeter also than syrup or honey from the comb." This bread of life is that which sustains us.

And it is this bread of peace and life the Lord sends the disciples to bring to the cities before Him in our gospel today. He tells them that as they declare peace to any house or town along the way, "If there is a peaceable man there, your peace will rest on him; if not, it will come back to you." And woe to those who do not welcome the reign of God these disciples bring in Jesus' name. Indeed, we hear that "the fate of Sodom will be less severe than that of such a town." If the Israelites were so open and welcoming to the Word of God read in their midst from the book of the law by Ezra the scribe, how much more welcoming should these people who have the emissaries of Christ Himself, sent to "cure the sick," be to receive the reign of God at hand? And how much more should *we* be open to receive His Word, who now know of the Lord's resurrection to glory and have the Holy Spirit in our midst by the authority given to His Church on earth? Brothers and sisters, we must hear and understand as well as they of Nehemiah's time, else what hope have we for celebration in Christ's glory? May His sweet words be in our ears and in our mouths, and so may we bleed with Him unto glory.

O. 26. Fri. (I)

Friday
(Bar.1:15-22; Ps.79:1-5,8-9; Lk.10:13-16)

"We have been disobedient to the Lord, our God,
and only too ready to disregard His voice."

Woe is upon us for our sin. We "have sinned in the Lord's sight and disobeyed Him," and so "the evils and the curse which the Lord enjoined upon Moses... cling to us even today." And if we do not recognize our sin, as Baruch does so beautifully in our first reading today, if we do not admit our failure to "heed the voice of the Lord," realizing and repenting of our going "after the devices of our own heart" rather than following in His holy way – if we do not accuse ourselves of "evil in the sight of the Lord," He will accuse us on the day of the judgment, as He does with Chorazin and Bethsaida in our gospel... and the woe upon us then shall be interminable, as we are "hurled down to the realm of death" with the cursed Capernaum. But if we turn to Him, if we cry out to Him as does Baruch, as does our psalm this day, declaring the evil and destruction that has come upon us for our sin, that same "reproach of our neighbors" which has "laid Jerusalem in ruins" will be removed from us – the Lord will "remember not against us the iniquities of the past," and we shall preserve our souls on the day of judgment.

"They have poured out their blood like water round about Jerusalem": great is the suffering which has come upon the Lord's wayward children. It seems at times the Lord will be angry forever for the sins committed by the perverse heart of man. But we know that His "compassion [will] quickly come to us," that His anger lasts but a moment, it is only for a time, and that He shall indeed "deliver us and pardon our sins." This has He done in Jesus, in His sacrifice, and word of it now is preached to the nations. If we accept it, we save our souls from destruction, from eternal damnation; if we reject the word of the Gospel, we reject Jesus, and we reject Him who holds the world in His creating hand – and so what hope of life have we, who have cast Life aside so wantonly… and so the wrath of the Lord our God can only "burn like fire" forever.

Let us reject sin while there is time. As His Word is still in our hearing, let us come to it and bare our souls before its truth "in sackcloth and ashes." The condition of this world of sin does not change, and it mounts up its punishment for judgment day. Let us come out of the world, humbly professing our sin, and listen now to the voice that leads us to forgiveness and grace, to exaltation "to the skies," standing at His side forever.

O. 26. Sat. (I)

Saturday
(Bar.4:5-12,27-29; Ps.69:33-37; Lk.10:17-24)

"He who has brought disaster upon you will,
in saving you, bring you back enduring joy."

That enduring joy which comes to us after this time of trial is our theme today. Not only does Baruch come to it in his exhortation for the people to "fear not" anymore but to turn to God and be glad, but it is David's song as well: "You who seek God, may your hearts be merry!" he exclaims as he assures us that "God will save Zion and rebuild the cities of Judah," which were once "left desolate" "for the sins of [her] children." Yes, as Baruch encourages Israel, "Fear not, my children; call out to God!" so David confirms that "the Lord hears the poor." And from all their sins He shall save them.

And does not our gospel tell us the same. In it we are told that "Jesus rejoiced in the Spirit" and gave the Father "grateful praise," saying, "What you have hidden from the learned and the clever you have revealed to the

322

merest children." To His children, to the humble, to the poor, He reveals Himself. And what can those who are blessed so, to see "what many prophets and kings wished to see" – what can we do but rejoice in His Spirit? For He has given us "power to tread on snakes and scorpions and all the forces of the enemy, and nothing shall ever injure" us. For sin no longer holds sway in our lives as it once did when we turned in the hardness of our hearts from the face of God and so were "handed over" to our foes. Though once we "forsook the Eternal God," we now return to Him; and so the "mourning and lament" suffered because of our sin now become joy in His eternal presence.

"Nevertheless, do not rejoice so much in the fact that the devils are subject to you as that your names are inscribed in heaven." We should rejoice not so much in the gift as in the giver, not so much in the power we have as in Him who gives the power. For great and wonderful as the overcoming of evil in this life certainly is, its entire purpose is to bring us into communion with the Lord in the New Jerusalem, in His heavenly kingdom. "Those who love His name shall inhabit it," so let us join with Jesus in the Holy Spirit to praise the Name of the Father and the great blessing of life He imparts to us. And we shall find redemption from the punishment of our sins and rejoice as children in His presence forever. Amen.

O. 27. Mon. (I)

Twenty-Seventh Week

Monday
(Jon.1:1-2:1,11; Jon.2:2-5,7-8; Lk.10:25-37)

"A Samaritan who was journeying along came on him
and was moved to pity at the sight."

First let me note that the book of Jonah is not a parable, not an imaginary story, as popular scholarship would have us believe. How do I know this? I have faith, yes, which those who would explain away any miracle of God so sorely lack; but I know it, too, by Scripture itself. For elsewhere the Lord compares Himself to Jonah, and states explicitly that the people of Nineveh – who had the faith to repent at the preaching of Jonah – will rise on the day of judgment and condemn those of Jesus' time, and us, for our failure to repent at the words of the Son of God. It is not possible that imaginary people could condemn others' souls (the very idea is absurd, of course, but such are our minds in this "enlightened" age), and this comparison would suggest that Jesus Himself is but imaginary, which seems not against the belief of the vain prophets of our day.

323

Ordinary Time

In today's gospel we have a parable: The Good Samaritan. It begins as the universal story all parables are – "There was a man..." ("a man," any man, every man), and its express purpose is to impart a lesson. And the lesson today is God's universal love. The dreaded "Samaritan" represents nothing but faithlessness and sin to the Jewish mind, but Jesus demonstrates that it is sinners He calls – and that those thought of as sinners indeed often show the greatest faith. We see this not only in our gospel, but also in our reading from Jonah, for notice how quickly the pagan mariners turned to their gods, who are no-gods, to seek deliverance from the "breakers" and "billows" which pass over them. Indeed, it is they who arouse Jonah, who has fallen asleep in the despair of his separation from the will of God, to pray to his Lord. And what horror overwhelms them when they hear how he has disobeyed the Lord's command – "How could you do such a thing!" Who has the faith here? Who convicts whom of sin?

Though Jonah is clearly different from Jesus in this his sin, he is like Him in a crucial way – he sacrifices his life for those in danger of death. Notice his words: "Pick me up and throw me into the sea, that it may quiet down for you." And so it does when he is finally cast forth – after remarkable, faith-filled prayer by these pagans; and so also these men "offered sacrifice and made vows" to the Lord, coming it seems to faith in God following Jonah's laying down of his life. And, of course, as Jesus will spend three days in the belly of the earth, so Jonah spends three days in the belly of the whale; and as the Lord will rise on the third day, so Jonah is "spewed upon the shore."

Brothers and sisters, the Lord heard Jonah's prayer from "the midst of the nether world," "from the belly of the fish." Do not doubt and test the Lord as the lawyer who seeks "to justify himself" in his pride. In your moments of darkness, come to the Lord as the humble servant He calls you to be, and He shall assuage your doubts, He shall be moved with pity looking upon you, and teach you of the love and compassion only He knows.

Tuesday
(Jon.3:1-10; Ps.130:1-4,7-8; Lk.10:38-42)

"He repented of the evil that He had threatened to do them;
He did not carry it out."

Nineveh is spared. Because "they proclaimed a fast and all of them, great and small, put on sackcloth," because they repented of their sin and called "loudly to God," He did not punish them for their iniquity but forgave them and withheld "His blazing wrath." And so this pagan city finds God's mercy through the preaching of Jonah.

We are all called to repent. We are all called to turn to the Lord and seek His forgiveness and grace to overcome and be spared of punishment for our falling short of His glory. Our psalm declares, "Let Israel wait for the Lord, for with the Lord is kindness and with Him is plenteous redemption." And so to find His mercy we must have faith and we must be patient. We must be as Mary in our gospel today, seated at His feet, listening to His words. We cannot remove ourselves from this place and hope to find salvation for our souls any more than the Ninevites could have taken a break from their sitting in sackcloth and ashes to have a snack and yet hoped to find the forgiveness they so desperately needed. Our fast must be total, our obedience complete. Do you think Mary had a mind to rise as she listened to her Lord? Do you think she was distracted by anything? Certainly not. And we in our prayer and in our work and in our lives must find the commitment she embodies if we hope to know the grace of God truly working in our hearts.

Indeed, the Lord "will redeem Israel from all their iniquities." Indeed, He hears the voice of all who cry to Him "out of the depths" of their sin. He will come and wash us clean; He will come and make us new. If we choose "the better portion," we "shall not be deprived of it" and its reward. But it must be our whole hearts that turn to the Lord, that are set on His word... that heed His preaching as it comes with its grace to our ears.

If we are short of prophets today, listen more closely, brothers and sisters. If it is difficult to find the Word preached with the power and blessing of Jonah, open your Bibles and turn to your hearts. Sit still before Him in silence and He will fill your soul with His light. And fail not to come into His presence where the people gather for Mass. The Word shall indeed fill you; His Bread shall indeed nourish you. And your soul shall be saved according to your commitment to Christ.

O. 27. Wed. (I)

Wednesday
(Jon.4:1-11; Ps.86:3-6,9-10,15; Lk.11:1-4)

"Your kingdom come."

"You are a gracious and merciful God, slow to anger, rich in clemency, loathe to punish." How beautifully Jonah speaks of God's blessed compassion on His people. And how poorly he is able to accept and live that grace. The Lord's forgiveness extends now to the ends of the earth; let us not be loathe to offer it unto all.

In our first reading, Jonah is angry with God for His mercy in forgiving Nineveh, the pagan empire and enemy of Israel. But the Lord teaches Jonah that He watches over these, too, not only Israel, signaling His universal call to salvation (which shall be fulfilled in the teaching of Christ). By comparing the city of Nineveh to the plant "that grew up over Jonah's head, giving shade that relieved him of any discomfort," the Lord instructs us that not only does He care for all nations, but indeed that all nations have a holy call, a blessed purpose, in which God Himself takes pleasure and comfort. He has raised *all* the nations and each is called as a member of His kingdom.

This word should give us great understanding of the graciousness of our God, and great joy in knowing that we are called by Him: "You, O Lord, are good and forgiving, abounding in kindness to all who call upon you." We can join with David in his prayer, knowing that God will "attend to the sound of [our] pleading" even as He does this blessed king of Israel; even as He listens to His chosen people, so He listens now to us, for the walls of division have been cast asunder and His love now extends to all.

But we must not be as Jonah shows himself to be today. We must "forgive all who do us wrong" or the Lord will not hear our prayer to "subject us not to the trial." If we harbor anger, it *will* mean our death; and the Lord will send "a burning east wind" and a sun to beat down upon us, too, to draw us from the hardness of our hearts and the condemnation we breathe in our souls. Our vision must be that of God, who sees that sinners "cannot distinguish their right hand from their left," or as Jesus says from the cross, "They know not what they do." And so we, too, must forgive.

Let us join in prayer today, brothers and sisters, that the Lord's kingdom may come to earth. Let us rejoice that His reign extends to all. For it is the Lord's desire to "forgive us our sins," and it is His will that all find refuge in the shade of His presence. And so we partake of "our daily bread" here in His Word and in His Sacrament; and so we live the kingdom of God.

O. 27. Thurs. (I)

Thursday
(Mal.3:13-20; Ps.1:1-4,6,40:5; Lk.11:5-13)

"For you who fear my name,
there will arise the sun of justice with its healing rays."

Both our psalm and first reading make clear the distinction between the blessed and the condemned: "The Lord watches over the way of the just, but the way of the wicked vanishes," our psalmist declares. The wicked are "like chaff which the wind drives away," while the just are "like a tree planted near running water, that yields its fruit in due season, and whose leaves never fade." Malachi proclaims the same. Where the Lord is healing rays of warmth to the just, for the wicked He comes "blazing like an oven... leaving them neither root nor branch." For one, His fire is holy and life-giving; for the other, it destroys.

And what is the sign that we "fear the Lord and trust in His name"? Malachi speaks of "going about in penitential dress" and states, "They who fear the Lord spoke with one another, and the Lord listened attentively." Our psalmist tells us the just "delights in the law of the Lord, and meditates on His law day and night." We must be repentant of our sins and come humbly before Him. We must recognize, as Jesus tells us, that we indeed are ones "with all [our] sins." This is first. But most importantly we must trust in Him and turn to Him, and *pray* in His Name. For "the heavenly Father give[s] the Holy Spirit to those who ask Him." He is not remiss in making them His own. He wishes all to be blessed and come before Him whole. But we must not fail to seek His will, to seek His way, to beg it of our God. *We* cannot be remiss in asking and seeking and knocking, for this persistence proves our love of Him and of His way, and by it we will find Him.

Brothers and sisters, there is nothing more important or more powerful than prayer. It is our way of coming to Him and becoming one with Him. It is at the heart of the distinction "between him who serves God, and him who does not serve Him." For all that we do will come to naught if not done in His presence, and it is only by prayer we enter the presence of His holy light. First and always we must have faith, yes. First and always we must believe. But now and ever we must seek Him; forever we must ask His grace to come into our lives. And He will hear. He will "give [His] children good things." So neglect not to remain in the presence of God and your reward will be assured, and you will know the blessed light of His face.

O. 27. Fri. (I)

Friday
(Jl.1:13-15,2:1-2; Ps.9:2-3,6,8-9,16; Lk.11:15-26)

"It is near, a day of darkness and of gloom,
a day of clouds and somberness!"

And we must be prepared. We must rend our hearts and not our garments. We must "spend the night in sackcloth," repentant of our sins. We must "proclaim a fast" and "cry to the Lord," "for near is the day of the Lord."

The prophet Joel sounds this alarm several hundred years before Christ, and in truth it proclaims the coming of Christ. For it is His coming that separates the wicked from the just; it is He who "judges the world with

327

justice" – it is by Him the names of the wicked are "blotted out forever and ever" and those who "declare all [His] wondrous deeds" find their salvation.

The day is coming and is already here, for the Lord declares in our gospel, "The man who is not with me is against me, and the man who does not gather with me scatters." He makes clear the works of Satan, which do not bring healing but only sickness and death, and the works of "the finger of God," which overpower and "cast out devils." Here the judgment is come; here it begins. In the end it shall be fulfilled and the great divide between evil and good will be set for all eternity, but here and in this time the Word of Truth goes forth, calling all souls to leave behind all sin.

But, brothers and sisters, our fasting must be complete; our weeping, our repentance, must be genuine. We must turn entirely from our sins and make place only for the Lord Jesus Christ to live in the houses of our souls. If the Lord lives in us, there is no place for darkness. If the Lord is within us, no devil can dwell there. But if in hypocrisy we pretend a conversion, we expand the space for the devil's dwelling in our homes. For the two are indeed mutually exclusive: the Lord has nothing to do with the devil, and the devil nothing to do with the Lord. And so if we hope to stand on the day when darkness covers the earth, "spreading over the mountains, like a people numerous and mighty"; if we hope to remain when the Lord returns with His myriad of angels to judge the earth and the thoughts of men's hearts... we must enter His grace this day – we must now call upon His Name. There is no other way, my brothers and sisters. You must be with Him or against Him. The choice between life and death is presented before you; for the day of darkness is nigh. Choose His eternal light!

O. 27. Sat. (I)

Saturday
(Jl.4:12-21; Ps.97:1-2,5-6,11-12; Lk.11:27-28)

"Near is the day of the Lord in the valley of decision."

And so, "blest are they who hear the word of God and keep it." For though "sun and moon are darkened and the stars withhold their brightness," though "mountains melt like wax before the Lord," "light dawns for the just," and for them "the mountains shall drip new wine, and the hills shall flow with milk." Yes, "the heavens and the earth quake, but the Lord is a refuge to His people."

Are we His people? Are our hearts set upon Him? Are we blest as our Mother with keeping the word of God and putting it into practice, giving our "yes" to all His words, and His commands? Are these commands sweet as honey; are they the new wine we drink each day? From Him do we find our daily bread? Though we are in His Church and have the blessed breasts of

328

this great Mother to nurse us, though we are here where the hills of the Lord "flow with [His] milk" – though we have at our hands the Body and Blood of the Lord and the true teaching, the Word of God, in our ears by His grace upon this House of God, do we truly appreciate these gifts He provides: do we eat and drink unto our salvation and keep His word as an ever flowing stream of life in our souls, at the heart of our beings? "The channels of Judah shall flow with water," as now they do. Do we wash ourselves clean in that water that "issue[s] from the house of the Lord"? Are we prepared for the day of decision?

Let us rejoice in Him, brothers and sisters. "Be glad in the Lord, you just, and give thanks to His holy name." With the psalmist let us raise our song and proclaim His justice to all the peoples. For what should we have but joy as we take refuge in His promise, as we come to the table of the New Covenant each day and share even now in the life He offers forth through His holy sacrifice? And let us pray to our Mother, Mary, that we shall be as she is, that we shall be so true to the Lord and serve as His handmaidens amongst the world. May she keep us close to the nourishing food the Church holds for all her children; and may our decision be as firm as hers as we give our unfailing "yes" to the Lord and so know His grace and blessing.

Twenty-Eighth Week

Monday
(Rm.1:1-7; Ps.98:1-4; Lk.11:29-32)

"You have a greater than Jonah here."

Greater than any prophet is He. Wiser than Solomon is the Lord who is the source of all wisdom. For it is He of whom the prophets speak; it is His promised coming "the Holy Scriptures record." The fulfillment of prophets and kings is in our midst. Our high priest is with us offering the sacrifice of Himself. Let us thirst for Him as the Ninevites did for Jonah's preaching and seek Him as the queen of the South for Solomon's wisdom. Let us listen to His servant and apostle Paul as he proclaims the Gospel of God and come to "obedient faith" with all the Gentiles "who have been called to belong to Jesus Christ." Salvation is upon us as it is all nations.

If Jonah's preaching was great, the Lord's is the greater. If he converted thousands, Jesus turns millions to the love of God. If Solomon was wise, our Lord is so much the wiser. For though this great king spoke well of all things of the earth by the grace of God, the Christ comes now with the wisdom of the richness of heaven. And so now we are all "called to holiness, grace and peace." It is these gifts which are imparted to us "from

God our Father and the Lord Jesus Christ." And by these blessings we become His children, greater indeed than any prophet or king of old.

Yes, the fulfillment has come. "The Lord has made His salvation known." "All the ends of the earth have seen the salvation by our God." His Word is brought forth even now, even this day to our hearts in the preaching of the Gospel that is Christ Jesus – "His resurrection from the dead" signals the redemption of all mankind. And so we celebrate. And so we "sing to the Lord a new song" as we, too, participate in His death and resurrection with the beloved apostle Paul, even as we come to the table set before us by His grace and holiness.

May that same "Spirit of holiness" which made Jesus "Son of God in power" now touch our souls and separate us from all that is unholy. May we respond in kind with the Ninevites to Jonah's preaching, that they might not condemn us on the last day for our lack of faith. May the wisdom which comes to us now by the grace poured forth from His lips sink into our hearts and find a place in our lives. For no greater than He shall we find; let us not be blind to this sign.

O. 28. Tues. (I)

Tuesday
(Rm.1:16-25; Ps.19:2-5; Lk.11:37-41)

"They stultified themselves through speculating to no purpose,
and their senseless hearts were darkened."

If these words do not refer to modern man most poignantly, then I imagine nothing can be said of anything. In ancient times, "they exchanged the glory of the immortal God for images representing mortal man, birds, beasts, and snakes" and bowed down to statues as if they were gods. The images man worships today are also the creations of his own hands, sometimes as physical as the idols worshiped before the time of Christ – who does not long to see his own image on one of our television sets, and who is held in greater esteem than those movie stars whom we have never met but know only of their image on a screen? – but perhaps most particularly they are the vain ideas, which reveal their utter absurdity to any mind with a modicum of common sense, but which are propounded as sacred by the elite thinkers of our day. Their numbers seem endless, and one wonders if man will rationalize himself out of existence, as perhaps he already has philosophically in the declaration that God is dead, and so often done in reality through movements such as Communism and Nazism.

Indeed, how relevant are all Paul's words today: "They certainly had knowledge of God, yet they did not glorify Him as God or give Him thanks"; "they claimed to be wise, but turned into fools instead"; "they

330

engaged in the mutual degradation of their bodies." But "the wrath of God is being revealed from heaven against the irreligious and perverse spirit of men who... hinder the truth." "These men who exchanged the truth of God for a lie and worshiped and served the creature rather than the Creator" cannot but come to naught, for "day pours out the word to day, and night to night imparts knowledge" – the Gospel goes forth "to the ends of the world" and Truth overwhelms all lies. As Jesus overturned the Pharisees who "cleanse the outside of cup and dish, but within... are filled with rapaciousness," so shall the mind of modern man be shown for all its absurdity in the clear light of day.

Time. There is but time to wait. Time for the Word to go forth and to pray for the conversion of the nations, of all peoples. And there is hope, hope that men shall turn from their absurdity and their perversity to embrace the light of the Gospel and the true teaching of love it brings. We pray the senseless will find faith and be led thereby to salvation.

O. 28. Wed. (I)

Wednesday
(Rm.2:1-11; Ps.62:2-3,6-7,9,13; Lk.11:42-46)

"Your hard and impenitent heart
is storing up retribution for that day of wrath
when the just judgment of God will be revealed."

"He will repay every man for what he has done... Yes, affliction and anguish will come upon every man who has done evil... But there will be glory, honor, and peace for everyone who has done good." This is the just judgment, and it comes only from God, not from sinful man.

And so we are chastised in preparation for that day, that from His wrath we may be spared. We should all wish to be "insult"ed by Jesus as are the Pharisees and lawyers in today's gospel, here, today, while there is still time. We should all desire His difficult words of instruction which would serve, if heeded humbly, to separate us from the sins of the world, the attachments of this life that cling to our soul and prevent our coming into His presence. Under His mighty hand we should all subject ourselves, that He might lighten our "impossible burdens," that He might take from us all that is not holy, all that is not true – that we might be freed from the judgment upon our souls and walk with Him in immortality. We must be ready for His day. But as it is the darkness is with us.

"Only in God is my soul at rest." With David we must sing this truth from our hearts. The emptiness of the flesh and its imagination must not possess us; vain pride must take no place in our lives... All our lusts must be set aside and we must know with certainty that only in God do we find our peace: He is our refuge and our strength. "He only is my rock and my salvation, my stronghold," we must cry, and "trust in Him at all times," or wandering from the truth we will find ourselves in the way of destruction.

"God's kindness is an invitation to you to repent." In His patience He gives you time to turn from sin and find His grace and mercy. Pray He will convict you of your sin in this time and you will not convict yourself by your judgment of others. Seek His redeeming hand at work in your life and do the good before Him. Then you "shall not be disturbed," when His Word has taken root in your soul, when you have left behind all the vanity of this world. Then the glory of God will be your own, and nothing shall remove it from you. Soften your heart to His blessed chastisement; it shall work for you against the day of judgment.

Thursday
(Rm.3:21-30; Ps.130:1-7; Lk.11:47-54)

"This generation will have to account for the blood of all the prophets shed since the foundation of the world."

And so shall it be with Christ's own blood, the fulfillment of all the martyrs' sacrifice; for these same scribes and Pharisees whom Jesus proclaims guilty of the prophets' murders will indeed devise the murder of the Son of God. And they prove the truth of His words immediately by their manifestation of "fierce hostility to Him" and their thus giving birth to the plot to crucify Him.

Perhaps most appropriate for today, with regard to Paul's epistle to the Romans, is the Lord's admonishment of the lawyers: "You have taken away the key of knowledge. You yourselves have not gained access, yet you have stopped those who wish to enter!" It is essentially the same message the Apostle teaches: "The justice of God has been manifested apart from the law... that justice of God which works through faith in Jesus Christ." It is not through "observance of the law" that justification comes; the works of the law – circumcision, animal sacrifice, dietary rules – which address the body, are useless in this regard. God is Spirit and it is spiritual means He uses to redeem us – we must come in *faith* to Him. And those who would restrict faith by the imposition of these laws serve only to impede the working of the Spirit and His grace. Paul states the question succinctly: "Does God belong to the Jews alone? Is He not also the God of the Gentiles?" If He is God of all nations, it is not meet to impose Jewish religious practice upon those apart from Jewish tradition. But these protectors, or rather "possessors" and defilers of the law – defiling it by their greed in seizing it, their pride in assuming it as their own and not God's –

cannot accept that "it is the same God," that the Gentiles are equal in grace with the Jews... and so to them this teaching is blasphemy.

At the root of the problem is the fact that these leaders are not as the psalmist in our readings today, who sings: "My soul waits for the Lord more than sentinels wait for the dawn." Nor do they cry "in supplication" "out of the depths" of their iniquity for God's forgiveness. If they had been so disposed, they would have seen who stood before them, they would have recognized His coming, and they would have fallen to their knees and found His grace.

Let us not be so hardhearted, for indeed the blood of Jesus is upon the hands of *all* who sin, just as His salvation is upon all who repent and believe in Him. Water alone will not wash us clean; we must recognize our lack of love, and find His Spirit working in us.

O. 28. Fri. (I)

Friday
(Rm.4:1-8; Ps.32:1-2,5,7,11; Lk.12:1-7)

"Happy is the man to whom the Lord imputes not guilt,
in whose spirit there is no guile."

All our sins shall be taken away by the Lord who watches over us and loves us, if we but believe.

We must lay bare our souls, brothers and sisters. We cannot hide from the eternal, piercing light of God. His hand is upon us at all times; His heart is open always for our entering in. It cannot be otherwise with the Lord of the universe, in whose sight "even the hairs of [our] head are counted." And He who surrounds us desires but our love, desires but our faith, desires but that we come into His presence confessing our sins, and He will take them away. And we shall not be "cast into Gehenna" but drawn into His kingdom.

His kingdom is coming. Jesus sees it as He gazes out at the dense "crowd of thousands" gathering before Him. He sees the kingdom coming as men's hearts turn to Him. And so He warns His disciples, who shall be the laborers to reap His harvest, "Be on guard against the yeast of the Pharisees, which is hypocrisy," for if they should take pride in their mission, if they should find in their deeds "grounds for boasting" and so forget the favor of God by which all are justified, they shall indeed tempt the fires of Gehenna. "Everything you have said in the dark will be heard in the daylight," for the Lord hears "what you have whispered in locked rooms." So, keep your hearts set on Him and His goodness, and the truth of the Gospel will be proclaimed to the world, and you shall save your immortal soul.

Jesus knows, too, that the faith of His disciples and their declaration of His Word to the world will bring persecution. He sees in this scene, too, the cross set before Him, and He knows those who follow Him shall share in it as well. And so He reassures His children that the Father is with them, that He treasures them even as He treasures His Son, and so the powers of this age will hold no reign over them, and that they should "not be afraid of those who kill the body and can do no more."

Yes, our soul is in His hands. He has power to forgive and to protect, if we but come to Him as children, if we but come to Him in faith.

Saturday
(Rm.4:13,16-18; Ps.105:6-9,42-43; Lk.12:8-12)

"All depends on faith, everything is a grace."

Faith is our father; it brings us to life for it makes us children of "the God who restores the dead to life and calls into being those things which had not been." By faith we entrust ourselves into God's hands and become as Abraham, who is "our father in the sight of God in whom he believed." "Hoping against hope, Abraham believed and so became the father of many nations," and insofar as we believe, we become his children before God. Indeed, it is through faith alone that we are born into His kingdom.

And having faith, we must acknowledge its presence in our lives by witnessing to the Son of God. If we are His disciples, as we must be, we will not hide His grace working in us but allow it to bear fruit in the profession of that faith before the world. And so, as we "come before synagogues, rulers, and authorities," as we stand before the face of this generation, as we do anything in this world, we must "not worry about how to defend [ourselves] or what to say." Jesus tells us, "The Holy Spirit will teach you at that moment all that should be said." And so by this trusting in Him we prove ourselves children of faith.

This is the manner in which I produce this writing. Trusting in Him as entirely as my faith allows, I am not concerned beforehand what I shall speak, what I shall write upon this page. In the measure that I am a child of grace, I prove it by my allowing Him to speak through me at this moment and in His way. This is what we must strive to do with all our work, in all our lives. All our lives are founded upon this faith, and the Lord calls us in an ever greater way to express that faith, to live that faith, by consecrating all we think and do to His will and desire. It is for us but to come into His presence, to remember He is here with us, and so to find His grace at work in our lives.

We must be prepared and be preparing ourselves always to stand before Him forever. As we place ourselves in His presence now, it is so that we die to ourselves and begin to live by His grace. More and more we must trust in that faith which joins us to Him and makes us children of the promise which "holds true for all Abraham's descendants... for all who have his faith." Faith alone will bring us to life, for faith alone brings us into the presence of Him who is life. Enter His grace, brothers and sisters, and find it working in your life.

Twenty-Ninth Week

Monday
(Rm.4:20-25; Lk.1:68-75; Lk.12:13-21)

"We should serve Him devoutly
and through all our days be holy in His sight."

For "this very night your life shall be required of you." Always and forever our faith is required of us, if we are to draw breath. Always and forever the Lord asks us what fruit we have produced. Always and forever we must be careful not to toil in vain, but to live according to His Word, believing in His promise. Else our lives will indeed be empty vessels.

Holiness befits His house. Adherence to His covenant is our call. Faith in the One who is "saving strength for us" is our necessity. We must indeed be as our father Abraham, who was "fully persuaded that God could do whatever He had promised," whose "faith was credited to him as justice." And if we have the same faith as Abraham, we will find the same justice, the same reward as he. "For our faith will be credited to us also if we believe in Him who raised Jesus our Lord from the dead." Jesus "was handed over to death for our sins and raised up for our justification" and only faith in Him as the fulfillment of the promise to Abraham will give us life.

Why do we turn to the things of this world and in them seek our fulfillment, and in them seek our rest, when they are so vain and when all the while Jesus calls to our souls to come to Him? Why is it we think that in the goods of this world we can find refuge, we can find strength? Why are we so blinded to believe that in them we can find our peace? "Relax! Eat heartily, drink well. Enjoy yourself." Here is the fruitless mantra of this materialistic world. Here is the epitome of our blindness to His will. Here is the belly seeking to take the place of the spirit.

Can we not see that it is only the spirit that gives life, that the flesh is of no avail, that the riches of this earth serve more as a distraction to finding the life and the peace we seek in the depths of our souls than to bringing a

335

fulfillment of this most human of desires? This desire cannot be satisfied except in Christ. We must not be as "the man who grows rich for himself instead of growing rich in the sight of God," or when these passing riches rot away or are taken from us, we will be left terribly empty. Rather, we should "avoid greed in all its forms" and dedicate ourselves to service of the Lord. Only in Him is life and peace made known, and only by holiness do we come there. At all times the Lord is calling to our soul; let us answer Him in faith.

Tuesday
(Rm.5:12,15,17-21; Ps.40:7-10,17; Lk.12:35-38)

"To do your will, O my God, is my delight,
and your law is within my heart!"

"May those who love your salvation say ever, 'The Lord be glorified.'" May we who love the Lord "exult and be glad" in Him. May we who take refuge in His grace sing aloud His praise. What greater gift could we have than Jesus Christ, whose "single righteous act brought all men acquittal and life. For truly we were dead in our sin," truly the offense of Adam had infected our souls, truly through this "one man's disobedience all became sinners" – but more truly "through one man's obedience all shall become just," for "His grace has far surpassed" the increase of sin. And so, what should we do but rejoice with David at the truth of Paul's instruction.

And what should we do but be ready, truly ready, really waiting, patiently, for the return of our Lord. "Be like men awaiting their master's return from a wedding." Set your hearts on His coming again, "so that when He knocks, you will open without delay." This is yet the greater blessing for us servants, that even in these dark days upon this earth, we stand ready for His return. Here is His grace at work within us, that our hearts are set on Him, that His presence, the coming of His kingdom, we know even now in anticipation of its arrival. No greater blessing could we hope for than to be "those servants whom the master finds wide-awake on His return." By this we know we have conquered sin; by this we see that we have overcome the darkness which surrounds us – if whether "at midnight or before sunrise" we are found prepared, if even in the darkest times we hold His light, if our eyes are like "lamps... burning ready" and our "belts [are] fastened around [our] waists"... we have all that we need in this world.

Be ready, my brothers and sisters, for the joy is coming; it will not delay. That happiness of life in His presence we sense even now, we taste even this day in our mouths, will come soon to fulfillment in the reign of our God. And so, "those who receive the overflowing grace and gift of justice

336

[will] live and reign through the one man, Jesus Christ," for whom we await, in whom we take our refuge, whose name we praise, His saving word etched upon our souls and bleeding in our hearts. In all we do we wait for His coming. He alone is our desire, and we shall not be disappointed.

O. 29. Wed. (I)

Wednesday
(Rm.6:12-18; Ps.124:1-8; Lk.12:39-48)

"Offer yourselves to God
as men who have come back from the dead to life."

If we have come back from the dead to life, should we then offer ourselves up to death again? As Paul questions, "Are we free to sin?" How absurd a thought! If we are sinners, let us give ourselves freely to sin, and find the condemnation which comes from this. But if we are men of justice, let us give ourselves to "obedience" of the teaching imparted to us, and find life firmly in our souls.

Jesus states quite clearly, "When much has been given a man, much will be required of him." Brothers and sisters, much has been given us simply by our release from the sin which once enslaved us. Indeed, "we were rescued like a bird from the fowler's snare," as David's psalm proclaims. The "raging waters" that "would have overwhelmed us," the "torrent [that] would have swept over us," has been calmed... For this alone we have much to be thankful; simply by this grace much has been entrusted to us. And what follows only adds to this initial blessing; for each day our souls are required of us, each day He puts in our hands and calls us to the work set aside for our souls to complete. Each day the gift of grace is increased within us. So should we then begin "to abuse the housemen and servant girls, to eat and drink and get drunk"? Should we then return to the slavery of sin which blinds our eyes to His eternal presence? Certainly not. Rather, we should "be on guard" at all times, vigilantly prepared for our master's return, employing the gifts He imparts to us each passing day.

We are no longer dead, brothers and sisters. We have the grace of our God at work within us, lighting our eyes and filling our souls with His holy food. We must now be holy as He. It is not for us to return to the death of sin, to subject ourselves to its chains once again, to have our eyes darkened and our souls destroyed. The grace, the light within us, must be diligently preserved. We must come to Him, come to His stewards to whom the most has been entrusted, who hold in their power sacramental grace, and confess our sins in His presence, and come and eat of His Body and Blood. Let us avail ourselves of these gifts these successors of the apostles hold and thus find the strength to give our own "bodies to God as weapons for justice" and not for sin.

Thursday
(Rm.6:19-23; Ps.1:1-4,6,40:5; Lk.12:49-53)

"The Lord watches over the way of the just,
but the way of the wicked vanishes."

The division is clear. The Lord Himself has stated, "I have come for division." Far from establishing "peace on the earth," His message makes clear the distinction between the evil and the good, the wicked and the just, drawn so well in our psalm today. He has "come to light a fire on the earth." It shall purify the just for the kingdom of God even as it burns up all the wicked.

Paul also makes clear the division between the evil and the good, between that which is of God and that which is of sin. "Formerly you enslaved your bodies to impurity and licentiousness for their degradation... But now that you are freed from sin and have become slaves of God, your benefit is sanctification as you tend toward eternal life." The distinction is certain: "The wages of sin is death, but the gift of God is eternal life in Christ Jesus our Lord." Indeed, the just "is like a tree planted near running water, that yields its fruit in due season, and whose leaves never fade," but the wicked "are like chaff which the wind drives away." This division is what the Lord's light and fire reveal; and this revelation is eternal.

It is painful, brothers and sisters. It is painful to undergo our own transformation to justice and light from the depths of depravity into which we have fallen, and will be painful to witness others destroyed by the hardness of their hearts. The Lord Himself expresses this pain when He says, "What anguish I feel till it is over!" He takes no pleasure in bringing the agony of division, which begins with His own agony in the garden and ends with His crucifixion. He suffers most to witness the sins of the masses so acutely. They wag their heads at Him even as He cries from the cross. What is to be done? Division must come. For the kingdom must come, the resurrection must take place, and sin cannot stand in its light – and so those who attach themselves to sin, to the works of the father of lies, will not stand in that day either. And even now the judgment comes, even now we must take sides – even now we choose death, or life.

Friday

(Rm.7:18-25; Ps.119:66,68,76-77,93,94; Lk.12:54-59)

"Why do you not judge for yourselves what is just?"

Do we not have the law of God at work in us now? Must we yet subject ourselves to the judge of this earth, who cannot but condemn us for our sin? If we cried out with our psalmist for the Lord to teach us His "commands," His "statutes," His "law," and His "precepts," His "promise" of "compassion" would be with us, His Spirit would come to us and instruct us on all matters. No longer "the prisoner of the law of sin in [our] members," we would be freed "from this body under the power of death." Not only would our "inner self agree with the law of God," but our actions would reflect, by the grace of Him who is at work within us, that law now written on our hearts. The "wisdom and knowledge" the Lord thereby imparts would be sufficient for the resolution of any problem in our lives, for there is nothing beyond the scope of the Spirit.

Both Paul and Jesus Himself encourage us to find the Spirit of Christ at work in our hearts. We as a community of believers would have no need to turn to the works of the world to resolve our problems if we followed well the teaching of the Lord and His Church. Should not the Church be our government? Should not the teaching of God, which transcends all earthly wisdom, be sufficient for our discerning right and wrong in any situation? Or is sin still at work in our members? Are we yet subject to this law and the condemnation and death it brings? Has the devil yet a hold upon us; does he yet cast us into darkness? Are we therefore too blind to see right from wrong?

Brothers and sisters, we must cast from our souls all vestige of sin; it cannot hold power over us any longer. We must find the light of Christ in our eyes and so be made able to judge all things in His justice. With our psalmist we must proclaim to the Lord, "Your law is my delight." If we yet take refuge in the law of sin, it will bring but judgment upon our lives. But if we turn to Him, true wisdom will be ours – and His compassion will save us.

All teaching the Lord puts into the hands of His apostles. Our Pope and bishops and priests continue, as His servants, to proclaim His truth and impart His grace. The Church is the home Jesus leaves us; upon it He places His Spirit. Let us follow the teachings of the Lord and find His power at work in our lives, and all things will be clear to our eyes. And so, condemnation we shall avoid as by the grace of God we judge all things rightly.

Saturday

(Rm.8:1-11; Ps.24:1-6; Lk.13:1-9)

"You will all come to the same end unless you reform."

We hear again today in our readings of the distinction between those who are of the flesh, and so of sin, and those who are of the spirit and justice. And since "the tendency of the flesh is toward death but that of the spirit toward life and peace," rightly does Jesus warn us that we will die in our sin if we do not repent and turn to Him. For indeed He and the Father, with the Spirit, are of life and have nothing to do with death, with sin.

Paul continues to make clear the difference, the separation, between those of flesh and those of spirit, and continues to encourage his reader to allow the body to die that the spirit might live: "If Christ is in you, the body is indeed dead because of sin, while the spirit lives because of justice." It is in Jesus that our salvation from sin has come, for when "God sent His Son in the likeness of sinful flesh, thereby condemning sin in the flesh," He made it possible for us to live no longer "according to the flesh," but "according to the spirit," for we know that "He who raised Christ from the dead will bring [our] mortal bodies to life also through His Spirit." Even now His Spirit brings our spirit to life, and on the last day our flesh shall also be joined to Him in heaven.

David's psalm questions, "Who can ascend the mountain of the Lord? Or who can stand in His holy place?" Only those "whose hands are sinless... shall receive a blessing from the Lord," and so, again, we must turn to Him, we must be of "the race that seeks for Him." "The Lord's are the earth and its fullness; the world and those who dwell in it" are of Him. But how our hearts have turned from Him in sin, and so, how shaken we have become, inviting death into our lives. And so only those who renounce their sin, who come by the power of the Spirit and the grace of Jesus' blood, shall attain to His presence. And only those who bear fruit in His Name will He preserve.

The end of our gospel makes clear that there must be fruit in our lives, brothers and sisters. This is indeed the sign that we are of the spirit – if we "bear fruit" in the Spirit. We cannot claim to be of the spirit and bear the fruit of the flesh, which is sin. Jesus will not fail to recognize the difference, however much we may fool ourselves or others. We will die in the flesh like any sinner if we do not live according to Christ and His Word.

Thirtieth Week

Monday
(Rm.8:12-17; Ps.68:2,4,6-7,20-21; Lk.13:10-17)

"All who are led by the Spirit of God are sons of God."

It is the Spirit of God that led the poor stooped woman in our gospel today to the synagogue to see and hear the teaching of Jesus the Lord, and to find a healing for her infirmity. "This daughter of Abraham... in the bondage of Satan for eighteen years" was by the Lord "released from her shackles" and became a daughter also of the Most High God. She is a sign of us all. For all, whether sons of Abraham by the flesh or not, are called into the presence of God to find healing for the sin and sadness and oppression of the devil which trouble us. On our own we cannot stand straight in the sight of God, but by the touch of Jesus we find our dignity and become sons of God with Him.

God is "the father of orphans and the defender of widows"; He "gives a home to the forsaken." And so we who were once under the "spirit of slavery" to sin may now find "a spirit of adoption through which we cry out, 'Abba!' (that is, 'Father')." Once having no father to watch over us, now "the Spirit Himself gives witness with our spirit that we are children of God." A greater blessing one could not find than to be a son or daughter of the Most High God. For "God is a saving God for us." Not only does He love us, but He shows that love even by dying for us, that we might live.

And it is so that "if we are children, we are heirs as well: heirs of God, heirs with Christ." And though it is by the death of Jesus that we are made heirs of the Father's glory, we only come into full possession of the riches of our glorious Lord by our own death, for we must "suffer with Him so as to be glorified with Him." It is this death of ours, a death to self, to flesh, to sin and the world, that brings us the life of Him "who controls the passageways of death" and so is able to free us from all death.

Day by day the Lord "bears our burdens." On all days, eternally, He is our Father and our Savior, waiting to heal us. Whenever we come to Him, we shall find Him ready to bless us. His Spirit He sends upon all, like a sun that never sets, calling us to His presence. We must but respond in humility and faith, and as we bow ourselves before Him, He will raise us up to the dignity He desires for all our lives. And we shall be His sons.

341

Tuesday
(Rm.8:18-25; Ps.126:1-6; Lk.13:18-21)

"Hoping for what we cannot see
means awaiting it with patient endurance."

We cannot see the coming of the kingdom of heaven. It comes so gradually; it rises imperceptibly, "like yeast which a woman took to knead into three measures of flour." It grows like the tiny mustard seed, which "became a large shrub and the birds of the air nested in its branches." A most fruitful reign is the reign of God, and well worth the wait. As Paul says, "I consider the sufferings of the present to be as nothing compared with the glory to be revealed in us." But wait we must. In hope we take our refuge. And as we hope, indeed we suffer, for "we ourselves, although we have the Spirit as first fruits, groan inwardly while we await the redemption of our bodies." With the rest of creation we groan "in agony" for the futility to which the physical universe has been subject. Yet hope have we, and it is this which gives us a sense of joy even as we wait so patiently.

"Those that sow in tears shall reap rejoicing." Our psalm gives us a picture of the joy that awaits us in the redemption of the just in the kingdom of God as it describes the happiness of the exiles' return from Babylon: "We were like men dreaming. Then our mouth was filled with laughter, and our tongue with rejoicing." The knowledge of the Lord's hand at work in the lives of these Israelites can only increase our hope, can only stir our faith that we too shall sing, "The Lord has done great things for us," that we too shall "come back rejoicing" after this time of trial which is our stay here on this earth. And the fact that we have the Spirit now as the first payment against the day of judgment and against the power of Satan in this dark world causes a sense of joy already in our bones, gives us even now a foretaste of the kingdom to come, and which comes to us indeed each day in every breath we breathe in His presence, and particularly in the food He leaves us to consume at the altar of His holy sacrifice.

Yes, we have His Word at work in us even now, brothers and sisters. Even as we speak (even as I write), the seed does grow into a tree, the yeast does cause the dough to rise. Though it take time and we hope most for its fulfillment, yet it is with us even now in this blessed growth we experience in the sight of our God, in the blood of our Lord. Our hope is not in vain, and the tears we shed now certainly nourish the growth of the kingdom within us and all around us. Even in these does our hope find fulfillment. Even in these tears do we taste surpassing joy.

Wednesday
(Rm.8:26-30; Ps.13:4-6; Lk.13:22-30)

"Lord, are they few in number who are to be saved?"

We question. We wonder. With the man who spoke to the Lord as He made His way toward Jerusalem, as He approached His own death, we ask Jesus, "Who will be saved?" particularly as we face our own imminent death. Jesus answers the man, and so He responds to us, too. His answer is simple: "Come in through the narrow door." His answer is wise, and comes with, and itself is, a warning to us not to take for granted the salvation by our God but to be diligent about our striving toward His kingdom, to be purposeful about our dying for Him. Those who walked with Him may have thought that this alone would be sufficient to ensure their entrance into heaven. But simply knowing Him, seeing Him, and even eating with Him will not do: He must know us. He must see us about His work as we see Him about the Father's work – He must come in and eat with us, nourishing our souls with His daily bread of labor in His Name, of life in His Word.

Brothers and sisters, we may come to His table every day. We may eat of His Body and drink of His Blood and hear His Word proclaimed to our ears; we may be members of His Church, sitting here in these pews; we may have since birth been graced with the blessings of the sacraments and teaching of our Catholic faith – but this alone does not assure our entering into heaven. We must *live* that faith. We must put flesh and blood to our belief. There is no other way we can be saved, because this is our life and our life is required of us by God. It will not magically occur at the moment of death if we have not spent our lives for Him.

O brothers and sisters, we must cry out with David, "Give light to my eyes that I may not sleep in death." We must sing to the Lord with him, "Let my heart rejoice in your salvation." We must seek Him, seek His life, with all our hearts, that the prophetic words of Paul might become our own, that our predestination "to share the image of His Son" the Father might accomplish in us. For the Lord does call us, and we must respond. As we respond, we shall be justified – He shall enter in and cleanse us of our sin. And remaining on this path of justification we shall soon find glory with God in His eternal kingdom.

Brothers and sisters, let the will of the Lord be accomplished in us. In our moments of doubt, when we have no words with which to come to God, let us turn to the Spirit who "intercedes for the saints as God Himself wills," "with groanings which cannot be expressed in speech." He truly is our help in weakness. He truly is our guard on this perilous journey. Only remaining with Him and in His Church do we find comfort in the knowledge that we are to be saved.

Thursday
(Rm.8:31-39; Ps.109:21-22,26-27,30-31; Lk.13:31-35)

"For your sake we are being slain all the day long."

And yet, "in all this we are more than conquerors because of Him who has loved us."

We die. Each day we die, we sacrifice our lives. We are "as sheep to be slaughtered." This is our call, to be as our Lord who was crucified – our King wears a crown of thorns. And yet in all this apparent weakness, in all those places where violence seems to reign, where death presumes dominion over us... it is void. It has no power. For God holds all the world in His creating hand, and He watches over us. So, indeed, "if God is for us, who can be against us?" If God fights for us, how shall we be conquered? We shall not, we cannot. "Christ Jesus, who died or rather was raised up... intercedes for us." And so the death He suffered, which led only to life, becomes our own, and only life is ours in Him.

The Lord would gather all His "children together, as a mother bird collects her young under her wing," but so many refuse. So many are disobedient. So many desire not the love of God. And so, death comes. Because of our sin, Jesus must suffer, Jesus *must* die. And we must die with Him if we are to follow Him through this world of darkness and sin into the kingdom of light. For the emptiness of the power of this world must be exposed. It must be shown for the nothingness it is. And only by dying does this become clear to our minds.

And so, Jesus does not shy away from death; He does not save Himself from its clutches. Freely He offers Himself for our sakes, that we might overcome the fear it produces in our fallen souls, that we might then be raised from darkness to light. The prayer of David is the prayer of Christ, standing in our stead, "I am wretched and poor, and my heart is pierced within me." The sword, which has no power over Him, nor over us now, He accepts in His side that new life might flow out from His broken flesh. The suffering which should be our own He takes and nails to the cross. And it is dead. And the power of Satan is nullified. And in His "generous kindness" the Lord has rescued us. And so as we suffer now with Him all the temptations of this earthly life, our heavenly king is by our side breathing upon us new life. Let us have no fear for any presumed power of this universe; the Lord is greater than them all.

Friday
(Rm.9:1-5; Ps.147:12-15,19-20; Lk.14:1-6)

"They could not answer."

The Pharisees are dumb. The leaders of the Jewish nation cannot speak as to whether a man should be healed on the sabbath. How far they have fallen from the presence of God.

We know the Israelites were God's chosen people. This is proclaimed clearly by both Paul and our psalmist today: "Theirs were the adoption, the glory, the covenants, the lawgiving, the worship, and the promises; theirs were the patriarchs, and from them came the Messiah"; yet when the Messiah, the Son, the fulfillment of all the gifts given them, stands before them... they are blind, they are dumb – they have no wisdom, no light. This is the nation whom the Lord has given "His statutes and His ordinances... He has not done thus for any other nation." And yet they are unable to judge that it is right for a man to be healed at any time, that this is God's will, that human life supersedes the mere observance of law, a law they have suffocated of its life.

And we? Again, being successors to the Jews we must always ask ourselves if we do the things which caused the promise to be taken from their hands. Do we proclaim the glory of this Word? Do we "speak the truth in Christ"? Or do we keep silent, too? And not the silence that bears all suffering as has our Savior upon the cross do I speak – I mean the death of the Word in our souls. The inability to discern His will. The fear to praise God by teaching the nations of the grace which has been granted us. "He sends forth His command to the earth; swiftly runs His Word!" But does that Word come through us, does it work through us who are the keepers of the New Covenant, or do we let it die in our throats?

"Blessed forever be God who is over all!" Paul shouts as despair he begins to detect for the failure of so many Jews to turn to Christ. And so we should ever praise our God whenever doubt or fear enters our soul. It is our only refuge. It is our only strength. Silence before the courts of this world which observe us closely will not do. Acceptance of our death, yes, but not fear of retribution should be ours. We must speak the truth in love, relying on the wisdom which comes from Him alone as we make our way through the challenges of this world.

Saturday

(Rm.11:1-2,11-12,25-29; Ps.94:12-15,17-18; Lk.14:1,7-11)

"The Lord will not cast off His people,
nor abandon His inheritance."

Today the gifts and call of the Israelites, which are "irrevocable," are spoken of beautifully in our readings.

Indeed, the majority of Jews rejected and even persecuted Jesus and His followers. But as Paul tells us, the Lord has always and will always leave a remnant among them to maintain His covenant with them. As Paul reminds us, "I myself am an Israelite." And of course so were all the apostles. God has not rejected His people, for "God's gifts and His call *are* irrevocable." The promise He has made to bless the Israelites stands to this day.

Paul explains clearly the wisdom of God and how He works through the transgressions of the Jews to bring the Gentiles to salvation. And how the Gentiles' conversion and the grace poured upon them shall lead the Israelite people back to the Lord: "Blindness has come upon part of Israel until the full number of Gentiles enter in, and then all Israel will be saved." Yes, all Israel will yet be saved; they shall yet come flowing to the mountain of God, to His Son, and find redemption, and find the honor bestowed upon them; and by their turning, how much all His holy people shall be blessed! "Judgment shall again be with justice, and all the upright of heart shall follow it." Alleluia!

But there is another lesson for us today, and it, too, has to do with the quality needed by the chosen. Jesus speaks of it clearly in our gospel, and it illustrates the difficulty the Jews have in coming to the Lord, and warns us against the same mistake. Jesus comes to dinner "at the house of one of the leading Pharisees" and witnesses the guests scrambling for the best seats at table. Quietly He speaks to them, gently He reminds them, that they are not called to exaltation of their own position, gifted as it may or may not be, but to humility before all, as He has indeed shown us. How unlike our Lord, who though in the form of God humbled Himself to become human and even to die on a cross (without uttering a word), are they. And here is the teaching of Christ: "Sit in the lowest place." The greater our call, the deeper should be our humility. This emptying ourselves as has Jesus is an indispensable virtue for any Christian. And only it will bring the Jew to realize the presence of Christ in his midst.

And should we who have been grafted to the kingdom's tree late in time boast of our gift, walk with haughty eyes in His house? By no means, lest we be cast off by Him. Let us rather treasure the grace the Lord has granted

346

us, preserve His call within us, and make our election permanent, beneath the shadow of His cross.

Thirty-First Week

Monday
(Rm.11:29-36; Ps.69:14,30-31,33-34,36-37; Lk.14:12-14)

"God has imprisoned all in disobedience
that He might have mercy on all."

I begin to see "how deep are the riches and the wisdom and the knowledge of God." For though I am far from knowing "the mind of the Lord," yet He does offer me a certain insight this early morning about Him whom Paul says, "From Him and through Him and for Him all things are."

It is in the complementarity of the readings the insight comes, particularly viewing the gospel in light of the first reading. Jesus instructs the chief of the Pharisees that when giving a banquet he should "invite beggars and the crippled, the lame and the blind" and to be "pleased that they cannot repay" him for his generosity, assuring him he "will be repaid in the resurrection of the just." Now, the Lord does not instruct us to be anything more or less than He and the Father are. So this instruction reflects God's own great desire and joy in giving to those who are not able to repay Him: it serves as a reminder that God is love, that He thrives, as it were, on mercy, on compassion.

Paul, in the first reading, states to the Romans, "God wished to show you mercy," and that for this reason the Jews "have become disobedient," as well as to fulfill God's longing that "they too may receive mercy" upon returning to Him who set them apart for Himself. Again we see the greatness of God's love, we glimpse His burning desire to show compassion to all creatures. Now, to the mind lacking wisdom (and love), it might seem as if God is somehow playing with us, causing our falling that He might lift us up again. But it is necessary to remember that God did not desire us to sin, that this was not His intention… and indeed that He did not need us to sin to show us His mercy and love. But our disobedience having come, God in His love is not conquered. This temporary and empty victory by the devil does not tie His hands. Rather, the Lord takes this opportunity to show in an even greater way the very mercy and love which are His essence – shown to us so clearly in the Person of our Lord Jesus Christ, who came to forgive men's sins – to show, really, His greatness, which has its source in this love.

And David's psalm speaks in the same line: "The Lord hears the poor, and His own who are in bonds He spurns not." In our affliction and pain we cry out and He comes with His "saving help"; He is pleased to "rebuild the cities of Judah," to return us to His side. It is not sin He desires, but the recognition of our dependence on Him for all things, that He might freely show us His love. For this love at His heart's core and which overcomes all – which is the essence of God and His creation – let us praise Him, brothers and sisters. "To Him be glory forever. Amen."

Tuesday
(Rm.12:5-16; Ps.131:1-3; Lk.14:15-24)

"Come along, everything is ready now."

Dinner is being served now in the kingdom of God. But are we prepared to sit down at table? Or do we turn our hearts to other things?

Jesus sets our place now in the kingdom of heaven. He has come. He has died. He has risen and sends now the Holy Spirit to invite us into His presence. And His presence is ever with us; He is ever knocking at the door of our hearts – His Spirit is always with us. But, again, do we hear His call, do we heed His call? Do we care to come into His presence and sup with Him, and receive His gracious gifts at His precious table, at His holy altar... or do we cling to what is evil, what is worldly?

How do we come to His kingdom? How do we find ourselves in His presence? Paul instructs us: we must simply do His will. Doing His will upon the face of this earth brings us to the kingdom of heaven. The teaching should be evident to all Christians: "One who is a teacher should use his gift for teaching... He who gives alms should do so generously... Rejoice in hope, be patient under trial, persevere in prayer..." Do all things as is meet for those things. It is not complex. There needs no genius to figure it out, or a scholastic degree to understand it. One need not travel miles to discover it. It is truth. It is Jesus. It is to suffer and die for Him as called by the Lord. "Your love must be sincere. Detest what is evil, cling to what is good." What more can be said? Find peace in the arms of the Lord. Say with our psalmist, "I have stilled and quieted my soul... like a weaned child upon its mother's lap." We must do as he proclaims: "I busy not myself with great things, nor with things too sublime for me." We must not complicate God's simple love for us and our call simply to love Him with all He gives us. We must, rather, heed His voice, and come into His presence when He calls.

The table is set. His Word is speaking to us. In silence we will hear Him; in quiet we will find His voice. In the vain activity of this world we become deaf. Only by hearing and doing His Word and will, will we come to sit at His table and partake of His heavenly banquet – only if this is the

348

true desire of our souls. Even now we taste Him in the Blessed Sacrament; even today we hear His Word proclaimed. Are we prepared to meet Him? Do we seek to do His holy will?

Wednesday
(Rm.13:8-10; Ps.112:1-2,4-5,9; Lk.14:25-33)

"Love is the fulfillment of the law."

Jesus tells us, "None of you can be my disciple if he does not renounce all his possessions," turning our backs even on father and mother, even on our very selves. Our psalm states of the happy man, "Lavishly he gives to the poor; his generosity shall endure forever." And Paul makes clear that we "owe no debt to anyone except the debt that binds us to love one another. He who loves his neighbor has fulfilled the law."

What is this love? Where is this generous spirit? How do we renounce all our possessions? In the cross of Christ we find our call. The cross of Christ means giving all, means laying down our lives for the Lord and our neighbor – the cross of Christ is love itself at work in this world in the death of self and the finding of the grace and the love of God in heaven.

Jesus wishes that you be sure about this. He desires that you understand what is required of you – your very life, your absolute love. Nothing short of total sacrifice will do; we must be entirely whole, utterly holy, to enter His gates, to follow Him into glory. This is greater and more significant than any war, than any project conceived by the mind of man, for it is our eternal soul that is at stake, whose weight cannot compare even to all the world. "Anyone who does not take up his cross and follow me cannot be my disciple." We all have a cross graciously placed upon our shoulders by our loving Lord to make us one with Him in His redemptive suffering and death, to make us one with Him in such utter love. How will we find heaven if we do not love? How do we come to that place which is only of love if we do not give ourselves to love completely?

"How can I do this?" you say. "The Lord asks too much." You must remember that it is only love He asks of you, and that it is His cross you carry – He who is only of love – and so He carries your cross with you, making it ever so sweet and light. Do you think the saints feared to die in the name of Christ? Do you think they shrank back even in the face of torture? None of this has any significance to the soul who is set on Christ; and without Christ a hangnail can seem overwhelming.

Love, brothers and sisters. It is simple as that. Love. Not this world, but His heart, His sacrifice, His cross. And you will see all brought to life before you; and you will find joy in your soul.

349

Thursday
(Rm.14:7-12; Ps.27:1,4,13-14; Lk.15:1-10)

"This man welcomes sinners and eats with them."

Since "every one of us will have to give an account of himself before God," who are we to "sit in judgment" or "look down on" a brother? Why are our eyes set upon others' sins instead of the Lord's glory? Why do we fall into this pit of condemnation?

Yes, Jesus welcomes sinners. For this has He come. How blessed are we that He makes such "a diligent search" to retrieve our souls from the grave of sin; how blessed are we when He finds us and puts us "on His shoulders in jubilation." In this forgiveness should we glory. In this grace we should praise the Lord, and seek to help others come to such blessing. But do we blind ourselves to the grace at work in our souls by setting our sights on the sins of others rather than the sacrifice of Jesus the Christ? Are we as judgmental as the Pharisees and as those Paul warns today against condemnation of others?

Brothers and sisters, we should rather be with David in his psalm and seek "to dwell in the house of the Lord" forever, and set our "gaze on the loveliness of the Lord and contemplate His temple"; we must not let our sights fall from heaven to earth and so lose ourselves in the judgment of others' sin. This is the great danger. This is the devil's temptation: "Look at him," he says, "see how evil he is." If he cannot get us to believe it about ourselves and so lose hope of redemption for our souls, he attempts to distract us with the sins of others, and so achieve the same ends. We must realize that "both in life and death we are the Lord's," that He loves us and desires our salvation, and that He loves and desires the salvation of all our neighbors. And so we must come to Him, take refuge in Him and in His love and forgiveness, and then we will "see the bounty of the Lord in the land of the living" and not die a miserable death.

Brothers and sisters, let each of us be that "repentant sinner" over whom the angels of God rejoice. The Lord welcomes us though we are sinners. Let us not forget His grace. And let us welcome others.

Friday
(Rm.15:14-21; Ps.98:1-4; Lk.16:1-8)

"The worldly take more initiative than the otherworldly
when it comes to dealing with their own kind."

What is the Lord teaching His disciples? What does He wish to tell them of their call? We need only look at the Apostle Paul, for here is a man, a child of God, who has taken the initiative the Lord would see wrought in us all.

Our first reading indeed speaks clearly of Paul's mission to the Gentiles. Not only has he covered a vast measure of the globe (particularly for that time), but his intense initiative is seen most acutely in his never going "to preach in places where Christ's name was already known"; rather, "they who received no word of Him" became Paul's audience. A greater example of taking initiative in the Spirit of Christ to bring His light to the world perhaps will never be known.

But it is required of all of us. We are not free to revel in complacency because Paul has been so industrious. It is still true that the Lord must make His salvation known "in the sight of the nations," and it is still so that we Christians of the Church militant have the responsibility to see that the Lord's work is accomplished. Each of us is called to take a measure of initiative, is gifted by God with the responsibility of bringing a portion of His kingdom to light – in our own way, in our own time... but invariably the call is there and must be answered. All must fulfill their role in salvation history before it can be truly and completely proclaimed: "All the ends of the earth have seen the salvation by our God."

The devious employee's heart was set thoroughly on the business at his hands, and he used his business wisdom, his worldly savvy, to save his skin. Where is our spiritual savvy? Where is the employment of our spiritual wisdom and insight to the salvation of others' souls, and our own? "I can take glory in Christ Jesus for the work I have done for God," Paul says quite freely. Are we able to say the same? Let us work industriously and with initiative to bring the spiritual kingdom to fulfillment. By God's grace, let the Spirit come.

O. 31. Sat. (I)

Saturday
(Rm.16:3-9,16,22-27; Ps.145:1-5,10-11; Lk.16:9-15)

"Let all your works give you thanks, O Lord,
and let your faithful ones bless you."

We are in the world, and amongst the wealth of this world. We have nothing to do with money and the world – "You cannot serve God and money," the Lord has told us, and so we cannot serve money... yet what have we to use but the riches of this world? And so "through use of this world's goods," by showing ourselves trustworthy with this "elusive wealth," we find and bring others to the "lasting" riches of heaven.

Ordinary Time

Paul at the end of his letter to the Romans lists all his "fellow workers in the service of Christ." Here are those who have been faithful with the elusive wealth of this world. They themselves have died, their bodies have been laid in the tomb, yet their works live on in the Spirit they have brought forth. Nothing of this world lasts long, yet these transitory things can and must be used, that "glory be given through Jesus Christ unto endless ages."

"Generation after generation praises your works and proclaims your might," sings David to the Lord. And with our voice, too, while we have breath, we must "speak of the splendor of [His] glorious majesty and tell of [His] wondrous works." Forever and in all our works we must praise and bless the Lord of all, that all we do leads unto the glory of the kingdom, that in all we serve God with all *our* might. We must join ourselves to Him, and we do this by the gifts He gives us, and by employing now what is at our disposal. So it is. So it has been back beyond the time of Paul, and so it shall be unto the coming of eternity.

Today we must think of how well we use this world's goods, how well we employ this Word of the Lord in the world. In the "little" things of our daily lives do we honor God, or are we unjust in some manner? For today begins the road to heaven; this time leads to eternity. And if we wish to find "lasting reception" with the Lord in heaven, we must be ever faithful in our works today. To God let us give thanks. May we who are the work of the Lord give praise to Him in all our works upon this earth.

O. 32. Mon. (I)

Thirty-Second Week

Monday
(Wis.1:1-7; Ps.139:1-10,24; Lk.17:1-6)

"Where can I hide from your spirit?
From your presence, where can I flee?"

Yes, "wisdom is a kindly spirit, yet she acquits not the blasphemous of his guilty lips." For the spirit of the Lord is everywhere and hears everything, listening closely to a man's inmost thoughts. "For the spirit of the Lord fills the world, is all-embracing, and knows what man says." And so it is that David sings, "If I ascend to the heavens, you are there; if I lie down in Sheol, you are there, too." How could we escape His encircling Hand and His omnipresent justice if, as David says, "Even before a word is on my tongue, Lord, you know it all"? And so, in heaven He is present to raise us to glory; but in hell, His presence condemns our sin.

We cannot sin, brothers and sisters. If we do, we shall not escape His hand. It cannot but be that the Lord condemns all evil, for "into a soul that

352

plots evil, wisdom enters not," and what hope have we of life if the spirit of wisdom guides us not? Indeed, we must "seek Him in integrity of heart." Yes, justice must be our love, and wisdom our treasure. This alone will bring us unto heaven. If our counsels are perverse and we cause sin to occur, leading others astray by our unjust words and actions, the Lord makes quite clear our fate in our gospel today: "It would be better for him if a millstone were put around his neck and he be thrown into the sea than for him to cause one of these little ones to sin." And there is a "little one" in ourselves, whom only the Lord – who probes our heart and mind – knows, and whom we condemn to destruction by our sin.

Rather, we must have faith. We must forgive others and have an abiding faith in Him, Jesus tells us. This faith will manifest itself in the great works done in His name, and in our following Him simply day to day. With such faith we cannot be shaken. Holding such faith, the light shining upon our souls by Him who sees all will purify us for the coming of His kingdom.

What can we say, brothers and sisters? The Lord hears us. Where can we go? He is with us. Either for evil because of our turning away, or for our good by our turning to Him, the Lord is ever present. It must be our desire to come to Him, in wisdom and in justice, in forgiveness and in faith... and hell we shall avoid as gratefully into His glory we fly, by the grace of our Lord Jesus Christ.

O. 32. Tues. (I)

Tuesday
(Ws.2:23-3:9; Ps.34:2-3,16-19; Lk.17:7-10)

"The souls of the just are in the hands of God,
and no torment shall touch them."

What does the Lord mean when He instructs us in our gospel to say, "We are useless servants," than that which David says in our psalm, "The Lord is close to the brokenhearted; and those who are crushed in spirit He saves," and that which the Book of Wisdom states in our first reading: "Chastised a little, they shall be greatly blessed, because God tried them and found them worthy of Himself"? For though we who serve Christ seem to be dead in the judgment of this world, and the laying down of our lives in service of Christ – who died upon the cross quite freely – seems to be nothing but "utter destruction," yet we know that it is precisely this death in Christ which brings life... and in His hands we shall be blessed.

"The Lord confronts evildoers, to destroy remembrance of them from the earth." Yet "when the just cry out, the Lord hears them, and from all their distress He rescues them." Yes, "those who trust in Him shall understand truth, and the faithful shall abide with Him in love: because grace and mercy are with His holy ones, and His care is with His elect." And "they shall judge nations and rule over peoples, and the Lord shall be their king forever." For they have given their service to the One who rules the universe, and so in His service they shall remain – death shall have no power over them. If "God formed man to be imperishable" and made him "the image of His own nature," what shall touch those who serve Him, who treasure that image of God upon them? How shall they die?

"We have done no more than our duty." This is the bottom line of our time on earth. And the accomplishment of our duty, the fulfillment of the Lord's Word at work in our hearts, is all that is needed to bring us to eternal life. And though it is not His obligation, though certainly no reward is due us who have but carried out the orders of our superior, the Lord will say to us in His grace on that day, "Come and sit down at table." And we shall sup with Him eternally, His gracious hand upon us for good.

Brothers and sisters, forget not your call to serve Him, to lay down your lives before Him, and He shall not neglect to hear you now, and to give you life eternal. Keep your "hope full of immortality" even "as gold in the furnace" your mettle is proven this day, and the day of the Lord shall be yours, when all torment shall have fled away.

O. 32. Wed. (I)

Wednesday
(Ws.6:1-11; Ps.82:3-4,6-8; Lk.17:11-19)

"Stand up and go your way;
your faith has been your salvation."

"This man was a Samaritan." Jesus chose the lowest of the low, not only a leper, the most ostracized of all individuals, but a Samaritan, a foreigner most despised by the Israelite nation, to reveal His mercy, to reveal the universal nature of His forgiveness, and so the universal call to salvation. He demonstrates that all may have faith in Him, and that it is for us to call all to Him.

Many are given power on this earth, power which was far from the Samaritan leper healed by Jesus. And Wisdom makes clear the responsibility that comes with that authority, the manner in which that judgment placed in the hands of princes must be effected. For the Lord shall hold accountable all to whom power is given; He shall "probe [their] works and scrutinize [their] counsels." And if they do not keep His law and "walk according to the will of God," great as the power given them shall be their punishment. "For the lowly may be pardoned out of mercy," as was the leper in our gospel today, "but the mighty shall be mightily put to the test."

354

I find it rather frightening to hear that "for those in power a rigorous scrutiny impends," for, brothers and sisters, we are all given a measure of power by the Lord, and so all shall be held responsible for their gifts. It can make us quake in our shoes to think that we are answerable to God, to the all-powerful Lord of the universe, for all we do. Do we "keep the holy precepts" well? Will we "have ready a response" when He stands before us, when He inquires of our actions? If we desire His words, we know that He will instruct us, but how can we who are so human and sinful be as faithful as we need to be? Our psalm warns us: "You are gods, all of you sons of the Most High" – we are all gifted greatly by our God to be as His children – "yet like men you shall die, and fall like any prince..." yet O how human we are, how subject to the elements of sin and death.

What shall we do? Our psalm indicates what our actions should be: "Defend the lowly and the fatherless; render justice to the afflicted and the destitute." And the blessed leper in our gospel reveals the attitude we should have toward our Lord: "He threw himself on his face at the feet of Jesus and spoke His praises." If we think ourselves any better than he or do anything differently, we shall not hear the Lord calling us to rise and go forth – we shall not find our salvation. Let us demonstrate our faith and the grace at work within us.

Thursday
(Ws.7:22-8:1; Ps.119:89-91,130,135,175; Lk.17:20-25)

"Let your countenance shine upon your servant,
and teach me your statutes."

Wisdom, who "is fairer than the sun and surpasses every constellation of the stars... reaches from end to end mightily and governs all things well." Wisdom "penetrates and pervades all things by reason of her purity," for she is "the refulgence of eternal light." How like the Lord she is, He whose coming "day will be like the lightning that flashes from one end of the sky to the other" and yet whose reign is "already in [our] midst." How we are filled with understanding when this light which "endures forever," which "is firm as the heavens," shines upon our simple minds, leading us to the grace of eternal glory.

Wisdom we need, brothers and sisters. The Lord's Word must be with us. "For there is naught God loves, be it not one who dwells with Wisdom." Else we shall be as those who "go running about excitedly" at every report of the Lord's being "here" or "there," at every proclamation of the end being near. The end is here; it is now the Son of Man "must suffer much and be rejected by the present age." The Lord has come, and so "the reign of God is already in [our] midst." Its fulfillment we shall not discern by "careful watching," by setting our sights on the things of the earth, but only with the "intelligent, pure, and very subtle" spirit of Wisdom. She alone teaches us of the kingdom, for she alone is "the spotless mirror of the power of God, the image of His goodness." Without her purity, our minds are dimmed. Without her surpassing light, we can but be blind. She alone knows, she alone leads holy souls into the truth of His presence. All words lacking her light are but vain speculation, which shall come to naught, which shall fall to the earth from which they are derived. Heaven alone is lasting.

Have we the light of Wisdom directing our thoughts and actions, brothers and sisters? Is her purity set firmly within us? Will we then stand on the day the lightning flashes, on the day the glory of the Lord is revealed? Do we carry that glory now within us? If not, let us turn to Wisdom, and she will teach us. Like a mother who cares for her children she will be. And led to the presence of the Lord we will be, where we will find our peace. Let us not fail to take her gentle yoke upon our shoulders; let the cross of Christ and the light of the coming kingdom be ever our guide.

O. 32. Fri. (I)

Friday
(Ws.13:1-9; Ps.19:2-5; Lk.17:26-37)

"Wherever the carcass is, there will the vultures gather."

It is so that "the heavens proclaim the glory of God and the firmament proclaims His handiwork." It is true that "from the greatness and the beauty of created things their original author, by analogy, is seen." Yes, "the things seen are fair," and speak even of the glory of our God... but they shall indeed all come to naught when He alone stands before us on the last day.

In the created world we exist. To an extent, in the created world we take refuge, discerning the hand of God at work in the things around us and coming by way of the knowledge presented to us in their beauty and wonder to that Hand which has created all. And so they can be beneficial to us. And so they can help to reveal God's presence to us who are so blind. But both the warning of our reading from Wisdom and Christ's own words in the gospel must be heeded: we cannot make "fire," "wind," or "mighty water" our gods; and we cannot be attached to our possessions. For these things of nature, as great as God has made them, and these things at our disposal, as much a blessing they may be to us for our time on earth, are passing away. Only God remains.

Brothers and sisters, we must look upon the stars of heaven, we must see the signs wrought in our midst... but we cannot be distracted by them from the God who made them. We must eat and drink, we must take husbands and wives... but we cannot get drunk or live in lust, allowing the earthly to overcome our spirits. Lot's wife turned to see what she'd left behind; she longed to return to her possessions and the carnal life of Sodom. Unable to understand or accept the grace of the angel of God who was leading her forth to a safer and more glorious land, she was turned to salt – all of worth was taken from her; only the carcass remained.

The day shall come when all we see shall be destroyed. And so, how important it is that our hearts not be set on all we see, else we shall be destroyed with it. Though with utmost respect we treat this world and even find joy in its beauty, we must ever keep in mind that its beauty is passing and is only significant if it leads to the eternal beauty of heaven.

Saturday
(Ws.18:14-16,19:6-9; Ps.105:2-3,5,36-37,42-43; Lk.18:1-8)

"He led forth His people with joy;
with shouts of joy, His chosen ones."

"They beheld stupendous wonders." Before their eyes, "out of what had been water, dry land was seen emerging." And so, sheltered by the mighty hand of the Lord, they crossed over, from the land of bondage to freedom. And in their joy "they ranged about like horses, and bounded about like lambs..." praising the Lord, "their deliverer."

This is the story of our own salvation; this is the way of our own redemption from the sin which holds us bound on this earthly plane. Our exodus, too, must come. The Lord shall return to earth. As He was faithful in leading the Israelites forth from the land of Egypt, where they had been slaves four hundred years, so He will not forget us who have been in the bonds of Satan upon this plane. Our deliverance, too, will come.

Yes, my brothers and sisters, God will "do justice to His chosen who call out to Him day and night." He will not "delay long over them" but will "give them swift justice." The vision of the Israelites at the Red Sea will be our own. Before our eyes we will see the dry land appearing. We shall rejoice at the Lord's hand guiding our steps out of this dark land. "An unimpeded road" we shall travel, moving toward His promised land. Yes, heaven will be ours. The first-born of Satan, the flower of evil, shall be destroyed in the stillness of the night, and truth and goodness and light will emerge victorious; and we shall be led forth, as it were, "laden with silver and gold," rejoicing in the abundant blessings of our Lord and God.

He does not delay. He will not delay. We wait, yes, and struggle with our faith... but He is ready – He does not have to be asked twice. But as our

Ordinary Time

hearts are weakened by sin, we must be encouraged, we must continue to pray, always, even in the face of darkness. Through the darkness the Lord's light shall come shining, if we remain faithful in our cries. So, "sing to Him, sing His praise... O hearts that seek the Lord!" for He is near in all our prayers, and shall lead us forth into His blessed kingdom. Alleluia!

O. 33. Mon. (I)

Thirty-Third Week

Monday
(1Mac.1:10-15,41-43,54-57,62-63; Ps.119:53,61,88,134,150,155,158; Lk.18:35-43)

"Terrible affliction was upon Israel."

O how the nation had become so blind. O how they had turned from their God. Some "preferred to die rather than be defiled with unclean food or to profane the covenant," but most ate freely of the poisonous fruit of the tree of abomination, and so became as the blind man begging by the side of the road – so spiritually bereft were they.

Our reading from Maccabees tells of a terrible time of persecution upon the Israelite nation less than two hundred years before the coming of Christ, and it shows that that persecution comes from within the community itself, as "men who were breakers of the law" sought alliance with the Gentiles and their pagan worship, thinking so foolishly that this would bring them blessing and comfort. How readily "they sacrificed to idols and profaned the sabbath." And the date is given here when "the king erected the horrible abomination upon the altar of holocausts," signifying Israel's complete turn from God and His laws to the vain worship of false gods.

Our psalm speaks repeatedly of "the snares of the wicked," "the oppression of men," the "malicious persecutors," the "sinners," the "apostates" who turn from the law and attempt to "twine" others about in their evil. This is man's sin from the beginning – attempting to form God of his own hands, refusing to be obedient to the ways the loving Father has imparted for his salvation, for his blessing. Man gives himself over to the lusts of this world and the imagination of a proud mind, and through such exaltation of self finds himself soon lost in the confusion that such vanity can only bring. But in the meantime he persecutes the just who hold to the way of truth; for a while he fools himself by the glamour of his idols. But soon the blindness sets in, and soon the salvation of the just shall come.

If we are in affliction because of the persecution of this world of sin that surrounds and closes in, we should consider ourselves blessed; this affliction is proof of our faith, and upon it the Lord looks with favor. If we are afflicted with the blindness of the nations wrought by our wallowing in sin,

358

we'd best cry out to the Lord as He passes us on the way to Jerusalem. He will hear us and He will stop, if we are persistent in our cries. And it is so that our faith will make us whole. Let us find our sight by the intercession of Christ and "giving God the glory" begin "to follow Him," whatever cross may await us.

Tuesday
(2Mac.6:18-31; Ps.3:2-8; Lk.19:1-10)

"I fear not the myriads of people
arrayed against me on every side."

Zacchaeus' running up ahead and climbing a tree in order to be able to see Jesus as He passed along the way may not be a witness on the order of Eleazar, who "declared that above all he would be loyal to the holy laws given by God" and went willingly to torture and death, "leaving in his death a model of courage and an unforgettable example of virtue not only for the young but for the whole nation," but the same faith inspired both. And perhaps this wealthy man giving half of his belongings to the poor does approach the heroism of Eleazar.

The principal figures in both our reading and gospel today indeed give witness to the faith in the salvation which Jesus has come to bring to all our houses. And both reflect the strength needed to overcome the myriad of obstacles set in our paths. "O Lord, how many are my adversaries!" David cries in our psalm. "Many rise up against me!" Eleazar is threatened by the systematic persecution of his faith and his people by the pagan king and his minions, but in the face of "the instrument of torture" this noble old man tells his persecutors "to send him at once to the abode of the dead," for he would not bring "shame and dishonor" on himself nor lead the people astray by giving in to an unlawful act. And in our gospel Zacchaeus finds himself surrounded by the murmuring crowd accusing him of being a sinner. But he stands his ground in the face of this persecution, justified or not, and proves himself worthy to be at the side of Jesus.

"The Son of Man has come to search out and save what was lost." It is His desire to bring us to salvation. Yet if we do not seek Him, He will not find us. If we do not call to Him, He will not hear us. And if we do not stand our ground and give witness to Him when put to the test for our faith, He cannot stand with us.

Temptations must necessarily come. We cannot escape persecution. But we must not listen to those who say, "There is no salvation for him in God." We must remember that God stands with us if we stand with Him, and that it is just such as us He has come to save.

Wednesday
(2Mac.7:1,20-31; Ps.17:1,5-6,8,15; Lk.19:11-28)

"He, in His mercy, will give you back both breath and life,
because you now disregard yourselves for the sake of His Law."

When the Lord returns "crowned as king" He will call all before Himself and judge each according to the profit he has made with his life. If we are like the seven brothers who suffered and died for the faith, if we have been like the good servants who invested wisely the gifts left with them by the Lord, we shall come into His reign. If we have wasted His talents or, God forbid, have persecuted, as Antiochus – who "contrived every kind of affliction for the Hebrews" – those who strive with the Lord to remain faithful to His call, we "will not escape the hands of God." He will come to judge; in justice He is known.

"On waking, I shall be content in your presence," sings David in our psalm, expressing the hope of those whose "steps have been steadfast" in the paths of God. And how this hope in the coming kingdom is embodied by the seven brothers with their mother "who were arrested and tortured with whips and scourges by the king" – how well they presage the suffering and death of Jesus, and the sword which pierces His mother's heart. The mother's words are particularly beautiful and wise as she witnesses to her sons that she was not the author of their lives: "It was not I who gave you the breath of life, nor was it I who set in order the elements of which each of you is composed," thus stirring them to faith in "the Creator of the universe who shapes each man's beginning" and holds the life of all in His hands. Hear her words of exhortation to faith spoken to her youngest son: "I beg you, child, to look at the heavens and the earth and see all that is in them; then you will know that God did not make them out of existing things." And so she encourages him to "accept death, so that in the time of mercy [she] may receive [him] again." Here, certainly, is our faith in essence. Here the hope we have in the Lord is lived.

The Lord has gone from us to the "faraway country" of heaven to receive His kingship and return for our souls. He has left with each of His servants gifts for the time of waiting. Today He and His heavenly kingdom are not far away for He is very present in His Church, in her priests and the sacraments, in the Word of God revealed to us, in the sky upon which we gaze to see His handiwork... in all things we know Him and for all our needs He provides. Let us not be afraid to live with Him and so to die for Him, to disregard our very lives in the employment of His talents... and the breath and life we do so cherish shall be ours forever in heaven.

Thursday
(1Mac.2:15-29; Ps.50:1-2,5-6,14-15,23; Lk.19:41-44)

"We will not obey the words of the king
nor depart from our religion in the slightest degree."

The King of heaven shall soon come into the city of peace, humble and riding on an ass, but today He weeps as He sees Jerusalem and knows of its imminent destruction for its sins. Yet He shall ride into Jerusalem, yet He shall be dragged outside its walls... and the death He proclaims upon all its children, He Himself shall know, He Himself shall undergo, that there may be means of escape for us all, for all who turn from the prince of this world and his seduction and seek to remain true to the commands of our God.

The persecution of the Jews some two hundred years before Christ's own we continue to hear of in our reading from Maccabees: "The officers of the king in charge of enforcing the apostasy came to the city of Modein to organize the sacrifices."   And though many go over to the enemy, Mattathias and his sons remain faithful, remain true to the Lord. Great is their zeal in the face of the threat and in the sight of the ways of the evil one. And flee the city and its abominations Mattathias did with all the righteous, to make a home apart in the desert. For he recognizes the time of visitation and the destruction of faith upon his city and his people; he has not "completely lost" vision of "the path to peace" but remains faithful even in time of persecution.

"Days will come upon you when your enemies encircle you with a rampart, hem you in, and press you hard from every side," Jesus prophesies as He weeps over Jerusalem. He wishes not to see the persecution come, nor to have to die Himself. But the people do not recognize with their hearts the love He offers forth... and so what can He do but die; and so what can they know but destruction. But His sacrifice shall prove redemptive for those who turn; a place in the desert He shall prepare for those who desire to be holy, to be set apart from the wickedness of this race.

"From Zion, perfect in beauty, God shines forth" and His "faithful ones" gather before Him. In their praise of His glory they fulfill their "vows to the Most High" and so the king of this world holds no power over them. In the New Jerusalem with the risen Lord they live, beyond the destruction of the old.

Friday

(1Mac.4:36-37,52-59; 1Chr.29:10-13; Lk.19:45-48)

"Let us go up to purify the sanctuary and rededicate it."

In both our reading and gospel today, we hear of the cleansing of the temple, and we see its purpose and fulfillment.

"My house is meant for a house of prayer," declares Jesus. A house of prayer, and a house for teaching: "He was teaching in the temple area from day to day." It is a house of music, for by the Israelites after the Maccabean revolution it "was reconsecrated with songs, harps, lutes, and cymbals." It is a place for humility: "All the people prostrated themselves..." and worship: "...and adored and praised Heaven." Praise is most fitting for the house of the Lord, for His holy temple, for it is this which unites us with our God. When we sing of His greatness – "Yours, O Lord, are grandeur and power, majesty, splendor, and glory. For all in heaven and on earth is yours" – we are joined to Him who is "exalted as head over all." For in proclaiming the truth of His "power and might" over all, we ourselves are cleansed and become as temples of the Lord, holy and radiant as gold.

"The entire populace was listening to Him and hanging on His words." To whom did the people listen but the Temple itself? What was begun by the Maccabee brothers is accomplished in Jesus. It had long been the hope and desire of the Israelites, and indeed the longing of all mankind, to have a holy place to worship God, to offer sacrifice to Him who is the greatest love of all hearts. And now He stands before them, now He speaks to them. And He effects the renewal of the temple not so much by His "ejecting the traders" who had made it "a den of thieves," as by His presence in their midst. For the temple exists not so much in the walls adorned "with gold crowns and shields" as in the flesh of Christ; and it is this Temple we become when we follow Him, when we hear and heed the words which issue forth like a cleansing stream from these sacred lips and heart, and when we eat His body and drink His blood.

The destruction of this Temple will come. Even now the leaders of the people are "looking for a way to destroy Him." But in three days the Temple will be rebuilt and dedicated forever in perfect purity for all who desire to enter there.

Saturday

(1Mac.6:1-13; Ps.9:2-4,6,16,19; Lk.20:27-40)

"The needy shall not always be forgotten,
nor shall the hope of the afflicted forever perish."

Death comes, yes. Death is upon us and surrounds us in this world. But the suffering we face in this life has its reward. Jesus has brought redemption: He has been resurrected, and we with Him. And this new life is eternal.

It seemed the Israelites were doomed. Antiochus had ruthlessly destroyed Jerusalem and the inhabitants of Judah. All hope seemed lost. But hope was not lost, and today we read of the return of the people to Jerusalem in strength and the defeat and death of their enemy, the king. Now Antiochus has become "sick with grief because his designs ha[ve] failed." Now he is "overwhelmed with sorrow" as he sees the evils he has committed overtake him and finds himself dying "in bitter grief, in a foreign land." While in Jerusalem the Israelites celebrate and sing praise to God: "My enemies are turned back, overthrown and destroyed before you."

And now such redemption is made eternal in the Person of Jesus Christ. What was but human and temporal, the fall and rise of empires and of temples, now becomes divine, now becomes everlasting in the coming of the Messiah in the flesh of God. Yet with Him there is death – but after His crucifixion it shall be no more. Yet with Him is new life – but with His resurrection it has no end. Now "those judged worthy of a place in the age to come and of resurrection from the dead... become like angels and are no longer liable to death." In His death He destroys death: He makes it bereft of all power. In His rising He draws all into the eternal presence of the Father. Now "all are alive for Him."

Brothers and sisters, may any "floods of sorrow" which afflict us now because of our sins or by the oppression of our persecutors not overwhelm us in this day. Let our sins be nailed to the cross with Him who is our salvation, and our hope of overcoming all the scourges of the evil one be made strong in the surpassing light of His glorious rising. With David let us "declare all [the Lord's] wondrous deeds," and our enemies will be left speechless.

(I must note today that the city bearing the name of this evil king – Antioch – would soon become the place where the followers of Christ were called "Christians" for the first time; and that the seat of the state which would next oppress the people of God – Rome – is now the place from which the Chair of Peter reigns. How God's redeeming Hand does work.)

Thirty-Fourth Week

Monday
(Dn.1:1-6,8-20; Dn.3:52-56; Lk.21:1-4)

"To these four young men God gave knowledge
and proficiency in all literature and science,
and to Daniel the understanding of all visions and dreams."

God is the giver of all good gifts; all is a gift from God. Whatever we give to Him can only seem paltry to Him "who look[s] into the depths from [His] throne upon the cherubim." But He makes any gift we give, anything we do, great by His heavenly grace.

All our offerings are as the widow's – but a couple of copper coins – even if we give vast wealth from our surplus. What is anything we offer in the sight of God, who owns the world and all that is in it, who sits "in the firmament of heaven"? So the size matters not. But when we give our paltry gift with a heart of faith, in answer to the love He gives us, how great our gift then becomes. For this He blesses. This He looks upon with favor. This He sees as He glances up; for it is the heart He looks upon and measures. It cannot but be that the widow gave her offering out of love, out of her deep faith in God. How could one become bereft of all riches if one did not believe in Him who surpasses all?

And is it not Daniel and the young men's faith which God does bless with His gifts of wisdom and prudence? Because "Daniel was resolved not to defile himself with the king's food or wine" sacrificed to his pagan gods, God first blessed him and his companions with exceptional health. Though they ate food that was poor as the widow's offering, yet "they looked healthier and better fed than any of the young men who ate from the royal table" – again, because all gifts, including that of health, are in God's hands and not in the things themselves. And God's gift of knowledge and understanding is a reward for their faith in Him as well; they give themselves to Him in obedience and He who holds all such light of wisdom in "the temple of [His] holy glory," who is "exalted above all forever" – which the young men readily recognize – grants them His favors by His grace.

What gift have we to give? What paltry sum have we to offer? Let it be as the two fish the boy offered in faith and generosity to the Lord (Jn.6:9), and with it He will feed five thousand. Let it be as the two coins jangling in the widow's pocket, and with it He will build a home for you in heaven. Let it be given in the faith of the four young men and God will bless it and reveal Himself at work in you.

Tuesday

(Dn.2:31-45; Dn.3:57-61; Lk.21:5-11)

"The iron, tile, bronze, silver, and gold all crumbled at once,
fine as the chaff on the threshing floor in summer,
and the wind blew them away without leaving a trace."

So shall the kingdom of this world be destroyed by "a stone which was hewn from a mountain without a hand being put to it"; so shall Jesus come – the Son of God, the King of kings – and make all things subject to Himself. And when shall this be? It has happened, and is happening, and will happen soon: fear not in your hearts. Simply praise the Lord of the universe.

There will be no trace of this world remaining when the Lord does come. He shall be the stone that "became a great mountain and filled the whole earth," which "shall break in pieces all these kingdoms and put an end to them." And by whose hand shall this be done? "The God of heaven will set up a kingdom that shall never be destroyed or delivered up to another people." And so, if accomplished by the hand of God and not by man, why do we look upon the "wars and insurrections," "plagues and famines," and become fearful, as if these shall bring the end? No, "the end does not follow immediately." We cannot state the time any more than could Daniel, the greatest of all interpreters of dreams and visions. So why are we misled when many come in the Lord's name saying, "I am He" or "The time is at hand," as if these could force the hand of God?

Let not the "fearful omens" and "great signs" perturb you, brothers and sisters. These are for those without faith as a warning to turn to God, but for those with faith they should prove no disturbance. Our souls should be set on Jesus, who surpasses all these things – even the temple "adorned with precious stones" – and whose coming we should see clearly in our hearts. Is He not at work in you? Are you not His children? Then why fear these things which are "bound to happen" to the earth? You should "praise and exalt" Him who is "above all" with the "angels of the Lord" and the "heavens." Let your hearts rise up to Him.

Yes, "the day will come when not one stone will be left upon another, but it will all be torn down." And in that day the Lord will reign supreme. Set your sights upon His majesty.

Wednesday

(Dn.5:1-6,13-14,16-17,23-28; Dn.3:59,62-67; Lk.21:12-19)

"You will be brought to give witness."

"Daniel was brought into the presence of the king." And what did this wisest of men have to say to this pagan king who ruled the earth? "You have rebelled against the Lord of heaven." He did not hesitate to tell him of the emptiness of his "gods of silver and gold, bronze and iron, wood and stone, that neither see nor hear nor have intelligence." And, remarkably, not a hair of his head is harmed; even this pagan ruler recognizes the truth of his words, and accepts that he will lose his kingdom.

"Before kings and governors" you will be summoned, "all because of my name," says the Lord. Yes, witness must be given to "the God in whose hand is [our] life breath and the whole course of [our] life." The world must come to know Him; light must be brought into the darkness. Is this an easy task? Certainly not. It may be glorious insofar as the Lord blesses our words, insofar as we trust in Him, not worrying about our "defense" beforehand – but the darkness resists the light; the world does not wish to hear of its sins, nor to be called to turn from them. Turning from sin is a painful process, and rather than endure its throes there will be those who would prefer to impose such persecution upon those who call to the depths of their hearts. Unwilling to suffer conversion, they make others suffer for their righteousness....

All the apostles but John underwent martyrdom: our Lord rules from a cross. But though we may not escape punishment from those to whom we are called to speak, as has Daniel the prophet, yet as Daniel surely "not a hair of [our] head will be harmed." For though we be killed for the Word of truth, yet our redemption awaits us: in heaven's light all is whole. And the rewards offered Daniel even by this pagan king will be as our own in paradise.

"I will give you words and a wisdom which none of your adversaries can take exception to or contradict," our Lord assures us. Let us trust in this gift of faith and witness, and praise with "sun and moon" and "stars of heaven" Him who is "exalted above all forever." Let us never fear to speak of our God and His hand at work in our lives.

O. 34. Thurs. (I)

Thursday
(Dn.6:12-28; Dn.3:59,68-74; Lk.21:20-28)

"Your ransom is near at hand."

"He is a deliverer and savior, working signs and wonders in heaven and on earth." And as "He delivered Daniel from the lions' power," so He shall save our souls from the destruction to come upon the face of the earth.

The king's prayer is answered: "To Daniel he said, 'May your God whom you serve so constantly, save you.'" And when the lions' mouths are closed because of David's innocence before God and men, Darius, in awe of the living God, writes to the nations that the kingdom of the God of Daniel "shall not be destroyed, and His dominion shall be without end." Another pagan king is brought to his knees in truth... "Praise and exalt Him above all forever"! Indeed, "let the earth bless the Lord."

But it is deliverance which is our theme today. Daniel is delivered from certain death in the lions' den, and our Lord speaks to us of the utter destruction of Jerusalem and the coming of the end of time – "Jerusalem will be trampled by the Gentiles, until the times of the Gentiles are fulfilled" – and of our means of escape from annihilation. Yes, we must flee the devastation that is near, flee to the mountains from the midst of the city, not linger behind in the land of Sodom as the angel comes to guide us to safety. Indeed, we must lift our heads to the sky even as its powers are shaken and all comes crashing to the ground but the strength of our God. For on that Day He will be made manifest, and on that Day, if we "stand up straight," our deliverance from sin and the powers of this world will be joyously known by our immortal souls. And we shall celebrate as did the king and Daniel upon the holy man's removal from the lion's den – and we shall praise the Almighty's name with "nights and days," with "lightnings and clouds," with all the elements of the Lord's universe. Alleluia!

Fear not, brothers and sisters, "in anticipation of what is coming upon the earth." Even as you are called, so you must be – to be "clever as snakes and innocent as doves" (Mt.10:16). Follow the saints' examples in simple obedience to the Shepherd's voice and, harboring no ill will toward your persecutors, be prepared to lay down your life if it be in the Lord's will, knowing full well that He will rescue you.*

* For this final thought I credit St. John Chrysostom and his wisdom, as found in this morning's Office of Readings.

Friday
(Dn.7:2-14; Dn.3:59,75-81; Lk.21:29-33)

"The beast was slain and its body thrown into the fire to be burnt up."

Daniel prophesies the coming of pagan empires in his vision of the four beasts. The vision is, in short, an overview of the coming salvation.

Notice that even as Daniel watches the beasts emerge with their horns and tusks and great iron teeth, even as he watches these terrible creatures devour and crush and trample in a kind of destructive euphoria... what does he see? "Thrones were set up and the Ancient One took His throne." The Lord God, the Eternal King, is there. (He is never far away.) And the arrogant horn is cast into eternal flame, and the other beasts lose their dominion, too, though they received "a prolongation of life for a time," indicating that a measure of the wickedness of such beastly empires – several of which we have seen very clearly in the last century – shall remain. But, nonetheless, there is "one like a son of man coming, on the clouds of heaven," and He indeed receives "everlasting dominion," a "kingship [that] shall not be destroyed." Like the Father in His eternal reign is the Son, who has come into our midst and even now winnows away the chaff of this world.

That even as evil presumes to reign the Lord is at work, is assuming His eternal reign in the heavenly kingdom, is evident in Jesus' words to the disciples in our gospel. He has told them to watch for the terrible signs which will come upon the earth and bring its destruction, and equates the recognition of these signs and wonders of the end time with the budding of a fig tree signaling the coming summer. Jesus is the fig tree, the peace that is born even in the midst of war, the love that grows though surrounded by hatred – the light that overcomes all darkness.

"The heavens and the earth will pass away, but my words will not pass away." Though the mountains fall into the sea, the Lord's heavenly reign but comes to fulfillment. Then all creatures, all "beasts, wild and tame," "everything growing from the earth" and all "seas and rivers" will "praise and exalt Him" whose kingdom lasts forever.

O. 34. Sat. (I)

Saturday

(Dn.7:15-27; Dn.3:59,82-87; Lk.21:34-36)

"The day I speak of will come upon all who dwell
on the face of the earth."

And so we must "pray constantly for the strength to escape whatever is in prospect, and to stand before the Son of Man."

The vision is explained to Daniel, and really it is quite simple: evil shall come, but good shall triumph in the end. Kingdoms of the Beast, of the evil one, "shall arise on earth. But the holy ones of the Most High shall receive the kingship, to possess it forever and ever," the angel tells Daniel, and reiterates this simple point: "All the kingdoms under the heavens shall be given to the holy people of the Most High, whose kingdom shall be everlasting." Yes, evil kingdoms shall rise and make war "against the holy ones," devouring the earth, beating it down, and crushing it... but the court of the Lord will be convened and the "final and absolute destruction" of the evil one is thus at hand. In Daniel's vision "the time came when the holy ones possessed the kingdom." And so it is; and so it shall be.

"Be on the watch," the Lord exhorts us in our gospel for this the final day of our liturgical year. We must indeed "be on guard," for if we do not watch, we will not be prepared for the coming day of the Lord which is ever at hand. Certainly we do not wish to be destroyed with the devil and his angels, but if our "spirits become bloated with indulgence and drunkenness and worldly cares," how shall we stand? And so it is that we must indeed pray constantly for the strength to withstand the coming chastisement – we cannot underestimate the devil's power to seduce us with his lies even as the grass grows beneath our feet. As the grass grows, so must our spirits grow, in truth and goodness and love. The Lord's peace must surround us to guard us against the sin which attacks us here as we live and breathe upon the face of the earth.

The day will come. Let it be our joy to be found waiting for the Lord.

(And so, Advent is now upon us.)

2. Year II

First Week

Monday
(1Sm.1:1-8; Ps.116:12-19; Mk.1:14-20)

"Hannah was childless."

And so she would "weep and refuse to eat," for it was "a constant reproach to her that the Lord had left her barren."

But He will not leave her barren long. Her husband's love for her despite her condition and her own prayers will soon be answered: she will give birth to the great prophet and priest, Samuel, who will anoint kings in Israel.

And her song of joy, which will foreshadow our Blessed Mother's own Magnificat, is here foreshadowed in our psalm in praise of the Lord's favor to His servants: "To you will I offer sacrifice of thanksgiving, and I will call upon the name of the Lord," as is her faithfulness in fulfilling her vow to offer her son entirely to God: "My vows to the Lord I will pay in the presence of all His people." All who have looked upon her shame and sorrow shall marvel at the blessing the Lord's "handmaid" will receive as He looses her bonds of emptiness and makes her fruitful in His eyes.

And in our gospel the Lord awakens the empty womb of the earth, stirring it to life. "The reign of God is at hand! Reform your lives and believe in the Good News!" He proclaims to a people in darkness. And children He brings forth from this barren country, the disciples He calls unto Himself, to be the first to share in His life. And they come forth, these pillars of the Church; they leave behind the world, all the world, to follow Him. Immediately, "on the spot," they "became His followers." "Along the Sea of Galilee," beside this simple body of water, the waves of grace call forth from the darkness the light that shall illumine all men.

"How shall [we] make a return to the Lord for all the good He has done for [us]?" How shall we poor sinners, barren of good works, unfruitful in His sight, thank Him for hearing our grieving cries? Simply, we must bear fruit in His name.

We are no longer childless.

Tuesday
(1Sm.1:9-20; 1Sm.2:1,4-8; Mk.1:21-28)

"May the God of Israel grant you what you have asked of Him."

For He holds all authority. "He gives orders to unclean spirits and they obey." "The Lord puts to death and gives life; He casts down to the nether world; He raises up again." All He wills, He does – nothing is beyond His reach and power. And His desire is to answer your prayer. If you are faithful as is Hannah, if you come before Him in such sincerity and truth, then what you ask shall be yours; for He Himself is sincerity and truth and goodness, and when you join yourself to Him, you join yourself to His authority... and find the answer to your prayer by His presence in your heart.

And so your heart shall exult with Hannah's. And so you shall see how "He raises the needy from the dust; from the ash heap He lifts up the poor." Indeed the prayer of the poor touches His heart and He "seat[s] them with nobles and make[s] a glorious throne their heritage." To heaven do they come, for heaven is their love.

How evident is the Lord's will and favor to those lowly ones who seek Him in the birth of Samuel – whose very name means "asked of the Lord" – to the barren wife Hannah. None could be poorer in blessing than she; ridiculed by the world is she for the Lord's lack of favor toward her. But as bitter as the fruit she must taste, she does not rebel against her God, but comes to Him in all humility and with a heart full of prayer and eyes filled with tears. And He loves His child. And one of the greatest men of the Old Testament becomes her son. And her song in praise of the Lord foreshadows Mary's own.

"Jesus entered the synagogue on the sabbath and began to teach." He comes to us now with His Word, His authority. Where Hannah sought Him, He now comes to us, offering freely the wisdom and power and grace which are His alone. And there is nothing which stands in the way of that Word. There is nothing to prevent its coming to our hearts and healing our souls of all injury, if we but listen, if we but seek His presence in our lives – if we but promise to give all to Him, He will give all we ask to us.

Wednesday
(1Sm.3:1-10,19-20; Ps.40:2-5,7-10; Mk.1:29-39)

"To do your will, O Lord, is my delight."

371

O how Samuel shows the "ears open to obedience" we all must have. For when called, even from sleep, he immediately and repeatedly rises and presents himself for service to the Lord. Even from his youth he is with the Lord and in His will. Such readiness to serve is also revealed in Peter's mother-in-law, who, when touched by Jesus, "immediately began to wait on them." She, too, rises quickly from bed (and sickness) to do the work of the Lord.

And certainly Jesus Himself is our greatest example of readiness to do God's will, for He and the Father are indeed one and all He does is according to the Father's word. After healing the "whole town" of their afflictions, working to exhaustion to arouse those imprisoned by the darkness of demons and bringing them into the light of God for service of the good, He rises "early the next morning" and goes "off to a lonely place in the desert," where "He was absorbed in prayer." When the disciples find Him, He is prepared to move on to the next town and the same exhausting work in service of the will of God, saying of the need to "proclaim the good news": "That is what I have come to do."

It is said of Samuel: he "grew up, and the Lord was with him, not permitting any word of his to be without effect." And so, well does this great prophet presage the coming of Christ – He who fulfills the will of the Father – and the faith of all those who follow Him. For all those who wait for the Lord, He stoops toward. To all those who say, "Behold, I come," He Himself comes, He Himself strengthens... His greatness He makes known through His children. So it is written in the scroll and upon our hearts: so is the will of God accomplished in our lives.

Only Him do we serve, brothers and sisters. His voice alone we must hear and heed. "Speak, Lord, for your servant is listening," must ever be our attitude toward the Creator of heaven and earth and the Savior of our souls. The Spirit's lead we must follow readily. And He will be with us to bless and give us the strength we need to work in Him beyond exhaustion, beyond sickness... beyond death. Life will be ours.

O. 1. Thurs. (II)

Thursday
(1Sm.4:1-11; Ps.44:10-11,14-15,24-25,27; Mk.1:40-45)

"Our souls are bowed down to the dust;
our bodies are pressed to the earth."

The Israelites suffer "a disastrous defeat" at the hands of their worst enemy. Not only do they lose thirty thousand men, but the ark of God – "who is enthroned upon the cherubim" which protect it – the tabernacle which holds the manna and the tablets of the Ten Commandments. This

372

most holy ark is taken into the camp of the Philistines. How can this be? The Israelites trusted in God's presence to save them, and they are beaten down. Our psalm addresses their plight directly: "You have cast us off and put us in disgrace, and you go not forth with our armies... those who hated us plundered us at will." And so the psalmist cries out with the defeated Israelites, "Why do you hide your face, forgetting our woe and our oppression?"

The Israelites – like the thieves on the cross either side of Christ, like us all – deserved their crushing defeat. They, again, as us all, turned their faces from the Lord of hosts to worship false and empty gods. There should be no question as to why the chastising hand of God is upon any of us. But our psalm is about more than this defeat of Israel or even our own punishment for sin. Written as the voice of Jesus Himself, it reveals the suffering of the innocent Lamb of God in our stead: "You made us the reproach of our neighbors, the mockery and the scorn of those around us." Jesus endures the scourging and the crown of thorns and the crucifixion for no other reason than to save our souls from similar fate, and more so, from condemnation. The sinless dove dies for the sinful flesh, which keeps us all in prison and pushes our faces to the dust. Though the sons of the high priest die in battle and are no more, Jesus lives, and through His death in battle for our souls, all now live.

In our gospel "a leper approach[es] Jesus with a request, kneeling down as he address[es] Him." Here we all are as sinners, symbolized by this outcast, coming earnestly to Jesus and humbling ourselves to the ground which, without God, is our place, is the dust from which we come and to which we return. Jesus is "moved with pity." Jesus "stretch[es] out His hand." Jesus "touch[es] him," and says: "Be cured." And the man is made whole.

Yes, this leper must be each of us, brothers and sisters. Humbly, our faces to the ground, knowing our sin and being repentant of it, we must come to Him. And He will raise our souls from the dust and our bodies from the earth into which they have fallen. This is why He has come; let us come to Him.

Friday
(1Sm.8:4-7,10-22; Ps.89:2,16-19; Mk.2:1-12)

"We have never seen anything like this!"

What the Lord can do, no one else is able to do – no king, no prophet, no priest. Though all may do in His name, nothing is done except through

Him. He alone forgives sins; He alone heals. He alone fights our battles, for He alone rules over us.

In asking Samuel to appoint a king over them, the Israelites reject the rule of God in their lives. If they but believed, the Lord would take care of all their concerns and they would keep all His blessings – their children, their animals, their land... as their own. But they do not trust in Him; rather, they fear the world, the surrounding nations, and seek to be like them, to fight as they do – to have one of their own to rule them. And thus they will lose what they have, for when we give all to God, He returns all we give with manifold blessing; but when we trust in man, giving ourselves to him, he swallows up our offerings.

Our psalm expresses well the attitude we should have toward God. It should be "in the light of [His] countenance" we walk. It should be "at [His] name [we] rejoice all the day." We should say with our psalmist: "To the Lord belongs our shield, and to the Holy One of Israel, our king." And so it is Jesus who must be our King; He alone must rule our lives, for He alone truly belongs to God; He alone is the Son of God.

The scribes were right to ask, "Who can forgive sins except God alone?" for God alone stood before them, forgiving the sins of His children. And it is now by His power, His presence, that our priests forgive men's sins in His name. "The Son of Man has authority on earth to forgive sins," and He does not take that power from the face of the earth upon His return to the Father's side in heaven: He multiplies that power – as well as the power to teach, to, in this sense, rule our lives – in His holy Church and its appointed leaders. What He granted to the Israelites because of their stubbornness of heart, He now brings full circle by blessing us with the presence of Christ: our king, our prophet, and our priest. No longer is it blasphemy for one to stand in God's stead, for the Lord has visited His people.

And should we not praise Him, therefore, for the wonders He accomplishes in our midst? Should we not shout for joy for His blessings? For now we have a king to rule us, a king greater than any other; now we need not fear the attacks of any nation. For even Satan He holds in His hands and casts him out at will; and so we are able to return to our land, to stand up and "go home." May "all give praise to God" for His goodness to us, turning our foolishness and sin to His grace and blessing before our very eyes.

Saturday
(1Sm.9:1-4,17-19,10:1; Ps.21:2-7; Mk.2:13-17)

"You are to govern the Lord's people Israel,
and to save them from the grasp of their enemies round about."

Tall and handsome, Saul gives every appearance of a king. And so God gives the people what they want in this "handsome young man" who "stood head and shoulders above the people." But with Saul the Lord shall indeed prove that it is not upon appearances He gazes. In the failure of Saul's reign will be revealed the emptiness of such outward attraction and our proclivity to desire what is appealing to the eye. For Saul shall not prove to be God's anointed; His Christ shall be quite another.

It is not of Saul our psalm of David sings when it speaks of the blessings of the king. The "majesty and splendor [the Lord] conferred upon him" is as passing as his beauty. The "crown of pure gold" is to be placed upon the head of Jesus Christ alone; it is He the Father has made "a blessing forever." His glory will be reflected in David, the ruddy shepherd youth whose son he is called, but will be fulfilled only in the Person of Jesus. It is He in whom all kings rejoice, in whom all find "the joy of [God's] presence," in whom all discover victory.

In our gospel, Jesus, the true king, comes, not with stately train, but "walking along the lakeshore." And crowds of people follow Him, people not of power and riches or reputation; rather, "many tax collectors and those known as sinners joined Him." This greatly disturbed the self-righteous scribes and Pharisees – it was not according to their vision of who He should be and what He should do. "Why does He eat with such as these?" they complain to His disciples. But He has a ready answer, one which cuts to the heart of us all and reveals the nature and purpose of this true king: "People who are healthy do not need a doctor; sick people do." And so the Savior comes into our midst, neither tall nor handsome nor desiring praise, to save us from our sin.

We are all sick, brothers and sisters! Make no doubt; have no question about it. We need Him! It is this king and the "goodly blessings" that flow from Him that must be our heart's desire, for He alone will bring us into the joy of the kingdom; He alone will save us from the sin into which we have all fallen. Let us follow Him as Levi, leaving behind our sinful station in life, and He will govern us well.

Second Week

Monday
(1Sm.15:16-23; Ps.50:8-9,16-17,21,23; Mk.2:18-22)

"Does the Lord so delight in holocausts and sacrifices
as in obedience to the command of the Lord?

The answer to the question Samuel puts to Saul is, in a word, "No."
"Obedience is better than sacrifice, and submission than the fat of rams."
Nothing does the Lord deem greater than our hearing and heeding His
Word, than our obedience to His will. And nothing will save us, nothing
will preserve our place in His kingdom like our doing what He asks of us.

Saul loses his kingship for his disobedience to the command of the
Lord. The Lord has told him to destroy the enemy he invades and all that
belongs to them. Saul retains some of the animals to bring back for sacrifice
to God. Why waste them? Why not honor God with them? Reasonable
thoughts to the human mind, but not the will of God. And in heeding these
thoughts is revealed the seed of Saul's rebellion against God, which will
lead to his attempts to destroy the king (David) the Lord has chosen to
replace him, and end in his own suicide.

How prone the human mind is to favor its own counsels against those of
God. How foolish seem submission and obedience, especially when they go
against our own logic. But David will show the humility God desires in
those He would bless. "To him that goes the right way I will show the
salvation of God," He promises us. David will be one who does not hate the
discipline of the Lord or cast His words behind his back. When all
justification is present for his killing Saul, who hunts down God's chosen
like an animal, he forgoes every opportunity, respecting his pursuer as
God's anointed. How different his attitude from Saul's, he who "rejected
the command of the Lord" by taking matters in his own soiled hands.

The blessing obedience is, the transcendent joy of joining oneself to the
will of the Lord, is evident in our gospel as well, in Jesus' teaching that
"new wine is poured into new skins" and not old. Fasting is a blessed
sacrifice provided by the law and by God. But as wholesome as this
practice, or any other religious observance, can be, it does not supersede
being present to the Lord. If we are not present to Him, all our works
become empty. The disciples are so close to Jesus, so happy to be in His
company, it is as if they have stepped into heaven – and so how can the
law's prescription for fasting touch them in a place where fasting is no
longer necessary? Indeed, they shall fast upon His death, and we know our
great saints have performed great fasts and sacrifices in the Name of the

Lord and for His glory... but first the grace of God must be with us all, or all becomes empty show.

It is the new wine we drink now, brothers and sisters; it is the Word become whole which is ours. Let us now be obedient to the Lord's command, and all we do will be joy for us and for our God.

Tuesday
(1Sm.16:1-13; Ps.89:20-22,27-28; Mk.2:23-28)

"Man sees the appearance but the Lord looks into the heart."

Indeed, how different the vision of God is from the vision of man, and how well the Lord illustrates this in His rejection of Saul and His choosing of David. When Samuel sees Eliab, whose appearance and "lofty stature" are reminiscent of Saul, even this great seer is blinded by his eyes and must be directed by God to look beyond what is apparent to his sight. All seven sons brought to the feast are rejected by the Lord, and the youngest, "who is tending the sheep," must be sent for. Jesse, his father, did not think David worthy of coming to the sacrificial banquet, but it is he who is the centerpiece of the celebration. This ruddy youth is the one chosen by the eyes of God.

And lest we think that there is some kind of diametrical opposition between physical beauty and interior loveliness, we must note that David is not ugly to behold and the Lord does not choose him for a poor appearance. He too was "handsome... and making a splendid appearance." But the beauty of David finds its source not in the skin but in a heart set on God, and it is this faithfulness and dedication to Him upon which the Lord gazes and, so, chooses, and not upon the curls falling around his face. David's appearance is beautiful because his soul is beautiful, and his soul is beautiful because it finds its life in God. And so, from the day of his anointing by Samuel, God's prophet, "the Spirit of the Lord rushed upon David" and there remained, for it had found its proper home.

In our gospel we have a quote like unto the one separated out for this day, and expressive of a similar lesson: "The Son of Man is Lord even of the sabbath," Jesus tells the Pharisees critical of His disciples picking, peeling, and eating heads of grain on the Lord's Day. For what do the Pharisees do but judge the law by its appearance alone, and fail to look into its heart? The law is indeed beautiful to behold and was made for man for his benefit, to draw him close to God; but how far from its purpose these leaders of the people have come, and so, how distant from the Lord they are – unable to recognize Him as He stands before them. The sabbath itself was made for man's rest and refreshment from labor, and yet when the disciples of Christ pick and eat to allay their hunger, to find refreshment for their failing bodies, these Pharisees deem it evil. Again one wonders how they can be so blind. Again it is apparent that they are unable to see beyond the surface. Empty indeed are their hearts.

As He has done for David, the Lord makes us strong, makes us fruitful and beautiful. He blesses our works as the works of this "highest of the kings of the earth," if those works are founded in Christ. If we truly say with David, "You are my father, my God, the rock, my savior," the Lord will hear us, and finding His presence in our hearts, He will bless us, even as His only Son.

Wednesday
(1Sm.17:32-33,37,40-51; Ps.144:1-2,9-10; Mk.3:1-6)

"You come against me with sword and spear and scimitar,
but I come against you in the name of the Lord."

"The battle is the Lord's" is the simple truth David proclaims to all those who stand in arms. To "all this multitude," he declares "that it is not by sword or spear that the Lord saves." Thus with David's defeat of the Philistine giant is emphasized what has already been revealed in the anointing of this ruddy youth as king and the loss of that kingship by the tall-in-stature Saul: the exalted are humbled and the humbled exalted. For God blesses those who make Him their "rock," trusting not in their own wealth or strength. "My refuge and my fortress, my stronghold, my deliverer, my shield, in whom I trust, who subdues peoples under me," David chants in praise of the Lord in his holy psalm. And so should we all take refuge in the Lord, and find strength in praising His Name.

And in "hoping to be able to bring an accusation against Him," do not the Pharisees come, too, with sword and spear against God's holy one today in our gospel? And do they not make this violence clear in their turning "to plot with the Herodians on how they might destroy Him"? They are defeated in battle by the Word of truth which issues forth and indeed is embodied by the Christ of God, Jesus, Son of David, Son of God. They cannot contradict the authority of His teaching or the blessing of the healing He brings from the Father on high, but yet they harden their hearts and close "their minds against Him," seeking to confirm their trust in the warring hand of this world in the capture and crucifixion of their Savior. But the battle *is* the Lord's, and their attempts to destroy Him shall prove the fruitlessness of such trust in violence – indeed, their killing Him with sword and spear shall be the instrument which leads to His resurrection, bringing the dawn of new life in whose light death itself, and the pride of man, shall be destroyed forever.

Let all know it is the Lord who fights for those whom He loves, those who trust in Him and His ways, who seek to do good and not evil, to "preserve life" and not "destroy it." The question Jesus poses to the Pharisees He presents to us: do we cherish the saving power of the Lord of life and take refuge and joy in Him, or do we reach for the weapons at our side to destroy Him? The posturing of this world is vain, for it is God who holds life and death in His Hand.

O. 2. Thurs. (II)

Thursday
(1Sm.18:6-9,19:1-7; Ps.56:2-3,5,9-14; Mk.3:7-12)

"Saul has slain his thousands,
and David his ten thousands."

And Jesus His millions. He slays an untold number of "unclean spirits [who] would catch sight of Him, fling themselves down at His feet, and shout, 'You are the Son of God.'" "A great crowd followed Him from Galilee, and an equally great multitude" from all the surrounding regions. So great were their numbers He needed a boat to escape the press upon Him. For He "cured many," and many more desired to be touched by Him.

The women sing of David's greatness upon his return from slaying the Philistine. Their rightful attribution of praise for David, through whom "the Lord brought about a great victory for all Israel" and so for its king (who had himself sought someone to stand against the giant Goliath), does nothing but provoke resentment and jealousy from King Saul. His anger even leads to his plotting to kill the man who has saved his kingdom; and though he sets aside his plan "of shedding innocent blood by killing David without cause" for the moment, the plot never leaves his heart and shall repeatedly surface with greater intensity. Thus Saul proves his inability to serve as king of the Lord's people. Thus his pride shall be his demise.

And rightfully does Saul claim of David that "all that remains for him is the kingship," for in fact he has already been anointed king in place of Saul by Samuel the prophet. And though as with the kingship of Jesus, who silences the demons from revealing "who He was," David's crown shall remain hidden for a time, inevitably – again, as with the Lord's reign – those who "press their attack against" the Lord's anointed shall be turned back and the true king shall "walk before God in the light of the living." It is inevitable for it is God's will, and neither the jealousy of Saul nor the plotting of the Pharisees – the jealous kings who would be overthrown by Jesus – can turn aside what God has ordained.

The Lord is with David. Though his "adversaries trample upon [him] all the day," he sings in praise of God in his psalm: "You have rescued me from death." And so we see how our psalms sing of Jesus Himself and why He is called Son of David. For the greatest victory the Lord God shall achieve will be the resurrection of His Son from the dead, and the redemption of the many souls who shall follow Him.

Friday
(1Sm.24:3-21; Ps.57:2-4,6,11; Mk.3:13-19)

"Sovereignty over Israel shall come into your possession."

Today we see David at perhaps his most humble and obedient in the sight of God – we see why he is the great king of Israel.

David is being hunted down by Saul once again in his jealousy. His psalm, our psalm today, is his cry for protection from the Lord in whom he trusts: "I call to God Most High, to God, my benefactor. May He send from heaven and save me." To the cave in which he hides, God sends his pursuer, vulnerable and at arm's length. But this man who will be king of the Israelites by God's ordination refrains from taking the sword into his hand to kill the man who would kill him. Why? Because Saul is yet the king, "the Lord's anointed," whom David even calls "a father to me" despite the threat he is to his life. Such an act of respect, such an understanding of the obedience due God and His will is unparalleled in Scripture. This is David. This is the king.

And how tragic a figure is Saul. Upon having his eyes turned inward to his very soul and the injustice he wreaks upon David, he weeps aloud in recognition of his sin: "You are in the right rather than I; you have treated me generously, while I have done you harm." It is he who speaks the words of our quote today, he who recognizes the truly kingly nature of David... Yet for all his penance and insight it shall not be long before his jealousy leads him to pursue David unrighteously once again. He cannot escape his envy for David's blessing.

And in our gospel we read of the blessed apostles of Christ, those "men He Himself had decided on," whom He summoned and "who came and joined Him." These "He would send to preach the Good News"; these would "have authority to expel demons." They are named for us today: here is the foundation of the Church in which God dwells. Here are His blessed kings of the New Jerusalem. Let us not be jealous of them. Let no man attempt to breach the authority given them; for pursue them as one would, none shall take their blessing away – it is they who are ordained by God for

His service. Humbly let us join them in their sovereignty over Israel. Obediently let us come into the Lord's kingdom.

Saturday
(2Sm.1:1-4,11-12,19,23-27; Ps.80:2-7; Mk.3:20-21)

"They mourned and wept and fasted until evening
for Saul and his son Jonathan."

For David's leading his men in mourning for Saul, it might have been said of him what was said of Jesus: "He is out of His mind." But even to the end David proves himself sincere in his respect for God's anointed, even slaying the man who claims to have dispatched the king upon Saul's request (after he had dealt himself a mortal wound). David is not anxious to claim the throne for himself, as so many around him suppose he should be. Like Christ, he does not grasp at what is his, but continually humbles himself before his Lord and God, and waits and accepts the will of the Father.

And so David weeps and fasts for the man who forever sought his life. And so he is given "tears to drink in ample measure." And so he cries with the Israelites, "fed with the bread of tears" at the death of their king. Jonathan, David truly loved. He was indeed better to him than any brother or any lover. For him his tears are understandable. Jonathan repeatedly saved David's life, to the point of provoking the wrath of his father against himself. But there is no explanation for his love of Saul, other than the Lord loved him and had blessed him. And so, David's love is as the love of God. His tears fall from on high.

And what shall we say of our gospel today? Jesus and His disciples are so pressed upon by the crowds of people, they made it "impossible for them to get any food whatever." We should remember this situation when we consider the Lord's family coming to "take charge of Him." We should understand their concern for His health when we interpret their statement that "He is out of His mind." They mean not that He is insane, but that He needs someone to look after His temporal needs, lest He tax Himself overmuch.

But the Lord's strength, like David's love, also comes from on high – it is not earthly. And His work is His food, and the Father will take care. His mourning and weeping and fasting and dying for us is blessed by His Father, and will bear fruit unto His kingship in heaven. If He did not live by the standards of heaven, there would be no hope for our salvation, for why should He die for sinners such as us, other than it is the Father's love?

381

Third Week

Monday
(2Sm.5:1-7,10; Ps.89:20-22,25-26; Mk.3:22-30)

"Whoever blasphemes against the Holy Spirit will never be forgiven."

How different are the scribes who come to Jesus from the Israelites who come to David to crown him king. "The tribes of Israel came to David in Hebron and said: 'Here we are, your bone and your flesh.'" So united would they be to him whom the Lord had said would "shepherd [His] people Israel," so well do they remember his leadership in war, that they wholeheartedly invite him to rule over them. They believe what God has said of His chosen king: "I have found David, my servant; with my holy oil I have anointed him," and they confirm his anointing among them.

But the scribes would drive Jesus from their midst. And as the Jebusites vainly threatened David before he took the stronghold of Zion and began his reign in Jerusalem, so these blind leaders of the people vainly attack Jesus before His entering and taking hold of the New Jerusalem. If David was anointed by God, how much more is the Father's anointing upon His only Son? If David's deeds in war deserved respect and praise, how much more Him who came to teach and heal the nation? And if these scribes should not only reject Jesus but designate the holy deeds He has worked among them as coming from the prince of demons, what hope have they but to join the prince of demons in eternal damnation? For if they call the good evil, how shall they come to accept the goodness of God and enter His reign? Shall they not rather fling themselves toward the fires of hell, as even they do here, taking the evil for good, led astray as they are by their pride and jealousy?

The Lord's hand is always with His Chosen One, "that [His] arm might make Him strong." It is in that strength we take refuge; it is in the blessing upon Him we find life. We must invite Him who is good to rule over us – His works must be our own. If we do not recognize the truth of His words and the grace in His deeds, what hope will we have of finding the fountain that washes us clean of our sins and prepares us for the holiness of paradise? What can these scribes do but "carr[y] the guilt of [their] sin without end," for they utterly reject Him.

Brothers and sisters, we choose life or we choose death. We choose to side with the good or turn to become one with the evil. Wickedness has no place with the grace of God and His goodness allows no evil to enter in. Jesus destroys evil: speak only the truth of this Word. The Spirit knows nothing of lies.

Tuesday

(2Sm.6:12-15,17-19; Ps.24:7-10; Mk.3:31-35)

"Lift up, O gates, your lintels;
reach up, you ancient portals,
that the King of glory may come in!"

In our first reading David leads all the Israelites in, "bringing up the ark of the Lord with shouts of joy and to the sound of the horn." "Dancing before the Lord with abandon," he brings the ark into Jerusalem and sets it within its tent or tabernacle. All celebrate this day as they surround the ark on its journey and as David "offers holocausts and peace offerings before the Lord," the ark having come to its place in the city of David. The Lord is in their midst, and so all the people rejoice.

In our gospel the ever present crowd of people is assembled, seated "in a circle" around Jesus. They surround the Lord as once the Israelites surrounded the ark – and how their hearts must celebrate at His presence in their midst. And how indeed their hearts must leap up to hear what is said of them: "These are my mother and my brothers." For thus the Lord gathers them into His arms; thus He feeds them better than with the meat of any holocaust – thus they are protected forever by His holy presence.

"Who is this King of glory? The Lord, strong and mighty, the Lord, mighty in battle." He blesses and protects all His children; He makes all who worship Him His own. And what need we do but celebrate; what need we do but shout for joy? For He is present before us. For He enters into us, into the New Jerusalem in which we dwell. Here in His Church we have His Blessed Sacrament to feed us on our way to Him. In this He is already with us, as He is in His teaching and in His priests and in all His brothers and sisters and mothers – "whoever does the will of God" becomes one with Him.

We love you, Lord our God, for your presence among us! We praise you, dearest Jesus, for your presence within us! O brothers and sisters, make room for His entry into your hearts and minds, bodies and souls, that you might enter in with Him to His heavenly kingdom. He stands and knocks at the door even now. Will you open and welcome Him into your home?

Wednesday

(2Sm.7:4-17; Ps.89:4-5,27-30; Mk.4:1-20)

"Your house and your kingdom shall endure forever before me;
your throne shall stand firm forever."

David seems intent on establishing the Lord's presence forever by building a permanent house in which He might dwell, but how well our God answers the great king's thoughts with the promise of making "his posterity endure forever." It is the Lord who establishes all, and so He states, "I will fix a place for my people Israel; I will plant them so that they may dwell in their place without further disturbance," to show that He thinks of us and loves us first. Though He approves and blesses our desires to care for Him and make Him known, as He shows by revealing to David that his son "shall build a house to [His] name," He cannot be outdone in His love for us.

Solomon will build the temple of the Lord, yes, and it will be a great house in which all shall worship God and through which all shall find blessing from God. But the true Son of David upon whom the Lord's favor rests eternally is Jesus Himself. It is His kingdom which "stands firm" forever. It is through Him the Lord will "destroy all [our] enemies" and grant us peace round about. He is the seed of David come to full growth, the promise of the king come to fulfillment. This is He whom the Israelites truly sought when first they asked for a king – this is God's blessed answer to their request for one of their own to rule them.

It is clear that David is as the seed "sown on good soil" which "yield[s] thirty- and sixty- and a hundredfold." Satan shall not come to carry off what is sown through him, nor shall he "wither for lack of roots" or be choked off by the cares of this world. For as the Lord says to him, "I have been with you wherever you went"; and so His nourishment, the Spirit of the Lord which rushed upon David from his first anointing, remains, too, upon this chosen king. And though he shall sin, and though his sons shall turn away from worship of the true God, yet the Lord's blessing remains. And in the enduring of the Lord's correction "with the rod of men and human chastisements," Jesus, the Son of David, the Son of God, by His crucifixion and death opens the way for all children of David, all children blessed by God, to return to the Lord of all and remain with Him forever. The kingdom of Jesus is now established; let us come to this Temple and be saved.

Thursday

(2Sm.7:18-19,24-29; Ps.132:1-2,3-5,11-14,Lk.1:32; Mk.4:21-25)

"If your sons keep my covenant and the decrees which I shall teach them,
their sons, too, forever shall sit upon your throne."

Yes, "the Lord has chosen Zion; He prefers her for His dwelling." His
blessings are upon His Church and its people, for "the Lord swore to David
a firm promise from which He will not withdraw: 'Your own offspring I will
set upon your throne,'" and Jesus completes that promise by establishing the
New Jerusalem in His Name. But we must exhibit the "anxious care" David
has shown for the preservation and promotion of the house which is ours
through this Son of David and fulfillment of God's promise.

If "the eye is the lamp of the body," as Jesus has said elsewhere in the
gospels (Mt.6:22), then we must say with David: "I will give my eyes no
sleep, my eyelids no rest, till I find a place for the Lord." Always our light
should be shining forth; always we should be looking to "make our call and
election permanent" (as Peter has elsewhere stated – 2Pt.1:10) – always we
must seek to serve Him, if we wish to dwell ever with Him. For as Jesus
says so poignantly to the crowd today: "Is a lamp acquired to be put under a
bushel basket or hidden under a bed? Is it not meant to be put on a stand?"
Thus He encourages us to bring our light "out into the open," to let it shine
forth for all to see. For then it shall be blessed.

"Listen carefully" now to what the Lord says further: "In the measure
you give you shall receive." Here is a golden rule which must be
understood and practiced. For it is so that the more we share the gifts the
Lord places in our hearts and at our hands, the greater these blessings grow.
As we share our faith, more faithful do we become. As we speak of Him,
the more do we understand of Him. In giving ourselves away for others and
the sake of the kingdom, we find ourselves present in His light. And so do
we grow. And so is our place in His house assured. And so we shall dwell
with Him forever.

Let us pray with David in our first reading, brothers and sisters: "Bless
the house of your servant that it may be before you forever," that what the
Lord has promised each of us through the Son of David may come to light.
As David simply asks the Lord to accomplish what He has graciously
vowed to do – "Confirm for all time the prophecy you have made
concerning your servant and his house" – let us beg the Lord to grant the
same to His Church for the salvation of all souls who worship Him in truth
and serve Him in strength. Alleluia.

Friday
(2Sm.11:1-10,13-17; Ps.51:3-7,10-11; Mk.4:26-34)

"The seed sprouts and grows without his knowing how it happens."

Jesus in our gospel tells us of the kingdom of God and of its gradual growth without our knowing. Seed is scattered, the Word is sown in our souls, and as we "[go] to bed and [get] up day after day," remaining in the presence of the Lord, good fruits little by little reveal themselves in our lives – till finally at the time of judgment we are gathered into the heavenly reign. Though small and humble seed, once we are sown in the Lord's grace, we "become the largest of shrubs, with branches big enough for the birds of the sky to build nests in its shade." And so this man made of dust may find life eternal in Jesus.

In our first reading there is another kind of gradual growth evident: the sin of David. It is the time of year "when kings go out on campaign" with their armies, but David remains at home – and so in this sin of sloth is sown that which will grow into adultery and murder. For one evening as the king "[rises] from his siesta and stroll[s] about on the roof of the palace," he sees the beautiful Bathsheba bathing, and lets his look linger upon her. Lust having taken hold of him, he takes her to his bed and has relations with her, despite her being another man's wife. In a vain attempt to cover his sin, he recalls the husband from battle that he might go in to his wife and believe the child David has conceived is his own. But the man is more faithful to the troops in battle than David is to his position as king, and remains apart from his home. Finally, David resorts to arranging for Uriah's death in battle.

O how sin has grown in the great king! From a small seed tremendous guilt is born. And now, what can the prince of the people do but seek the mercy of the Lord. In his famous psalm of repentance David begs God, "Turn away your face from my sins, and blot out all my guilt." He calls out, "Thoroughly wash me from my guilt, and of my sin cleanse me." Recognizing his plight as a member of the fallen human race: "In guilt I was born, and in sin my mother conceived me," the king shows genuine humility, and so finds the forgiveness of God – but now the sword shall be upon his house. Though there shall be peace in the time of the son he will later conceive with the wife of Uriah, it shall not remain. Only in Christ will God's blessing truly return again.

Brothers and sisters, from small seeds indeed great trees come. We must be ever diligent about the seed we sow, remaining always in the light of the Lord and nourished by the Spirit. When "the time is ripe for harvest," all we have done shall be exposed; until then, let us trust in His presence alone.

Saturday
(2Sm.12:1-7,10-17; Ps.51:12-17; Mk.4:35-41)

"I have sinned against the Lord."

David is the man who "took the poor man's ewe lamb and made a meal of it for his visitor." To feed his lust he has feasted on another man's wife. And he sees the injustice of this; he recognizes his guilt when his sin is exposed. But why has he done it? "As the Lord lives, the man who has done this merits death!" And so David, too, has need of the true King and His cross to redeem him.

What does the Lord say to David as he "lie[s] on the ground clothed in sackcloth," praying for the dying child he has conceived by his sin? We know what *he* says to God, for we have Psalm 51 to eternally express the misery of this sinner, and all sinners. We know he cries out: "Free me from my blood guilt, O God, my saving God." But how does God respond? Is He with him? We know the Lord forgives David – Nathan tells him so – but yet "the sword shall never depart from [his] house," and he shall have his sin later exposed in broad daylight by his own son, Absalom, who lies with David's wives in the public eye. Much woe remains with David long after his fall, and really throughout the history of Judah and Israel. He is assured: "You shall not die," but though his house remain and is fulfilled in the coming of Christ, what pain must be with the king in this time.

If he had called upon the Lord, as He rebukes the wind and the sea in our gospel: "Quiet! Be still!" so would God have calmed his lust upon a word from his mouth. But he "utterly spurned the Lord." How is it such a humble and obedient king could do such a thing? How is it the *disciples* are so "lacking in faith" at the specter of the violence of the sea? Why do they become so "terrified"?

Would not we all, brothers and sisters? Have we not all sinned and fallen short of the glory of God? Do we not all become awed by Him whom "the wind and the sea obey"? Yet we must come to Him. Yet we must beg His pardon. Yet we must seek the strength of His Spirit, of His Word within us. Yet we must fall to our knees before our priest and cry out to our God – "A clean heart create for me, O Lord, and a steadfast spirit renew within me." Thus we all have need of cleansing this side of heaven; we have all brought forth children unto death.

Fourth Week

Monday
(2Sm.15:13-14,30,16:5-13; Ps.3:2-7; Mk.5:1-20)

"Many are saying of me,
'There is no salvation for him in God.'"

Today David's sins rise to his neck, and he is persecuted for them. But in accepting the persecution as chastisement from the hand of God, David regains his kingly stature, becoming once again humble and obedient to the Lord.

David's son Absalom has successfully led a rebellion against him among the Israelite nation under David's command. The king is forced to flee, and as he leaves, his son will lie with the wives and concubines he has left behind upon the same roof where David first spied the bathing Bathsheba. How his sins come to visit him!

But it is in mourning David flees Jerusalem and climbs the Mount of Olives – the hill upon which Christ's own passion shall begin in the garden where He is taken by the sword. David "wept without ceasing. His head was covered and he was walking barefoot." Repentant is the king in remembrance of his sins and the punishment now come upon him. And his sincerity he exhibits profoundly again, for as Shimei curses and stones him, though he is surrounded by soldiers he does not exact retribution or seek to stop him. Despite the fact this kin of Saul has no right to act toward the king in this way, yet David is struck to the heart by the truth of his words: "Now you suffer ruin because you are a murderer," and leaves all in the hands of God, responding to his soldier, "Suppose the Lord has told him to curse David; who then will dare to say, 'Why are you doing this?'" Open is David about the fact that even his own son is seeking his life, and so what standing can he expect to have with his enemies. As he endures his trial, he hopes only it shall be purgatorial: "Perhaps the Lord will look upon my affliction and make it up to me with benefits for the curses he is uttering this day." And so he does not "fear the myriads of people arrayed against him on every side," for he rediscovers his faith in God.

And as the Lord casts out the legion of demons from the possessed man of Gerasene, so He shall purge David of his sin. To whatever extreme our afflictions have grown, the Lord is present to save. For if this man who could not be secured with chains, who "uninterruptedly night and day amid the tombs... screamed and gashed himself with stones," could be found by a word from the Lord "sitting fully clothed and perfectly sane," what have we to fear of all the devils who accuse us of our sins? Jesus is mightier than them and there is no telling "how much the Lord in His mercy" can do when we fall on our faces before Him in homage. True repentance brings salvation to all sinful souls.

Tuesday
(2Sm.18:9-10,14,24-25,30-19:3; Ps.86:1-6; Mk.5:21-43)

"Hearken, O Lord, to my prayer,
and attend to the sound of my pleading."

Today in our readings we hear of desperate pleas made to the Lord. In our gospel there are at least two "earnest appeal[s]": Jairus "fell at [the] feet" of Jesus and begged Him to heal his dying daughter; and without words the woman "who had been afflicted with a hemorrhage for a dozen years" makes her appeal by working her way through the crowd simply to "touch His clothing" and be well. The woman is healed "immediately" and hears from the Lord, "It is your faith that has cured you." Her He sends in peace, but peace and the same faith He does not find as He approaches Jairus' house after having been told his daughter is dead. There is "the noise of people wailing and crying loudly on all sides." Theirs seems to be a kind of pleading, but the Lord's answer to such prayer they reject and mock, and so must be put out of the house – only those of faith can know of healing.

And so Jesus takes only Peter, James, John, and the girl's parents into the room where the child lies, for they are able to heed His teaching: "Fear is useless. What is needed is trust." And so when He reaches out His hand to the little girl and speaks to her, "Talitha, koum," she indeed rises and walks about. The prayer of a true heart is always answered in the power of God.

What can we say of David's "weeping and mourning for Absalom" in our first reading? Again a father cries out for his child. But here it is not an innocent "child of twelve" for whom the prayer rises up, but for a son who has rebelled against his father "with evil intent," seeking indeed to overthrow David's kingdom and put him to death. David's cry, "My son, my son Absalom! If only I had died instead of you, Absalom, my son, my son!" stands in opposition to what is expected of him as he is informed of the "good news" that his enemies have been defeated and their leader killed. But here again the king knows it has been his own sin which has led to such disruption in his house. And so it is as much for himself he cries as for the child of his loins. And though Absalom shall not be raised from the dead, perhaps the Lord hears the sorrow of David's heart and will later comfort him.

"To you I call all the day," O Lord. "I am afflicted and poor," but "you, O Lord, are good and forgiving." Heal me as I cry out to you. Look upon my weeping and mourning with your kindness; raise me from the dead by your word and feed me with your Body and Blood.

O. 4. Wed. (II)

Wednesday
(2Sm.24:2,9-17; Ps.32:1-2,5-7, Mk.6:1-6)

"I acknowledged my sin to you;
my guilt I covered not."

The Lord can heal only those who believe in Him, who turn to Him in their guilt to be saved.

David has sinned against the Lord once again. His kingdom had been blessed by the Lord and was flourishing in His sight. Rather than accept the blessings the Lord poured upon him and so find their increase, by numbering the people who had been the Lord's gift to him the king sought control over that which should have been left in the hands of God. And so now their number shall be decreased in his sight.

But David regrets his sin, acknowledging it before the Lord and begging His pardon: "I have sinned grievously in what I have done. But now, Lord, forgive the guilt of your servant, for I have been very foolish," and he throws himself on the mercy of God. The Lord does destroy some seventy thousand in the kingdom, but relents at David's intercession for the sheep under his rule who have done no wrong – the king entreats, "Punish me and my kindred," and then offers an appeasing sacrifice to God.

David's sin is severe and has serious consequences, but the Lord is faithful in forgiving him when he calls out to Him. However, when "Jesus went to His own part of the country," as shown in our gospel, their hearts were closed against Him and He could share no grace. Were they any less sinners than David? Had they any less need of His forgiveness, of His healing? Their hardness of heart itself proves otherwise, but, sadly, "they found Him too much for them"; and "their lack of faith," which distressed the Lord, prevented them from knowing the mercy found by their ancestor David. Ironically, it is their own closeness to Him and His human family that keeps them from recognizing the greatness of the grace which works through Him. Would they disown David, him whose sons they claim to be, if he had come to them in such a way? And yet Jesus they reject.

Brothers and sisters, our sights must be set on heaven and the mercy that falls from there through the Lord. We have all sinned as David in our foolishness. We must acknowledge it as he has, with faith that the Lord can heal us, that He walks amongst us as a brother to cure all our ills and teach us the way to love. If we listen without acceptance of Him in faith, "no miracle" will be worked in our lives – and it is a miracle we most need, for we simple servants must lay down our lives.

Thursday
(1Kgs.2:1-4,10-12; 1Chr.29:10-12; Mk.6:7-13)

"Yours, O Lord, is the sovereignty;
you are exalted as head over all."

Solomon begins his reign, and the apostles begin their mission. But how different is their manner of rule. Solomon sits in sovereignty upon a throne, while the apostles are sent in poverty to all towns. Solomon's reign is of the physical universe, with the riches of the world at his disposal; whereas the twelve apostles rule in the kingdom of heaven, shown by the Lord's "giving them authority over unclean spirits." They go forth with "no food, no traveling bag, not a coin in the purses in their belts," "preaching the need of repentance," the dust upon their feet. Solomon remains within the walls of his palace, well-guarded and with all "riches and honor," seemingly of "grandeur and power, majesty, splendor, and glory."

Now let us not think that the riches themselves are evil, for these are a gift from God (rewarding Solomon for his initial desire for wisdom above all else); but it must never be forgotten that, as David declares to God at the time of his son's anointing: "Riches and honor are from you." His *always* are the majesty and the glory. If Solomon would remember this, if he would heed the Lord's words to David's sons to "remain faithful to [Him] with their whole heart and with their whole soul," observing always His commands – his kingship would be blessed. But Solomon, too, shall sin, and worse than his father: he shall turn to worship of other gods. And the sons that follow shall only continue the decline, necessitating the reign of Christ to enter in.

So, humbly do the disciples of the Lord go forth, though with the greatest of power. They call for the repentance of all proud souls, possessed of the throne of this unholy world. The Twelve "expelled many demons, anointed the sick with oil, and worked many cures," thus bringing the kingdom of God to this world; and we are called to follow them, in the same poverty. None of this can we do if our hearts are set upon the riches of this world. Empty must we be of the desire for the food of earthly security – into the Lord's hands we must utterly place our lives. Only then will we be rich in Him "from eternity to eternity."

Splendor awaits us all, brothers and sisters, in the cross we carry upon this dusty earth.

Friday

(Sir.47:2-11; Ps.18:31,47,50-51; Mk.6:14-29)

"Herod feared John,
knowing him to be an upright and holy man."

O how the Lord has given power to His great men. It is He who "gave great victories to [the] king." David "called upon the Most High God, who gave strength to his right arm"; and as David "made sport of lions as though they were kids," as he "slew the giant" and his "tens of thousands" in battle, so John the Baptist slays the sins of the multitude, even striking great fear into the heart of King Herod by the simple words: "It is not right for you to live with your brother's wife." And though it is John who is beheaded, it is Herod who shakes in his boots long after the Baptist is gone. As our gospel relates today, "On hearing of Jesus, Herod exclaimed, 'John, whose head I cut off, has been raised up!'" This king's guilt remains, as do the words of the Baptist in his heart.

"He is a shield to all who take refuge in Him," David declares so knowingly in our psalm today. Indeed, the Lord's blessed protection has been continually with his king, who has ever taken Him as his Rock. Of David, Sirach writes, "With his every deed he offered thanks to God Most High, in words of praise. With his whole being he loved his Maker and daily had his praises sung." What tremendous witness the wise man gives to the Lord's chosen king. And perhaps most poignant and most significant is his statement that "the Lord forgave him his sins and exalted his strength forever." David does not lose his kingship because of his failures – as does Herod, who is already dead by his wickedness – but in fact has the establishment of "his throne in Israel" fulfilled in the coming of Christ.

The Lord's power is upon His chosen. To each He gives the grace needed to offer lives of sacrifice. As David's life was "like the choice fat of the sacred offerings" and John's death a holocaust that rises yet unto God, so all our lives may be enriched and blessed, and made whole in His sight; so will they be as "sweet melody," if we but entrust them to the Lord our God. And then none shall be able to stand before the power that is with us, for His holiness conquers all.

Saturday

(1Kgs.3:4-13;   Ps.119:9-14;   Mk.6:30-34)

"He began to teach them at great length."

"Who is able to govern this vast people of yours?" Solomon asks in his plea to God for wisdom. And "upon disembarking Jesus saw a vast crowd" who "were like sheep without a shepherd," our gospel tells us. The apostles have just "returned to Jesus and reported to Him all that they had done and what they had taught," how they had managed to enter into His mission, and now it is time for rest in a deserted place. But the crowds hasten on foot to fill that deserted place, and what can the Lord do but feed those who thirst so much for His presence and His word.

In our first reading Solomon reflects his father David's humble obedience before God: "O Lord, my God, you have made me, your servant, king to succeed my father David; but I am a mere youth, not knowing at all how to act." And so he makes the request for wisdom that so pleases the Lord. And so God grants his request: "I give you a heart so wise and understanding that there has never been anyone like you up to now, and after you there will come no one equal to you," and adds the greatest of riches and glory to it. Solomon it is who composes proverbs, who judges the most difficult of cases, who is able to answer any question – it is he who rules the great kingdom of Israel in peace. And all this he is able to do because his soul is as our psalmist's today; he sings with him, "With all my heart I seek you; let me not stray from your commands," and, "In the way of your decrees I rejoice, as much as in all riches." But when the king strays, he shall lose the great promise which has been so marvelously revealed in his reign. He, too, shall show that he is but human.

Only the Lord teaches, brothers and sisters! Only the Lord is able to rule! All teaching and all governance come only from Him and not our own souls. As great as the wisdom of Solomon was, apart from the Lord it becomes nothing but vanity. For it is He who grants it to the king, according to his humble request. And it is He who can only take it back again, upon separation from Him.

Let us keep to His words, brothers and sisters. Let us remain under His Spirit's tutelage, within the walls of Mother Church. Here we shall be taught. By His wisdom we shall come to know. In His Word we shall find the salvation of our souls. Come now to your Shepherd and hear His voice imparting the grace of wisdom, the food that sustains you, to your mind and heart. Enter into His call.

Fifth Week

Monday
(1Kgs.8:1-7,9-13;   Ps.132:6-10;   Mk.6:53-56)

"Let us enter into His dwelling,
let us worship at His footstool."

"Advance, O Lord, to your resting place, you and the ark of your majesty." Yes, in our first reading, "the elders of Israel and all the leaders of the tribes" come to bring the ark of the Lord into the temple Solomon has built in Jerusalem. "For the occasion [they] sacrificed before the ark sheep and oxen too many to number or count." When the ark was in its place in the holy of holies, "the Lord's glory... filled the temple" in the form of a cloud. The Lord's presence had come to rest in this "princely house." But this shall not be a dwelling "where [He] may abide forever," as Solomon says; for the eternal Temple is Jesus.

In our gospel "crowds scurried about the adjacent area and began to bring in the sick on bedrolls" when the Lord and His disciples tied up their boat in Genessaret. Here as everywhere He went "they laid the sick in the marketplaces and begged Him to let them touch just the tassel of His cloak." Mark tells us, "All who touched Him got well." Here is the true Temple at work, a place where prayers are answered, where healing is known. As the ark was placed "beneath the wings of the cherubim in the sanctuary," so the Father has the angels spread their wings over His Son, guarding and blessing His every step. As when the ark is brought in to the holy of holies, the Lord's glory fills the temple, so when He comes to us, when we but touch Him, we are filled with His presence and made whole. As the Israelites crowded into the temple to offer sacrifice, so now all in need surround the Lord to share in the holy sacrifice of His Body and Blood.

Here is the Temple not made by human hands, brothers and sisters. Here is the Lord's eternal dwelling place. Here is Jesus, the Son of God. In all the tabernacles of all the churches throughout the world He rests, His presence abides. Let us flock to Him. Let us receive Him into our hearts and bodies. Let us know His healing touch upon our souls. Let us pray with our psalmist, "May your priests be clothed with justice; let your faithful ones shout merrily for joy." For here is His holy presence; here is the glory of the Lord. Here He hears our prayers as we call upon His Name and worship before Him each day. Here He enters in and makes His home with us, and so we, too, become temples of the Lord.

Tuesday
(1Kgs.8:22-23,27-30; Ps.84:2-5,10-11; Mk.7:1-13)

"Can it indeed be that God dwells among men on earth?"

Well does Solomon do in stating, "If the heavens and the highest heavens cannot contain you, how much less this temple which I have built!" For though the Lord will heed Solomon's prayer and "listen to the petitions of [His] servant and of [His] people Israel which they offer in this place," He indeed will only "keep [His] covenant of kindness with [His] servants who are faithful to [Him] with their whole heart." When they do as the Pharisees and "disregard God's commandment and cling to what is human tradition," when they hold fast only to the walls of the temple and neglect to keep His Word, the blessing He provides through the temple they built shall be removed from their midst – the walls themselves shall crumble (as even they do, not many generations from Solomon's time).

The Pharisees indeed sin by clinging to the walls, by a scrupulous observance of care for the body even as the soul rots. They carefully wash hands and food and "cups and jugs and kettles" but forego the cleansing of their hearts within. And so they "nullify God's word in favor of the traditions [they] have handed on"; they ornament the walls of the temple, but God is not within. They indeed fulfill Isaiah's prophecy: "This people pays me lip service but their heart is far from me."

Brothers and sisters, do we pray in truth? Do our "heart and [our] flesh cry out for the living God"? Can we say with our psalmist, "My soul yearns and pines for the courts of the Lord," for His holy presence? If it is so that we treasure the Lord above all, then we shall be as "the sparrow [who] finds a home, and the swallow [who has] a nest in which she puts her young" – then we shall dwell happily in the house of God and He shall hear our prayers. For in truth the Lord Jesus has come to dwell among men on earth; the true Temple walks among us. No longer need we be separated from God or anxiously fear the loss of His presence. The temple walls and the traditions developed to protect us from uncertainty no longer must be clung to, for here are the temple walls in the flesh of Christ, and here is the cleansing we need in the shedding of His blood. And His Church now is alive in the Spirit of God and is moving everywhere. Let us enter its eternal walls and find true reverence there. In this place He shall answer all our prayers.

Wednesday

(1Kgs.10:1-10; Ps.37:5-6,30-31,39-40; Mk.7:14-23)

"The mouth of the just man tells of wisdom
and his tongue utters what is right."

Today in our readings we have a passage to illustrate the great extent of the wisdom and riches of King Solomon. "The queen of Sheba, having heard of Solomon's fame, [comes] to test him with subtle questions." She had not believed the report she'd heard of him, but having "witnessed Solomon's great wisdom" in the answers he gave to every one of her questions – "nothing remained hidden from him that he could not explain to her" – and having seen "the palace he had built" and all the amenities that surrounded him... "she was breathless." And rightly does this pagan queen attribute the blessings Solomon enjoys to the Lord, who "has made [him] king to carry out judgment and justice."

How true it is that the Lord blesses him who holds "the law of God in his heart." And rightly does David declare in our psalm that if we "commit to the Lord [our] way... He will make justice dawn for [us] like the light." We shall shine "bright as the noonday," bright as Solomon's temple, if we "trust in Him." If Solomon's servants were happy, how much happier should we be to "stand before [the Lord] always and listen to [*His*] wisdom." For having eaten at the table of such grace and glory, what could come from our mouths but the same? And what shall we be called then but wise men?

But the same mouth which utters wisdom may also utter evil. For though the good man from the treasure of his heart speaks only good, it is also so that "wicked designs come from the deep recesses of the heart" as well. Here one may find murderous plots and malicious intent. We shall find soon that Solomon's heart will change and that what "emerges from within" him will bear little likeness to wisdom. And so, should we not all heed the Lord's words of warning in our gospel today and take care what comes from within our hearts, that we ourselves are not rendered "impure"? Let the wisdom of the Lord and His holiness always issue forth from our hearts in all our words and actions. Then we shall know the blessings of the eternal King.

Thursday
(1Kgs.11:4-13; Ps.106:3-4,35-37,40; Mk.7:24-30)

"It is not right to take the food of the children
and throw it to the dogs."

Jesus speaks these words to a foreign woman, a pagan Greek, who "beg[s] Him to expel the demon from her daughter." They seem harsh. Some may interpret them so. After all, in our gospel we find Jesus traveling to the northernmost part of Israel where "He retired to a certain house and wanted no one to recognize Him." And here comes this foreign woman to beg at His table... Can He find no peace? But though the Lord may be weary, He is not angry. He but tells the truth: He has come for the lost sheep of Israel; it is only after He is gone that His followers will bring His salvation to the ends of the earth. First, "the sons of the household" must be fed. All in proper order. Notwithstanding this, the woman's great faith prevails upon the Lord – and probably greatly heartens Him – and her prayer is answered.

It is in the application of the quote to King Solomon that it becomes harsh, for is this not what David's son has done? Has he not taken the greatest of blessings the Lord has heaped upon or will heap upon any man, and turned them over to the devil? Solomon, the wisest and richest of all kings, "did evil in the sight of the Lord," and that unreservedly – and that without compunction. It is only for the sake of his father David that the Lord does not wrest all His gifts from him that very day. You say, "But didn't David sin greatly in committing adultery and murder?" Yes, the servant of the Lord did sin. But this king humbled himself ever before his God. He repented with a whole heart, and did not return again to his sin. Solomon recognizes no sin. Scripture says nowhere he is sorry; his repentance is lacking. And his sin is of the most grievous, the most deeply rooted kind: he turns to worship of other gods. In his reign and by his leadership, the people "sacrificed their sons and their daughters to demons," taking thus the very flesh and blood of the children of Israel and throwing it to the dogs.

For this "the Lord grew angry with His people, and abhorred His inheritance." For they perform abhorrent acts under him who had become a most abhorrent king. This king who had received six hundred and sixty-six gold talents a year in regular payment showed himself comfortable with the mark of the beast unto whom he had turned his heart. "His foreign wives who burned incense and sacrificed to their gods" he preferred to the love of the Lord; and so it is he who is cast from the Lord's presence.

397

Ordinary Time

Our psalm says of the Israelites, "They mingled with the nations and learned their works"; the great works of sin known in the darkness of this world became their own. But in our gospel it is a foreign woman who humbles herself before the True King. What of us, brothers and sisters? Where does our allegiance lie? For His Word does now travel to the ends of the earth; one can now no longer hide.

Friday
(1Kgs.11:29-32,12:19; Ps.81:9-15; Mk.7:31-37)

"My people heard not my voice,
and Israel obeyed me not;
so I gave them up to the hardness of their hearts."

The Lord has said, "There shall be no strange god among you nor shall you worship an alien god," but the people did not listen. Led by their corrupted king, "they walked according to their own counsels" and took to themselves the perverse gods worshiped by the nations of the world. And so it is that the prophet must remove his "new cloak" and tear it "into twelve pieces," one for each of the tribes of Israel. How sad that the great kingdom which had so recently been united and so greatly been blessed by peace round about under the reign of the wise Solomon, now is to be torn asunder. Only a remnant will be left to David, out of respect for the Lord's promise to him; and now, we are told: "Israel went into rebellion against David's house to this day."

"If only my people would hear me, and Israel walk in my ways..." The psalmist's words come as a lament for the deafness of the nation. If they would but listen and turn to Him, their amazement would go "beyond all bounds," as does that of the people who brought Jesus "a deaf man with a speech impediment and begged Him to lay His hand on him." They, too, would exclaim, "He has done everything well! He makes the deaf hear and the mute speak!" For Israel is this deaf man. All of us are this man impeded in his speech. All need desperately to turn to Him, to have Him pray over us – to seek the words of His lips. And so all will know the blessing that comes thereby: "At once the man's ears were opened; he was freed from the impediment, and began to speak plainly."

Hear the voice of the Lord, brothers and sisters. Listen to it in the deep recesses of your heart. This voice comes to heal, like light to the very drums upon which the vibrations beat. Such purity could be yours. Such grace could be known in *all* the world, healing the rifts that divide nations and peoples, if all would but come to Jesus in the same faith as this deaf man and his friends. And then would we speak plainly of what the Lord has done. No deceit upon our lips, we would declare Him Lord... and the amazement at the peace He brings would extend to the corners of the earth. Let your ears "be opened!" to His voice; with a soft heart turn to Jesus the Christ.

Saturday

(1Kgs.12:26-32,13:33-34; Ps.106:4,6-7,19-22; Mk.8:1-10)

"Whoever desired it was consecrated
and became a priest of the high places."

For this sin "the house of Jeroboam... was to be cut off and destroyed from the earth." Not only will their king be so punished, but the whole Israelite nation will find the wrath of the Lord for such idolatrous action. Not learning from their forefathers, whom the Lord had a mind to wipe entirely from His book of life and the promise He had given Abraham, again "they exchanged their glory for the image of a grass-eating bullock." Led by Jeroboam, who from selfish anxiety for the power the Lord had given him made two calves of gold and set them up for the people to worship – by the ministration of priests not chosen by God – they sinned grievously; as Solomon had done, they broke the most essential command to love God above all else. And this sin will stain the nation for perpetuity and lead in time to their exile.

Only those so ordained by God may serve at His temple. Only in the place He assigned is sacrifice and worship to be offered. And only He is to be worshiped and adored. No man, no king, can take any of this in his own hands. Trust in God and obedience to His will is necessary. All must go up to Jerusalem.

It is clear that our gospel today is a foreshadowing of the Mass, wherein Jesus' Body is the bread we eat. After teaching the people at length, the Lord desires to share with them food that will nourish them for their journey home. But the disciples had but seven loaves of bread. Yet in an action foretelling the consecration of the Holy Eucharist, "taking the seven loaves He gave thanks, broke them, and gave them to His disciples to distribute." And the leftovers of this miracle reach down to us this day; from "the seven wicker baskets" the disciples gathered after four thousand had eaten, we yet feed. And it is a wonderful paradox that the more we eat of the Lord's blessed Body, the more there is for others to share.

But this feast is not eaten under every green tree. None can build high places and make priests for themselves. Only those ordained by Christ distribute His bread. And so we must come up to the Church He has founded to receive Him, the Church within whose walls His sacred body rests each day. Only this Temple is our Jerusalem.

Sixth Week

Monday
(Jas.1:1-11; Ps.119:67-68,71-72,75-77; Mk.8:11-13)

"Count it pure joy when you are involved in every sort of trial."

How well James explicates the wisdom of the cross. First he encourages us to "realize that when [our] faith is tested this makes for endurance," and then to "let endurance come to its perfection so that [we] may be fully mature and lacking in nothing." This is the wisdom of our suffering on earth; this is the blessing of the cross.

It is the same wisdom our psalmist propounds when he sings, "It is good for me that I have been afflicted, that I may learn your statutes." If the Word of the Lord and the promise He offers is "more precious than thousands of gold and silver pieces" to us, then we must undergo many afflictions to prevent our going astray into the vain things of this world. For these flowers of the field droop and die under the scorching heat of the sun, but what is of the Lord lasts forever, and thus to join Him we must be trained to endure.

How different is the wisdom found in suffering beneath the cross; how different is this school from the one found in this world. The exact antithesis is our King to those who rule here in vainglorious power. For this King preaches death, and dies for us in humble poverty – this would be the shame of the one who finds his teaching in the seeking of riches and fame. And this is why the Pharisees cannot see Jesus and the sign He is before their eyes. Their minds are closed to the cross and its wisdom, for their hearts are set on the vain illusions of earthly life. But He is heavenly and all the sign we need; following in the shadow of His cross will lead us to all our hearts do seek.

Brothers and sisters, be not like the Pharisees, seeking some momentous occurrence to tantalize your eyes. The Word is within you, it is of you; and shouldering His cross you will find it growing all your life. Hold the wisdom of the cross, ask it in faith of the generous God who will give all to you, and find the beauty of His way as you are afflicted, and comforted again. The Lord chastises those whom He loves, and His love is pure joy, while those who would stray He leaves to die, following their sinful ways. Come to Him and His cross, and live.

Tuesday
(Jas.1:12-18; Ps.94:12-15,18-19; Mk.8:14-21)

"He wills to bring us to birth with a word spoken in truth."

But how deaf we are to His speaking.

The disciples exhibit a remarkable degree of ignorance in our gospel today. It would be comical were it not so usual, were it not such a defining trait of us humans. Preoccupied with their forgetfulness to bring bread for their journey, when the Lord mentions the word "yeast" in a chastising instruction, their minds go immediately to the bread they now lack by their negligence. Able to go no deeper than the surface of the words, and able not to see beyond their immediate concerns, they are as blind to the truth Jesus would teach them as so often we weak humans are. For those still struggling with the text at hand, Jesus is telling us that man does not live by bread alone but by every word that comes forth from the mouth of God. Has not the Lord shown this quite directly by feeding the thousands by virtue of a blessing spoken over a few loaves?

Our hearts should not be set on the bread of this world as are the Pharisees', whose yeast is a pride in self that rises to condemnation. It is pride that blinds us and concern for the body that produces ignorance. "Keep your eyes open!" the Lord commands. Do not let your minds be darkened by the cares of this world – the body is useless! It is the spirit that gives life. Open your hearts to the teaching of the Spirit, the great gift that Jesus imparts. "Happy the man whom you instruct, O Lord, whom by your law you teach," our psalmist sings, and so should all blessed to hear the Word of the Lord join his chorus.

James tells us in our first reading that God does not tempt us to sin. "Rather the tug and lure of his own passion tempts every man"; only "genuine benefit comes from above, descending from the Father of the heavenly luminaries." Do we seek His gifts that are worthwhile, or are our hearts fixed on things below? It may be hard to listen to His Word, to be brought to birth by His truth, but "happy the man who holds out to the end through trial!" "The crown of life awaits... those who love" the Lord, and He is near to sustain us as we climb.

Brothers and sisters, once the Spirit fell upon the apostles, no longer did they experience such ignorance. Is not the life-giving Word at work within us this very day? Then our eyes should be open to His light.

Wednesday
(Jas.1:19-27; Ps.15:1-5; Mk.8:22-26)

"Jesus laid hands on his eyes, and he saw perfectly."

What is it to see perfectly but to be as "the man who peers into freedom's ideal law and abides by it"? For to see perfectly is to see as God sees, not looking upon the surface of things – that which is reflected in a mirror – but to see the light of God reflected off the souls of His children. And not merely to speak of such things, but, as James states so forthrightly, to "act on this word," to let the Lord's light take "root in you"... to "humbly welcome the Word," and then to "put it into practice."

Does Jesus not put the word of God into practice in our gospel today? James says we should be "looking after orphans and widows in their distress," and Jesus shows this concern for the poor and needy by taking "the blind man's hand and [leading] him outside the village," there to anoint his eyes and grant him vision to "see everything clearly." With all His life Jesus gives example of how we must put flesh to the word of God, for He Himself is the Word made flesh. If we have not flesh to the laws we hold, to the teaching we receive, we have not Christ, and our faith is worthless. "He who walks blamelessly and does justice," he it is that is acceptable in God's sight.

"Can you see anything?" Jesus whispers to all of us as He works to illumine our vision. *Do you know my touch upon your eyes?* If we see people "like walking trees," He will touch us again, for He does not tire of serving our needs. And must we not be the same? Mustn't we never harm but always help our "fellow man"? Must we not be men as Jesus? He is the mirror in which we see ourselves.

And O to gaze into His face when we awake! O to even now know His flesh in our bones and His blood flowing through our veins! O to be a Christian! A Christian! A man living as Christ... What joy is ours as He gives light to our eyes and we see ourselves walking with Him! Let it be so for all eternity.

Thursday
(Jas.2:1-9; Ps.34:2-7; Mk.8:27-33)

"You are not judging by God's standards but by man's!"

This is a most important statement Jesus makes; it really cuts to the heart of His teaching, and to His sacrifice for our sins.

He has just finished asking His apostles, "Who do you say that I am?" and for perhaps the first time heard their belief that He is the Messiah. This is a critical moment. But there is no time to sit back and enjoy it, for "He then beg[ins] to teach them that the Son of Man ha[s] to suffer much, be rejected by the elders, the chief priests, and the scribes, be put to death, and rise three days later." He knows they will not understand. He knows they will not hear "rise three days later" but "suffer" and "death" and be appalled that the Son of God should be treated so. The sacrifice is here beyond their comprehension. And He knows, too, that Peter does not only speak for all when he declares Jesus the Messiah, but also when he "remonstrates with Him." And so the Lord turns around from where Peter had led Him privately, and makes a point of "eyeing the disciples"; for in His reprimand of Peter as a "satan," He reprimands them all. Their minds must be utterly changed; they must see things as God – they must look upon heaven and not earth.

James, of course, speaks of the same matter in his discourse condemning favoritism or the judging of others by appearance. For if we favor the rich man with the gold rings, we are showing our preference for the mark of the beast "who blaspheme[s] that noble name which has made us God's own." If we judge against the faith of the poor in favor of the wealth of the rich and powerful, what are we saying? That we desire the riches and power of this world and not the treasure God holds in store for us in heaven. We are indeed "as judges who hand down corrupt decisions," for we are nothing but false to the faith we profess.

Again we must ask ourselves what our hearts are set upon. The Lord's challenge to our souls is severe. Is it Satan's realm we prefer, or are we as "the lowly" of whom David sings, who find salvation in glorifying the Lord? It is a clear choice with which we are presented: to judge as God or to judge with the limited and ultimately deadly vision of man fallen under the sway of the devil. It is from just such judgment the Lord has come to release the apostles, and all His Church, in His Name.

O. 6. Fri. (II)

Friday
(Jas.2:14-24,26; Ps.112:1-6; Mk.8:34-9:1)

"Faith without works is as dead as a body without breath."

How dead indeed is a body without breath; how short a time we can go without breathing before dying. And so, how much our faith is dependent on works to remain alive.

Brothers and sisters, we are human, we have bodies – of the earth, of flesh and bone, we are. We are not angels. And having bodies we must use

403

what God gave us, what we are: it is in such action we prove the worth of
our salt. We cannot sit by idly while another suffers and call ourselves
Christian; we cannot prove our faith other than by actions. We must work
out our call. We must "take up [our] cross and follow in [Christ's] steps."
Sitting by the side of the road will get us nowhere. Just as Abraham showed
His belief in God by taking his son to be sacrificed, so must we move as the
Lord calls.

   And He calls us to service, He calls us to love. He calls us to lay down
our lives for the sake of others. And this not just in thoughts or words, but
in deeds. We must be as He who "dawns through the darkness, a light for
the upright" and conduct our "affairs with justice." If we are ashamed of
Jesus and the doctrine of the cross He preaches, if we hide our light under a
bushel basket afraid to speak or act in His name, He makes quite clear that
He will be "ashamed of [us] when He comes with the holy angels in the
Father's glory." Profession of faith alone is not sufficient to enter "the reign
of God established in power"; we must practice what is preached.

   Was not Jesus of flesh and bone? Did He not perform great works in
our midst? And does He not still perform great works through us His
Church; or are we now angels flying at heaven's gate? Flesh of His flesh
and bone of His bone we *must* be, or we are nothing worth. We eat His
body and drink His blood and shoulder His cross to find "the wealth and
riches [that] shall be in His house," that will live eternally.

   (It occurs to me that the quote could be reversed to be phrased more
literally: "Faith without works is dead as breath without a body," wandering
aimlessly; but it would not get across the dire need for works quite so
forcefully.)

O. 6. Sat. (II)

Saturday
(Jas.3:1-10; Ps.12:2-5,7-8; Mk.9:2-13)

"He hardly knew what to say,
for they were all overcome with awe."

O brothers and sisters, how like Peter we should be in the presence of
God and among one another. So conscious of the Lord's wondrous being in
our midst should we ever remain. Then we would not sin with our tongue,
but listen to His holy word instead. For our tongues are indeed "like a fire
[that] is enkindled by hell," but His words are "like tried silver, freed from
dross, sevenfold refined."

   In our first reading today, James presents clearly with strong analogy the
dangers of the tongue. Though "a small member" it serves to guide the rest
of our bodies like the bit in the mouth of a horse or the rudder of a ship.

And how difficult to control it is! "The tongue defiles the entire body" so easily. "It is a restless evil, full of deadly poison" which so soon infects our members. How shall we find the means to control it? Only by obedience to the Lord and silence in His presence.

"A cloud came, overshadowing them, and out of the cloud a voice: 'This is my Son, my beloved. Listen to Him.'" O the voice of God and the words of His Son! O how our ears and our hearts must be attuned to this Word, to this voice speaking to us! This is He; you are not He. Listen – do not speak. Know what "the Scriptures say of Him." He is the One. Only His words matter.

Notice, too, what Elijah and Moses do when they appear with the Lord: "the two were in conversation with Jesus." What holy speech this can only have been! And do we dare speak as they converse? And does not God converse with His Son and with His creation at all times? Does He not call to us in all sounds? And do we listen – are our ears open to His voice? Or are we too busy cursing men, men "made in the likeness of God"? Certainly, "this ought not to be, my brothers."

"May the Lord destroy all smooth lips, every boastful tongue, those who say, 'We are heroes with our tongues; our lips are our own, who is Lord over us?'" Only "if a person is without fault in speech [is he] a man in the fullest sense." Let your tongue be controlled and so your whole body. Let your thoughts be pure, then so will your actions be. But if you speak falsehood, you are inclined to damnation.

Be silent before the wonder of God. Let His Word steer your ship.

Seventh Week

Monday
(Jas.3:13-18; Ps.19:8-10,15; Mk.9:14-29)

"The command of the Lord is clear,
enlightening the eye."

What is the wisdom of which James speaks in our first reading but this enlightening of the eye and the mind by following the command of the Lord? It is the words and the wisdom of Jesus, reflected clearly in the Lord's own life, James relates to the waiting ear this day. What does he instruct but to practice "a humility filled with good sense" and to "cultivate peace," not to "nurse bitter jealousy in [our] hearts" but to "refrain from arrogant and false claims against the truth"? We must be as "innocent" as the Lamb of God, and as forgiving. Then we will realize that "the decree of

405

the Lord is trustworthy, giving wisdom to the simple," for "wisdom from above" will then fill us, and lead us by its sacred light.

How clear the command of the Lord is in our gospel, and how powerfully it enlightens the eye. As He comes down from the mountain where He has been transfigured before His principal apostles, "a large crowd... on catching sight of Jesus" is immediately "overcome with awe. They [run] up to greet Him." Being presented with the boy possessed by a spirit that often "throws him into the fire and into water," Jesus "reprimand[s] the unclean spirit by saying to him, 'Mute and deaf spirit, I command you: Get out of him and never enter him again!'" And the boy is healed; he is freed from bondage to the devil, and now in his right mind, he can see.

Though perhaps not always so dramatic, every command of the Lord casts out just such darkness which pervades our souls. Coming in faith before Him as the father who trusts in God and in His Son, the same healing do we know. Following His words, our eyes and ears are opened, too, and we discover that indeed "the law of the Lord is perfect, refreshing the soul." So, brothers and sisters, let us pray with David today: "Let the words of my mouth and the thought of my heart find favor before you, O Lord, my rock and my redeemer," that we might remain ever in His enduring purity and light.

O. 7. Tues. (II)

Tuesday
(Jas.4:1-10; Ps.55:7-11,23; Mk.9:30-37)

"In the city I see violence and strife;
day and night they prowl about upon its walls."

The violence this world holds is known most poignantly, of course, in "the Son of Man... [being] delivered into the hands of men who... put Him to death," but exists most pervasively and fundamentally in our own bodies, insofar as they are conformed to the spirit of the world. For as James asks so pointedly, "Where do the conflicts and disputes among you originate? Is it not your inner cravings that make war within your members?" It is indeed the evil desire in our bones, the "envy," the "love of the world [that] is enmity to God" which causes us to "quarrel and fight," which is the source of all sin, and so death, and so war.

That "the spirit He has implanted in us tends toward jealousy" is evident even in the apostles, whom we find in today's gospel "arguing about who was the most important." Even these, who have yet to receive the "greater gift" – the Holy Spirit of God who serves to cleanse His children of the evil

406

in them – even these are divided by the cravings that make war in our members. Even these contribute to the crucifixion of Christ.

Brothers and sisters, if you would "find shelter from the violent storm and the tempest" at work in you and about you, you must "cast your care upon the Lord, and He will support you." "Submit to God; resist the devil and he will take flight." "Purify your hearts" of all that is not in conformity with the Spirit of God and you will find safe haven from the violence of this world and the violence of your own hearts. For "never will He permit the just man to be disturbed."

And both James and the Lord teach what it is to be just, what it is to excel before God. If you desire the goodness of the Lord, rend your hearts; "be humbled in the sight of God and He will raise you on high." You cannot raise yourself, for you are but dust; and dust you must be if you desire holiness in the presence of the Most High: "If anyone wishes to rank first, he must remain the last one of all and the servant of all," as is Jesus, the suffering Son crucified for the sins of each of us.

Brothers and sisters, let our hearts be so docile as to welcome His children openly – as His humble children we ourselves must be. For then we shall welcome Him; for then we shall be sons of the Father, free from sin and so no longer subject to the violence known in the city that is this world of sin. May our own members and all the members of the Church be cleansed of all strife by the power of the Holy Spirit.

O. 7. Wed. (II)

Wednesday
(Jas. 4:13-17; Ps.49:2-3,6-11,Mt.5:3; Mk.9:38-40)

"Anyone who is not against us is with us."

And whoever is not with the Lord is against Him. There are only two ways by which a man may walk. We choose to place our lives in the hands of God, or we worship the things of this earth.

Indeed, anyone who "perform[s] a miracle in [His] name" is with Him, for a tree is known by its fruit. If indeed we commend our lives into the care of the Lord, saying, "If the Lord wills it, we shall live to do this or that," then we shall find His blessing at work within us, and we shall be His children, doing His will. And demons shall be expelled at our words. And we shall never "fear in evil days when [our] wicked ensnarers ring [us] round."

But if instead we "make arrogant and pretentious claims," boasting reprehensibly of the profits this earth shall bring us by the power of our own hands, we are in utter danger of the destruction we think can never touch us. For "in no way can a man redeem himself, or pay his own ransom to God."

If we "have no idea what kind of life will be [ours] tomorrow" – and who knows the turns this earth does take? – what can we do at all by our own will? We are, in fact, utterly dependent upon God for each breath we draw, and He may withdraw such life from us at any moment.

What fool is there among you who "trust[s] in [his] wealth"? Who are they for whom "the abundance of their riches is their boast"? Have you no eyes in your head? Is there no sense in your mind? "Hearken, all who dwell in the world, of lowly birth or high degree, rich and poor alike," and from all lands and of all times – it is in Jesus alone that you find strength to draw your next breath; it is He alone who brings light to your eyes. Your riches will rot. Even prophecies will cease. There will not be a stone here left upon another. Consecrate yourself now to the Lord of all and begin to find His grace at work within you. And each day renew the power of God at work in you for that day. In His name do all things, and you shall be with Him, and He shall not leave you.

O. 7. Thurs. (II)

Thursday
(Jas.5:1-6; Ps.49:14-20,Mt.5:3; Mk.9:41-50)

"You lived in wanton luxury on the earth;
you fattened yourselves for the day of slaughter."

"You rich, weep and wail over your impending miseries," James warns all those who trust in their wealth. For though they were "contented with their lot," to find which they "condemned, even killed, the just man," yet "like sheep they are herded into the nether world," where "quickly their form is consumed." "Your wealth has rotted, your fine wardrobe has grown moth-eaten, your silver and gold have corroded" – all these things in which the fool has trusted will not only die of themselves but also "devour [his] flesh like a fire," for so greatly has he placed his heart upon them that with their destruction he is also destroyed.

"See what you have stored up for yourselves against the last days." The rich man fattens himself for "Gehenna, where 'the worm dies not and the fire is never extinguished.'" Thus does Jesus call us to repentance in such severe terms, for lacking of it indeed how "quickly [our] form is consumed." It is not the body which matters, or this earth; heaven is all that matters, and so our souls. Therefore, it is indeed better to cut off hand or foot or tear out one's eye than to "enter Gehenna with its unquenchable fire." For what are these things, what are all the riches of the world, in comparison with the kingdom of God and its eternal riches? Do not, therefore, be led astray by your earthly passions; store up treasures for heaven.

"The shouts of the harvesters have reached the ears of the Lord of hosts." "The wages you withheld from the farmhands who harvested your fields" are known to God. And as "it would be better if anyone who leads astray one of these simple believers were to be plunged in the sea with a great millstone fastened around his neck," so much better would be your fate than to suffer eternally the fires of hell. For what shall your unjust wealth benefit you there? From whom shall you steal among your fellow prisoners in chains?

"The nether world is their palace," those who grow rich on the backs of the poor and oppressed of this world. For ultimately "death is their shepherd, and the upright rule over them." They "shall never more see light"; but peace shall reign in the hearts of all God's children.

Friday
(Jas.5:9-12; Ps.103:1-4,8-9,11-12; Mk.10:1-12)

"Merciful and gracious is the Lord,
slow to anger and abounding in kindness."

And we must be like Him.

James makes clear that we must "not grumble against one another, nor swear an oath, any oath at all," but rather simply speak "in the name of the Lord": "Let it be 'yes' if you mean yes or 'no' if you mean no. In this way you will not incur condemnation." And as a sign of the endurance we must have to find the Lord's blessing, he reminds us of "the steadfastness of Job" and "what the Lord, who is compassionate and merciful, did in the end."

"As your models in suffering hardships and in patience, brothers, take the prophets." And, of course, Jesus is the fulfillment of the prophets, and His suffering in silent servitude the sentence of crucifixion is the fulfillment of their endurance of persecution. And in our gospel today, does He not give example of the patience we all must hold and the clarity with which we all must speak? For when the Pharisees "ask Jesus whether it was permissible for a husband to divorce his wife," how do they intend their question but "as a test"? But the Lord does not take offense at their temptation; He simply answers them, clearly and to the point: "At the beginning of creation God made them male and female; for this reason a man shall leave his father and mother and the two shall become as one." And lest there be any doubt that He is saying no to divorce, He continues, "They are no longer two but one flesh. Therefore, let no man separate what God has joined." And even when "the disciples beg[i]n to question Him about this" again later, He remains patient and gives direct answer: "Whoever divorces his wife and marries another commits adultery."

The question would seem a simple one and the answer easy to understand, but is it not this question that is at the heart of man's disobedience, of his grumbling against God? Is it not this answer man seeks most to change, thus leading to his greatest sins, and really to the destruction of society? Yet the Lord's love is greater than our profligacy, and as the father so readily forgave the prodigal son, so He waits for us to turn to Him – to His presence, to His truth. As David sings of God: "He redeems your life from destruction, He crowns you with kindness and compassion"; and so He longs to "put our transgressions from us" "as far as the east is from the west." Indeed Jesus "pardons all [our] iniquities, He heals all our ills" – for this has the Savior come. And if we but bless Him for "all His benefits" and share in His love in our relationships with others, we shall find the merciful Lord enabling our endurance of all on this earth and making firm our place with Him in heaven.

O. 7. Sat. (II)

Saturday
(Jas.5:13-20; Ps.141:1-3,8; Mk.10:13-16)

"Let my prayer come like incense before you;
the lifting up of my hands, like the evening sacrifice."

"The fervent petition of a holy man is powerful indeed." For indeed Elijah "prayed earnestly" and "no rain fell on the land for three years and six months." Then "when he prayed again, the sky burst forth with rain." And now greater things are accomplished by prayer, especially of "the elders of the Church," our priests, who, in union with Jesus the Lord, "reclaim the one who is ill" and bring "forgiveness" to the sinful soul. Redemption itself is at our hands through the Anointing of the Sick and Confession, and all the other blessed sacraments. And prayer by all souls is a constant guard and reclaimer of lives gone astray.

And in our gospel it is made clear what our disposition should be when we pray, when we come to Jesus. The Lord encourages the little children to come to Him and states unequivocally: "Whoever does not accept the kingdom of God like a little child shall not enter into it." We must always come to Him as children – with faith, in innocence, of truth – if we hope to gain a hearing in His sight, brothers and sisters. If when we call upon Him we do not have the pure faith of a child, how can we expect to communicate with Him who dwells in absolute light? If our prayer and our song fall short of the love and joy of innocent praise, then we fall short of reaching Him. But if in such innocence and with such faith and of such truth we come to Him, know that He will treat us just as the children who come to Him today: "He embraced them and blessed them, placing His hands on them." Yes, then His holy hand will be upon our lives, and His great power we will find at work within us and through us.

> "Toward you, O Lord, my eyes are turned."
> Please "hearken to my voice when I call upon you."
> "In you I take refuge; strip me not of life,"
> but make me as your child of light.

Our prayer comes like incense before the Lord when it is united with the sacrifice of the Son. Anointed by the Lamb's blood, all our cries rise unto the Father of Life.

Eighth Week

Monday
(1Pt.1:3-9; Ps.111:1-2,5-6,9-10; Mk.10:17-27)

> "Go and sell what you have and give to the poor;
> you will then have treasure in heaven."

"You may for a time have to suffer the distress of many trials," for even if you are not a rich man with "many possessions" to give up, all that you have that is of the world must die before you will find "birth to an imperishable inheritance incapable of fading or defilement, which is kept in heaven for you." You can have no pride, you can have no greed, you can have no lust in your heart if you are to find the kingdom of God. Your faith must be like "fire-tried gold" whose "genuineness [will] lead to praise, glory and honor when Jesus Christ appears."

Jesus' question to the rich young man: "Why do you call me good? No one is good but God alone" is, I think, often misunderstood. The Lord is not saying not to call Him good because that title is reserved only for God, for He *is* God and deserves every title of praise we can utter. Rather, He is testing the young man, who kneels at this moment at His feet, to find out if he truly recognizes that He is "good", that He is the Son of God.

This is borne out by the Lord's response as to what the young man should do "to share in everlasting life." Jesus first lists only the latter commandments, which refer to love of neighbor, which the young man rightfully states he has kept well. "Then Jesus looked at him with love and told him," in essence, of his need to keep the first three commandments, those which refer to love of God, in a more complete fashion. For what is He telling him in our quote above but to have no false gods, to love the Lord with heart, mind, soul, and strength – and how is this accomplished but in

Ordinary Time

His instruction: "Come and follow me"? As we give up the idols which spring from the earth, as all our possessions and our trust in them are taken from us, we find the "birth unto hope which draws its life from the resurrection of Jesus Christ from the dead." By such death we follow Him unto heaven.

Brothers and sisters, "there is cause for rejoicing here," for on this strait path, through this "needle's eye," we are "achieving faith's goal, [our] salvation." Let us "give thanks to the Lord with all [our] heart in the company and assembly of the just." Let us "rejoice with inexpressible joy touched with glory" because God "has sent deliverance to His people; He has ratified His covenant forever." And "He will ever be mindful of His covenant" – always He will be at our side by the grace of Jesus Christ and the power of the Holy Spirit to lead us to the "salvation which stands ready to be revealed in the last days." Endure now the sadness and distress of the death of this life, and find therein the fulfilling of your hope for the treasures of heaven.

O. 8. Tues. (II)

Tuesday
(1Pt.1:10-16; Ps.98:1-4; Mk.10:28-31)

"Set all your hope on the gift to be conferred on you
when Jesus Christ appears."

"The Lord has made His salvation known: in the sight of the nations He has revealed His justice." That "which the prophets carefully searched out and examined" but was hidden from their eyes, that into which "angels long to search" is now indeed made known "by those who preach the Gospel to you, in the power of the Holy Spirit sent from heaven." Yes, "the divine favor which was destined to be [ours]," "the sufferings destined for Christ and the glories that would follow" spoken of in all Scripture by the Spirit of Christ, are now come into our midst; and it is these we wait to see fulfilled.

And as we await our salvation we must "become holy... after the likeness of the holy one who called" us. As we stay, we must share in His sufferings to find His glory. "Obedient sons" of the one Father, we must pattern ourselves after His only Son. "The desires that once shaped [us] in [our] ignorance" must be absolutely abandoned as we become holy as He.

And the same Peter who instructs us in the salvation prepared for us from all ages and the holiness which alone befits it, exclaims to Jesus in our gospel today, "We have put aside everything to follow you!" as if to plead, "Have we done enough?" And the Lord assures him all that he gives up for the kingdom's sake shall return to him a hundredfold, and "in the age to come" he shall have "everlasting life." For indeed, as the Lord has been, so

412

the apostles have followed, and in these same steps we must walk – to this same cross we must come.

Here we stand at the end of salvation history, as the last in a long line of the children of God. But first we can be, with the Spirit as our guide and conformed to the sufferings of Christ. Being at the end of this line we have the benefit of all the prophecy and teaching that has prepared this time; greater fullness of truth is ours than at any time before. And so, more so are we called to be like our Savior; impossible is it become for us to hide in ignorance. "All the ends of the earth have seen the salvation by our God," the light of Christ has been cast upon all hearts, and to continue in sin becomes yet a greater torture – for our eyes are so much less blind. Now must the earth become obedient to His voice, calling so clearly in its soul; condemnation awaits otherwise. Now the simple word of truth spoken by God at the heart of Scripture must be our sure guide: "Be holy, for I am holy," and our expectations will soon be fulfilled in Him.

Wednesday
(1Pt.1:18-25; Ps.147:12-15,19-20; Mk.10:32-45)

"The Son of Man has not come to be served but to serve –
to give His life in ransom for the many."

As Jesus and His apostles make their "way up to Jerusalem, where the Son of Man will be handed over to the chief priests and scribes," He tells them that these elders of the people "will condemn Him to death and hand Him over to the Gentiles, who will mock Him and spit at Him, flog Him, and finally kill Him." He then adds, "But three days later He will rise." Here is the Gospel in short. Here is "the living and enduring Word of God," the "indestructible seed" which brings us to life by our "faith and hope" centered upon it. Yes, "by Christ's blood" we "were delivered from the futile way of life" that sin wrought in us; this blood is "the blood of a spotless, unblemished Lamb chosen before the world's foundation and revealed for [our] sake in these last days." Christ has died, Christ is risen, and in Him we come to life again.

And we must "drink the cup" He drinks; we must "be baptized in the same bath of pain." There is no other way to His glory. Our lives on this earth must be joined in sacrifice with Him. Never are we to "lord it over" others; but always we "must serve the rest." So Jesus instructs His apostles in this most weighty moment filled with "wonderment" and "fear," as He stands at the precipice of His sacrifice. And Peter tells us the same when He counsels us to "love one another constantly from the heart." Jesus' blood is the greatest love and it is in this river we must swim; in this ocean we shall be cleansed – "by obedience to the truth you have purified yourselves for a genuine love of your brother," the Lord's principal apostle declares to all his faithful readers.

"He has proclaimed His word to Jacob, His statutes and ordinances to Israel," and all these are summed up in the blood of the Lamb of God. "Swiftly runs His word" to all who seek redemption from God; swiftly it comes to pierce our hearts. And though by it we ourselves bleed with Him, by it "He has granted peace in [our] borders" – through Jesus we are "believers in... the God who raised Him from the dead and gave Him glory," and His same glory is ours as we die with Him now. Let this Word be inscribed upon your heart.

O. 8. Thurs. (II)

Thursday
(1Pt.2:2-5,9-12; Ps.100:2-5; Mk.10:46-52)

"Be as eager for milk as newborn babies –
pure milk of the Spirit to make you grow unto salvation."

Does not the "blind beggar Bartimaeus" show his eagerness for the milk of the Spirit, for the blood of Christ upon his soul, when he persistently calls out "Jesus, Son of David, have pity on me!" despite those who "were scolding him to make him keep quiet"? And was his ready desire to meet with the Lord not revealed most clearly when "he threw aside his cloak, jumped up and came to Jesus." All else becomes as nothing as even in his blindness he strains forward to find the Lord.

Brothers and sisters, should we not "come to Him, a living stone, rejected by men but approved, nonetheless, and precious in God's eyes," just as this beggar? Are we not "'a chosen race, a royal priesthood, a consecrated nation, a people He claims for His own to proclaim the glorious works' of the One who called [us] from darkness into His marvelous light"? Is it not so that "once [we] were no people, but now [we] are God's people"? Once we were blind as Bartimaeus, without mercy for our souls, "but now [we] have found mercy." And O how we should treasure such grace – even as a newborn child treasures its milk.

Who better than Peter, our high priest, to let us know that we "too are living stones, built as an edifice of spirit, into a holy priesthood, offering spiritual sacrifices acceptable to God through Jesus Christ"? Having been cured of our own blindness, having been purged of our "carnal desires," we join this blessed Rock of the Church at the altar on high, sharing in the sacrifice of our Risen Christ. Should this thought not cause us to "serve the Lord with gladness"? Should it not make us ever eager to serve Him more, to draw ever closer to Him as He passes by? Is it not our desire to be with Him forever?

"Get up! He is calling you!" Do not be afraid for "He made us" and we are "the flock He tends." The gentle Lord desires nothing more than to heal your troubled soul. See that you now "follow Him up the road" in joy, growing daily in the new life and light of the Spirit of God.

Friday
(1Pt.4:7-13; Ps.96:10-13; Mk.11:11-26)

"The consummation of all is close at hand.
Therefore, do not be perturbed;
remain calm so that you will be able to pray."

As at the time Jesus walks the earth the end of the Israelite nation is at hand – a consummation signified in "the fig tree withered to its roots" at His command, a consummation that will be fulfilled in the crucifixion of the Messiah but whose coming is already evident in the fact that the temple has been turned into "a den of thieves" – so at the time of Peter's writing, that end is about to be realized in the destruction of the temple. And more than this, the "trial by fire" occurring in the midst of the disciples refers greatly to the death of this world we face in becoming Christians, to the persecution faced by all His children and felt most genuinely at the hands of the Romans.

But as all around is cast into the sea at the command of the Lord, we should not fear. This is the time to "put [our] trust in God," to pray in faith, to put [our] gifts at the service of one another" and "let [our] love for one another be constant." Rather than be sad, we must "rejoice instead, insofar as [we] share Christ's sufferings." For it should be our joy to see the temple cleansed, to have our hearts purified of all that is not holy – to witness the power of the hand of God at work. "For He governs the peoples with equity" as "He comes to rule the earth," so indeed "the heavens [should] be glad and the earth rejoice."

"In all of you God is to be glorified through Jesus Christ." His "house is to be called a house of prayer for all peoples." We are His House now; we hold His promise – and we come to His glory as we share in the trials He has known. If the end is close at hand, if the world is already dead, if the devil's illusions are about to fade... what can this bring us but joy to know the Truth is about to be revealed and all His faithful ones are about to be gathered into His kingdom? Remain steadfast in love and prayer, and "a multitude of sins" shall indeed be covered; and the new life which has

415

sprung from the withered roots of the fig tree shall soon be fulfilled in your sight.

Saturday
(Jd.17,20-25; Ps.63:2-6; Mk.11:27-33)

"Welcome the mercy of our Lord Jesus Christ
which leads to eternal life."

"As [Jesus] was walking in the temple precincts the chief priests, the scribes, and the elders approached Him." They come to Him who is the true Temple here in the place where He teaches, but they do not come "praying in the Holy Spirit" or "persever[ing] in God's love." Their questions rather are those which hold condemnation. If they had come seeking truth, they would be able to speak truth when asked by Him of John's baptism. But, far from seeking the grace of God, they desire only political advantage. And so they think among themselves, "If we say..." and "Can we say..." instead of simply baring their souls before Him who could save them. And so, answering, "We do not know," indeed do they close themselves off from knowledge of the "authority" and "power" given to Jesus the Christ.

This cannot be our faith, brothers and sisters. Our faith must be as that sung of so beautifully by David in our psalm today: "O God, you are my God whom I seek; for you my flesh pines and my soul thirsts like the earth, parched, lifeless and without water." With all our beings we must strive to know Him whom our soul loves. Knowing our own emptiness apart from Him who is Truth, we indeed turn our "[gaze] toward [Him] in the sanctuary," we indeed long for His love and mercy. And instead of speaking ill against Him or looking to condemn Him, rather we bless Him with all our souls, singing with His servant David: "Lifting up my hands, I will call upon your name... and with exultant lips my mouth shall praise you."

The baptism of John was divine and Jesus is its divine fulfillment. He is the "One who can protect [us] from a fall and make [us] stand unblemished and exultant in the presence of His glory" if we but say, "Glory be to this only God our Savior, through Jesus Christ our Lord." His indeed are "majesty" and "might"; He indeed "correct[s] those who are confused" and "snatch[es] others from the fire." He has rescued us from sin and poured the water of the Holy Spirit upon us to slake our thirst for Him. And so, "as with the riches of a banquet shall [our] soul be satisfied." By the mercy of our Lord Jesus Christ, heaven is now ours.

416

Ninth Week

Monday
(2Pt.1:2-7; Ps.91:1-2,14-16; Mk.12:1-12)

"I will deliver him and glorify him;
with length of life I will gratify him
and will show him my salvation."

So the Lord speaks of us through prophecy of His only Son. So the Lord seeks to accomplish in everyone who "acknowledges [His] name." So indeed He has sent "the Son whom He loved" for our salvation. So He prays with Peter, the Rock of His Church, "May grace be yours and peace in abundance through your knowledge of God and of Jesus, our Lord." For "by His own glory and power... He has bestowed on us the great and precious things He promised, so that through these [we] who have fled a world corrupted by lust might become sharers of the divine nature."

Brothers and sisters, "that divine power of His has freely bestowed on us everything necessary for a life of genuine piety through knowledge of Him." He has come into this world, He has entered the vineyard despite the threat of death, and has indeed been "beat[en]," "treated shamefully," and "killed," all that He might found His Church among us; and His grace is for us "marvelous to behold." Should we not then "make every effort" to employ the gifts He provides by the Holy Spirit and the Church He has made? Should gift not build upon gift so that in this house of ours we grow from the foundation of faith unto the divine love of all?

Let us not be like those tenant farmers who acted out of jealousy, who could only say of the Son: "Here is the one who will inherit everything. Come, let us kill Him, and the inheritance will be ours." For the Lord has indeed "come and destroy[ed]" these faithless servants "and turn[ed] His vineyard over to others." We are those others. And we "inherit everything" with the Son if we "say to the Lord, 'My refuge and my fortress, my God, in whom I trust.'" Yes, brothers and sisters, it is we who "dwell in the shelter of the Most High, who abide in the shadow of the Almighty." Let us be most conscientious in our work in His name; let us be ever ready to provide Him "His share of produce from the vineyard." For the vineyard is all His, and we are all His, and He is with all of us and with all we do and are – and He will deliver us and glorify us in the eternal life to which He has come to lead us. In His Son is our salvation.

Tuesday
(2Pt.3:12-15,17-18; Ps.90:2-4,10,14,16; Mk.12:13-17)

"Give to Caesar what is Caesar's
but give to God what is God's."

"Some Pharisees and Herodians were sent after Jesus to catch Him in His speech." These "two groups" seem to come one from God and the other from Caesar. But their devious plotting shows the only party present of God is Jesus Himself.

And to whom do we belong? Peter makes it abundantly clear in his letter today where our allegiance should lie. He exhorts us to "look for the coming of the day of God and try to hasten it!" We must not set our hearts on things below but on things above, where God dwells; for "the heavens will be destroyed in flames and the elements will melt away in a blaze." It is "new heavens and a new earth" we must await, where "the justice of God will reside."

What is of Caesar will return to the earth, just as God "turn[s] man back to dust, saying, 'Return, O children of men.'" (For where is Caesar today? And where is the coin that was in their hands?) But the Lord is "from everlasting to everlasting"; "a thousand years in [His] sight are as yesterday... or as a watch of the night." For He exists "before the mountains were begotten and the earth and the world were brought forth." These indeed He created; and these are destroyed by His hand.

Brothers and sisters, as our years "pass quickly and we drift away," let us listen to Jesus, who indeed "teach[es] God's way of life sincerely." Let us listen to His servant Peter, who tells us, "Be on your guard lest you be led astray by the error of the wicked." The wicked surround us here on this earth, but even here our hearts must be set on God and we must "be found without stain or defilement, and at peace in His sight." Here we must pray that the Lord will "fill us at daybreak with [His] kindness," that when He comes we shall know His glory... but also that even in these decaying earthen vessels we shall find His grace and see His work accomplished. "Glory be to Him now and to the day of eternity!" May He make us His own.

Wednesday
(2Tm.1:1-3,6-12; Ps.123:1-2; Mk.12:18-27)

"He has robbed death of its power
and has brought life and immortality into clear light
through the Gospel."

It is this Gospel which Paul exhorts his "dear child" Timothy to serve, to preach and to teach "with the strength which comes from God, bear[ing] [his] share of the hardship which the Gospel entails." Paul has suffered for the sake of the Gospel – and suffers "present hardships" till the end – and he would see his favored disciple carry on in his way. And so he encourages him: "The Spirit God has given us is no cowardly spirit but rather one that makes us strong, loving, and wise." For of the life Christ brings, the world must know, and who shall preach it if we don't? And so, through his letter Paul calls us all to be as he is, "an apostle of Christ Jesus sent to proclaim the promise of life in Him."

Does Jesus not bear well His hardships today in our gospel? Does He not stand strong and speak of life everlasting even before those who "hold there is no resurrection"? The Sadducees question Him: "At the resurrection, when they all come back to life, whose wife will she be" – she who has married so many? Again a trap is laid, and again it is shown so futile, for what word can stand before the word of God? And that Word answers simply and directly: "When people rise from the dead, they neither marry nor are given in marriage but live like angels in heaven." These Sadducees "fail to understand Scripture or the power of God," and so they are terribly blind in their mistaken thinking, which sees nothing beyond the present time. (Yet the present, too, they do not understand, for they do not recognize Him who stands before them.)

Brothers and sisters, we are called to live like the angels of heaven, and not only to live as such, but to preach this life as our Savior has done, as Paul has done, as Timothy. We must keep "our eyes on the Lord, our God," "confident that He is able to guard what has been entrusted to [us] until that Day" when we join Him who is "enthroned in heaven." And so let us "stir into flame the gift of God"; let us speak His Word of life without fear for the hardships the Gospel entails. The Light that lasts forever has come into our midst, and before Him death has no dominion.

419

Thursday

(2Tm.2:8-15; Ps.25:4-5,8-10,14; Mk.12:28-34)

"Guide me in your truth and teach me,
for you are God my Savior."

Brothers and sisters, "Remember that Jesus Christ, a descendant of David, was raised from the dead." He is our Lord. He is our God. He is our Savior who speaks only truth. Listen to Him and walk in His way, "following a straight course in preaching the truth."

After Jesus proclaims the greatest of all commandments today, finally, "no one ha[s] the courage to ask Him any more questions." Finally the traps cease to be set to catch Jesus in His speech and the leaders of the people "stop disputing about mere words." For who can argue with the Son of God when He makes known the clear path to God, when He exposes the heart of the law and the prophets in absolute terms? Only silence can follow such Truth. No vain utterance can stand in the face of such Love.

For the command is love, and Jesus is love – and this Paul has come to preach, "even to the point of being thrown into chains." His only concern is for "those whom God has chosen, in order that they may obtain the salvation to be found in Christ Jesus." For this he preaches the Gospel unto death, that all might hear and know of the love of God... and should we not join him? Should the Church not be a speaker of the truth in love, "a workman who has no cause to be ashamed"? Should she cower to declare Christ Jesus risen from the dead and fear offending those on the path to destruction? Should she stand by idly as false gospels are preached and docile lambs are led to the teeth of wolves in sheep's clothing? Does she not care for the flock as does Paul, as does Paul exhort Timothy? Should it not be she who "guides the humble to justice" and "teaches the humble His way"?

Brothers and sisters, "there is no chaining the word of God!" and there is no place for falsehood to stand in its light. God is love and we must love others. We do not love by nodding as others fall into error – this is not our call in the Lord. We must teach the truth with Jesus our Lord with "heart," "mind," "soul," and "strength," His Spirit of love and truth upon us. Then will all lies fall silent. Then will light shine. Then will His love be known and all come to the "eternal glory" He holds.

420

Friday

(2Tm.3:10-17; Ps.119:157,160-161,165-166,168; Mk.12:35-37)

"Princes persecute me without cause
but my heart stands in awe of your word."

The Word of God and persecution are our topics for today. On the one hand, Paul tells Timothy, "All Scripture is inspired of God and is useful for teaching," and Jesus uses a passage of Scripture (Psalm 110) to refute His persecutors and verify that the Son of God, the Word of God made flesh, is indeed greater than David – being David's Son insofar as the flesh is concerned, but truly begotten of God the Father and one with Him from all eternity. And on the other hand, Paul states categorically, "Anyone who wants to live a godly life in Christ Jesus can expect to be persecuted," and our psalmist sings, "My persecutors and my foes are many." But these two hands become one hand, working in the one Body of Christ, revealed in the passage Jesus quotes: "The Lord said to my Lord, Sit at my right hand until I make your enemies your footstool." For by the power of the Word of God in Scripture and made flesh in Christ we His children conquer with Him all our enemies… these persecutors become as so much empty wind.

Brothers and sisters, never lose awe for the Word of God spoken in Holy Scripture. Be like Timothy who "from [his] infancy" knew "the sacred Scriptures, the source of the wisdom which through faith in Jesus Christ leads to salvation." Treasure this gift at our hands, "inspired by the Holy Spirit" as it is for our instruction. And I pray your teachers will always be as Paul, so faithful to the Lord in knowing His Word and living it with "resolution, fidelity, patience, love, and endurance, through persecutions and sufferings." Then your path will be straight on the way to God; then will your hearts and minds be filled with light. There are many "evil men and charlatans" about who, "deceived themselves" and "deceiving others," fail to drink of the undrainable waters of Scripture, and who avoid the Lord's cross at all costs… listen not to these.

"I turn not away from your decrees," our psalmist declares, and so he finds "great peace" despite any trial. Brothers and sisters, for us who love the Lord and are like the crowd in today's gospel who "heard [His words] with great delight," "there is no stumbling block." All our persecutions but add to our ever increasing knowledge of our Savior, drawing us ever closer to the kingdom of God, where Jesus reigns forever.

Saturday

(2Tm.4:1-8; Ps.71:8-9,14-17,22; Mk.12:38-44)

"Put up with hardship, perform your work as an evangelist,
fulfill your ministry."

In final words to his blessed disciple, Paul exhorts Timothy with all the strength he is able to muster "to preach the word, to stay with this task whether convenient or inconvenient – correcting, reproving, appealing – constantly teaching and never losing patience." He even invokes "the presence of God and of Christ Jesus, who is coming to judge the living and the dead," to emphasize the seriousness of his charge. Clearly the end approaches for Paul. He himself states: "The time of my dissolution is near" – and so it is with great urgency he desires his preaching task to go forth, for Timothy's own sake, that he might share the "merited crown" that awaits his father in the faith, and for all who look "for [the Lord's] appearing with eager longing."

Paul sees as he draws nigh to the Day of the Lord what has perhaps never been known so clearly as today, that "the time will come when people will not tolerate sound doctrine, but, following their own desires, will surround themselves with teachers who tickle their ears." He prophesies so well what is true of every age but is magnified so greatly in the dark time in which we live: "They will stop listening to the truth and will wander off to fables." More have died in war in the last century than in all the rest of human history; and the martyrs' blood has never mounted as high to heaven as in this atheistic age wherein all hearts turn away from true doctrine to enshrine the workings of their own hands and minds. (May the smoke of Satan be blown from the confines of the Church and the devil's veil of illusion be lifted from all minds!)

But we must not be as the scribes "who like to parade around in their robes and accept marks of respect in public, front seats in the synagogues, and places of honor at banquets." The prideful adulation that sparks the unholy fire of the cults so prevalent in our glamorous time is not what must call to our hearts or be the leaven for our souls. We must but praise the Lord! With our psalmist we must sing to our Lord and our God, "the Holy One of Israel": "My mouth shall be filled with your praise, with your glory day by day." We must "give [Him] thanks with music on the lyre," with our body's every fiber.

Brothers and sisters, we must "always hope and praise [God] ever more and more." Ever we are called to draw closer to the Lord. We have not yet been as the widow who "gave from her want, all that she had to live on"; we have not yet been "poured out like a libation" as has Paul; we have not yet shed blood with Jesus on the cross. We cannot yet say, "I have fought the good fight, I have finished the race, I have kept the faith"; for there is much race yet to be run, and to the end our faith must endure and grow ever stronger day to day. Indeed our ministry must be fulfilled, all our strength spent in witness to the Word of Truth.

Tenth Week

Monday
(1Kgs.17:1-6; Ps.121:1-8; Mt.5:1-12)

"My help is from the Lord,
who made heaven and earth."

It is He whom we seek when we "lift up [our] eyes toward the mountains." And what do we find but that "the Lord is [our] guardian; the Lord is [our] shade; He is beside [us] at [our] right hand."

Does the Lord not watch over those who trust in Him? Take Elijah for your example. He is led into exile under the stars, separated far from his people, yet he finds "the sun shall not harm [him] by day, nor the moon by night." He finds, in fact, his needs are met in a most marvelous way, for "ravens brought him bread and meat in the morning, and bread and meat in the evening, and he drank from the stream." At the Lord's command even these birds of the air serve to provide the needs of those who take refuge in Him. And His refreshing waters are always at our side.

Brothers and sisters, what do we see when we lift our eyes to the mountain? Do we not see the Lord sitting, teaching us His way? Are our hearts not nourished by His Word and our souls refreshed by His Bread? He speaks to us only truth, assuring us that "blest are the poor in spirit: the reign of God is theirs." He tells us what we indeed find as we live our lives under His wings. If our refuge were the world, how could sorrow and lowliness bring us blessing? Would our hunger and thirst not then be for the riches of this world, and we find ourselves fatted thereby for the day of slaughter? But being "single-hearted" and with a "hunger and thirst for holiness," we find ourselves more than satisfied; we find that we "shall see God." What more need has the devout soul than to dwell in the light of the Lord?

"The Lord will guard your coming and your going, both now and forever"; He shall not "suffer your foot to slip," for "He neither slumbers nor sleeps" but is ever diligent in the protection He provides His holy ones. And so what should you do but "be glad and rejoice, for your reward is great in heaven." As long as you remain with Him, He shall watch over you; and to His blessings there is no end, for all is held in His sacred hands and His desire is always to shower His mercy upon your soul.

Tuesday
(1Kgs.17:7-16; Ps.4:2-5,7-8; Mt.5:13-16)

"The jar of flour shall not go empty,
nor the jug of oil run dry,
until the day when the Lord sends rain upon the earth."

Again today we see in our readings that the Lord provides for His children's needs, that indeed He is with us until the end of the age – yes, "the Lord does wonders for His faithful one."

As "the brook where Elijah was hiding ran dry," the Lord instructed him to go to Zarephath of Sidon, a pagan territory, saying, "I have designated a widow there to provide for you." Elijah is obedient and the Lord is faithful to His word, for just "as he arrived at the entrance of the city, a widow was gathering sticks there." (Indeed, how wonderful it is to see the word of the Lord fulfilled!) Elijah does not hide the Lord's prophecy from his benefactress, and she, too, believes the word the Lord has spoken. And so she and her son and the prophet were "able to eat for a year" from a jar and a jug that were all but empty.

Brothers and sisters, our psalmist David sings in joy to the Lord today, "O Lord, let the light of your countenance shine upon us!" And how certain it is that He gives light to those who seek Him, those who have faith in Him. For "when [we] call... [He] relieve[s] [us]... in distress... [and] put[s] gladness into [our] heart[s], more than when grain and wine abound." For the light of the Lord is greater than the bread we eat; it is His love alone which provides all and alone brings joy to our souls.

And we are called to share in that light, to be "the light of the world." It is into us He places His light and then invites us to "set it on a stand where it gives light to all in the house": "Your light must shine before men so that they may see goodness in your acts and give praise to your heavenly Father." As He is Light, we must be light; as He provides for the needs of all, we must provide for the needs of all. And we must believe that, as "the jar of flour did not go empty, nor the jug of oil run dry, as the Lord had foretold through Elijah," just so the light He gives our lives shall not dim and the salt which draws it forth shall not lose its savor – we must believe that He indeed will provide for us, even to His second coming. And it shall be so. His love shall ever grow and this Bread be shared more and more with those He calls out of the world. Though famine be upon the land, He feeds us with the finest wheat, and calls us to feed others.

424

Wednesday
(1Kgs.18:20-39; Ps.16:1-2,4-5,8,11; Mt.5:17-19)

"If the Lord is God, follow Him;
if Baal, follow him."

Today "the only surviving prophet of the Lord" comes to reveal to the people that "the Lord is God!" Elijah seeks to open the Israelites' eyes to the presence of God, to bring them "back to their senses." And how evident it becomes that "they multiply their sorrows who court other gods," and that those "who set the Lord ever before" themselves are able to declare with David in faith: "With Him at my right hand I shall not be disturbed."

The great futility, the absolute emptiness of following false gods is shown in clear focus in the four hundred and fifty "prophets" who "hopped around the altar" and "called on Baal from morning to noon, saying, 'Answer us, Baal!'" How well our first reading summarizes the response of gods who are no gods: "But there was no sound, and no one answering." After "Elijah taunted them: 'Call louder, for he is a god and may be meditating, or may have retired, or may be on a journey. Perhaps he is asleep and must be awakened,'" they compounded their worship to utter absurdity as they "called out louder and slashed themselves with swords and spears, as was their custom, until blood gushed over them."

From this exercise of futile worship Elijah calls the people, saying simply, "Come here to me." And they move from this macabre circus scene over to the altar of the Lord the prophet prepares. And here the power of the Lord is unveiled beyond doubt to open the wayward hearts of God's chosen ones. Water upon water is poured upon the evening sacrifice, but the Lord's fire comes at the word of Elijah and consumes all.

"Lord, God of Abraham, Isaac, and Israel, let it be known this day that you are God in Israel." Let it be understood that your law must be followed and not the wicked contrivances of the human heart. Let be known the truth of your Son's words: "Whoever breaks the least significant of these commands and teaches others to do so shall be called least in the kingdom of God. Whoever fulfills and teaches these commands shall be great in the kingdom of God." For we shall only know the "fullness of joys in your presence" if we keep to your way, following Him who has come "to fulfill" "the law and the prophets." Let us never "court other gods" but with your humble king call out ever, "My Lord are you."

Thursday
(1Kgs.18:41-46; Ps.65:2,10-13; Mt.5:20-26)

"You have visited the land and watered it;
greatly have you enriched it."

"There is the sound of a heavy rain." The Lord is speaking. The Lord is teaching. Jesus is revealing the strait path of holiness that leads to the Father, and His words and His Person come like a fruitful rain upon a drought-stricken land.

O Lord, "thus have you prepared the land: drenching its furrows, breaking up its clods, softening it with showers, blessing its yield." By your speaking, by your teaching... by your bleeding on the cross for us "you have crowned the year with your bounty, and your paths overflow with a rich harvest." But will we receive these rains? Will we accept His chastisements which lead to life, which are the only way to the kingdom of God?

Here are the Lord's words, the commands of His mouth: "Everyone who grows angry with his brother shall be liable to judgment; any man who uses abusive language toward his brother shall be answerable to the Sanhedrin, and if he holds him in contempt he risks the fires of Gehenna." To what extent has He increased the prescriptions of the law! For He calls us to a holiness that surpasses the holiness of the law. He calls us to the kingdom of God, and great rains are needed to foster its life. And so He demands that we "be reconciled with [our] brother"; and so He warns us to "settle with [our] opponent." For we are on our way to His holy court, and not even the smallest sin will stand there.

The eyes of Elijah see but "a cloud as small as a man's hand rising from the sea." It is but the shadows the prophets knew as "the sky grew dark with clouds and wind." But it was enough to recognize the coming presence of the Lord that would relieve the drought upon the land, upon the nation of Israel. We, brothers and sisters, are those upon whom "a heavy rain fell," for now Christ has come; now He calls to us in Person from the cross and from His throne in heaven. If you wish to come to where He is, you must go where He has been: the cross is the heavy rain which brings the sweet smelling flower of heaven.

"God's watercourses are filled" and "rejoicing clothes the hills." Listen to His words now. Be obedient to His command. It is the driving rain which breaks up the ground and prepares the soul for holiness.

Friday
(1Kgs.19:9,11-16; Ps.27:7-9,13-14; Mt.5:27-32)

"Of you my heart speaks; you my glance seeks."

"Your presence, O Lord, I seek. Hide not your face from me," David sings in our psalm; and it is the presence of the Lord that is made known to Elijah in our first reading. And that same presence stands most openly before us in the teaching of Jesus in our gospel.

Elijah comes to the mountain of God to find shelter against the persecutions of his own people, for as he says, "I alone am left, and they seek to take my life." He alone holds the word of God, and so with what zealousness his life is sought. God promises to show Himself to His lone prophet, but neither in the "strong and heavy wind" nor in "the earthquake" nor in "the fire," which come before Elijah with great power as he stands upon the mountain, does the prophet find God. By none of these is he moved. But in "a tiny whispering sound" the presence of the Most High God is made known ("it is not by sword or spear..." 1Sm.17:47); it is this still, small voice that instills the fear of the Lord in his pierced soul and causes him to "hid[e] his face in his cloak and [go and stand] at the entrance of the cave," now seeking shelter from the power of God.

And is not this quiet Word made known in fullness today in the presence of Jesus, He who came "humble and mounted on an ass" (Mt. 21:5)? Does His simple teaching, do His gentle words not rend our hearts in twain? Here is the power of strong wind, earthquake, and fire all together in the voice of the Son of a carpenter; here in this unassuming flesh is God Himself made known.

And what does He teach us? And how difficult is it to hear! How we must cower at His words as they reach into our heart! For He tells us that our glance must seek God alone, that our heart must speak, our actions must reveal, His love only. Else what can we do with our eye but to "gouge it out and throw it away"? What can we do with our hand but "cut it off and throw it away" if it will not do the will of the Lord? For all else is waste, and to pursue in blindness the mere pleasures of the flesh, to look upon the vanity of the world with longing, will but bring us to Gehenna – this the gentle Lord would prevent with all His might, with even His death upon a cross.

Do not turn your look upon the sins of this degenerate age. Do not throw in your lot with those "who have forsaken [the Lord's] covenant, torn down [His] altars, and put the prophets to the sword." "Wait for the Lord with courage; be stouthearted and wait for the Lord," and you "shall see the bounty of the Lord in the land of the living" – and you shall be wed in truth

427

Ordinary Time

to Him who is all love, and you shall be called to anoint kings and prophets, to do the will of the Father in fullness as His holy children.

Saturday
(1Kgs.19:19-21; Ps.16:1-2,5,7-10; Mt.5:33-37)

"I will follow you."

Elisha gives His "yes" to Elijah, and so to God. He "kiss[es] [his] father and mother good-bye" and weds himself to the prophet who has thrown "his cloak over him." And he shall not turn back, shall not fall short of giving his entire self to the service of God, and so shall be greatly blessed. All he leaves behind. His very livelihood he slaughters, and gives these twelve oxen "to his people to eat." For he shall not return to work for them anymore.

"You are my inheritance, O Lord," David sings; "my allotted portion and my cup, you it is who hold fast my lot." All his soul trusts in the Lord in whom he "take[s] refuge," and what more does the Lord's king need? "My heart is glad and my soul rejoices, my body, too, abides in confidence": all his being finds peace in the presence of God, for all his being is set upon Him.

So it is, brothers and sisters, that to the extent we give ourselves to God, to the degree that we give our "yes" to the Lord, even so will we find our place secure. For making our home in heaven with Him, there is nothing to keep us from His grace. All else falls short of His glory. Heaven and earth shall pass away, and the hairs on our heads are numbered: only the New Jerusalem is lasting; only heaven is secure, for only in heaven is God.

We must be with Him. We must give ourselves to Him. Why should anything less hold sway in our lives? Why should we hesitate to follow Him with our whole heart? For there is nothing else that has importance – heaven is all that matters, and giving our lives to this place which is all life, how protected we are from "the evil one" who would dilute our love of God. And how certain our "yes" to our God is a "no" to this adversarial devil.

Honor your mother and father, children; give to all the love that is due. But give to God your very soul; let your spirit rest in Him alone, and you will be blessed forevermore.

Eleventh Week

Monday
(1Kgs.21:1-16; Ps.5:2-3,5-7; Mt.5:38-42)

"I will obtain the vineyard of Naboth the Jezreelite for you."

How divergent are the paths of Jezebel and Jesus. This Queen of Israel, wife of Ahab, holds the philosophy that if someone won't give you what you ask for, take it by force; whereas the Lord says if someone wishes to take something from you, give it and more.

Here are the way of the world and the way of heaven in stark contrast. When as a petulant child Ahab refuses to eat after not getting what he wants, his wife plots the death of Naboth to obtain the king's desired land. She truly is among "the bloodthirsty and the deceitful the Lord abhors." Jesus and those who follow Him are they whom the Lord loves. Far from stoning the righteous man to death, they themselves are the righteous who shed blood freely at the hands of their enemies. Both the wicked Jezebel and the just Jesus go beyond the old law: "An eye for an eye, a tooth for tooth." She takes an eye and a tooth when none has been taken from her, going thus below the law; but Jesus says, "Offer no resistance to injury," going thus above the law. Where He fulfills the law in love, she makes a mockery of God.

We hear these mutually exclusive paths spoken of even literally today. Jesus instructs His disciples: "Should anyone press you into service for one mile, go with him two miles," encouraging His followers on the same way of suffering He models for all – a way revealed most clearly in His carrying of the cross to the hill of Golgotha; and our first reading tells us that "on hearing that Naboth was dead, Ahab started off on his way down to the vineyard of Naboth the Jezreelite, to take possession of it," walking quite a different path of blood.

Brothers and sisters, it should be obvious that God "delight[s] not in wickedness; no evil man remains with [Him]." He indeed "destroy[s] all who speak falsehood" – the justice of God they shall not escape. But let it be equally obvious that we must follow the Lord's words in turning the other cheek. His are not mere platitudes but necessary instructions for finding the way to God He Himself walks. If we do not walk where He has walked, how can we come to the place He now is? Do not think you will come to heaven along an easy path, much less a wicked one. You will obtain the vineyard of heaven only by drinking the blood of Christ where you are, only by laying down your very life here in this world.

Tuesday
(1Kgs.21:17-29; Ps.51:3-6,11,16; Mt.5:43-48)

"Thoroughly wash me from my guilt
and of my sin cleanse me."

We have hope, brothers and sisters; we have hope that the very depths of our sin and depravity against the Lord shall be forgiven, and we shall be made new, washed in His blood. For the Lord "sends His rain on the just and the unjust," and this He proves today in our readings.

The Lord forgives David his "blood-guilt," he who has committed the dual sins of adultery and murder; and Ahab, too, of whom it is said, "No one gave himself to the doing of evil in the sight of the Lord as did Ahab," finds a measure of His mercy. Indeed, if there is reconciliation of these sinners with the Lord God, then even we must have hope of the Lord's grace at work within us.

The Lord is He who loves even His enemies, whose "sun rises on the bad and the good" alike, whose arm is not shortened, whose love knows no bounds – for has He not gone so far as to die on the cross as a common criminal, as the worst of sinners, to redeem all from their sins? But to receive such grace and mercy how must we come to Him?

It is clear both in our first reading and in David's great psalm that forgiveness is not obtained in a casual manner. To find it, we must imitate our sinners in their repentance as we have mirrored them in our sin. For Ahab when he heard the condemnation of the Lord upon his house "tore his garments and put on sackcloth over his bare flesh"; he did not hesitate to "acknowledge [his] offense" before the Lord and all the people. And recognizing that his "sin is before [him] always," David comes begging the Lord, "Turn away your face from my sins, and blot out all my guilt," seeking the compassion he knows only God holds. And this trust in His mercy the Lord sees; this declaration of sin the Lord hears. It is because Ahab "humbled himself before [Him]" and because David proclaimed openly his guilt that God has mercy on their lives. And we must join them just so in our own repentance to find that same mercy and kindness.

More than this, brothers and sisters. To more than this are we called now, my friends. For like the Lord Himself we are commanded to be – to show such mercy as He. The blood of Christ now outpoured, and it having poured upon our souls, we must now see that it is shared with all. We do that by shedding our own blood, by sharing that same love with everyone, indeed even with our enemies, as with us the Lord has done. And so our freedom from sin is made complete in His heavenly presence.

Wednesday

(2Kgs.2:1,6-14; Ps.31:20-21,24-25; Mt.6:1-6,16-18)

"As they walked on conversing,
a flaming chariot and flaming horses came between them,
and Elijah went up to heaven in a whirlwind."

Jesus instructs us in our gospel, "Whenever you pray, go to your room, close your door, and pray to your Father in private." This prescription the holy prophet Elijah fulfills in our first reading when he miraculously crosses the Jordan River and enters the wilderness, out of the sight of the prophets who remain standing on its other side. Elisha, too, he would have remain apart, but this holy man determines to stay with his father in faith. And so as their prayer becomes secret, as their conversation of God becomes hidden and private, even then Elijah is taken in flames of holy fire from the sight of men; even then he ascends to heaven. And though the scene is so otherworldly, the eyes of Elisha witness the hand of God lifting the prophet from our midst.

Brothers and sisters, can you see that this is as what happens with us when we pray to God in our private rooms? David in his psalm declares, "How great is the goodness, O Lord, which you have in store for those who fear you, and which, toward those who take refuge in you, you show in the sight of men." When we "hide... in the shelter of [His] presence... screen[ed]... within [His] abode," He reveals Himself to us in His glorious might, He lifts us up to heaven where He dwells. As He blesses those who keep their alms secret and repays those whose fasting is hidden, so He anoints the prayers of His children who find Him in the recesses of their hearts. From this wilderness, from this desert place, He lifts us to see the encompassing shining of holy light.

The quiet place is within your soul; the kingdom of heaven is within you. Converse with the Lord quite readily, quite faithfully, in this hidden place, and all shall be revealed to your eyes. Stay with Him; do not leave His side, and all your requests shall be filled in His blessed generosity. And His cloak He shall place upon you, His cross He shall lay across your shoulders, and the great blessings of heaven will be your own.

"Love the Lord, all you His faithful ones!
The Lord keeps those who are constant."
And all humble souls He raises
to the throne of God.

431

Thursday
(Sir.48:1-14; Ps.97:1-7,12; Mt.6:7-15)

"Your kingdom come,
your will be done
on earth as it is in heaven."

Our psalm sings of the greatness of our God; in our first reading we hear of how this greatness was revealed in the prophets Elijah and Elisha; and in the Lord's Prayer we call for this greatness to be present in our midst.

"Fire goes before Him and consumes His foes round about," our psalmist declares in praise of God. "His lightnings illumine the world." How great indeed is He: "The mountains melt like wax before the Lord, before the Lord of all the earth." Nothing stands before His glance, for "justice and judgment are the foundation of His throne," and this world is held in His all-powerful Hand.

And how well this greatness is brought to bear by His holy prophets. We are told, "Like a fire there appeared the prophet Elijah whose words were as a flaming furnace." The consuming power of the Lord is indeed revealed in him, for "by God's word he shut up the heavens and three times brought down fire." He "brought a dead man back to life from the nether world, by the will of the Lord... sent kings down to destruction," and finally was "taken aloft in a whirlwind, in a chariot with fiery horses." How the Lord blesses His holy ones! How He reveals His greatness in them! And of Elisha it is said, "Nothing was beyond his power... In life he performed wonders, and after death, marvelous deeds."

There is no end to the power the Lord provides to His children, for there is no end to His power, and this power He would share with all. Thus does the Lord encourage us to call upon the majesty of God our Father to be with us, to feed us each day, that His Name might indeed be praised, that His holiness might be revealed in His chosen ones. And to avoid His wrath, and to share in His power, what must we do? What is the central call of this all-powerful, all-holy Lord? Forgiveness. His grace is power, and grace and mercy we must share with all to share that power which has no end.

Trust in Him who holds you in His Hand, brothers and sisters. And His mighty Hand you shall see at work in the course of your day, and the fire of His grace shall pour upon your soul.

Friday

(2Kgs.11:1-4,9-18,20; Ps.132:11-14,17-18; Mt.6:19-23)

"The eye is the lamp of the body.
If your eye is good, your body will be filled with light;
if your eye is bad, your body will be in darkness."

And "how deep the darkness" is upon Athaliah. For her eye is evil, her "light is darkness," as so desperately she seeks to "lay up for [herself] an earthly treasure" by unjust and murderous means. Seeing that her son, the king of Judah, has died, she attempts to hold on to his crown by killing all the rightful heirs to his throne, caring more for the things which "moth and rust corrode" than for the righteousness of God. And she succeeds, though only briefly, as, true to the words of our gospel today, "thieves break in and steal" the kingship she has herself stolen away. And how great is her woe upon seeing all she has so anxiously and vainly sought removed from under her sight. How deep indeed is her darkness, deeper than the death she is about to endure.

In our psalm today we are reminded of the promise the Lord has made with David, king of all Israel: "If your sons keep my covenant and the decrees which I teach them, their sons, too, forever shall sit upon your throne." For in Zion the Lord vows to "place a lamp for [His] anointed," and declares that upon His chosen one His "crown shall shine." This crown, this lamp, is for all the Lord's children to receive, to shine forth in His holy presence. All who keep to His ways shall know such blessing. But, clearly, those who turn away lose the light the Lord deems to give to us as followers of His One Light, Jesus Christ. And however boldly or by whatever anxious means we attempt to hold on to it, it shall be removed from us like the passing day. Only remaining in Him are we saved.

In our first reading the people, led by Jehoiada the priest of God, renew the covenant "by which they would be the Lord's people." Terribly they have fallen from it and its grace and seek to regain what has now, and so often, been lost. Continually, in fact, the Israelites fell away from the Lord's command and so were abandoned to their sins – thus necessitating the coming of Christ – but continually the Lord returns them to the light when they return to Him, until finally Jesus does come.

Let us not be as the Israelites have been, brothers and sisters, so easily led into darkness and error, so easily seeking to look upon the evil of this earth. The Lord has come now to lead us away from just such things and give us a light that never fades. It is for us to remain with Him. Let your eye be sound, and so let His wisdom shine through you, O blessed one.

Ordinary Time

Saturday

(2Chr.24:17-25; Ps.89:4-5,29-34; Mt.6:24-34)

"Because you have abandoned the Lord,
He has abandoned you."

How quickly Joash the king of Judah, who so recently had restored true worship in the temple at Jerusalem, "transgress[es] the Lord's commands." After Jehoiada the priest died, the people "forsook the temple of the Lord, the God of their fathers, and began to serve the sacred poles and the idols." And so, "wrath came upon Judah and Jerusalem." So great is their apostasy that not only would they "not listen to [the prophets'] warnings" when they were sent "to convert them to the Lord," but when Zechariah the son of Jehoiada stood up in their midst to call them back to the Lord, "they stoned him to death in the Lord's temple." And so the central place of worship becomes a place of murder.

How truly Jesus speaks in today's gospel: "No man can serve two masters. He will either hate one and love the other or be attentive to one and despise the other." How clearly we see the hatred of God at work in Judah as she embraces false and empty gods. And so Judah becomes like her profligate sister in the Northern Kingdom of Israel. She who is set aside to preserve the temple and the holy city of Jerusalem, who is given yet a share in the inheritance promised David, turns boldly from her call and blessing to despise that which is most her own. And now does her hatred grow. And though she may escape the chastising hand of God a longer time than her sister, God's promise: "If [David's] sons forsake my law and walk not according to my ordinances, if they violate my statutes and keep not my commands, I will punish their crime with a rod and their guilt with stripes," will not be set aside forever, and they shall follow their sister into exile.

Brothers and sisters, we must choose the master we shall serve: if the world and its spirit, then you court God's condemnation; if the Lord, then remain faithful with your whole heart and follow His Son unto heaven. It is to heaven He desires your soul to come, but you must trust in Him and remain faithful to His call. For if you leave Him, He cannot but leave you; but if you hold fast to His love, He can do nothing but bless you.

Today Jesus, the Son of the Father in heaven, stands up to warn you against the traps of this world and call you into full, living worship of the One God. Will you enter into His love?

434

Twelfth Week

Monday
(2Kgs.17:5-8,13-15,18; Ps.60:3-5,7,12-13; Mt.7:1-5)

"In His great anger against Israel,
the Lord put them away out of His sight."

Jesus instructs His disciples today, "If you want to avoid judgment, stop passing judgment." In other words, "Judge not and you shall not be judged." Here is the prerequisite not only for avoiding judgment and condemnation at the hand of God, but also for assisting and healing others, as is our call. If we wish to serve as Christians and remove the speck of sin from others' eyes that they might see in the clear light of the Lord Jesus Christ, first it is certainly necessary that we ourselves see so clearly, that we come to the Lord and have our great sin removed from our souls. Otherwise our desire to help others in their frailty will indeed but turn to judgment of them; first we must recognize the great sinners we ourselves are – and so, that we cannot judge another – before we can find the grace from God to bring Jesus' mercy to others. God alone judges, brothers and sisters, for God alone is good, God alone is pure... the Lord Jesus alone is free from every speck of sin.

And God will judge. Believe this. He will send His apostles and prophets forth to bring remission of sins – He has sent His Son to die on the cross that we might be cleansed in His blood – but failing the acceptance and embracing of the call of the Lord, indeed what hope have we of salvation? There is but His righteous judgment remaining for our souls; there is but His chastising Hand to be placed upon us.

That God does judge, that He does cast sinful man from His sight, is made evident in exemplary fashion in the fate of our ancestors, the Israelites. "Because the Israelites sinned against the Lord, their God," He cast them into exile at the hand of their enemies. "The Lord warned Israel... by every prophet and seer, 'Give up your evil ways and keep my commandments and statutes'"; He sought to turn them from their sins by those whom He had touched, but "they did not listen... They rejected His statutes, the covenant which He had made with their fathers, and the warnings, which He had given them." And so, His pure eye unable to look upon them anymore, He removed them from before Himself.

"O God, you have rejected us and broken down our defenses," David cries, and begs the Lord's return to the Israelites' ranks... And how often this must be our prayer because of our foolishness in the sight of the Lord. Brothers and sisters, we have a greater covenant now with the Lord than did

435

the ancient Israelites, for we have a greater than David or Moses or Abraham with us now. And more demanding is He of our purity, of our virtue before Him. For what threatens us now is not mere exile, but the fires of hell; what awaits those who turn from Him now is eternal damnation, and so let us remain faithful to our God. Indeed let us remove the log from our eye that we "will see clearly to take the speck from [our] brother's eye" and so effect the building up of the kingdom of God. The time is now upon us; let us do all we can to remain in His sight.

Tuesday
(2Kgs.19:9-11,14-21,31-36; Ps.48:2-4,9-11; Mt.7:6,12-14)

"I will shield and save this city for my own sake,
and for the sake of my servant David."

Brothers and sisters, "renowned is He as a stronghold," the Lord our God. And faithfully does He watch over His chosen one.

Our psalmist proclaims, "Great is the Lord and wholly to be praised in the city of our God." He extols the glory of Mount Zion, of Jerusalem, "the city of the great King," for the blessings of God upon it. Here is His temple and so here it is we "ponder [His] kindness"; here it is we take refuge, finding "the narrow gate" that leads to Him and to His salvation.

In our first reading today the Lord gives evidence of the way in which He protects His children; He reveals that He will not "give what is holy to dogs or toss [His] pearls before swine." The king of Assyria has indeed "laid waste the nations and their lands," including the Northern Kingdom of Israel. He has acted with seemingly invincible power, and now he has come to the Lord's chosen city to destroy it as well. And though this Jerusalem, where His temple does dwell, and the chosen tribes of Judah (through whom His Savior shall come) shall not be protected forever... though this earthly tent shall so soon be ransacked and taken into exile itself, today the Lord shows how His promise, His covenant with them, will never be taken away. Though the temple's walls be one day destroyed, His spiritual kingdom, His New Jerusalem is eternally blessed in heaven.

Hezekiah indeed "enter[s] through the narrow gate" of prayer. Taking the threatening letter from Sennacherib in his hand, "he [goes] up to the temple of the Lord, and spreading it out before Him, he pray[s] in the Lord's presence." He calls out, "O Lord, our God, save us from the power of this man, that all the kingdoms of the earth may know that you alone, O Lord, are God." And the Lord listens. He takes pity on His "virgin daughter Zion... for out of Jerusalem shall come a remnant, and from Mount Zion, survivors." And by the hand of the Lord the king of Assyria is turned back.

Brothers and sisters, "Jerusalem will not be handed over" to the king of this world. Upon His Church His blessed protection remains. Through Judah and David, the king whose city is Jerusalem, Jesus has come – the Lord's promise is fulfilled and the remnant now does thrive. Here is the Temple not made by human hands; here is the narrow gate through whom all must enter paradise... here is "the joy of all the earth," God's "holy mountain" in our midst; and on His heights and in these walls, we are shielded and saved forever.

Wednesday
(2Kgs.22:8-13,23:1-3; Ps.119:33-37,40; Mt.7:15-20)

"Lead me in the path of your commands,
for in it I take delight."

The people of Judah and Jerusalem have been unfaithful to God and to the covenant made with Him, and so the time of their exile draws near: soon this remaining tribe of Israel shall join the others in being cast from their promised land. But today we hear of a faithful king, Josiah, who makes a kind of final effort, a final sign of faithfulness among the people, as he seeks to restore what has been so sorely lost by the nation.

King Josiah recognizes that Judah has sinned against God and so lost His blessing; and this truth is brought home to him in the clear light of "the book of the law," which has been uncovered in the temple of the Lord, dusted off of its many years of neglect, and read in his presence. Hearing the commands of the Lord, the Word which gives life to its hearer, the king tears his garments in penitence for what has been lacking to the kingdom, and declares: "The anger of the Lord has been set furiously ablaze against us because our fathers did not obey the stipulations of this book, nor fulfill our written obligations." To his great credit he seeks now to fulfill these stipulations, making "a covenant before the Lord that they would follow Him and observe His ordinances, statutes, and decrees with their whole hearts and souls, thus reviving the terms of the covenant which were written in the book." The covenant made through Moses he looks to restore.

"And all the people stood as participants in the covenant"; a measure of the blessing does return to God's chosen as they "turn away [their] eyes from what is vain" and find life in the ways of the Lord. Here is a final harvest of good fruit before the tree turns rotten and so must be uprooted from the Lord's sight.

Brothers and sisters, it is adherence to the Word of God which gives all life; it is faithfulness to His call that is our bread of life. If we do not remain in Him and walk in "the way of His statutes," we are no better than the "false prophets" who are but "wolves on the prowl" and shall be burned in the fires of Gehenna. If we are faithless how shall our tree grow? And if no growth, then no God have we, and we shall but rot.

In His light let us remain, seeking the nourishment of His Word and the Bread we break and offer at His altar. And we shall need fear no exile from the Promised Land, from the Temple that is our risen Christ... We shall be led ever in the way of Truth and grow each day unto Life.

O. 12. Thurs. (II)

Thursday

(2Kgs.24:8-17; Ps.79:1-5,8,9; Mt.7:21-29)

"The rains fell, the torrents came,
the winds blew and lashed against his house.
It collapsed under all this and was completely ruined."

Yes, "the officials of Nebuchadnezzar, king of Babylon, attacked Jerusalem, and the city came under siege," and "Jehoiachin, king of Judah, together with his mother, his ministers, officers, and functionaries, surrendered to the king of Babylon, who... took him captive... None were left among the people of the land except the poor"; and these, too, shall soon be struck.

Yes, the nations "have defiled [the Lord's] holy temple, they have laid Jerusalem in ruins." And why has such destruction come? Our first reading tells us simply of Jehoiachin, "He did evil in the sight of the Lord, just as his forebears had done"; and now finally the day of reckoning has come. And now the nations "have poured out their blood like water round about Jerusalem, and there is no one to bury them." Now does the Lord's "jealousy burn like fire."

And what shall be left when that fire is passed? Who shall stand on that day of reckoning that shall come to all souls, to peoples of all nations? Will you stand before the Lord and recount the great deeds you have done before Him who holds all the world in His holy hand? Will you attempt to justify yourself before Him who justifies all? Will your heart truly be set upon such vain pursuit? Truly then the Lord will "declare to [you] solemnly, 'Out of my sight, you evildoers'"; for all you have done will be as a grain of sand in His sight, and that grain will be blown from His hand for your lack of humility, for your pride before whom none can stand.

How shall it be then that your house be "solidly set on rock"? How will you avoid the fate of His chosen city Jerusalem? If *it* has been destroyed, do you not think that you, too, are liable to be struck from His sight? Or do you find yourself perfect? You must cry out as our psalmist, "Deliver us and pardon our sins for your name's sake." You must heed the words of Christ

438

and consider yourselves unworthy servants (Lk.17:10), unfit as you are to stand before His eyes, to dwell in His light. Then He may have pity on your wretched soul. Then He might make you strong. Your tongue silent before His majesty, there will be hope that you shall remain.

Remember, brothers and sisters, this is He who "taught with authority" before whom you stand. Do not lose the awe of His presence. And perhaps the great collapse of your house will not be necessary; perhaps you shall find His great love which washes away all sin. Let the rains He sends but be cleansing. Endure them gracefully.

O. 12. Fri. (II)

Friday
(2Kgs.25:1-12; Ps.137:1-6; Mt.8:1-4)

"Then Nebuzaradan, captain of the guard,
led into exile the last of the people remaining in the city."

And so the exile is complete. Not a soul remains in the holy city. And their captors "burned the house of the Lord, the palace of the king, and all the houses of Jerusalem." Not a stone is left standing one upon another. Not even the government appointed by the king of Babylon could remain. And they even "tore down the walls that surrounded Jerusalem."

Now she is utterly exposed. Now she who was his precious pearl is cast out and trampled underfoot. And so our psalmist can but lament, "By the streams of Babylon we sat and wept, when we remembered Zion." And so his songs of joy are silenced in this "foreign land." But in his lament today do we not find a kind of hope? Does not his abiding love for the holy city of God bring expectation of a better day? Listen to his faith: "If I forget you, Jerusalem, may my right hand be forgotten! May my tongue cleave to my palate if I remember you not, if I place not Jerusalem ahead of my joy." Even as we hear of the utter destruction of the temple and the city of God, we are given a sense of the faith that will build it up again.

And on the day we hear of the completion of the exile of Judah and Jerusalem to Babylon, we hear of the healing of one who is completely ostracized by society. The leper comes begging for a cure, seeking to join his fellow men upon the land, and the Lord answers him: "Jesus stretched out His hand and touched him and said, 'I do will it. Be cured.'" Should this not give us hope in all our travails? Does this not signal not only the return of the exiles in seventy years, but our utter redemption and return to the Lord in the coming of the Person of Jesus? For upon heeding the Lord's instruction to "show [himself] to the priest and offer the gift prescribed," the leper will be welcomed into the Church and society – his exile will be ended.

Ordinary Time

We all stand exiled by sin. We are all utterly bereft of the blessing of the Lord. But there is hope. We are told that even in this exile to Babylon "some of the country's poor" remained to till the land. And has not Jesus just come from the mountain where He has taught His disciples, "Blest are the lowly; they shall inherit the land"? If we humble ourselves before Him as has the leper, if we remain meek in His sight as have the poor of the land, the blessing of the Lord shall come to us and never leave. For He indeed wills it so. He indeed desires our return from exile. Do we have a heart to come to Him? Do we remember where we have been?

O. 12. Sat. (II)

Saturday
(Lam.2:2,10-14,18-19; Ps.74:1-7,19-21; Mt.8:5-17)

"It was our infirmities He bore,
our sufferings He endured."

And O how deep are those sufferings; "great as the sea is [our] downfall." And graphically are they seen in the destruction of Jerusalem; sharply they pierce the flesh of the Son.

Yes, the Lord "has torn down in His anger the fortresses of daughter Judah… On the ground in silence sit the old men of daughter Zion; they strew dust on their heads and gird themselves with sackcloth. The maidens of Jerusalem bow their heads to the ground." And the children and infants "faint away like the wounded in the streets of the city, and breathe their last in their mothers' arms." And so the prophet Jeremiah is "worn out from weeping"; and so his "gall is poured out on the ground because of the downfall of the daughter of [his] people."

And is this weeping not Jesus' own? Does He not shed tears over Jerusalem for the suffering it has known, and its suffering to come? Does He not indeed die for our sins? Listen to the description of the destruction of the holy city offered by our psalmist today: "With chisel and hammer they hack at all the paneling of the sanctuary." Are these not the blows Jesus suffered; are they not the nails which pierced His hands and feet and side? "They set your sanctuary on fire; the place where your name abides they have razed and destroyed." Is not Jesus the Temple of the living God, crucified by the hands of lust and greed and jealousy? Have we not done such violence to our Lord? And has He not endured all for our salvation?

Let the priest and all the children note the cause of such destruction of God's chosen ones, the suffering of His only Son. Is it not the prophets who proclaimed "false and specious visions," who "did not lay bare [the people's] guilt, to avert [their] fate"? And note the Lord's own words and attitude toward those who follow Him, to the children of Israel who press

440

upon Him: "The natural heirs of the kingdom will be driven out into the dark. Wailing will be heard there and grinding of teeth." Does Jesus fail to show those in His care the narrow gate? And so should we continue to coddle faithless hearts unto their destruction?

He indeed bears all our infirmities, all the sickness our sin has wrought. But we must indeed see ourselves as the centurion's servant boy, "in bed paralyzed, suffering painfully," to find His word of healing. We must come with the faith of the centurion to know His saving touch. For destruction indeed awaits the land, and so we must cry out to Him, "Turn your steps toward the utter ruins; toward all the damage the enemy has done in your sanctuary," if we hope to be redeemed by His blood.

Thirteenth Week

Monday
(Amos 2:6-10,13-16; Ps.50:16-23; Mt.8:18-22)

"Consider this, you who forget God,
lest I rend you and there be no one to rescue you."

What we should realize from our readings today is that the Word of the Lord is severe. Old Testament, New Testament, Psalms, etc. – His chastising hand is upon us in the words He speaks to our sinful hearts. He does not nod and smile as we walk our errant ways, but calls us onto the strait path He treads.

In our first reading and psalm the Lord recounts the sins of the people, "drawing them up before [their] eyes"; and for their crimes He declares, "I will not revoke my word" – they shall not escape His punishing hand. They who "sell the just man for silver, and the poor man for a pair of sandals," who "trample the heads of the weak into the dust of the earth," will themselves be "crush[ed]... into the ground as a wagon crushes when laden with sheaves." The sheaves of their sins are indeed heavy, and will duly lie upon their backs. Those, too, who are thieves and adulterers, who give their mouths "free rein for evil" and "harness [their] tongue for deceit," will not their fate be the same? And you, brothers and sisters, "when you do these things, shall [the Lord] be deaf to it?" He is not evil as yourselves, and so cannot stomach your iniquity.

And do you think with Jesus you will be able to continue in your sin? Because He bears your sins upon His shoulders, because He is crushed to the ground for your sakes, do you find thereby the right to go on sinning? Do you somehow believe the way of Christ is easier than that presented through Amos? Listen to His demand: "Follow me, and let the dead bury

441

their dead." This He says to a seemingly willing disciple who desires to remain with his family a while, not to a notorious dictator or a profligate heathen. And do you still wish to follow Him who "has nowhere to lay His head," Him whom the world wishes dead – Him who will be whipped and beaten and crucified for the sins of mankind? This is your fate. This is your fate, O Christian. In it will you find your joy?

The Lord has come to rescue us, indeed to exalt us on high, "and to him that goes the right way [He] will show the salvation of God." But your sins are not forgotten by Him who sees all things; they are no light matter in His sight. And following Him is not an easy road, for He is God.

Tuesday
(Amos 3:1-8,4:11-12; Ps.5:4-9; Mt.8:23-27)

"The lion roars – who will not be afraid!
The Lord God speaks – who will not prophesy!"

Yes, the Lord prophesies against Israel today like a lion rending and roaring: "You alone have I favored, more than all the families of the earth; therefore I will punish you for all your crimes." He brings upon His chosen "such upheaval as when God overthrew Sodom and Gomorrah: [they are] like a brand plucked from the fire." In no uncertain terms does He cry out through Amos – "Prepare to meet your God, O Israel."

A frightening prospect indeed it is which is presented to us in our readings. Here is the Lord God coming to take vengeance on His people. This is He before whom "no evil man remains," who "destroy[s] all who speak falsehood." And against His own who turn from Him, He reserves greater punishment.

How shall we react, we who are now become His chosen children? What should we do before such an awesome prospect as the Lord's hand coming with power? With David we should "bring [our] plea expectantly before [Him]"; with the disciples we should make "our way toward Him" and call out: "Lord, save us! We are lost!" And if we have the faith and humility of the Lord's king, who declares, "I, because of your abundant kindness, will enter your house; I will worship at your holy temple in fear of you, O Lord," then with his same confidence we may believe that the Lord will wake and take "the winds and the sea to task" – that what besets us because of our sin and separation from Him will be appeased by the same voice which threatens our destruction thereby. For indeed the Lord is abundantly kind and speaks to us as His own, and chastises us as His own. He raises His voice that we might return to Him; He places us in the fire that we might be purged. Let us find our strength in a holy fear.

442

And let us join His voice. Let us call out with Him to His blessed children, that all might return to Him who is their maker and protector – that all might be rescued from harm. The Lord would not see us caught in the snare laid for the wicked, and so He has sent His only Son to appease the wrath He has justly spoken forth. Let the lion's mouth not close upon our heads, but may we be awakened by its voice and open our own mouths to declare the mercy of our God.

Wednesday
(Amos 5:14-15,21-24; Ps.50:7-13,16-17,23; Mt.8:28-34)

"Hear, my people, and I will speak;
Israel, I will testify against you."

The chastising continues in our readings today. Against the people's vain sacrifices and "noisy songs," both Amos and our psalmist speak in the Lord's name. In need of healing as the two men "possessed by demons" do we find ourselves in the sight of God.

"Why do you recite my statutes, and profess my covenant with your mouth, though you hate discipline and cast my words behind you?" comes the warning from the Lord. And is it not a word we who pray must keep constantly in our hearts? For how easy it is to fall into empty worship; how readily do we begin to offer mere lip service to our God, when it is our very souls He demands. And not for His sake does He instruct us to "let justice surge like water, and goodness like an unfailing stream" – to put into practice the words we speak. He commands us to "seek good and not evil," for "then truly will the Lord, the God of hosts, be with [us] as [we] claim."

Indeed we claim His presence in our lives; we presume His blessing upon us as we attend Mass and read His words, each day receiving His Body and Blood and hearing His instruction. But continually we must check ourselves, for blindly do we fall into separation from the Lord, even in His house, and so may hear from His mouth: "I hate, I spurn your feasts... I take no pleasure in your solemnities."

At these times we must come "out of the tombs" as do the demoniacs today. We must cry out to the Lord as we realize our sin. And He will be faithful to us. As He healed even these, He will cast the devils from us, too, and quickly. But first we must realize that His "are the world and its fullness," that He needs nothing from us. First we must see that all our sacrifices do *Him* no good – only us. Then He "will have pity," when we have humbled ourselves. Then He will gather us into His fold, when our hearts are set on His justice.

Ordinary Time

Let the devil be cast from your mocking lips; accept the chastising Word of God, and new life at His feet you may find, possessed of the breath of His Spirit. Then will your offerings find favor in His eyes.

Thursday
(Amos 7:10-17; Ps.19:8-11; Mt.9:1-8)

"The Son of Man has authority on earth to forgive sins."

Amos says of himself in our first reading: "The Lord took me from following the flock, and said to me, Go, prophesy to my people, Israel." And so he can say, "Now hear the word of the Lord!" And so he can speak for God. And so he can reveal the Lord's will to the people, calling them to return to His presence.

Like the prophets is the law, of which David, another shepherd called by God – himself to be king – sings today in our psalm: "The law of the Lord is perfect, refreshing the soul." As the prophets' chastisement would bring healing to those who listen and obey the word of the Lord they impart, so the law of God is meant to bring a "fear of the Lord [which] is pure, enduring forever," so it, too, would bring blessed healing to the wayward child, "rejoicing the heart" and "enlightening the eye."

But the people did not listen to the prophets; they refused to obey the law of the Lord. His words they cast aside, unable to swallow them, unable to make them an enduring part of their lives. Like a cloud which passes, so ephemeral, so abstract and therefore unknown they would too often become. And so the Father sent His Son.

"Have courage, son, your sins are forgiven," Jesus says to the "paralyzed man lying on a mat"; and this word He has come to make real in all our hearing – to all He brings forgiveness for their straying hearts. Even the stiff necks of the scribes the Lord would bring healing. The sins of the past He comes to wash away, advocating to the Father for us that we knew not what we were doing before His arrival, and come now He has to make real for us God's presence in our midst, to take away our ignorance of the Father's love... to enable us to stand up and walk "toward [our] home."

Indeed, "a feeling of awe" should come over us as it did over the crowd that witnessed Jesus' power, for the same authority resides with us now in His Church – He has not left His people abandoned. And so, come to the Lord and confess your sins, for the Lord in His grace gave "such authority to men" to act in His stead as does Christ. And now find the courage and conviction to live your life led by the Incarnate Word of God. May your soul be in the hands of the Good Shepherd.

Friday

(Amos 8:4-6,9-12; Ps.119:2,10,20,30,40,131,Mt.4:46; Mt.9:9-13)

"Many tax collectors and those known as sinners
came to join Jesus and His disciples at dinner."

It is just such as these that Amos prophesies against in our first reading; it is sinners such as Matthew whom he addresses when he declares, "Hear this, you who trample upon the needy and destroy the poor of the land!" For the apostle the Lord calls today is a tax collector, one of those famous for extorting money from his fellow Jews even while standing in the stead of their occupiers, the Romans. And so are he and his kind not like those who can't wait for an end to the Lord's sabbath that they might "fix their scales for cheating," greedily proclaiming, "Even the refuse of the wheat we will sell"? And so is it any wonder the Pharisees complained, "What reason can the Teacher have for eating with tax collectors and those who disregard the law?"

Our psalm itself supports the importance of following the law of the Lord, stating, "Happy are they who observe His decrees, who seek Him with all their heart." And so, how unhappy, how lacking in God's blessing must Matthew be to live apart from His word. And so, are not the Pharisees correct in their assessment that such as he deserve but condemnation?

They are correct. It cannot be denied. But what they cannot see is that they just as guilty. What they do not understand, as these others do, is that before their eyes the Lord's prophecy through Amos is being realized: "I will make the sun set at midday and cover the earth with darkness in broad daylight," our God makes known – and it is the sinners they condemn who are the ones who "mourn as for an only son"; it is they who now "gasp with open mouth in [their] yearning for [the Lord's] commands"... it is they who recognize the famine "for hearing the word of the Lord" that is upon the earth and upon their souls, and turn to the Son who feeds the hungry even as He joins them at table. What these Pharisees do not see is that the justice of the Lord is not the judgment in their hearts, else all, including themselves, would be condemned.

Brothers and sisters, open your eyes to the emptiness of your soul and come to His table this day with open mouth and open heart to hear His Word and receive His Body and Blood. For it is repentant sinners such as you whom the Lord feeds quite freely.

Saturday
(Amos 9:11-15; Ps.85:9,11-14; Mt.9:14-17)

"I will bring about the restoration of my people Israel."

Of the city of David, the Lord promises, "I will wall up its breaches, raise up its ruins, and rebuild it as in the days of old." Beautiful imagery is given indeed through the prophet Amos to illustrate the renewal of the land now fallen: "The juice of grapes shall drip down the mountains, and all the hills shall run with it." Indeed, in His great grace the Lord vows, "Never again shall they be plucked from the land I have given them." And so we have prophecy of the New Jerusalem.

Our psalm continues such prophecy of the kingdom to come, declaring, "He proclaims peace to His people, and to His faithful ones... The Lord Himself will give His benefits; our land shall yield its increase." Justice and truth shall be known in fullness, even as salvation walks "along the way of His steps."

And these steps have been trodden in our midst. Jesus is coming and has come, bringing in Himself the new wine of the New Jerusalem, which courses like a river through all this City's streets. Indeed His Blood flows in our veins now. Indeed we become the new wineskins that hold His abundant goodness, and so are lifted to the kingdom of heaven. John's disciples do not yet understand. If the Lord's own followers have difficulty seeing, it should not be surprising that those who have yet to be baptized in the fire of the Holy Spirit still find themselves preoccupied with the stipulations of a law that is passing away, a law – so embodied by the Pharisees – which is to be subsumed by the greater Law of love Jesus comes bleeding to bring into our midst.

But they shall. There can be little doubt that these followers of John and his baptism will come, with the Lord's own disciples, and be washed in the blood that makes all things new. There is certainty that these, as even some Pharisees, shall "drink the wine" of the New Covenant, even as we do this day.

Brothers and sisters, this new wine is upon our altars this day; before us is set the Blood that washes all clean. It is for our restoration the Lord provides this feast. Let us not refrain from partaking of what He has died to bring into our midst, but let us be indeed the new wineskins filled with His Word and His Blood, and declare His salvation unto the nations.

Fourteenth Week

Monday
(Hos.2:16-18,21-22; Ps.145:2-9; Mt.9:18-26)

"When the crowd had been put out
He entered and took her by the hand,
and the little girl got up."

How like Hosea's prophecy today is the Lord's raising of the synagogue leader's daughter in our gospel. For the Lord speaks through His prophet, saying, "I will lead her into the desert and speak to her heart," and Jesus does this when He puts the crowd out of the house before whispering to the little girl to arise. And as the Lord declares in our first reading, "I will espouse you in right and in justice, in love and in mercy," so Jesus takes the hand of the child, wedding His Spirit to her own; and so, as the redemption is promised Israel in her again calling the Lord, "My husband," so the daughter of the synagogue leader stands and walks in the light of Christ.

"She shall respond there as in the days of her youth," it is said of the Lord's chosen nation. With the faith of a child all shall be raised. And as the Savior covers the "woman who had suffered from hemorrhages for twelve [full] years" with the edge of His cloak, taking her into His wedding chamber and so immediately healing her flow of blood, so Jesus would make us all His own; so in His grace and love He would enter all our souls and make us one with Him. And so would all find themselves "restored... to health," His blood alone coursing through our veins.

"I will espouse you in fidelity, and you shall know the Lord," our God declares. And knowing the Lord, being wed unto Him in the depths of our hearts where He speaks, promising us His love, what can we do but "praise [His] name forever and ever" with David His king? What can we do but "speak of the splendor of [His] glorious majesty and tell of [His] wonderful works"? For "great is the Lord and highly to be praised," and His Spirit wed to our own we are overwhelmed by the glory of His presence and cannot help but declare our love for Him who has loved us above all.

Listen to His voice, brothers and sisters; let Him enter your hearts and make you His own. And you shall be raised from the death of sin unto His glorious majesty. Yes, may news of His grace circulate among all; let us "publish the fame of [His] abundant goodness and joyfully sing of [His] justice," for He speaks now to our souls.

447

Tuesday
(Hos.8:4-7,11-13; Ps.115:3-10; Mt.9:32-38)

"Our God is in heaven; whatever He wills, He does.
Their idols are silver and gold, the handiwork of men."

In Israel, the people have turned from worship of the living God and "with their silver and gold they made idols for themselves, to their own destruction." As the golden "calf of Samaria" is "destined for the flames," so they "shall be like them, everyone who trusts in them." So empty are the lives of those who worship wood and stone, and to inevitable destruction do they come. That which we make rots; only what is made by God endures.

How the Lord Jesus contrasts with the false and empty gods worshiped by the nations: where they are dead, He is alive. He alone is able to see and hear and smell and feel. He alone walks the earth with a heart that is "moved with pity." He alone reveals the living God and enables us thereby to see and hear and smell and feel. He alone gives us strength to walk this earth and do His work. Their gods are mute – "they have mouths but they speak not." But He takes the "mute who was possessed by a demon" and enables him to speak. It is He who gives us our souls, who renews our spirit.

"Nothing like this has ever been seen in Israel!" the crowds exclaim as they witness the glory of God in their midst. It is as if they shout, "God is alive!" and come to faith in His presence. For here He breathes upon them; here His heart beats in their hearing. In Jesus all see the wonders of the Father in heaven come to earth and made real before their eyes. Such is God's will – to bring heaven to earth. Such is His great grace – to send us His only Son. And what can we do but rejoice at the works of the Lord; what can we do but join Him in such labor?

"He shall remember their guilt and punish their sins," those who harden their hearts against Him and trust in the wisdom of their own minds and the works of their own hands. For only the works wrought by *His* hands, through His living Spirit, are genuine, are true – are alive. All else dies. So let us leave off any empty sacrifice, any false worship not accomplished in the House of God. There is but one God and one Church through which He works, and only by what He has established will we know the grace and freedom of the living Lord of all. Only in Jesus' Body and Blood do we find the life that yields lasting grain.

Wednesday
(Hos.10:1-3,7-8,12; Ps.105:2-7; Mt.10:1-7)

"Jesus sent these men on mission as the Twelve."

And in these men the Lord founds His Church, choosing "first Simon, now known as Peter," as the Rock upon whom the Building rests, and in like fashion all the twelve apostles, upon whom He places His Spirit. And so the foundation is set. And so none can separate themselves from these and their teaching, for in them and in this Church, Jesus Himself resides. It is in their place the bishops stand; it is through these, priests are ordained. In His holy Catholic Church we find the New Jerusalem.

The Lord chose Abraham and his son Isaac, and placed His blessings upon the twelve tribes of Jacob and their descendants. He does not remove this blessing, does not break His covenant. And the Lord set up in Jerusalem His place of worship. This, too, does not change. Regardless of how corrupt the priests or kings may have been throughout the history of Israel and Judah, these remain His chosen people, and here is His temple. And when another would rise up to take the place of what God had anointed, as typified by Jeroboam's setting up the golden calf in Samaria that the people might worship there and so not go up to Jerusalem, this pride the Lord curses. In our first reading He vows, "The king of Samaria shall disappear, like foam upon the waters. The high places of Aven [Iniquity] shall be destroyed, the sin of Israel; thorns and thistles shall overgrow their altars." Yes, "God shall break down their altars and destroy their sacred pillars" for "their heart is false." It is not these upon whom His Spirit rests.

Brothers and sisters, "it is time to seek the Lord," to come into the House His hands have made – not a separate Church set up apart from His covenants but standing in fulfillment of them with the coming of Jesus as the Christ and Messiah – and realize that "the reign of God is at hand." Here in His New Jerusalem you shall find His presence; here you shall hear His teaching transmitted through the apostles and receive the Bread of His sacrifice at their holy hands. Know that "He, the Lord, is our God" and "throughout the earth His judgments prevail." "Glory in His holy name; rejoice, O hearts that seek the Lord," for now He has come to "the lost sheep of the house of Israel." Now through His apostles, through those who "seek to serve Him constantly," He gathers all into the New Jerusalem – upon this House His favor remains.

Thursday
(Hos.11:1,3-4,8-9; Ps.80:2-4,15-16; Mt.10:7-15)

"I am God and not man,
the Holy One present among you."

And He comes to us as do the disciples today, blessing each home as He enters. And "if the home is deserving, [His] blessing will descend upon it. If it is not, [His] blessing will return" to Him. Be careful to receive the blessing of the Lord, for if you reject Him, He will leave you, shaking the dust from His feet, and "it will go easier for the region of Sodom and Gomorrah on the day of judgment than it will" for you.

In days past the Lord loved Israel as "a child," drawing him "with human cords, with bands of love." And though "they did not know that He was their healer," though they rejected Him, His "pity [was] stirred" and He did "not give vent to [His] blazing anger." He withheld His "flames" of wrath and offered them forgiveness. Thus Jesus is sent into our midst. For we, as Israel, have sinned. All have spurned the love of God and gone astray. But here comes the Holy One to heal us once again.

But now if we should reject Him, now if we should spurn His Son present to us, how shall we be saved? What more can the Lord God do to draw us home to His loving arms? The Lord has heard the psalmist's plea to "look down from heaven and see," to "take care of this vine, and protect what [His] right hand has planted." He comes to His children wholly offering Himself for their sakes. Like the apostles, like His saints who come without money or goods but possessing everything they need and giving all this blessing freely to any who would receive it, so the Lord comes to us this day – and do we receive Him?

There is nothing more the Lord can do to save our souls: He has died for us. He has given all He has freely for our redemption. His Son walks amongst us. Enter His reign today. Accept His blessing. The day of judgment is not far from you.

Friday
(Hos.14:2-10; Ps.51:3-4,8-9,12-14,17; Mt.10:16-23)

"O Lord, open my lips,
and my mouth shall proclaim your praise."

Hosea instructs the Israelites, "Take with you words, and return to the Lord," and this David does in his psalm of sorrow. In "sincerity of heart" he begs the Lord's forgiveness for his sin and finds that the Lord creates "a

450

clean heart" for him. "In [Him] the orphan finds compassion," and so the humbled king receives the Lord's cleansing grace.

Because the Lord does "forgive all iniquity, and receive[s] what is good," so we find that Hosea's prophecy – "He shall strike root like the Lebanon cedar, and put forth his shoots" – is fulfilled in His Church today. We indeed "blossom like the vine": the vine of Christ covers the earth. And though "straight are the paths of the Lord," though Jesus' blunt words to His disciples – "You will be hated by all on account of me" – are realized in all who are "brought to trial before rulers and kings, to give witness before them and the Gentiles"... though persecution, the cross, be an inevitable part of every Christian's life, yet through it all the Church is strengthened, growing "like a verdant cypress tree." For always it is the Lord who strengthens us; always it is "the Spirit of [our] Father... speaking in [us]." It is He who opens our lips; it is His praise we proclaim with all our words, and so what can He do but bless us? We "say no more, 'our god,' to the work of our hands," and so no more do we sin. Taking refuge in the love of God, "because of [Him we] bear fruit."

"Your Holy Spirit take not from me," O Lord. "A willing spirit sustain in me," that your wrath might ever be "turned away," that I might forever be purified by your grace – that the pangs I suffer never be the result of my sin but rather the blessing of sharing your cross in this world. Come, O Son of Man, and find your sheep suffering all for you. Your Word keep upon our souls.

Saturday
(Is.6:1-8; Ps.93:1-2,5; Mt.10:24-33)

"'Holy, holy, holy is the Lord of hosts,'
they cried one to the other.
'All the earth is filled with His glory.'"

Hear the angels' song. It is their praise, which fills the heavens like fragrant incense, that our psalmist proclaims: "The Lord is king, in splendor robed; robed is the Lord and girt about with strength." Exalted is the majesty of the Father in heaven, upon whom no eye can gaze, and so of His Son. And rightly does the prophet Isaiah – "a man of unclean lips, living among a people of unclean lips" – fear having seen "the Lord seated on a high and lofty throne, with the train of His garment filling the temple."

And should we not fear Him, too? Should we not fear the glorious Son in whose light we dwell and in whose steps we follow? Do we realize His Majesty? Do we somehow presume to outrank our teacher, or are we as the pupil who is "glad to become like his teacher, the slave like his master"? If humbled before the Lord of all, we shall fear nothing of this world. Fearing Him who "can destroy both body and soul in Gehenna," any power of the devil becomes as nothing in our sight. For we know our God holds every "single sparrow" in His Hand, and we "are worth more than a flock of sparrows."

The Lord sends "one of the seraphim" to touch the lips of the prophet with "an ember which he ha[s] taken with tongs from the altar." (So holy is the Lord that even the angels cannot touch His fire with their hands.) And so Isaiah's "wickedness is removed, [his] sin purged." And so he is sent, in turn, to proclaim the Word of God. First he must be purified; first we all must be purged of sin, for indeed "holiness befits [His] house" – holiness alone may stand in His presence, and only the tongue cleansed of stain can "speak in the light" the truth of our God. And as the prophet speaks, as the psalmist sings, so are we sent to proclaim the glory of "the King, the Lord of hosts."

"Your throne stands firm from of old; from everlasting you are, O Lord." You alone are holy. What can we pray but that the earth be filled with your glory, but that we shall enter your house and praise your name all the days we are blessed with life? Make us holy as thou art.

O. 15. Mon. (II)

Fifteenth Week

Monday
(Is.1:10-17; Ps.50:8-9,16-17,21,23; Mt.10:34-11:1)

"Your hands are full of blood!
Wash yourselves clean!"

Elsewhere in Scripture we read, "The Lord chastises those whom He loves" (Heb.12:6), and this truth is made evident in our readings today. The Lord commands us through the prophecy of Isaiah, "Put away your misdeeds from before my eyes; cease doing evil; learn to do good." Our psalm continues the same theme, declaring again in the voice of God, "You hate discipline and cast my words behind you." And the lesson is fulfilled in Jesus' own admonishment: "Whoever loves father or mother, son or daughter more than me, is not worthy of me."

How difficult for many to hear Jesus' words: "My mission is to spread, not peace, but division." How in conflict with their image of a pleasant Jesus placed so neatly in a politically proper box. How they would anesthetize themselves against the suffering of the cross. But the same Spirit who speaks through Isaiah, proclaiming, "Hear the word of the Lord, princes of Sodom! Listen to the instruction of our God, people of

Gomorrah!" is He who speaks through the Son, who Himself condemns the towns that do not receive His preaching and presence to a worse fate than these infamous cities. Our Lord is no less offended by "worthless offerings" and "octaves with wickedness." He is no more deaf to our disobedience or blind to our sin. In fact, as He is the fulfillment of the love of God in the forgiveness and grace He offers all, so He is the fulfillment of God's justice in the ultimate judgment of every soul.

"I will correct you by drawing [your sins] up before your eyes," the Lord declares through our psalmist. And does not Jesus call the Pharisees "a brood of vipers" (Mt.12:34)? Does He not call Peter "Satan" (Mt.16:23)? Does He not open all our eyes to the sin upon our souls to save us from final damnation? If He did not do this, could He say He loves us? Is it not by this cross placed firmly upon our backs that we rise from the sin weighing down our hearts? Otherwise, would we not drown in sorrow?

Brothers and sisters, do not try to ration away your cross by vain supposition. They are wolves in sheep's clothing who would convince you there remains no place for the wood, for the blood. The world is ever and more a place of sin, and the devil ceases not to lead souls to perdition. Be warned by the Lord of all. Stand chastised in His love. Wash yourselves clean of all pride and vanity; be not as he who "brings himself to ruin." You are called to be the Lord's image in the world; and the Word made flesh ends His life on earth fixed to a cross. Accept His gift of love.

Tuesday
(Is.7:1-9; Ps.48:2-9; Mt.11:20-24)

"Unless your faith is firm
you shall not be firm!"

"Take care you remain tranquil and do not fear; let not your courage fail." For "great is the Lord and wholly to be praised in the city of our God" and "renowned is He as a stronghold." But the faithless shall be as the rebellious nations which came against the Lord and His anointed: these "shall not stand" but "shall be crushed." Though "the kings assemble, [though] they come on together" against the "city of the great King," they shall be seized with "quaking," with "anguish, like a woman in labor." They shall be "stunned, terrified, routed."

And so Jesus proclaims His rebuke of Capernaum and the other "towns where most of His miracles had been worked." So His severe reproach echoes to all faithless hearts, hearts which have refused His mercy, who have turned from His wonders: "I assure you, it will go easier for Sodom than for you on the day of judgment." Sodom was burned with fire. There

453

is no city greater known for sin than this profligate place which sought even the rape of the angels. And so, what shall be the fate of those who turn now from the preaching of Jesus, from His holy presence among us? What shall indeed become of the baptized who reject the grace at work in their souls? One can only shudder to think of the horrors built up by such turning away, by such "failure to reform."

O Lord, how often I have turned from you; how little of your grace I have treasured in my soul. How little faith have I. And so, how I fear your mighty hand, your perfect, absolute light. Who shall stand in the purity of your love? Who can know your holiness? My heart condemns me of my sin; "in sackcloth and ashes" I come before you, seeking the strength found only in your touch. Send me not "down to the realm of death" but lift this faithless soul to your side. Let me fear no attack of the world. Enable me to stand in your light.

Wednesday
(Is.10:5-7,13-16; Ps.94:5-10,14-15; Mt.11:25-27)

"Shall He who instructs nations not chastise,
He who teaches men knowledge?"

Again we learn the basic teaching of the Lord: The exalted are humbled and the humbled exalted. In our first reading "the Lord of hosts" promises to "send among His fat ones leanness" – condemning Assyria for the pride it takes in its "own power"; and in our gospel Jesus "offer[s] praise" to His "Father, Lord of heaven and earth," declaring, "What you have hidden from the learned and the clever you have revealed to the merest children." "Judgment shall again be with justice," for the Lord shall raise those who have been "trample[d] down" even as He topples the pride of the wicked.

Assyria boasts, "I am shrewd" and proclaims itself "a giant." But truly he is a fool who exalts himself above the power of the Lord and does not see that all things are done only in Him. Yes, with what wisdom Isaiah speaks when he questions: "Will the axe boast against him who hews with it?" and, could a rod "sway him who lifts it, or a staff him who is not wood"? How clearly he exposes the foolishness of the vain boasting of those who are mighty in their own eyes.

And how well his lesson leads to Jesus' own. "Everything has been given over to [Jesus] by [His] Father": all power is in our Lord's hands. And when He states, "No one knows the Son but the Father, and no one knows the Father but the Son – and anyone to whom the Son wishes to reveal Him," what is He saying but that no one comes to the Father, no one receives any blessing of the Father's power and love, unless He humbles himself before Jesus who is the Chosen One? Nothing of God can anyone know, nothing of His power can we share – no salvation is found at all unless we come to Him as a child.

"Shall He who formed the ear not hear? Or He who formed the eye not see?" Do you believe your vision greater than His own? "Understand, you senseless ones among the people; and, you fools, when will you be wise." For though these puffed-up souls "murder" "the fatherless" with their tongue, though "widow and stranger they slay" in their wicked deceit, the truth shall not escape them: justice shall indeed come. And as "the upright of heart... follow it" – follow the Lord of all to eternal glory – for those who take pride in their own power, "instead of His glory there will be kindling like the kindling of fire." Know this, you who are slow to believe.

Thursday
(Is.26:7-9,12,16-19; Ps.102:13-21; Mt.11:28-30)

"The Lord looked down from His holy height,
from heaven He beheld the earth,
To hear the groaning of the prisoners,
to release those doomed to die."

Yes, "we cried out in anguish under [His] chastising. As a woman about to give birth... we conceived and writhed in pain, giving birth to wind." Empty were our works; dead in sin were we. But the Lord took pity on His people. Though "oppressed by [His] punishment" and as prisoners in chains, the time arrived for Him to "arise and have mercy on Zion." And so He sent His Son.

"My soul yearns for you in the night, yes, my spirit within me keeps vigil for you." Because even in death His faithful set their hearts on Him and make Him the "desire of [their] souls," He comes. "He has regarded the prayer of the destitute, and not despised their prayer." Though we are afflicted by sin, the Lord looks upon our tears; and His heart breaks with ours, and the light walks among us... and Jesus comes. And Jesus comes.

Hear the words of our Lord: "Your souls will find rest." He promises us His peace. Though heavy burdened with the weight of this dark world, He is here to save us. How do we find such peace? How do we find release from the prison in which we are confined? Heed His instruction; "take [His] yoke upon your shoulders and learn from [Him]." And what is this yoke in which you will find your freedom? It is nothing else but the cross.

The Lord has looked down from heaven; He has sent His Son forth from His throne. And what does He come bearing "to release those doomed to die"? Yes, it is a cross He carries. Our sins and our pain He takes upon

Himself. Only through this instrument of salvation, only through the flesh of Christ fastened to the wood – only by the nails which pierce His hands and feet are we brought life. For He cries with us in anguish: He dies with us in pain. And the Lord's pity is realized, the mercy of God fulfilled... and washed are we in this blood from sin, and our cry is thus taken away.

And we must do the same as He. We must die, too. We must unite ourselves to His cross, and let Him take all pain from our souls. And so we shall be whole. And so the cry shall be no more. And so we shall never die. "Awake and sing, you who lie in the dust," for your "corpses shall arise."

O. 15. Fri. (II)

Friday
(Is.38:1-8,21-22; Is.38:10-12,16-17; Mt.12:1-8)

"Hezekiah turned his face to the wall
and prayed to the Lord."

"When Hezekiah was mortally ill, the prophet Isaiah, son of Amoz, came and said to him: 'Thus says the Lord: Put your house in order, for you are about to die.'" When the Jewish race was about to perish for lack of love, Jesus Christ, the Son of God, came to the Pharisees and declared, "It is mercy I desire and not sacrifice." And if they heed not His word, they indeed shall die.

But will what occurred "in those days" with the king of Judah recur with these leaders of the Jews? Will they, too, turn their face to the wall and cry out to the Lord? For there is a greater threat than "the hand of the king of Assyria" upon their race now. Here is a greater threat than death. The condemnation they cast so freely upon "innocent men" now begins to overshadow their souls.

"To the gates of the nether world I shall be consigned for the rest of my years," Hezekiah cries out; and indeed his fears shall be realized in these Pharisees. For they "shall see no more the Lord in the land of the living" if they refuse to see Him here as He stands before them. They shall know no longer the mercy that sustains all life if they harden their hearts to Him who holds that mercy in His flesh and blood.

The Lord seeks to open their eyes and their hearts to the power and love of God. By their own Scripture and history and law He proves their judgment wrong, asking, "Have you not read what David did when he and his men were hungry...? Have you not read in the law how the priests on temple duty can break the sabbath without incurring guilt?" But yet would they condemn King David and the temple priests, placing their own judgment over the law of the love of God.

456

I fear for them, brothers and sisters, as for all who are obstinate of heart. For here are the chosen of God. Here are those graced with the Lord's promise. But what shall become of their blessing if they reject the Promise when He stands before them? What shall become of those who turn the grace of God to empty wind? O how their bones shall rot! O how the fears of Hezekiah shall be fulfilled! O that they could hear the words the Lord speaks to His repentant king: "I have heard your prayer and seen your tears. I will heal you." O that they would know the mercy of God.

To Him may all come, for He who stops the sun and moves it back upon its course indeed holds all in His loving hands. The Temple of the Lord is here.

Saturday
(Mic.2:1-5; Ps.10:1-4,7-8,12,14; Mt.12:14-21)

"When the Pharisees were outside
they began to plot against Jesus
to find a way to destroy Him."

Is it not of these David sings when he declares, "He lurks in ambush near the villages; in hiding he murders the innocent; his eyes spy upon the unfortunate"? And though He withdraw from them this day, though He will silently subject Himself to torture and death at their hands, be assured that the Lord is "planning against this race an evil from which [they] shall not withdraw [their] necks."

"Woe to those who plan iniquity, and work out evil on their couches." And what greater woe can there be than for the one who plots disaster upon the head of the Chosen One? These are they who would "cheat [the] owner of his house, a man of his inheritance"; for here is the One of whom Isaiah prophesies in the name of the Lord: "Here is my servant whom I have chosen, my loved one in whom I delight." Yet by "cursing, guile, and deceit" these would steal the inheritance of the only Son. But the Lord shall not "stand aloof" forever, and over these soon "shall be sung... a plaintive chant: 'Our ruin is complete, our fields are portioned out among our captors.'" What the Lord has promised He has accomplished in wresting the House of God from the disobedient and placing it in the hands of His children of light.

Now the Lord does "proclaim justice to the Gentiles." And we who suffer with Him, we "the afflicted, who are caught in the devices the wicked has contrived," rejoice in the knowledge that "judgment is made victorious" in Him – "on [Him] the unfortunate man depends," and his fortunes are made prosperous as the Lord's own.

457

Ordinary Time

"'There is no God,' sums up his thoughts," the evil one who turns from the Lord. But the One they kill is God Himself, whose patient endurance of their crown of thorns shall bring the wicked to ruin. Caught in their own snares, "misery and sorrow" shall be theirs forever, even as the Lord and His anointed find release from the plots of men and are gathered into the kingdom of heaven.

The beast is slain by a word from His mouth, opened on that Day; though silent now, His redeeming Word goes forth to the ends of the earth, setting free all suffering prisoners.

O. 16. Mon. (II)

Sixteenth Week

Monday
(Mic.6:1-4,6-8; Ps.50:5-6,8-9,16-17,21,23; Mt.12:38-42)

"The Lord has a plea against His people,
and He enters into trial with Israel."

"God Himself is the judge," brothers and sisters. And so He declares: "Gather my faithful ones before me, those who have made a covenant with me by sacrifice." All are brought before His throne, and all must "present [their] plea" in His presence.

And what shall we say on that Day? Will you "come before Him with holocausts, with calves a year old? Will the Lord be pleased with thousands of rams, with myriad streams of oil?" Hear His word to His people: it is not these the Lord desires. It is not the sacrifices offered in the temple built by human hands the Lord seeks of His chosen ones. The temple He has destroyed, and with it the vain works of the flesh. It is now the Lord's desire that you but "walk humbly with your God." And so He promises: "To Him that goes the right way I will show the saving power of God," and proclaims, "He that offers praise as a sacrifice glorifies me."

O how we should praise Him! He who is "greater than Jonah" and "greater than Solomon." O how we should repent and reform our lives at His preaching! O how we should walk in the light of His wisdom! But are we not too often like those who offer vain sacrifice and seek to have our eyes impressed by some extraordinary sign? The sign stands before us. But all too often we are as faithless and blind as the scribes and Pharisees in our gospel today.

What a terrible thought that we might be condemned for our lack of faith by the "citizens of Nineveh" and "the queen of the South," who needed so little, really, to believe in the greatness of the Lord. Has He not "brought [us] up from the land of Egypt"? Has He not released us from "the

458

place of slavery"? Why do we so soon forget what the ancients knew by much less? Is not Jesus in our midst this day?

Let us not be blind to His presence, and let us not offer our sacrifice unworthily. For here before us stands the Lord of all; into our souls and bodies we receive Him by Word and by Sacrament. All He asks of us is our faith. And will we believe Him? Or is our worship only on the tongue and not burning in our heart? Let Him not find you faithless this day.

Tuesday
(Mic.7:14-15,18-20; Ps.85:2-8; Mt.12:46-50)

"Then extending His hands to His disciples, He said,
'There are my mother and my brothers.'"

The Lord's blessing rests upon all who worship Him in spirit and in truth, and it comes to us primarily through the forgiveness of our sins. For the Lord extends His hands to His disciples first of all to "cast into the depths of the sea all our sins." This is His principal work, He whose name means "God saves." And by such compassion poured upon us, by His "treading underfoot our guilt," we are drawn into His holy fold; we become "the flock of His inheritance" by the death that brings us life.

"Who is there like you, the God who removes guilt and pardons sin for the remnant of His inheritance?" Who indeed is like Jesus? For He dies and we live. He washes us clean of sin, and we become His children. Though we deserve His "burning anger," He abandons not us but "[His] displeasure against us." He "does not persist in anger forever, but delights rather in clemency," a clemency that not only forgives but redeems – for Jesus also extends His hands to His disciples to gather them into the Father's arms.

"You have favored, O Lord, your land; you have restored the well-being of Jacob. You have forgiven the guilt of your people; you have covered all their sins." How shall we thank you, Lord, who "grant us our salvation"? How shall we praise you, Lord, whose "kindness" has made us your own? "Shall not your people rejoice in you?" Will we not sing of your glory forever? Will we not stand in your presence and serve you for all ages to come? "You have withdrawn all your wrath." You "will again have compassion on us." In you we take refuge always, as your blessed daughters and sons.

O Mother in heaven, pray for us,
that children of the Lord we shall ever remain,
doing the will of the Father as thou hast done.

Wednesday
(Jer.1:1,4-10; Ps.71:1-6,15,17; Mt.13:1-9)

"O God, you have taught me from my youth,
and till the present I proclaim your wondrous deeds."

So does the seed grow, and bear fruit in the sight of the Lord.

Our psalmist declares, "On you I depend from birth; from my mother's womb you are my strength." Indeed we are planted in our mother's womb and we grow by the grace of the Lord. And as our bodies grow so gradually from the womb of our mother, so our spirits, too, grow from the womb of our Mother, the Church, in whose womb the Lord plants us and nurtures us with His water, the Holy Spirit. For it is the Lord who prepares the ground for our planting. As He declares to Jeremiah, "Before I formed you in the womb I knew you, before you were born I dedicated you." So even before we are planted as seed the Lord holds us in His Hand, and that Hand of love shall never leave us.

And what does the Lord expect of the seed He plants and nurtures but that it sprout and bear much fruit? What does He do but call us forth to proclaim His Word with our lives: "To whomever I send you, you shall go; whatever I command you, you shall speak" – what He requires of Jeremiah He requires of us all. As "the Lord extended His hand and touched [the prophet's] mouth, saying, 'See I place my words within your mouth!'" so He reaches out to us all, planting His Word within our hearts and expecting it to grow and blossom forth. Into the light our works must come to reveal His heavenly presence.

"The crowd stood along the shore" as rows of plants in an ordered garden, and Jesus watered them with His teaching. And in whom would His Word take root? Who would grow unencumbered in His light? Who would bear fruit unto the kingdom of God? "Let everyone heed what he hears!" Make the Lord your "rock of refuge" and He will "rescue [you] from the hand of the wicked" and nurture you with His Bread and the Word of Life. And your "mouth shall declare [His] justice, day by day [His] salvation" as you come gradually and invariably – you know not how – to the kingdom our Savior prepares with His Blood.

Thursday
(Jer.2:1-3,7-8,12-13; Ps.36:6-11; Mt.13:10-17)

"They look but do not see,
they listen but do not hear or understand."

O how "sacred to the Lord was Israel, the first fruits of His harvest." And O how they loved the Lord "as a bride," following Him so closely. But O how they have forgotten "the devotion of their youth" and turned from Him! For when He "brought [them] into the garden lands to eat its goodly fruits," they did not seek Him from whom all their blessings flowed, but rather "entered and defiled [His] land," and "made [His] heritage loathsome." So blindly "they have forsaken [the Lord], the source of living waters [and] have dug themselves cisterns, broken cisterns, that hold no water." And so, how empty of life they have become.

And so Jesus echoes Isaiah's prophecy upon the people today, declaring it now fulfilled: "Listen as you will, you shall not understand, look intently as you will, you shall not see." Though the Son of God stand before them, though their blessing is complete in their midst, strain as they might they cannot see what is so obvious – for "sluggish indeed is this people's heart." Too long have they turned their sights away from Him, and now what shall refresh their vision?

Should they not sing with David of the Lord's glory – "How precious is your kindness, O God"? Should they not "take refuge in the shadow of [His] wings"? Does He not spread them above them this day? In Jesus should they not "have their fill of the prime gifts of [His] house"; does the Lord not "give them to drink" from this "delightful stream"? Then why are their mouths closed to receiving this precious gift offered upon His altar? Is He not the holy sacrifice of the covenant renewed? Is it not so that in drinking His blood all find life? Is He not the source of living water?

O Lord, "with you is the fountain of life, and in your light we see light." Awaken our hearts to see your face; let us "turn back to [you]" that you may "heal [us]." For you are Light and Life itself, and all our blessings flow from you and from your Son's Body and Blood offered for our sakes. In Him may we find again our home; may our hearts be open to understand your love present in our midst.

Friday
(Jer.3:14-17; Jer.31:10-13; Mt.13:18-23)

"At that time they will call Jerusalem the Lord's throne;
there all nations will be gathered together
to honor the name of the Lord at Jerusalem."

I would like today to focus the attention particularly of the Lord's chosen race on the following prophecy of the great Jeremiah: "They will in those days no longer say, 'The ark of the covenant of the Lord!' or miss it, or make another." For I must in obedience to the Spirit of Truth ask the

461

question: If the temple of the Lord has been destroyed, how is it Judaism can be said to yet exist? With the discontinuance of the sacrifices, does the heart of the Mosaic Law not undergo a certain transformation? To the point: Does the sacrifice of Christ *not* supplant – even as it fulfills, perfectly – the Old Covenant? Is His blood poured upon the altar now and sprinkled upon all our souls, is it not this which gives birth to the New Jerusalem, where "they shall come streaming to the Lord's blessings"?

And does not the destruction of the temple so soon after the death of Him who prophesied it in tears not substantiate His claim as the Temple not built by human hands? And does the fact that the ancient walls have remained in ruins for some two thousand years not indicate its permanent end? Would the Lord really wish it to be built again? And do you think He would leave you alone for so long a time? Has He not come?

My brothers, my sisters, should not he who has the deepest "roots" be the strongest tree reaching to the greatest heights? Is He not? And should you not be as this quintessential Jew, suffering for the sake of all at the hands of those who breathe condemnation? (Here is a message to those who would take the Lord's justice in their violent hands – you shall not escape condemnation for your sin. Whatever good may seem to result from your prideful persecution, though His chosen may turn at your threat, yet *your* sin will be remembered.)

"Shouting, they shall mount the heights of Zion." This word is for all who understand "the message about God's reign" Jesus comes to sow in receptive hearts. And so, "hear the word of the Lord, O nations, proclaim it on distant coasts" to all God's "rebellious children," to all who yet walk "in their hardhearted wickedness" – for all may now "become fruitful in the land." (And you, brother Catholic, do you know the blessing that is upon you; do you see that you stand in the New Jerusalem?) But still the chosen are called first of all; still the Lord waits for those most blessed, to pour His new graces upon them.

Let no man's soul be choked by "worldly anxiety"; let all come now to the Lord's glorious throne, here in the heavenly Jerusalem.

Saturday
(Jer.7:1-11; Ps.84:2-6,8,11; Mt.13:24-30)

"Reform your ways and your deeds,
so that I may remain with you in this place."

We hear again today of the failure of "the temple of the Lord" and its sacrifices to bring the Israelites to the eternal presence of God. For though the Lord "sowed good seed in His field," though He made His temple a house of prayer, it has become "a den of thieves" in the eyes of His chosen. And the Lord "see[s] what is being done." And because they "steal and murder, commit adultery and perjury, [and] burn incense to Baal," the Israelites break the covenant upon which the temple is founded, and it can but fall to ruin. The Lord spells out what they must do to preserve the integrity of His temple: "If each of you deals justly with his neighbor; if you no longer oppress the resident alien, the orphan, and the widow; if you no longer shed innocent blood in this place, or follow strange gods to your own harm..." but though He repeatedly warns them of what it takes to maintain His presence in their midst, yet they repeatedly turn from His blessings and the words the prophets offer. Unable to "thoroughly reform [their] ways and [their] deeds," they cannot but lose the temple.

But, again, there is hope. For what has not been preserved on earth shall be made permanent in heaven. Though "an enemy came and sowed weeds through His wheat," and though in this world they are not rooted out from our midst – though our worship fall short of the Lord's eternal glory, yet Jesus comes to perfect God's will in us, drawing us to the Temple not made by human hands... and with Him the weeds are no more. Yes, because of our sin we lose His blessing; but by His grace our worship is made whole in His sight.

"My soul yearns and pines for the courts of the Lord. My heart and my flesh cry out for the living God." In the heart of Jesus I would dwell; in His flesh we find the Temple. And His Temple we become as we eat His Body and drink His Blood. As we follow this Word made flesh, we are redeemed and our home with God blessed permanently. And so in truth and with His love welling up in our souls, we cry with our psalmist: "I had rather live at the threshold of the house of my God than dwell in the tents of the wicked"; and so, "happy" indeed we are. Praise the Lord for His eternal goodness, for in Him "even the sparrow finds a home."

O. 17. Mon. (II)

Seventeenth Week

Monday
(Jer.13:1-11; Dt.32:18-21; Mt.13:31-35)

"You were unmindful of the Rock that begot you.
You forgot the God who gave you birth."

So Moses says of the people he led through the desert. So Jeremiah is told of the Lord's chosen at the time of the Babylonian exile. So it is with those who are deaf to Jesus' parables. And so we, too, forget the Lord whenever we turn from Him in sin.

So close were the Lord's children to Him and His blessings: "As close as the loincloth clings to a man's loins, so had I made the whole house of Israel and the whole house of Judah cling to me, says the Lord." The God of earth and heaven calls them "my people, my renown, my praise, my beauty." He has set them aside to be His own, to make them holy in the eyes of the world. "But they did not listen." But they did not remain faithful. Going after "strange gods to serve and adore them," they showed themselves to be "sons with no loyalty in them." And so they became "rotted, good for nothing."

How sad is sin. "What a fickle race [we] are." For all we need the Lord provides, yet we "walk in the stubbornness of [our] hearts" a path away from Him, apart from His love. And now Jesus "announce[s] what has lain hidden since the creation of the world." In parables He speaks of the kingdom of God. But how many hearts are closed to His teaching? How many "refuse to obey [His] words?" And should the Lord not therefore be "filled with loathing and anger toward His sons and daughters"?

The kingdom of heaven cannot grow in us if we separate ourselves from Jesus. As Israel and Judah were cast off, so shall we be, if we do not heed His commands. Following the "vain idols" of the nations will not bring us to *His* kingdom, but only make us abominable in His sight. And what horror to lose His blessing, to turn our renown and beauty to an everlasting curse.

It need not be so. To Him we can return, with open ears and understanding hearts and light thus filling our eyes. Remaining ever in His presence, remembering His Name, He who has planted us as seed "in His field," He who has given birth to new life within us, will see that each day we grow. And on the last Day we shall be formed in His image.

O. 17. Tues. (II)

Tuesday
(Jer.14:17-22; Ps.79:8-9,11,13; Mt.13:36-43)

"Remember not against us the iniquities of the past;
may your compassion quickly come to us,
for we are brought very low."

If the prophet's "eyes stream with tears day and night, without rest, over the great destruction which overwhelms the virgin daughter of [his] people, over her incurable wound," how many more tears will there be "at the end of the world" when the "weeds are collected and burned"? For in our first reading Jeremiah sees "those slain by the sword" and "those consumed by hunger," suffering enough to bring tears – but this "blow" struck by the Lord is not one which "cannot be healed." "A time of healing" shall indeed

464

come as the nation is brought back from exile only seventy years after its being taken; and soon Jesus shall come to "free [all] those doomed to death," to set prisoners free... to make permanent the compassionate deliverance of the Lord God. But at the end of the age, when Jesus comes again and finally, the sentence that is passed against those who have sinned shall have no means of repeal; the death upon souls shall be everlasting.

In our gospel today Jesus speaks in plain terms as He explains "the parable of the weeds in the field." This is no mere fable but the delineation of the harvest time that shall come upon all. To heaven or to hell all shall go, and there shall be no more changing: no more opportunity for redemption for those set upon evil, and no more faltering into wickedness for those set upon good. Great shall be the eternal gifts showered upon the blessed, but what of the wailing then... what of the wailing?

"We have sinned against you." "We recognize, O Lord, our wickedness." We pray you shall "remember your covenant with us," and from all our sin set us free. "Deliver us and pardon our sins" and we "will give thanks to you forever; through all generations we will declare your praise." Keep us safe from your judgment on the Last Day. Do not "cast [us] off completely," but raise our lowly hearts unto your kingdom.

Wednesday
(Jer.15:10,16-21; Ps.59:2-4,10-11,17-18; Mt.13:44-46)

"If you repent, so that I restore you,
in my presence you shall stand."

The Lord called Jeremiah even from before he was formed in his mother's womb, but it seems he falls short of fulfilling that call, for the Lord says to His prophet today, "If you bring forth the precious without the vile, you shall be my mouthpiece." Indeed it seemed Christ's words in His parable today – "The reign of God is like a buried treasure which a man found in a field" – had been realized in Jeremiah, who declares, "When I found your words, I devoured them; they became the joy and the happiness of my heart." Yet it appears the prophet struggles to heed the Lord's instruction to "put up for sale all he had," to give up all else to receive fully the gift of God's gracious presence.

Jeremiah complains to God, "Why is my pain continuous, my wound incurable, refusing to be healed?" And what is this pain but the persecution he continually finds as "a man of strife and contention to all the land"? The Lord has called him to be a continual sign of contradiction toward His rebellious house, and the difficulties of this cross he must bear move the prophet toward despair.

What is the "vile" matter of which Jeremiah must "repent" to become "a solid wall of brass" in his mission for God? It is, I believe, the "indignation" he says he has toward his fellow people, who, though evil in the sight of God, must be borne with patience, according to the Lord's call. It is his failure to be as really only Christ is – able to forgive His persecutors even as He stands nailed to the cross. Jeremiah must accept his weakness and trials, as does Paul later, but struggles greatly in this time before the coming of the Son.

Yet the Lord promises to "free [him] from the hand of the wicked, and rescue [him] from the grasp of the violent." Yet the Lord is with him to answer his prayer when he cries out as has David, "Rescue me from my enemies, O my God; from my adversaries defend me." And yet he will know what David proclaims: "You have been my stronghold, my refuge in the day of distress." For whoever cries out to Him from the cross, the Lord hears; and to him He brings the greatest treasure of all – His own presence within him.

(If you would find this "pearl" of greatest value, brothers and sisters, in a word, learn to love thy enemy.)

O. 17. Thurs. (II)

Thursday
(Jer.18:1-6; Ps.146:1-6; Mt.13:47-53)

"Like clay in the hand of the potter,
so are you in my hand, O house of Israel."

"I went down to the potter's house and there he was, working at the wheel." According to the Lord's word Jeremiah goes, and a marvelous sign is provided him. For there in the hands of the potter and in his work, he sees the Lord huddled over His creation. And what in particular does he witness in this vision? "Whenever the object of clay which he was making turned out badly in his hand, he tried again, making of the clay another object of whatever sort he pleased." Are we not indeed like this clay in the potter's hands? Does He not send His only Son to remake us in His image? And so, should we not be as pliable as clay in the holy hands of our Lord and God?

And are we not as those caught in the net of the fishermen who, having "collected all sorts of things... put what was worthwhile into containers. [But] what was useless they threw away." Yes, at the end of the world "angels will go out and separate the wicked from the just," and then the hand of the Lord will be at work in its fullness. So, while there is yet time, let us do all we can to be remade in God's image, that we might avoid "the fiery furnace" – let us not be hardened in our sin. For once cast in this kiln, what shall they do but "wail and grind their teeth"?

466

Brothers and sisters, do you not see that it is the Lord "who made heaven and earth, the sea and all that is in them"? It is the Lord who holds all in His holy hands, and does what He will with the universe. And so, should you not take refuge in Him? "Put not your trust in princes, in men, in whom there is no salvation." What is man who "when his spirit departs he returns to his earth"? When God removes His breath from man, indeed he becomes as nothing but clay in a potter's hands. But "happy he whose help is the God of Jacob, whose hope is in the Lord, his God." For the one who trusts in Him, He shall remake in His own eternal image; upon this clay His breath shall remain. And so his soul shall ever "praise the Lord."

O. 17. Fri. (II)

Friday
(Jer.26:1-9; Ps.69:5,8-10,14; Mt.13:54-58)

"No prophet is without honor,
except in his native place, indeed in his own house."

How consonant are our readings today, all speaking of the persecution the prophet of God must bear in bringing the truth to His people. (Indeed I had thought to refer to the incident in our gospel before having even come to it, while still reading the words from Jeremiah, for elsewhere in the gospels the same quote of Jesus written above causes His people to lead Him to the brow of a hill, intending to throw Him down.)

As Jesus was rejected when He "went to His native place and spent His time teaching in their synagogue," so when Jeremiah is obedient to the Lord's command to "stand in the court of the house of the Lord and speak to the people of all the cities of Judah who come to worship in the house of the Lord ... all the people gathered about [him]," not to "listen and turn back, each from his evil way," but to join with "the priests and prophets [who] laid hold of him, crying, 'You must be put to death!'" And David bemoans the same treatment in our psalm: "I have become an outcast to my brothers, a stranger to my mother's sons," as for the sake of the Lord he "bear[s] insult."

What does the prophet come to do; what does Jesus speak to His people but truth? They themselves recognize that He has great "wisdom and miraculous powers." With these He would save their very lives; His sword of truth would incise every cancerous growth of sin from their souls – He would heal them with the Word of God. In fact, it is their health He is so zealous to effect. But "because zeal for [the Lord's] house consumes [Him]... the insults of those who blaspheme [God] fall upon [Him]." As they do upon Jeremiah. As they do upon David... As they do upon every faithful prophet of God.

Those who "disobey [God], not living according to the law [He] placed before [them] and not listening to the words of [His] servants the prophets," do not wish to hear of their sin: foolishly, they would be left to die in their rebellion. And so they kill the prophet, attempting vainly to destroy His message. And it must be those of the Lord's own house that reject His word, that kill the Christ, for it is only they who know His voice speaking in their hearts.

"This city shall be desolate and deserted." Hear these words, brothers and sisters. Let them sink deeply into your ears and take root in your hearts. Be not afraid of the death that must come to this earthen vessel. Nor reject the word because it comes from one who is your own brother. It is this sword of truth alone that will save you.

O. 17. Sat. (II)

Saturday
(Jer.26:11-16,24; Ps.69:14-16,30-31,33-34; Mt.14:1-12)

"In truth it was the Lord who sent me to you,
to speak all these things for you to hear."

Jeremiah speaks to the people in the Lord's name, even as he is threatened with death: "Reform your ways and your deeds; listen to the voice of the Lord your God, so that the Lord will repent of the evil with which He threatens you," he declares at his trial – he does not hide the truth. And the words of David's psalm are proven genuine: "His own who are in bonds He spurns not"; for the prophet's words find a hearing in the people, and Ahikam advocates for his release.

It is the truth which John the Baptist, the greatest of prophets, comes to declare most boldly. Even from Herod's dungeon this voice crying in the wilderness continues to proclaim the sinfulness of the king's taking his own sister-in-law to wife, repeatedly telling him, "It is not right for you to live with her." He, too, does not back down in the face of trials, in the dark of prison, and he, too, is released from bonds – though bonds of a different kind. He, too, is "rescued from [his] foes, and from the watery depths... The pit [does not] close its mouth over [him]." For though he be beheaded, though death at the hands of his persecutor he does not escape, yet it is his message which lives and has power, power shown now in the presence of the Truth walking the earth in the Person of Jesus Christ – a power which causes the evil king to shake in his boots at the voice which still comes to his ears. Indeed, John yet lives. In Jesus he makes his home.

"I will praise the name of God in song, and I will glorify Him with thanksgiving." For all His "lowly ones" He sees; all who "seek God" are known to Him. And these shall be released from all bonds of this earth, even as they speak His truth.

The party shall soon be over, the dance of the daughter of lust come to an end. And who shall stand justified then? Who shall hear His soothing words? And who shall be condemned? Turn to Him in your hearts this day. Listen to His voice.

Eighteenth Week

Monday (A)
(Jer.28:1-17; Ps.119:29,43,68,79-80,95,102; Mt.14:22-36)

"Let those turn to me who fear you
and acknowledge your decrees."

Hananiah does not fear the Lord; he cares nothing for His decrees. And so he prophesies that the Lord will bring "the vessels of the house of the Lord and all the exiles back from Babylon" within two years, though the Lord has not said this. And he refuses to turn to Jeremiah – who does acknowledge the Lord's decrees and speaks only truth – hardening himself against the word and the will of the Lord even unto his death. How foolish to have "false confidence," to have no fear of God and His prophets. "Rebellion against the Lord" can but bring destruction to the proud soul.

And what of the fear the disciples exhibit throughout our gospel today: the fear of the boat "being tossed about in the waves raised by strong head winds"; their terror at seeing Jesus "walking on the water" in the middle of the night ("'It is a ghost!' they said."); Peter's fear of sinking in the water... Is this the fear the Lord desires of His chosen ones? No. For this is the fear of a faithless soul disturbed by the distractions the devil might raise, not the fear of the Lord. The fear the Lord requires we see after Jesus "had climbed into the boat, [and] the wind died down." Here read of the fear of the Lord: "Those who were in the boat showed Him reverence, declaring, 'Undoubtedly you are the Son of God!'"

Acknowledge Him we must. To His feet we must bring all our sickness, all our blindness. Knowing that by His word alone we are saved, that in His presence alone do we find our home, our harbor in this storm – this is the fear which must burn in our hearts. There is no other way. There is no other word which has weight. Only His hand reaches out and lifts us up from drowning in the waves. And for this we honor Him. For the law of His mouth we praise His name. For what does He speak but our salvation? What does He come across the lake bringing us but assistance in our exile

469

here? And so, what should we do but reverence His eminent grace? Let the Lord be praised!

Monday (B,C)
(Jer.28:1-17; Ps.119:29,43,68,79-80,95,102; Mt.14:13-21)

"Take not the word of truth from my mouth,
for in your ordinances is my hope."

The word of truth is what Jeremiah speaks in the face of the lies of Hananiah. The false prophet declares in the name of God: "I will break the yoke of Nebuchadnezzar, king of Babylon, from off the neck of the nations," even as he takes "the yoke from upon the neck of Jeremiah" (which he wore to symbolize the exile to which Judah was fated) and breaks it "in the presence of all the people." A dramatic action and a prophecy all would gladly consume. But a lie. To Hananiah, Jeremiah prophesies the truth: "By breaking a wooden yoke, you forge an iron yoke!" as well as the false prophet's own death, which comes in but a few months. And yes, it is seventy years the exile shall last, not two.

And is it not the word of truth by which the Lord feeds the five thousand today? Using human logic the disciples suggest to Jesus that He "dismiss the crowds so that they may go to the villages and buy some food for themselves." But it is with the word of truth Jesus states: "Give them something to eat yourselves." How? they respond. "We have nothing here... but five loaves and a couple of fish." How does the Lord multiply these loaves and fish? How can He feed five thousand with barely enough food for fifty? It is not possible except by the word of truth, which can move mountains. Is it not His looking up to heaven and blessing and breaking the food that causes it to be multiplied in the sight (and eating) of all? Does not the Father give the Son all for which He asks? Is His prayer not true?

Brothers and sisters, if the ordinances of the Lord are our hope, what can we not do? What food can we not multiply? What ailing hearts can we not heal? For trusting in Him and in His Word all is ours for the asking. But making our own words and our own desires our way in this world, what can we come to but death? What shall we find but an iron yoke upon our necks?

Yes, the yoke of the Lord is light, for it is formed by the word of God, and in its truth we are buoyed up unto heaven. And all our words are justified. And we are fed with the bread of life.

470

Tuesday (A)

(Jer.30:1-2,12-15,18-22; Ps.102:16-23,29; Mt.15:1-2,10-14)

"Every planting not put down by my heavenly Father
will be uprooted."

Is it not these Pharisees of whom Jeremiah speaks when he prophesies, "Incurable is your wound, grievous your bruise"? Truly there is "no remedy for [their] running sore, no healing for [them]." Blind shall they ever be, for they do but harden their hearts when their sin is brought up before their eyes.

And so, though Jesus comes to "restore the tents of Jacob," "when the Lord has rebuilt Zion and appeared in His glory," where shall they be? Where are they now as He brings this to pass in their very presence? Is it not so that they cannot see? And so, as "the peoples gather together, and the kingdoms, to serve the Lord," they can only remain outside His house knocking so vainly...

"It is not what goes into a man's mouth that makes him impure; it is what comes out of his mouth." With this simple declaration the Lord turns the eyes of all ancient religions – set so much on the letter of the law, witnessed in the washing of hands and the preparation of food for the body (which shall but die one day) – in upon themselves. With this essential challenge all are forced to examine their faith and discover upon what it rests. Is it truly upon the Almighty God, who is "heavenly," who is Spirit? Or is it upon their own belly? It is a hard look that must be taken if one is to be drawn into the renewed covenant and anointed by its blood. (How else shall one stand in the overwhelming light of His glory?)

It shall be so that "all your lovers have forgotten you": anything upon which you set your heart that is short of the Almighty God shall indeed but rot, shall be exposed for all its vanity. And though it seems at this time that the Lord has "struck you as an enemy would strike," that He has "punished you cruelly," know that it is "because of your great guilt, your numerous sins, [He has] done this to you," that He might uproot these from your midst – that you might not be uprooted from His presence.

Tuesday (B,C)

(Jer.30:1-2,12-15,18-22; Ps.102:16-23,29; Mt.14:22-36)

"His assembly before me shall stand firm."

The words of the prophet Jeremiah are fulfilled in the Apostle Peter and in the Church, for upon this Rock we have our firm foundation.

471

Ordinary Time

"The Lord looked down from His holy height, from heaven He beheld the earth"; and when the time had come, He sent His only Son. And that Son, in all His wisdom, chooses those who would follow Him, making certain thereby that indeed "the children of [His] servants shall abide, and their posterity shall continue in [the Father's] presence," thus fulfilling the word of the Lord: "You shall be my people, and I will be your God."

Yes, Jeremiah declares of the New Jerusalem, the "city [that] shall be rebuilt upon [the] hill": "His leader shall be one of his own, and his rulers shall come from his kin." Jesus is of our kind, a man like each of the Lord's children, and so is the apostle He chooses – and all who likewise follow. All bishops and priests, all the descendants of Peter and the apostles in the ministry of the Word and the ministry of the flesh of Christ, all come from our midst and are our very brothers. And the Church is ruled by them in the power of the Holy Spirit.

In the beginning of our gospel today we find Jesus much as He was the night before choosing His apostles – "He went up on the mountain to pray, remaining there alone as evening drew on." John the Baptist has been killed and the time has come now for our Lord's mission to increase, and so He prepares Himself for this next step in His ministry. And so it becomes His primary concern to be sure that when the time comes for Him to die, His successor shall be readied. And so the test and teaching He brings His Rock, Peter.

"When I summon him, he shall approach me; how else should one take the deadly risk of approaching me? says the Lord." Again Jeremiah's prophecy is fulfilled, for Peter does not come to Jesus on his own, but first states, "Lord, if it is really you, tell me to come to you across the water," and waits for the Lord to exclaim: "Come!" And what happens now, what miracle? "Peter got out of the boat and began walking on the water, moving toward Jesus." Yes, our Rock walks miraculously with the Lord! Then why does he begin to sink? you say. It is the Lord's will to teach our leader, and all of us, of our dependence on Him alone and our need to cry out, "Lord, save me!" (O how sweet and instructive are the words Jesus whispers loudly into the apostle's ears – "Why did you falter?")

O may the Lord ever bless His Church with the firmness of faith found only in Him! May we ever stand in His presence, unshaken by the winds of the world and our own human weakness. Yes, may we be His children.

O. 18. Wed. (II)

Wednesday
(Jer.31:1-7; Jer.31:10-13; Mt.15:21-28)

"Shouting, they shall mount the heights of Zion,
they shall come streaming to the Lord's blessings."

In our first reading Jeremiah prophesies the restoration of "all the tribes of Israel" to the grace and "age-old love" of their Lord and God. The Lord promises His virgin daughter: "Carrying your festive tambourines, you shall go forth dancing with the merrymakers." He will "turn their mourning into joy" as this "remnant" returns to the holy heights of Mount Zion, as he "gathers them together" as His chosen once again.

And in our gospel the Lord makes clear it is for the lost children of Israel He has come. Here in the mission of the Christ, Jeremiah's prophecy is fulfilled. But more than the restoration of the nation of Israel do we hear of today. What we find is that not these alone shall come streaming to the Lord's blessings, but indeed all the nations shall find Him whom their hearts desire. And it is the Canaanite woman who leads the way for all Gentile people to receive the grace and favor of the One God.

On her knees she comes, crawling like a dog, this mother of all us not born of Jewish blood, to be grafted to the kingdom's tree. Here is a sign of the humility we all must have. And when rebuffed she does not answer, Who are you? and leave in anger, but drops further on her face, pleading for "the leavings that fall from [the] master's table." And so she shows the Lord the "great faith" even we Gentiles can exhibit; and so she wins a hearing not only for herself but all people of foreign nations who, like Ruth, are able to say in truth: May your God be my God (see Ru.1:16). And so her daughter finds the healing touch of the Lord.

Brothers and sisters, the promise given the people of Israel is now for all of us to share, if we have but faith – if we but have the love of God burning in our hearts. And so, "rise up, let us go to Zion, to the Lord, our God" and "enjoy the fruits" He offers forth for all His many sheep. This Canaanite woman came "shouting after" Him and found the ear of the God of the universe; let us now "shout with joy for Jacob" and with Jacob, as we celebrate the glory of the Lord here present in our midst.

O. 18. Thurs. (II)

Thursday
(Jer.31:31-34; Ps.51:12-15,18-19; Mt.16:13-23)

"I will make a new covenant with the house of Israel
and the house of Judah."

Do not the days come to pass, is not this promise made through Jeremiah fulfilled, when the Lord declares to Peter, "On this rock I will build my Church, and the jaws of death shall not prevail against it"? Does Jesus not hereby wrest the covenant from the hands of the leaders of the Jews and thus make His people anew, here founding His New Covenant and His new Church upon Peter and the apostles? Does not all that has been

Ordinary Time

declared to the Chosen now come to pass in the Christ and in those who follow Him? Are we not, as it were, true and complete Jews, basking in the light of the Messiah?

And what is it this New Covenant is like? The Lord says, "I will place my law within them, and write it upon their hearts; I will be their God and they shall be my people." Indeed, all shall "know the Lord." And how shall this come about? Is this not the answer to David's heartfelt prayer when drowning in the midst of sin: "A clean heart create for me, O God, and a steadfast spirit renew within me"? Is it not by His cleansing us of all our transgressions that He shall "remember [our] sin no more"? Is it not in this way our hearts are prepared to receive Him, and He comes to make His home with us? Is this not why Jesus has come?

"Your Holy Spirit take not from me," David cries out, and his "heart contrite and humbled" the Lord responds to. For upon Peter and His Church He places His Holy Spirit, never to be removed, and all who dwell within this House shall indeed never be "cast... from [His] presence." Later He shall breathe upon the apostles; later the Spirit shall fall mightily on them. Now He is still teaching them to make "God's standards" their own; now He is still making room for His love in their hearts. But still, here is the declaration that His Church shall be, and shall grow unto eternity.

May we all take refuge within the blessed walls formed by the Lord's hands, anointed by His Spirit. May our hearts all be set upon Him. And His power shall be in our hands; and we will be His own... and the New Covenant of love will be known.

Friday
(Nah.2:1,3,3:1-3,6-7;   Dt.32:35-36,39,41;   Mt.16:24-28)

"It is I who bring both death and life,
I who inflict wounds and heal them."

When the Lord comes indeed "He will repay each man according to his conduct." And the justice and judgment that are the Lord's alone are evident in His work amongst Israel and their enemies, spoken of in our first reading and psalm today.

"The flame of the sword, the flash of the spear, the many slain, the heaping corpses, the endless bodies to stumble upon!" such is the graphic description of the horrors inflicted by the "bloody city" of Nineveh, of Assyria, whose nation is "all lies, full of plunder, whose looting never stops!" And that which they have visited upon the nations, and upon the children of Israel, shall come to rest upon their own heads. For "surely, the Lord shall do justice for His people" and prove to the evildoers that it is He alone who "will sharpen [His] flashing sword"; it is He whose "hand shall lay hold of [His] quiver." For vengeance is with the Lord alone and it is He who "will repay [His] foes and requite those who hate [Him]."

All those who take up the sword, what can be said of them? "Close at hand is the day of their disaster, and their doom is rushing upon them." Like Nineveh they shall be "destroyed, and who can pity [them]?" Are they not like he who has "gain[ed] the whole world and ruin[ed] himself in the process?" And shall not all who trust in "horses a-gallop, chariots bounding, cavalry charging," themselves hear "the rumbling sound of wheels"? As the Lord has duly repaid those on earth, so He will more greatly repay all on the Day of salvation.

But even as death is visited upon the sinner, life dawns upon the righteous. For them, "the bearer of good news [comes], announcing peace." Those who are pierced to the heart by the cross of Christ in this life, those who bear its weight through this forsaken land, walking in the footsteps of the Lord – even these shall "see the Son of Man come in His kingship." For "whoever loses his life for [God's] sake will find it," and it shall be preserved unto eternity.

Brothers and sisters, though wounded here, the Lord Himself shall heal us. Let death come to all sin, and salvation shall be assured.

Saturday
(Hb.1:12-2:4; Ps.9:8-13; Mt.17:14-20)

"They trust in you who cherish your name,
for you forsake not those who seek you, O Lord."

"Why could we not expel it?" the disciples asked Jesus regarding the boy so severely possessed by a demon. "'Because you have so little trust,' He told them."

Brothers and sisters, is it the Lord who "delays"? Is it He who fails to cast wickedness and misery from our midst? Or is it not rather we who fail in faith? We complain and ask, When will the Lord act? but is the Lord not quick to act, as He does in our gospel today, whenever we call upon Him in truth? Does He not give us the power to do all in His Name? Does He somehow withhold His grace?

Certainly not. "He has not forgotten the cry of the afflicted," and it is eternally true that "the just man, because of his faith, shall live." The wicked man shall not "keep brandishing his sword to slay peoples without mercy"; and of the fool who "sacrifices to his net" for the fish that come through it – failing to see the God who provides all things and who alone deserves our trust... how long shall such vanity last? It shall disappear with the coming dawn.

"The vision still has its time, presses on to fulfillment, and will not disappoint." He who is here in our midst is coming to us, and we know "He judges the world with justice; He governs the peoples with equity." And His time is soon fulfilled. But how we must trust in Him! How our faith must be purified! How our hearts must be taken from the empty things of this world and our eyes set entirely on the Lord. Only this will save us; and this is what He teaches.

> Trust in Him and in His Name;
> it is only He who saves us.
> He forsakes not His children.

Nineteenth Week

Monday
(Ez.1:2-5,24-28; Ps.148:1-2,11-14; Mt.17:22-27)

"His majesty is above earth and heaven."

Gleaming like gold or silver, shining forth like burning fire, splendorous as "the bow which appears in the clouds on a rainy day" – "such was the vision of the likeness of the glory of the Lord" given the prophet Ezekiel. And this is but His likeness; nothing could describe the glory of the One who has beneath His feet the four living creatures whose wings beat "like the roaring of mighty waters, like the voice of the Almighty." These eyes cannot see God.

But His only Son we can see, for He whose greatness is as the Lord's own has deigned to walk amongst us in human form. Though His place is at the throne of the Almighty God, though His glory is itself exalted above earth and heaven, yet the Son of God becomes also the Son of Man. And not only does He walk in our skin, but even dies for our sin. How humble is our glorious God!

And though He Himself is the Temple of God, though it is by His hands only the temple on earth has been built, yet He does not presume exemption from paying tax to those who are but its caretakers. For He subjects Himself entirely to our laws, as well as to our scourges. (And notice that the coin Peter will find in the mouth of the fish is "twice the temple tax," to pay simultaneously for himself and Jesus. Thus is Peter equated with the Lord in the exemption of sonship, in authority over the temple – for it is he who shall be at the helm of the new Temple.)

476

The disciples are "overwhelmed with grief" at hearing of their Lord's coming crucifixion. They have known the glory of God so wonderfully as wedding guests, as the best men of the bridegroom – as the blessed disciples of the Son – and now the thought of His dying is beyond their comprehension. (So much so that they do not even hear that "He will be raised up on the third day.") They want to maintain the glory they have known, which is indeed heavenly. But Jesus' humbling of Himself is not complete, as neither is His glory. Remain on this earth He cannot, but must return to the right hand of the Father. And the only way to this fulfillment of glory is through the cross – only this will bring Him to resurrection, and bring us all from our sin.

"Praise the name of the Lord, for His name alone is exalted." Let all that lives and that breathes praise our Savior, Jesus. For it is He who brings us to the majesty of our Father.

Tuesday
(Ez.2:8-3:4; Ps.119:14,24,72,103,111,131; Mt.18:1-5,10,12-14)

"How sweet to my palate are your promises,
sweeter than honey to my mouth!"

And is there a sweeter promise or a sweeter teaching than that which Jesus gives today in our gospel? In answer to the disciples' question, "'Who is of greatest importance in the kingdom of God?' He called a little child over and stood him in their midst and said ... 'Whoever makes himself lowly, becoming like this child, is of greatest importance in that heavenly reign.'" And He goes on to assure them that none of His children is forgotten by the Father – each He searches out diligently. Always they shall behold the absolute sweetness of His countenance... forever they shall look on His presence. O to be as that innocent child in the Lord Jesus' arms!

"Yes, your decrees are my delight; they are my counselors." O Lord, "I gasp with open mouth in my yearning for your commands." Let us be as your prophet Ezekiel, to whom you bring the written scroll and command, "Open your mouth and eat what I shall give you." Let us "eat what is before [us]"; let us "eat this scroll." Let us consume your words and commands and "feed [our] belly and fill [our] stomach" with your teaching and your promises. For all your words are "sweet as honey in [the] mouth." All that comes from you is grace and peace and joy. And though the words may be sour in our stomach, though we may have to declare "lamentation and wailing and woe!" to those who turn from your law – though suffering may indeed follow in accomplishing your will, yet the sweet knowledge that all comes from your hand shall sustain us; we shall never forget your blessing.

Nothing is sweeter, nothing is more wonderful, than fulfilling the word of God in our lives. Nothing is greater than coming to His table to eat. And now this Word made flesh is in our midst, and of its sweetness we daily partake. Of His presence we cannot receive enough; to His love there are no bounds. And children before Him we constantly become as we ever consume His promises, listening to His Word and eating and drinking His Body and Blood. And so, let us rejoice as we receive from the "hand stretched out to [us]."

Wednesday
(Ez.9:1-7,10:18-22; Ps.113:1-6; Mt.18:15-20)

"Where two or three are gathered in my name,
there am I in their midst."

And so the four living creatures, the cherubim gathered beneath the feet of the Lord, "rise from the earth" and move "straight forward," the breath of the Spirit animating every beat of their wings. And so the angels called forth by the voice of God protect or destroy the inhabitants of His city, according to His command. And so Jesus can assure His disciples, "Whatever you declare bound on earth shall be held bound in heaven, and whatever you declare loosed on earth shall be held loosed in heaven." For He is in our midst.

"Who is like the Lord, our God, who is enthroned on high and looks upon the heavens and the earth below?" The answer is, of course, no one. And yet the answer is everyone, everyone whom the Lord touches – everyone He ordains to do His will. For the Lord does not work in a vacuum but anoints all His chosen to serve as His hands and arms, His feet and legs... His tongue and soul on earth and in heaven. We are not left alone, but become as He is. Though "above the heavens is His glory," yet to the earth has He come down and walked amongst us, making us as His appointed angels. His work must be accomplished in us.

Raise your voice unto Him, brothers and sisters; with angelic blessings we are called to dwell. For He is here in our midst, He who is above the angels' realm. So, may our hearts beat with the breath of the Spirit; may He animate our every thought and movement. May the will of the Lord be done in His Church, that all shall be prepared to receive His mark, that all will be prepared for the last Day... when the Lord passes through His "city," when He comes to save and destroy. Now let men be taught what is right and what is wrong; now let us gather in His Name. "From the rising to the setting of the sun is the name of the Lord to be praised."

Thursday
(Ez.12:1-12; Ps.78:7,56-59,61-62; Mt.18:21-19:1)

"As captives they shall go into exile."

"The prince who is among them shall shoulder his burden and set out in darkness, going through a hole he has dug in the wall, and covering his face lest he be seen by anyone." O the woe of the "rebellious house"! How their sins eat away at their souls like hands digging holes in a wall; how they must hide their faces from the light of day and from the Lord's glorious face. Into what hell they cast themselves with no means of escape, their burden too heavy to bear.

The house of Israel "turned back and were faithless like their fathers," and so the Lord "surrendered His strength into captivity, His glory into the hands of the foe." And just such a fate awaits all who are hardened by sin, who have no forgiveness in their hearts. For all owe the Lord "a huge amount" and all have "no way of paying it"; and so all deserve to be sold into slavery. Only the mercy of God preserves us from such a fate. But can a heart know mercy which shows none? Can a soul receive forgiveness if it continues in sin? Does not this house remain in exile from its God? And what shall become of the one who spurns the love of God as does the wretched servant? Shall he not be like him whom "the master handed... over to the torturers until he paid back all that he owed'?

There is only woe for the soul so set in opposition to the loving will of God. There is only banishment from His sight. As the Lord "was enraged and utterly rejected Israel," His chosen children whom He had loved and blessed and forgiven so much, so all shall die in their sin who refuse to turn to Him... for there is no place for the evil with the good.

From darkness let us come, brothers and sisters. Exile from the Lord let us avoid. May we, too, learn from Ezekiel's sign and open our eyes to the danger upon us. On our knees let us come to our confessor, who has been instructed by his Master to forgive "seventy times seven times," and so wash ourselves clean of our rebellion – and then share the same with others. To the Lord let us return.

Friday
(Ez.16:1-15,60,63 or Ez.16:59-63; Is.12:1-6; Mt.19:3-12)

"I will remember the covenant I made with you when you were a girl, and I will set up an everlasting covenant with you."

Ezekiel first "make[s] known to Jerusalem her abominations," telling the people, "You were thrown out on the ground as something loathsome, the day you were born." And though by the Lord's blessing they "grew and developed"; and though when they were "old enough for love" He "spread the corner of [His] cloak over [them]"; and though when He "swore an oath to [them] and entered into a covenant with [them]" they became His, the recipient of all the bride's gifts and graces – "You were adorned with gold and silver; your garments were of fine linen, silk, and embroidered cloth. Fine flour, honey, and oil were your food" – yet they took the beauty with which the Lord had endowed them, and turned to harlotry. The wisdom of the Lord, His laws and decrees with which He favored no other people, which were the source of their glory, they spurned in favor of the wickedness of the nations.

The hardness of the hearts of the Israelites we find well illustrated in our gospel today; their attitude toward the marriage covenant reveals their level of faithfulness to the Word of the Lord. A covenant is made binding for all generations, yet the Lord relates the truth to those who question Him: "Because of your stubbornness Moses let you divorce your wives." Never was it meant to be so. This promise, this sacrament Paul later tells us mirrors the love of God for His Church, was ever meant to be lasting. But how weak is the faith and the love of even His chosen, causing even the disciples to marvel at all that is asked of them.

But the covenant the Lord made with His people in their immaturity, the marriage He called them to when they were but profligate children, He now comes to make everlasting through the grace brought by His only Son. He forgets us not in our sin and weakness; He remembers our humble origins.

Now may we "be utterly silenced for shame when [He] pardon[s] all [we] have done"; now may we declare, "God indeed is my savior" and rely entirely upon His strength and the word from His mouth. "Great in your midst is the Holy One of Israel!" and He comes now to wed you to Himself forever.

O. 19. Sat. (II)

Saturday
(Ez.18:1-10,13,30-32; Ps.51:12-15,18-19; Mt.19:13-15)

"Cast away from you all the crimes you have committed,
and make for yourselves a new heart and a new spirit."

"A clean heart create for me, O God, and a steadfast spirit renew within me," David cries out in his psalm. Ezekiel speaks of the same cleansing needed to find the life of God. And Jesus amongst the children reveals the purity to which we are all called.

"Turn and be converted from all your crimes, that they may be no cause of guilt for you," the Lord exhorts us through his prophet today. Through Ezekiel it is revealed that we are judged "each one according to his ways" – the sinner according to his sin and the virtuous according to his "right and just" acts. And the sinner "because he practiced all these abominations... shall surely die," while the just "shall surely live." This is the Word of the Lord God.

But the Word continues. Ezekiel also reveals that the Lord God "takes no pleasure in the death of anyone who dies," that it is His desire that all should live. And so he cries out, "Return and live!" for the Lord is a forgiving God and will indeed wash clean all who turn from their sin.

"My sacrifice, O God, is a contrite spirit; a heart contrite and humbled, O God, you will not spurn." Here is the truth of our Lord: He does not desire to cast us "out from [His] presence," but wishes us to come as children before Him, to know His love, to discover the kingdom of God which belongs to "such as these"... for these are as He is – humble as Jesus, the Child of God. Marvelously our sins He shall wash away, and we shall live! We shall know "the joy of [His] salvation" as children in His sight.

O Lord, we pray that "sinners shall return to you." We pray that none shall die. We pray that you take our own lives and let them witness what it is to be a virtuous child of God. In your hands may our hearts be: "a willing spirit sustain in me." Lay your hands upon our heads before you leave this place; let all our sin be cast away.

O. 20. Mon. (II)

Twentieth Week

Monday
(Ez.24:15-24; Dt.32:18-21; Mt.19:16-22)

"Son of man, by a sudden blow
I am taking away from you the delight of your eyes,
but do not mourn or weep or shed any tears."

A striking similarity there is between our first reading and our gospel: as Ezekiel's wife dies, and so his most valuable treasure is taken from him by the Lord, so the rich young man is told by Jesus, "Go, sell your possessions, and give to the poor," thus calling him to give up his treasure. But an ironic contrast also exists: Ezekiel is asked by the Lord not to mourn his loss, though custom and conscience and righteousness would inform him otherwise, while the young man goes away in sadness when really he should be rejoicing that the Christ is calling him to follow Him. For the death of a

481

loved one we should rightfully weep – for here is a life taken from us – but our possessions, what are they?

And more so should we weep when it is our sins which have caused our loss to befall us, as is the case with the Israelites. The Lord teaches them that He shall remove Jerusalem and its temple from their sight, for they have forgotten God and "angered [Him] with their vain idols," and so He is "filled with loathing... toward His sons and daughters." But will they cry out to Him for the loss their sin has brought about? Will they turn and seek Him in prayer and fasting? No. He tells them, "You shall not mourn or weep, but you shall rot away because of your sins and groan one to another." The hardness of their hearts shall keep their tongues from crying out, and so they shall not find the grace of God.

And O the sad fate of the rich, who likewise are prevented from entering the realm of God, in this case by their wealth of possessions. These vain things should mean no more than the dust of the earth, and when called from them and the anxiety they produce, what should one do but rejoice to approach the gates of heaven? But rather than this, the soul is made sad. It is a twisted world which only the grace of God can remedy. But who of this "fickle race" will come to the font of life and drink in the Word of salvation? Who will mourn in earnest the loss of life granted by God and have no care for the dead things of our earthly existence? And who shall continue the wicked twisting?

Tuesday
(Ez.28:1-10; Dt.32:26-28,30,35-36,39; Mt.19:23-30)

"Only with difficulty will a rich man enter the kingdom of God."

Yes, "close at hand is the day of their disaster, and their doom is rushing upon them!" – those like the prince of Tyre who are "haughty of heart, and say, 'A god am I! I occupy a godly throne in the heart of the sea!'" What condemnation they mount up for themselves, those who by their "great wisdom applied to [their] trading... have heaped up [their] riches," for "the most barbarous of nations... shall draw their swords... [and] run them through [their] splendid apparel." These shall be "thrust down to the pit, there to die a bloodied corpse in the heart of the sea." How else shall they learn that they "are a man, not a god"? How else might they find the humility necessary for the kingdom of heaven?

It is tragic how riches and power turn men's hearts away from truth, making them "a people devoid of reason, having no understanding." For what do such as these say of their state but, "Our own hand won the victory; the Lord had nothing to do with it," thus blinding themselves to the fact that all comes only from God? And so the Lord's warning against those inflated by the riches of this world; and so "it is easier for a camel to pass through a needle's eye than for a rich man to enter the kingdom of God." For how their swollen pride makes it impossible to squeeze through the gates which admit only the humblest of children.

Brothers and sisters, store not up for yourselves a heap of treasure which serves but to block the light of the Son of God. Use not "your wisdom and your intelligence... [to make] riches for yourself." This is not the proper end for the gifts God gives, and will serve only to bring the destruction of your haughty soul, along with the riches themselves. If you desire to "inherit everlasting life," it is upon this your heart, your wisdom, your desire for riches, must be set. For the heavenly treasures from the hand of God do not fail and cannot be run through by the sword of the nations; and in this kingdom "the last shall come first."

O. 20. Wed. (II)

Wednesday
(Ez.34:1-11; Ps.23:1-6; Mt.20:1-16)

"I myself will look after and tend my sheep."

How grateful we should be that "the Lord is [our] shepherd," for with Him we want for nothing. Indeed, our "cup overflows" and "only goodness and kindness follow [us] all the days of [our] life"; for it is He who watches over our every step, and He is only goodness, He is only kindness – His mercy endures forever.

How the Lord's hand contrasts with the false shepherds' of the house of Israel. These "pastured themselves and did not pasture [the Lord's] sheep." They "fed off their milk, wor[e] their wool, and slaughtered the fatlings," but the sheep they allowed to be "scattered over the whole earth, with no one to look after them or to search for them." But where these shepherds "lorded it over [the sheep of Israel] harshly and brutally," the Lord Himself is "generous." Though under them the sheep "were scattered for lack of a shepherd, and became food for all the wild beasts," the Lord, the owner of the vineyard, the Good Shepherd, goes forth at all times of day seeking every straying sheep, gathering all into His fold and seeing that we have wages enough to feed each of our families.

And whether the laborer works many hours or few, yet he is provided all his needs. Here, of course, is notice that the Gentiles, who come late to salvation history, enter the kingdom before the Jews, who have always been in the Lord's house. Here is word that the generosity of our God extends to all, that His loving arms will not be shortened. And we may learn, too, from the response of the workers to the owner's questioning why they have been

483

"idle all day" – "No one has hired us" – that the Lord looks upon the heart and pays us not so much for the work accomplished but for the intention of our will. For these would have worked all day had they earlier been approached.

"In verdant pastures He gives me repose." In the Lord's loving arms we all find our home. Had He not come Himself to shepherd us, still we would be wandering alone. But as it is we work now in His vineyard, sharing in the very blood of the Son. As it is we are well cared for by a Father whose generosity knows no bounds. He whose mercy alone could redeem us has come with His staff to guide us on the "right paths" that lead to His kingdom. And so we say, gratefully, "Thank you, Jesus, for your kindness."

Thursday
(Ez.36:23-28; Ps.51:12-15,18-19,Ez.36:25; Mt.22:1-14)

"Cast me not out from your presence,
and your Holy Spirit take not from me."

The Lord desires to "prove the holiness of [His] great name," which has been "profaned among the nations" by the children of Israel. And so He determines to "gather [them] from all the foreign lands," to bring them back from their exile from His sight, and bless them again upon their "own land." He will "cleanse [them] from all [their] impurities... a new heart and... a new spirit within" them, and they shall be "careful to observe [His] decrees": "You shall be my people, and I will be your God."

But when the time comes for the reign of God to be fulfilled in their midst, when all is prepared and they are invited to the "wedding banquet for His Son"... when indeed the Lord would wed the Israelites to Himself by the grace and blessing of the Messiah – they refuse the call. "Come to the feast," He cries out; eat your fill of my delights. But they make excuses and even kill those by whom the invitation comes (laying hands even on the only Son). And so the chosen city having rejected His offer, the Lord tells His servants to "go out into the byroads and invite to the wedding anyone [they] come upon." So do the apostles preach the Gospel to the ends of the earth; so are all now called to the wedding feast. But will all be prepared?

To "the chief priests and elders of the people" Jesus addresses His parable of the wedding banquet today, for it is these who refuse to hear Him – it is they who reject the call of the Lord. And so, indeed, to the nations does His voice go; the Gentiles now hear the call. And we, we who though founded firmly upon the rock of Judaism are in such great number of Gentile races, do we heed the call of the Lord and prepare our hearts to receive His food? We are now the chosen city and the banquet table is now spread before us each day: His Body and Blood is the greatest food of which we could ever hope to partake. But have we the wedding garment necessary to remain in His banquet hall, in His Church, or do we wander in ignorance of the gift and graces before us?

Brothers and sisters, we must pray not to be cast from the Lord's holy presence. We must seek the purity of heart we need to receive His blessing, to partake of the food of His altar and grow in His grace. We shall only avoid being thrown "out into the night" if we nurture the light that is with us and prepare well to meet our Jesus. Only then will the Holy Spirit here remain.

Friday
(Ez.37:1-14; Ps.107:1-9; Mt.22:34-40)

"I will open your graves and have you rise from them,
and bring you back to the land of Israel."

The commentary in the missal I read states: "The lesson here is return from captivity, not life after death." And so the speaker proves once again the limited vision of so many of our scholars – indeed, how like the Pharisees and the Sadducees and the lawyers of Jesus' time these faithless are, how blind... how dry their bones without spirit.

Certainly the prophet Ezekiel speaks to the exiles of their return to Israel: to these he is sent, and of this redemption they must hear. But if this were all the Scripture says, what lesson would we take from it – this passage why should we bother to read? And if this were all God intended even for these scattered children, what an ineffective God He would be. (As limited in vision as so many of our leaders today.) For what is the land upon which any find life but the kingdom of heaven? And how do we come there except through death, the death of our attachment to this earth? Vain all is if we have not the resurrection of Jesus within us; we must rise from our graves before anything has meaning in life.

That the Lord speaks of more than the return to Israel in Ezekiel's prophecy of the dry bones today is indicated clearly in our psalm, which equates "the redeemed of the Lord" with those "gathered from the lands, from the east and the west, from the north and the south." Is it not so that the Psalms, though greatly written a millennium before Christ (and hundreds of years before even Ezekiel's time), speak of Christ, and even in the voice of Christ? Is it not Jesus who speaks even to Ezekiel himself? Listen to our psalm. It speaks of the Israelites' wandering "in the desert wilderness." It says they were "hungry and thirsty" and that "their life was wasting away within them." Certainly they lacked food and water in this arid place – but

485

is this all of which the psalmist speaks! Do they not rather fail to drink from the spiritual rock which follows them? Is their hunger not for Christ? And the "inhabited city" to which the Lord leads them, is it but the land beyond the Jordan River? Is it the dust of this earth that will satisfy their dry bones? No. They "give thanks to the Lord... because He satisfied the longing soul and filled the hungry soul with good things" – things of the spirit, not merely the body.

"On these two commandments the whole law is based, and the prophets as well," Jesus says of the love of God and neighbor. Here is the Spirit! Here is the Life! Here is what nourishes the dry bones and makes them stand upright: the Love of God! This is in every passage of Scripture – every prophecy, every psalm... This Word is the lesson we must always find: Jesus Christ is risen from the grave!

"From the four winds come, O Spirit, and breathe into these slain that they may come to life." May the Spirit of love open all eyes.

Saturday
(Ez.43:1-7; Ps.85:9-14; Mt.23:1-12)

"The temple was filled with the glory of the Lord."

Certainly the vision of Ezekiel is fulfilled in the coming of Jesus and His founding the Church, the New Jerusalem, here amongst us. In this Temple He has "set the soles of [His] feet"; here He "dwell[s] among the Israelites forever." For though the temple in Jerusalem shall be restored, it shall again be destroyed, and forever. In the Catholic Church now does His presence remain. Through it and through its teaching "the earth [has] shone with His glory."

"Truth shall spring out of the earth": Jesus is born in our midst and walks among us; "justice shall look down from heaven": through Him the light of God shines upon us, bringing salvation to all souls. And it is in His Church truth and justice remain, "glory dwelling in our land."

And "like the roaring of many waters" is His teaching, which comes with power, which comes with authority. And this teaching He leaves in the apostles' hands. As "the Pharisees have succeeded Moses as teachers" and Jesus has succeeded these, so do the apostles succeed Jesus; thus we must "do everything and observe everything they tell us" – the Spirit is upon the Church, which does not teach in error despite the sins of its members. These must be respected; it is upon these, and so upon Jesus' teaching, the Catholic faith is founded.

And what if some refused to enter into this Temple and share in His glory present in His Church? What if they did not share the wholeness of

His thought or receive His precious Body and Blood, offered each day in the New Jerusalem? Their eyes would be as blind and their vision as limited as those who quote our gospel today to prove that the Church should not call its priests "Father". They would not be able to see that what Jesus teaches His disciples in telling them to avoid "marks of respect in public and of being called 'Rabbi'" is to avoid having themselves inflated with pride. If these blind souls were correct, then no one could be called "teacher" either, for this is more the word the Lord wishes us to avoid. And they would have to condemn Paul for calling himself "father" of the Church in Corinth (1Cor.4:15). Such absurdity ensues when one has not the wholeness of Truth, but looks only on appearances.

Brothers and sisters, where would we be without the teaching of the apostles? In a word, we wouldn't have Jesus. It is from Him their teaching comes, bringing His glory to the ends of the earth. In this Temple let us dwell, His Word and Sacrament sustaining our lives.

Twenty-First Week

Monday
(2Thes.1:1-5,11-12; Ps.96:1-5; Mt.23:13-22)

"Which is more important, the offering
or the altar which makes the offering sacred?"

The Pharisees in their blindness taught: "If a man swears by the altar it means nothing, but if he swears by the gift on the altar he is obligated." Indeed, "How blind [they] are!" For what do they do but exalt that which is secondary beyond that which is primary? What do they do but invert logic?

And what is the significance of their blindness? Why does it bring them "an evil day"? What the Pharisees essentially do in their thinking and their teaching is place the created ahead of the Creator, themselves before their God. For we are the gift upon the altar and the Lord Jesus the altar that receives and consumes our offering. It is He who makes us holy, and not we Him; it is we "who belong to God our Father and the Lord Jesus Christ," and not vice-versa. He is above; we are below. The divine order of things must not be skewed. Yes, "the Lord made the heavens" and we who dwell below the heavens, and we must bow down before Him and praise His name.

"Awesome is He, beyond all gods." Above every created thing He stands, He towers, for all these things, including our souls, are in His almighty hands. "All the gods of the nations are things of naught," idols of so much dust and sand, devised alone by human hands and serving to inflate

Ordinary Time

the pride of those who make them. These we must leave aside. Our false ideas we must abandon. To Him alone must we come.

"Tell His glory among the nations," brothers and sisters, "for great is the Lord and highly to be praised." It is He who is "seated on [the] throne" of heaven, He alone who merits our songs of praise. So let our song rise up to Him from our place upon His altar; let our offering be acceptable in His sight. Let us pray "that our God may make [us] worthy of His call, and fulfill by His power every honest intention and work of faith," that "the name of our Lord Jesus may be glorified in [us] and [we] in Him, in accord with the gracious gift of our God and of the Lord Jesus Christ." May He make us holy.

O. 21. Tues. (II)

Tuesday
(2Thes.2:1-3,14-17; Ps.96:10-13; Mt.23:23-26)

"He shall rule the world with justice
and the peoples with His constancy."

"Brothers, stand firm." Be not "easily agitated or terrified" "on the question of the coming of our Lord Jesus Christ and our being gathered to Him." This should not preoccupy your thoughts because this is not in your mind to know or your hands to control. The day and the hour are with God alone. Rather, you should pray that the Lord will strengthen your hearts "for every good work and word." This is what is in your power, and effectively accomplishing the Lord's will thus, all fear will be removed from your souls.

Brothers and sisters, be not like the scribes and Pharisees, the "blind guides" who "strain out the gnat and swallow the camel!" Distracted by the details, they inevitably neglect "the weightier matters of the law, justice and mercy and good faith" – those for which the Lord calls us above all to be concerned. And so their vision and their actions are not whole, and they are not holy. Failing to see as God sees and to do as God does, they indeed become blind guides frittering the life of the Lord away in anxiety for external matters. Let this not be the fate of your soul.

Children, know of a certain that "our Lord Jesus Christ Himself... loved us and in His mercy gave us eternal consolation and hope." We must make this hope our own. For "the Lord is King. He has made the world firm, not to be moved," and we must be as immovable as He in our faith and in our work. We should not doubt that "He governs the peoples with equity," that in fairness all are looked upon in His sight, and so, that if we strive to do His will with all our hearts He will indeed bless us.

488

Friends, we should know that, though not complete, though He does not stand before us in final judgment yet, still it is so that "the day of the Lord is here," in our midst today. His rule has always been and has come to us in this place. And what we do now leads only to that day – the kingdom should be growing within us at all times. If we know not His justice and His constancy at work in our days, then indeed we have reason to fear and should heed the Lord's rebuke. But if we strive with Him for holiness, any fear itself will be holy and lead us only to the joy that makes "the heavens... glad and the earth rejoice." For each day we rejoice with them in the presence of our God.

O. 21. Wed. (II)

Wednesday
(2Thes.3:6-10,16-18; Ps.128:1-2,4-5; Mt.23:27-32)

"You shall eat the fruit of your handiwork."

"Anyone who would not work should not eat" was the rule laid down by Paul among the Thessalonians. A man must earn his bread. And as on earth, so in heaven. For who shall come to the fruits of the kingdom if they are not as Paul, who has labored "to the point of exhaustion" for the sake of the reign of God? This is the "straight path" laid down for us by all the apostles: in the Lord's name we must walk "day and night." It is work which produces fruit.

And what fruit will the scribes and Pharisees know? Their work is to "erect tombs for the prophets and decorate the monuments of the saints," those who have been murdered by their forefathers. Yet they join these "in shedding the prophets' blood," thus making the tombs they erect all the more vain; yes, they shall "fill up the vessel measured off by [their] forefathers" by crucifying the Christ, the only Son of God. And this work they do shall have its fruit as well – it shall lead their souls to the gates of hell, where only the same blood they shed will save them.

We will be judged according to our deeds, brothers and sisters. All is seen by God who looks upon the heart and whose eyes are everywhere. Let not your works be empty, or just so empty will be your heart, will be your place in the reign to come. Each day our souls are required of us; ever the Lord seeks fruit upon our tree. So, if you wish to "see the prosperity of Jerusalem all the days of your life," if you long to know always the blessing of God, then "walk in His ways." "Fear the Lord" who holds your life in His hands and do as He commands. Then "happy shall you be, and favored"; then the fruits of the kingdom you shall taste even here. And even the death you die and the blood you shed shall not remove this favor – by it "the grace of our Lord Jesus Christ" will be fulfilled in you. Amen.

489

Thursday

(1Cor.1:1-9; Ps.145:1-7; Mt.24:42-51)

"He will strengthen you to the end,
so that you will be blameless on the day of our Lord Jesus Christ."

Brothers and sisters, "you lack no spiritual gift as you wait for the revelation of our Lord Jesus Christ." The Lord provides all you need, generously and faithfully. You "have been consecrated in Christ Jesus and called to be a holy people" and so "have been richly endowed [by God] with every gift," that you might fulfill the call He places upon your soul, that by His grace you might indeed be holy. And so you should realize "the favor He has bestowed on you in Christ Jesus" and "call on the name of our Lord Jesus Christ" to gain all the blessings the Lord God is ready to pour forth upon you.

Brothers and sisters, "keep a watchful eye and [do] not allow [your] house to be broken into." "Be prepared" for the Lord's coming. Let His every gift be at work in you, that readiness will ever be yours. Do not think as the foolish and worthless servant, "My master is a long time in coming," and turn thus away from His light, sagging into the world's darkness. Such a thought brings only death and the punishment of the Lord. For never is He long in coming. Always is He present to us; ever is His Spirit here within us when we remain faithful to Him. He it is who is of life and light – it is we who grow blind to His grace and are slow to come to His eternal presence. Forsake not His gifts, which sustain us at all times.

Here is cause for rejoicing. Here is the reason David sings, "Every day I will bless you, and I will praise your name forever and ever" (revealing thus the newness of life which is ever upon us): "God is faithful, and it was He who called [us] to fellowship with His Son, Jesus Christ our Lord." No more than this need we know. For this reason "generation after generation praises [His] works" and "publish[es] the fame of [His] abundant goodness." It is this which brings His praise to our throats. For indeed in His grace He has called us to be as His only Son, and of course He is faithful to His call. And so by faithfulness all is ours in the Lord, and on that Day His blessings shall be full. Remaining in His light, growing in His gifts and favors, there shall be no "wailing then and grinding of teeth" for our souls – no, "happy that servant whom His master discovers at work on His return!"

490

Friday

(1Cor.1:17-25; Ps.33:1-2,4-5,10-11; Mt.25:1-13)

"The world did not come to know Him through its 'wisdom'."

"I will destroy the wisdom of the wise, and thwart the cleverness of the clever," says the Lord God. And in its place we find the Gospel, "the message of the cross," which is "complete absurdity to those who are headed to ruin, but to us who are experiencing salvation it is the power of God." It is this wisdom which saves us, even as the wisdom of the world falls to dust.

The wisdom of the world tells us to take our rest, to find our pleasure in the things of this life; the wisdom of God instructs us to "keep [our] eyes open" for the coming of the kingdom of God, wherein we shall find eternal rest. The wisdom of the world has only the torch to offer; like the foolish bridesmaids, it brings no oil for its lamp, for it can see nothing beyond its eyes – its immediate physical concerns are its preoccupation. The wisdom of God knows that all depends on the oil of the lamp, and so it calls us to find our souls in the Word of God, which is a flask whose contents never recede but rather increase with use and preserve the soul's burning brightly before its Creator. The wisdom of the world is "wordy," is empty rambling with no foundation in truth; God's wisdom is founded in silence, pregnant with the power and authority of all ages.

"The Lord brings to naught the plans of nations; He foils the designs of peoples." What can stand that is not rooted in Him? What has purpose that is not spoken by His mouth? Apart from Him nothing comes to be or lasts. And does not the Lord thwart the ideas of the human mind most perfectly in the crucifixion of His Christ? Making "Christ the power of God and the wisdom of God" turns the vain strivings of men upside down and exposes them in all their emptiness. Here is my Word, He says; here is my Love. To this sacrifice does He call us all, that we might celebrate at His wedding feast and not be barred outside in the cold world. For indeed all that is of the world comes to nothing, "but the plan of the Lord stands forever; the design of His heart, through all generations." And it is His design that we become children of light, shining forever in the light of His wisdom, not burning to ashes in the deceit of our hearts.

In the cross all our empty words fall to naught as we are confronted with the truth of our sin and the love of our God. Thus our eyes are opened. May they remain so, fixed on this lamp which shines in the darkness of the night. By no other means will we come to know God and the meaning of our lives.

491

Saturday
(1Cor.1:26-31; Ps.33:12-13,18-21; Mt.25:14-30)

"He called in his servants and handed his funds over to them
according to each man's abilities."

All comes from the hand of God. Yes. Do you see this? God it is who provides any talent you possess on this earth and "God it is who has given you life in Christ Jesus." Not yourself. It is not from you any power comes. God has proven His power by choosing "the lowborn and despised, those who count for nothing," and making them strong. This is you. You are nothing; and yet you have all things in God.

Brothers and sisters, "mankind can do no boasting before God." How could they? It is He who looks down from heaven and "sees all mankind"; it is He who chooses "His own inheritance." It is He who places in our hands the "silver pieces" we employ on this earth – and it is He who expects us to use well that which we have been given. To Him we must answer for all things. And if we are "industrious and reliable" in our service, it is He who will declare, "Since you were dependable in a small matter I will put you in charge of larger affairs." On earth as it is in heaven... If our work is done well here, it shall lead to the greater fruits, and we shall "share [our] Master's joy!" But it is always His joy to which we come and not our own.

God is all things to us. "He has made [Jesus] our wisdom, and also our justice, our sanctification, and our redemption." All that we have is from Him, and without Him we could not live. And should you be resentful of so great a gift? Should you return the gift of Himself He lays before you on your table? Or should you not rather take it up, make it your own, and by it produce fruit according to the abilities He has shared with you? This is all He expects of you: that the graces He shares with you, you share with others.

"In His holy name we trust." Yes, "our soul waits for the Lord" and "in Him our hearts rejoice." For He does not fail us. What He gives He does not take back: it is we who reject His love; it is He who increases the yield within us. "Brothers, you are among those who are called," and so be among "those who hope for His kindness." For His kindness shall but enrich you each day as you make His will your own and find your "boast in the Lord." Praise Him for His gifts and for His grace, for by His grace the gifts He provides become eternally fruitful in our lives. Alleluia!

Twenty-Second Week

Monday
(1Cor.2:1-5; Ps.119:97-102; Lk.4:16-30)

"Your faith rests not on the wisdom of men
but on the power of God."

Paul comes to the Corinthians with preaching that has "none of the persuasive force of 'wise' argumentation, but the convincing power of the Spirit," and with them he determines to "speak of nothing but Jesus Christ and Him crucified." Similarly, when "Jesus came to Nazareth where He had been reared," in the synagogue He simply read the passage from Isaiah which prophesies the coming Messiah, sat down before the eyes of all, and stated, "Today this Scripture passage is fulfilled in your hearing." I AM here. I AM He. This is the day of salvation. Period. And here even at the beginning of His ministry we see how the crucifixion is already near, as His townspeople attempt to kill Him for the truth He speaks.

Upon what is this simple wisdom, this power of the Lord, based but the Word of God? The psalmist, whose "meditation all the day" is the law of the Lord, declares in truth and in joy: "Your commandment has made me wiser than my enemies." It grants him "more understanding than all [his] teachers" and "more discernment than the elders," because all genuine wisdom comes from the Word spoken by the mouth of God and not through human learning. We have seen that Scripture is the foundation of the teaching of Jesus Himself, who is the Word of God made flesh. Yes, He speaks much more through "the appealing discourse which came from His lips." Yes, there is oral tradition as well (for the Word of God is living and active); but on Scripture He begins His instruction, and continually He refers to the Word. Whether rejecting the devil's temptations, rebuking the Pharisees and scribes, or enlightening the people – as He tries to do today by referring to Elijah's having to go to Zarephath and Elisha's healing only the Syrian, to show how prophets are not accepted in their native place – the Lord's words are founded in the Word of God, in Scripture.

And, of course, an integral part of that Word is the suffering the Christ must undergo. But notice that even as the people intend "to hurl Him over the edge" of the hill of Nazareth, just as directly as He has spoken truth to them, so directly and with the power of God He "went straight through their midst and walked away." For the Word is as a sword which pierces all the dark limits of the world, and even through death it shall lead all to salvation.

Brothers and sisters, let your faith rest on this Word that is Christ found in Scripture and living in the Church, for the Spirit does not die with the devices of the human mind. This Spirit holds eternal life.

Tuesday
(1Cor.2:10-16; Ps.145:8-14,17; Lk.4:31-37)

"We have the mind of Christ."

The demon has been cast from us and we see the Lord as He is: "Good to all and compassionate toward all His works." "The glorious splendor of [His] kingdom" is before our eyes, and it is this which gives us light. We have bowed ourselves down before Him, the demon has thrown us "to the ground before everyone's eyes," and we have found that "the Lord lifts up those who are falling." No longer "the natural man" who finds "what is taught by the Spirit of God" complete "absurdity," filled with His Spirit we now "recognize the gifts He has given us." And in these gifts we rejoice, for we have become as He is.

"The Lord is faithful in all His words and holy in all His works," and so what should we who are His works do but "discourse of the glory of His kingdom and speak of His might," brothers and sisters? Should not all our words and all our works give Him due glory? How can we do otherwise, knowing now how "gracious and merciful" God is and that His "kingdom is a kingdom for all ages"? "All generations" must be called into His holy presence.

"He commands the unclean spirits with authority and power, and they leave." Here is the Good News in action; here is the glory of God come among us. All the evil that possesses the soul of man is cast out by a word from His Son's mouth. And so is paved the way to the kingdom.

Brothers and sisters, embrace the Spirit of God at work in the world. Put on the mind of Christ. "The Spirit we have received is not the world's spirit but God's Spirit," and so should we not teach as we have been taught? If indeed the light of the Lord is upon us illumining our minds and hearts, is it not but just that we should be compelled to impart that same Spirit to others that they might not be in darkness but might also be able to "appraise everything" "in a spiritual way," that they too might know "the mind of the Lord"?

Devils, be gone! Be silenced before the Son of God! All the evil of the world shall be struck and destroyed by the all-powerful Word of God. All His children sharply shine His saving light.

Wednesday
(1Cor.3:1-9; Ps.33:12-15,20-21; Lk.4:38-44)

"To other towns I must announce the Good News of the reign of God, because that is why I was sent."

"And He continued to preach in the synagogues of Judea." And He continues to preach to all hearts through His blessed apostles, and His Church continues to grow. To the ends of the earth the kingdom progresses, and we each have a hand in its rising.

Yes, "he who plants and he who waters work to the same end," but "neither he who plants nor he who waters is of any special account, only God, who gives the growth." As Paul has said to the Corinthians: "Who is Apollos? And who is Paul? Simply ministers through whom you became believers, each of them doing only what the Lord assigned him." As great as the work of any apostle may be, yet it is God alone through whom progress is made. He alone causes "His cultivation, His building" to grow; it is yet Jesus who announces salvation in any of our lives.

Indeed, no matter how big our work, it is God who accomplishes all – but also no matter how small. For all are called. And even as Paul and Apollos plant and water by their great gift of preaching, so we are told of Simon Peter's mother-in-law that once Jesus had cast the fever from her, "she got up immediately and waited on them," entirely ready to perform her work for the upbuilding of the kingdom of God. As with the sick the Lord "laid hands on each of them and cured them," and as He taught with authority, so all in their way are invited to offer their service to the only God and thus become built into His kingdom. It *is* God who builds the House, but indeed "we are God's co-workers" and must cooperate with His grace.

And how we should know Him and His working among us and through us! The demons declared, "You are the Son of God!" for they "knew that He was the Messiah" – they knew well He who had come to destroy them. Why is it we whom He has come to build up do not know Him just as well, or even more? Truly it is "He who fashioned the heart of each [of us], He who knows all [our] works"; it is He "who is our help and our shield," and "in Him our hearts [should] rejoice" – and through Him we should accomplish all. Do we know His presence with us so well? Do we rejoice in Him and do His works and become His work...? Brothers and sisters, let it be indeed that the Good News is announced clearly to all through the Lord working upon our soul.

Ordinary Time

Thursday
(1Cor.3:18-23; Ps.24:1-6; Lk.5:1-11)

"Amazement at the catch they had made
seized him and all his shipmates."

What a truly remarkable scene! Here upon the call of the apostles, the first of apostles, Simon Peter, "fell at the knees of Jesus." Here in his barque, boats once desolate now suddenly fill to bursting with fish flopping about everywhere, unable to be contained... This is a painting for the ages, this blessed moment! It is this image which drives the Church forth, filling the barque of Peter with blessed, saved souls. "From now on you will be catching men," the Lord says to His Rock – and so the Church is called, on this sunlit day.

Yes, "the Lord's are the earth and its fullness; the world and those who dwell in it." And how wonderfully that fullness that is the Lord's is revealed in these boats continually filled "until they nearly sank," and how clearly these abundant fish represent we who dwell in God's world. Even literally our psalm is fulfilled: "He founded it upon the seas," David sings; and as He founded the world, so here He finds the Church, His renewal of the world, here upon the Sea of Galilee. Here He sends out His call to those who "stand in His holy place"; and through His apostles all will find the strength and purity to "ascend the mountain of the Lord." Here is the faith firmly rooted, here in the barque of Peter. The race that "seeks the face of the God of Jacob" shall find Him now, shall see Him even as clearly as Peter looking up at Him from here at His knees on this marvelous day.

"All things are yours," Paul declares, "and you are Christ's and Christ is God's." Indeed, the fullness of heaven and earth are at our hands through Jesus and the ministry of His apostles. All the apostles are ours, the world is ours, life and death are ours, the present and the future... Why? Because we are in Christ, in the boat in which He sits, surrounding our leader on our knees – all is ours because we leave everything to become His followers.

After the Lord's resurrection this scene shall repeat itself, and so the call be fulfilled. Here it begins though, here in "nets [that] were at their breaking point," here in boats that are filled – here in one man falling to his knees, all come before the Lord of all.

Friday

(1Cor.4:1-5; Ps.37:3-6,27-28,39-40; Lk.5:33-39)

"The salvation of the just is from the Lord."

"For the Lord loves what is right, and forsakes not His faithful ones." And so He comes. He comes bearing a new garment; He comes with the blood of a New Covenant, His own blood, to wash us clean and make us whole as He is. Drinking this new wine indeed we are made holy.

It is not as "John's disciples" or as "the disciples of the Pharisees" we shall find our salvation – only as disciples of the Son of God, only by "commit[ting] to the Lord [our] way" will "justice dawn for us like the light." And that His way, His covenant, is whole we see in His teaching that "no one tears a piece from a new coat to patch an old one," for this indeed "will only tear the new coat, and the piece taken from it will not match the old." What foolishness this would be. No, the New Covenant founded in the blood of Jesus Christ, though absolutely in accord with the Old, is whole unto itself and serves to redeem and fulfill the covenant that has come before. One cannot take pieces of it as it might suit one's judgment – it must be received entire as grace from the Lord. Then, "bright as the noonday shall be your vindication," and feast with the bridegroom you shall.

Brothers and sisters, "the Lord is the one to judge," and His Word must be accepted in full. Only "He will bring to light what is hidden in darkness and manifest the intentions of hearts," for only His eyes see all things. And so, do not attempt to judge for yourselves the worth of a person or even yourself. Paul says, "I do not even pass judgment on myself," not because he is innocent, but because God alone knows his heart. And as we cannot judge one another, so we cannot (as James has said elsewhere – 4:11) judge the Law of God. We must simply live under His Law, seeking to obey the Word of His covenant. We must only make it our concern to "turn from evil and do good, that [we] may abide forever." For when the Lord comes again, when the New Covenant is fulfilled in our midst, "at that time, everyone will receive his praise from God."

Neither praise nor condemnation from the mouth of man has worth. Trust not in this. "Trust in the Lord and do good, that you may dwell in the land and enjoy security." Commit yourself entirely to His Word and Blood, and a new skin to receive His grace you shall find.

Saturday
(1Cor.4:9-15; Ps.145:17-21; Lk.6:1-5)

"God has put us apostles at the end of the line,
like men doomed to die in the arena."

"Up to this very hour we go hungry and thirsty, poorly clad, roughly treated, wandering about homeless," the great Apostle Paul tells us of the persecution and slander all the Lord's apostles must undergo. And yet "when we are insulted we respond with a blessing," for this is our call in the Lord: to love even our enemies, that we might show the love of God to all, that we might indeed become "a spectacle to the universe, to angels and men alike" – "fools on Christ's account," yet bearing all patiently that the Gospel might truly be fulfilled and the last shall be shown to be first in the eyes of God.

It is this birth to which Paul brings the Corinthians, his "beloved children." And though it seem a difficult fate to call down upon a people, yet we know that David's psalm is true, that "the Lord is near to all who call upon Him, to all who call upon Him in truth"; and so through all trials He leads us and comforts us, making any suffering a light burden to bear. And just as Paul is father to this people, so the Father of all is there always to watch over all His children, for it is "in Christ Jesus" the Apostle has begotten them; and as the Father has heard the cry of His Son upon the cross and brought Him to resurrection, so "He hears [all His children] cry and saves them."

In our gospel the Lord's disciples are hungry, and so, in the hot sun, "walking through the standing grain" with Jesus, He feeds them: all around is food at their hands. Truly their prayer does He answer; their need does He see. But instead of seeing that the Lord "fulfills the desire of those who fear Him," all the Pharisees can do is ask, "Why are you doing what is prohibited on the sabbath?" Thus the very men who should be present to bless and comfort and guide the followers of the Holy One can but call them into the arena of persecution with the rest of the fallen world. Thus the shepherds who are called to feed the sheep would remove the food from their hands and see them perish. Instead of becoming apostles themselves, they become their bane. For they cannot comprehend that God's love transcends God's law, that "the Lord keeps all who love Him" and this is what makes Him "just in all His ways and holy in all His works," and not the mere precepts to which they hold so desperately, so blindly... so jealously. Thus the chosen of God become in their eyes "the world's refuse, the scum of all." And what can they be but crucified?

498

All must come to the holy Lord and "all flesh bless His holy name forever and ever." And though war be brought upon our souls, we must always "try conciliation" – peacemakers covered with blood and spittle is the state to which we are called. No other way will the world come to know that the love of God transcends all, and all call upon Him from their hearts.

Twenty-Third Week

Monday
(1Cor.5:1-8; Ps.5:5-7,9,12; Lk.6:6-11)

"Let us celebrate the feast not with the old yeast,
that of corruption and wickedness,
but with the unleavened bread of sincerity and truth."

For indeed, "Christ our Passover has been sacrificed"; indeed, the new Sabbath has come. And on the Day of the Lord only goodness remains.

"Get rid of the old yeast to make of yourselves fresh dough," Paul commands the Corinthians as he chastises them for their "boasting" and self-satisfaction even while tolerating a professed sinner in their midst. He writes here to insist that they should be "grieving and getting rid of the offender," both for the sake of the community and that the sinful man's "spirit may be saved on the day of the Lord." For, as David makes quite evident in his psalm, God "delight[s] not in wickedness; no evil remains with [Him]." And as for the vain pride of the community: "the arrogant may not stand in [His] sight."

It is not an unkind exaggeration to say that the Lord "hate[s] all evildoers." The sharp line dividing evil and good Jesus would make clear as He confronts the scribes and Pharisees in the synagogue on the sabbath, "a man whose right hand was withered" standing before Him: "I ask you," He says, "is it lawful to do good on the sabbath – or evil? To preserve life – or destroy it?" Then He heals the man, much to the chagrin of the scribes and Pharisees who deem this unlawful work for the day. But in the Lord's House and on His Day good is always and only done – and certainly this healing is a blessed act. And since only the good remain in His House, just as the man who is "living with his own father's wife" will be purged from the Corinthian community at Paul's urging, so by the word of our Lord Jesus Christ these false leaders who harbor such distrust and jealousy will be cast from within the walls of the Lord's Church; for "the bloodthirsty and deceitful the Lord abhors," and indeed the blood of the Son is upon their hearts, and will be upon their hands.

But we, brothers and sisters, we have the new feast, the new Sabbath before us now. We come now into His House to eat His Body and drink His Blood. Each day, in fact, we may celebrate the greatness of God's glory and the grace of His presence in our midst. And so, let us celebrate with a pure spirit, with His cleansing blood upon our hearts, that our goodness may be preserved and we who "love [His] name" and "take refuge in [Him]" may "be glad and exult forever."

O. 23. Tues. (II)

Tuesday
(1Cor.6:1-11; Ps.149:1-6,9; Lk.6:12-19)

"You have been washed, consecrated, justified
in the name of the Lord Jesus Christ and in the Spirit of our God."

Yes, "power went out from Him which cured all." And as all were "healed of their diseases" and "those who were troubled with unclean spirits were cured" by His touch, so we, too, are made whole in His sight; so we now become His holy children of light. For "the unholy will not fall heir to the kingdom of God," and His kingdom being the desire of our hearts, we come with "the whole crowd... trying to touch Him," trying to reach His presence upon the mountain of God.

And He calls His apostles; He selects the Twelve. And the power to teach and to heal He bestows upon them and upon their descendants. His wisdom and His grace He imparts upon those to whom His Father leads Him; and this same power rests upon all those baptized in His name into His Spirit. And so, as these Twelve who are the foundation stones of the New Jerusalem sit in judgment of the twelve tribes of Israel, so it is that the redeemed of the Lord are, as Paul tells us, "to judge angels." Yes, "the believers will judge the world." This power which is the Lord's alone He gives to all in the world to come, for all are to be infused with His wisdom, and His love.

And so are we not therefore "up to deciding everyday affairs"? "If the judgment of the world is to be [ours], are we to be thought unworthy of judging in minor matters?" And not only in cases "between one member of the Church and another," but in all the details of our lives. If we are to judge with the wisdom and grace of God in heaven, we must here be able to see clearly the right from the wrong, or we have not His Spirit upon us – or we stand in opposition to His Truth and to His Church. "Do not deceive yourselves: no fornicators, idolaters, or adulterers, no sodomites, thieves, misers, or drunkards, no slanderers or robbers will inherit God's kingdom." If your conscience tells you otherwise and you do these things or fail to condemn these things, you are sadly misinformed; and rather than judge the nations with the Lord and His apostles, you shall be judged by them.

Come only unto His Word, brothers and sisters; come only unto His Hand. And you shall be cleansed of all evil and be made able to stand here in this world as in His kingdom. And you shall sing His "praise in the assembly of the faithful" and with them "exult in glory" before your "maker" and "king." "This is the glory of all His faithful"; His holy song is sung by all the redeemed.

Wednesday
(1Cor.7:25-31; Ps.45:11-12,14-17; Lk.6:20-26)

"The world as we know it is passing away."

And so, "hear, O daughter, and see; turn your ear, forget your people and your father's house," for the King is calling you from this passing world to the heavenly marriage feast – "He is your Lord, and you must worship Him." This call is for every chosen soul, for who is the Lord's virgin daughter, who is His Bride but the Church? It is she who is called, even as the Virgin Mother who has preceded her to heaven, and each of our souls must be wed to Him alone. And we who leave all behind to follow Him "shall be filled" and "shall laugh" on the Day of our marriage, for "the reign of God" will be ours.

It is not in this world we take our "consolation" – how sad those who do so. For the riches of this world will rust and rot, and its laughter shall prove so hollow. Thus Paul instructs the wise: "Buyers should conduct themselves as though they owned nothing," for in truth they have nothing at all: of what worth is that which does not last? Only an illusion are the temporary pleasures and vain accolades of this dying earth. The trials we find are all that should cause us to "rejoice and exult, for [our] reward shall be great in heaven" if we endure our exile well.

To those who consider marriage, Paul gives the instruction: "[You] will have trials in this life, and these I should like to spare you." Certainly marriage is not sinful, and is even a fruitful sacrament, but even this which can be such a blessing is but passing in the eyes of God. And the attachment we find to our spouse, again, though blessed by the Lord, is a union that is also passing – one which must ultimately be left as well. Since only our marriage to the living God is that which endures, Paul in his wisdom offers this word: "Those with wives should live as though they had none"; for this beauty, too, shall fade, and it is not in it we are called to make our home.

Yes, "the time is short," brothers and sisters. The time is always short because time itself is passing – only eternity remains. And so, set not your

501

hearts on the fading things of this life. The Lord who has died now prepares a place for you in His heavenly kingdom. And "all glorious is the King's daughter as she enters; her raiment is threaded with spun gold." So, to His palace be "borne in with gladness and joy"... join now the song of all His saints in our heavenly homeland.

Thursday

(1Cor.8:1-7,11-13; Ps.139:1-3,13-14,23-24; Lk.6:27-38)

"The measure you measure with will be measured back to you."

And what is your measuring stick, brother? Is it the ruler of this earth, limited by eyes of flesh? Or is it the yardstick of heaven, which reaches unto the Lord's side and finds us in His sight? Do you toil on this plane alone, or do you climb the mountain where He sits, where He teaches? Do your ears hear only of the debits and credits recorded in the book of this world; or are they open to the word the Lord speaks, and the generous outpouring of His grace?

In our first reading Paul states: "'Knowledge' inflates, but love upbuilds." What he means is that our knowledge of earthly things can do little but inflate our pride, and thinking that this is true knowledge makes us blind. The "knowledge" that we should seek is the love of God, which comes from God and teaches us all things. "If anyone loves God, that man is known by Him," and living thus in His sight, in His light, we see all with heavenly vision. With this wisdom we understand that "there is no God but one" and that "an idol is really nothing": all the idols man makes upon this earth are empty and vain, and all the teaching which comes from such has no resonance, falls short of truth.

Yet we are called to be patient with the weakness of others, with their failures in faith. We must "not be an occasion of sin" for others but always be prepared to pardon and love even those who hate us. For if someone does violence to us, what do we teach these who cannot measure beyond earthly passion if we do them violence in return? If we answer with violence, what language do we speak but that of the world? But we are called to converse with heavenly tongues, even with the word of our Lord, and cannot rightly be called His sons if we do not do so. "If you love those who love you, what credit is that to you? Even sinners love those who love them." And you are thus but saying that you are a child of the earth and not heaven, living in the flesh and not the spirit.

"Truly you have formed my inmost being; you knit me in my mother's womb," is David's song of joy to God. He gives thanks that he is "fearfully, wonderfully made." And if made by God should we not reflect God and the love He has revealed in the Lord Jesus Christ? Should we not be as His Son? And so, should we not with David call upon the Lord to "probe" us and to "know [our] heart" and our "thoughts," that He might straighten out our "crooked" ways and set us on the path His love prepares? Do we not desire the overflowing joy He brings? Then we must measure as He, with the heavenly yardstick that reaches up to where the Trinity is.

Friday
(1Cor.9:16-19,22-27; Ps.84:2-6,8,12; Lk.6:39-42)

"Although I am not bound to anyone,
I made myself the slave of all so as to win over as many as possible."

How like His Lord is Paul in his declaration, "To the weak I became a weak person with a view to winning the weak." For as Jesus descended from heaven to take on flesh and save those corrupted by its sin, so the Apostle has made himself "all things to all people," stepping inside their skin "in order to save at least some of them." Indeed, Paul proves himself to be "on a par with his teacher" in sacrifice and fruitfulness, for how well he serves "to remove the speck from [his] brother's eye" that he might see Jesus in the clear light of day.

The Apostle has been "entrusted with a charge," that of "preaching the Gospel." And doing so willingly he finds his "recompense." And what is this recompense but that he receive nothing in return for his work, nothing here on earth except of course the blessing of persecution such work for the Master entails? Then why engage in such toil, and why call others to such a life of self-sacrifice? Ah yes, because of the "crown that is imperishable" which awaits the runner of such a race. This heavenly blessing, too, is found when one does all "for the sake of the Gospel."

"My heart and my flesh cry out for the living God," our psalmist intones today, and goes on to proclaim the happiness of those "who dwell in [God's] house." "Continually they praise [Him]... They go from strength to strength," for "grace and glory He bestows." This is the goal Paul has in mind when he says, "I do not run like a man who loses sight of the finish line." All his tribulations never distract him from his final destination; the kingdom of heaven remains ever upon his heart. And ever does he strain forward that he and so many others might attain that crown for which "our soul yearns and pines."

Brothers and sisters, we must "discipline [our] own body and master it"; we must "remove the plank lodged in [our] own [eye]" if we hope to join Paul in the place where "even the sparrow finds a home and the swallow a nest in which she puts her young." And our young we, too, must bring there

– all those in our charge must know of the kingdom of God. And so let us join Paul and our holy Lord in here becoming slaves of all, enduring our exile bravely that we might draw others to the eternal home found on the altar of the living God.

Saturday
(1Cor.10:14-22; Ps.116:12-13,17-18; Lk.6:43-49)

"Is not the cup of blessing we bless a sharing in the blood of Christ?
And is not the bread we break a sharing in the body of Christ?"

The Body and Blood of Christ we have upon our altar and in the Word of His teaching. It is these which set a firm foundation within ourselves, these by which we bear fruit in His Name – these by which we come to be as He is.

Paul tells the Corinthians today "to shun the worship of idols," not because they are real, for they are not, but because these sacrifices are made "to demons and not to God" and we, as sons and daughters of a jealous God, "cannot drink the cup of the Lord and also the cup of demons" nor "partake of the table of the Lord and likewise the table of demons." As "a good tree does not produce decayed fruit any more than a decayed tree produces good fruit," so evil has no place with good and demons no place in the house of God. Partaking of this table is like building a "house on the ground without any foundation" and will only serve to weaken and eventually destroy our faith in the Lord.

And so we should have no share in the things of the world or in the decayed fruit which such mammon bears. This unholy food and drink is but to be vomited out in the sickness it produces. And calling upon the name of the powers of the earth and the air will but cause us to choke in an unholy fear. We must "call upon the name of the Lord" and upon His Name alone build our home. It is "the cup of salvation [we must] take up" and drink of the blood that is sanctified by the sacrifice of our Lord and God. And what does our psalmist mean when he sings, "My vows to the Lord I will pay in the presence of all His people" but that, as Jesus Himself instructs us in our gospel, we must "put into practice" the promises we make unto God? Else our words are empty; else our words are evil, for else our words will bear no fruit and our worship will be in vain.

A great call have we, brothers and sisters: to be like the Lord. And this call is within our reach. His Body and Blood are upon our table; His words are ringing in our ears. We have but to eat; we have but to listen... we have but to accept these gifts and *do* His will, and even the torrents of death shall not shake our souls. For we shall be as "the man, who, in building a house, dug deeply and laid the foundation on a rock"; we shall stand solidly with unshakable trust in the eternal Lord. For like Him we shall have become by sharing in His sacrifice.

Twenty-Fourth Week

Monday
(1Cor.11:17-26,33; Ps.40:7-10,17,1Cor.11:26; Lk.7:1-10)

"Just give the order and my servant will be cured."

By a word from His mouth what cannot be done? For those who have faith this is all that is needed.

Listen, brothers and sisters, to the centurion's explication of "the meaning of an order": "I say to one, 'On your way,' and off he goes; to another, 'Come here,' and he comes; to my slave, 'Do this,' and he does it." Do you see faith at work? Do you understand the power of a word? And if a mere centurion in the Roman army possesses such power and gains such loyalty by his commands, do you think the Lord's words shall fall short or His servants be found lacking in obedience?

"I am not worthy to have you enter my house" are the words the centurion speaks to Jesus before our quote for the day, and they are of course the sentence we utter just before we receive the Lord in Holy Communion. That same sacrament of Communion is described for us by Paul in his letter to the Corinthians; he tells us of the Christ's words and actions upon its institution "on the night in which He was betrayed." "This is my body," Jesus says; and, in Paul's phrasing, "This cup is the new covenant in my blood." And so do we partake of the Lord's Body and Blood even as we remember His sacrifice for our sins; and so, like the centurion's servant, we are healed of our ills.

Yet there are "divisions among [us]" regarding this central sacrament of our faith. Perhaps "there may even have to be factions among [us] for the tried and true to stand out clearly." But the Lord is never pleased with a lack of faith. And if He decries the lack of "faith among the Israelites," what is His thought on Christians who cannot believe in His presence in the Sacrament? Does the Lord not also have "soldiers under His command" like the centurion? Do they not also carry out His orders? Or is the word He gives them not powerful enough to carry out His will? Is it somehow impossible for the Lord to make Himself present (as He has promised) by the intercession of His apostles, His priests – even as by the intercession of the Jewish elders the centurion gained his request from the Christ? Does your faith not fall short if you thus limit the power of God, of His Word, of the power given His apostles? "I received from the Lord what I handed on to you," Paul states succinctly as he speaks to his disciples of the Lord's Supper. And this meal shall last till the end of time; and it shall ever feed us body and soul with the presence of Christ.

"Behold, I come," says the Lord. To do the Father's will is the Son's "delight" and the delight of all who follow Him. In body He comes and in body He remains, upon our altars and in His sons. This "justice" we "announce in the vast assembly"; we do "not restrain [our] lips." For His faithfulness to us, we His slaves and soldiers well know; and for such love we can but proclaim: "The Lord be glorified"! For by a word from His mouth uttered through His priest – "This is my body" – He is in our midst.

Tuesday
(1Cor.12:12-14,27-31; Ps.100:1-5; Lk.7:11-17)

"A great prophet has risen among us."

A great prophet, yes, and so much more; for here is He who is Himself the "one body" upon whom the "one Spirit" rests, and in whom all find their home.

"The body is one and has many members; but all the members, many though they are, are one body; and so it is with Christ." Christ is all things: He is apostle sent by the Father, prophet speaking for God, teacher instructing all on the narrow path that leads to heaven, miracle worker raising the dead, healer of body and soul causing the deaf to hear and the blind to see, assistant washing the feet of His disciples, administrator apportioning the gifts and graces which are His own, and speaker in tongues upon whom the flame of the Spirit eternally rests and whose Word goes forth to all nations. We are not all apostles, prophets, teachers, miracle workers, healers, and speakers in tongues – but He is. He is all these things for He is whole; He is the only Son of God, and we are "His people, the sheep of His flock" who share in His power according to our baptism in His Name.

And so should we not "sing joyfully to the Lord" for the Savior who has been raised from among us? Should not all "lands," all members of His blessed body "serve the Lord with gladness," that all might tend to the glory of God? In our gospel "a considerable crowd of townsfolk were with" the widow, and "a large crowd accompanied" Jesus. These met at "the gate of the town" called Nain. When the Lord raised the son of the widow from the dead, "fear seized them all and they began to praise God." Is not this scene of celebration like that which should encompass the body of Christ? Should not such joy in recognition of the greatness of God course through all our veins, strengthening all our muscles? For we know more than they. We know this Man is more than a prophet – we know it is the Messiah who is among us. And so, let us "enter His gates with thanksgiving, His courts with praise" as we "set [our] hearts on the greater gifts" at work within us now as members of the body of the only Son.

Alleluia! He raises us all from the dead to speak in the power of the Spirit.

Wednesday
(1Cor.12:31-13:13; Ps.33:2-5,12,22; Lk.7:31-35)

"We piped you a tune but you did not dance;
we sang you a dirge but you did not wail."

"Like children squatting in the city squares and calling to their playmates," seeking to have them comply with their own selfish will, so are "the men of today" according to our Lord. And so is their song not "a noisy gong"? Do they not lack of love? Could they be more "rude," more impatient and unkind, than to declare of John the Baptizer, "He is mad!" and of the Son of Man, "Here is a glutton and a drunkard"? Could they any more "rejoice in what is wrong," utterly shutting out the truth?

And why? Why is it they do so lack of love? Why are they so ungodly? Is it not that they fail to realize and state with the Apostle Paul: "Our knowledge is imperfect and our prophesying is imperfect"? Is it not because they trust in their own minds that they do not come to the wisdom of God?

And what is "God's wisdom"? It is what Paul speaks of so well today: God is love, and without God we are worth nothing. Yes, God is love. Love is the heart of the Law even as God is the heart of the Law, and without the heart the body is useless. But knowing God is love, hearing it repeated over and over, is not sufficient for our salvation. Certainly, "of the kindness of the Lord the earth is full." The Lord ever pours forth His grace, His love upon all His creatures – but how do we come to have that love, how do we come to accept it? Again, the key is in Paul's statement, "My knowledge is imperfect now." It is in understanding that, even though "we put childish ways aside," yet "we see indistinctly." It is in the realization that we are not God, that we need God and His love; in a word, it is in repentance. Genuine repentance is the attitude that brings us to the love of God. And the need for it is constant!

I think there is a kind of divine equation to our relationship with the Lord: the more we recognize our misery, the more He shares His mercy; the more we acknowledge our lack of His wisdom and love, the more He fills our desire for them. Marvelous is the justice of God!

Brothers and sisters, "give thanks to the Lord on the harp; with the ten-stringed lyre chant His praises." It is ours to "speak with human tongues and angelic as well"; we must employ "the gift of prophecy," "feed the poor," and be ready to "hand over [our] body to be burned." But all we do must be driven by His will, must be founded in His love. Our song must be set in His holy key and reflect His eternal harmony, or we have nothing to fill our emptiness.

Thursday
(1Cor.15:1-11; Ps.118:1-2,16-17,28; Lk.7:36-50)

"I am the least of the apostles."

Brothers and sisters, "little is forgiven the one whose love is small." And it is in the sweet tears of repentance that we discover the love held in the merciful heart of the Lord.

Paul speaks the truth of himself when he claims that he does "not even deserve the name" of apostle because he has "persecuted the Church of God." "But through the favor of God" he has "worked harder than all the others," preaching the Gospel of the Lord. As small as he is and as undeserving as he is, so great is the Lord's blessing upon him. In the measure he recognizes his sin, the Lord pours His grace into him, and through him to others.

And what grace pours forth through the woman in our gospel today! In her we see our own encounter with the Lord. Here is she who is "known in town to be a sinner" standing and kneeling in tears before her God. And the Lord knows well "who and what sort of woman this is that touches Him – that she is a sinner," and He knows well, too, her repentant heart. While the others at table see neither their own sin nor the woman's repentance, He allows Himself to be touched by both (her sin and her repentance) – it is for just such a moment as this He has come. And how well the Lord speaks the truth in His detailed description of the woman's repentance; how well we see His love reflected in her... and how blest is she to hear these words for which every heart does long: "Your sins are forgiven." And how her tears increase at this word come forth from the mouth of the Holy One. And so, while the others argue blindly among themselves, He reaches out His hand, touches her face, and whispers to her soul: "Your faith has been your salvation. Now go in peace."

"O my God, I extol you... You have been my savior." Indeed, your "mercy endures forever," and now I know that "I shall not die, but live, and declare the works of the Lord." This is the song the woman must sing; this is the song of St. Paul. This is the song of every soul redeemed by the love of the Lord. So let us all "stand firm" in the Gospel preached to us by those who have seen Him, from Peter to this wretched Paul; we "are being saved by it at this very moment if we retain it" in its purity. And here is the Word simply put: "That Christ died for our sins in accord with the Scriptures; that He was buried and, in accord with the Scriptures, rose on the third day." What grace is ours, we the least, we poor sinners – we who know the greatness of His love.

Friday
(1Cor.15:12-20; Ps.17:1,6-8,15; Lk.8:1-3)

"Christ has been raised from the dead,
the first fruits of those who have fallen asleep."

This is the heart of our faith. This is the "Good News," the Gospel preached in our midst. This is our firm belief. Upon it all our hopes stand. Christ has been raised, and His disciples will follow Him. As surely as we accompany Him here in His mission on earth, so surely will we find ourselves in His presence in heaven. Dying in Him means rising in light.

But "if our hopes in Christ are limited to this life only, we are the most pitiable of men." We could then be said to have truly wasted our time, for then the very heart of our faith would have been torn out, and what but scoffing would we have to hold? A dead Christ we would carry in our arms, and we "the deadest of the dead" with Him.

Paul speaks of this quite pointedly; he pulls no punches in this regard, declaring openly: "If Christ has not been raised, our preaching is void of content and your faith is empty too." Yet there are those today, as then, who "say there is no resurrection of the dead," that "Christ was not raised" – and these would call themselves Christian. And in the same manner there are many who do not truly believe the resurrection, yet wear the Christian nametag. If we have doubt in our hearts, or, worse yet, if we preach against the core of the faith, what do we do but kill ourselves? What do we do but work against the very Gospel of Christ? And how then do we merit the name of Christian?

Brothers and sisters, we must know in our hearts and be assured that Jesus is risen from the dead. We must realize that God has "attend[ed] to [David's] outcry," that He has "hearken[ed] to [his] prayer" – that the most urgent longing of our souls has been answered by the "savior of those who hope in [Him]." With David, we of faith should say with his resolve: "On waking, I shall be content in your presence." Has the resurrection not been indicated in the "women who ha[ve] been cured of evil spirits and maladies" and who now accompany Jesus? Does not Mary Magdalene, "from whom seven devils had gone out," give clear example of hope in Christ fulfilled? For she is not at all as she was, and this woman once so completely possessed by death itself is the first to see the Lord risen.

We must know the resurrection in our lives on earth; this is the only way we will comprehend it in heaven. Release from sin allows us to see already the eternal fruits of the kingdom. Accompanying Him now, our sins behind us, already upon heaven's road we tread. And we know for certain we shall pass through these "towns and villages" even unto His kingdom.

Saturday
(1Cor.15:35-37,42-49; Ps.56:10-14; Lk.8:4-15)

"Just as we resemble the man from earth,
so shall we bear the likeness of the man from heaven."

It is not difficult to recognize our earthly bodies. They are with us always, and make themselves known in the "weakness" that befalls us. Adam's sin is upon us his children and reminds us always that we are human, of the earth.

But as we know this body of the earth so "subject to decay," so "ignoble" in itself, so we should know the "spiritual body [that] comes up" as this "natural body is put down" by us. Here is the meaning of Jesus' teaching that we must lay down our lives, that we must die to this world to be raised up in His presence. For the earthly form we know so well by the weakness and sin inherent in its confines we must set aside, not nourish in its passions, that ever the Spirit might take shape in our lives... that we might take on the likeness of Christ. And so even our corrupted nature may bring growth and fruit of great significance when we sow it in the ground, when we place it back whence it has come. In this death is life.

"A farmer went out to sow some seed." This farmer is, of course, Jesus, the spiritual Man who casts seed of the Spirit for all waiting hearts to receive and nourish to growth as a "full-blown plant" in the Father's light. If we heed the Word He proclaims to us with exclamation, if we become ourselves as "the seed sown on good ground," given rebirth in the Gospel of Christ, resurrection of our weakened form we will know; even now it shall begin to mature within us. But if we are empty as "those on the footpath" or rootless as "those on rocky ground" or stifled as "the seed fallen among briers," how then shall we escape the natural body and its corruption and reach up to the kingdom of heaven? It cannot but be that we shall die – and in this death there will be no resurrection to life.

O brothers and sisters, let us be as David, who declares in faith, "Now I know that God is with me" and asks with such confidence, "What can flesh do against me?" How indeed can the flesh hold us down, pressed to the earth though it may be, if we have God's Word in us growing so surely? In God let us "trust without fear," and on the day of full growth, when this "earth formed from dust" has died completely and the Man of Spirit has His kingdom revealed, we shall rejoice with David and sing: "You have rescued me from death... that I may walk before God in the land of the living." Then the Spirit so really we shall know.

Twenty-Fifth Week

Monday
(Prv.3:27-34; Ps.15:1-5; Lk.8:16-18)

"The curse of the Lord is on the house of the wicked,
but the dwelling of the just He blesses."

Light fills the house of him "who walks blamelessly and does justice; who thinks the truth in his heart and slanders not with his tongue," for he who does these things is as light itself, having no part with darkness. He knows that "to the Lord the perverse man is an abomination," and so he "env[ies]" not the lawless man and choose[s] none of his ways" but chooses always the way of God and so finds the "friendship" of the Lord which is with "the upright," which is as light shining upon him and through him.

As for the wicked, "he who has not will lose even the little he thinks he has," for the Lord is not with him; and all he has gained by "usury" and by "bribe[s] against the innocent" shall be revealed in all its emptiness on the day the Lord shines His encompassing light – he will indeed be left with nothing, for nothing he truly has. He who has "plot[ted]... evil against his neighbor" and "quarrel[led]... with a man without cause" will never be able to stand in the light of the Lord, for he has made his home in darkness, and in darkness he shall remain. Certainly this "reprobate is despised" by the Lord, for his rebellion puts him in opposition to the kingdom of God.

And so we must "take heed, therefore, how [we] hear" the Lord's instruction, for His instruction is as light itself and brings the light of salvation to the receptive soul. This light we must make our own and place it "on a lampstand so that whoever comes in" – whoever approaches the house in which we dwell – "can see it" and can share in it freely. All shade of sin must be removed from our souls so that without hindrance and without hesitation our light will shine forth and all will know the abiding love of the Lord. "He who does these things shall never be disturbed." He who does these things, who reflects the Lord's justice and love all his days, cannot but be blessed by the Lord, for he himself becomes His own.

511

Ordinary Time

"When He is dealing with the arrogant, He is stern, but to the humble He shows kindness." And so, having his deeds "brought to light" is as a curse for the wicked, but to the just it means eternal blessing.

Tuesday
(Prv.21:1-6,10-13; Ps.119:1,27,30,34-35,44; Lk.8:19-21)

"My mother and my brothers are those who hear the word of God
and act upon it."

Our readings today are filled throughout with one line pearls of wisdom culminating with Jesus' above instruction in our brief gospel. And though each individual proverb or paean to the command of the Lord seems a separate entity distinct from the others which surround it, in fact, all speak of the same sword of truth that separates the way of the wicked from that of the just. In even thousands of proverbs there is but one word – that we must be hearers and doers of the word of God.

"Like a stream is the king's heart in the hand of the Lord; wherever it pleases Him, He directs it." O that such blessed obedience could be all our own! O that we would follow Him so perfectly, for "happy are they whose way is blameless, who walk in the law of the Lord"; and they become as His only Son. "To do what is right and just" must be our constant aim, our eternal prayer. "Lead me in the path of your commands," we must beg of our God, for in it alone we know the light of His grace; in His way alone we find all our "delight." Only in observing His decrees, walking in His love, do we become brother and sister and mother to the Christ.

For the wicked shall not enter His embrace, shall not be counted among His family. "Haughty eyes and a proud heart" the Lord will not countenance, for "the tillage of the wicked is sin" and with sin the Holy One has no relation. Thus we may be certain "there is One who brings down the wicked to ruin." As grandiose as his plots may seem and as adamantly as he may pursue them with "a lying tongue," he is but "chasing a bubble over deadly snares" and shall be caught in the trap he himself has laid.

"When the wise man is instructed, he gains knowledge"; he draws ever closer to the light of the Lord as he drinks in His Word. Let us be as those who "meditate on [the Lord's] wondrous deeds." Let us beg Him with our psalmist: "Give me discernment, that I may observe your law and keep it with all my heart." When Jesus speaks let us be quick to listen and follow in His way, that truly we may become His blessed family, one in the Church modeled by the Mother of God.

Wednesday
(Prv.30:5-9; Ps.119:29,72,89,101,104-105,163; Lk.9:1-6)

"Take nothing for the journey."

How can he who takes nothing with him for his journey be provided for? Does not such action contradict the wisdom of the king who asks in his book of Proverbs – "Give me neither poverty nor riches"? Is it not poverty the Lord recommends to His disciples?

The evangelical counsel of poverty practiced by the religious communities and striven for by all true members of the Christian faith is not the same as that which our author of Proverbs wishes to avoid (no more so than the riches he would keep far from himself are those of the heavenly kingdom). For those whom Jesus sends out never find themselves "in want," the want which would lead the desperate to steal and so sin; rather, the only "want" His disciples have is for an increasing understanding and practice of the word of God. And the poverty they practice is meant to feed this hunger for the greatest of food.

Proverbs itself gives us answer to the means by which the Lord's disciples taking "no bread, no money" are fed: "He is a shield to those who take refuge in Him." The Lord is always our food. Cannot He who "endures forever," whose word is "firm as the heavens," care for the small needs of His creatures here below? Will not he who labors for Him have all he needs to accomplish his work? Certainly! For though the disciples *take* nothing, it does not follow that they *have* nothing – for they have the Lord with them, and that is everything.

Indeed, it is because the first of the wise king's requests of God – "put falsehood and lying far from me" – has been answered in them that this second is accomplished. "Remove from me the way of falsehood," our psalmist echoes, and for the Lord's disciples this has been done. They "add nothing to His words" as "from every evil way [they] withhold [their] feet"; and so "the law of [His] mouth," which resounds from their own mouths as they "proclaim the reign of God," "is to [them] more precious than thousands of gold and silver pieces" and feeds them abundantly.

The Word of the Lord will be received by those who seek His truth, and in turn feed the speaker as it does the hearer. So let us be wary of "being full" of the things of this world, lest we find no room for God, and let us make our psalmist's declaration truly our own: "Falsehood I hate and abhor; your law I love." Then all things will be provided for.

513

Thursday
(Ec.1:2-11; Ps.90:1,3-6,12-14,17; Lk.9:7-9)

"See, this is new!"

Here is He who is "new under the sun." For it is not so that "John has been raised from the dead," nor that "one of the prophets of old has arisen": He has not "already existed in the ages that preceded us." He is the Christ! He is the Messiah! He it is who has come to "fill us at daybreak with [His] kindness, that we may shout for joy and gladness all our days." In Him the dark of the night veiling our eyes is banished from our midst.

O Qoheleth, pursuer of your passions in all their vanity, why do you race to catch up with the sun as if it should stand and wait for you? What makes you think you could hold the wind in your hand? Why would you see end of the rivers' path to the sea? Why do you toil so blindly, taking your refuge in created things and frustrated when you cannot control them to your own ends, when they betray the peace you seek? "Back to dust" you shall indeed return, and the sun and the wind and the sea still stand; and above them all does reign our God, for whom "a thousand years... are as yesterday, now that it is past." In Him you should have taken refuge.

O Herod, drowning in your debauchery, do you, too, now begin to see its ends; does its emptiness now overtake your soul? Do you remember the words the prophet delivered to your ears? What is the cause of your curiosity, and will you listen now to the voice echoing through your halls? The kingdom of the world crumbles before our eyes and no "profit has man from all the labor which he toils at under the sun," unless it is the Lord who "prosper[s] the work of our hands for us." Dead we are and alone will ever be in our profligacy, the emptiness upon us.

Qoheleth, your words are proven wrong: it is not so that "there is no remembrance of the man of old," for we read your thoughts with diligence today; and three thousand years after your time you teach us still of the dark vision of life without the Christ. And of Him who has come after thee there is great remembrance, and more than this, for His breath is now upon us. In Him is "the ear filled with hearing" and the eye "satisfied with seeing," for now truth and light do walk with us, even under the sun. And though our body "by evening wilts and fades" as of old, our soul "at dawn springs up anew." For "the gracious care of the Lord [is] ours" and He "teach[es] us to number our days aright, that we may gain wisdom of heart." And this wisdom is true; this wisdom is new: this wisdom bears us light to transcend the vanity of a worldly life and come to the kingdom of heaven.

Friday
(Ec.3:1-11; Ps.144:1-4; Lk.9:18-22)

"He has made everything appropriate to its time,
and has put the timeless into their hearts."

Yes, "there is an appointed time for everything, and a time for every affair under the heavens"; and there is a time for time to cease and the timeless to come to the fore – a time for the things above the heavens. And that fullness of time has come upon the earth, for the Son of Man has known His "time to be born"; and in man's discovering "the work which God has done," no time for vain toil is there anymore. The time has come to make Him our "refuge and [our] fortress," our blessed "rock" of truth.

"One day when Jesus was praying in seclusion and His disciples were with Him," the time had come for Him to "put the question to them": "Who do you say that I am?" And now it was Peter's "time to speak," to declare the faith of the Church: "The Messiah of God." And though it was not then time "to tell this to anyone," for the Son of Man had yet to know His "time to die," soon the time would come for the Son to rise, and then there would be no more "time to be silent."

That time has come upon us now, brothers and sisters. Now is only "a time to plant" and "a time to build" – a time to raise the kingdom of heaven here on earth, a time to labor to complete God's Church. For timelessness now has its time; life eternal overtakes us. And so we have only "time to love," having broken the wheel of sin by the sacrifice of Christ and so come out from under the shadow of hatred. No return to the vanity of the things of this world is there for us, for we must do all as if doing nothing.

It is true: "Man is like a breath; his days, like a passing shadow," but it is also so that the Lord "take[s] thought of him." And in this earthen vessel He has placed the Spirit of life – and that Spirit is now known in full in our Lord and Savior Jesus Christ. It is "time to embrace" Him and know the "time of peace" He breathes eternally upon His creatures, letting all shadow pass away as we walk in His holy light and proclaim His holy name.

Saturday
(Ec.11:9-12:8; Ps.90:1,3-6,12-14,17; Lk.9:43-45)

"The dust returns to the earth as it once was,
and the life breath returns to God who gave it."

"As a watch of the night" is our life, passing unnoticed while souls slumber. "You make an end of them in their sleep," Psalm 90 prophesies (as we hear the same verses of this same psalm for the second time in three days); indeed man lies unaware of his coming death, ignorant of the day which passes. For though in our youth we "follow the ways of [our] heart, the vision of [our] eyes," and seem to "ward off grief" at will, yet "the next morning [we] are like the changing grass"; so quickly does our flower fade. And so little of this do we see.

In our gospel the Lord speaks again to His disciples of His imminent death, and so, really, the death we all must undergo; but though He makes a clear point that they should listen carefully, saying, "Pay close attention to what I tell you," yet they seem unable to hear His words. Our gospel tells us, "They failed... to understand this warning; its meaning was so concealed from them they did not grasp it at all." He repeats what He has said before in no uncertain terms, and yet they are deaf to His word; yet they are blind.

How like us all the disciples are. When confronted with the coming of death how easily we shut our eyes. Though it draw upon us inevitably, how desperately we hold to the vanity of these passing things, unwilling to hear of the day when "the sun is darkened... and the strong men are bent... and the sound of the mill is low." "Man goes to his lasting home, and mourners go about the streets" – so Qoheleth paints the image of the time when "the clouds return after the rain." How compelling his verses are, and how ominous... and of this darkness we must hear. It is not wise to remain blind to the passing of this life, or with it we shall die when it ends. Though none of this should touch our souls, yet we must learn to let the body go.

O Lord, "you return man back to dust, saying, 'Return, O children of men,'" yet you hold each of us in your loving hands. And so we cry unto you this day, "Return, O Lord! How long? Have pity on your servants!" For we wait with expectant hearts for Him who has risen from the dead to come to us again. Let your Spirit breathe upon us now and turn this dust into the image of your Son. May it be your Day which comes to us, even as we die.

O. 26. Mon. (II)

Twenty-Sixth Week

Monday
(Job 1:6-22; Ps.17:1-3,6-7; Lk.9:46-50)

"Naked I came forth from my mother's womb,
and naked I shall go back again."

In the beginning and in the end, we have nothing: and so should be our attitude toward all things we are given – that they are not our own, that we do not possess them... that they shall pass from us unto eternity again. As shall we all.

In our first reading we begin to hear of Satan's temptation of Job, of whom the Lord's own words witness: "There is no one on earth like him, blameless and upright, fearing God and avoiding evil." But Satan in his jealousy responds, "Is it for nothing that Job is God-fearing?" and recounts all the blessings the Lord has bestowed on His "servant." The adversarial angel then wins from God permission to tempt Job by removing all his blessings.

And the persecution is strong. All in a day Job loses his multitude of livestock, his servants, and his children. Four messengers come, each with catastrophic news, each the sole survivor of the tragedy of which they speak, and each following the previous "while he was yet speaking." In a moment all but his life is taken from Job. But Job proves God's assessment of his character true by proclaiming, "The Lord gave and the Lord has taken away; blessed be the name of the Lord!" thus properly putting all things in God's hands, and praising His glory even in such tragedy. We are told, "In all this Job did not sin, nor did he say anything disrespectful of God." He is as the child Jesus sits beside Himself in our gospel today.

Satan has failed in his effort to get Job to curse God; he will not do so even at his wife's prompting. But Job, so Christlike in his suffering the abandonment God's Servant knows so fully upon the cross, shall fall short of the Christ in one respect: this innocent child will not be able to keep from decrying his state or withstand the accusations of others that he must be guilty of sin. He will not be able to suffer in silence, not opening his mouth to defend himself (taking this unwarranted persecution upon himself to redeem others, as Jesus has done) but will declare his "just suit" to the Lord, begging Him to "attend to [his] outcry," saying with David in our psalm: "Hearken to my prayer from lips without deceit." He shall not be able to keep from stating his innocence, from saying, "Though you test my heart, searching it in the night, though you try me with fire, you shall find no malice in me." And in this way Satan shall break him; in this manner he shall fall short of the perfect humility of Christ. (Though the Lord shall justify and reward his faithful servant in the end.)

Brothers and sisters, do not act with jealousy, as even the disciples seem to do today in trying to stop one "not of [their] company" from healing in Jesus' name. Do not even think among yourselves of who is the greatest. This is an abomination before God. Have the attitude of Job toward all things – that they are but gifts from the Lord and that we are nothing in ourselves. Then you will be like His little child and so know His blessings forever.

517

Tuesday

(Job 3:1-3,11-17,20-23; Ps.88:2-8; Lk.9:51-56)

"My soul is surfeited with troubles
and my life draws near to the nether world."

After sitting in silence seven days, scraping the boils from his skin, finally, "Job opened his mouth and cursed his day." Finally he cried out against all his troubles, asking, "Why did I not perish at birth, come forth from the womb and expire?" Only so much can mortal man bear, and so Job seeks now only the tranquility of death, wherein "the weary are at rest."

How well our psalm today describes Job's state, he who is among those "whose path is hidden from them, and whom God hemmed in." For he truly finds himself now "numbered with those who go down into the pit... a man without strength" from whom all blessing has been taken. His "couch is among the dead, like the slain who lie in the grave, whom [God] remember[s] no longer and who are cut off from [His] care." And so he prays for an end to his misery; so he seeks the forgetfulness of death to remove its pangs from his body and his heart.

And is it not these same pangs James and John would inflict upon the Samaritans who refuse to welcome Jesus: "Lord, would you not have us call down fire from heaven to destroy them?" Would they not plunge them "into the bottom of the pit, into the dark abyss" where Job sits in his innocence? Is it not right that God's "wrath lies heavy" upon such as these? Let God's "billows" "overwhelm" them, they declare.

But Jesus has another answer. He would not see even the guilty suffer the fate of the righteous Job. For He is now "firmly resolved to proceed toward Jerusalem," where His crucifixion awaits. He is now upon the fulfillment of His mission here on earth, and it has nothing to do with punishing the sins even of His persecutors – it has only to do with His death. It is He upon whom God's wrath shall be heavy, He who will be plunged into the pit... He who will suffer all punishment for sin. Even for these Samaritans (even for you and me), the Lord shall suffer and die, taking upon Himself the punishment James and John see rightly due them, rightly due to all. His cross completes the pangs inflicted upon Job. And through this cross the troubles shall be overcome.

Brothers and sisters, let us no longer cry for relief from our suffering, for that relief is at hand now in the cross of Christ; He has suffered all these things already, and we must but give them to Him to be drawn from the nether world and set in His glory.

Wednesday
(Job 9:1-12,14-16; Ps.88:3,10-15; Lk.9:57-62)

"Why, O Lord, do you reject me;
why hide from me your face?"

The cry of our psalmist certainly reflects that of Job, who in his travails asks, "How can a man be justified before God?" who realizes that the Lord "does great things past finding out" and that "should He come near [us], [we] see Him not." But it also reflects Jesus' treatment of those who might follow Him, and could easily be their cry as well.

"If I appealed to Him and He answered my call, I could not believe that He would hearken to my words." Such a seemingly hopeless attitude may be understandable in one suffering such a plight as Job. For he is as "the mountains [removed] before they know it"; he is shaken as "the earth out of its place." He is as one suddenly confounded by God, who is "wise in heart and mighty in strength." Before such power how can he speak, or expect to be heard? And so, rightly in silence he must remain. Certainly he could cry out to the Lord, "Will you work wonders for the dead?... Do they declare your kindness in the grave, your faithfulness among those who have perished?" and in justice be saved from "the land of oblivion." But the test Job undergoes passes beyond justice to the suffering of the innocent before the mighty power of God.

And what of those who would be Christ's disciples spoken of in our gospel today? To them why does the Lord speak so severely? Why does it seem they, too, are unable to come before His face – why does He seem to reject them? Is He not of love, this Son of Man, unlike the judgmental God? Does He not welcome all with open arms? Then why such sharp words to those who approach and those He calls to "come away and proclaim the kingdom of God"? The Lord does not reject them, but puts them to the test as He has with Job to see if their hearts are truly set upon Him alone, as indeed they must be. It is, of course, for the great glory to which He calls them that all His disciples are chastised so vehemently.

Think not that He rejects you, brothers and sisters, when He hides His face from you. Know that you are never hidden from Him, and that should He remove Himself from your presence, it is only to grant you clearer vision of His face. None is more blessed than Job for none has known so fully the awesome power of God and given himself over to it so completely. None but Christ and His followers, who give up all things, who suffer all persecutions innocently, silently, in order to know the surpassing might and tender mercy of God. Indeed His "wonders [are] made known in darkness," for then they most clearly shine.

Thursday
(Job 19:21-27; Ps.27:7-9,13-14; Lk.10:1-12)

"I know that my Vindicator lives,
and that He will at last stand forth upon the dust."

"The hand of God has struck me!" Job exclaims as he begs pity from his friends who "hound [him] as though [they] were divine," reminding him unendingly of the Lord's justice and ever accusing him of having sinned against his Maker. Job defends himself and wishes "that with an iron chisel and with lead" his "words were written down." And truly his prayer is answered, for here are his words "inscribed in a record... cut in the rock [of Scripture] forever."

And what has this poor soul to say? Reflecting David's own call for pity from the Lord and his own desire to know his God – "Of you my heart speaks; you my glance seeks" – Job declares, "My inmost being is consumed with longing"; his heart, too, is set upon God. And as David proclaims in great hope, "I believe I shall see the bounty of the Lord in the land of the living," so Job makes known his faith and hope in the Lord: "My own eyes, not another's, shall behold Him." What testimony from a man in such travails!

And in our gospel we see that his (and David's) hope is not in vain, for here now stands the Lord forth upon the earth, Himself having taken the form of our dust and multiplying His presence among us as He "send[s] workers into His harvest." And He comes to bring peace; His disciples declare, "The reign of God is at hand." And every "peaceable man" receives now this gift of grace from the Lord Most High, this realization of His presence before us. No longer does He hide His face.

And now we wait again, for the Lord to return once more to our towns; now we long for the Day when with our "flesh [we] shall see God," when we shall gaze upon Him forever and know His everlasting peace. Now He comes to heal us; now He sends forth His Word and His workers to prepare His way... and so now we should make straight His way, for His reign is upon us.

May He never have cause to "shake the dust" of our town from His feet – may He never regret having come among us. But let us, brothers and sisters, "wait for the Lord with courage" and perseverance, with a blessed hope born in faith. Let us with Job know that our Vindicator lives and He shall not be long in coming... indeed, He is already here. "Be stouthearted, and wait for the Lord." Welcome His Spirit into your home.

520

Friday

(Job 38:1,12-21,40:3-5; Ps.139:1-3,7-10,13-14,24; Lk.10:13-16)

"I put my hand over my mouth."

When the Lord speaks, what can we be but silent? When He chastises us for our pride and sin, we can only be ashamed. No defense have we before Him who holds us and all the world in His mighty hand and who comes to us with His redeeming love. We can but bow before Him.

The Lord has "commanded the morning and shown the dawn its place"; He has "entered into the sources of the sea [and] walked about in the depths of the abyss" – He has "comprehended the breadth of the earth" and the highest heavens. And so, if we "take the wings of the dawn, if [we] settle at the farthest limits of the sea," He is there. If we "go up to the heavens" or "sink to the nether world," He is present. He is present everywhere, and everywhere we are, we are subject to His hand. For He has "formed [our] inmost being"; He has "knit" us all "in [our] mother's womb." And He alone knows "the dwelling place of light" and "the abode of darkness," and to which place our souls shall come. There is nothing we can say before the Creator and Judge of all the earth except, "I am fearfully, wonderfully made; wonderful are your works," as we humbly give thanks to Him who scrutinizes all our ways.

And when He comes to us with His love, when He has wrought forgiveness in "the miracles worked in [our] midst" by the grace of the only Son... when redemption for all our sin He offers by a merciful hand, what must we do but accept it? For how shall it be for us on "the day of judgment" if we reject the Word of God walking among us and speaking to our hearts? It cannot but "go ill" with us if we fail to reform our broken lives when the Almighty Creator of heaven and earth stands before us with love in His arms, blood pouring from them as He hangs upon a cross.

Should not our hands be over our mouths at such a sight, brothers and sisters, at such a witness of undying love? Should it not convict us of our sin and make our hearts burn with a spirit of repentance and cry silently to God as our prideful tongues cleave like stone to our palate? What hope have you if you yet dare to speak before Him? Rather, bow your heads and fall to your knees and beg the forgiveness of Him who has made you and who loves you to the heights and depths, with all the breadth of His Spirit.

Lord, like Job, I have "no more" to say; I am yours.
(Blessed silence before the Lord may we all come to know.)

Saturday

(Job 42:1-3,5-6,12-16; Ps.119:66,71,75,91,125,130,135; Lk.10:17-24)

"I watched Satan fall from the sky like lightning."

O how our readings conspire together today to bring heavenly light to our eyes. Truly by them the Lord would say to us what He says to His apostles, what is so evident with Job: "Blest are the eyes that see what you see." For what more could we hope to behold than the defeat of Satan and the power of the Almighty at work in our lives?

"I had heard of you by word of mouth, but now my eye has seen you," Job declares unto the Lord who stands before him. Could there be a greater blessing than this for him who has longed for just this moment? For just in this moment comes to him who has suffered so greatly at the hands of Satan the vindication of the Lord's servant, the justice that is in the hand of God. Truly is Satan now cast down before the Lord of all, and truly do the eyes and the heart of Job witness this power of the Most High. For truly is he set free from the evil one's clutches and blessed so abundantly. Job's eyes see the return and the increase of his myriad of animals; they witness the great blessing of seven sons and three daughters, of whom it is said, "No other women were as beautiful as the daughters of Job." These eyes behold "his children, his grandchildren, and even his great-grandchildren," yes, but the greatest of all visions for which Job is truly blessed and which brings any and all other blessings is that his eye has seen the Lord: he knows now Him who has made him and rejoices sublimely with the apostles that his name is "inscribed in heaven," indeed that it cannot be blotted out; for Satan has done all he could to accomplish this, and failed.

"It is good for me that I have been afflicted, that I may learn your statutes" – our psalmist's words could be Job's own, for indeed in the Lord's faithfulness He has afflicted Job to "teach [him] wisdom and knowledge." And what knowledge the seventy-two disciples receive this day in our gospel; a knowledge hidden from all ages, a power residing only with God, is given over unto their spirits. Satan himself and all his minions are now subject to their command. What falls short of the light in their eyes; what do they now lack? And so, what can they do but rejoice greatly? For even Jesus Himself rejoices "in the Holy Spirit"; even the Son of God gives "grateful praise" to the Father for the power and wisdom granted His "merest children." Brothers and sisters, the blessings of the Lord are overwhelming... and we do not yet even see heaven!

"The revelation of your words sheds light," O Lord, "giving understanding to the simple." Let us hear what you wish to teach us this day. That which "prophets and kings wished to see... and hear" you reveal to us at this time – that the power of your Word casts out sin and Satan, and that your own glory you share with your little ones on earth. Bless us here with your gifts, O Lord. Remove from our hearts all fear. Let us know with certainty that you have destroyed the evil one, and draw us now inextricably to your kingdom.

Twenty-Seventh Week

Monday
(Gal.1:6-12; Ps.111:1-2,5,7-10; Lk.10:25-37)

"Teacher, what must I do to inherit everlasting life?"

Do you really want to know? Do you really seek to hear of the Gospel of Christ? Do you really desire the Word of God, which is "reliable forever and ever, wrought in truth and equity" and which "came by revelation from Jesus Christ?" If so, listen to what He speaks to you today; do not go on "so soon deserting Him who called you in accord with His design in Christ" – be not as the priest and the Levite who, coming upon the man "stripped" and "beat[en]," "saw him but continued on." For He shows Himself to you this day. He lies before you like "the man who fell in with the robbers," and He calls you to love.

You know what to do, brothers and sisters, just as the lawyer knew so well the Shema, the great command to love God and neighbor. The answer to the question of "who treated the man with compassion" is obvious. We see the love of God, we know the love of God, and we know that we are called to practice the love of God. "Then go and do the same," Jesus says. "Go and do the same." Here is the Gospel in short, in this short phrase: love others as I have loved you. Lay down your life; die to yourself and live for God and others if you wish to inherit eternal life. Such inheritance comes only after such death, and love is all that will bring you there.

"If anyone preaches a gospel other than the one you received, let a curse be upon Him!" This exclamation by Paul is also one of love. For to love does not mean "to win man's approval," "to please" or "ingratiate" oneself to others that all might speak well of us who have spoken well of them – to love means to speak the truth, for only by such truth is love preserved. There is no Gospel but the Gospel of love spoken by the mouth of the Lord, one which calls us not to an easy compliance with the world, a nod of the head and a sidestep around the wounded bodies before us... it is that which calls us to lay down our lives along this road of ours. This is what is from God, shown most clearly by the death of His Son.

523

Brothers and sisters, "holy and awesome is His name" and His call. "His praise endures forever" in our mouths for "He has ratified His covenant forever"; and the love of Jesus is all we need to know. Can you do all the Samaritan has done for the stranger? Then everlasting life is indeed close to your heart. Follow in His way.

O. 27. Tues. (II)

Tuesday
(Gal.1:13-24; Ps.139:1-3,13-15,24; Lk.10:38-42)

"The time came when He who set me apart before I was born
and called me by His favor
chose to reveal His Son to me."

Paul speaks of his conversion to the faith today. But before he changed and became the Lord's great Apostle, he tells us, "I made progress in Jewish observance far beyond most of my contemporaries, in my excess of zeal to live out all the traditions of my ancestors," and that he "went to extremes in persecuting the church of God and tried to destroy it." Now, isn't Martha as Paul was? Is it not her own zeal for observance of Jewish tradition which makes her so anxious and blinded to truth? We hear that she "was busy with all the details of hospitality," a venerable Jewish custom and requirement of the law; but does not her own "excess of zeal" for this observance lead her even to persecute the Church of God, as it has with Paul? For is her sister not as the Lord's Church, as His holy Bride seated at His feet? And what does Martha intend to inflict upon her when she asks in her presumption, "Lord, are you not concerned that my sister has left me all alone to do the household tasks? Tell her to help me," but by such public humiliation to draw her from the blessings of Christ into her own anxiety? But as Paul has heard the call of the Lord, so now Mary does as well, and nothing shall remove such favor from her. And instead of the drawing of Mary from the Lord, it is the Lord who calls Martha from her chores to listen to the voice of God.

Martha shall heed the Lord's call, we know, for it is she who shows such great faith at the tomb of her brother Lazarus, she who hears the Lord's most wonderful revelation: "I am the resurrection and the life." And so she, like Paul, like her sister, finds herself chosen by the Lord. And so must we all, brothers and sisters! So must we all. We all must know the call of Him who "formed [our] inmost being," by whom our "soul" and our "frame" were "made in secret, when [we were] fashioned in the depths of the earth," in our "mother's womb." We must all come to that place where He will speak to these very depths of our being – where only He probes – and know the "wonderful" call of the Lord, that as it was said of Paul, "He who was

524

formerly persecuting us is now preaching the faith he tried to destroy," so it will be said of us that all doubt and fear we have left behind and the Lord's will is our only occupation. We must hear His voice and we must speak His NAME, or all we do will be in vain.

"My journeys and my rest you scrutinize, with all my ways you are familiar," O Lord. And so I pray that all my rest will be taken in you and all my work you will bless. Bring us all to the quiet place within our souls, where you speak in silence, where your will is revealed to waiting hearts... let us be seated always before you.

O. 27. Wed. (II)

Wednesday
(Gal.2:1-2,7-14; Ps.117:1-2,Mk.16:15; Lk.11:1-4)

"He who worked through Peter as His apostle among the Jews
had been at work in me for the Gentiles."

And that same Spirit, that same God, that same Lord and Creator is at work in all His holy apostles, and is the Father of all who call upon His Name.

"Father, hallowed be your name." You are great and you are glorious, and you bless all your children, your children of light. From every nation you call us by the power of your Word. Jesus, you send out apostles as you sent out Paul, to the ends of the earth. You gather all your children together at your one table to feast upon your Body and your Blood, and you speak to the heart of all creation. We your people you call to pray; your disciples you teach to call upon your Name. To the depths of our souls you breathe your Spirit, and so you make us your own. Like you we would be, O Lord! Like you, dear Jesus, in your devotion to our Father.

Help us, O Lord; teach us to forgive, teach us to love. Teach us not to draw away from others, but to join with all who heed your call. Let us always be "straightforward about the truth of the Gospel," always breathe it and speak it with all our lives – with all our strength let us love and welcome all, especially the poor. And let us present ourselves to your "recognized pillars," to the leaders of your Church. Let us not go off on our own, with our own thoughts, pursuing our own goals, but let us be ever obedient unto those in whose hands you have placed your teaching ministry... let us lay down our lives "for their scrutiny" as has even the Apostle Paul. For none can work without your approval, without the blessing that comes in "the handclasp of fellowship" your Church extends. And so, in your Church, under its guidance, and in absolute love of all, what shall we then lack?

Ordinary Time

"Praise the Lord, all you nations, glorify Him, all you peoples!" For the Lord comes to you now – He teaches you His sacred way to the Father of all. Heed but His Word; speak and do but His work. Love always Him and all His people and you shall know how wonderfully "the fidelity of the Lord endures forever"; His children you shall indeed become, and He shall work through you as He has Peter, as He has Paul... as He has His only Son. Say amen to His Spirit. Amen.

O. 27. Thurs. (II)

Thursday
(Gal.3:1-5; Lk.1:69-75; Lk.11:5-13)

"I can't get up to look after your needs."

Does Jesus ever speak these words to us? Does He ever deny our petitions, failing to bring them to His heavenly Father? Do we ever find ourselves empty-handed when we come to Him "in the middle of the night"? Does He ever tire of serving us, of saving us from our sins? Then neither should we turn our back on our brother's needs; neither should we fail to hear his cry and give him food.

Brothers and sisters, is it not "you before whose eyes Jesus Christ was displayed upon the cross?" Have you not seen for yourselves the miracle in which we have found "salvation from our enemies and from the hands of all our foes"? And so should you not "serve Him devoutly and through all [your] days be holy in His sight"? If we do this, if we wake in the night to answer the needs of those who call, if we make ourselves available always as does the Lord, then even as we rise from rest Jesus will be with us – in this very action we will know His salvation present in our hearts. For as we lay down our lives, as we die with Him in service of others, the light of His resurrection already becomes present to our eyes.

Though the burden is made light by the Lord, this way is not easy – but we should not tire of imitating Him. Does Paul tire of teaching and preaching the faith, of correcting his wayward children who seem so foolishly to stray? Just as the heavenly Father would never give His son "a snake if he asks for a fish, or hand him a scorpion if he asks for an egg," so the Apostle, too, knows the needs of his flock and works constantly to feed them with the Word of God. Though it weary him no end, yet he ever pours himself out as a libation for their sakes. He is ready for heaven, ready to die and unite with God, yet he gets up in the night, yet he remains present to his children, to provide the food that is due them. And we must be the same as this Apostle.

A great assurance the Lord gives us: "Whoever asks, receives; whoever seeks, finds; whoever knocks, is admitted." If we "have faith in what [we

526

have] heard," we shall indeed find "that God lavishes the Spirit on [us] and works wonders in [our] midst." For He is faithful and forgets not His promise to us. Yes, "He has raised a horn of saving strength for us in the house of David His servant," and our Savior is ever present to answer all our needs. But who shall carry out His Word? Who shall know the cross of Christ and its redeeming grace in their own flesh? Who shall serve Him and be thus as His children? Those who rise to look after others' needs, they shall be bone of His bone.

O. 27. Fri. (II)

Friday
(Gal.3:7-14; Ps.111:1-6; Lk.11:15-26)

"All who believe are blessed along with Abraham,
the man of faith."

But those who do not believe cannot be called "sons of Abraham," in whom "all nations shall be blessed," for they have not the faith of the father of many nations. For those who do not proclaim the Lord's "renown for His wondrous deeds," but rather say of His "gracious and merciful" acts: "It is by Beelzebul, the prince of demons, that He casts out devils," there is only a curse. They curse themselves and scatter their own salvation to the winds by the evil thoughts of their hearts. "The reign of God is upon" them, and they say it has come from hell. Have such as these faith? Have they even eyes in their head? Then how shall they be saved? How shall they be called Abraham's children? Rather, the devils will return to them "to find [their] house swept and tidied," prepared by the emptiness of their hypocrisy for these to take up eternal residence there.

"He has given food to those who fear Him... He has made known to His people the power of His works." All those of faith see that this is the Messiah and "give thanks to the Lord with all [their] heart in the company and assembly of the just." All these are blessed. They live in a house guarded by "a strong man fully armed," and their "possessions go undisturbed." For the devil cannot break into the house of God, and he has no key to enter; but the Lord breaks down the doors of the evil one and all his weapons are removed from his hands. And so we are free... We are free because the Lord has redeemed us, and in His house we are protected from sin.

Brothers and sisters, the Savior has been "hanged on a tree... that through Christ Jesus the blessing bestowed on Abraham might descend on the Gentiles in Christ Jesus, thereby making it possible for us to receive the promised Spirit through faith." This faith itself is redemptive. In this faith is the blood of Christ. It is this blood which fills our hearts and makes room

527

Ordinary Time

there for the Holy Spirit to come in. There no devils can enter, for our doorposts have been anointed by Him. And so, what can such souls dwelling in this house of faith do but sing out with our psalmist, "Great are the works of the Lord, exquisite in all their delights"? What can we do but declare His "majesty and glory" as we see that "His justice endures forever" and His justice is founded in love? For by our faith He has made us whole; we who once grumbled against Him are now sons of Abraham. He has taken all our sin away, and it shall not return again.

O. 27. Sat. (II)

Saturday
(Gal.3:22-29; Ps.105:2-8; Lk.11:27-28)

"Each of you is a son of God
because of your faith in Christ Jesus."

Praise God! "Glory in His holy name; rejoice, O hearts that seek the Lord!" For He has come among us. Born of the womb of Israel, the Messiah is in our midst. And so we should "sing to Him, sing His praise, proclaim all His wondrous deeds." For now by faith in Him we live, and are truly blest.

Brothers and sisters, "before faith came we were under the restraint of the law... the law was our monitor until Christ came to bring about our justification through faith." Under the law we lived in sin, for who could fulfill all the demands of the law? "But now that faith is here, we are no longer in the monitor's charge." We have found One who has fulfilled the demands of the law, and who is perfect in the eyes of God; and He makes us as Himself, as sons of the living God! And so what can we do but rejoice? We "who have been baptized into Christ Jesus have clothed [our]selves with Him." And so we stand naked to the world no more. And so we hide no longer from the sight of God, for our sin before Him has been taken away, and with it the law.

Listen attentively to the preaching of Paul, that "there does not exist among [us] Jew or Greek," that it is faith in the Lord that saves us all. It is the same lesson Jesus teaches in our gospel today. For "the womb that bore you" refers to Israel; it is the breasts of the Chosen that have given Him suck, that have nourished Him well – it is of them He comes. But not for this is the people blest; we cannot boast of our heritage. Rather, we shall be judged worthy of blessing only by how well we "hear the word of God and keep it," as our Blessed Mother has done in preeminent fashion. She, as Paul, does not boast in her Jewish upbringing. She knows that it is not even for her great work of bearing the Son of God that she found favor with Him. Rather, all favor, the highest favor and grace, comes to her for the love she

528

bears Him and the service she performs eternally in His Name... for her absolute faith.

We must "seek to serve Him constantly" as does our Blessed Mother, as does our Mother, the Church, in faith. Then truly we shall be "descendants of Abraham, His servants, sons of Jacob, His chosen ones!" And we shall rejoice to see His Day.

Twenty-Eighth Week

Monday
(Gal.4:22-24,26-27,31-5:1; Ps.113:1-7; Lk.11:29-32)

"At the judgment, the citizens of Nineveh
will rise along with the present generation,
and they will condemn it."

Paul's words to the Galatians today sound much like a parable: "Abraham had two sons, one by the slave girl, the other by his freeborn wife." He himself states pointedly, "All this is clearly an allegory: the two women stand for the two covenants." But though Hagar may be seen as the mother of all "children [born] to slavery" and Sarah may be compared to "the Jerusalem on high," which is free, the allegorical significance notwithstanding, both Hagar and Sarah were flesh and blood human beings who walked the face of the earth along with the father of their children, Abraham. So, though the life of anyone may be seen in an allegorical light, it does not mean the life itself is but an allegory.

And yet the scholars of our day would turn the life of Jonah into a mere allegory – as they would, it seems, with Jesus. They say that Jonah did not exist, that the book written of him is but a story, a parable. And so they say that the Lord would compare Himself to a parabolic figure: "Just as Jonah was a sign for the Ninevites, so will the Son of Man be a sign for the present age." And so they say we will be judged by fictional characters.

The Lord's words remain ever true: "This is an evil age." It is given a sign, the greatest of signs, and it denies it. It seeks further sign with a heart only to deny once more. Why? Because it has no faith. And without faith one cannot reason; without faith one can see nothing. Truth remains ever hidden from one's eyes. And so those with empty minds stumble blindly through their theorems, the products of a diseased imagination. And so those without faith seek at every turn to tear down the faith, which ever eludes their clawing grasp. But they shall be judged. What shock will be theirs when the ones they have sought so vainly to make into fictional characters stand before them to condemn them to death. Perhaps then they will see. Perhaps then there will be an end to "the yoke of slavery" they would place upon the "freeborn" children of God.

Beware the faithless soul, dear children. Remember only, "From the rising to the setting of the sun is the name of the Lord to be praised." Indeed, "high above the nations is the Lord; above the heavens is His glory," and He shall lift you "lowly from the dust" to be with Him. As He tears down those who exalt themselves and reveals their children to be so vain, He will bring your fruits to light and you will bear many. The works of all will be exposed on that Day.

O. 28. Tues. (II)

Tuesday
(Gal.5:1-6; Ps.119:41,43-45,47-48; Lk.11:37-41)

"Any of you who seek your justification in the law
have severed yourselves from Christ
and fallen from God's favor!"

Brothers and sisters, "it is in the Spirit that we eagerly await the justification we hope for, and only faith can yield it." The works prescribed under the testament of old have had their day and their time is passed. Circumcision, the central act of the law, along with the temple and its sacrifices, has been rendered useless. Physically there may yet be benefit to this practice, and so it is employed widely, but spiritually it is now without merit. All that is of the old law has been subsumed by the new, and to set our hearts on what is now dead will leave us but as empty and dead ourselves.

Now there is baptism in the name of the Lord. Now there is Jesus and His Body, the Church. Now there is the Holy Sacrifice of the Mass. With these in our midst all else pales, for these are set upon the Rock of eternal life; these are founded in the Spirit which does not pass, nor can be destroyed – and these are known only by faith. Truly, "in Christ Jesus neither circumcision nor the lack of it counts for anything; only faith, which expresses itself in love." Now that love has overcome the law, now that it has fulfilled it, why should we be concerned with the cutting of flesh? It is our hearts that must be circumcised.

What is inside is what matters. Jesus has said this repeatedly and He declares it again today to the Pharisee who is so preoccupied with physical washing, with the need to "cleanse the outside of the cup and dish." This is slavery! Indeed it is born of an attachment to the things of this earth and places our neck under its yoke. If we do not "give what [we] have as alms," if we do not open our hearts to love of the Lord and love of neighbor, all the scouring of our skin will be utterly useless – in this way we shall never touch our souls. We must have love, we must have faith, and do the outside things only as necessary.

"Let your kindness come to me, O Lord, your salvation according to your promise." Though I am no longer under the law of old, yet I see how weak I am, how reliant on my works, and how ignorant and blind to your presence I can become. And so I pray that you "take not the word of truth from my mouth." I pray you enter my house and recline at my table, and that my heart will be set on love of you above all... and that all things else will but serve this love. Let me not fall from your favor, from your love.

Wednesday
(Gal.5:18-25; Ps.1:1-4,6,Jn.8:12; Lk.11:42-46)

"Since we live by the spirit,
let us follow the spirit's lead."

"Happy the man who follows not the counsel of the wicked nor walks in the way of sinners, nor sits in the company of the insolent"; these indeed follow not the spirit's lead but the dictates of the flesh. And all their "licentiousness" and "drunkenness," all their "hostilities" and "envy," shall but lead to their doom. For "those who do such things will not inherit the kingdom of God!" When they die – as already they are dead – the grave alone shall be their home, with the tortures that are found there. But "those who belong to Christ Jesus have crucified their flesh with its passions and desires" and so know the "fruit of the spirit" and not the flesh. "Love, joy, peace" and all the precious gifts are theirs in this life, and shall remain with them forever. The Spirit leads us to such blessing.

As for the Pharisees in our gospel today, they prove themselves children of the flesh and not the spirit, for though they "pay tithes on mint and rue and all the garden plants," though they are so careful about the details of the letter of the law, their worship is in vain for they do all "while neglecting justice and the love of God," thus tearing out the very heart of the law of God they presume to follow. And so their path is the one which leads but to the grave. They clearly are even now dead, "like hidden tombs over which men walk unawares." Here are "the insolent" the just must avoid. Here are those who build pretense of holiness but have nothing of the spirit inside. And so their decaying souls shall crumble from within, and "like chaff which the wind drives away," so shall their remains be scattered like dust by the truth of the Spirit, which exposes and destroys all lies.

"The way of the wicked vanishes," brothers and sisters. It cannot stand, for there is no foundation, there is no truth on which it rests. It is but empty, illusory, passing. But we who claim to be sons and daughters of the living

Ordinary Time

God, redeemed by the blood of Jesus Christ and following the lead of the
Holy Spirit, must have nothing to do with the fruits of this way. Our
worship must be true, must be genuine, must be that in which the flesh is
crucified and the spirit allowed to breathe, that none of us will be crushed
under the burden of sin but all be set free to walk in liberty now and forever.

Thursday

(Eph.1:1-10; Ps.98:1-6; Lk.11:47-54)

"It is in Christ and through His blood
that we have been redeemed and our sins forgiven."

Oh, brothers and sisters, "so immeasurably generous is God's favor to
us." He "has bestowed on us in Christ every spiritual blessing in the
heavens!" In Christ we are chosen "to be holy and blameless in His sight, to
be full of love... to be His adopted sons." In our midst the Lord fulfills the
plan "to be carried out in the fullness of time: namely, to bring all things in
the heavens and on earth into one under Christ's headship." And He does all
this by the shedding of His blood.

"God has said, 'I will send them prophets and apostles, and some of
these they will persecute and kill.'" "From the blood of Abel to the blood of
Zechariah, who met his death between the altar and the sanctuary," to the
blood of Christ, who died within the sanctuary – who is the sanctuary and
whose blood is poured out upon every altar until this day – the sacrificial
blood of the martyrs has been poured forth. And all the blood shed until His
time, and all the blood shed by His faithful until His Day... all is the blood
of the Christ who redeems us all who shed that blood by our sins. And we
should but desire to add our own blood to fill up what is yet lacking in the
sacrifice of the Lord, that all the chosen may enter His kingdom.

Brothers and sisters, no longer is "the key of knowledge" kept from us;
we now have access to enter into His reign. For "God has given us the
wisdom to understand fully the mystery" of the plan of His salvation. And it
speaks to us in Christ's blood. And in His blood we should rejoice; we
should "praise the divine favor He has bestowed on us in His beloved." For
"the Lord has made His salvation known: in the sight of the nations He has
revealed His justice." And His justice is this: that though the devil accuse us
rightly of our sins, though the blood of the prophets be on our hands, though
none is worthy of the kingdom and all should be justly thrown into hell – yet
"all the ends of the earth have seen the salvation by our God," yet there is
One who has died in our place to wash us clean from our sins, to measure
off the justice due us... yet the devil's hope for our condemnation is
thwarted by the One who loves us immeasurably. And so we can enter in

and "with trumpets and the sound of the horn sing joyfully before the King, the Lord." And so we may know fully the blessings of Christ's blood.

Friday
(Eph.1:11-14; Ps.33:1-2,4-5,12-13; Lk.12:1-7)

"What you have whispered in locked rooms
will be proclaimed from the housetops."

What we have whispered and what has been whispered to us, the teaching of the Lord, the truth of the Spirit, is destined to grow unto praise of God – to be proclaimed to the ends of the earth. What begins here in a small way in Jesus the Messiah, shall proceed in His disciples to all nations. In the dark, first it is but whispered. It sinks deep into the locked rooms of our guarded hearts. There the truth finds a home, takes root, and grows. And all the world shall know... All the world shall know all that is spoken in your heart.

Brothers and sisters, "when you heard the glad tidings of salvation, the word of truth, and believed in it, you were sealed with the Holy Spirit who had been promised." In Him and in His truth whispering in your heart you found "the pledge of our inheritance, the first payment against the full redemption of a people God has made His own to praise His glory." Though a tiny spark at first, concealed in the dark, this flame has burned intensely, and now becomes the fire of praise unto God. "We were predestined to praise His glory"; this was the Lord's desire from the first moment He touched us with His Word. And now His plan must be fulfilled.

As Jesus looks about in our gospel and sees "a crowd of thousands had gathered, so dense that they were treading on one another," He realizes how the flame has already begun to grow. And so He warns His disciples to be true to the Word He has labored to plant in their minds and hearts and souls. He knows that they will be tempted by "the yeast of the Pharisees, which is hypocrisy," that they may be inclined to speak what will tickle the public's ear in order to gain their approval and support. Thus does He say, "Do not be afraid": do not be afraid of what the truth may bring or that you might be killed for speaking it. Remain true to what I have whispered to you in our locked rooms, for the Word must go out to the ends of the earth. Their mission upon them, He calls His friends to fulfill it.

And so let all our voices resound with the praise of God who has saved us, for "praise from the upright is fitting." "Exult, you just, in the Lord... for upright is the word of the Lord, and all His works are trustworthy." Now all must know that "of the kindness of the Lord the earth is full," so fail not to "chant His praises," to proclaim His truth to all the world. It is here we are called to do so.

Saturday
(Eph.1:15-23; Ps.8:2-7; Lk.12:8-12)

"Whoever acknowledges me before men –
the Son of Man will acknowledge him before the angels of God."

We are only very small, less than a speck of dust in the eyes of God. Beholding His heavens, "the moon and the stars which [He] set in place," should we not cry out to God with David in our psalm: "What is man that you should be mindful of him, or the son of man that you should care for him?" Truly we are but miserable creatures. And yet the Lord of all has deigned to make man "little less than the angels, and crowned him with glory and honor"; and yet through Jesus Christ He raises him up to His heavens.

How like the acknowledgment the Lord promises is Paul's acknowledgment of the Ephesians: "I have never stopped thanking God for you and recommending you in my prayers." For their "faith in the Lord Jesus and [their] love for all the members of the Church," rightly do they gain honor from the Lord's Apostle, and from the Lord Himself. And all who are like them shall know "the wealth of glorious heritage to be distributed among the members of the Church." "Like the strength [God] showed in raising Christ from the dead and seating Him at His right hand in heaven," so will be the strength and grace Jesus shows in raising us up to be one with Him and His Father among the angels of heaven.

"He has put all things under Christ's feet and made Him head of the Church, which is His body." And all who acknowledge His greatness, all who serve the Lord and His members, become part of "the fullness of Him who fills the universe in all its parts." Indeed they will be lifted up with Him who is "high above every principality, power, virtue, and domination, and every name that can be given in this age or in the age to come." For the body shares in the blessing of its head; the oil poured upon our Lord flows down upon all His members through the power of the Holy Spirit.

And, yes, the Spirit is with us, brothers and sisters, defending us always and teaching us at every moment just what we need to do and say, if we have but faith. He gives us all the "wisdom and insight" we need to know the greatness of our call in Him and to accomplish all His works, if we but call upon the Lord's Name. Acknowledge Him always in all you do; be among the "babes and sucklings" who praise His majesty and glory, and His blessing you shall know to the depths of your soul, and the heights of heaven.

Twenty-Ninth Week

Monday
(Eph.2:1-10; Ps.100:2-5; Lk.12:13-21)

"It is owing to His favor that salvation is yours through faith.
This is not your own doing, it is God's gift."

Brothers and sisters, salvation is no "reward for anything [we] have accomplished." It is nothing we make by our own hands, but comes only by God's "kindness to us in Christ Jesus."

"God is rich in mercy." Here is the great truth; this is our great hope: "Because of His great love for us He brought us to life with Christ when we were dead in sin." By our own hands we had but built up our condemnation and so "deserved God's wrath." Like the foolish rich man, we thought we could take our refuge in the things of this earth, that in them we would "have blessings in reserve for years to come." But however much we "pull down [our] grain bins and build larger ones," filling them with all the "grain" and "goods" of the world, yet we will have nothing; yet will we be empty and in need. For our life is in His hands alone. "He made us" and not we ourselves; "we are truly His handiwork," and so, dependent on Him for all things. And if not for His mercy we would still be dead in our sin.

Brothers and sisters, we must not "live at the level of the flesh"; we cannot give our "allegiance to the present age and the prince of the air" and remain in the favor of God. "Following every whim and fancy of our own" will but lead us down a dark road, and all the "piled-up wealth" we can amass will give us no light for the night ahead. Truly we must realize that we are "created in Christ Jesus to lead the life of good deeds which God prepared for us in advance." Now that by His mercy He has saved us, has lifted us from the mire into which we'd sunk, it is ours to "serve the Lord with gladness" and "come before Him with joyful song."

"In Christ Jesus [God] raised us up and gave us a place in the heavens, that in the ages to come He might display the great wealth of His favor." And should we not but accept this gift from Him "whose kindness endures forever"? Should we not humble ourselves before our Holy Lord and "enter His gates with thanksgiving"? All He requires of our souls is to accept the salvation He brings us, and to grow "rich in the sight of God."

Tuesday
(Eph.2:12-22; Ps.85:9-14; Lk.12:35-38)

"You who were once far off
have been brought near through the blood of Christ."

We who "were excluded from the community of Israel," who were not of His chosen people upon whom His Spirit rested and so were "without hope and without God in the world," now are "fellow citizens of the saints and members of the household of God" by the great grace of the cross of Christ. Now, "in Him [we] are being built into this temple"; now all "have access in one Spirit to the Father."

"He came and 'announced the good news of peace to you who were far off, and to those who were near" – to us who were far off, we of the nations apart from "the covenant and the promise," that the promise might be ours as well; but also to those who were near, those to whom the covenant had been given. For those who were near were also far off; they too were blind to His presence in their midst and needed their eyes opened by the living Christ. For though the word and the sacrifice were at their hands, far was He from their hearts, and so the blessed coming of the Messiah is for these, of course, as well. He came, in fact, for them first of all.

"Near indeed is His salvation to those who fear Him." Gentile or Jew, it does not matter. Now there is but one race: Christian. Now there is but one Savior for all. For now indeed there is "glory dwelling in our land," and any who come to it become children of its light and are fitted into the House of the Lord. "He proclaims peace" now unto all, that all might know "His benefits."

And are we ready for His coming again? Do we heed our Lord's exhortation in our gospel today? Do we serve Him constantly, ever keeping a place for Him in our hearts and at our tables, that when He comes the great promise He makes to His servants – "He will put on an apron, seat them at table, and proceed to wait on them" – we will know? Will we be gathered into His heart and His home? Brothers and sisters, "become a dwelling place for God in the Spirit." Realize the blessing that is ours now through the cross. If under its blessed shade we take refuge, if we heed the call to come from our former residences so distant from Him and draw near to the love of the Lord, then already we will sense "the master's return" upon us, and holy light it will bring to our souls.

Wednesday
(Eph.3:2-12; Is.12:2-6; Lk.12:39-48)

"When much has been given a man,
much will be required of him."

Yes, "more will be asked of a man to whom more has been entrusted," and today we see two of the men to whom the most has been entrusted. First, of course, is Peter, who queries the Lord and to whom the Lord addresses His question, "Who in your opinion is that faithful, farsighted steward whom the master will set over his servants to dispense their ration of grain in season?" knowing full well it is to the blessed Rock of His Church He speaks. And Paul tells us how "through the gift God in His goodness bestowed on [him] through the exercise of His power, [he] became a minister of the Gospel." Paul has been "given the grace to preach to the Gentiles the unfathomable riches of Christ and to enlighten all men on the mysterious design which for ages was hidden in God, the Creator of all." The Rock of the Church and its great Apostle – how much has been entrusted to these two men!

And what has been entrusted to these is entrusted to all who follow in their wake, to all "the holy apostles and prophets" to whom "the mystery of Christ" is "revealed by the Spirit." And so the same responsibility is upon them as well. The Lord has promised, "With joy you will draw water at the fountain of salvation," and how can the faithful find such life-giving water if the Lord's priests and preachers do not offer it forth freely as it has been given them? If they withhold the children's food and their tongues cleave to the roofs of their mouths, how shall the Church be fed, how shall she be instructed in the way she should walk? If the guardians of the truth are not vigilant, but rather begin "to abuse the housemen and servant girls, to eat and drink and get drunk," feeding only themselves, their own bellies... what shall become of the Body of Christ? And what shall become of those who have allowed the Lord's House to be broken into?

"Sing praise to the Lord for His glorious achievement; let this be known throughout all the earth": that "God indeed is [our] Savior," and all are called unto Him. Brothers and sisters, we all share in the priesthood of Peter and the evangelical ministry of Paul, and so, "drawing near Him with confidence," we must all "among the nations make known [the Lord's] deeds." All have been given a measure of the Lord's grace and power, and all are responsible for fulfilling the "master's wishes" with regard to our call. This is our gift from God, to share in His work of service, in His cross. Let us embrace it as readily as have Peter and Paul.

537

Thursday
(Eph.3:14-21; Ps.33:1-2,4-5,11-12,18-19; Lk.12:49-53)

"Do you think I have come to establish peace on the earth?"

Strong contrast we find in our readings today. Jesus speaks of the division He has come to bring by the fire of truth He lights on this earth – fire like a sword separating even the closest of family members one from another; whereas Paul speaks of "the breadth and the length and the height and the depth of Christ's love" and the great oneness found in "the Father from whom every family in heaven and on earth takes its name." How does one reconcile this apparent contradiction? Is the Lord of peace or division?

Brothers and sisters, there is no contradiction here. Paul speaks of the "glory in the Church and in Christ Jesus" which exists "through all generations" and which we share "with all the holy ones" for whom "charity [is] the root and foundation of [their] life." As our psalmist proclaims, "Happy the nation whose God is the Lord, the people He has chosen for His own inheritance." In the House of God is peace. In His Church is the oneness of perfect love, and all its members "experience this love which surpasses all knowledge" and "attain to the fullness of God Himself."

Then whence the division the Lord emphasizes? The division exists here on earth, as He Himself states. When the light of truth comes up against the darkness that is this world, when the holy ones of God meet up with the children of this evil age, there is necessarily division. Despite the best efforts of the just to bring peace to all, how often is our offering of peace rejected – how frequently is Christ nailed to the cross. So, though we yet hold love for all as the disciples of our living Lord, it cannot but be that many will cling to darkness and so find an enemy in the light. And thus division comes. Though in heaven and in the Church there is nothing but peace, the world breeds only division.

Brothers and sisters, "may Christ dwell in your hearts through faith." "May [the Father] strengthen you inwardly through the workings of His Spirit" as you undergo the anguish of the baptism His Son has known. May He keep you in peace and "bestow on you gifts in keeping with the riches of His glory." For soon division will be gone and His peace will be all that is known.

538

Friday
(Eph.4:1-6; Ps.24:1-6; Lk.12:54-59)

"Make every effort to preserve the unity
which has the Spirit as its origin
and peace as its binding force."

Is this not what Jesus instructs the crowds in saying, "When you are going with your opponent to appear before a magistrate, try to settle with him on the way"? Do not both Paul and Jesus speak of the love we must have one for another, even for those who may seem our enemies? Again, in the House of God there is unity, there is peace. Among His children there should be understanding, there should be grace. We must make every effort to have no enemies – to hate no one, to bear no grudge against any – in this life or the next.

Brothers and sisters, we are called to live as one, "bearing with one another lovingly," for "there is but one body and one Spirit" in Christ; "there is one Lord, one faith, one baptism," which we all share, and so we should live as children of the "one God and Father of all." On our oneness in the Lord our hearts should be set, and nothing should disturb the peace we find in Him. We see so many other things, we understand so much of the world and its ways... why do we not understand this? Why do we not know and practice God's way?

"The Lord's are the earth and its fullness; the world and those who dwell in it." This David tells us: all are one under the Lord God. But only those "whose hands are sinless, whose heart is clean," "may stand in His holy place." We cannot "ascend the mountain of the Lord" if we are not made perfect as He. And so the Lord warns us of the necessity of settling all our accounts here, now, while there is time – while we yet have breath and eyes to see – lest we come to the judge at the end of time with the darkness of sin upon our soul. Now is His mercy offered forth, and we are called in turn to offer it freely to others. Then will be grave punishment for sin, for failures to love and maintain unity.

"A blessing from the Lord" awaits us all. He "that seeks the face of the God of Jacob" shall receive his reward. Even now the Spirit of the Lord grants us a foretaste of such grace. But we must be ever diligent to maintain it. We must be ever ready to forgive one another if we are to remain in Him. And so I ask: forgive me, brother; forgive me, sister, any wrong I have done you... and be assured of my forgiveness.

Saturday

(Eph.4:7-16; Ps.122:1-5; Lk.13:1-9)

"Each of us has received God's favor
in the measure in which Christ bestows it."

Paul reminds us today of Scripture: "When He ascended on high, He took a host of captives and gave gifts to men." Christ Himself "descended into the lower regions of the earth," coming to the place where we lowly humans dwell, and then "ascended into heaven, that He might fill all men with His gifts," that those to whom He comes here on earth might know the riches of heaven to which He draws us all.

"It is He who gave apostles, prophets, evangelists, pastors, and teachers in roles of service for the faithful to build up the body of Christ." Yes, He gave us these leaders such as Paul to guide us to all truth, but He no less has given us each a share of His heavenly glory and bestowed upon each of us the gifts that are our portion from Him. None is without gifts, and none can fail to employ these gifts. It is necessary that the Body of Christ has "the proper functioning of [its] members joined firmly together by each supporting ligament" if it is to grow in love as it is called to do. All our gifts must be employed to the full; each must fulfill his role.

The Lord makes clear the call upon each of our souls to utilize the gifts He grants to each of His members. Listen to the words of the vinedresser in His parable: "For three years now I have come in search of fruit on this fig tree and found none." Who is that vinedresser but Jesus Himself and who is that fig tree but we who claim to be His disciples? And finding no fruit on the fig tree, what does the vinedresser say? "Cut it down. Why should it clutter up the ground?" Why indeed should we drag down the Body of Christ struggling to grow in love in this world; if we are dead members, what place have we in His kingdom? And unless we reform in the short time we are given, what shall become of our souls?

Brothers and sisters, do we not wish to "go up to the house of the Lord," to rejoice in the heavenly Jerusalem, to "form that perfect man who is Christ come to full stature"? Then our tree must bear fruit in His name and serve to build up the Body in love; "if not, it shall be cut down," and we shall be separated from the glorious presence of the Lord. See the great graces and gifts the Lord showers upon you; pray for their fulfillment, for their growing more and more – "profess the truth in love" and the favors you have been given will bear their fruit, for your benefit and that of the whole world.

540

Thirtieth Week

Monday
(Eph.4:32-5:8; Ps.1:1-4,6,Eph.5:1; Lk.13:10-17)

"There was a time when you were darkness,
but now you are light in the Lord."

Brothers and sisters, remember always that "God has forgiven you in Christ." Once you "walk[ed] in the way of sinners," but now you are as he who "delights in the law of the Lord." And so as God has shown His mercy to you, so should you do unto others; we must "be imitators of God as His dear children." As when Jesus saw the woman who "was badly stooped – quite incapable of standing erect," for eighteen years afflicted by her infirmity, He had pity for her, called her to Him and "laid His hand on her" so that "immediately she stood up straight and began thanking God"... so should our hearts go out to all those in need, all those afflicted by infirmity and sin, that all might be as well as we have become, that all might praise God as we do.

"Make no mistake about this: no fornicator, no unclean or lustful person – in effect an idolater – has any inheritance in the kingdom of Christ and of God." Brothers and sisters, how many of us have been guilty of the deadly sins of which Paul speaks today? (And if not these, what others?) How many of us have deserved to be barred from the kingdom? In truth we must say that all of us have fallen short of God's glory and found ourselves in desperate need of the salvation only Christ brings. And so should we hold out no hope for those who commit such sins now, who are as we have been? Certainly "there are sins that bring God's wrath down on the disobedient" and put them in danger of dying; but do we instruct these to "have nothing to do with them," do we offer light to those in such darkness... or do we presume their condemnation?

The Lord left not the stooped woman in Satan's clutches, despite the "indignant" attitude of the leaders of the synagogue – whose own inability to stand erect is so much more difficult to cure. No, the Lord saw a soul in need and reached His hand out to her; and should we not do the same with those we see suffering affliction, if not with a healing touch of our hand at least with the healing touch of devout prayer? The well-being of others must always be our concern. We must ever "be kind to one another, compassionate, and mutually forgiving." For if our hearts stoop to jealousy and judgment as does the leader of the synagogue's, what hope shall there be for us then of entering God's kingdom? We must ever be children of

541

light, dispelling all darkness, if we are truly to be the "dear children" of our Lord.

Tuesday
(Eph.5:21-33; Ps.128:1-5; Lk.13:18-21)

"To what shall I compare the reign of God?"

Jesus Himself compares it to a mustard seed which grows so steadily into a "large shrub," and to yeast which makes "the whole mass of dough" rise. And Paul tells us of the marriage union that it "refers to Christ and the Church." These images should lead you, brother, to understand the glorious kingdom that is beyond all image.

"The husband is head of the wife just as Christ is head of His body, the Church," and husbands should "love [their] wives, as Christ loved the Church," giving themselves "up for her" as the Lord has done for us. A wonderfully beautiful call; a marvelous image which is to bring the Lord so really into our midst: love between husband and wife – the love of love upon this earth, which indeed brings the fruit of new life. "A man shall leave his father and mother, and shall cling to his wife, and the two shall become one flesh." Here is a word of truth incomparable to others in the joy it brings the ear and the heart open to its call. For by it is promised great happiness to those "who fear the Lord, who walk in His ways." Yes, the obedient man will find that his "wife shall be like a fruitful vine" and his "children like olive plants around [his] table"; great is the blessing upon those who wed in love, the true love of the Lord.

But a greater promise than this does this word bring, for in it is indeed "a great foreshadowing"; in it we see not only the fruitful love of man and woman, but of God and His people. For does not Jesus leave His Father in heaven and cling to us? Does this not bring the great knowledge that we shall be made one with Him and with His Father in heaven? If "he who loves his wife loves himself," does this not emphasize the absolute oneness of husband and wife? And if such marriage foreshadows Christ's love for us, can we not conclude that we will be as He is?

O to what glory we are called! To be as the only Son of God, to be one with Him. Indeed "we are members of His body" even now, certainly. Has Jesus not asked Saul why he was persecuting Him, referring to His Church (see Acts 9:4); and has He not said what we do unto the least of our brothers we do unto Him? We are one with Him even now, but yet we are growing, yet we are rising. And the immeasurable glory to which we come is beyond even the most poignant image to depict. It is absolute fullness, absolute

542

union with our Lord and God. Alleluia! "The prosperity of [the New] Jerusalem" is ours.

Wednesday
(Eph.6:1-9; Ps.145:10-14; Lk.13:22-30)

"Do God's will with your whole heart
as slaves of Christ."

These words Paul addresses to the slaves of his time, instructing them to "obey [their] human masters with the reverence, the awe, and the sincerity [they] owe to Christ," but they apply well to us all, who are in all things to serve the Lord. Always we should "give [our] service willingly, doing it for the Lord rather than men." This is as "the narrow door" of which our Lord speaks; this is what will bring us into His heavenly kingdom. For it is certain that "each one, whether slave or free, will be repaid by the Lord for whatever good he does."

Brothers and sisters, the Lord's "kingdom is a kingdom for all ages, and [His] dominion endures through all generations." It matters not when we live or where, or what position we have in society – none of these things pertain to the reign of God. For those who are to be saved shall indeed come from the four corners of the universe and from every period of time, and as Paul says to masters of their slaves: "You and they have a Master in heaven who plays no favorites." So if you think that any honor or preference of this earth will smooth your way into the kingdom, you are surely mistaken and risk the grave disappointment of discovering that "some are first who will be last," or finding yourself barred from His House for failing to serve the Lord with all your heart in all the things of the world. For He has come to serve and not to be served, and He "lifts up all who are falling and raises up all who are bowed down."

Jesus goes "through cities and towns teaching – all the while making His way toward Jerusalem." Even unto the cross He offers instruction to those who would follow Him. He is as the fathers Paul instructs to "bring [their children] up with the training and instruction befitting the Lord." But we must heed His words; we must honor and obey the Lord as children are expected to honor and obey their parents. For His words are wise and they carry the greatest promise: "That it may go well with you, and that you may have long life," not so much upon this earth, but in the heavenly kingdom.

Do all things in His name, brothers and sisters. Honor Him. Obey Him. Serve Him well that He might see you and "know where you come from" and thus honor you "at the feast in the kingdom of God."

543

Thursday

(Eph.6:10-20; Ps.144:1-2,9-10; Lk.13:31-35)

"Today and tomorrow I cast out devils and perform cures,
and on the third day my purpose is accomplished."

"Blessed be the Lord, my rock, who trains my hands for battle, my fingers for war," King David sings, for the Lord is the "shield... who subdues peoples under [him]"; He is the "stronghold" by whom "victory" is his.

The same image of battle is used by Paul as he encourages us, "Put on the armor of God so that you may be able to stand firm against the tactics of the devil." But "our battle ultimately is not against human forces" – in war against nations or even any individual enemy – "but against the principalities and powers, the rulers of this world of darkness, the evil spirits in the regions above." It is spiritual warfare we engage in, and in it we must "pray constantly and attentively for all in the holy company," for the attacks against us are constant and we must ever with our brothers and sisters resist the evil one and "stand [our] ground." Heed Paul's summary of the strength we must draw from the Lord for our mission: "Stand fast, with the truth as the belt around your waist, justice as your breastplate, and zeal to propagate the gospel of peace as your footgear."

Does not the Lord do just this? Does He not witness fully to the courage we must have in the battle of earthly life? For though the Pharisees come with the warning, "Leave this place! Herod is trying to kill you," Jesus "proceed[s] on course" in firm resolve. Though "Jerusalem... slay the prophets and stone those who are sent to [her]," yet the Lord's face is set like flint to enter there. In every step along the way, on every day that leads there, He conquers the devil valiantly, displaying His great power over all darkness of this world by His Word of truth; and when He comes to the cross the war will have been won – the evil one will have no weapon remaining.

"Blessed is the one who comes in the name of the Lord." Blessed is Jesus the Christ, and blessed all those who follow in His way, who fight unto death the evils that beset us here. Brothers and sisters, faith in God will deflect all "the fiery darts of the evil one." "The helmet of salvation" will protect you from all harm; and by "the sword of the Spirit, the word of God," you shall conquer mightily with the Lord. "Pray in the Spirit." Pray always. Pray for the Church militant that she proclaim the Gospel and come quickly to the Lord's salvation.

Friday
(Phil.1:1-11; Ps.111:1-6; Lk.14:1-6)

"My prayer is that your love may more and more abound."

Paul's prayer is addressed to the Philippians, who "have all continually helped promote the Gospel from the very first day" he came into their midst preaching. He overflows with love for them himself and finds them present "to a man" sharing in his "gracious lot," even as he "lie[s] in prison" far from their land. And so he prays that always "with a clear conscience and blameless conduct [they] may learn to value the things that really matter," and is confident that "He who has begun the good work in [them] will carry it through to completion, right up to the day of Christ Jesus."

And Jesus' prayer for the Pharisees is really the same. Though they treat Him as Paul has so often been treated, though He is "summoned to defend the solid grounds on which the Gospel rests" before eyes that observe "Him closely" for any misstep upon which they could capitalize – yet His desire for them is the love of God; yet He would teach them of the ways of the Lord Most High, who cares at every moment for the well-being of even His smallest creatures. Thus does He ask them, "If one of you has a son or an ox and he falls into a pit, will he not immediately rescue him on the sabbath day?" to open their eyes to the innate concern they have for those in their care, that they might see the love of God for all. And though they are not like the Philippians, though they do not accept His word with joy and put it into practice immediately, there may come a time when they will listen, when at least some of them will hear and follow His teaching.

"Majesty and glory are His work, and His justice endures forever." This is what every heart must proclaim of the "wondrous deeds" of God. It is not only Paul's wish but the wish of the Lord Himself that all of us "may be found rich in the harvest of justice which Jesus Christ has ripened," which He has brought to maturity in His blood, in His love. "He has given food to those who fear Him"; this food of love is for all who reverence God to share. More and more it should abound in our midst, even as it does in all our churches and on all our altars this day. Alleluia!

Saturday
(Phil.1:18-26; Ps.42:2-3,5; Lk.14:1,7-11)

"When you are invited by someone to a wedding party,
do not sit in the place of honor
in case some greater dignitary has been invited."

At the feast of the marriage of Christ to mankind, we are the lesser party, and must act humbly before our God.

Jesus comes among us as a guest to eat a meal in our house; He humbles Himself to sit at our table. And this guest who sits in the lowest place among us is in fact the Host of the banquet of which all are invited to partake. Though the Lamb that is slaughtered for all to eat, He the sacrifice rules at the altar of our worship.

Listen carefully to what Paul says to his beloved Philippians; see how his own attitude mirrors that of the humble Christ, and how it must be imitated by us all. He says quite openly, "I long to be freed from this life and to be with Christ, for that is the far better thing." In the choice of living or dying, he would opt for the latter, "for, to [him], 'life' means Christ; hence dying is so much gain." As the psalmist sings in comparing his soul to "the hind [that] longs for the running waters": "When shall I go and behold the face of God?" When shall he know full union with the Lord? Only in death, the dawn of perfect day. But though "strongly attracted" to death, Paul has equal attraction to life, and accepts that he must "go on living in the flesh" for the "productive toil" it means; and so he will "persevere with [his disciples], for [their] joy and [their] progress in the faith." He will remain "with the throng" that he might lead them "in procession to the house of God... amid loud cries of joy and thanksgiving," though he himself is already prepared to enter the festival gates.

Do you not see how this attitude is as Christ's own? Would not the Lord Jesus have preferred to remain in the heavenly kingdom with the Father? Would this not have been better for Him by far? And yet He comes among us, and yet He remains with us. And yet He takes on flesh which is as the cross itself and bears it with all patience for our benefit. He gains nothing by sitting with us at table as a dishonored guest, but we gain life eternal as we eat the Bread He feeds us.

And so, listen to the Lord's teaching. Pray that "when your Host approaches you He will say, 'My friend, come up higher.'" Let His sweet words of humility and sacrifice be in your ears and in your heart – and upon your lips, lived through your body – that with Paul you will "have full confidence that now as always Christ will be exalted through" your own humility; then you will find the same "conviction that this will turn out to [your] salvation." If here you sacrifice your life, at the wedding party of our Lord and our souls you will be given your due place of honor at table in the kingdom.

546

Thirty-First Week

Monday
(Phil.2:1-4; Ps.131:1-3; Lk.14:12-14)

"Let all parties think humbly of others as superior to themselves,
each of you looking to others' interests rather than his own."

The key to Christianity is to see others, even the blind and the lame and the crippled beggar, as superior to ourselves, and place ourselves at their service in love. As Christians we can never look down upon another individual; if our heart is proud and our "eyes haughty," we are certainly set up for a fall, for the Lord who sees all and humbles Himself before all will certainly humble our proud souls. Rather, we must maintain the "fellowship in spirit, compassion, and pity" of which Paul speaks, "possessing the one love, united in spirit and ideals" and thus always giving one another the "encouragement" we owe in Christ.

Jesus would teach this humility and unity of spirit to the chief of the Pharisees today. He would have him adopt a truly Christian attitude, expecting nothing in return for his feeding of the sheep, concerned only for the welfare of the poorest in his midst. Thus He would convert him to the faith by wiping the mocking smile from his face in a spirit of genuine compassion. He tells him, "Whenever you give a lunch or dinner, do not invite your friends or brothers or relatives or wealthy neighbors." He should not be concerned simply with those of his blood and the people of means, for certainly these would "invite [him] in return and thus repay" him. No, quite a novel idea has the Son of God for the head of the Jewish Church: expect your recompense at "the resurrection of the just," not on earth. Set your heart on things that are above, not below. And go beyond your blood to invite all into the hall of the Lord, especially those most in need, those most outcast. Such a call must have been shocking to the sensibilities of this Pharisee, as indeed it remains shocking to most even today. But He only calls us to do as He has done – empty ourselves completely for the good of others.

"Make my joy complete by your unanimity," Paul begs the Philippians; and unanimity in the Lord encompasses all. In it there can be no "rivalry or conceit" because in it there are no factions: all are one in the Lord. To this unity, found only in humility, the only Son does call us all, for He knows it is there we shall find our peace; in such humble service we find our eternal rest upon the lap of our Father.

Tuesday
(Phil.2:5-11; Ps.22:26-32; Lk.14:15-24)

"The lowly shall eat their fill."

Yes, "happy is he who eats bread in the kingdom of God." Indeed, he shall have his fill. But who shall partake of such grace? Who shall come to the feast when the Master calls?

Brothers and sisters, our "attitude must be as Christ's: though He was in the form of God, He did not deem equality with God something to be grasped at." Rather, He made Himself lowly, as we are lowly. And now He is exalted; now He prepares the banquet of salvation for all lowly souls.

Who are the lowly souls? The lowly souls are they who bow down before the Lord. "At Jesus' name every knee must bend in the heavens, on the earth, and under the earth." If one does not bend the knee before our Savior, he is not humble, he is not lowly – rather, he stands in his vain pride.

And these proud souls shall not come to the table in the kingdom. If when He calls they turn away unto their own affairs, spurning the only appointment which carries importance, they lose their place in the Banquet Hall. And listen to the command of the "master of the house" to his servant: "Go out quickly into the streets and alleys of the town and bring in the poor and the crippled, the blind and the lame." The Jews having rejected the invitation which was most especially theirs, we the outcast Gentiles now hear the call of the apostles of the Lord, a call that goes out to the ends of the world. All the poor souls are now invited.

Brothers and sisters, "all the ends of the earth shall remember and turn to the Lord; all the families of nations shall bow down before Him. For dominion is the Lord's, and He rules the nations. To Him alone shall bow down all who sleep in the earth," all in the heavens, and all on earth. None shall be deprived of hearing the call to the feast the Son prepares; all shall stand before Him and have opportunity to bend the knee, to realize our lowliness before Him whom every tongue does praise. So "let the coming generation be told of the Lord that they might proclaim to a people yet to be born the justice He has shown," that all forever might bow their hearts before His majesty and proclaim: "JESUS CHRIST IS LORD!" In such humble praise they shall eat their fill of the blessings of the kingdom.

Wednesday
(Phil.2:12-18; Ps.27:1,4,13-14; Lk.14:25-33)

"Work with anxious concern to achieve your salvation."

Strive we must always to attain the kingdom of God, setting our hearts on salvation alone, and trusting in the Lord all the while.

"If one of you decides to build a tower, will he not first sit down and calculate the outlay?" And do you think the outlay for being a follower of Christ is any less important to consider? For what is required of the soul on the path to the kingdom is nothing less than all he owns, and the work involved is the laying down of his very life. And so we must be prepared; and so we must act with conviction, to dispel any "fear of laying the foundation and then not being able to complete the work."

It certainly cannot be said of St. Paul, "That man began to build what he could not finish," for he states with absolute conviction to his beloved Philippians, "Even if my life is to be poured out as a libation over the sacrificial service of your faith, I am glad of it and rejoice with all of you." He is prepared to die to accomplish the work the Lord has set for him, and he shall. But he witnesses the fruit of his efforts: "As I look to the day of Christ, you give me cause to boast that I did not run the race in vain or work to no purpose." In his disciples he sees the faith he has planted grow. And now throughout all the earth do his words go forth, bearing the fruit of Christ among all who listen.

And so, brothers and sisters, set your hearts on accomplishing the work the Lord places before you. Let no doubt or fear cause you to stumble on the way. Proclaim with David, "The Lord is my light and my salvation, whom shall I fear?" Have this same confidence and commitment to His grace. For "it is God who, in His good will toward you, begets in you any measure of desire or achievement." It is His work you do and so He will surely bless it. Know that your King is able to do battle with any enemy, that none holds any sway over Him, and be as He is, giving yourselves entirely to His mission, His cause. And you shall "gaze on the loveliness of the Lord and contemplate His temple"; and you shall certainly achieve your salvation. Onward, soldiers of the Lord.

O. 31. Thurs. (II)

Thursday
(Phil.3:3-8; Ps.105:2-7; Lk.15:1-10)

"I have come to rate all as loss
in the light of the surpassing knowledge of my Lord Jesus Christ."

Paul tells us, "Those things I used to consider gain I have now reappraised as loss in the light of Christ." The "legal observance" he grasped so tightly – having been "circumcised on the eighth day," "a Hebrew of Hebrew origins," himself a Pharisee – he now looses to the wind, desiring only to be among those "who worship in the Spirit of God and

549

glory in Christ Jesus," and "seek[ing] to serve Him constantly." What matters but Jesus and His love, and "the judgments He has uttered"?

But this justice those who remain as Paul was cannot begin to consider, for they say to themselves as Paul once said of himself: "I [am] above reproach when it [comes] to justice based on the law"... yet do they hold tightly to their fine legal observances, looking down upon those who are below their reproach and judging them all as loss, as wayward sheep destined for the fires of Gehenna. And this Man eats with them! But what is loss in their eyes becomes great gain in the eyes of God, for there is "more joy in heaven over one repentant sinner than over ninety-nine righteous people who have no need to repent"; and the angels sing in praise as they see the Son of Man sitting and ministering to these sinners, drawing them, as He has been sent to do, into the kingdom's gates.

The Lord "light[s] a lamp and sweep[s] the house in a diligent search" for straying souls. When He succeeds, He calls us all, saying, "Rejoice with me because I have found my lost sheep." And will we be jealous of the Lord's discovery, as the Pharisees and scribes, or will we realize that we all have need of repentance, that we are all that lost sheep, that lost coin which the Lord treasures so once He holds it in His hand again?

Brothers and sisters, it is in the Lord's hands we must always place ourselves; this is to be in the light of the surpassing knowledge of Christ. By our own hands, in our own wills – "putting our trust in the flesh" – what do we make but corruption, even as our first parents who desired so to hold the apple in their hands and eat it at their pleasure? In things themselves, and our willful manipulation of them, we find only a knowledge that brings death, that leads to darkness. And who will lead us out of such darkness? Jesus, who is Light. In trust in Him we realize we do not know the good we do, for all of any worth is of *His* making. And so all our desire is for knowledge of "the wondrous deeds that He has wrought" and forgetfulness of our sinful selves. Rejoice in the Lord's salvation!

O. 31. Fri. (II)

Friday
(Phil.3:17-4:1; Ps.122:1-5; Lk.16:1-8)

"We have our citizenship in heaven."

Brothers and sisters, we are not among "those who are set upon the things of this world." Always we must remember this. Though surrounded by worldly things, our hearts are not set upon them; rather, "we eagerly await the coming of our savior, the Lord Jesus Christ." Our hearts are set upon heaven.

Then what are we to do with "this lowly body of ours" as we long for the Lord to "remake it according to the pattern of His glorified body"? What purpose have we of heaven here upon this earth? Is there nothing for us to do with this old form that has been afforded us? Is emptiness all we are to know here?

We must know and remember, brothers and sisters, that in this dark world we are called to light; we are called to "go up to the house of the Lord" even here where we stand. Is the Church not with us? And has not the Lord left His sacraments with her, that even now we may be transformed into the new creation He makes us? We do not wait in vain for our Savior to come; we do not sit empty here as we long for His Day. He is here now with a measure of His grace; "His power to subject everything to Himself" is already evident in our midst... and we must join with that power and work diligently to transform not only ourselves into the image of Christ, but the dark world we see around us as well.

"Be imitators of me," Paul encourages his brother Philippians. In warning them against those who "go about in a way which shows them to be enemies of the cross of Christ," he exhorts them to be the cross's friend – to prove their mettle as they continue "to stand firm in the Lord." There are those for whom "their god is their belly, and their glory is in their shame," and the "devious employee" of whom Jesus speaks may well be among these. But though we are called in no way to imitate his wickedness, yet we must see that he is given "credit for being enterprising" by the owner, despite the fact that he had been "dissipating his property." "Why?" indeed. And how can the Lord use an example such as this to teach us of the kingdom?

Here the Lord employs great wisdom, and calls us to do the same. For He reveals to us how even in one destined to condemnation there is yet the spark of intelligence. ("I have it!" he declares, after taking consideration.) And should not this light of intelligence, which comes only from our Maker, be in us who are to be found entirely of light? And should we not bring the light of salvation through the gifts the Lord provides us even to those like this employee who are most in darkness? Should the devil control the things around us, the things here at our King's feet, or should we? Our citizenship in heaven requires us to employ its light here on this earth. There is much we owe our Master. Wise as serpents and harmless as doves let us be.

Saturday

(Phil.4:10-19; Ps.112:1-2,5-6,8-9; Lk.16:9-15)

"Well for the man who is gracious and lends."

"Lavishly he gives to the poor; his generosity shall endure forever; his horn shall be exalted in glory." Such is the man who knows the proper use of this world's goods, that is, to give them all as "a fragrant offering, a sacrifice acceptable and pleasing to God." This shows that he "fears the Lord," that his heart is not set on the things of earth but the riches of heaven; and so to these shall he come.

"Make friends for yourselves through your use of this world's goods," Jesus instructs His disciples, "so that when they fail" – when the goods of this world have faded into eternity – "a lasting reception will be yours" in the kingdom which does not pass away. Our life on this earth serves indeed as a kind of test. The Lord needs to see if He "can trust [us] in little things," in the passing things of this passing day; then He will know that He "can also trust [us] in greater," in the eternal graces of our heavenly homeland. How well shall we prove ourselves?

The Philippians prove their generosity well. The Apostle Paul commends them for their repeated gifts to supply his needs as he preaches the Gospel. Here we see a perfect example of wise use of this world's goods, of their being given in service of God and man. And because of their generosity, there is "an ever-growing balance in [their] account," not of silver and gold, but of the "magnificent riches in Christ Jesus." As they empty themselves of what they have, as they give of their riches on this earth, the Lord gives them all they might desire of the true riches; as Paul says as he assures them he has been "fully paid" by the fruits they have offered: "My God in turn will supply your needs fully."

"No servant can serve two masters." We either amass wealth for our own benefit in this world – and toward our own condemnation – or we give what we have for the benefit of God and others. We love God or we love money; there are no two ways. "The Pharisees, who were avaricious men, heard all this and began to deride Him." Does your heart tend to deride the generosity to which the Lord calls you, as do these? Is there yet mockery upon your tongue and lips against the preaching of the emptiness of this world's possessions? Do you also "justify yourselves in the eyes of men"? Know indeed that "God reads your hearts" and "what man thinks important, God holds in contempt." And if you would have it go well with you in the heavenly kingdom, you must practice the abounding generosity that is the heart of that kingdom (shown in our Lord's limitless mercy upon our souls), here with what is at your hands.

Thirty-Second Week

Monday
(Ti.1:1-9; Ps.24:1-6; Lk.17:1-6)

"Who can ascend the mountain of the Lord?
Or who may stand in His holy place?"

"He whose hands are sinless, whose heart is clean, who desires not what is vain."

Of priests and holy men our readings speak, yes, but most especially of bishops, who are most entrusted with the Word of God, with the preaching of the Gospel of eternal life... and how silence in this regard leads but to condemnation.

Paul sets the standard for the "servant of God." He presents himself "as an apostle of Jesus Christ for the sake of the faith of those whom God has chosen and to promote their knowledge of the truth as our religion embodies it." Here is the bishop in sum. Here is the priest in sum. Here is the sum of any sent to teach in His name: increase the faith and knowledge of the flock. And in this service certainly a priest must be "irreproachable," and "the bishop as God's steward must be blameless." He must be "steady, just, holy, and self-controlled. [And] in his teaching he must hold fast to the authentic message, so that he will be able both to encourage men to follow sound doctrine and to refute those who contradict it."

But how many of our leaders hold to Paul's words? How many encourage the keeping of sound doctrine, and, perhaps more to the point, how many refute error? Worse yet, how many travel merrily along with the error of the day? "If your brother does wrong, correct him," Jesus says. But how many tell their flock, "You should not fornicate or commit adultery" or "You should not abort a child or contracept him" or "You should not be 'self-willed or arrogant, a drunkard, a violent or greedy man'"? And how many freely engage in sins such as these themselves? Yes, Jesus says, "If he repents, forgive him" (even "seven times a day") of the brother in your care; but how can he repent if he knows nothing of the wrong he does, and how can you instruct him if you are committing the same sins as he? And so where is true forgiveness?

"Scandals will inevitably arise, but woe to him through whom they come." It is a terrible warning the Lord gives today, particularly to those entrusted with much, for how great will be their punishment for the abuse of their call. And of course, the source of such travails in the wayward soul is simply a lack of faith. Not "the size of a mustard seed" or a speck of dust is the faith of too many. If even it could be detected with a microscope it

553

would show itself in good works. But it is not there. And so, who indeed shall climb the mountain of the Lord? How many vainly grovel at its base? And if our leaders do not climb, how shall any follow? So, who shall come to holiness?

Let us awaken to the call of our God! Let the Church serve as His presence in this world. Let us be "the race that seeks for Him," putting holiness before all else. And let the ordained among us lead us in this way.

Tuesday
(Ti.2:1-8,11-14; Ps.37:3-4,18,23,27,29,39; Lk.17:7-10)

"Live temperately, justly, and devoutly in this age."

Brothers and sisters, be "eager to do what is right" as servants of the Most High God. "Trust in the Lord and do good, that you may dwell in the land and enjoy security." For "the Lord watches over the lives of the wholehearted; their inheritance lasts forever."

Paul gives instruction to all on how to live a godly life here on this earth. He "tell[s] the older men that they must be temperate, serious-minded, and self-controlled"; the older women that they must give "good example" to the younger women, teaching them thus "to love their husbands and children, to be sensible, chaste, busy at home, kindly, submissive to their husbands"; "the young men to keep themselves completely under control"; and those who teach to "have the integrity of serious, sound words to which no one can take exception." Then "no opponent will have anything bad to say about us"; then we will have given right witness to Christ in this age.

And "when [we] have done all [we] have been commanded to do" by the Lord and His apostles, when we have fully served Him and one another in our life on this earth – when we have finished "prepar[ing] [His] supper" and "put[ting] on our apron and wait[ing]" on our brothers – what should we do but say in all humility and in all truth: "We are useless servants. We have done no more than our duty"? For this is what will assure us that we will "abide forever"; this will prove that we are as our Lord, "who sacrificed Himself for us," and so, with "the just [we] shall possess the land, and dwell in it forever."

Our God has come "to redeem us from all unrighteousness and to cleanse us for Himself as a people of His own." Let us show we are that people by ever being "sound in the faith, loving, and steadfast," doing all for the Lord and our neighbor. In this way we indicate that even upon the dust of this earth "we await our blessed hope, the appearing of the glory of the

great God and of our Savior Jesus Christ." In this way we attain to the age
to come, where we shall be seated at His table.

Wednesday
(Ti.3:1-7; Ps.23:1-6; Lk.17:11-19)

"Jesus, Master, have pity on us!"

Such is the cry of the ten lepers standing at a distance from the Lord.
And such is the cry that wells up in all our hearts when we realize we must
keep ourselves far from His company for the sin that festers like a disease in
our souls. Desiring no longer to be outcasts from His love, we call out...
and He answers.

Do you think you are something different than these lepers? Do you
think your status with God is somehow raised above these poor souls?
Beware. Heed the words of Paul: "We ourselves were once foolish,
disobedient, and far from the faith; we were the slaves of our passions and
of pleasures of various kinds." Was our soul not then in a diseased state?
And was it any work of our own that brought us healing, that brought us to
"baptism of new birth and renewal by the Holy Spirit"? No. Rather, "when
the kindness and love of God our Savior appeared, He saved us, not because
of any righteous deeds we had done, but because of His mercy." So, by
rights we should yet be in the mire of our sin; we should yet be as lepers
outside the gates of salvation. But His "Spirit He lavished on us through
Jesus Christ our Savior, that we might be justified by His grace and become
heirs, in hope, of eternal life." And do we appreciate what He has done for
us?

Indeed the Lord indicates today that most of us are ungrateful wretches
when He asks, "Were not all ten made whole? Where are the other nine?" at
the sight of the single leper returning to give praise to God. "Where are the
other nine?" Only one of ten falls "on his face at the feet of Jesus"; and to
how many of us does this lack of thanksgiving speak? And so, how many of
us remain with more than a trace of our leprosy?

"He refreshes my soul," David sings in humble appreciation of the
blessings of the Lord he finds before himself in all things. It is He who
gives "repose"; it is He who "anoints [our] head with oil"... it is He who
cleanses our soul. And if we fail to realize this grace at work within us, then
a measure of pollution remains, and still we need to cry out to our God, and
fall on our knees in praise for His answer. Ever is He our Master; ever are
we His slaves – ever do we need His mercy to live in righteousness each
day.

Thursday
(Philm.7-20; Ps.146:7-10; Lk.17:20-25)

"The reign of God is already in your midst."

Brothers and sisters, Jesus the Christ has come, He has "suffer[ed] much and be[en] rejected by the present age"... and He has risen. This is all you need to know. There is no need for "careful watching when the reign of God will come," for it is not "a matter of reporting that it is 'here' or 'there'" – it is among us today. And when it shall be fulfilled, you will never know.

"Through you the hearts of God's people have been refreshed," Paul writes to Philemon: does the kingdom of heaven not come through this man? "Refresh this heart of mine," the Apostle adds – does he not call for an increased manifestation of the kingdom? A slave has stolen from his master and run away. Paul has discovered him and now calls him, "My child whom I have begotten during my imprisonment." The slave has run to the prisoner and found freedom; does not the kingdom of God come to this place? And certainly Philemon will accept his slave back as a brother in the Lord, his arms open like the father of the prodigal son... how the Lord does work among us.

And our psalm presents a litany of the Lord's work: yes, "the Lord sets captives free," as we see in our first reading; but whenever the eyes of the blind are opened or the widow and the stranger are cared for, whenever justice is secured and the hungry are fed... the Lord is at work, His kingdom comes. This world *is* in His hands, after all, and whenever love is "freely bestowed" by any of us toiling upon this earth, the Lord shows Himself indeed in the beat of our heart and our arms open wide. It is not difficult to see.

You must remember, my brothers and sisters, that all prophecy has been fulfilled; all revelation is complete in the coming of the Son of God, in His death and in His resurrection. There is nothing left to await but the final day, a Day about which false prophets conjecture and faithless souls run anxiously about to find, only moving themselves further from its presence. "The Son of Man in His day will be like the lightning that flashes from one end of the sky to the other" – don't worry, you will not miss it; nor can you mistake it. Your purpose in the meantime is to spend yourself bringing His kingdom to this earth in the love you share with your neighbor. In such love come only from Christ, the kingdom is already here.

Friday
(2Jn.4-9; Ps.119:1-2,10-11,17-18; Lk.17:26-37)

"Anyone who remains rooted in the teaching
possesses both the Father and the Son."

While "anyone who is so 'progressive' that he does not remain rooted in the teaching of Christ does not possess God." Rather, he possesses but the emptiness of this earth.

And what is this teaching so necessary for our salvation, for knowing and possessing the Lord our God? It is indicated clearly in John's request of the Lady to whom he writes (whom we may take as the Church herself): "Let us love one another." Here is the commandant we "have heard from the beginning," which we need to find rooted in our hearts – this "commandant is the way in which [we] should walk." For "happy are they... who walk in the law of the Lord... who observe His decrees, who seek Him with all their hearts"; for they shall find Him, and they shall possess Him forever.

Love has come, brothers and sisters: Jesus Christ has "come in the flesh." And though the people in the days of Noah and in the days of Lot were particularly wicked and meriting condemnation from the Lord, they at that time did not have the Son of God come in their midst. And so if their punishment was great for turning from the way and the call of God, how much greater will be our own if we set our hearts on the possessions of this land and thereby lose Him whose love knocks upon the door of our hearts? It is now among those who deny Him as if they stand under the brightness of the noonday sun and say, "I see no light. I feel not its heat." If we refuse to open our eyes to what is so obvious, what punishment will be enough for our souls?

Learn the lesson of the two men sleeping and the two women "grinding grain together." Though they lie and sit or stand in close proximity to one another in this place, seeming no different one from the next, yet "one will be taken and the other left." While one flies up to the reaches of heaven, the other will rot like a carcass on earth. And why? Who can tell which one says within his heart, "I treasure your promise, that I might not sin against you," and which has turned his heart from the Lord? "On the day the Son of Man is revealed," so will be the thoughts of all hearts. And He who is Love alone will know who owns the love He alone imparts. He will say who has walked in His teaching.

Saturday
(3Jn.5-8; Ps.112:1-6; Lk.18:1-8)

"When the Son of Man comes,
will He find any faith on the earth?"

So beset by weakness are we on this earth, brothers and sisters. So doubtful, so fearful... so seemingly without help, alone. And so our faith does falter, and so we do fall. And we wonder, "Where is God?"

But the Son asks us today where we are. He emphasizes "the necessity of praying always and not losing heart." Why should we think that God does not listen to us? If the corrupt judge can give justice to the widow who begs him constantly for her "rights against [her] opponent," "will not God then do justice to His chosen who call out to Him day and night?" Do we make Jesus a liar by failing to believe in the Lord's "swift justice"? Is this corrupt judge more reliable than He?

And listen to what John writes to Gaius. He says to him, "You demonstrate fidelity by all that you do for the brothers." He has "testified to [his] love before the church" by caring for its members. And John now asks this beloved disciple to support those who pass through his neighborhood carrying the message of the Gospel to the nations, to "help them continue on their journey." And we can be assured that this child of God does continue to demonstrate his generosity, that "he is gracious and merciful and just" toward his brothers in their need. And if this man "dawns through the darkness, a light for the upright," shall the Lord Himself then leave us alone when we call out to Him in *our* need?

Why are we of such little faith? Why do we so easily falter in our trust of the Lord's protection, of His grace at work upon our souls and His providential hand in our lives? If weak human beings can give aid to those in distress, cannot God? Are not all "wealth and riches... in His house"; does He not hold all the world and all our souls in His loving hand? Then why should we be afraid? Why should we think He does not answer our prayer? It is not because He is not listening that we have not the good we desire – this lack is from our lack of faith.

Brothers and sisters, be encouraged by the Lord today to never give up hope, to never give up our petitions to the Lord. He does not need to be worn down, but is ready at every moment to help us. Seek but to believe in Him.

Thirty-Third Week

Monday
(Rv.1:1-4,2:1-5; Ps.1:1-4,6,Rv.2:7; Lk.18:35-43)

"Jesus of Nazareth was passing by."

"A blind man sat at the side of the road begging. Hearing a crowd go by the man asked, 'What is that?'" And he was told that "Jesus drew near," that all he could possibly ask for was upon him – and so he cried out with the greatest sincerity he could muster.

And as the end of the Church year approaches, we hear from the Lord's beloved "servant John" "the revelation God gave to Jesus Christ"; he "bears witness to the word of God and the testimony of Jesus Christ," telling us truly that "the appointed time is near," that He "who is and who was and who is to come" is passing by the way. It is time to call to Him, and know His healing touch.

To the church in Ephesus specifically, the Lord instructs His apostle to speak today, to commend the disciples there on their "patient endurance" and their lack of tolerance for "wicked men," and to call them back to their "early love... the heights from which [they] have fallen"; thus do they need to "repent," to call out themselves to the Lord for renewal of their innocent hearts and their burning love for God. You see, all have their own reason to cry to Jesus as He passes by.

What need have you to call upon the Lord's Name as He passes by here at the end of days? Do you walk at every point in "the way of the just," or are you somehow blind to His presence, or are you in some way cold in your love? Or have you any of innumerable other sins that keep you from His kingdom? Be careful. The time is indeed short, and we are indeed sinners – and Jesus is indeed still passing by to heal us. Do not be afraid to cry out to Him, to leave "the company of the insolent" and find His redeeming graces. Let the light of faith burn in your soul that you might know "the One who holds the seven stars in His right hand and walks among the seven lampstands of gold." His holy light is coming now upon the earth, and you must join yourself to it.

"Jesus, Son of David, have pity on me!"

Tuesday
(Rv.3:1-6,14-22; Ps.15:2-5,Rv.3:21; Lk.19:1-10)

"Today salvation has come to this house."

Ordinary Time

To two of His houses, two of His seven churches, does the Lord speak today, calling them both to repentance, that they might know the salvation Zacchaeus has found.

In no uncertain terms does the Lord call the churches in Sardis and Laodicea, chastising both dearly, telling the first: "I know the reputation you have of being alive, when in fact you are dead!" and the second (who think themselves "so rich and secure that [they] want for nothing"): "How wretched you are, how pitiable and poor, how blind and naked!" In Sardis there are only "a few persons who have not soiled their garments"; and the Laodiceans, who are "neither hot nor cold," are promised by the Lord, "I will spew you out of my mouth!"

All the unfaithful, all those who have lost their fervor and who pride themselves on their own works shall be spewed from the Lord's mouth, shall be cast from His presence. All He calls to "wake up," to "repent," to "buy white garments in which to be clothed, if the shame of [their] nakedness is to be covered." All He summons to rouse themselves in the sharpest and truest of words, for "whoever is dear to [Him] [He] reprove[s] and chastise[s]" – for He knows that only by the jettisoning of our sin will we find the salvation He so dearly desires for each of our lives.

Brothers and sisters, the Lord "stand[s] knocking at the door. If anyone hears [Him] calling and opens the door, [He] will enter his house." And He will sup with him, and will sit him on His own throne. Listen to the promise our Lord makes: "The victor shall go clothed in light. I will never erase his name from the book of the living, but will acknowledge him in the presence of my Father and His angels." And see how the promise is fulfilled in Zacchaeus, who in his great fervor "climbed a sycamore tree which was along Jesus' route, in order to see Him"; who in his great generosity promised "to give half of [his] belongings" to the poor – and who has had the Lord in to sup in his home and has heard the blessed words spoken over him: "Today salvation has come to this house."

And so, strive with all you have to be as "he who walks blamelessly and does justice, who thinks the truth in his heart and slanders not with his tongue." Let His chastisement bear blessed fruit in your life; turn from your sin... and you too will know the victory the Lord Himself has won for all faithful souls.

O. 33. Wed. (II)

Wednesday
(Rv.4:1-11; Ps.150:1-6,Rv.4:8; Lk.19:11-28)

"O Lord our God, you are worthy
to receive glory and honor and power."

"A man of noble birth went to a faraway country to become its king." And of this faraway country and of its king, whom "everything that has breath" should praise, John has vision today.

"Above me there was an open door to heaven"; and a "trumpetlike voice" called the great Evangelist, "Come up here and I will show you what must take place in time to come." And so, "caught up in ecstasy" he sees the "One whose appearance ha[s] a gemlike sparkle," the Lord of all, seated on His throne. And on twenty-four thrones surrounding this King he sees the elders, "clothed in white" with "crowns of gold on their heads," sharing in their Master's Kingship. And the four living creatures are at the center, singing, "without pause": "Holy, holy, holy, is the Lord God Almighty!" And ever do the elders worship Him and join in the song of praise which rises continually to the One through whom all things "came to be."

"Praise the Lord in His sanctuary... praise Him for His sovereign majesty," for He reigns justly over all and is indeed worthy of all praise. "With the blast of the trumpet... with lyre and harp... with clanging cymbals" – with every instrument that is placed in our hands, with all the talents He provides here as we wait for His return, we must join in the song of the angels and the saints in the heavenly kingdom and praise His holy Name. For He will seek "to learn what profit each [has] made" when He returns to us from His journey. He will "send for the servants to whom He [has] given" His possessions, and call them to account in His love. Will our deeds then praise "His mighty deeds"?

Glorious is the kingdom of the Lord, and blessed are they who join Him in such marvelous glory. These He puts in charge of His cities; with these He shares His crown and His throne. And everywhere He has a right to reap, for only *He* does so in love – and there is nowhere He has not sown. All are invited into His radiant presence: to all He gives gifts that will bring them there. And but for their employment does He wait, that they might learn to praise His glory.

Follow Him as He continues "with His ascent to Jerusalem," and the cross He meets in this city will lead you to the light of paradise.

O. 33. Thurs. (II)

Thursday
(Rv.5:1-10; Ps.149:1-6,9,Rv.5:10; Lk.19:41-44)

"Do not weep. The Lion of the tribe of Judah,
the Root of David, has won the right by His victory
to open the scroll with its seven seals."

"Jesus wept over" Jerusalem "because [she] failed to recognize the time of [her] visitation"; and so she will be destroyed, and so her enemies will "leave not a stone on a stone within" her walls. And John "wept bitterly because no one could be found to open or examine the scroll" "in the right hand of the One who sat on the throne." The scroll "had writing on both sides and was sealed with seven seals." How wonderful it must be! But "who is worthy to open" it?

The tears of both will be appeased, both by the One. For whom does John see appear at the throne of God but "a Lamb standing, a Lamb that had been slain" – Jesus, our Savior! who is on His way even in our gospel today to conquer death, to receive the wounds John witnesses, that by His blood He may purchase for God "men of every race and tongue, of every people and nation"… that He might take the destruction of Jerusalem upon Himself and thus redeem her from annihilation. Because of His sacrifice, He is able to read the wisdom of the ages to all waiting hearts, for that wisdom is known only in such dying, only in His redeeming love.

And so, let us join with the elders who fall "down before the Lamb." Let our prayer unite with "the prayers of God's holy people," which rise up like "aromatic spices" before the throne of the One on high. Let us sing the new hymn unto the Lamb who was slain for our sins and so saved us from all tears. "Sing to the Lord a new song of praise in the assembly of the faithful." Weep no more but "let the high praises of God be in [your] throats" and "praise His name in the festive dance."

How great is our God! How profound is the revelation of His wonders in our midst! What joy do we find in His blood! His wounds bring us victory over death, and we reign now in the New Jerusalem as priests in the service of our King, joining ourselves ever to His sacrifice, finding ever the wisdom only He brings.

O. 33. Fri. (II)

Friday
(Rv.10:8-11; Ps.119:14,24,72,103,111,131; Lk.19:45-48)

"I gasp with open mouth
in my yearning for your commands."

In our first reading, John is told to "take the open scroll from the hand of the angel" and to "eat it." In his mouth "it tasted as sweet as honey." And now he who has eaten of the blessed word of God "must prophesy," must speak the words upon the scroll, despite the sour stomach, the persecutions, it will inevitably bring.

In our gospel we hear that "the entire populace was listening to [Jesus] and hanging on His words" as He taught daily in the temple. The Lord has cleansed the temple of the impure forces at work within it, and for this and for His speaking the irresistible words of Truth He shall know the sour stomach of persecution – the cross is now quite close on the horizon as the leaders of the people seek "a way to destroy Him."

O Lord, "how sweet to my palate are your promises, sweeter than honey to my mouth!" "The law of your mouth is to me more precious than thousands of gold and silver pieces." "Your decrees are my delight," "the joy of my heart," and despite the cross I find in consuming and then having to proclaim them, I shall not cease to eat of your glorious presence. Day to day you come to me. Moment to moment you whisper in my ear. You speak to my heart your wondrous promises, instilling faith and hope in my soul, and I shall not turn back from loving you. May all "peoples, nations, languages, and kings" know of your greatness; may all embrace the inheritance you offer by the death of sin in our lives.

Open your mouth, brothers and sisters, and He will fill it. He will feed you with the food that comes without cost; the sweet Bread of Heaven shall be yours. Even at His altars and from His pulpits it is today offered forth. Eat, and it will bring life to your soul, life that lasts beyond the destruction of the world.

O. 33. Sat. (II)

Saturday
(Rv.11:4-12; Ps.144:1,2,9-10; Lk.20:27-40)

"After three and a half days,
the breath of life which comes from God
returned to them."

And these his two witnesses "went up in a cloud as their enemies looked on" "in sheer terror." For it seemed they had "conquer[ed] and kill[ed]" the Lord's prophets. Their corpses had lain "in the streets of the great city, which has the symbolic name 'Sodom' or 'Egypt,' where also their Lord was crucified." Fire had "come out of the mouths of these witnesses to devour their enemies," but now it seemed the truth had been overcome and sin and death had won the day. And so "the earth's inhabitants gloat[ed] over them and in their merriment exchange[d] gifts." But their death, as with the death of the Lord, was not to last, was only to show the absolute power of the God of life.

And fire comes from Jesus' mouth today to silence the evil conjurings of the enemies of life. His word is truth and cannot be answered, cannot be gainsaid by even the most unbelieving mind. And what He tells all today is that "the dead rise again," that death has no dominion in the kingdom of the living God. The Lord is "the God of Abraham, and the God of Isaac, and the God of Jacob," and these fathers of the faith along with the prophets and saints of any and all time "are alive for Him," for He is but Life: in His reign

563

all His children "become like angels and are no longer liable to death. Sons of the resurrection, they are sons of God." This truth cannot be denied, will not be conquered.

"Blessed be the Lord, my rock, who trains my hands for battle, my fingers for war." It is He who is "my shield, in whom I trust, who subdues peoples under me." As He was with His only Son, giving Him victory in every battle and final victory over death; as He was with His witnesses who devoured their enemies' lies and rose from the dust after three and a half days; so He is with all who put their trust in Him, enabling them to conquer all doubt and fear, all surrounding sin and death. For Jesus crucified sits now at the right hand of God, and His witnesses with Him; and all who take their refuge in His power, though they die, cannot but rise to life. Yes, they will hear "a voice from heaven say to them, 'Come up here!'" and will again have the breath of life. Alleluia!

(Note on "three and a half days": more than its obvious similarity to the three days the Lord spent "in the heart of the earth" (Mt.12:40) may be an allusion to His approximately thirty-five years spent on this earth (which is half the span of a human life – "seventy is the sum of our years" (Ps.90:10)), itself a kind of death for Him.)

Thirty-Fourth Week

Monday
(Rv.14:1-5; Ps.24:1-6; Lk.21:1-4)

"They are pure and follow the Lamb wherever He goes."

Here is answered most definitively the question David sings: "Who can ascend the mountain of the Lord? Or who may stand in His holy place?" In John's vision, the Lord Jesus, the Lamb of God "was standing on Mount Zion, and with Him were the hundred and forty-four thousand who had His name and the name of His Father written on their foreheads." Here are they who are worthy to stand with the perfect and pure One, for their "hands are sinless, [their] heart is clean": "on their lips no deceit has been found; they are indeed without flaw." And so they "receive a blessing from the Lord, a reward from God [their] savior." The greatest blessing of all is theirs – remaining in His presence forever.

And these holy ones play the thunderous song of praise "on their harps," "singing a new hymn before the throne in the presence of the four living creatures and the elders." They indeed have found their place as firstfruits of the kingdom of heaven, singing a hymn no one else could learn. And again, it is their purity, their perfection in the sight of God, that brings them to this holy place. All they have given over to the Lamb, and so He makes them like Himself.

And in our gospel we see in the simple widow indication of the spirit necessary to enter God's presence. She holds nothing back from the Lord, but gives "every penny she ha[s] to live on." Yes, brothers and sisters, every penny must be paid; all we have and all we are must be given to Him. If we are like this widow and like the holy ones who stand before the throne and give all while here on the face of the earth, we shall come quickly to heaven and find our place in His presence prepared. If not, the purgatorial flames await to take away any flaw in our soul, to remove any selfishness from our hearts – to bring us then to give up all that we yet have to Him, that with Him we might truly be. But the saints tell us these flames are not pleasant. In fact, they say they are much the same as the fires of hell, though they shall come to an end.

So let us here and now offer all we have to the Lord; let us seek to serve Him with all our lives, that we might by His grace avoid the cleansing fire and come immediately before Him. Only those in absolute purity follow Him and stand in His place.

O. 34. Tues. (II)

Tuesday
(Rv.14:14-19; Ps.96:10-13; Lk.21:5-11)

"Use your sickle and cut down the harvest,
for now is the time to reap."

Brothers and sisters, you will "hear of wars and insurrections," and "there will be great earthquakes, plagues, and famines in various places, and in the sky fearful omens and great signs." "These things are bound to happen first, but the end does not follow immediately." The end does not follow immediately from the signs, so do not set your hearts upon them – "take care not to be misled" by those whose seed has no root and so jumps up at any indication of travail. There has been travail throughout human history and the end, which is upon us every moment now, will only be fulfilled at the angels' cry. When this will be, be assured you do not know.

In John's vision, at the first angel's cry "the one sitting on the cloud wielded his sickle over all the earth and reaped the earth's harvest." At a second angel's cry another "wielded his sickle over the earth and gathered the grapes of the earth... [and] threw them into the huge winepress of God's wrath." And so the end comes. But does John see the future only, the past or the present as well... or a time that exists quite apart from our own? And even the angels did not know the time had come until they obediently acted upon the word of their God. And would you yet listen to the anxious rantings of those without eyes, those whose vision does not approach the heavenly reality?

The Lord "shall rule the world with justice and the peoples with His constancy" when "He comes to rule the earth." This you can know even now; of this you can be assured. But when "the heavens [shall] be glad and the earth rejoice... [and] the sea and what fills it resound," none can say – this word is in His mouth alone, and when the Mighty One shall pronounce it is known to His Heart alone. He has spoken once at the coming of Christ, but when He shall speak finally cannot be ascertained; it is but for us to be prepared for that Day. For He will come again, we know, and the angels' sickles shall be sharp, and separate with certainty the wheat from the chaff. The time of harvest is at hand.

(In the harvest of the wheat and the grapes of the earth at the end of the age is made perfect this Body and Blood of Christ we eat and drink from our altar today. The saints' flesh and blood become the Lord's own.)

O. 34. Wed. (II)

Wednesday
(Rv.15:1-4; Ps.98:1-3,7-9,Rv.15:13; Lk.21:12-19)

"By patient endurance you will save your lives."

Jesus tells His disciples bluntly: "People will manhandle and persecute you." Some will be "put to death" as they are "brought to give witness on account of" His name – "All will hate you because of me." Yet in their witness He promises to provide "words and a wisdom" to serve as an impenetrable defense against their enemies... and in the end, after persevering through all suffering, eternal life shall be theirs.

John's vision in our first reading reveals the fulfillment of the Lord's promise. Even as "seven angels holding the seven final plagues" of "God's wrath" stand ready to cast these culminating tribulations upon the earth, the Evangelist sees "those who had won victory over the beast and its image" – over the illusory power of the evil one – "holding the harps used in worshiping God," and singing "the song of the Lamb" who was slain but now lives forever: "Mighty and wonderful are your works, Lord God Almighty! Righteous and true are your ways, O King of the nations!... You alone are holy."

Brothers and sisters, let us "sing to the Lord a new song, for He has done wondrous deeds; His right hand has won victory for Him, His holy arm." Yes, "the Lord has made His salvation known," and as those who stand "on the sea of glass" give praise to God with harps in hand, so does "the sea and what fills it resound," so do "the rivers clap their hands, [and] the mountains shout with them for joy." Let us join their holy song "before the Lord, for He comes, He comes to rule the earth"; His everlasting "justice" is upon us. And though we may have to suffer for a time in this world of darkness and sin, where light is shunned by the sons of men, yet even in our persecutions this eternal joy should take hold of our souls so that we know not the suffering from the rejoicing – for both are done in His name, and soon the former shall pass away.

Indeed, the song of the Lord is already upon our lips; we wait now only for its eternal resonance before His throne.

Thursday
(Rv.18:1-2,21-23,19:1-3,9; Ps.100:2-5; Lk.21:20-28)

"These indeed will be days of retribution,
when all that is written must be fulfilled."

The destruction of the world and the coming of the kingdom is our clear theme today. It is what is written. It is what must be fulfilled.

"Fallen, fallen is Babylon the great!" that "dwelling place for demons," cries out an angel by whose authority and glory "all the earth was lighted up." He calls down the destruction of the evil empire that is the city of this world. And the "assembly in heaven" sing loudly, "He has condemned the great harlot who corrupted the earth with her harlotry," exulting in the salvation and glory and might of the One God, whose "judgments are true and just!" For though "the blood of His servants... was shed by her hand," "the great city" is "hurled... into the sea" like "a huge millstone," "cast down" with such "violence" that it shall never rise again. And so, "happy are they who have been invited to the wedding feast of the Lord," who sing "Alleluia!" to the great and wonderful presence of our God in the kingdom that is to come.

And in our gospel Jesus warns of the coming destruction of the city of Jerusalem, and of the final destruction of the earth. Yes, "Jerusalem will be trampled by the Gentiles." Indeed its "devastation is near," a mere thirty-five years from the death of the Lord. But the devastation of Jerusalem will last beyond its destruction by Rome, by the whore of Babylon, around 70 A.D. – it will continue "until the times of the Gentiles are fulfilled," until the nations' drinking of the cup of evil to its dregs, and the consequent end of this world brought about by the mighty hand of God. And so the blood of His servants continues to be shed, even as the kingdom is on the horizon.

"Those in the heart of the city must escape it." Here is a grave warning. You must rise from the mire of the sin into which the world leads you. For "the powers in the heavens will be shaken"; the walls of the city will be torn down, and you will be exposed and alone. "Flee to the mountains" of holiness; take refuge in "the country," where the Lord pastures His sheep. Do not give yourself to the ways of this world or the mark of the beast – lust not for the gold in its hands. For she is "a cage for every filthy and disgusting bird"; though the appearance may be otherwise, though the cage may be gilded, the horror within shall be revealed in the last days.

Brothers and sisters, we must find ourselves standing with those who "sing joyfully to the Lord," who "enter His gates with thanksgiving, His courts with praise." On the last day we must not fear "the roaring of the sea and the waves" because of our complicity with evil, but "stand up straight and raise our heads," ready for our ransom to come at the hands of our Lord. Let His goodness which "endures forever" be fulfilled in our souls. (With arms open upon the cross, we shall find our song.)

O. 34. Fri. (II)

Friday
(Rv.20:1-4,11-21:2; Ps.84:3-6,8,Rv.21:3; Lk.21:29-33)

"The heavens and the earth will pass away,
but my words will not pass."

Indeed John tells us of his vision that once "the former heavens and the former earth had passed away, and the sea was no longer," he saw "new heavens and a new earth," which are, of course, founded on the Word of God, given life by the breath of His mouth alone.

Yes, in the great Evangelist's vision there was "One who sat on" "a large white throne," and "the earth and the sky fled from His presence until they could no longer be seen." Even as the dead whose names are "not found inscribed in the book of the living" are "hurled into the pool of fire," even as they cannot stand before the judgment seat of the Lord, neither can this earth we walk upon or the heavens upon which we gaze, for they too have become as corrupted as their inhabitants: all that has been spoiled by sin must be cast into darkness, into eternal death. For all that is wicked must join the prince of wickedness, whom the angel of God chains up and hurls "into the abyss, which he close[s] and seal[s] over him." And any release from this dungeon is only illusory and brief, for this is the home prepared from the foundation of the world by the Word of God for him and those who serve him.

But O the wonder of the "New Jerusalem, the holy city, coming down out of heaven from God, beautiful as a bride prepared to meet her husband." It is she whom He has indeed prepared for Himself, purifying her as a precious jewel, even from the time she was first conceived in His mind, even since His breath first came upon her. And so it is our "soul yearns and

568

pines for the courts of the Lord," and is not happy until it rests in His house – yes, our soul is like a sparrow which finds its home in Him, and like the swallow which in His altars makes a nest for her young.

"Happy they who dwell in your house! Continually they praise you." And in our midst we see your fig tree bloom in the shoot that is your only Son, and your peace does come to reign upon us now. To nothing of this world let us hold but let all corruption pass, that your judgment we may endure, and be found worthy of new life in the Word you speak eternally.

O. 34. Sat. (II)

Saturday
(Rv.22:1-7; Ps.95:1-7,Rv.21:20; Lk.21:34-36)

"Remember, I am coming soon!"

And when He comes what blessings there shall be for those who have been faithful to Him. They shall eat of "the trees of life which produce fruit twelve times a year," which grow either side of "the river of life-giving water, clear as crystal" flowing from "the throne of God and of the Lamb." Healed entirely shall they be by the medicine of their leaves.

Then, brothers and sisters, if we wish to eat of this blessed, holy fruit, let us not now "become bloated with indulgence and drunkenness and worldly cares." For the bitter fruit of this earth will only poison our souls with sin and so prevent our tasting the food of the heavenly kingdom. "Nothing deserving a curse shall be found there," so let us remove all of this world's bitterness from our tongues.

O my dear brethren, the promise is great for those who "serve Him faithfully," who "acclaim the Rock of our salvation," the Lord, the "great God," and Jesus Christ His Son. Listen to what our blessed brother John imparts to us today, for "these words are trustworthy and true," and O so beautiful: "They shall see Him face to face and bear His name on their foreheads. The night shall be no more. They will need no light from lamps or the sun, for the Lord God shall give them light, and they shall reign forever." Do you hear these words? Does the promise take root in your hearts? O let your heart be upon His light! Let the glory of His face be all you aspire to, for it is not far from you.

"Come, let us bow down in worship; let us kneel before the Lord who made us." For "the Lord, the God of prophetic spirits, has sent His angel to show His servants what must happen very soon." Let us listen to His words. "Happy the man who heeds the prophetic message of this book!" who eats the Bread God provides. His dawn is on the horizon.

IV. LENT

Lent

A. First Five Weeks

Ash Wednesday
(Jl.2:12-18; Ps.51:3-6,12-14,17; 2Cor.5:20-6:2; Mt.6:1-6,16-18)

"Even now, says the Lord,
return to me with your whole heart,
with fasting, and weeping, and mourning."

"We implore you, in Christ's name: be reconciled to God!" Paul exclaims; and the people of God today raise a cry, rending their hearts, begging His forgiveness… turning from their sins to find His healing grace.

The trumpet is blown in Zion; the people are gathered as one. Now "let the bridegroom quit his room, and the bride her chamber. Between the porch and the altar let the priests, the ministers of the Lord, weep." For now is the time of mourning, now is the time of prayer… now is the time to cry with David, "Thoroughly wash me from my guilt and of my sin cleanse me." For now as we "acknowledge [our] offense" we find how "gracious and merciful is He"; now "the joy of [His] salvation" returns to us as "a clean heart" He creates for us, as His Holy Spirit He instills in our souls. Yes, "Now is the acceptable time! Now is the day of salvation!" And so let us cry out to our Lord: "Spare, O Lord, your people!"

The Lord will hear us, brothers and sisters; He will be quick to respond, as long as we are careful "not to receive the grace of God in vain." As Jesus said to His disciples, so He says to us: "Be on guard against performing religious acts for people to see." Only such vanity will prevent our finding the "recompense from our heavenly Father." Yes, we must give alms. Yes, we must pray. Yes, we must fast. But listen to the Lord's instruction to "keep your deeds of mercy secret," to "pray to your Father in private," and to make sure "no one can see you are fasting but your Father who is hidden." For then indeed "your Father who sees what is hidden will repay you" for your sacrifice. But if your offering is one to impress the eyes of man, be sure the eyes of God do not look upon it and it shall find no blessing in His sight.

The time has come, the time of great mercy. As we call upon our God, "in the greatness of [His] compassion [He will] wipe out [our] offense." In Jesus and in His sacrifice for our sin we might now "become the very holiness of God." May we find now the Lord "stirred to concern for His land and [taking] pity on His people." May we find His grace at work in our souls as we give ourselves to Him.

Thursday after Ash Wednesday

(Dt.30:15-20; Ps.1:1-4,6,39:5; Lk.9:22-25)

"The Lord watches over the way of the just,
but the way of the wicked vanishes."

In our first reading, Moses makes clear the choice we all must face: "I have set before you life and death, the blessing and the curse." "By loving the Lord... heeding His voice, and holding fast to Him," the Israelites will be blessed with "long life" in the Promised Land; they "will live and grow numerous" by "loving Him and walking in His ways." This will be life for them. "If, however, [they] turn away [their] hearts and will not listen... [they] will certainly perish." The promise to them will soon die if they walk "in the way of sinners."

Life and death. The blessing and the curse. The just and the wicked. To the Israelites the promise that they would be "like a tree planted near running water" if they followed the commandments of the Lord referred quite literally, quite physically, to the blessing of long life and enjoying the fruits of the earth. It showed itself in the numbers of people in the nation and the land they were given to occupy. When they were cursed, their kingdom was torn down and the land taken away from them. They became "like chaff which the wind drives away" when they were forced into exile from the lands of Judah and Israel.

What is the land we must so treasure today, brothers and sisters? What place are we called to preserve by following in the way of the Lord? For now he "who gains the whole world" will likely "destroy himself in the process." Now our sights, our hopes, can no longer be set on the physical universe. Jesus has come. The Son of Man walks in our midst. And His presence, His flesh, makes the heavenly homeland our desire – it is this which is now our Promised Land. It is the number born into this kingdom which now causes our hearts to rejoice. It is this blessing that now comes to him "who delights in the law of the Lord and meditates on His law day and night."

And the Lord makes clear what "the way of the just" now entails. Our gospel tells us "Jesus said to all" – not just to His disciples, but to *all* who would find the blessing, would find life – "Whoever wishes to be my follower must deny his very self, take up his cross each day, and follow in my steps." And His steps include enduring "many sufferings," being "put to death" and then being "raised up on the third day." Now it is death that leads to life. Now this world must be left behind. Now, though we love all – even our enemies – and everything upon it, we must leave the earth we have held so dear. The command is the same (to renounce all sin and love

573

God), but now the prize is much greater, and so the way there much more narrow. But the Lord blesses our every step toward Him.

Friday after Ash Wednesday
(Is.58:1-9; Ps.51:3-6,18-19; Mt.9:14-15)

"Would that today you might fast
so as to make your voice heard on high!"

Brothers and sisters, in this day of fasting and penance, first we must "acknowledge [our] offense" as David in our psalm. We must cry out to our God: "Against you only have I sinned, and done what is evil in your sight." This is our leaven of truth. "A contrite spirit, a heart contrite and humbled" the Lord cannot resist. It is this heart the Lord answers; it is prayer of this soul He hears – to this "cry for help... He will say: Here I am!"

"When the day comes that the groom is taken away, then they will fast." We "go in mourning" when Jesus is no longer in our midst. What does this then say of our fast? For though the Lord may be with us always in the power of the Spirit, yet He is physically taken from us now till the end of time. Our fast must therefore be a permanent condition all the while we walk this earth. And so true is this if we understand the Lord's definition of a fast as revealed in our first reading from Isaiah: "This, rather, is the fasting that I wish: releasing those bound unjustly... sharing your bread with the hungry, sheltering the oppressed and the homeless, clothing the naked... and not turning your back on your own." And what sense it makes that this be our fast now that Jesus is gone, for are we not His children here, called to carry out His mission in this world? Are not these the very things He instructs us to do in His stead for the least of His brothers who suffer now? On this earth here at the end of the age we should be engaged in fasting always.

And if we pray with a sincere heart, and if we do the will of the Lord in all things, what promise He makes to us: "Your light shall break forth like the dawn, and your wound shall quickly be healed... The glory of the Lord shall be your rear guard." All we ask shall be given us; all we seek we shall find in Him. And so, what shall our fasting be for us but pure joy, even as we become one with the Lord our God?

A blessed call is upon us now, one which makes our voices known to Him. Let us "remove from [our] midst oppression, false accusation and malicious speech." Let us denounce any "quarreling and fighting" that keeps us from Him, and see that His will is done in our lives. Then indeed He shall hear us; then by this death to sin we shall come to the glory of our God.

Saturday after Ash Wednesday
(Is.58:9-14; Ps.86:1-6,11; Lk.5:27-32)

"'Repairer of the breach,' they shall call you,
 'restorer of ruined homesteads.'"

"Levi gave a great reception for Jesus in his house," but it is Jesus who invites him, and all sinners, "to a change of heart" and to join Him in the home He makes for us all in heaven. As Levi (or Matthew) has done, so must we all: we must leave our "customs post," that which roots us to this world – we must stand up and follow Him.

"You, O Lord, are good and forgiving, abounding in kindness to all who call upon you." David makes his prayer in our psalm, coming to the Lord as one "afflicted and poor," begging the Lord's pity upon his soul. And there is confidence that his cry is answered, that his soul is gladdened; for the promise has been made through Isaiah that "He will renew [our] strength," that we "shall be like a watered garden, like a spring whose water never fails." All that He has broken down in His anger against us and against our sins shall be raised up again: "The ancient ruins shall be rebuilt for your sake, and the foundations from ages past you shall raise up." As we turn to Him and "call the sabbath a delight... not following [our] ways, seeking [our] own interests, or speaking with malice," we shall indeed "delight in the Lord" and in His inheritance; He shall indeed "nourish [us] with the heritage of Jacob" – the food He gives us will far surpass the bread upon the table at Levi's banquet. For it is upon His own Body we shall feed, and so find ourselves renewed in spirit and strengthened for the kingdom of heaven.

The Lord comes to invite all "sick people" to His healing grace. All who turn from their sins shall be acceptable to Him. And in His House they shall find a place, and be nourished well. "Even on the parched land" they shall find the water of life, for His grace extends to all places and all peoples. And with the bread we bestow on the hungry we ourselves shall be fed, for by this labor we shall unite with Him. "The mouth of the Lord has spoken." Let us find the mercy His words desire for us.

First Week

Sunday (A)
(Gn.2:7-9,3:1-7; Ps.51:3-6,12-14,17; Rm.5:12-19; Mt.4:1-11)

"Just as through the disobedience of the one man
the many were made sinners,
so, through the obedience of the one,
the many will be made righteous."

And what obedience Jesus shows in His temptations. For He was weakened, "He was hungry" after His forty-day fast in the desert, and the devil came at Him with all his power. But He does not falter as did the first man; He remembers the Word of God and His command. And by His faithfulness the sin of Adam is washed clean.

See how the Lord atones for our sins; see how directly His temptations parallel those presented to Eve. As she is shown the goodness of the food before her, that it is "pleasing to the eyes," so the devil tempts Jesus with bread that will sustain His life. As Eve ventures to take the food despite the command of God, listening to the serpent's words: "You certainly will not die!" so Satan would lead Jesus to cast His weakened body down from the parapet of the temple, with the encouragement that the angels will protect Him. And as Eve is seduced by the devil's promise, "You will be like gods," so he tries the same promise of power over "all the kingdoms of the world" with Jesus. In the first two temptations Jesus struggles as He will later under the weight of the cross, sweating and bleeding under the devil's test; but in the third, perhaps with understanding that the end of the temptations is at hand, He now exclaims, "Get away, Satan!" apparently revived – and His words are a most cutting blow to the prince of darkness: "The Lord, your God, shall you worship and Him alone shall you serve"; for it is the great sin of Satan to presume to be as the Almighty God.

And so the prayer of David, found so poignantly in our psalm: "Have mercy on me, O God, in your goodness; in the greatness of your compassion wipe out my offense," is answered. And so the sin that has been "before [us] always," since Adam fell in the garden, is now to be cleansed from our souls. For now the angels do come to minister to Him; and now He begins the ministry that leads directly to the cross and the redemption of mankind in His sacrifice. Now the die is cast for the salvation of our race. Soon the devil will hold no dominion.

Sunday (B)

(Gn.9:8-15; Ps.25:4-9; 1Pt.3:18-22; Mk.1:12-15)

"I set my bow in the clouds
to serve as a sign of the covenant between me and the earth."

In times past God made a covenant with Noah and his sons once they had come from the ark "that the waters shall never again become a flood to destroy all mortal beings," that they and those who would descend from them, indeed all races of men, should experience such devastation no more. And the sign of the rainbow He has given "for all ages to come," that His covenant shall not be forgotten.

This promise is a reassuring one, even if not by water but by fire we know this earth shall yet be destroyed. But a greater promise than this certainly we have, one for which this covenant is but a shadow. For now we have "Jesus Christ, who has gone into heaven and is at the right hand of God, with angels, authorities, and powers subject to Him." Through His resurrection from the dead He now shines in the firmament more brightly than any rainbow, and indeed in Him *all* races of men meet again and find their hope, not only that they shall not be destroyed from the earth, but that they shall know everlasting salvation in heaven. Even "the spirits in prison, who had once been disobedient when God patiently waited in the days of Noah during the building of the ark," have this word preached to them.

"The kingdom of God is at hand." Yes, the salvation of the Lord has been set firmly in our hearts, even as the rainbow God set in the heavens. He has remembered His "love" and "compassion" which "are from of old" and in His "goodness" has fulfilled them in His only Son. Though Jesus has had to suffer death for our sakes, yet death is remembered no more as we gaze upon His resurrected form – as the bow after the rain, so does His glory shine after the death of this flesh. And though the flood "prefigured Baptism," yet Baptism in the name of the Lord and into His death and resurrection is so much more, for "it is not a removal of dirt from the body but an appeal to God for a clear conscience," with which we are blessed now.

And so, brothers and sisters, let us find the "life in the Spirit" to which our Savior, come from the desert of our sin, now leads us. Let us fix our eyes upon His resurrection glory, even as we experience the death of the body.

577

Sunday (C)
(Dt.26:4-10; Ps.91:1-2,10-15; Rom.10:8-13; Lk.4:1-13)

"To His angels He has given command about you,
that they guard you in all your ways."

Can there be any doubt that the Lord God will bear Jesus up through His temptations in the desert, that He "will deliver Him and glorify Him"? For if "everyone who calls on the name of the Lord will be saved," will the Father leave His Son "in distress"? If He has rescued David from "the lion and the dragon," will He not also "set [Jesus] on high," apart from any danger? If the Israelites say: "We cried to the Lord, the God of our fathers, and He heard our cry" – and so delivered them from the "affliction" and "toil" and "oppression" of Egyptian slavery – will the deliverance of the Holy One from Satan's clutches be long in coming? Indeed the angels watch over Him, for His name is joined to that of the Father.

And indeed it is His name we now call upon in our need. As Paul tells us, "If you confess with your mouth that Jesus is Lord and believe in your heart that God raised Him from the dead, you will be saved." And so He who has been preserved from the devil's temptation now becomes the source of our own salvation – we find ourselves now protected as He, blessed by our faith in the Lord of all.

I notice again how the temptations present in our gospel are indicated, and answered, in our first reading and psalm. Of course, the devil himself attempts to use our quote from Psalm 91 to bring the Lord to ruin – showing how Scripture can indeed be twisted to perverse ends – foolishly failing to see that the quote would prove ultimately true. And the Israelites' bringing their tithe to God, saying, "I have now brought you the firstfruits of the products of the soil which you, O Lord, have given me," reveals the sacrifice that verifies that "one does not live by bread alone"; while Moses' instruction that they then "bow down in [God's] presence" confirms that "Him alone shall [we] serve."

O devil, all your temptations will be in vain; can you not see the fruitlessness of your acts? You cannot harm Him who holds your life in His hands, and so why do you not turn and, as the faithful angels, learn to love and serve the Holy One? Brothers and sisters, it is too late for this "viper" to come to truth, but not for any man who will confess that Jesus is the Christ. So let us preach to the ends of the earth by the power of deliverance from sin won by our Lord that *"No one who believes in Him will be put to shame."* O that all souls would be saved!

Monday

(Lv.19:1-2,11-18; Ps.19:8-10,15,Jn.6:63; Mt.25:31-46)

"As often as you did it for one of my least brothers,
you did it for me."

"You shall love your neighbor as yourself." Such is the golden rule and the second of the greatest commandments, which is like unto the first: Love God. And the union of the two is made evident by Jesus in our gospel today; He makes clear that what we do to others we do to Him, and so to love God and neighbor become one and the same. So tied is the Lord to His creation by the incarnation of His Son.

And how blessed are all His commands to us, all of which are summed up in love, and all of which give us life. "Refreshing the soul... giving wisdom to the simple... rejoicing the heart... enlightening the eye... enduring forever" – such is the Word of God to the obedient soul. All He speaks is just and all He speaks is holy and brings life, for all He speaks is of the Spirit of love. And of that Spirit we must be, if we hope to attain to eternal life where He sits in glory.

"Let the words of my mouth and the thought of my heart find favor before you, O Lord, my rock and redeemer," is David's prayer after extolling the virtues of the law of the Lord in his psalm today. And such should be our prayer. For if our hearts are set upon Him, and if our mouths speak truth, we can be assured that our actions will follow and we will please the Lord in all we do. For being of the Lord, we can only feed the hungry; seeking His will, we can only welcome Him and all His children into our lives. If we are founded upon this Rock, all will find in us the love of God.

For He is love, brothers and sisters, and all He asks of us is love. Love does "not steal." Love does "not lie." Love does "not defraud" or "curse the deaf" or "act dishonestly" in any way. In a word, if you are of love as He is love, "you shall not bear hatred for your brother in your heart." And all are our brothers, even the least of these; the Lord has made this known. All are our neighbor and so none can "stand by idly when [his] neighbor's life is at stake." All are called by love to lend their hand, His hand, to others in need. For then we help Him.

Would we not help the Lord if we saw Him wanting? Is it not our desire to ease His pain? We have opportunity ever to do this in those around us. When we do, we fulfill His command and find life for our souls, for then we are holy as He.

Tuesday

(Is.55:10-11; Ps.34:4-7,16-19; Mt.6:7-15)

"Give us today our daily bread."

Our daily bread comes from the mouth of God; it is His Word that nourishes us. His Word "water[s] the earth, making it fertile and fruitful, giving seed to him who sows and bread to him who eats." By His Word our spiritual lives are anointed with holiness; the breath of His mouth makes us whole, and so we become fruitful in His Name.

Yes, we are sharers in His Word; it is His Word the just speak in their time of need. "Crushed in spirit" before Him like holy seed, their cry comes to His ears and the rain He sends upon them saves them from all sin, "deliver[s] [them] from all fears." Jesus, the Word made flesh, is true, and His words are true: "Your Father knows what you need before you ask Him"; and so the Father is quick to hear when we enter into His Word and call upon His Name in all humility. It is this humility which makes us fertile earth, this trust in His will that lifts our faces toward His light, that we "may not blush with shame." "Look to Him that you may be radiant with joy," O sinner. "Glorify the Lord" and "extol His name," for with you He shares His Spirit; in you He plants the Word that grows to eternal life.

Father in heaven, you alone are holy, and your Name is life to us. Let "your kingdom come," let "your will be done," for apart from you we wither and die. Make our earth your heaven; bring to us all the blessings you know we need to live ever in your light. Feed us with your bread, feed us with your Word – your Son is all the food we need. And for all "the wrong we have done," as He has taught us, let us find our forgiveness by releasing from all bondage those who have done wrong to us, by loving our enemies. In the end we pray, O Lord, that temptation be taken from our path; though we treasure your chastising Hand, let us not falter anymore – "deliver us from the evil one" who lurks in this world seeking the ruin of our souls.

O Lord, our lives are in your hands. Our hearts are given life by you. In our prayer let us not imitate the vain words of the pagans, but let us join in the Spirit with your Son and become one in the Word with you. (Help me to remember your Name.)

(I witness here that however many times I speak the Lord's Prayer, as however many times I attend Holy Mass, by the grace that comes through the Spirit, it is ever new and alive with the blessings that come from above. These words are a gift to us we must cherish in our souls.)

Wednesday

(Jon.3:1-10; Ps.51:3-4,12-13,18-19; Lk.11:29-32)

"At the preaching of Jonah they reformed."

Let us learn from the people of Nineveh, who heeded the message of repentance given Jonah.   At Jonah's cry they "believed God; they proclaimed a fast and all of them, great and small, put on sackcloth." Even the king "laid aside his robe, covered himself with sackcloth, and sat in the ashes" in hopes of averting the destruction he knew God held in hand for his wayward city. He decrees that "every man shall turn from his evil way" and "call loudly to God." Such utter repentance! Such turning from sin! And this from a pagan king and a pagan nation.

If Nineveh has so believed in God, if it has so recognized its sin before Him and turned so dramatically back to Him, pleading for His mercy, what should we not do, brothers and sisters, in this time of Lent set aside for the cleansing of *our* sins, we who have Jesus' preaching now ringing in our ears and calling to our hearts? Indeed, we must again and continually cry out with David to God for His mercy to come upon us. Ever with "a contrite and humbled heart" we must sit before Him recognizing our sin. For always our sin is with us, however much we might be ignorant of our guilt as we live our lives in vain. "Cast me not out from your presence, and your Holy Spirit take not from me," must be our eternal plea, for we are in continual danger of going away from Him.

Let us not be afraid to humble ourselves before God and man. Let us seek nothing else but the wisdom of Christ, the call of the cross to our souls. In humility, in sackcloth and ashes, let us prostrate ourselves before the true king who will come at the judgment to discern the worth of all souls. Perhaps He will have mercy. Perhaps He will "withhold His blazing wrath." Perhaps the punishment we deserve He may avert and "we shall not perish." Upon the soul He finds His cross inscribed, He shall take pity, my friends.

O Lord, we have sinned and done what is evil in your sight. In your infinite mercy look upon our broken hearts, and help us to reform our lives. For you alone are God.

Thursday

(Est.C:12,14-16,23-25; Ps.138:1-3,7-8; Mt.7:7-12)

"My Lord, our King, you alone are God.
Help me, who am alone and have no help but you."

In our gospel we have today a few of our Lord's most famous words: "Ask, and you will receive. Seek, and you will find. Knock, and it will be opened to you." Jesus encourages us to faithfulness in prayer, assuring all that our "heavenly Father [will] give good things to anyone who asks Him." How beautiful are His words, and how true.

And how well Queen Esther illustrates the faithful prayer of one who has "recourse to the Lord." She comes to the Lord in all humility, as an obedient child before her father, and opens her heart to God with a sincere plea for her fellow Jews, threatened with extinction by the enemy. She says of her forefathers, proclaiming herself a daughter of Abraham, "You fulfilled all your promises to them," and comes now seeking the same answer from the "King of gods and Ruler of every power." Such prayer for salvation before the God she recognizes "know[s] all things" cannot but be answered by the loving Father. He will give her the food she desires.

In our psalm we hear David's song of thanksgiving for the prayers the Lord has been faithful in answering for him: "I will give thanks to you, O Lord, with all my heart, for you have heard the words of my mouth," thus proving the truth of Jesus' exhortation to His disciples, and indicating that Esther will also find answer to her prayer – and so, that we all should have assurance of God's loving desire to heed all *our* sincere pleas. David, too, acknowledges the greatness of God: "You have made great above all things your name and your promise," and so comes to the place where the "kindness and [the] truth" of the Lord will be known to him. And his faith in the Lord's promise to be with him and hear him lasts for perpetuity: "The Lord will complete what He has done for me."

Praise the Lord, who answers all prayers. Praise the loving God who knows all things. It is in His heart to feed us with the best of wheat, and this He does each day for those who "worship at [His] holy temple and give thanks to [His] name." "Forsake not the work of your hands," dear Lord. Be with us always to hear our humble prayers, that we might witness always your loving faithfulness to all who call upon you in truth.

L. 1. Fri.

Friday
(Ez.18:21-28; Ps.130:1-8; Mt.5:20-26)

"Settle with your opponent while on your way to court with him."

We are all on our way to court, brothers and sisters. The judgment of the Lord awaits us all on the Last Day, and the Last Day is upon us here at the end of the age. There is no time to lose; we must be "reconciled with [our] brother"; we must turn from sin today and find the Lord's grace. "With the Lord is kindness and plenteous redemption; and He will redeem

Israel from all their iniquities" – but "out of the depths" we must cry to Him "in supplication" to find His blessed forgiveness; and from sinful paths we must turn our feet to know His salvation.

"If a wicked man, turning from the wickedness he has committed, does what is right and just, he shall preserve his life." It is a great promise that comes to us through the prophet Ezekiel, that none of our crimes shall be remembered by God when we return to Him. For the Lord does not "derive any pleasure from the death of the wicked," He "rather rejoice[s] when he turns from his evil way that he may live"; for the Lord wishes life for us all, wishes Himself, who is Life, for every soul, and gives it freely, and quite naturally, when we follow His ways.

It is really rather simple: as when a wicked man turns to good things he is no longer wicked but good and so lives in the Lord, so "when a virtuous man turns away from virtue to commit iniquity, and dies, it is because of the iniquity he committed that he must die." Evil brings death, and righteousness and justice (goodness) bring life. The Lord desires life for us all and so He calls us to repentance, to repentance from even what might seem to our minds the smallest of sins – for so greatly does He wish life for us. And clearly does He know that which we cannot see, that death holds sway over us by every sin on our soul.

Let us avoid the fires of hell and the pains of purgatory, brothers and sisters. Let us call out to the Lord this day and find His "plenteous redemption" even as we turn from our sins. And there shall be no prison into which we are thrown, as we forgive one another, and the Lord forgives us, our sins.

L. 1. Sat.

Saturday
(Dt.26:16-19; Ps.119:1-2,4-5,7-8; Mt.5:43-48)

"You will be a people sacred to the Lord, your God."

The promise made to the Israelites through Moses is also a command, and is fulfilled in the command of Jesus.

In our first reading Moses tells the people the Lord will raise them "high in praise and renown and glory above all other nations," but makes it clear that this shall be so only as long as they "walk in His ways and observe His statutes, commandments, and decrees" – only if they "hearken to His voice." For His law is as food to the body and light to the mind and must be observed carefully, "with all [our] heart and with all [our] soul," to maintain the presence of God in our lives. If "He is to be [our] God," we must do as He commands.

Lent

Thus our psalmist sings of the happiness of those "who observe His decrees, who seek Him with all their heart." Thus does he cry out in longing, "Oh, that I might be firm in the ways of keeping your statutes!" for he knows in them is life. To "walk in the way of the Lord" is his joy.

And that joy is made complete, our life is made whole, by the new command of love Jesus imparts to our soul. The Lord fulfills the Law of Moses, which gave light to the people, by commanding us not to love only our "countryman" but all: "Love your enemies, pray for your persecutors." Here is His challenge for us to "prove that [we] are sons of our heavenly Father," to love as He loves, to know the greatness of His glory, therefore, in our very lives. If the psalmist cried out in such joy at the blessing found in following the Law of Moses, what indescribable joy is ours when we follow Jesus' words. What greater call can we have than to "be made perfect as [our] heavenly Father is perfect"? What greater merit and blessing could there be? None. For He is Life itself, and here we are called to live with Him.

"His sun rises on the bad and the good, He rains on the just and the unjust." Nothing dims God's holy light or stems the blessings He showers upon all. In absolute light, in absolute love, the Father dwells, in the heavenly kingdom; and if we can love as He loves, as Jesus has loved, we shall know such blessing. Love even those who hate you and you will be as the Father, who knows only love, and you will become sacred to Him – you will be saints in His kingdom.

L. 2. Sun. (A)

Second Week

Sunday (A)
(Gn.12:1-4a; Ps.33:4-5,18-20,22; 2Tm.1:8b-10; Mt.17:1-9)

"Rise, and do not be afraid."

Here in the midst of the darkness we drink in during this Lenten Season comes a light shining to assure our hearts of the promise that is ours. The Lord's Transfiguration is presented to us this day to lead us through all the tribulations of the cross to the resurrection, which is our holy goal.

"Beloved: Bear your share of hardship for the gospel with the strength that comes from God," Paul says to his special child Timothy, and so the Lord speaks to us all, reminding us that "He saved us and called us to a holy life." It is "up a high mountain by themselves" Jesus leads His principal disciples Peter, James, and John, to reveal to them the glory to which they are called – thus signifying the cross we must all carry along the rough terrain of this world to reach our place in heaven. In seeing that "His face

584

shone like the sun and His clothes became white as light" and then hearing the voice of the Father overshadowing them, they are overawed... but the hand of the Lord touches them, and strengthens them for the road ahead.

Our call is like that of Abraham, the father of all those of faith: "Go forth from the land of your kinsfolk and from your father's house to a land that I will show you." We all must leave behind the security this world holds and go according to God's word, to travel in a land foreign to our souls. But His assurance is with us, His blessing is upon us, and so the darkness of the night should not make us afraid. For "the eyes of the Lord are upon those who fear Him, upon those who hope for His kindness, to deliver them from death and preserve them in spite of famine." And so, however difficult the walk, however steep the climb, our hearts should never waver; for we have always at our side "our Savior Christ Jesus, who destroyed death and brought life and immortality to light through the gospel."

And so, brothers and sisters, as we travel through the heart of the sacrifice this Lenten time invites us to share, let it be that "our soul waits for the Lord, who is our help and our shield," and let our prayer be as David's: "May your kindness, O Lord, be upon us, who have put our hope in you." For Jesus is before us to lead us to our home.

L. 2. Sun. (B)

Sunday (B)
(Gn.22:1-2,9-13,15-18; Ps.116:10,15-19; Rom.8:31-34; Mk.9:2-10)

"You shall offer him up as a holocaust
on a height that I will point out to you."

"Take your son Isaac, your only one, whom you love," the Lord instructs Abraham, calling him to sacrifice even as an animal his beloved child, upon whom God's promise rests. To a mountain he is led, with his son carrying wood in tow.

And arriving at the place God had told him to go, "Abraham built an altar there and arranged the wood on it... and took the knife to slaughter his son." The angel comes to stay his hand, but Abraham is prepared to do as the Lord commands.

The Lord prevents Abraham from making this sacrifice because it is not *his* son who is to die; only the Lord's Beloved could be offered as such a holocaust – only His Son is called upon to die. "Christ Jesus it is who died," no one else, for only His death brings life.

And on Mount Tabor today we see the life that will come by the Lord's sacrifice; already we glimpse the rays of heaven. Jesus is as engulfed in flames, holy fire of the most blessed holocaust; and – like the three young men in the furnace, like the bush before Moses on Mt. Horeb – by these flames He is not burned: by these flames His purity is made to shine.

How good indeed it is for these apostles to behold this blessed vision! In it we all find hope that the death of Christ is not for naught, and neither shall our own death be. For all who die in Christ, die as Christ, a death that brings only eternal life. And so, comprehending here the majesty to which we are called, all disciples of Jesus, all children of the God of Life, are strengthened for all trial.

God "did not spare His own Son but handed Him over for us all," not because He loved Him not, but because He loves us all. And now "will He not also give us everything along with Him?" Will He now seek to condemn those whom He has justified at such a massive cost?

"It is God who acquits us," brothers and sisters, by the death of His Son. And now "precious in the eyes of the Lord is the death of [all] His faithful ones"; do not be afraid to serve the Lord. For by your sacrifice, to a great height He will draw you, even as He has His Son, who "is at the right hand of God" this day. With Abraham, He "will bless you abundantly."

Sunday (C)
(Gn.15:5-12,17-18; Ps.27:1,7-9,13-14; Phil.3:17-4:1; Lk.9:28-36)

"A cloud came and cast a shadow over them,
and they became frightened when they entered the cloud."

As darkness thus covered the three apostles, so "a trance fell upon Abram, and a deep, terrifying darkness enveloped him." Both find themselves surrounded by darkness and filled with fear. In just this way the Lord brings His revelations. For as the Lord is about to pronounce beyond doubt that Jesus is the Messiah, so He is about to send "a flaming torch" to pass between Abram's offerings and so confirm his taking possession of the Promised Land. The Lord must act in such manner to cleanse all foolishness from our souls, that we might hear His most pure Word.

But light comes out of the darkness: indeed, "the Lord is [our] light and [our] salvation" – He Himself is not darkness. And so as the fire of the torch pierces the dark night upon Abram's mind, so the chief apostles are privileged to see Jesus' glory, to witness in fullness the Light the Son of God is. And the Lord God leaves no doubt with them that it is of Jesus He says, "This is my chosen Son," for though the greatest men of Jewish history had also "appeared in glory" with Jesus, now He is "found alone" – and the apostles are left speechless.

It must pass to the marrow of our bones, the Truth of Christ's salvation. If in any way superficial or "occupied with earthly things" is our vision,

Him we have not known. He alone stands as our "life's refuge"; in Him alone do we find God's presence – Him alone should our "glance" seek. But as we pray, "Hide not your face from me," we should realize how profound is the prayer we make. For the Lord indeed "will change our lowly body to conform with His glorified body" when He appears at the end of the age, but consider for a moment what it will be like to have that power of refinement upon ourselves. Very much like the darkness which envelops the apostles and Abram today; very much like the dark night of the soul of which our great saints speak. Are you prepared to have the Lord separate soul from spirit with His sword of Truth? Do you know this piercing, fiery process even now? Then even in this world you shall begin to behold His face, and find yourself ready on that Day to be taken from earthly to heavenly tents.

Monday
(Dn.9:4-10; Ps.79:8-9,11,13,103:10; Lk.6:36-38)

"Deliver us and pardon our sins for your name's sake."

It is a cry for forgiveness our psalmist makes to our compassionate God. "Remember not against us the iniquities of the past," he begs, seeking release from sin's prison for himself and his people. And Daniel does the same; acknowledging with full throat the sins of Judah and all Israel, he seeks the merciful hand of the Lord upon the people, interceding in their stead. Though he himself is an upright man, he cries out, "We have sinned, been wicked and done evil," praying thus for the rebellious nation which has been scattered to "all countries" for their failure to heed the command of the Lord.

Well do our Old Testament figures embody Jesus' teaching in our gospel, summed up simply: "Be compassionate, as your Father is compassionate." For they "do not judge" or "condemn" those individuals primarily responsible for the apostasy and so the destruction of the kingdom and the covenant, but rather seek earnestly to heal the rift that has come by giving generously of themselves and their love for God and others, in Christlike fashion standing in the breach. And so they earn the titles of prophet and psalmist of God; and so they foreshadow the heavenly compassion Jesus calls all His followers to pour forth in His name. (And so we can be assured their compassion has been "measured back" to them by the Lord.)

Jesus on the cross dies for the sins of all people, and this is His central call to all our souls: to imitate Him is our blessed goal. For insofar as we die for God and others, insofar as we lay down our lives in His truth, thus far we shall find His "compassion quickly come to us" and so live in the heavenly glory which is now His place. To us all He calls this day to pardon and forgive, for in doing so we shall find the reconciliation of the Lord even with our enemies, and secure for ourselves a room in His heavenly home.

He who knew no sin was made sin for our sake. He has humbled Himself to carry the sins of the nation... Let us, brothers and sisters, die with Christ on the cross, that all sin might be taken away in His Name.

L. 2. Tues.

Tuesday
(Is.1:10,16-20; Ps.50:8-9,16-17,21,23; Mt.23:1-12)

"To him that goes the right way
I will show the salvation of God."

"Put away your misdeeds from before my eyes; cease doing evil; learn to do good." For it is only following in the way of the Lord we shall be saved; for mere words, vain pretense, the Lord has no patience.

Indeed it is so, what Isaiah proclaims: "Though your sins be like scarlet, they may become white as snow." Forgiveness is offered forth generously by the Lord to the nation that goes astray. But we must be "willing, and obey" the word "the mouth of the Lord has spoken." If we "hate discipline and cast [His] words behind" our backs, if we but "recite [His] statutes" as the Pharisees whose "works are performed to be seen," whose mouths profess the covenant but whose deeds are far from Him, how is it we shall find salvation? For the Lord is not blind and deaf as we to the heart of man; and unlike our own, His word is true, and His command must be followed – we must serve Him and our neighbor. We must humble ourselves in His sight if we hope to be exalted to His kingdom.

"Make justice your aim: redress the wronged, hear the orphan's plea, defend the widow." Over and over we hear from the mouth of the prophet and the psalmist and the Son Himself – the Lord has compassion on the poor and lowly, and we must *do* as He calls... we must be His arms and legs in this world. Unlike the Pharisees who "will not lift a finger" to carry even the lightest burden, whose "deeds are few," we must take up the full weight of the cross. It is not "places of honor" and "marks of respect in public" for which we hunger; but when we teach and as we serve, our hearts must be set on the salvation of souls, which can only be accomplished by living the way of the Messiah, by following His example.

What has Jesus not done for us? What teaching has He left lacking flesh and blood? And so, rightly is He called "Rabbi"; and so, truly is He the only Son of the one Father in heaven. Brothers and sisters, we must go the way He leads – we must follow the humble path to the kingdom. In this our sins shall become "white as wool," washed in the blood of the Lamb.

Wednesday
(Jer.18:18-20; Ps.31:5-6,14-17; Mt.20:17-28)

"Can you drink of the cup I am to drink of?"

Do you know what He asks, brothers and sisters? And do you know where it leads?

In our gospel today, Jesus is very deliberate in His instruction to His apostles. As He starts out "to go up to Jerusalem," where the chief priests and scribes "will condemn Him to death" and the Romans crucify Him, He takes "the Twelve aside on the road" to speak clearly to them of the fate which awaits Him. (So objective are His words that He refers to Himself in the third person.) Of course, the apostles are yet far from understanding His message, as shown by their soon dissembling into jealous indignation regarding the question of the power and importance of each. And the Lord must teach them again that He has come "to give His own life as a ransom for many"; He "has come, not to be served by others, but to serve," and that those who "aspire to [the] greatness" that is His must necessarily "serve the needs of all."

We know that Peter is the first among equals "for whom it has been reserved by [the] Father," as the Lord has indicated earlier, and not James or John – though both of these shall have prominent place in drinking of the cup of Christ: James as the first apostle martyred and John, the beloved, whose martyrdom shall be white, coming in the endurance of a long life – but all of us who seek to follow Jesus indeed share in the selfsame cross, and so shall receive of the selfsame blessings of Him who is raised up "on the third day." All are called to drink of the cup of suffering and service in Jesus' stead. We must be clear on this essential point of faith.

And does not Jeremiah's persecution at the hands of the citizens of Jerusalem show that the cross of Christ extends even to the time before He had come in the flesh? Do not the words spoken against the prophet: "Let us destroy him by his own tongue; let us carefully note his every word," echo exactly the plottings of the Pharisees against Jesus, whom they repeatedly sought to entrap? And all this though He does "speak in their behalf, to turn away [the Father's] wrath from them." And David in our psalm chants the same refrain: "They consult together against me, plotting to take my life."

Brothers and sisters, as it was for David and Jeremiah and Jesus, following in the ways of the Lord will bring us persecution. You may well

589

Lent

ask, Must good be repaid with evil? but the Lord will answer, "Let it be for now." For "from the clutches of [our] enemies and [our] persecutors" He rescues those who trust in Him. Take heart that the humbled shall be exalted as you drink deeply of His cup.

L. 2. Thurs.

Thursday
(Jer.17:5-10; Ps.1:1-4,6,40:5; Lk.16:19-31)

> "He is like a tree planted beside the waters,
> that stretches out its roots to the stream."

"Blessed is the man who trusts in the Lord, whose hope is the Lord." For he shall be like the tree "that yields its fruit in due season, and whose leaves never fade." He shall never be "like a barren bush in the desert" or "like chaff which the wind drives away." Never shall he know the "place of torment," for "the heat when it comes" shall do him no harm. This man "follows not the counsel of the wicked nor walks in the way of sinners," but rather "meditates on [God's] law day and night." His faith and his hope are the roots that stretch out to the living water of the living God who nourishes all by His Word and in His flesh.

Brothers and sisters, we must never "trust in human beings" as do the Pharisees, or be as the rich man who "seeks his strength in flesh," "dressed in purple and linen and feast[ing] splendidly every day." This earth itself holds not our food. Notice that it is to the Pharisees Jesus addresses His parable in our gospel today. How closely the rich man parallels these leaders of the people. The bounty of God's wisdom is bestowed upon them, but they use it to feed their bellies rather than to shepherd those in need. They claim Abraham as their father and the Law of Moses as their guide, but they neither have the faith that makes Abraham the father of all, nor do they follow the instructions Moses conveys. Only in the flesh are they Abraham's sons; and though they see him from the hell to which they come, they cannot touch him, they cannot reach past him to the Father in heaven, who gives Abraham his blessing. Dwelling but in their "father's house" as the rich man who gorged himself on the pleasures of the flesh, they come not to the Father's House on high, for their roots penetrate not to the living water that is found in faith, and now Lazarus cannot even "dip the tip of his finger in water to refresh [their] tongue." Dead as the stone upon which the commandments were written do they become.

Notice, too, brothers and sisters, the connection between thoughts and actions, between faith and works, between the word and the flesh in our first reading, and present throughout Scripture: "I, the Lord, alone probe the mind and test the heart, to reward everyone according to his ways, according

590

to the merit of his deeds." Only the Lord, who is Himself the living water, knows if His Word of life dwells in a man, and that faithful spirit is reflected directly in the just man's deeds – for by these the Lord judges. And Jesus is the just man; He is the Word made flesh in whom the Spirit dwells, in whom all find life. He is the undying tree, one with the Father, whom all must imitate. His words are living water; His flesh is food we eat: He alone is perfect in word and deed, for in Him spirit and flesh meet. Let our hearts be set on Him, and we, too, shall be blessed; and we shall know that He is risen from the dead.

Friday
(Gn.37:3-4,12-13,17-28; Ps.105:5,16-21; Mt.21:33-43,45-46)

"They sold Joseph to the Ishmaelites for twenty pieces of silver."

"The stone which the builders rejected has become the keystone of the structure." Hear what Scripture says. As he who was "sold as a slave" by his brothers became "lord of [the king's] house and ruler of all his possessions," so He whom the elders of the people could call "our brother, our own flesh," whom they "seized... dragged... outside the vineyard, and killed," has become the very foundation of the New Jerusalem.

How parallel are our first reading and gospel today. Jacob, Israel, sends the son he loves best, he who is "the child of his old age," to the brothers who are tending their father's flock, to bring them food to nourish them in their labor. The Father in heaven sends Jesus, His beloved Son – who is Child of His old age both in His existing with Him before time and in His coming here at the end of the age to His brothers – to those to whom He has entrusted the care of His vineyard, through whom He feeds all the people, with the greatest of nourishment to sustain them unto heaven itself. For their jealousy over the favor granted their brother, Israel's sons strip Joseph of his long and princely tunic and cast him into a cistern "which was empty and dry" as their souls. Out of the same jealousy and in the desire for His inheritance, the chief priests and Pharisees will soon arrest the Lord and see that He is stripped and nailed to a cross.

And, brothers and sisters, the outcome of each story shall be the same. As his brothers must come on their knees to their brother to find grain to keep themselves from dying of famine on the parched earth once Joseph has taken his place as ruler of the king's possessions in Egypt, so the elders of the people and all of us who bear responsibility for the death of Christ by our continual sins against Him shall have to come on our knees before Him who sits on the throne of heaven robed in glory, to find nourishment for our

591

Lent

journey here in His sacred Body and Blood, and to find a place at table in
the kingdom to come.

There is much to be pondered in the rejection of Jesus, as is so with the
betrayal of Joseph. It is not only the Pharisees – who answer so well the
Lord's question regarding the fate of the tenant farmers, yet have not the
faith to match the words God puts on their lips – who must look inside
themselves and recognize their anger and jealousy and greed. The Lord
invites each of his brothers to examine his conscience this day, in this time.
In particular, are we showing ourselves to be the nation the Lord has given
the kingdom of God? Do we "yield a rich harvest" for Him who was sold
for thirty pieces of silver? Or have our souls gone bankrupt? May from us
the Lord "obtain His share of the grapes."

L. 2. Sat.

Saturday
(Mic.7:14-15,18-20; Ps.103:1-4,8-12; Lk.15:1-3,11-32)

"While he was still a long way off,
his father caught sight of him and was deeply moved."

"He ran out to meet him, threw his arms around his neck, and kissed
him." Amen. Such is the forgiveness of the Lord, that even while we are
far from Him, yet while we are sinners, He sees our hearts turn to Him and
welcomes us into His embrace.

We have all "sinned against God," brothers and sisters. We are all as
the Prodigal Son who has "squandered his money on dissolute living." But
O the forgiveness of our God, who "with kindness and compassion"
"redeems [our] life from destruction," who in "pardon[ing] all [our]
iniquities" raises us from the death of sin to sit with Him in heaven. Does
not the father in our parable say as much of the sinner? "This son of mine
was dead and has come back to life." Is it not so that when we were still
sinners Jesus died for us, to raise us with Himself to new life?

"Who is there like you, the God who removes guilt and pardons sin for
the remnant of His inheritance?" the prophet Micah asks in our first reading,
wondering at the infinite grace of our Father. "As the heavens are high
above the earth, so surpassing is His kindness toward those who fear Him,"
sings David in our psalm. And so, how joyous we should be, how our souls
should "bless the Lord... and forget not all His benefits." For indeed, "not
according to our sins does He deal with us, nor does He requite us according
to our crimes." Rather, even though we deserve damnation, even though the
most we could hope for is to be treated as one of His hired hands, yet does
He remember His love for us. Beyond all human reason, He graces us with
"the finest robe" and calls us in to "eat and celebrate" at the heavenly

592

banquet, where there shall be "music and dancing" to the Name of our God, where all the gifts of the Spirit poured forth through the blood of Christ are ours as we become one with the Father, as we return to Him "in good health." Is there anything more remarkable?

And let us not sin as the elder brother. Let us not begrudge God, the loving Father, His infinite generosity to all His sons. Let us not presume to stand in judgment against those the Lord deigns to forgive, but share His forgiveness and His grace toward all. Then truly the father's words to the elder son (which are a noticeably kind word to the Pharisees, whom this son represents) will be our own: "You are with me always, and everything I have is yours." Let us know the truth of this, God's will for all our souls, and accept the gracious forgiveness which brings us to it as we come "to [our] senses" and turn to Him with all our hearts this day. He is calling us home.

L. 3. Sun. (A)

Third Week

Sunday (A)
(Ex.17:3-7; Ps.95:1-2,6-9; Rom.5:1-2,5-8; Jn.4:5-42)

"Everyone who drinks this water will be thirsty again;
but whoever drinks the water I shall give will never thirst."

What is this "spring of water welling up to eternal life" but the Holy Spirit come upon us, the Truth of God in our midst through the blessed sacrifice of the Son for us "while we were still sinners." Brothers and sisters, "the love of God has been poured out into our hearts through the Holy Spirit who has been given to us," even as Jesus' words of spirit and truth are poured into the ears of the Samaritan woman. Do we know His grace? Do we hear His voice and leave our water jar at the old well as we go to tell others about the Christ?

In our readings today is the juxtaposition of the physical and the spiritual, and the call to enter into the Spirit of God. In our first reading, the Israelites "in their thirst for water" while wandering in the desert cry out against God and Moses and long to return to their slavery in Egypt, that they might but be able to eat and drink. The Lord would teach them to depend on Him, to trust in the Spirit and His love, and He will provide for all their needs, as He does this day, but they are blinded to the Hand of God. "Though they had seen [His] works," they continually tested Him, unable to find rest in Him, and for their hardness of heart virtually none shall themselves enter the Promised Land. And the source of their lack of faith is ever their bellies.

593

In our gospel twice we see the inability to understand the Spirit speaking because of the belly's grumbling. The Samaritan woman confuses the life-giving water of which Jesus speaks with the passing water she came to draw from Jacob's well: "Sir, give me this water, so that I may not be thirsty or have to keep coming to this well." And the disciples think someone else has brought the Lord something to eat when He says, "I have food to eat of which you do not know," at their urging Him to eat the food they have in hand. But as He speaks to the woman of the Holy Spirit, He speaks to them of our daily bread – "to do the will of the one who sent [us] and to finish His work." Indeed, as He awaits the return of the sinful woman with her Samaritan neighbors, He prepares them for the mission that must now go forth even to "foreigners." It is the Spirit of God He desires them to eat that they might be fortified for their call. And it is the Spirit found in the Body and Blood He has shed for our sakes of which we all must partake to slake our thirst and find the strength to do the work which leads us to the kingdom of God. His is a kingdom for all; and it lasts forever.

L. 3. Sun. (B)

Sunday (B)
(Ex.20:1-17; Ps.19:8-11; 1Cor.1:22-25; Jn.2:13-25)

"The fear of the Lord is pure,
enduring forever."

Is it not fear of the Lord, Jesus would instill in the people as He makes "a whip out of cords" and drives those who buy and sell out of the temple? Is His great zeal not to purify His Father's House of all corruption? And will the Temple He will raise up not endure forever?

David tells us that "the law of the Lord is perfect," and it is so; and so our worship of the Lord should be perfect as well – it should match the perfection of the Lord and His Word. Thus does the Lord give us His commandments, to refine us in His light and make us like Himself. Thus should we rest on the sabbath day as He has done, and indeed do all things according to His way, having "no other gods besides" Him. He alone is worthy of our worship, and He alone is worthy of imitation. His words alone will enlighten our eye.

And how do we know this "wisdom of God" except by the blessed presence of His Son? And how do we know it most fully but in His crucifixion? Here is the wisdom of God upon the cross, calling us to what is far beyond us – beyond this world and our lusts. "Human nature" He knew quite well, assuming it in all but sin as He has, and so He knows it must be nailed to the cross if we are to gain redemption. And what wisdom is greater than that which effects salvation? To what greater place could we be led than the kingdom of heaven?

And "Christ crucified" reveals not only the wisdom of God but "the power of God" as well, for what makes the devils tremble more than our Savior on the cross? What forces them to realize the vanity of their efforts to destroy man than to see Him dead, and know that He shall live again? (And we with Him... and we with Him.) "The weakness of God is stronger than human strength," and here God's weakness comes to full power. And with absolute force it shall drive all evil from the world, and from our souls.

"Destroy this temple and in three days I will raise it up," are the Lord's prophetic words. The Temple of His Body once destroyed now is made to last forever, for it can never be destroyed again. Now that He is raised from the dead, death has no more dominion. Purified of all darkness and sin is the kingdom; and in awe of the Lord's humble majesty we come there with open eyes and hearts on fire, to dwell with Him in eternal life.

Sunday (C)
(Ex.3:1-8a,13-15; Ps.103:1-4,6-8,11; 1Cor.10:1-6,10-12; Lk.13:1-9)

"The Lord secures justice
and the rights of all the oppressed."

Thus does the Lord God appear to Moses and call him to rescue the Israelites from the Egyptians. He has "witnessed the affliction of His people"; He has "heard their cry of complaint against their slave drivers" and "know[s] well what they are suffering." And so, by the hand of Moses, He will lead them to "a good and spacious land, a land flowing with milk and honey."

Yes, brothers and sisters, the Lord "has made known His ways to Moses"; His "kindness and compassion" He has revealed to His people. The great I AM (YHWH), He who is and who will always be, has come and shown Himself to His servant on the "holy ground" of Mount Horeb. In a "bush [that] is not burned" though flaming with fire, He opens Moses' eyes to His presence. And He tells him His glorious NAME, by which He is "to be remembered through all generations" – that it is He who is Life. And, of course, the life He brings is one of mercy and healing.

Yet, though the Lord is certainly "merciful and gracious," He is also just; thus does Paul remind us that though all the Israelites "were baptized into Moses in the cloud and in the sea" in their exodus from slavery, though all ate and drank from "the rock [that] was Christ... God was not pleased with most of them, for they were struck down in the desert." So the blessings they had gained by the mercy of our God, they soon lost by their own disobedience. And so could we all lose the grace of Christ at work in our lives if we "desire evil things, as they did." For God is merciful, but God is just, and will not have His kindness presumed upon.

Thus does Jesus Himself also warn us, even as He warns the people who question Him this day that they are no better than those "whose blood Pilate had mingled with the blood of their sacrifices," that we are not without guilt ourselves. Thus does He proclaim, "If you do not repent, you will all perish as they did," as all sinners do. And thus does He warn us by parable that if we do not bear fruit in His name, we shall be cut down and thrown in the fire – for there is no wasted ground in the kingdom of God.

If you cry out to Him, He will hear you, for it is He who "redeems your life from destruction" and your salvation is His desire. But justice insists that if you turn back to your sin, you choose to remove yourself from His loving arms.

L. 3. Mon.

Monday
(2Kgs.5:1-15; Ps.42:2-3,43:3-4; Lk.4:24-30)

"There is no God in all the earth, except in Israel."

"There is a prophet in Israel," brothers and sisters, and this prophet is God. Jesus Christ has come, salvation from the Jews. Do you recognize Him? Will you accept Him?

It is only in "the waters of Israel" that we are made clean. As wonderful as may be the waters of our native land, it matters not, for it is these alone that are blessed; these alone will make our flesh again "like the flesh of a little child." For a little child has come through these waters, has been baptized in this River, and it is His blood which baptizes us all and makes us clean as the flesh of God.

"Bring me to your holy mountain, to your dwelling place," our souls should sing with our psalmist as they seek "the running waters" of "the living God" that alone will satisfy all our needs. O to "behold the face of God," to "go in to the altar of God" in "gladness and joy"! How we should search for His grace and His presence! Like Naaman, who came from a distant land upon the word of a servant girl, so should we obediently seek the grace that comes only from God, the God of Abraham, Isaac, and Jacob – the Word made flesh in Jesus Christ. He is our dwelling place, the Temple of God.

"No prophet gains acceptance in his native place," Jesus proclaims to those of His hometown. And His prophecy is true. For though salvation is from the Jews and they are Jews who serve as its foundation stones, yet the Church shall be constituted greatly by those of other lands. The Jews who follow Him shall be greatly persecuted by their own, and the Word shall bear fruit to the ends of the world before the eyes of the Chosen shall be opened to the living water, the healing grace, in their midst.

Come in faith, brothers and sisters, to this holy mountain where the Lord does dwell, to find the cleansing of your sins. Through none else does salvation come; in no one else is the Word made known. The flesh of God is Jesus alone.

Tuesday
(Dn.3:25,34-43; Ps.25:4-9; Mt.18:21-35)

"With contrite heart and humble spirit let us be received."

The Lord "guides the humble to justice, He teaches the humble His way," and so it is the prayer of these He receives; upon them He showers His mercy. For His mercy is His justice and it is known by those who humbly share the same.

Azariah makes his prayer for mercy for his people Israel, who suffer the purgatorial fires of their exile from the Promised Land, even as he himself stands in the quite literal fire of the furnace of the king of Babylon for his faithfulness to the living God. He begs the Lord: "Do not let us be put to shame, but deal with us in your kindness and great mercy," and as he comes humbly and with great faith interceding for others and not himself, and thus exhibiting the mercy he desires of the Lord, he is well protected from the flames by the angel of God. The Lord's justice is known to him who "follow[s] [Him] with [his] whole heart."

And Jesus makes quite clear the great mercy God holds for all who humble themselves before Him – "seventy times seven times," eternally, He forgives. His reign is like the king who "wrote off the debt," though it was "a huge amount," of his servant who begged his mercy. For the Lord is "moved with pity" at our contrition for our sins. But the same forgiveness we must offer to others if we are to prove that His blood runs in our veins. The master tells his wicked servant: "I canceled your entire debt when you pleaded with me. Should you not have dealt mercifully with your fellow servant, as I dealt with you?" And indeed the fires of hell and purgatory await those who break their bond of justice and mercy with the Lord by failing to manifest the same grace that has been revealed to their souls. We are sinners and must see ourselves so. The Lord forgives and we must accept His grace. Others seek our mercy and we must grant it to them. This is how the kingdom works. Those who do not follow the Lord's way of compassion do not enter there.

Lent

Brothers and sisters, we must be as Azariah, who "stood up in the fire and prayed aloud." For all, we must humbly intercede before our merciful God even in this dark world. And for the contrition we show for our sins and those of others, the Lord holds an eternal reward. As our priests, as Peter, as God Himself, let us forgive one another; if we receive one another humbly and mercifully, the Lord will receive us in His grace, in His justice.

L. 3. Wed.

Wednesday
(Dt.4:1,5-9; Ps.147:12-13,15-16,19-20; Mt.5:17-19)

"What great nation has statutes and decrees
that are as just as this whole law?"

"He has proclaimed His word to Jacob, His statutes and ordinances to Israel." The Lord in His grace "sends forth His command to the earth; swiftly runs His word!" And as the snow and the rain come down to nourish the land, to bring life to the earth, so His Word is food and life to all who listen to it. By His Word He "strengthen[s] the bars of [our] gates," giving us protection against the tribulations of this world, and by it He "bless[es] [our] children within" us, making fruitful all our endeavors. By fulfilling and teaching His commands, we find life eternal in the kingdom of God; by breaking them and leading others to do so, we court death.

And so why should the Word be withheld from the ears of the flock? By his silence does not a priest give credence to the breaking of the law? And then are not the results upon his soul? Has the devil so blinded his eyes to the truth that he cannot see the life-giving water the Word of God is, that His commands are not burdensome but bring release from labor under the weight of sin? By withholding such nourishment does he hope to increase his flock? O but it is so hard to open my mouth, you say, so difficult to speak the truth. Better you die to self now than to find your soul dead to the kingdom of heaven.

Brothers and sisters, it is fulfilling "the smallest letter of the law... the smallest part of the letter," that brings us to perfection, that brings us to life that is our God. Ignorance shall not bring you there. As Moses instructs of the commands of the Lord, "Observe them carefully, for thus you will give evidence of your wisdom and intelligence to the nations." For they are a great gift made known to souls; they are the fountain of life, fulfilled in the flesh of Jesus. So neither practice them in vain "nor let them slip from your memory as long as you live," for they hold life, and should you lose them, you shall lose the Christ.

Do you desire holiness? Do you wish to be whole? Do you long for the presence of God, thirsting for His truth? Then follow the Word He speaks

598

in your presence today and teach others to do so: Abortion is wrong. Contraception is wrong. Euthanasia is wrong. Premarital sex is wrong. Love of money and goods is deadly. We have the word in our Church – our mouths must speak it, or we shall die. By our Baptism we are all made priests in the sight of God and are called to live and to preach the Word of God. "What great nation is there that has gods so close to it as the Lord, our God, is to us whenever we call upon Him" or whenever we come to His table of sacrifice to receive Him? In love make His Word and presence known.

Thursday
(Jer.7:23-28; Ps.95:1-2,6-9; Lk.11:14-23)

"They walked in the hardness of their evil hearts
and turned their backs, not their faces, to me."

The Lord calls His people to "listen to [His] voice," to "walk in all [His] ways," that they "may prosper." But with whom is there obedience? How many harden their hearts against Him!

Of the people of Jeremiah's time the Lord says, "Faithfulness has disappeared; the word itself is banished from their speech." They, as all, should "bow down in worship" and "kneel before the Lord who made us," but they, as we, do not recognize that "He is our God, and we are the people He shepherds, the flock He guides." They pay no heed to the voice of the prophet.

And this hardness of heart is fulfilled in the opposition of the faithless to Jesus. In our gospel He casts out a devil that a dumb man may speak and some say, "It is by Beelzebul, the prince of devils, that He casts out devils." Indeed, the hardness of heart does not get any greater than this. And so for this sin against the Holy Spirit and His ways there can be no forgiveness. They call good "evil" and presume that the evil they speak is a good – but they are utterly lost in darkness. "The reign of God is upon" them, and they desire to dwell in the realm of the devil who is being cast from their midst. What can save such a soul? For all prayers the Lord answers.

Brothers and sisters, it is a dark world and a difficult age in which we dwell. But the response of our hearers is not our concern; we must speak as called regardless of the reaction – we must live our vocation despite any opposition. Note the Lord's words to Jeremiah: "When you speak all these words to them, they will not listen to you either; when you call to them, they will not answer you." For as with all the prophets, and as with ourselves, he speaks to "the nation which does not listen to the voice of the Lord, its God, or take correction." To these it is our duty to call; to darkness we must bring light. And realize, too, the fate of Jesus, who will die on the cross for His work to bring salvation to the world. It is this same cross to which we are all called, for it is by this same cross *we* have been called; and those who are yet to be gathered in must hear our voice. Let us stand with the Lord and gather in His grain, despite the stiffened necks we might find. There shall be others like us who hear the cry of Jeremiah and cling to the saving power of Jesus. Test Him not with your own hardness of heart.

L. 3. Fri.

Friday
(Hos.14:2-10;   Ps.81:6-11,14,17;   Mk.12:28-34)

"Hear, O Israel! The Lord our God is Lord alone!"

"There is no other than He," and so what should we do but "love the Lord [our] God with all [our] heart, with all [our] soul, with all [our] mind, and with all [our] strength"? What promise the Lord makes to us if only we would return to Him and love Him: "If only my people would hear me, and Israel walk in my ways, I would feed them with the best of wheat, and with honey from the rock I would fill them." Indeed, then we would be "not far from the reign of God," even here on earth.

Brothers and sisters, we "have collapsed through [our] guilt." We have had "strange god[s]" among us and said, "'Our god,' to the work of our hands." Why should we continue so blind? Why should we continue stumbling as sinners – why do we find the straight paths of the Lord so difficult to walk? He will "forgive all iniquity" and strengthen us in justice; if we turn to Him, He will "heal [our] defection" and "love [us] freely." "In distress you called, and I rescued you," He says in the words of our psalmist, and His words are true. Turning away His wrath, He shall become "like the dew for Israel." And with His living water to nourish us, we "shall blossom like the lily... blossom like the olive tree." We "shall dwell in His shade and raise grain," our "fragrance like the Lebanon cedar." We must but love God and our neighbor, and we shall "bear fruit."

"Let him who is wise understand these things; let him who is prudent know them." There is no God in all the world but the Lord, and it is He in whom "the orphan finds compassion." Why should you continue in your vain pursuits when love awaits your turning to Him? What refuge can you find in your false gods? In them and in your pride you indeed will find yourself orphaned, cut off from the love that only the Father holds. But He loves the orphan, brother, and so He calls to your soul to return to Him with all your heart. In this is true wisdom; in Him you will find strength.

There is no further question when the love of God is known. When His presence is revealed we fall silent, for nothing can be said in the face of Truth. Listen, brothers and sisters; but listen – and then do.

Saturday
(Hos.6:1-6; Ps.51:3-4,18-21,Hos.6:6; Lk.18:9-14)

"As certain as the dawn is His coming,
and His judgment shines forth like the light of day!"

It is night. There is darkness. In this world of sin we are afflicted on account of our guilt, for our failures to love God. And so David cries out in our psalm, "Have mercy, O God, in your goodness"; and so the tax collector in our gospel "beat[s] his breast and say[s], 'O God, be merciful to me, a sinner'"; and so with all the afflicted, in the words of Hosea, we should "return to the Lord, for it is He who has rent, but He will heal us."

Brothers and sisters, we must "strive to know the Lord," for "He will come to us like the rain, like the spring rain that waters the earth" to cleanse us of our sin and make us fruitful again. To us the Lord will "be bountiful... by rebuilding the walls of Jerusalem." He will grant us a place for worship and again "be pleased with due sacrifices, burnt offerings and holocausts." Our prayers shall again come before Him. But if our piety is not to be "like a morning cloud, like the dew that passes early away," we must come to know and love God. And the first step to knowing God and showing our desire for His love is the recognition of our own sinfulness before Him, for "he who humbles himself shall be exalted."

Yes, brothers and sisters, "in the greatness of [His] compassion [He will] wipe out [our] offense." "He will revive us after two days; on the third day He will raise us up." But first we must die. We must die to the sinful pride that afflicts our souls and leads us from the light that shines, that awaits all our coming to Him in blessed humility. For He desires to show us mercy, but mercy we must have. He longs to bring us light, but light we must seek to find. His judgment, which is just, must be our desire, and it will come to us and wash us free of all our sin. And we shall know Him. And His love shall be our own. And only light will shine in our souls.

It is night, brothers and sisters. There is darkness. Our sins are with us still. But the Lord is coming: the light is upon us. Turn to it now, and live.

601

Fourth Week

Sunday (A)
(1Sm.16:1b,6-7,10-13a; Ps.23:1-6; Eph.5:8-14; Jn.9:1-41)

"I am the light of the world."

And by that light alone we see. By this light which comes from God we who were born blind, who were born into sin, have our eyes opened. And so having escaped the darkness we "live as children of light."

When David was presented before Samuel, immediately the prophet's eyes were opened to the one on whom God's favor rested. His eyes which had first "judge[d] from… appearance," now with the Lord look "into the heart." How clearly he hears the Lord speak to him, "There – anoint him, for this is the one!" And how readily he takes "the horn of oil in hand" and anoints the new king. And how wonderfully "from that day on, the Spirit of the Lord rushed upon David."

Here is our own baptism in the Lord foretold. Here is our own anointing with the oil of Christ presaged. And as "Jesus made clay and anointed [the] eyes" of the blind man, so in our baptism we find our own anointing, an anointing which washes us clean of original sin, an anointing which prepares our hearts to receive Him – an anointing which opens our eyes to His light. The eyes of our heart now see. Our souls cry out from their depths of the light which has entered in and made them clean. And so we say with the blind man in the presence of Jesus, "I do believe, Lord," and we, too, worship Him as our "cup overflows" with "the goodness and kindness" of God.

"Christ will give you light." For this He has come into the world, "that those who do not see might see." In the words of Scripture, Paul entreats us today: "Awake, O sleeper, and arise from the dead." The Lord has come to give us light. As long as we say, "'We see,' so [our] sin remains"; we must be blind, we must recognize sin's darkness encroaching upon our souls… and then we would "have no sin," for then Jesus would remove from us our sin – then He would bring us light.

"Everything exposed by the light becomes visible," and so we must bring our sins before Him, and from the dead we shall rise… and with His light we shall shine. May the Lord anoint us all with the oil of Christ, and may we be faithful to that anointing.

(Note: In Confession as in Baptism we are washed clean of our sins by Christ, and light is thus brought to our eyes. Constant recourse we have to this preservation of our souls.)

Sunday (B)
(2Chr.36:14-16,19-23; Ps.137:1-6; Eph.2:4-10; Jn.3:14-21)

"By the streams of Babylon we sat and wept."

For "practicing all the abominations of the nations and polluting the Lord's temple," the people of God "were carried captive to Babylon." For all their "infidelity" they were forced to watch as "their enemies burnt the house of God [and] tore down the walls of Jerusalem." And so did their "tongue[s] cleave to [their] palate[s]" in a foreign land; so they "hung up [their] harps"; so their "right hand[s] [were] forgotten"... They could not sing the praises of the Lord; they could not strum to His glory – all the works of their hands were stilled. They could but weep in desolation.

So are we like them in our sins. So do our transgressions silence our tongues and make us lame and ineffective. So were we dead as these before Christ Jesus came to save us. And as the Israelites were called back to the city of peace and entreated to build the Lord's house there once again, as they found their release from exile by the king of Persia speaking in the name of God... just as these could enter in once more to the "song of the Lord," so we now find our freedom from the chains which bound us, and to the Lord's temple come proclaiming His gracious salvation.

No more should we cry, brothers and sisters. No more should we sit idly as the streams of this world pass us mockingly by. No, now we must come resolutely to the Christ of God, for the word has gone forth to the ends of the earth that all who love Him should come into His light. "By grace [we] have been saved"; by the Lord's immeasurable kindness we have been redeemed – in His love we must now sing our song. "For we are His handiwork, created in Christ Jesus for the good works that God has prepared in advance," and so our work must now be accomplished in Him.

"Whoever lives the truth comes to the light, so that his works may be clearly seen as done in God." And so "saved through faith" we must now bring before Him the offering of our lives. There is no longer cause to hide. There is no longer need to weep for our sin, to find the oppression of the world and the devil too much to bear. No, the gates of Jerusalem are opened once again, and the Lord God has "seated us with Him in the heavens in Christ Jesus." Here in this light let us now find our home. Here in His presence let us begin to live the Lord's eternal salvation. Our tears of sorrow, with our condemnation, have passed.

Sunday (C)
(Jos.5:9a,10-12; Ps.34:2-7,9; 2Cor.5:17-21; Lk.15:1-3,11-32)

"Today I have removed the reproach of Egypt from you."

As the Israelites now realize their redemption from slavery in Egypt as they step into the Promised Land, so the prodigal son comes to his own redemption, his own release from slavery as a hired hand in a foreign land, as he returns to his father's house. Yes, as the Israelites "ate of the produce of the land" for the first time after the feast of Passover, so the prodigal son feasts on the "fattened calf" slaughtered for him by his merciful father. And the redemption of both is a redemption from sin.

Today we hear quite clearly "the message of reconciliation" proclaimed throughout our readings. It is a call to all souls and a thanksgiving to God, "who has reconciled us to Himself through Christ." And will we come to the water and drink? Will we leave behind "the pods on which the swine fe[e]d" and come to His table to eat? Will we too come to our senses and, realizing the mercy the Father holds for all His children, return to the House of God and feast in the land to which He leads us?

It seems certain, and simple, that we should join David in his song of praise, that we should heed him as he entreats our souls: "Glorify the Lord with me." For as "from all his distress He saved him," so from all our distress He saves us; and so nothing should fill our hearts but joy. "He was lost and has been found," the Lord declares in jubilation over every poor sinner who returns to His fold. And so, should we not respond gratefully to the appeal of Paul and all those entrusted with "the ministry of reconciliation" to indeed "be reconciled to God." In faith let us confess our sins and know the gracious blood of our Redeemer pouring upon our souls.

"For our sake He made Him to be sin who did not know sin, so that we might become the righteousness of God in Him." And now He waits on the road before His House for our return. Now He longs to open the doors of forgiveness and let us into His dwelling. Now He would see the sacrifice of His Son bear fruit, that we all might be as He is. Accept His removal of sin like a sword in the depths of your soul, and enter into His kingdom.

Monday
(Is.65:17-21; Ps.30:2,4-6,11-13; Jn.4:43-54)

"You changed my mourning into dancing."

Here in the midst of Lent we find the purpose of all our suffering, the hope to which we all are called. "At nightfall, weeping enters in, but with the dawn, rejoicing." And thus does this time of penance and fasting lead to the abundance found in Easter joy. For what is darkness but the world in which we dwell, and what is the dawn but the coming of Jesus to our hearts, the kingdom of heaven within us? And even in the midst of this darkness, the light begins to shine. "Lo, I am about to create new heavens and a new earth," the Lord says. And today we hear that reassuring voice speaking to our waiting souls.

In our gospel today we find a marvelous sign of the light that follows the darkness, of the joy that follows sorrow. A royal official, a man in darkness for his lack of faith in God – and whose darkness is compounded by his position of authority under a faithless king – comes to the true King of the Jews, the Light of God. In sorrow he mourns the imminent death of his son... and so the darkness is quite complete. But the man's son shall not die, and neither shall his hope of salvation. For it is great faith he shows. Enlightened by the One he seeks, he believes, and so his son is saved by the Son of the Most High, and so he enters the fold of Heaven. What greater joy could he have hoped to find? For not only is his son "brought... up from the nether world," but indeed he (with the unbelievers he represents) is "preserved... from among those going down into the pit." No greater words of joy could we read than these: "He and his whole household thereupon became believers."

Brothers and sisters, the Lord has made us to be a people of "rejoicing and happiness." He tells us so today through the prophet Isaiah: "I create Jerusalem to be a joy and its people a delight." This is our destiny; this is our call. If we must suffer for a time in this land of darkness, in this time of penance, let us be assured of the fullness of joy that comes Easter morning: "No longer shall the sound of weeping be heard there, or the sound of crying." Yes, how particularly marvelous it is to hear of this light before us even as we stand in the midst of the darkness; what even greater joy do we feel!

The Lord conquers all. He wishes only life for our soul. And that life is upon us even this day. At the wedding feast we shall dance: "sing praise to the Lord, you His faithful ones, and give thanks to His holy name."

L. 4. Tues.

Tuesday
(Ez.47:1-9,12; Ps.46:2-3,5-6,8-9; Jn.5:1-3,5-16)

"There is a stream whose runlets gladden the city of God,
the holy dwelling of the Most High."

Brothers and sisters, Jesus is our living water.

Lent

In our first reading, Ezekiel speaks of his heavenly vision of the river of God which runs from His holy temple. The water, which increases as it flows further from its source, eventually "empties into the sea, the salt waters, which it makes fresh." Along both banks of the river are trees whose "leaves shall not fade, nor their fruit fail... for they [are] watered by the flow from the sanctuary." Their fruit nourishes and their leaves heal.

What is this river and this temple? What is this sea and what are these fruit trees revealed to the eyes of the prophet? Brothers and sisters, that Jesus is the river, the healing water, is made poignantly clear in our gospel. The sick man struggles daily to plunge himself into the healing pool at Bethesda but is never able to find the assistance he needs. When Jesus asks him if he wants to be healed and the man explains his plight, the Lord immediately states: "Stand up! Pick up your mat and walk!" The healing waters have come to him, and he is cured.

Yes, Jesus is the living water, and the cross is as the temple from which His healing blood flows. Upon us all who have prepared the cross and set it in place by our sins – which have made *our* water undrinkable – His grace pours to make us whole... and so we are the salt sea made fresh. And so the trees on the river's banks, bearing fresh fruit each of the months, do we become, as we walk in the paths of the twelve apostles... who are first to know His redemptive power, and with whom God becomes "our refuge and our strength."

"Come! behold the deeds of the Lord, the astounding things He has wrought on earth." For by the river that flows from His pierced side He has prepared a people and a kingdom. And all shall see what Ezekiel sees; all shall know what the prophet is shown – the water of the Lord flows out now to the ends of the world, making all whole and fruitful by His presence.

L. 4. Wed.

Wednesday
(Is. 49:8-15; Ps.145:8-9,13-14,17-18; Jn.5:17-30)

"Just as the Father possesses life in Himself,
so He has granted it to the Son to have life in Himself."

Here the great mystery of the unity of Father and Son is revealed, and so also our salvation.

God is life. The Father is the great I AM, He who will be what He will be and do what He will do – He who holds the world and all its wonders in His creating Hand. And Jesus is as He is. He shares absolutely in the Life that is the Father. "Speaking of God as His own Father, [He is] thereby making Himself God's equal." And this perfect union is most clearly evident in the fact that "the Father has given over to Him power to pass

606

judgment." For who can judge the soul of man but God, and so, who is Jesus but God Himself?

And this union of Father and Son in the absolute love that gives proof of the Spirit's presence, and thus completes the Holy Trinity, is the key to our readings today. Thus, though the thrust of the Word is our own salvation from sin and death, this is only effected in the love of the Father for the Son – for it is in our own union with Jesus and in His washing us clean from sin by standing in our place upon the cross that we find union with the Father, that we find the Life to which we all are called... in whom we find our home of love.

The Lord says, "I will cut a road through all my mountains, and make my highways level." Jesus the Son is that road by which the Father "comforts His people and shows mercy to His afflicted" by leading them back to Him, guiding them "beside springs of water" that "they shall not hunger or thirst" but "find pasture" in His arms. For "can a mother forget her infant, be without tenderness for the child of her womb?" Greater than any mother's love is the Lord's love for us, and this He makes known through His only Son.

Brothers and sisters, "the dead shall hear the voice of God's Son, and those who have heeded it shall live." Even now the Lord is "saying to the prisoners: Come out! To those in darkness: Show yourselves!" Out from the tombs He calls us, for He is "compassionate toward all His works" and desires in His perfect will that all share in His holiness, in His Life. Let us do right in Him, and as His Son we, too, shall live.

L. 4. Thurs.

Thursday
(Ex.32:7-14; Ps.106:4,19-23; Jn.5:31-47)

"If you believed Moses you would then believe me,
for it was about me that he wrote."

As Moses wrote, so Jesus speaks. As Moses wrote, so Jesus is. The eternal life to which the Scriptures testify is now in our midst. The Word has come to life; the Law is now fulfilled. The "form [we] have never seen" now stands before us. The "voice [we] have never heard" now speaks to our ears. But do we "have His word abiding in our hearts"? Do we "believe the One [the Father] has sent"? "The works the Father has given [Jesus] to accomplish" "testify on [His] behalf." Let us exult in their light.

The Lord "had done great deeds in the land of Egypt," "wondrous deeds" and "terrible things" in the sight of the Israelites through His servant Moses. But "they forgot the God who had saved them," "making for themselves a molten calf and worshiping it" instead of the living God. They could not wait for the Word to come to them; their hearts were not set on Moses' return from the mountain with the Law of God. And so, for their lack of faith God "spoke of destroying them." The fire of wrath the Lord would have "blazed up against them to consume them" – such was the thought of His heart.

But Moses "withstood Him in the breach." "Let your blazing wrath die down; relent in punishing your people," he begs. And so, because of Moses' intercession, "the Lord relented in the punishment He had threatened on His people" for their lack of faith in Him. And now it is Jesus who stands in the breach made by our sins, preventing our eternal punishment at the hands of a righteous God. For by all accounts we deserve death for *our* lack of faith; but in His grace the chasm between us and God He fills by stretching out His arms on the cross.

Brothers and sisters, let us believe in His redemptive sacrifice. Let it never be said of us, "You do not have the love of God in your hearts," for such a state would mean the end of our days. But God has promised: "I will make your descendants as numerous as the stars in the sky." About this Moses writes, and the words speak of Jesus, He who is our salvation. Let us not forget the One who saves us in His love, "on whom we have set [our] hopes."

L. 4. Fri.

Friday

(Ws.2:1,12-22; Ps.34:17-21,23; Jn.7:1-2,10,25-30)

"He calls blest the destiny of the just
and boasts that God is His Father."

And for such He shall be persecuted; for such He shall be killed. For to the wicked "He is the censure of [their] thoughts; merely to see Him is a hardship" for those who stray from the Lord's commands. And so, in vain attempt to spare themselves the just judgment of the Lord, in their jealousy they say to one another: "With revilement and torture let us put Him to the test"; and so they "condemn Him to a shameful death," tempting the Lord God to watch over Him.

Evil are their thoughts and wicked are their ways. But the one "they want to kill," the one "they tr[y] to seize," escapes their grasp, for indeed the Lord "watches over all His bones; not one of them shall be broken." And they cannot take hold of Him unless He so wills it; so, frustrated are their efforts "because His hour ha[s] not yet come."

Even when His hour comes and He is delivered into the hands of the prince of darkness, still their violence will not touch Him; yet will He be protected by the Lord, as are all who follow Him. Yes, David sings of what he knows: "The Lord is close to the brokenhearted; and those who are crushed in spirit He saves." And so, even in distress, even in death, the Lord is near to His chosen ones. The Son of God shall ever be delivered from the grasp of those whose "wickedness blind[s] them."

Jesus stands up in the temple and cries out: "I was sent by One who has the right to send... it is from Him I come." He declares openly that He is the Son of God, and the wicked who would hide their sins seek to destroy Him for bringing such light. But it shall indeed be proven that He is the Son of the Most High, that God is His Father. The "recompense of holiness" shall be witnessed by all eyes. In subjection to their evil plots, in dying upon the wood of the cross, and in His subsequent resurrection, Jesus shall utterly destroy all the power of wicked men and reveal the one true light that shines, that cannot be overcome by darkness.

"We know where this man is from," they say, and so they are blind. For God the Father is not of this dark earth, and neither is His just Son.

Saturday
(Jer.11:18-20; Ps.7:2-3,9-12; Jn.7:40-53)

"Let us destroy the tree in its vigor;
let us cut him off from the land of the living,
so that his name will be spoken no more."

With these words "they were hatching plots against" Jeremiah, and in the same way against Jesus. And so, "like a trusting Lamb led to slaughter," "like the lion's prey, to be torn to pieces, with no one to rescue" are they. But "the malice of the wicked [shall] come to an end."

"The upright of heart" are ever persecuted. Even Nicodemus, "one of their own number," a member of the Pharisees who are seeking the life of the Lord, was "taunted" when he "spoke up to say, 'Since when does our law condemn any man without first hearing him and knowing the facts?'" But the Lord "sustain[s] the just" "because of the innocence that is" theirs. In Him do they "take refuge," and He will not leave them a prey to their teeth.

Even the temple guards recognize the power of the word that comes from Christ. "No man ever spoke like that before," they state as the reason that "no one laid hands on Him." "He is the Messiah," it is sure, and only the hardest of heart are able to blind themselves to the authority that issues forth from His lips. But the Lord is the "searcher of mind and heart," of "heart and soul"; He is the just Judge, the just God, and so even as He rescues the innocent from trial, so He "punishes day by day" the evil man.

Their plots shall come to naught; in vain do they pursue Him. For though He shall allow them "to apprehend Him," He will be eternally free from their clutches. Indeed, He will be fixed to a cross. Indeed, like an innocent lamb He shall not open His mouth to protest or to call upon the angels for assistance. And they shall think that He is theirs. But rise from the dead He will, and His Name will be spoken to the ends of the earth. For nothing can destroy the power of the Word of God.

L. 5. Sun. (A)

Fifth Week

Sunday (A)
(Ez.37:12-14; Ps.130:1-8; Rom.8:8-11; Jn.11:1-45)

"I am the resurrection and the life;
whoever believes in me, even if he dies, will live,
and everyone who lives and believes in me will never die."

"You shall know that I am the Lord, when I open your graves and have you rise from them, O my people!" says the Lord God through the prophet Ezekiel. "The one who raised Christ from the dead will give life to your mortal bodies also, through His Spirit dwelling in you," says St. Paul. And our psalm sings of the Lord's "plenteous redemption," that "He will redeem Israel from all their iniquities"; and so, "more than sentinels wait for the dawn, let [us] wait for the Lord," who dispels all darkness, all death, by His Word, by His presence among us. Let us but believe in Him, and we shall live.

The dawn comes to Bethany, to Martha and Mary, and to Lazarus. It comes to us all in this powerful sign of the Lord's conquering of all darkness and death, "that [we] may believe." Wrapped in burial cloth is Lazarus, laying in the sealed tomb four days. The tears of a people are shed for the loved one who has died, and Jesus joins their weeping. Deeply human is the Lord, and so, "perturbed and deeply troubled" He becomes at the sorrow we all know when death is near. He longs ever to cry out to us not to mourn, but believe, and now we hear His voice call upon the Father's name; and now as He "crie[s] out in a loud voice, 'Lazarus, come out!'" we see that what He says is true: He is the resurrection and the life. And so, believing in Him, no longer does the Christian fear death.

Death is of the flesh, but we are "in the spirit." "The body is dead because of sin," but "the spirit is alive because of righteousness." And so, as we rise from the graves opened by the powerful word of the Lord, as we rise from our iniquities unto eternal life, we know His Spirit at work within us, the Spirit of Christ that is only life. In Him let us take refuge; in Him let us believe. He is here with us to keep us from death, to release us from all darkness – to free us all from sin. Let us remain with Him and so have eternal life.

Sunday (B)
(Jer.31:31-34; Ps.51:3-4,12-15; Heb.5:7-9; Jn.12:20-33)

"Father, glorify your name."

Jesus cries out in supplication to Him who is "able to save Him from death," but He prays not to be saved from death, not to be saved from the sacrifice He must make, but only that in His death the Father might glorify His name. His "hour has come," He knows. He hears from His apostles of the Greeks who seek Him, and He knows it is now time for Him to return to the Father and for His apostles to take over the work He has begun – to carry His salvation to the nations. And though He is "troubled," knowing "the kind of death He would die," knowing that it is the only path to the Father, yet He does not ask to be saved "from this hour." His only desire is to fulfill the Father's will by being "lifted up from the earth" in crucifixion and resurrection that He might "draw everyone to [Him]self" and to the glory in the Father He knows.

And of course "He was heard because of His reverence." Because His cry is sincere, is a laying down of His life in perfect humility and perfect love, the Father readily answers His prayer. Even in "a voice c[o]me from heaven" He responds, speaking not for the sake of His Son – who needs no such assurance, who is dead to Himself and serves the Father perfectly – but for those whom the Son would save by His "fall[ing] to the ground" in death. For them, for us, the Father answers, for this is the Son's wish.

And if we are holy as He, we "all, from least to greatest, shall know" the Lord our God just as He knows Him – we shall have our prayers answered as readily as the cries of supplication of our Savior. And so we shall be saved; and so we shall be preserved from death... and so we, too, shall glorify the Father's name. As the Lord listens to David when he cries out in his penitent psalm, so shall God come and make our hearts clean: so shall He come and write His name upon them as we cry out to Him. And we shall be blessed as Jesus, and we shall stand just as steadfast. Renewed in spirit, our offenses wiped out, we shall stand in the Son's stead upon the cross and in the kingdom.

"Your Holy Spirit take not from me," O Lord, for it is the proof of your presence within me; it is the seal of your Son and His blood upon my soul. By your Spirit I know I shall be protected from death; by His touch I am led to my salvation. Father in heaven, glorify thy name in me as in thy Son.

611

Sunday (C)

(Is.43:16-21; Ps.126:1-6; Phil.3:8-14; Jn.8:1-11)

> "Forgetting what lies behind
> but straining forward to what lies ahead,
> I continue my pursuit toward the goal."

In times past the Lord opened "a way in the sea" for the Israelites to pass through, while Pharaoh's army He "snuffed out and quenched like a wick." Afterward, He "brought back the captives of Zion" from the lands to which they had been scattered to rebuild the temple in Jerusalem. "Great things" the Lord has done for His people, but through the prophet Isaiah He enjoins all to "remember not the events of the past," to "consider not" these mighty and wondrous deeds. For as marvelous as His deeds once were, now He proclaims, "See, I am doing something new!" And indeed, something new is in our midst.

We see perfect evidence of this surpassing work in the apostle Paul, who has "accepted the loss of all things" – including any righteousness this former Pharisee may have had by the law – that he may "gain Christ and be found in Him," for he knew that all good things are to be found in Jesus the Lord. And now he is but "depending on faith to know Him and the power of His resurrection."

Here is the *new thing* which is done: the only Son has died and been raised from the grave, never to die again. And so Paul seeks to share "of His sufferings," to be "conformed to His death," that he too "may attain the resurrection from the dead." Nothing else is worth our time or our breath in this world; only this "one thing" calls us upward to God.

And see how this new thing has affected the adulterous woman, the sinner who represents us all. She is brought forward in all her abomination, deserving death for the act she has knowingly committed... yet she leaves Christ's presence an entirely free woman. Free not merely to go as she pleases, but free from the sin which should have spelled her condemnation.

Here is the new thing as it affects every human soul: the forgiveness of our sins. And what joy this should bring us! For if Jesus who is to judge the heart of all sentient beings does not condemn us, who shall stand with stone in hand to punish our transgression? But heed, my brother, my sister, the Lord's due warning, if you would truly know the grace of this new thing – "from now on do not sin anymore" – or what is new and bringing refreshment will become old and stale very soon. Forward we must strive all the days of our lives, leaving well behind our sins; only in heaven will we take full hold of Him who has taken possession of us by His mercy.

Monday (A,B)

(Dn.13:1-9,15-17,19-30,33-62; Ps.23:1-6; Jn.8:1-11)

"Let the man among you who has no sin
be the first to cast a stone at her."

"Then the audience drifted away one by one, beginning with the elders."
And no one was left to accuse her.

In both our gospel and our first reading a woman is accused of adultery, one justly, the other unjustly. Yet both are freed. For under the old law the innocent were to be set free, but under the new, even the guilty. In the blood of Christ sinners are saved from the fate they deserve; the Lord does not condemn us, and only He has power to do so – for it is always against Him that we sin.

It is curious to note that in both reading and gospel the accused woman is brought before the man against whom she is principally accused of sinning. In the case of Susanna, it is her husband Joakim to whom the people come with their difficult questions, "because he was the most respected of them all"; and the woman in the gospel is brought before Jesus, the Lord and the bridegroom of us all. It is only wed to Him that we find salvation, and He does not disappoint the repentant adulteress today. Nor shall He condemn any of us who stand before Him weeping for our sins against His pure love.

There is a "dark valley" through which we all must walk. One day we shall all stand before the Judge. Some will be persecuted only for righteousness' sake, accused of that which they have not committed; others will stand in the full light of their sin. But all before Christ might find forgiveness, if they but realize their faults and who it is stands before them. For the love of God is unimaginable; it is not something we humans can put our fingers upon. The love of God and the grace and mercy He holds forth will never be deserved by our race. Yet they are there. Yet we are washed clean. Yet the Truth will set us free.

Let no man condemn another; "the angel of God waits" "to receive the sentence from Him" – none of us is able to move His hand. And so, always we must forgive to find His grace alive in our souls.

Monday (C)

(Dn.13:1-9,15-17,19-30,33-62; Ps.23:1-6; Jn.8:12-20)

"Judgment of mine is valid because I am not alone.
I have at my side the One who sent me, the Father."

613

"It is laid down in [the Mosaic] law that evidence given by two persons is valid." Thus does the assembly condemn Susanna to death, because the two elders testify as one against her. But then "God stirred up the holy spirit of a young boy named Daniel," and so we find a better pair of witnesses – the Spirit and Daniel – to refute the lies of the wicked elders. And so Daniel, empowered by the Spirit, separates these evil men; and so the lack of integrity and unity in their testimony is exposed; and so "an angel of God shall receive the sentence from Him and split [them] in two" – the "fine lie" they have told will cost them their heads.

And can there be any truer witness of two than that which is known in the Father and the Son, both of whom testify, in the Spirit, that Jesus is "the light of the world"? This great truth cannot be hidden, and so those whose witness is most perfect must speak it, that "no follower of [His] shall ever walk in darkness" but "shall possess the light of life." This is the will of God, whose Word is true; and this revelation shall be accomplished despite any deceptions devised by those who walk in darkness.

Brothers and sisters, be comforted that the Lord is "at [your] side, with [His] rod and staff that give [you] courage." With Him and with His Spirit you shall be saved from all evil. Be as Susanna in your time of trial: "Through her tears she looked up to heaven, for she trusted in the Lord wholeheartedly," and He will strengthen you and "spread the table before [you] in the sight of [your] foes." Taking Him as your witness, you cannot be denied. And the same justification she has known will be your own.

All wicked men shall meet their end, for lies cannot stand and the "past sins" of the false judges shall "come to term." There is but one Judge whose verdict is true and lasting, and all those who find refuge in Him and His Father shall stand as He does unto eternity.

L. 5. Tues.

Tuesday
(Nm.21:4-9; Ps.102:2-3,16-21; Jn.8:21-30)

"From heaven He beheld the earth,
to hear the groaning of the prisoners,
to release those doomed to die."

As the Lord has said to the Pharisees: "You belong to what is below; I belong to what is above." And truly, how could we come to where He is unless He reached down to lead us there?

The Israelites show just how much they are of this world below when they reject the food of the heavens in utter bitterness: "We are disgusted with this wretched food!" they say of the manna the Lord has provided.

And punishment comes to them in the form of a serpent for their cursing the hand of God.

And the Pharisees are the same. They have the living bread from heaven standing before them, teaching them, yet they cannot grasp what He says and with mockery ask, "Who are you, then?" when He tells them, "I AM." And so they too "will surely die in their sins" for their rejection of the great I AM.

But still there is hope. For the Israelites, Moses "make[s] a serpent and mount[s] it on a pole," and those who gaze upon it are healed from the serpent's deadly bite. And, of course, Jesus Himself will mount the wood of the cross and be fixed there – and the Pharisees and we who gaze upon our sins (which, as with the serpents, have caused this punishment), we who see what we have done and repent thereof, shall be healed, restored, forgiven.

"When you lift up the Son of Man, you will come to realize that I AM," says the Lord. And now we look up at Him who has died for us and pray He will take us where He has gone, that our cry will come to Him, that He will regard "the prayer of the destitute" and lift us up to heaven with Him as we share in His cross.

Wednesday
(Dn.3:14-20,91-92,95; Dn.3:52-56; Jn.8:31-42)

"The truth will set you free."

Sin binds. Like the cords with which "the strongest men in [Nebuchadnezzar's] army bind Shadrach, Meshach, and Abednego," sin fetters our souls and casts us "into the white-hot furnace." "Everyone who lives in sin is the slave of sin." But for those like these three faithful servants who "will not... worship the golden statue that [the king of this world] set up," there is freedom. For the Lord who is "praiseworthy and exalted above all forever," who sits "on the throne of [His] kingdom... in the firmament of heaven," "can save us from the white-hot furnace and from [the king's] hands." For those who "yielded their bodies rather than serve or worship any god except their own God," sin holds no sway. And so we find them "unfettered and unhurt, walking in the fire," the angel of God at their side.

God sits on His "throne upon the cherubim," but He "look[s] into the depths." And so He sends His Son to walk among us and set us free from slavery to sin. As Jesus says, "I came forth from God, and am here." Here *is* the Son; here is the true reflection of the Father. Here, indeed, is Truth itself, by whom we are all set free.

How Jesus strove to bring the truth to "those Jews who believed in Him" but struggled in their acceptance. But the Lord does not pull punches; He does not gloss over the truth, however harsh it may seem. He tells them plainly, "You are trying to kill me," and so they do the works of Satan – and so do they sin. In their pride they deny their sin, and the envious plots in their hearts: "Our father is Abraham," they argue, and not the evil one. "We are no illegitimate breed!" But the truth is that they are, and though it mean His death, Jesus must deliver this truth unto them… for it is all that will set them free.

How little it seems the truth is brought to the people today, and so, how few it seems are set free. As sin goes merrily along, the devil sits laughing… But God is still God, and the Son is still the Son, and all who give themselves to Him and not the idols of this earth will still find themselves set free. Brothers and sisters, "if the Son frees you, you will really be free." Confront your own sin, and entrust all to Him.

L. 5. Thurs.

Thursday
(Gn.17:3-9; Ps.105:4-9; Jn.8:51-59)

"Before Abraham came to be, I AM."

Abraham is a great man, the blessed patriarch, to whom God made the promise: "I will maintain my covenant with you and your descendants after you throughout the ages as an everlasting pact, to be your God and the God of your descendants after you." So Abraham becomes "the father of a host of nations," not just by lineage, but by faith in the promise God has given him and the keeping of the covenant with Him. Abraham is father to all who believe in the one God: the sons of Israel, the Jews; the sons of Ishmael, the Muslims; and all who worship the living Lord and "seek to serve Him constantly."

Yet as great as Abraham is, as fertile as he has become, Jesus is the greater and the more prosperous, for He Himself is the LORD our God, from whom Abraham receives his promise and so his greatness. "Abraham rejoiced that he might see [Jesus'] day. He saw it and was glad." For here come to us is the only Son of the God before whom he "prostrated himself"; here is the LORD of all the nations of whom Abraham is father.

Jesus is equal with the Father, coeternal and all-powerful. He does not make Himself so but receives such glory from the Father, with whom He is always. How hard it is for the Jews to hear this. Though according to their faith they have been waiting for just such arrival of the Holy One, of the Messiah, yet their hearts are unable to accept such divine wonder. And so

616

"they picked up rocks to throw at Jesus" upon His solemn declaration of His divinity.

Is it not just so hard for all of us who call ourselves believers to come to terms with the awesome majesty of Jesus our God? It seems something so far beyond our belief, that God could walk in our midst. And yet HE IS; and so we must see how much greater than any man He is. For though fully a man born in time and murdered upon a cross, yet He is God, living forever as LORD of all. So great a gift, so wonderful a presence, is all that assures us that we "shall never see death" but be as He is, alive in the kingdom as He has promised. Keep His word, and the Word of Life will be with you.

L. 5. Fri.

Friday
(Jer.20:10-13; Ps.18:2-7; Jn.10:31-42)

"He has rescued the life of the poor
from the power of the wicked."

As Jeremiah's persecutors surround him on every side but are "put to utter shame" when he calls out to the Lord, so as the Jews "again tried to arrest Him," Jesus again "eluded their grasp." And so when "the breakers of death surged around [us], the destroying floods overwhelmed [us]..." so when our sins seemed to have conquered our souls, the Lord came to save us.

Evil is all around. Always there is "terror on every side!" and those who would shout, "Denounce! Let us denounce him!" because of our missteps, because of our stumbling into sin. Ever the devil is on the watch to trap us with his wiles and cast our souls into "the nether world." But always, too, the Lord is present, and when to Him we entrust our cause, saying with David, "O Lord, my rock, my fortress, my deliverer," whenever we call upon His name, He hears and saves us from "the snares of death." "Praised be the Lord, I exclaim, and I am safe from my enemies," David sings. "Sing to the Lord, praise the Lord," Jeremiah echoes, and he, too, is safe. All who call upon Him He hears, and affords them His salvation.

"The Jews reached for rocks to stone Him," but still He called to their hearts: "Many good deeds have I shown you from the Father. For which of these do you stone me?" Still He invites them to look upon the good works He has done in His Father's name to see that He is indeed the Son; still He desires their salvation. The signs He performs are recognized by many people who thus "come to believe in Him," but the hardness of heart of these the leaders continues to blind their eyes to the truth of what John the Baptist said and what He is. This ignorance shall find its ultimate expression soon in the crucifixion of the Son of God; but even from this the

617

Lord shall deliver Him – and by this sacrifice we shall all be saved. And many more will come to know thereby that He is God.

The Lord rescues all our souls when we cry out to Him. Let us put all trust in His saving grace.

Saturday
(Ez.37:21-28; Jer.31:10-13; Jn.11:45-57)

"My sanctuary shall be set up among them forever."

Jesus is the fulfillment of God's promise to "gather [His people] from all sides to bring them back to their land"; He is the "one prince for [us] all" by whom God makes complete the "everlasting covenant" with us: "I will be their God, and they shall be my people." It is He "who make[s] Israel holy," who makes us all one in Himself. And so, "no longer shall [we] defile [our]selves," but we "shall live by [His] statutes and carefully observe [His] decrees" now written upon our hearts by the power of the Spirit upon His flesh and blood.

In our gospel the Sanhedrin fear the loss of the Jewish nation on earth when they say, "The Romans will come and sweep away our sanctuary and our nation" because of the wonders Jesus performs and the power He has over all people. So when Caiaphas asks, "Can you not see that it is better for you to have one man die for the people than to have the whole nation destroyed?" it is of the protection of the temple and its worship he speaks and which is his concern. But, of course, he unwittingly prophesies the salvation of all in the eternal, heavenly Temple of the New Jerusalem, where Jesus "gather[s] into one all the dispersed children of God."

Yes, "Jesus would die for the nation"; He would give Himself that all might live. The plan "to kill Him" He shall allow to bear fruit; though all are on the lookout to apprehend Him, yet He shall come to the feast to offer Himself as the spotless Lamb of Passover, to purge the nation of its sins and protect it from final damnation. And so, "He who scattered Israel, now gathers them together, He guards them as a shepherd His flock." And so we should "come streaming to the Lord's blessings: the grain, the wine, and the oil" – so we should come now and consume His Body and His Blood. For the New Covenant is now set in place; His sanctuary is here among us. And forever He is seated in the heavenly kingdom to make intercession for us and for the purging of our sins, to draw into the presence of the Father all His holy children.

He is "likely to come to the feast," brothers and sisters, for the feast would be nothing without Him. It is His sacrifice alone which "turn[s] our mourning into joy," which "shall make [all] merry and dance" in the sanctuary of God's love.

B. Holy Week

Passion (Palm) Sunday
(Is.50:4-7; Ps.22:2,8-9,17-20,23-24; Phil.2:6-11;
Mt.26:14-27:66 or Mk.14:1-15:47 or Lk.22:14-23:56)

"His blood be upon us and upon our children."

"The whole people" cry out for the death of Jesus. "Let Him be crucified," they shout ever more loudly. The sins of us all demand the death of the Son. And though He would have us not bear such guilt – "My Father, if it is possible, let this cup pass from me" – and though even after we have succeeded in our lust for innocent blood, He forgives... yet bear such a burden we must, to find release from its punishment under the shadow of His cross, where, upon the opening of our eyes in the fear of our crimes and the power of Him whom we have crucified, we shall proclaim, "Truly, this was the Son of God!"

Yes, it is an irony that the blood of this "King of the Jews," the Chosen of the chosen, the Messiah, the Son of God, is upon our souls both for condemnation for the great crime all commit in crucifying the Lord always by our sins; and, of course, for our salvation by its cleansing the same sin from our souls through our belief in Him Who Is. And so He accepts our mockery. And so He remains silent before our accusations against Him. And so He "set [His] face like flint," enduring "buffets and spitting"; as "many dogs surround" Him and "a pack of evildoers closes in," He endures all for our sakes, knowing only this will bring us to open our eyes and see the light that is the love of God. "They have pierced my hands and my feet; I can count all my bones." Could more of a sacrifice be made for sinful man? Could greater than this be accomplished in the name of God? What more need you to believe? O let His blood pour upon you!

Brothers and sisters, Christ Jesus "emptied Himself, taking the form of a slave, coming in human likeness... becoming obedient to the point of death, even death on a cross." God has come among us and suffered all for our sake, that we might be washed clean of all the evil within us by His gentle acceptance of all our hatred, of all our doubt and fear, of all the violence we could mount, saying to our heart: I love you still, and my Father, too... that we might return to the grace that is ours in Him. Let us not be ashamed to bend the knee "at the name of Jesus." Let "every tongue confess that Jesus

619

Lent

Christ is Lord, to the glory of God the Father." "You who fear the Lord, praise Him; all you descendants of Jacob, give glory to Him; revere Him all you descendants of Israel." Let His blood pour upon your soul.

L. Holy Week. Mon.

Monday
(Is.42:1-7; Ps.27:1-3,13-14; Jn.12:1-11)

> "I formed you, and set you as a covenant of the people,
> a light for the nations."

He has come "to open the eyes of the blind, to bring out prisoners from confinement, and from the dungeon, those who dwell in darkness." "He establishes justice on the earth," and this justice is His bringing light to our darkness. But He could not release us from the dungeon unless He Himself had entered the dungeon. How else could light penetrate the darkness? And so He not only enters the veil of flesh, humbling Himself to be born as a man, but also gives Himself up to the death we all must die – in our own form He pays the wages of our sin, that we might be released from its prison.

How could we "be stouthearted" "when evildoers come at [us] to devour [our] flesh," we who are so weakened by the scourges of sin, if He had not strengthened us by standing in our stead? How could we truly say with David, "Though war be waged upon me, even then will I trust," if He had not defeated the enemy that comes against us? We can say, "The Lord is my light and my salvation; whom should I fear?" only because Jesus has brought God's justice into our very midst, to our flesh and to our bone, by entering into the world of darkness we have created and taking upon Himself the death we deserved.

Lazarus, who sits at table with Jesus a week before His own death, is a sign of our release from the dungeon, from the tomb of our sin. As "Jews were going over to Jesus and believing in Him on account of Lazarus," so should all be drawn to the promise of new life which the Lord shall fulfill now in His death and resurrection. And as we enter Holy Week, as we prepare ourselves for the great mysteries of our faith, how appropriate for Jesus to sit at table "in the land of the living" with this dead man. See that He will sit with us all just so in the kingdom of heaven.

Now the light comes; now justice is done. The aromatic fragrance of His holy sacrifice fills this house, and darkness shall be banished forever.

Tuesday
(Is.49:1-6; Ps.71:1-6,15,17; Jn.13:21-33,36-38)

"I am made glorious in the sight of the Lord,
and my God is now my strength!"

The Lord is with His servant, with Israel, with Jesus, the Son of David, the Son of Man, the Son of God: "From my mother's womb you are my strength... O God, you have taught me from my youth." And to this "sharp-edged sword" the Lord has concealed "in the shadow of His arm," to this "polished arrow" He has hidden in His quiver, God says: "I will make you a light to the nations, that my salvation may reach to the ends of the earth." He who was called from birth, given His name in His mother's womb, prepared before all the ages, now comes to reveal the glory of God.

And how is it "the Son of Man [is] glorified and God is glorified in Him"? We see in our gospel the moment the glorification begins; we see in our gospel the path by which it comes. At table at the Last Supper Jesus grows "deeply troubled," for the time of His betrayal has come. Judas eats the morsel of food dipped in the dish and "immediately after, Satan entered his heart." Then, "no sooner had Judas eaten the morsel than he went out," and, we are told, "It was night." And immediately upon Judas' leaving, the Lord proclaims His glorification has begun.

Here begins the Passion. Here begins the first of the three days Jesus will spend in the belly of the earth. How unlike the days the Servant spent in His mother's womb these days shall be! And yet it is precisely these days and in this way that what God has prepared for Him and for all creation shall come to its fulfillment. Now shall the arrow be sharpened fully and shot forth to pierce all men's hearts with truth – even as the nails pierce His hands and the sword His side. Through the depths of such absolute darkness, light shall shine forth, and this light shall in time reach to the ends of the world.

Now the time has come. Now all shall abandon Him. Now by the Suffering Servant shall all be saved.

Wednesday
(Is.50:4-9; Ps.69:8-10,21-22,31,33-34; Mt.26:14-25)

"The Son of Man is departing, as Scripture says of Him."

Of Him in Scripture we read, "Morning after morning He opens my ear that I may hear; and I have not rebelled, have not turned back." Even as death approaches, even as His betrayer goes forth (perhaps especially at this

621

dark time), He sets His face "like flint" to confront those who oppose Him, those who would destroy Him. In His own voice He speaks to us in the first reading and the psalm of His trial and His resolve: "I gave my back to those who beat me, my cheeks to those who plucked my beard," though "they put gall in my food, and in my thirst they gave me vinegar to drink." And He stands alone before such blasphemy – "I looked for sympathy, but there was none; for comforters, and I found none."

Though only one of the Twelve betrays Him, all but John abandon Him in His brokenness; none stands by His side as He "bear[s] insult" in the Name of God. But the Father does not desert Him: "See, the Lord God is my help." "For the Lord hears the poor, and His own who are in bonds He spurns not." And when He cries from the cross, it is not His fate He bemoans, but our own, whose dark separation from God He takes upon Himself as our guilt He bears.

Yes, He must depart in this way; He must suffer at our hands. But that it is written so, and that by this our souls are made whole, in no way nullifies that we have sinned – sin remains the evil it is. As for Judas, yet it would have been "better for him if he had never been born," for the fires of hell are real; and as for the souls who abandon Him, as for *all* His disciples, it is only through similar darkness that we shall come back to His light.

Tears will fill our eyes as we look upon Him whom we have pierced. Yet, fear not, for the Lord hears the cry of the "lowly ones... who seek God"; and Scripture speaks just as faithfully of the third day.

L. Triduum. Holy Thurs.

Holy Thursday
– Mass of the Lord's Supper –
(Ex.12:1-8,11-14; Ps.116:12-13,15-18,1Cor.10:6; 1Cor.11:23-26; Jn.13:1-15)

"This cup is the New Covenant in my blood."

For this cup holds the Blood of our Lord. And, "Seeing the blood, I will pass over you," says the Lord. "When I strike the land of Egypt, no destructive blow will come upon you." As the Israelites mark each of their houses with the blood of a lamb, so our bodies are marked by the Blood of the Lamb; and so we are saved by the Lord our God and become temples of His Spirit.

"How shall I make a return to the Lord for all the good He has done for me?" the psalmist cries in joy. Each day we "offer sacrifice of thanksgiving," taking up "the cup of salvation" and "call[ing] upon the name of the Lord": each day we partake of His blessed Body and Blood. And sharing in this celebration of the Eucharist we "proclaim the death of the Lord until He comes"; and so, into our midst He comes.

"He poured water into a basin and began to wash the disciples' feet and dry them with the towel around his waist" as "a model to follow": "as I have done for you, you should also do." He says to His brothers in the upper room the night "His hour had come to pass from this world to the Father": "You ought to wash one another's feet." And so by this teaching, and so by His masterful lead, He multiplies His presence in the world through His twelve apostles. And so shall these souls by whom the Bread of Life is multiplied, by whom we have inheritance with the Lord, wash the feet of all His followers by their witness and the ministry they shall bring to the ends of the earth. And so shall all who have bathed in His Blood be made clean for the Holy Day.

And we, as they, as the Lord, find the strength to lay down our lives in service of one another by being as our Jesus, who was "fully aware that the Father had put everything in His power and that He had come from God and was returning to Him." Any power that any have comes only from the Father, and comes only through the Son, and is known only in His Blood – which all must share, by which all must be anointed, if we are to be preserved until the coming of the Christ again into this world of darkness.

L. Triduum. Good Fri.

Good Friday
– Celebration of the Lord's Passion –
(Is.52:13-53:12; Ps.31:2,6,12-13,15-17,25,Lk.23:46; Heb.4:14-16,5:7-9; Jn.18:1-19:42)

"He shall be raised high and greatly exalted."

Here is your king: "Jesus the Nazarene, the King of the Jews," Pilate has written upon His cross. Here He is lifted up, where "many were amazed at Him – so marred was His look beyond human semblance and His appearance beyond the sons of man." Yet "shall He startle many nations; because of Him kings shall stand speechless." The Scripture passage is fulfilled: "They will look upon Him whom they have pierced." And there they shall see that He who "was spurned and avoided by people... one of those from whom people hide their faces," held in "no esteem" as He was... this same "lamb led to the slaughter" "shall divide the spoils with the mighty"; for as He has been lifted up on the cross, debased beyond all others, so He shall be raised on high in His kingdom, one with the Father in heaven. Here they "wove a crown out of thorns and placed it on His head." Here they "clothed Him in a purple cloak, and they came to Him and said, 'Hail, King of the Jews.' And they struck Him repeatedly." But there no mockery shall He know; there all shall see that He is the Son of God.

Brothers and sisters, "we have a great high priest who has passed through the heavens, Jesus, the Son of God." Our weaknesses He has known in full, and now He brings us "light in fullness of days." Though on earth "He offered prayers and supplications with loud cries and tears," now has He become "the source of eternal salvation for all who obey Him." For all the tears He shed, all the scourging He underwent, all the humiliation He experienced and the death He knew, were all for our sake. "It was our infirmities that He bore, our sufferings that He endured." And having suffered in our stead for the sins of those by whom He is condemned, now He has come unto what is His own, and invites us there as well.

"He shall take away the sins of many, and win pardon for their offenses." The guilt of the nations is removed by Him who had "no guilt in Him," and is known by all who "take refuge" in His wounds. And so, "take courage and be stouthearted, all you who hope in the Lord"; though we, too, may be "an object of reproach" in this world of sin, He awaits us all in His heavenly kingdom. And for this we call this Friday "good."

V. EASTER

A. Octave of Easter

Easter Vigil

(Gn.1:1-2:2; Ps.104:1-2,5-6,10,12-14,24,35 or Ps.33:4-7,12-13,20-22; Gn.22:1-18;
Ps.16:5,8-11; Ex.14:15-15:1; Ex.15:1-6,17-18; Is.54:5-14; Ps.30:2,4-6,11-13; Is.55:1-
11; Is.12:2-6; Bar.3:9-15,32-4:4; Ps.19:8-11; Ez.36:16-17a,18-28; Ps.42:3,5,43:3,4;
Rom.6:3-11; Ps.118:1-2,16-17,22-23; Mt.28:1-10 or Mk.16:1-7 or Lk.24:1-12)

"He is not here."

The women come faithfully to the tomb early Easter morning. What do they find but that the stone is rolled back from its gaping mouth; and angel(s) in white deliver unto them the message of the ages: "He has been raised."

This night, this early morning, we are led through salvation history, through our own history as human beings made in the image of God here upon the face of the earth, souls coming unto heaven. "Our soul waits for the Lord, who is our help and our shield," is the song of the Old Testament. From the beginning of Creation our hearts are set on Him. Along the way "Abraham took the wood for the holocaust and laid it on his son Isaac's shoulders," prefiguring the Father's own sacrifice of His Son for our sins and our salvation. Moses led the Israelites out of Egypt, out of the land of sin, through the Red Sea, "with the water like a wall to their right and to their left," prefiguring our Baptism as Christians; and they "sing to the Lord for He is gloriously triumphant," prefiguring our own joy.

Always we are reminded by the prophets of old: "The Lord calls you back, like a wife forsaken and grieved in spirit." And he who heard the call even then sang, "O Lord, you brought me up from the nether world; you preserved me from those going down into the pit." Yes, repeatedly the Lord calls out through His prophets: "Come to the water!... Come, without paying and without cost, drink wine and milk!" He promises, "With joy you will draw water at the fountain of salvation." We who "have forsaken the fountain of wisdom" by the sin that plagues our inheritance are called back to "the One who established the earth for all time... before whom the stars at their posts shine and rejoice"; we are called to cling to the Word of God, to Wisdom: "Turn, O Jacob, and receive her: walk by her light toward splendor." For the sake of His Name, the Lord who "scattered them among the nations" now beckons His children home. And those of faith sing with David, "Send forth your light and your fidelity; they shall lead me on and bring me to your holy mountain, to your dwelling place."

Brothers and sisters, we know that "we who were baptized into Christ Jesus were baptized into His death," the death to sin. And having been "buried with Him," we are also raised with Him this night, this morning, that "we too might live in newness of life." Now His holy dwelling place is here among us with the purest of light that rises this day. Let us be children of this holy Light. No longer in the tomb let us dwell.

Easter Sunday
(Acts 10:34a,37-43; Ps.118:1-2,16-17,22-24; Col.3:1-4 or 1Cor.5:6b-8; Jn.20:1-9 or Lk.24:13-35)

"Everyone who believes in Him will receive forgiveness of sins
through His name."

"His mercy endures forever," brothers and sisters, and it is for us to "declare the works of the Lord": that Jesus was "raised on the third day," that He lives, that He still is "healing all those oppressed by the devil." With Peter and the apostles we must "preach to the people and testify" that "the right hand of the Lord is exalted." Yes, "they put Him to death by hanging Him on a tree," but "the stone which the builders rejected has become the cornerstone." Yes, we all bear guilt for the death of the Son, but in His rising He brings about the death of our sin.

Brothers and sisters, "you were raised with Christ" and should have nothing more to do with sin. "Christ is seated at the right hand of God," and we must be seated there with Him. To Him should we raise our eyes for our "life is hidden with Christ in God." "Therefore, let us celebrate the feast, not with the old yeast, the yeast of malice and wickedness, but with the unleavened bread of sincerity and truth." No more should sin find place in us or grow within us unto death, but now that new life has come, we should find our place with Him.

Peter and John ran to the tomb upon hearing the news that Jesus was not there. Upon entering, they "saw and believed," they "understood the Scripture that He had to rise from the dead." Upon believing, death no longer held dominion over them; and soon they would proclaim to all the world the Gospel of life and peace. Soon the cornerstone of truth would take hold of all who heard their words, and grow in time unto heaven. And His kingdom shall not be removed.

Brothers and sisters, each day the Lord opens the Scriptures to us as we gather as His children. Each day we recognize Him in the breaking of the bread. Each day we are called to make known the glory of the resurrection we hold in "our hearts burning within as He [speaks] to us on the way." Here at His table we receive Him each day in Word and in Sacrament. May all men know the gift of life that is ours through the forgiveness of sins He offers. Let us pray that all will believe.

Monday

(Acts 2:14,22-33; Ps.16:1-2,5,7-11; Mt.28:8-15)

"You will not abandon my soul to the nether world,
nor will you suffer your faithful one to undergo corruption."

"It was impossible that death should keep its hold on Him." And so "the paths of life" we now walk; "joy in [His] presence" is ours – "in confidence" we abide forever. For God has "raised Him up again," this Jesus, our Lord. Let us be witnesses of His truth to the ends of the earth. Like Peter, our Holy Father, let us be faithful to the Word at work within us.

As the women "ran to carry the good news to [Jesus'] disciples" that He, the Lord, was no longer in the tomb, in the belly of this earth, the guards ran to the chief priests, who concocted a lie. See how the ways diverge between truth and lie. And see today the power with which Peter, inspired by the Holy Spirit, the Spirit of Truth, stands up even amongst those who had Jesus crucified, and proclaims the truth of the risen Lord. And God is with Him. He has heard the Lord's words: "Peace!" and "Do not be afraid!" He knows full well that his soul will never be abandoned to the nether world; he has life at work in him, the life that comes from "the resurrection of the Messiah." And so he witnesses in strength, as do our popes to this day.

Let us "live on in hope," brothers and sisters, "half-overjoyed and half-fearful," though only with the fear of God which overwhelms our souls, and He will be before us always, speaking words of peace; and we will see Him walking in the places He was wont to walk on earth… and we will see Him walking everywhere we walk. For by our side will He be constantly in the power of the Spirit to lead and guide us always unto Life, the life that is already with us and will never leave us.

The Lord is risen, alleluia! The powers of death and hell shall never touch us, for in Him alone do we "take refuge," He alone is our "allotted portion and cup" – in Him alone do we believe, and so we "shall not be disturbed" even by the darkness of night. The Light has dawned; in Him let our souls rejoice.

Tuesday
(Acts 2:36-41; Ps.33:4-5,18-20,22; Jn.20:11-18)

"Let the whole house of Israel know beyond any doubt
that God has made both Lord and Messiah
this Jesus whom you crucified."

Brothers and sisters, we are all as Mary Magdalene who "stood weeping beside the tomb," and like the Jews who were "deeply shaken" by the words of Peter. Though it is to the Chosen people "that the promise was made," it extends "to all those still far off whom the Lord our God calls." To all sinners, to all who ask His apostles, "What are we to do, brothers?" the Lord responds: "Reform and be baptized... in the name of Jesus Christ, that your sins may be forgiven"; indeed, then we "shall receive the gift of the Holy Spirit" – then our eyes shall be opened to His presence among us as we turn to Him in tears.

"She turned around and caught sight of Jesus standing there," this greatest of sinners become most faithful disciple. And as He speaks the name of her who cares only for Him – "Mary!" – so He calls by name "each one" of us who come to Him in our desperation; so He cares for all sinners who love Him and seek Him with all their heart. And the same joy that she has known shall also be ours; we shall declare, "I have seen the Lord!" to all who wait to hear of Him.

"Save yourselves from this generation which has gone astray," Peter urges his fellow Jews on Pentecost day, and "some three thousand" accepted his message and were baptized. Here is where the Church begins to grow, here among those who crucified the Lord – here among His own brothers in the flesh. And though the message is primarily to them this day, indeed it is for all who would be grafted to this tree of life, to this race of whom Jesus is come. For, indeed, it is so that all are sinners, that all bear the guilt of His crucifixion; and so to all who hear His call for repentance, forgiveness may come, and the Spirit follow.

"The eyes of the Lord are upon those who fear Him... to deliver them from death." What was sung of under the Old Covenant is even truer today; and so let what was true of those faithful under the Old be so with us now. Let it be that "our soul waits for the Lord." Let us declare, "Upright is the word of the Lord," and the Word in its fullness shall be ours, and the tears we cry shall be answered quickly by our Lord and Savior who calls us each by name.

Wednesday
(Acts 3:1-10; Ps.105:1-9; Lk.24:13-35)

"The Lord is risen! It is true!"

And how it is proven this day! The two disciples find their "hearts burning inside" as He "explain[s] the Scriptures" to them on the road to Emmaus, and then they come "to know Him in the breaking of bread." "The Eleven and the rest of the company" of disciples rejoice in Jerusalem because "He has appeared to Simon." And the crippled beggar at the Beautiful Gate is pulled up by Peter "in the name of Jesus Christ the Nazarean," and he goes "into the temple with [Peter and John] – walking, jumping about, and praising God." "Rejoice, O hearts that seek the Lord!"

Brothers and sisters, the Church is as this crippled beggar at the temple gate; it is as these confused disciples sojourning for answers to their deepest questions and fears – it is the whole company assembled and astounded and declaring with joy the truth of God's presence among us. To the beggar the Lord says with Peter, "Look at us!" To those on the road to Emmaus He says, "How slow you are to believe!" And to all He appears in the breaking of the bread. The beggar He heals; in the seeker He instills faith; and to us all He leaves His Blessed Sacrament, the greatest proof of His presence.

"Sing to Him, sing His praise, proclaim all His wondrous deeds." And as great as His healing may be, as wonderful as His teaching is, the greatest of these is the table He sets before us and the Body and Blood with which He nourishes us. Here is His love most known, here where we "give thanks to the Lord" and "invoke His name." For in this we are healed, in this His teaching is made real – until the end of time this shall stand as proof of His presence... in this is ever declared, "The Lord is risen!"

"He remembers His covenant which He made binding for a thousand generations." Never shall this blessing leave us, brothers and sisters. Always we have His Word at work within us, and always we share His Body and His Blood. Here He remains "powerful in word and deed in the eyes of God and all the people." Let us not fail to declare all He has done for us; let us never be afraid to proclaim His truth. For then all shall be "struck with astonishment"; then all shall know the Risen Lord.

Thursday

(Acts 3:11-26; Ps.8:2,5-9; Lk.24:35-48)

"In His name, penance for the remission of sins
is to be preached to all nations, beginning at Jerusalem."

And so Peter begins the preaching at the temple: "When God raised up His servant, He sent Him to you first to bless you by turning you from your evil ways," he announces clearly to the Jews, those first to hear of the Savior, Jesus. And again he speaks boldly and repeatedly of their sin: "You disowned the Holy and Just One... You put to death the Author of life," for it is absolutely essential that they recognize their guilt if they are to find their salvation. How can they repent of what they do not see? How can "a season of refreshment be granted" through Jesus if they do not know that they are despoiled? And brothers and sisters, it is certainly no different for us. We *must* recognize our own complicity in the Lord's death or we shall have no place with Him in life. Hear the message of His apostle: "Reform your lives! Turn to God, that your sins may be wiped away!" If you have nothing to reform, how are you a hearer of the Good News? And if your repentance falls short of knowing the blood of Christ upon your hands, how ineffective it will be.

"All the prophets... have announced the events of these days." "God has brought to fulfillment by this means what He announced long ago: that His Messiah would suffer." What Peter proclaims, Jesus confirms in His own teaching to the disciples, "It is written that the Messiah must suffer and rise from the dead on the third day," as "He open[s] their minds to the understanding of the Scriptures." What must be has been, and now is – Jesus has died and risen. "Look at my hands and my feet; it is really I," He says to His incredulous apostles. And so in "flesh and bones" the Truth has become known, and this same flesh we eat each day.

The disciples' same "sheer joy and wonder" we should share, brothers and sisters. For what is theirs is ours, too. Though "out of ignorance" we crucified Him, in grace we now know Him. And so should we not cry out, "O Lord, our Lord, how glorious is your name over all the earth"? Should His blessed care for this sinful man not make us incredulous with joy? For though man is guilty of the Lord's own death, yet He has "made him little less than the angels, and crowned him with glory and honor." How little we deserve the Messiah, now glorified in heaven, to be with us; but O how generous He is! No "power or holiness of our own" has brought us to life – it is His forgiveness that has made us whole.

Friday
(Acts 4:1-12; Ps.118:1-2,4,22-27; Jn.21:1-14)

"Jesus is 'the stone rejected by you the builders
which has become the cornerstone.'"

What Peter has proclaimed to the people, he now proclaims even more boldly to their leaders: "There is no other name in the whole world given to men by which we are to be saved." Jesus, whom they crucified, is the Messiah. And the same quote Jesus offered the Pharisees after making it clear to them they would lose dominion over God's vineyard – over His people, over His Church – Peter invokes before the high-priestly class today... for here standing before them is the new authority on earth.

And so, here the Church is gathered, under Peter and the apostles. This day of preaching in Jesus' name by the power of the Holy Spirit has brought about five thousand children to God, and there shall be no stopping the power of the Word which goes forth to draw in all believers. On the Church goes "proclaiming the resurrection of the dead in the person of Jesus."

Our gospel today is the perfect parallel to our first reading, and reveals just from where the power of the apostles' preaching comes. First, it shows Peter as the clear leader. He says among the seven – the number of fullness – disciples assembled: "I am going out to fish." And they reply: "We will join you." All night they toil in vain. Why? Because they lack the cornerstone who comes to them in the morning. (Notice in our first reading Peter and John are put in jail for the night to await their trial in the morning. But, ironically, this night is less of a prison than the one spent toiling in vain on the sea... for this day they have been most fruitful; for by this time they have been anointed by the Spirit.)

In the morning Jesus stands upon the shore and instructs them where to cast their net, much as He did when first He called His fishermen apostles. And like that morning, their catch is overwhelming. John cries, "It is the Lord!" and Peter jumps into the water to swim to his Jesus as the others tow the net and fish behind him. Once all have come to land, it is Peter who goes "aboard and haul[s] ashore the net loaded with sizable fish" and drops it at the Lord's feet. But it is the single fish Jesus has prepared which is most important, with which they must begin their feast. For Jesus is that fish Himself, the cornerstone upon whom the tallest of buildings stands. And see how He feeds them as at the Eucharistic table: "Jesus came over, took the bread and gave it to them, and did the same with the fish." Here the Bread of Life is distributed to those who shall impart it to all others.

One hundred and fifty-three (the number of Hail Marys in a full Rosary, pre-Mysteries of Light) fish are gathered by the disciples in a net beyond the point of breaking. Five thousand men are drawn into the fold by Peter and John's fearless speaking. God's Church is here built up on the cornerstone that is Jesus; and so we exclaim with our psalmist today: "O Lord, grant salvation! O Lord, grant prosperity! Blessed is He who comes in the name of the Lord; we bless you from the house of the Lord. The Lord is God, and He has given us light." Amen.

Saturday
(Acts 4:13-21; Ps.118:1,14-21; Mk.16:9-15)

"Go into the whole world
and proclaim the good news to all creation."

How faithfully Peter and John accomplish the Lord's command, and with what strength, so much so that our first reading tells us, "The priests and elders were amazed as they observed [their] self-assurance" – for these "were uneducated men of no standing." How can this be? they must have queried inside. "Then they recognized these men as having been with Jesus." And so the answer had come: it is from Him all power derives. In His Spirit all God's disciples "declare the works of the Lord."

And how wonderfully silenced the leaders of the people are: "When they saw the man who had been cured standing there with them, they could think of nothing to say." For the works of the Lord speak for themselves, and the power of the Spirit cannot be denied. And though these priests of the Old Covenant attempt to silence the glory of God, telling Peter and John "that under no circumstances were they to speak the name of Jesus or teach about Him," these first of apostles declare confidently, "We cannot help speaking of what we have heard and seen." Indeed, "a remarkable show of power [takes] place in them."

And what have they heard and seen? Our gospel tells us: "Jesus rose from the dead early on the first day of the week." From Mary Magdalene, to whom He first appeared, "they heard that He was alive and had been seen by her." And the same "good news" is announced to them by the two disciples who had sojourned to Emmaus. And though "they refused to believe it," and though when "Jesus was revealed to the Eleven," when they saw His risen presence for themselves, He chastised them "for their disbelief and their stubbornness" – though the doubt from human corruption still clings to them, it shall no longer be so (as evidenced by Peter and John) when Pentecost has come. In the descent of the Holy Spirit upon the apostles, the Word shall be preached and believed in strength and power.

"The right hand of the Lord has struck with power." "The joyful shout of victory in the tents of the just" has come now in fullness to all His

Easter

children who hear and see and declare that the Lord is risen. "My strength and my courage is the Lord, and He has been my savior," sing all the redeemed. As the psalmist "give[s] thanks to the Lord" and the people who had witnessed the great work wrought through the apostles "were praising God for what had happened," so joy is unbounded for all who enter the "gates of justice" and know in their bones the power of the Spirit at work through the resurrection of Jesus the Christ. Brothers and sisters, let your joy be known by all; declare the good news to all the earth, that light may come to a world in darkness.

E. Oct. Sun. (A)

Divine Mercy Sunday (A)
(Acts 2:42-47; Ps.118:1-4,13-15,22-24; 1Pt.1:3-9; Jn.20:19-31)

"Blessed are those who have not seen and have believed."

Jesus comes to the disciples, repeatedly appearing to them after His Resurrection, to make certain there is absolutely no doubt in them: "Do not be unbelieving, but believe." He invites them even to put their fingers in His hands and their hands into His side. To Thomas He speaks, yes, but them all He teaches. For He is commissioning them to go forth in His name in word and sacrament to bring forth life to souls who are dying, to preach the salvation from sin by His resurrection from the dead. "Peace be with you," He says to His Twelve. "As the Father has sent me, so I send you." And so He breathes on them the Holy Spirit, giving them power even to forgive men's sins. Now, those to whom they shall proclaim that God "in His great mercy gave us a new birth to a living hope through the resurrection of Jesus Christ from the dead" will not have had the benefit of seeing the Lord. And so, how can one expect them to believe just by the word of another if the speaker of that word is not completely convinced of its truth? Their witness, their commitment, must extend even to the grave – as it shall – if it is to go beyond the grave.

And the strength of the apostles' witness and the fruit it has borne – which, in turn, becomes a faithful witness unto others – is greatly evident in our reading from Acts. Here we are told the first disciples "devoted themselves to the teaching of the apostles and to the communal life, to the breaking of bread and to the prayers." Sharing all in common, their lives were centered on daily prayer and the Eucharistic meal, the feast of thanksgiving. And "with exultation and sincerity of heart, praising God and enjoying favor with all the people," they lived their lives in truth, they lived their lives in faith. What Peter ascribes to the disciples of Christ we find in these: "Although you have not seen Him you love Him; even though you do not see Him now... you rejoice with an indescribable and glorious joy, as

634

you attain the goal of your faith, the salvation of your souls." How effective his and the other apostles' witness has been.

Brothers and sisters, "His mercy endures forever." The apostles' words reach down to us this day and the sacraments of their hands are still in our midst. And so "the joyful shout of victory in the tents of the just" we too should know. We too should sing, "My strength and my courage is the Lord, and He has been my savior." Though the Church has been made to suffer persecution and been dispersed to the ends of the earth, this is but to bring the Word forth, and through all suffering to make it perfect within us. For ultimately the kingdom is not in this place; heaven we cannot completely see. Only faith will lead us to the Lord's risen presence.

Divine Mercy Sunday (B)
(Acts 4:32-35; Ps.118:1-4,16-18,22-24; 1Jn.5:1-6; Jn.20:19-31)

"His mercy endures forever."

Our psalmist "was hard pressed and was falling, but the Lord helped" him. The disciples were locked in their rooms for fear, but "Jesus came and stood in their midst and said to them, 'Peace be with you.'" Thomas was hardened in unbelief, but His God appeared to him and said, "Bring your hand and put it into my side." We are all sinners, but to us each, Christ offers mercy.

From that side into which Thomas placed his hand "blood and water" poured forth for the cleansing of souls and the realization of new life. The institution of Baptism and the Eucharist had come, and so the Church is born from the side of its Savior. And so all souls are justified; and so all souls find new life. And so all of the "community of believers" become "of one heart and mind."

This is Divine Mercy Sunday, so proclaimed by the Spirit who testifies through Holy Church, and that to which the Spirit testifies is truth. God's encompassing mercy our Mother and our Lord would have us celebrate this day – of that which Jesus thirsts to share with us, she and He would have us drink. Let none be unbelieving. Let none despair. Let all be blessed to own that faith which "conquers the world," that makes us "children of God." The Lord is ready to forgive men's sins; He is desirous of this above all things. He has given power to His disciples to forgive in His name... Let all come and share in His mercy.

Let us love God and one another, my brothers and sisters. Let us love the Father by accepting the grace that comes from His Son, and let us love one another by sharing that grace and mercy with everyone. We keep His Word when we share in His mercy, when we swim in the ocean of love the water and blood from His side create. And new life will be our own as it was for the first disciples; there is nothing lacking for "those who have not seen but believed." In fact, more blessed may we be now, for we must have the greater faith.

Forever the Lord's mercy endures. Every day it is poured forth. And today we declare in truth its great graces, that all might be one in the Lord.

E. Oct. Sun. (C)

Divine Mercy Sunday (C)
(Acts 5:12-16; Ps.118:1-4,22-27; Rv.1:9-13,17-19; Jn.20:19-31)

"When I caught sight of Him,
I fell down at His feet as though dead."

But Jesus "touched [John] with His right hand and said, 'Do not be afraid.'" Thomas exclaimed, "My Lord and my God!" as he humbled himself at the sight of the risen Christ who had appeared before him, and so he was blessed with faith. The first believers "carried the sick out into the streets and laid them on cots and mats so that when Peter came by, at least his shadow might fall on one or another of them." And the sick and possessed brought forth "were all cured." All "those who fear the Lord" know His eternal mercy!

Brothers and sisters, let us not be afraid to humble ourselves in awe before the mighty Lord and the apostles He sends forth in His name and with the blessing of the Father. We must set our hearts on "the first and the last, the One who lives," and let nothing keep us from the path to His grace, to the glorious vision of His holy face. He waits. He waits in expectation for all humble souls to turn to the blood poured out by the nail marks in His hands and the wound in His side. He wishes not to have died in vain, and so with power He sends the Spirit out through the ministry and the sacraments of His Church on earth.

"Many signs and wonders were done among the people at the hands of the apostles," and these same wonders and more are offered for our edification and our salvation this day. The time of fulfillment is upon us and the Lord Jesus is not remiss with His graces: generously the fount of mercy gushes forth. And as John was surrounded by water on the island of Patmos in the day of his divine vision, so are we surrounded with the blessings of the Lord, if we but come to His presence. He is near. He is waiting. Do not doubt; but believe – and whatever ailment of body or soul, heart or mind, which seems to obstruct your reception of the glory of God, will be removed in an instant, if you but fall down at His feet in awe.

Dead before Him we must be, dead to sin and sadness. Alive in the Spirit we must remain, keeping His peace within us. With John let us share "the distress, the kingdom, and the endurance we have in Jesus," and the distress will disappear and the kingdom come, even as we endure all in His name. God's "peace be with you."

B. Weeks 2 – 7

Second Week

Monday
(Acts 4:23-31; Ps.2:1-9; Jn.3:1-8)

"No one can see the rule of God
unless he is begotten from above."

"Princes conspire together against the Lord and against His anointed," we are told in our psalm as well as our first reading. But their rule shall be shattered "like an earthen dish" by the power of the Spirit and God's anointed One, to whom He gives "the nations as an inheritance." And in the Book of Acts we see the apostles begin to collect such inheritance "in the name of Jesus," the "holy Servant" of the Sovereign Lord, the King He has set up "on Zion, [His] holy mountain." All stream to Him upon seeing the "cures and signs and wonders" worked through them by the Holy Spirit.

In our gospel, it is these undeniable signs of God's presence which lead a member of the princes who will crucify the Christ to seek understanding from Jesus. And how sad is the question Nicodemus whispers in the night to our Lord: "How can a man be born again once he is old?" It is sad not only because of the futility of his interpretation to "return to his mother's womb," but mainly because this is all he can see. He is so of the flesh he cannot understand anything but the flesh; and this sense extends even to the Pharisees' grasp of the law, which has become as an empty shell void of meaning – bereft of the Spirit as they are. There is hope Nicodemus will hear the words of Jesus; there is possibility other leaders of the people will come to life. But first they will have to leave their vain pursuits behind.

"The wind blows where it will... but you do not know where it comes from, or where it goes." So it is with the disciples as by the powerful wind of the Holy Spirit "the place where they were gathered shook as they prayed"; and so, filled with the Holy Spirit they "continued to speak God's word with confidence." They are born from above. They have new life in the name of Jesus. All their lives are sacrificed with Him to the will of God. And so the princes have no power over them, but to make them rejoice at the persecution they find at their empty hands.

"You must all be begotten from above," brothers and sisters. None is to be left behind with the carcasses that gather beneath the eagles' circling flight. Take refuge in the Lord of Life; be born now in His Spirit.

Tuesday
(Acts 4:32-37; Ps.93:1-2,5; Jn.3:7-15)

"The community of believers were of one heart and one mind."

This oneness is itself of heaven, is itself the sign that they are "begotten of the Spirit." And this oneness is reflected in a very real manner in the fact that "none of them ever claimed anything as his own; rather, everything was held in common." This sharing of goods, of "lay[ing] them at the feet of the apostles to be distributed to everyone according to his need," is but an earthly thing. It is easy to see; it is easy to know, for it deals indeed with the things of the earth. But if like Nicodemus this earthly matter is beyond our comprehension, if we say such living as one on this plane is impossible, how far short we will fall of understanding the oneness that exists on the heavenly plane. For do you not see that one not only reflects the other, but in fact leads to the other? How can one be as the wind which "blows where it will," how can one's origin and destination be said to be unknown if one is unduly placed, indeed rooted, in the houses, in the property of this earth? And so Barnabas is indeed a "son of encouragement," because by selling his entire farm and laying the money derived therewith at the apostles' feet he is saying: I no longer live here on earth. My home is in heaven.

How tied we can be to earthly things. How blinded by them. And yet they can be a means to heaven, if one gives them to the Lord. For then already here in this world we will begin to see and know the life of heaven. Even now the Spirit shall move within us and our eyes will be opened to see "that all who believe may have eternal life" in Jesus. Yes, by the giving up of our goods, by dying to self in this real way, we may transcend this earthly plane.

"Holiness befits your house, O Lord, for length of days." Do you not understand this matter, brothers and sisters? Do you not see that you are called here on earth during your limited length of days to live as though in heaven? Do you not know that it is but this which will lead to the unlimited number of days lived in holiness in heaven? Do not think that one is somehow separated from the other, as if heaven can be kept apart, as if its power is not all-encompassing. Here you must begin; even here you must find yourself on that eternal road. For such has Jesus been lifted up, to show you the emptiness of your earthly self. To such oneness with Him and His disciples does He call you – to be a child of heaven. Let us walk together in the Spirit of the Lord and love one another with the love that comes only from God.

Wednesday
(Acts 5:17-26; Ps.34:2-9; Jn.3:16-21)

"He who acts in truth comes into the light,
to make clear that his deeds are done in God."

Jesus is "the light [that] came into the world," and "happy the man who takes refuge in Him." None shall fear anymore who love the Lord, for He shall answer all his cries. And newness of life shall be ours.

The Sadducees, who do not believe in the resurrection of the dead, "arrested the apostles and threw them into public jail." They attempted to hide the truth in darkness, to kill the light of the Spirit. "During the night, however, an angel of the Lord opened the gates of the jail [and] led them forth," telling them to preach again in the temple "about this new life." And so, "they went into the temple at dawn and resumed their teaching." Do you see the resurrection at work here, brothers and sisters? Do you see how the Word is rescued from the darkness of night, from the prison into which the world would cast it, and brought into the clear light of dawn? The Truth cannot be chained and death shall never overcome life.

And what do the apostles preach but the words Jesus whispers into the waiting ears of Nicodemus in the middle of the night – bringing him, too, out of the darkness into the Lord's marvelous light: "Yes, God so loved the world that He gave His only Son that whoever believes in Him may not die but may have eternal life." Eternal life! This is the Word come from God through His only Son, begotten in love for us all. The high priest and the Sadducees would hide this; but here one of the leaders listens. He does not question anymore how this can be. And so the seed of eternal life is planted in his heart.

That seed must be planted in all hearts, and so the apostles repeatedly return to preaching, unafraid of the consequences. For how clearly it has been shown them that "the angel of the Lord encamps around those who fear Him, and delivers them." How well they believe their own words, that in Jesus is found eternal life. In their hearts burns the faith, and so, openly they speak. And though they shall see just how much "men loved darkness rather than light," yet they shall seek the salvation of all: unto death they shall stand in the light of truth, confident in the resurrection to follow.

May all believe "in the name of God's only Son" and thus avoid condemnation. May all stand confidently in the Light of the new day, for the darkness of sin and death is banished when we call upon His Name.

639

Thursday
(Acts 5:27-33; Ps.34:2,7,9,17-20; Jn.3:31-36)

"The One whom God has sent speaks the words of God;
He does not ration His gift of the Spirit."

And thus it is that Peter and the apostles, sent by the Lord to speak His words, can boldly proclaim to the Sanhedrin's chastisement for continuing "to teach about that name": "Better for us to obey God than men!" In no way do they ration the Spirit as they testify that God "has raised up Jesus whom [they] put to death," that it is "He whom God has exalted at His right hand as ruler and savior," that He is "to bring repentance to Israel and forgiveness of sins." The praise of God and of His Son is "ever in [their] mouth," for indeed they know the happiness of "the man who takes refuge in Him."

And they know, too, the folly of those who deny the Truth of God's presence in Jesus the Christ. For as He Himself says to Nicodemus in our gospel, "Whoever disobeys the Son will not see life, but must endure the wrath of God," and as David states in his psalm, "The Lord confronts evildoers, to destroy remembrance of them from the earth," so the blessed Rock and his fellow apostles convey to the high priest and the Sanhedrin as they are persecuted by their hands. Their declaration that not only do they testify to Jesus as the Messiah but "so too does the Holy Spirit, whom God has given to those that obey Him," is a clear indictment of those to whom they speak, those who are deaf to the Spirit's words. And it is for this implication that they lack the truth that the Sanhedrin "were stung to fury and wanted to kill them."

But it is they who shall be killed. It is their rule which shall not last, which shall be overcome by the Just One and the Spirit of Truth upon Him and His own. It is Peter, who speaks for all the apostles, who shall lead the New Jerusalem, the holy Church of God. Such chastisement the leaders cannot bear, save perhaps for Nicodemus; the testimony of "the One who comes from heaven" they cannot accept, and so they fail to "certif[y] that God is truthful." What then shall be left to them?

Brothers and sisters, though the just man find himself "brokenhearted," "crushed in spirit," and with many "troubles," know that "out of them all the Lord delivers him." And He shall deliver you, if you but speak His truth. Find strength in the witness of the apostles, in the saints and martyrs of all the ages, and in the Lord Himself. He is with the one He sends and so will bless him as he speaks the truth without fear. "The Father loves the Son and has given everything over to Him," and He, in turn, gives to those whom the Spirit inspires. Trust in Him with all your lives.

Friday
(Acts 5:34-42; Ps.27:1,4,13-14; Jn.6:1-15)

"I believe that I shall see the bounty of the Lord
in the land of the living."

Seeing the vast crowd following Him up the mountain as He seeks to sit with His disciples, Jesus asks Philip, "Where shall we buy bread for these people to eat?" In honesty the disciple answers, essentially, "It is impossible." Ah, but nothing is impossible with God.

Brothers, is it not their seeing "the bounty of the Lord" that causes the apostles to leave the Sanhedrin and the whipping they received at their hands "full of joy that they had been judged worthy of ill-treatment for the sake of the Name"? And is not this bounty revealed most clearly here "in the land of the living" in the Bread of Life Jesus provides for us at His Eucharistic table? And so should we not rejoice every day in this miracle?

"Wait for the Lord with courage; be stouthearted, and wait for the Lord." Are not David's words the ones Jesus speaks to His children in the feeding of the five thousand? Should the apostles not but sing, "The Lord is my light and my salvation; whom should I fear?" as they stand each with one of the "twelve baskets full of pieces left over" from the miracle brought about at the Savior's hands? Does He not here convey their mission of feeding His sheep?

And filled by the food at their hands, should not our own reaction be in accord with the joy expressed by the people in that green field, "This is undoubtedly the Prophet who is to come into the world"? For does He not come into us each time we receive Him?

But king He shall not be made, not in this world. No, this world cannot contain His Kingship, for we have a greater than David here. The land of the living will ultimately be not upon this grass beneath our feet, but upon the clouds of Heaven. Thus the persecution comes, you see. Thus those who go about "fighting God Himself" scourge and crucify the Word they cannot bear and the messengers who bring it to their ears. But the ill-treatment that comes by their jealous hands brings no fear but only encouragement to the hearts of His apostles.

Brothers and sisters, let us be as they who "day after day, both in the temple and at home... never stopped teaching and proclaiming the Good News of Jesus the Messiah," making always this world as one with the kingdom of God.

641

Saturday

(Acts 6:1-7; Ps.33:1-2,4-5,18-19,22; Jn.6:16-21)

"The eyes of the Lord are upon those who fear Him,
upon those who hope for His kindness."

Alleluia.

As the apostles set out to cross the lake, "it was dark, and Jesus had still not joined them; moreover, with a strong wind blowing, the sea was becoming rough." As they struggled to row and keep afloat, "they sighted Jesus approaching the boat, walking on the water." They had not expected their prayers for assistance and their wishes that Jesus was with them to be answered so remarkably, and so they must have wondered if He was a ghost. But He assures them, "It is I; do not be afraid." (And these eternal words of comfort and peace come to rest upon His Church.) The disciples of the Lord now were ready "to take Him into the boat, but suddenly it came aground on the shore they had been approaching." He is with you, brothers and sisters, be assured, and will bring you to the home you seek, despite the storms you may face.

In our first reading, the eyes of the widows must have been looking to the Lord, wishing that He was with them to provide for them. In this case, "the Twelve assembled the community of disciples," and though they do not enter the boat themselves, do not "wait on the tables" to address the tumult that had arisen between the factions, they provide what is needed to calm the winds and see this boat ashore by laying hands on "deeply spiritual and prudent" men chosen from their own. And so, "the word of God continued to spread" through the apostles' concentration "on prayer and [their] ministry," "while at the same time the number of the disciples in Jerusalem enormously increased." So the widows are fed as the Word is spread; so the boat comes aground on the land it approaches.

Jesus is with us, brothers and sisters. In all things He is there, working. He ministers to us always as the head of His Church through the hands and hearts and voices of all His disciples. And each to his own call, and this ship shall find its port assured. And all shall sing His praises as they see in us and we know in Him that "upright is the word of the Lord, and all His works are trustworthy."

His eyes are upon us. Do not be afraid.

Third Week

Sunday (A)
(Acts 2:14,22-33; Ps.16:1-2,5,7-11; 1Pt.1:17-21; Lk.24:13-35)

"God raised this Jesus; of this we are all witnesses."

Peter stands up "with the Eleven" and proclaims to all the Resurrection of the Christ, that He who was crucified has been released "from the throes of death." David "foresaw and spoke of the resurrection of the Christ, that neither was He abandoned to the nether world nor did His flesh see corruption." The women who went to His empty tomb early Easter morning saw "a vision of angels who announced that He was alive"; this they declared to His apostles. And as for the two sojourning to Emmaus, "He was made known to them in the breaking of bread," whereupon they "returned to Jerusalem where they found gathered together the Eleven and those with them who were saying, 'The Lord has been raised and has appeared to Simon!'" All reports converge. The earth cries out of the presence of the living God. He is risen!

"As you see and hear," you who "invoke as Father Him who judges impartially," "exalted at the right hand of God, [Jesus] received the promise of the Holy Spirit from the Father and poured Him forth." This truth is evident in all the words of Scripture, in all His holy witnesses, and in this bread and wine made the Body and Blood of our Lord. Do you not see? Do you not hear? Do you not know that "you were ransomed from your futile conduct... with the precious blood of Christ as of a spotless unblemished lamb"? Is it not you "who through Him believe in God who raised Him from the dead and gave Him glory"? Is it not so that "your faith and hope are in God"? Do you not see? Do you not hear? Do you not know Him even as these witnesses? And do you witness with them?

Let us cry out with the words of our psalm, "O Lord, my allotted portion and my cup, you it is who hold fast my lot," even as we approach His altar today. As we receive Him, let our eyes be opened to recognize His presence. Our hearts should burn as He speaks to us and with His witnesses "open[s] the Scriptures to us," and in His breaking of the bread we should see Him. And then we should go forth, inspired as Peter, inspired as the women, inspired as the two disciples and all those gathered in His name, to proclaim that He is risen, that He is with us – that we see Him and know Him. Let all hear and understand that "He was known before the foundation of the world but revealed in the final time" for the sake of all. Yes, "the Lord has truly been raised."

643

Easter

Sunday (B)
(Acts 3:13-15,17-19; Ps.4:2,4,7-9; 1Jn.2:1-5a; Lk.24:35-48)

"He is expiation for our sins."

Brothers and sisters, "we have an Advocate with the Father, Jesus Christ the righteous one." For us this Savior has come; for our sins He has died on the cross. Even as it is written of Him in Scripture, so all has been accomplished in His Name.

And so we need fear no more. We need not be "startled and terrified" at the sight of Him in our midst. He has come to us and has taken His place among us, even as He sits at the right hand of God. And His place among us is the cross, even as God announced – "that His Christ would suffer" – and by His sacrifice He has been greatly blessed, and we greatly blessed with Him. Now His blood, once shed by our own hands, pours upon us for "the forgiveness of [our] sins."

David once cried, "When I call, answer me, O my just God, you who relieve me when I am in distress," and so in Christ his prayer is answered; for in this Jesus, our greatest distress – that inflicted by our transgressions – has been washed clean from our murderous souls. He lives. He lives now, brothers and sisters, to make intercession for our sins "and for those of the whole world." Let us all come to Him in truth and find "the light of [His] countenance shin[ing] upon us!"

The light the Lord is, the salvation He affords to each of our souls, must "be preached in His name to all the nations"; all must come to know the blessing embodied in the risen Christ: all must see Him, that in His redemptive wounds all might take refuge. It is the will of God that all sins "be wiped away," that all hearts be converted to truth and light, that all might live before Him in eternal peace.

Do not delay your repentance in His sight; freely forgiveness pours from His side. For this alone He has died, but to receive His mercy you must reform your lives.

Sunday (C)
(Acts 5:27-32,40b-41; Ps.30:2,4-6,11-13; Rv.5:11-14; Jn.21:1-19)

"You changed my mourning into dancing."

Throughout our readings today we witness the glory the risen Lord effects by His sacrifice, the change of fate that comes by the Savior.

In our first reading, though the apostles are brought before the Sanhedrin for persecution, they leave their presence rejoicing, happy to have "suffer[ed] dishonor for the sake of the name." In our psalm David sings the praise of the Lord for His having brought him "up from the nether world," turning his weeping into joy. In our second reading, John sees and hears "every creature in heaven and on earth and under the earth and in the sea, everything in the universe, cry out" the "blessing and honor, glory and might" of "the Lamb that was slain" – perceiving thus the ultimate fulfillment of the Lord's living sacrifice. And in our gospel, though the apostles had toiled in vain all the night within their boat, and were tired and hungry and disillusioned as morning approached, Jesus stood upon the shore... and at His instruction they caught more fish than they could carry, and were fed by His hand.

The light follows darkness, inevitably. "At nightfall, weeping enters in, but with the dawn, rejoicing." It is the maxim of the universe, epitomized by the death and resurrection of the Christ. And so, though Jesus calls Peter from the freedom he has known in youth to the bondage that shall be his as he "grow[s] old," it is understood that, indeed, by this "death he [will] glorify God," and thus joining his death with the Lord's own, shall know the same glorious morn Jesus does now own, and to which He leads all His followers.

Darkness can never overcome the eternal light of our God; of the glory of the Lord the angels and all living creatures sing in heaven even now. And we shall join their voices, we shall stand in the ranks with Peter and John and David and all His holy ones very soon. Once we have finished giving thanks to the living God for the suffering we are graced to endure here in His name, we will come to the joy that is ours in Him in heaven. Then we shall dance and sing forever.

Monday
(Acts 6:8-15; Ps.119:1,23-24,26-27,29-30; Jn.6:22-29)

"This is the work of God:
have faith in the One whom He sent."

It is this faith that moves Stephen; it is this work upon which he sets his heart. And so he was unmoved when "the people, the elders, and the scribes... confronted him, seized him, and led him off to the Sanhedrin" and "brought in false witnesses" against him. Surely the words of our psalm are fulfilled in him as they had been in the Lord: "Though princes meet and talk against me, your servant meditates on your statutes." Thus it is that throughout his persecution, "Stephen's face seemed like that of an angel" – through it all it is the voice of the Lord to which he listens. And one wonders if the members of the Sanhedrin had not "stared at him [so]

645

intently" because they had seen that face of an angel not long before in the One whom they had crucified, the One who stood before them like a sheep before its shearers. And this one, too, they will sacrifice.

"You should not be working for perishable food but for food that remains unto life eternal, food which the Son of Man will give you." It is this food, which those who persecute him cannot see, that Stephen eats. If he were seeking to get his "fill of the loaves" which satisfy the stomach, he would not suffer the trial upon him, and not in such peace. Only Jesus gives this food, brothers and sisters. It is nourishment the world cannot touch, and to it there is no end. We need eat nothing else to sustain ourselves.

"Yes, your decrees are my delight; they are my counselors." O Lord, what voice can compare with thine own? What word can stand where yours is spoken? For yours is "the way of truth," and the truth cannot be shaken, cannot be changed over time. It is not subject to the corrupting forces present in our flesh; it is of the spirit. And so, in the Spirit let us be, called before your throne. Though we stand accused before the tribunals of this barren land, may your food be ever within us to sustain us – in your presence ever let us rest.

On this unshakable foundation we shall remain, even as the world passes away.

Tuesday
(Acts 7:51-8:1; Ps.31:3-4,6-8,17,21; Jn.6:30-35)

"No one who comes to me shall ever be hungry,
no one who believes in me shall thirst again."

"I myself am the bread of life," Jesus declares, and it is in this Bread we take refuge. It is by this Bread we are fed.

Do you think that Stephen is at all hungry as he lives again the trial, way of the cross, and crucifixion of the Lord in our first reading today? No, even in this time, and perhaps especially in this sacrifice, the Lord feeds him with Bread from heaven. Even as he is stoned to death, the Lord God hides him "in the shelter of [His] presence from the plottings of men."

Yes, in our first reading we have Jesus again chastising the elders and indeed all the people for their betrayal and murder of the Word of God. Here we have again Jesus being dragged "out of the city" and killed at the hands of those "who received the law through the ministry of angels [but] have not observed it." And here again we have forgiveness offered with His last breath. Here is the persecuted Church found in the person of Stephen; here is Jesus. Recall Jesus' words to Saul upon his conversion: "Saul, Saul, why do you persecute me"(Acts 22:7)? And here is that same Saul overseeing this first "act of killing," this first martyrdom of the Body of Christ.

But all the while Jesus is there, not only in the persecution, but quite evidently in His glory. "I see an opening in the sky, and the Son of Man standing at God's right hand," Stephen exclaims. And notice that it is not until this moment, not until they hear this declaration – despite their "shouting aloud, holding their hands over their ears" – that the people are moved "as one man" to destroy that voice. Stephen's chastisement "stung [them] to the heart" and made them "ground their teeth in anger," but it is this Truth of the presence of the Lord which they simply cannot stand. And what is the significance of Stephen's vision being the impetus for his own death? It does bring his stoning, but simultaneously it prepares him for such martyrdom, for now truly the Lord is with him. Before this he would not have been able to bear so completely this cross. And without this Bread he would not have been killed.

"God's bread comes down from heaven and gives life to the world." That bread of life is in Stephen's trust in the Lord and in his echoing the words of David's psalm, which are Jesus' own: "Into your hands I commend my spirit." For even as he dies, he is most alive. It is this same faith we need, brothers and sisters, and we shall never be hungry, and we shall never be without the Lord, but shall declare His love and His truth to all, happy to be called His own. The Lord's "face shine[s] upon [His] servant[s]," and they always have the Bread they need.

Wednesday
(Acts 8:1-8; Ps.66:1-7; Jn.6:35-40)

"Let all on earth worship and sing praise to you,
sing praise to your name!"

And why should there be such exultant joy among all the peoples of the earth? What should cause all men to "shout joyfully to God"? It is Jesus' profession that "everyone who looks upon the Son and believes in Him shall have eternal life." Nothing but life everlasting can bring such absolute joy, and we have the assurance from the Lord's own lips that He "shall lose nothing of what [the Father] has given" Him, that all who come to Him He "will raise up on the last day." Alleluia! Let us come to Him.

How evident the universal call of the Lord is in our first reading. Upon the persecution which follows the death of Stephen, Philip, a Greek-speaking Jewish Christian "goes down to the town of Samaria" – where the Jews intermarried with the pagans of the land – "and there proclaimed the Messiah." And we are told that "without exception, the crowds that heard

Philip and saw the miracles he performed attended closely to what he had to say" and that "the rejoicing in that town rose to fever pitch." Here we see the fulfillment of Jesus' prophecy to the woman at the well, that all who worship Him will worship in spirit and in truth and not in any particular place; here we see the realization of the Lord's parable of the Good Samaritan, that all men truly are our neighbors. For now *all* are called into His holy fold. All now come to know the glory of the Lord. And, of course, he who leads the persecution against the growing Christian community, he who "entered house after house, dragged men and women out, and threw them into jail"... this same Saul we hear of today will soon become the great Apostle Paul, who travels to all the nations of the world converting waiting souls.

Yes, brothers and sisters, "He has changed the sea into dry land; through the river they passed on foot." As the Israelites passed through the Red Sea, so now all God's children pass through holy Baptism and have the way made straight before them. "The glory of His name" is upon us all, upon all who believe in His Son, and now we who were "paralytics or cripples" – who were unable to move for not having heard of His Name or who had had our limbs disjointed for having forgotten His Law – all, Gentile or Jew, are now welcomed into the Father's eternal home. For "no one who comes will [the Son] reject." In Him all find their dwelling, and so, what should we do but "rejoice in Him" and "proclaim His glorious praise"?

E. 3. Thurs.

Thursday
(Acts 8:26-40; Ps.66:1,8-9,16-17,20; Jn.6:44-51)

"No one can come to me
unless the Father who sent me draws him."

How evident it is in our first reading that the Father draws all believers unto Himself. For though it is clear that the Ethiopian eunuch is in search of God, has a desire for God, and welcomes God – He is coming from pilgrimage to Jerusalem, is reading Holy Scripture, and "invite[s] Philip to get in and sit down beside him" – which is necessary for belief as well, it is most certain that the Lord is leading him to Himself. The angel of the Lord directs Philip to the Ethiopian. The Spirit specifically instructs him to approach his carriage, and then inspires His disciple to speak to the eunuch of the Word of God and lead him into the waters of baptism (snatching Philip away immediately upon the completion of his task).

Also evident in our first reading is Jesus' quotation of the prophets: "They shall all be taught by God." For indeed it is God that, through Philip, enlightens the Ethiopian eunuch regarding the Suffering Servant spoken of by Isaiah, and all of Scripture, "telling him the good news of Jesus." It is "not that anyone has seen the Father," for the Father is not visible to our human vision. But the Father has sent the Son, "the one who is from God," and "He has seen the Father," and He knows Him. And now through the power of the Holy Spirit, the Son sends His disciples forth as His own flesh and blood, with the same Spirit that inspires Him, to reveal the Father's love to a waiting world.

"The bread I will give is my flesh, for the life of the world." We are those who have heard His Word, who have been instructed in His way, and who have received His Body and His Blood. And so, having eaten "the bread that comes down from heaven," we indeed become flesh of His flesh, bone of His bone. Wed we are to the Son of Man by the power of His Word and the blessing of His Sacrament. We have responded to the Lord's call; He who draws all to Himself and to the Father has become our "living bread," our life-giving water. And now at His command we must draw all men to the Son, who brings all to the Father.

The Light of the world shines in our midst, and we are drawn as moths to this flame, to Him who "is deprived of His life on earth." And though we die in our turn as this Sheep who "was led to the slaughter," yet "of His posterity," and so our own, all the world will speak... and be drawn to Him who has been lifted up from the earth upon a cross, to Him who dwells with the Father in heaven.

E. 3. Fri.

Friday
(Acts 9:1-20; Ps.117:1-2,Mk.16:15; Jn.6:52-59)

"My flesh is real food and my blood real drink."

And "the man who feeds on this bread shall live forever."

The truth is simply stated to those who wonder at His words today in our gospel. As the Israelites in the desert asked, "What is this?" when presented with manna as their food, so now the Jews say, "How can this man give us His flesh to eat?" For those who do not believe, it is impossible; but for those who believe, it is *the* gift of God.

Here is the Bread of Life in our midst, as real as the Light which shone around Saul and knocked him off his horse; as real as the voice which spoke aloud to his soul. This bread and wine on the table of the Lord, this great grace upon His altar of sacrifice, is indeed that which feeds us, that which sustains us – that which makes Him most present to us. Our first reading says of Saul that "his strength returned to him after he had taken food." For three days he had fasted in darkness, experiencing the absolute blindness of his life as persecutor of the Church. Then Ananias laid his hands on him and he recovered his sight. Then he was baptized. Then he could come to the table of the Lord our God and gain the strength "to proclaim in the synagogues that Jesus was the Son of God." Yes, the Scripture refers in fact but to ordinary food, but indeed it indicates the "real food" Saul shall soon come to know and find his spirit through.

"The man who feeds on me will have life because of me." He will become one with the Son as He is with the Father. And him, too, the Lord will be speaking of when He asks, "Why are you persecuting me?" By this Bread we become so one with our God, and with Him we suffer for His Name. "I myself shall indicate to him how much he will have to suffer for my name," Jesus says to Ananias. And so the disciple is convinced that this man who has done nothing but harm to God's holy people is truly being called to come to the Lord of all. It is through such suffering that discipleship comes, as it is through His sacrifice we have this food upon our table.

Eat His Body, dear brothers and sisters. Drink His Blood. Let us share together this day this gift of oneness with our God. And let us be strong; and let us bleed with Him upon the cross, to bring His Name to all. "The fidelity of the Lord endures forever," and He shall never leave us orphaned. He shall feed us forever.

E. 3. Sat.

Saturday
(Acts 9:31-42; Ps.116:12-17; Jn.6:60-69)

"We have come to believe."

Yes, Peter professes for the Twelve (except Judas, of course), "We are convinced that you are God's holy one." They have heard His words and seen His works, and despite the difficulty of this latest and most challenging of words – that they must eat His flesh and drink His blood – their faith is not shaken as is that of so many others, as is the faith of so many even today regarding the same teaching. Peter declares, "You have the words of eternal life," and he knows by Jesus' words all things are possible, for "it is the spirit that gives life" to the flesh. And so Peter and the apostles can sing with our psalmist, "The cup of salvation I will take up, and I will call upon the name of the Lord," and by this invocation – "This is my body... This is my blood" – the Lord's words are proven true: His presence is with us, and of Him we eat.

And in our first reading, faith comes, too, through the blessed healing of two disciples. We are told that through the healing of one, "All the inhabitants of Lydda and Sharon, upon seeing him, were converted to the Lord"; and upon the raising of the other, "Many came to believe in the

Lord." Truly here is evidence that the Church "was being built up and was making steady progress in the fear of the Lord." Whereas in our gospel we see a pruning of the faithful to discover those who truly believe, here we see those so refined, today in the person of Peter, serving to increase the numbers of those who believe.

"You have loosed my bonds." What appropriate words from our psalmist today for those cured by Jesus through Peter's intercession to sing in praise of God. For one is released from paralysis and the other from the very bonds of death. But how much more appropriate these words are for the others to sing, those who are set free from a lack of faith – those who come to believe in Jesus. For here truly is the greatest freedom, the greatest healing there is, to be able to declare with the whole of His faithful: "To you I will offer a sacrifice of thanksgiving, and I will call upon the name of the Lord." O that all might come to life in the Spirit of our Lord Jesus Christ!

As Jesus did, so do the apostles. As he healed, so do they. As Jesus told the paralytic to take up his mat and go home (Mt.9:6), so Peter says, "Get up and make your bed." As Jesus said, "'*Talitha, koum*', which means, 'Little girl, I say to you, arise!'" (Mk.5:41), so Peter says, "Tabitha, stand up." And as surely as these are raised by the words spoken in Jesus' name, so when the apostles speak the Lord's words of spirit and life – "This is my body... This is my blood" – over the gifts of bread and wine, so truly do they become His flesh and blood. I pray all shall come to believe.

E. 4. Sun. (A)

Fourth Week

Sunday (A)
(Acts 2:14a,36-41; Ps.23:1-6; 1Pt.2:20b-25; Jn.10:1-10)

"Whoever enters through the gate is the shepherd of the sheep."

Jesus says in earnest to the Pharisees, "I am the gate for the sheep... Whoever enters through me will be saved, and will come in and go out and find pasture." But they are as the thief who "comes only to steal and slaughter and destroy."

Today, too, brothers and sisters, the thief is among us, those teachers who do "not enter a sheepfold through the gate but climb over elsewhere." For neither seeing nor caring to seek the wholeness of Scripture, that it is here that God speaks, they attempt to enter another way, relying on their own devices. So it says in the commentary of the missal I read: "the author of the First Letter of Peter" and "the author of John's gospel," for the author here shows he knows not the Word of God. Like the Pharisees who were so preoccupied with the words of the law that they could not see the Author of

651

Life standing before them, so these are blind to the voice of Jesus and His apostles speaking in this Holy Book. As they piece together the fragments of supposed facts gleaned by their fanciful imaginations, the wholeness of the Word, holiness itself, entirely escapes them. How can they hear His silence amongst such chatter?

And so the false shepherds strip the "verdant pastures" and pollute the "restful waters" of Holy Scripture. On wrong paths for their own sakes they lead others into the "dark valley" with no "rod" or "staff" of the Lord to give "courage." Only coming before the Word of God as children will they "receive the gift of the Holy Spirit" and so see the truth of prophecy – but this is entirely too shameful to their pride. By their own minds must they live; in their reason alone they seek their refuge, caring not to "dwell in the house of the Lord" and have His "goodness and kindness follow" them. They need this not – they are quite self-sufficient.

Brothers and sisters, my prayer is that you "save yourselves from this corrupt generation," that you "run away" like sheep at the "voice of strangers," saying, "The Lord is my shepherd; I shall not want." And as for these blind guides, I pray that they shall cease their vain effort to crucify the Lord again by making Him and His Word into a metaphor, a symbol – an empty construct of the human imagination – rather than the flesh and blood of God He Is. May they be "cut to the heart" as those at Peter's preaching, and like the rest of the faithful who "had gone astray like sheep" now return "to the shepherd and guardian of our souls." Entering through the gate that is Jesus, may they recognize the voice of God as He speaks through His Rock and His Beloved.

E. 4. Sun. (B)

Sunday (B)
(Acts 4:8-12; Ps.118:1,8-9,21-23,26,28-29; 1Jn.3:1-2; Jn.10:11-18)

"There is no salvation through anyone else."

Do not "trust in princes" or in any man; it is by Jesus alone "we are to be saved." Though "the builders rejected" Him, though the princes of this age saw fit to crucify the Lord – yet "God raised [Him] from the dead" and exalted Him above every power on earth and in heaven. And so He is indeed now the foundation of our salvation, the only shepherd who will lead us to the Father... the one who "lays down His life for the sheep."

Many wolves there are who fat themselves, scattering the sheep to desolate places. Their care is for the "pay" they receive and not the welfare of the flock they fail to tend. Only Jesus cares for the human race; only the Christ serves His sheep in love – only He dies that we might live, that we might indeed become members of His flock.

And so, "blessed is he who comes in the name of the Lord"; "what love the Father has bestowed on us" in Jesus, His only Son, for now we can be like Him – now we are God's holy children. Taking "refuge in the Lord" by His Son, we come at once to our salvation. O what glory is ours following in our Savior's wake! Listen to what our Good Shepherd states: "I know mine and mine know me, just as the Father knows me and I know the Father." Realize to what union with the Father of all you are called by the Child He has borne to us for our redemption. O how "wonderful in our eyes" this should be! And consider if you will that one day we His children "shall see Him as He is." How shall our souls bear such blessing?

Brothers and sisters, like the cripple seemingly doomed to a life of incapacity are we all. But what Peter has effected by a word in Jesus' name is now ours by that same name and through the ministry of His apostles. How? you say. How shall I discover such salvation? How shall this lame man leap like a stag? Faith. Faith in the Son draws the Father's mercy from above. And if I must tell you further, I shall, you wayward soul. Confess your sins! Kneel before the priest the Lord has ordained as His instrument of salvation and bare your heart to God on high. What graces are yours if only you have faith in the Lord and the Church He alone has founded. Turn from the wolves that besiege you, and come to Him who "is good."

E. 4. Sun. (C)

Sunday (C)
(Acts 13:14,43-52; Ps.100:1-3,5; Rv.7:9,14b-17; Jn.10:27-30)

"The Lamb who is in the center of the throne will shepherd them
and lead them to springs of life-giving water."

Joy is our promise in the Lord, brothers and sisters. Absolute, eternal, universal joy. And though we may suffer persecution now, "the time of great distress" upon us but provides the means, the water, by which all saints "have washed their robes and made them white." "The blood of the Lamb" is necessary to bring us to the kingdom of God.

Paul and Barnabas suffer "violent abuse" today for proclaiming the word of the Lord. But from it comes their turn to the Gentiles, who delight in joy at this call to the kingdom. And these disciples themselves "were filled with joy and the Holy Spirit," despite being expelled from the territory to which they'd come. All is joy in the Lord!

In our second reading, John depicts all the saints who "stand before God's throne and worship Him day and night in His temple." Here they are utterly protected from harm, the harm that afflicted them while on earth. No trials exist anymore in this everlasting shelter, for the Lord has "wipe[d] away every tear from their eyes." These tears, too, are water which cleanses the soul, which makes us robed in white before the Lord.

And Jesus assures us, to our great exultation, that "no one can take [us] out of the Father's hand," or His own. He and the Father are one, and no greater power is there under or above the sun. Though threats of robbery besiege our souls as we travel through this world, let us make the Lord's assurance our own, and have faith that nothing will remove us from His arms.

Our psalmist exalts in the joy that should reflect the song in all our souls: "Sing joyfully to the Lord, all you lands; serve the Lord with gladness; come before Him with joyful song." So let us search our hearts to find that joy within us and overflowing from us. Let me ask you, brother, sister, did John see you present in his "vision of a great multitude, which no one could count, from every nation, race, people, and tongue"? Is the life-giving water of the Lamb washing you clean for that day? Then joy should be yours even where you stand, for even now you stand with Him.

Monday
(Acts 11:1-18; Ps.41:3,42:2-3,43:3-4; Jn.10:1-10 or Jn.10:11-18)

"God has granted life-giving repentance even to the Gentiles."

In his vision Peter sees "an object like a big canvas... lowered down to [him] from the sky by its four corners." Upon it he discerns "four-legged creatures of the earth, wild beasts and reptiles, and birds of the sky." Like Noah's ark it seems to contain all the animals upon it. But these animals he sees are not for the good Jew to eat: they are unclean. And so Peter protests when instructed to "slaughter, then eat." But he is assured (and three times), "What God has purified you are not to call unclean," and "the canvas with everything in it [is] drawn up again into the sky."

What is this shepherd to do – he who has been told by the Lord, "Feed my sheep"? When the uncircumcised come to him seeking salvation, how can he turn away? And so, as the canvas which came from the sky and returned to the sky, we learn that everything comes from God and returns to Him, and He calls whom He will. And so the Gentile man whose home Peter enters by the Spirit's direction is "saved, and all [his] household." "As [Peter] began to address them the Holy Spirit came upon them," for they, too, "believed in the Lord Jesus Christ."

Yes, even these thirst for God "as the hind [who] longs for the running waters," and so are led to the Lord's "holy mountain, to His dwelling place"; even these "go in to the altar of God." For these unclean creatures are made as the pure and obedient sheep of Israel, heeding the Good Shepherd's voice. Here are "the other sheep that do not belong to this fold" of which Jesus speaks, whom He leads, too, by His loving word.

All that He calls shall come to Him who lays down His life for the sake of the fold, by whom all "have life and have it to the full." All living creatures are His own, for it is He who is the living God; and all who live, live for Him and through Him alone. The Son has come from the Father that we might know Him as He knows Him, and so that we might indeed have life. As good sheep let us follow in His way, and lead those behind us also to salvation. Let us all "go and behold the face of God" as we turn from anything that makes us unclean in His sight and listen for His voice leading our pure hearts.

Tuesday
(Acts 11:19-26; Ps.87:1-7,117:1; Jn.10:22-30)

"Of Zion they shall say:
'One and all were born in her.'"

"I tell of Egypt and Babylon among those that know the Lord; of Philistia, Tyre, Ethiopia," sings our psalmist today. Yes, "when the peoples are enrolled" in the kingdom of heaven, when it is noted: "This man was born there," it shall not be to the soil of Jerusalem to which the angels refer, but to birth in the spirit of the place, in the Holy Spirit Himself, who leads all into the New Jerusalem. For all nations are called, and it matters no more the land of your origin.

This impotence of place and importance of the Spirit is made clear in Jesus' words to "the Jews gathered around Him" "in the temple area, in Solomon's portico." To those here in the heart of the city of Jerusalem He says, "You are not my sheep." They "refuse to believe" that He is the Messiah and so they prove that they are no sons of Abraham, that they have no faith. Only those of faith hear the voice of the Shepherd, and only these are admitted into the kingdom. This He tells them plainly. For what is He saying when He declares, "The Father and I are one" but that He dwells with the Father in heaven, and not upon this earth. The earth to which they cling shall pass away, but the kingdom shall last forever.

"My sheep hear my voice," Jesus says, and how that voice does work among all souls. (For this let us praise the Lord!) We are told in our first reading that at first "the community who had been dispersed by the persecution that arose because of Stephen went as far as Phoenicia, Cyprus, and Antioch, making the message known to none but Jews." Here, even though the Word is spread far, it is kept for those born of the land of Zion. But then the change occurs, and the truth of the Word, which goes beyond all borders, becomes known, for "some men of Cyprus and Cyrene among them who had come to Antioch began to talk even to the Greeks, announcing the Good News of the Lord Jesus to them." The church in Jerusalem, the protector of the faith – whose seat is now in Rome – sends Barnabas to investigate. He finds "the evidence of God's favor" and rejoices to realize the Lord's sheep come from near and far. Here "in Antioch the disciples were called Christians for the first time." Here it becomes clear that there is a new Church being formed, one that finds "eternal life" in following Jesus.

"The gates of Zion" "the Lord loves," and to this holy mountain He brings all, through the Gate that is Jesus. And "no one shall snatch them out of [His] hand," for this mountain cannot be shaken, this Temple cannot be torn down. It is of the life of heaven "all shall sing, in their festive dance" when they proclaim: "My home is within you." And this land shall endure forever.

E. 4. Wed.

Wednesday
(Acts 12:24-13:5; Ps.67:2-6,8; Jn.12:44-50)

"Set apart Barnabas and Saul for me,
to do the work for which I have called them."

These words came to the church at Antioch "while they were engaged in the liturgy of the Lord and fasting"; spoken by the Holy Spirit, they show how intimately the Church and her apostles are connected to the Lord Jesus and His Father.

In John's gospel, Jesus proclaims, "The Father who sent me has commanded me what to say and how to speak." Jesus is sent by the Father. He is the Image of the Father: "Whoever looks on me is seeing Him who sent me." In the same way, Barnabas and Saul are "sent forth by the Holy Spirit" through the ministry of the Church, who "imposed hands on them and sent them off" to proclaim the word of God. Jesus is sent by the Father. Jesus speaks in the Holy Spirit the words of everlasting life. Hearing these words His children, His Church, go forth to the ends of the earth. There is absolute unity in the Church and all its members, as long as we are as obedient as Jesus, our Head, who declares, "Whatever I say is spoken just as He instructed"; as long as we are as faithful to the Spirit's prompting as Jesus is to the Father's will, we shall reflect His glory as He reflects the Father.

And what is the glory of the Son of God but to bring light to this dark world: "I have come to the world as its light, to keep anyone who believes in me from remaining in the dark." The words He speaks, the instruction He offers and the sacrifice He makes, indeed bring spirit and life to those who listen and obey. He is true when He says He has not come to condemn but to save, for the world is already condemned by its sin and His words would bring it to life. And so, if we reject His words, we reject the lifeline He provides, and what hope can there be for us? If we do not ask that "He let His face shine upon us" and celebrate in joy the salvation that comes "among all nations," if we do not seek the holy light of God... where else shall we find eternal life? "His commandment means eternal life"; all other words lead to destruction. We must follow the Lord and His way.

Brothers and sisters, it should be obvious to us that we are called even as Barnabas and Saul and the first Christians in the city of Antioch. The Spirit of God remains upon the Church, and He would send us forth in Jesus' name to do the work and will of the Father. Do not reject His call upon your soul; put faith in Jesus and in Him who sent Him, and the Spirit will lead you forth.

E. 4. Thurs.

Thursday
(Acts 13:13-35; Ps.89:2-3,21-22,25,27; Jn.13:16-20)

"He who accepts anyone I send accepts me,
and in accepting me accepts Him who sent me."

And who is this Jesus who sends apostles like Paul forth traveling from Syria to Cyprus to Asia Minor? Who is He of whom Paul rises to speak in this distant synagogue? Two quotes I offer for your consideration. First is the Baptist's declaration, "I am not worthy to unfasten the sandals of His feet." The second is the mere statement of fact that Jesus "washed the feet of the disciples." And so with two questions I will tell you who He is: Tell me, who is worthy to unfasten His sandals? Then tell me, whose feet does He not wash? Mary washed His feet with her tears and her hair and knew herself nothing but unworthy to touch Him (see Lk.7:38). Jesus stoops to cleanse the feet even of Judas, His betraying apostle, who will kiss Him on the cheek, but to whom He shall turn the other one. He heals lepers; children come to Him – none is beyond His humble reach. Yet this man with the towel around His waist is none other than the Son of God.

The Israelites awaited His coming. Hundreds of years they expected Him. Paul tells us that "God testified, 'I have found David son of Jesse to be a man after my own heart who will fulfill my every wish," and in this Son of David the Father's every wish is indeed fulfilled. Here is the "Savior for Israel." It is of this Christ the Lord speaks when He says, "With my holy oil I have anointed Him, that my hand may be always with Him, and that my arm may make Him strong." And He in turn says of the Lord, "You are my

Easter

Father, my God, the Rock, my Savior." So obedient is Jesus to the Father that there is none for whom He will not die; for all He shall drink the cup the Father offers, that the whole world might know the Father's love. Here is the great "I AM", "the fulfillment of Scripture," the WORD made flesh, the image of the living God: Jesus, Son of David, Son of God – God Himself dwelling among us. And as He was Chosen, so He now chooses, instructing men to go forth.

Do "you know all these things"? Do you see who He is and hear the words He speaks? Then "blest will you be if you put them into practice." For in humble service of the Name of God, with Him you shall "be exalted." Bring forth His message of love.

E. 4. Fri.

Friday
(Acts 13:26-33; Ps.2:6-11; Jn.14:1-6)

"You are my Son;
this day I have begotten you."

This same verse appearing in both our first reading and our psalm is spoken also by Jesus in our gospel when He says, "I am the way, and the truth, and the life; no one comes to the Father but through me," for such is the Son begotten of the Father.

How comforting are Jesus' words in our gospel, and how enlightening Paul's speech. The disciples' hearts are troubled at the Lord's speaking of His imminent departure; that He must die begins to sink in to them. But the only Son tells them, "In my Father's house there are many dwelling places," and, "I am indeed going to prepare a place for you." Not only this, He also promises, "I shall come back to take you with me, that where I am you also may be." The words come like a river of peace, like a wind of love breathing upon them, and upon us. And the same message is spoken by Paul to "the children of the family of Abraham and [all] others who reverence our God." His is "this message of salvation," that though the rulers condemned Him to death and "laid Him in a tomb," "yet God raised [Jesus] from the dead." And now His witnesses, those to whom He appeared thereafter, declare the Good News of His resurrection, and our own. "The words of the prophets which we read sabbath after sabbath" and "what God promised our fathers He has fulfilled for us, their children, in raising up Jesus." This is the word Paul brings to the waiting ears of his Jewish brothers, and which should be heard by us all.

"Do not let your hearts be troubled," brothers and sisters. The Lord is near and is calling us to His home. Even as we speak He is preparing a place for us. The death that you experience day to day is passing away, and

658

all that will be known is the truth, the life of God the Father. The Lord declares, "I myself have set up my king on Zion, my holy mountain," and Jesus is that King for all ages and all peoples. With His truth He shatters kings, and so death itself, "like an earthen dish"; He takes "the nations for an inheritance and the ends of the earth for [His] possession." He has died, but He is risen, and now all must "serve the Lord with fear, and rejoice before Him." There is no breaking in to the place He prepares for us to dwell.

The devil has been defeated by the Son begotten of the Father; his house has come crumbling down. We need but follow the way Jesus is to find our home in the New Jerusalem. Death no longer holds dominion, for the Son is now come.

Saturday
(Acts 13:44-52; Ps.98:1-4; Jn.14:7-14)

"I have made you a light to the nations,
a means of salvation to the ends of the earth."

In the preaching of Paul today is fulfilled the words of our psalm, "All the ends of the earth have seen the salvation by our God." Rejected by the Jews to whom he comes, he "now turn[s] to the Gentiles," and – fulfilling the words of our psalm which read, "Sing joyfully to the Lord, all you lands, break into song; sing praise" – our first reading tells us "the Gentiles were delighted when they heard this and responded to the word of the Lord with praise." Thus does the light of the Lord's salvation go out to the ends of the earth.

And our gospel makes clear just how salvation comes to all. First Jesus declares with wonderful clarity the oneness of the Son and the Father. When asked by Philip, "Show us the Father," Jesus responds, "After I have been with you all this time, you still do not know me?" Notice that Philip's request refers to the Father but Jesus' response refers to the Son, as if to ask of one is to ask of the other. The Lord then states the truth of His oneness with the living God in plain terms: "Whoever has seen me has seen the Father." There is no separation here, and all that Jesus does is done by the Father, so the living Lord of the universe is at work in absolute fashion through the Son's words and works. In Him the Father's will of love, His desire to save His children from sin and death, is accomplished.

But more than this is made evident of the working of salvation, for the Word must reach to the ends of the earth. How is this accomplished? The Lord again declares with absolute clarity the oneness now of Himself and His disciples. In order "to glorify the Father in the Son," He makes them the solemn promise, "The man who has faith in me will do the works I do." And the oneness of Jesus and His disciples is made more poignant in His definitive statement: "Anything you ask me in my name I will do." Who does these works of the Lord? Who brings His salvation forth? We do the works, do we not? We are those still on this earth with flesh and bone and voices. Yet He says "I will do" them to show how *He* works through us in all we do, to reveal our oneness with Him and the Father.

Our first reading tells us, "Almost the entire city gathered to hear the word of God" when Paul and Barnabas were in Antioch in Pisidia. In this simple line is shown both that the salvation of the Lord is going forth to all, and that it is occurring through His disciples. For it is indeed "the word of God" that Paul the apostle speaks and not his own, and in its truth and love this Word is irresistible to all hearts open to hear the voice of Him who speaks, for this Word brings only joy.

Fifth Week

Sunday (A)
(Acts 6:1-7; Ps.33:1-2,4-5,18-19,22; 1Pt.2:4-9; Jn.14:1-12)

"Let yourselves be built into a spiritual house to be a holy priesthood
to offer spiritual sacrifices acceptable to God through Jesus Christ."

Peter tells us in his letter that we are "a chosen race, a royal priesthood, a holy nation, a people of His own." Quoting Scripture, he calls us to "'announce the praises' of Him who called [us] out of darkness into His wonderful light." The house we become, the priests we are, and the sacrifices we offer are evident throughout our readings today.

First, in our gospel Jesus tells the disciples very directly, "In my Father's house there are many dwelling places" and that He is going "to prepare a place" for them, and so for us, there. And even now He draws us to that place He is with the Father, each to our own room, each with his own ministry. For, second, the priesthood all share in Christ is pictured in our first reading from the Acts of the Apostles. As the community of disciples grows in Jerusalem, so do the functions prescribed to its members. It becomes clear that the Twelve and their successors are to "devote themselves to prayer and to the ministry of the word," so in order to care for the particular concerns surrounding such matters as the daily distribution of food, they ordain "respectable men" to "serve at table," thus instituting the ministry of the deacon. And, finally, the spiritual sacrifices all offer to God are sung of by David in our psalm: "Exult, you just, in the Lord; praise from the upright is fitting." As this humble servant "give[s] thanks to the

Lord on the harp" placed in His hands by God, so all have their place in the kingdom founded on Jesus; all have their lives to offer in praise of God by the instruments He provides.

"Whoever believes in me will do the works I do." Yes, the Lord's works in great abundance are given to us to accomplish through Him who now sits with the Father. The way to His heavenly kingdom has been made clear by the ministry and the sacrifice of Jesus, and we must follow in His footsteps, for we are now the Body of Christ here on this earth. In Him and through Him we offer ourselves and all we do to draw all to the House which He prepares in light, to proclaim with our beings that "of the kindness of the Lord the earth is full." Today we are encouraged to hear that "even a large group of priests were becoming obedient to the faith," that the priests of the Old Covenant were now finding themselves true priests under the New. And so we should realize the manner in which we are all called to service in the Temple of the Lord as members of His own Body, giving praise to the Father of us all through His only Son.

Sunday (B)
(Acts 9:26-31; Ps.22:26-28,30-32; 1Jn.3:18-24; Jn.15:1-8)

"Let the coming generation be told of the Lord..."

Let the vine that is Christ continue to grow; let its branches extend to the ends of the world. Anointed by the Spirit, let all His children proclaim the name of Jesus, that "all the ends of the earth shall remember and turn to the Lord," that in our midst the call upon the Church of God shall be fulfilled.

Brothers and sisters, we should all be like Paul, who "spoke out boldly in the name of the Lord." Though it brought him the threat of death, he did not mind; his sole concern was for greater growth of the people of God – that all might become branches of the vine of Jesus. And so, by apostles like Paul, "with the consolation of the Holy Spirit [the Church] grew in numbers" and spread to the four corners of the world, and "a people yet to be born," including ourselves, have heard of the salvation that comes only by the Lord.

And so this growth must continue. Those who are still yet to be born, whether because they are still in their mother's womb or because their hearts have not been touched by the Spirit of God, must also come to be grafted upon the holy vine. And so, can we fail to speak of Jesus our God? Can we fail to perform the deeds to which our Father calls us? Would you see any deprived of the blessing of "the true vine"? "By this is [the] Father glorified, that [we] bear much fruit and become [His Son's] disciples," bringing others to that same discipleship, that the house of the Lord might be filled to overflowing. "The lowly shall eat their fill," hearts hungry for the word of God shall find their joy, only if we "fulfill [our] vows before those who fear the Lord," only if we do the will of Him who sends us forth.

Brothers and sisters, let us "remain in Him, and He in [us]"; let "the Spirit He gave us" preserve us in His love... Let it be His blood which courses through our veins as we drink His cup. And let us call all souls to share in this cup, that we might be assured all our "descendants shall serve Him." Lord, let your Church be built up in your truth and your love. May all believe in your name.

Sunday (C)
(Acts 14:21-27; Ps.145:1,8-13; Rv.21:1-5a; Jn.13:31-33a,34-35)

"Behold, God's dwelling is with the human race."

This is the promise on which we set our hearts, this vision of John. This is the word which encourages us to look forward to the coming of our God in the fullness of His presence amongst us. How we long to be His bride in heaven!

John indeed sees the "new Jerusalem, coming down out of heaven from God," His holy bride. And his ears hear the promise that "He will wipe away every tear from [our] eyes." No more shall there be "death or mourning," no more "wailing or pain" – these things which beset us here shall all pass away. On this glory we must set our sights, for as long as we toil upon this earth there will be tests and trials that can only be overcome with this vision of God.

In our first reading we hear that Paul and Barnabas have accomplished the rounds of their mission journey and "made a considerable number of disciples." We witness how God "opened the door of faith to the Gentiles" and so to the world at large. All men of all times are now called into the kingdom of God. And here is cause for great rejoicing. Yet the message of these apostles, borne out by their own experience, is that we must "undergo many hardships to enter the kingdom of God," for though the Spirit of the Lord fall on Christ's disciples, still these disciples are in this world, where the coming of the kingdom has yet to be fulfilled, and weeping at the darkness remains part of our condition.

In this world there shall be persecution, no doubt. Though God's "kingdom is a kingdom for all ages, and [His] dominion endures through all generations," though Jesus has come and lived and died among us and sent His Spirit for rebirth, though indeed His presence is very much in our midst – yet the evil one enters in; yet he lurks in hiding. And we must be prepared

662

to conquer him, and even to find our salvation by enduring the suffering he devises.

In Jesus we see well the way in which God is with us here and how we come to Him in heaven. The Lord says as His hour of death approaches: "Now is the Son of Man glorified, and God is glorified in Him." Even as Judas leaves to fetch the instruments of His death, Jesus sees His glory come. In His crucifixion He shall destroy the devil and come completely to the Father – and even on the cross, God is with Him.

Here we must endure, brothers and sisters, knowing God is with us; and soon we shall come to the fullness of His presence, to "the glorious splendor of [His] kingdom." Soon the Lord will "make all things new," as new as our spirits have already become.

Monday
(Acts 14:5-18; Ps.115:1-4,15-16; Jn.14:21-26)

"May you be blessed by the Lord,
who made heaven and earth."

"Anyone who loves me will be true to my word, and my Father will love him; we will come to him and make our dwelling place with him." Thus are we blessed, by keeping the word of the Lord. Thus we know His love, for thus we accept the love He offers by His instruction and by His presence.

It is this blessing of "the living God, 'the one who made heaven and earth and the sea and all that is in them'" that Paul and Barnabas would bring to the hearts of the Gentiles to whom they preach. It is in the name of Jesus, Paul brings healing to the lame man who "used to sit crippled, never having walked in his life." Indeed, the same healing he would bring to all the pagans before him who also have been crippled all their lives by the folly of worshiping "idols [that] are silver and gold, the handiwork of men" and the products of human imagination. Never have they walked in the true light of the Lord. In fact, their limitations are most evident in their desire to sacrifice to Barnabas and Paul themselves, as Zeus and Hermes; "even the priest of the temple of Zeus... wished to offer sacrifice to them," and Barnabas and Paul must shout at them "frantically": "We are bringing you the Good News that will convert you from just such follies as these"!

"Not to us, O Lord, not to us but to your name give glory" is our psalmist's refrain today, and the same is exclaimed by Barnabas and Paul: "We are only men, human like you." Worship the living God! is their exhortation. And Jesus Himself speaks in the same humility and with the same deference to the Father: "The word you hear is not mine, it comes from the Father who sent me." All comes from the Father and must return to Him; and so we are all encouraged to make our home with Him alone.

"Our God is in heaven; whatever He wills, He does." He wills to love all, to bless all, to make His home with all. To find our homes with Him, to know the blessed love the living God has for all His creatures, we must listen to the instruction of His Son, to the Holy Spirit the Father now sends in His name, and to the ones who are sent to preach the truth of the living God. May the light of His face shine upon you.

E. 5. Tues.

Tuesday
(Acts 14:19-28; Ps.145:10-13,21; Jn.14:27-31)

"We must undergo many trials if we are to enter into the reign of God."

"With this instruction" Paul and Barnabas "gave their disciples reassurances, and encouraged them to persevere in the faith." Their apostolic journey has been a witness that the road to the Lord is wrought with difficulties, but that it bears great fruit. These apostles are pursued from towns in which they have preached by those who would destroy them and their word. Paul is stoned, seemingly unto death. But their trials do not dissuade these apostles from retracing their steps through the very towns from which they have been ejected and installing elders, priests, in each one, "commend[ing] them to the Lord in whom they had put their faith." And so they arrived again at the place "where they had first been commended to the favor of God for the task they had now completed." Now they are able to relate in joy "all that God had helped them accomplish, and how He had opened the door of faith to the Gentiles," perhaps the greatest feat of the growing Church, the Body of Christ on earth.

Of course, Jesus' words to His disciples are the same as Paul's: "'Peace' is my farewell to you, my peace is my gift to you," Jesus says, and adds, "I do not give it to you as the world gives peace." For the peace Jesus gives is deeper and abides eternally; it remains through any trial of the world for it is not dependent on the consolations that come from earthly things. And so He can assure them, "Do not be distressed or fearful." He can freely invite them into the peace He possesses and to which He returns, as *He* retraces His steps back to the Father from whom He has come, whence He had first been commended to the favor of God for *His* mission. He knows they will suffer, even as He is about to suffer death at the hands of "the Prince of this world." But He knows the devil's power "has no hold" on Him, and would have us know Satan has no power over us either. For we are with Jesus; we are with the Father in heaven. And though we be as Paul in his persecutions, though we be stoned and "dragged... out of town" and left for

664

dead, the Lord's angels will surround us as Paul's disciples surrounded him – as they come to Jesus in the tomb – and like Paul, and like our Lord, "before long" we shall get up and return to our call; and ultimately we shall rise from the dead to eternal life with Jesus, coming to the home He now prepares.

"I go away for a while and I come back to you," Jesus assures His disciples, and asks them to be joyful that He returns to the greatness of the Father, whose "dominion endures through all generations." And so, brothers and sisters, may our "mouth[s] speak the praise of the Lord" all our days; "may all flesh bless His holy name forever and ever." Let us do as He commands and "discourse of the glory of [His] kingdom and speak of [His] might," and that power will enable us to endure all things, and we shall be brought at last into His reign.

Wednesday
(Acts 15:1-6; Ps.122:1-5; Jn.15:1-8)

"I am the vine, you are the branches."

And within Him we must remain; nurtured by the Church He has planted we must always be. We must have His blood flowing in our veins and His Word inspiring our souls. There can be no separation from Him and from His teaching if we are to bear fruit abundantly, as is the Father's desire.

Paul and Barnabas bear fruit abundantly. As "the church saw them off... they made their way through Phoenicia and Samaria, telling everyone about the conversion of the Gentiles as they went." And to each branch of the vine they went, "their story caused great joy among the brothers." Here is the vine's growth evident, the blood of the Lord coursing through its veins. "When they arrived in Jerusalem they were welcomed by that church," too, and there they "reported all that God had helped them accomplish" to the apostles. Why have they come here to Jerusalem? Because "in it are set up judgment seats." As great as their work had been, yet they knew the necessity of being obedient to the structure of the vine the Lord tends by His hand. And so when a controversial question arises, Paul and Barnabas "go up to see the apostles and elders in Jerusalem" to find answer.

Why Jerusalem? Because the Church, the New Jerusalem, is "built as a city with compact unity," and still at this time the Rock, Peter, and the foundation stones, the twelve apostles, reside in this place. If one separates oneself from the roots of this vine, one effectively separates oneself from Jesus and becomes "like a withered, rejected branch, picked up to be thrown in the fire and burnt." "No more than a branch can bear fruit of itself apart from the vine, can you bear fruit apart from me," Jesus instructs His disciples. And Paul and Barnabas know the order that must be preserved if the vine is to remain whole, if their work is to be truly fruitful. So here as to the question of circumcision, the first major controversy in the early Church, "the elders accordingly convened to look into the matter."

"If you live in me, and my words stay part of you, you may ask what you will – it will be done for you." The Lord's promise is great. But to receive such grace we must keep our feet firmly planted within the gates of the New Jerusalem, in the one, holy, catholic, and apostolic Church He has founded. We should rejoice to "go up to the house of the Lord," for there we shall find Jesus, there we shall find His vine spreading faithfully to the ends of the earth – in it we shall always be nourished by truth.

Thursday
(Acts 15:7-21; Ps.96:1-3,10; Jn.15:9-11)

"We are saved by the favor of the Lord Jesus."

We are told of the Council of Jerusalem, convened to determine if the Gentiles need be subject to circumcision and the Mosaic Law, "After much discussion, Peter took the floor," and that after he had finished speaking, "the whole assembly fell silent." What is there to say after the Rock of the Church has spoken? And how marvelously his declaration mirrors Jesus' own simple command to His disciples, "Live on in my love."

I am certain that before he stood to speak in the midst of the din of argument that pervaded this first assembly of God's people, Peter heard the words of Jesus speaking to his heart: "Simon, son of John, feed my sheep." He remembers his call and the Spirit the Lord has placed upon him as keeper of the keys of heaven. He remembers, too, the vision the Savior of mankind brought to his mind, instructing him not to discriminate in his sharing of the Word of God. He therefore reminds his brothers that God "reads the hearts of men," and particularly of how "He showed His approval [of the Gentiles] by granting the Holy Spirit to them," just as He had done to those gathered in this assembly. God "made no distinction... but purified their hearts by means of faith also." And would they then place undue burden upon what God has wrought by His own hand?

Yes, Peter in his pronouncement sings of the "new song" of the Lord and by doing so encourages all to "sing to the Lord; bless His name." He hereby "announce[s] His salvation," that His glory might be told "among the nations; among all peoples, His wondrous deeds." Here he demonstrates how the Lord "governs the peoples with equity." The righteous judgment that James makes, now shared in harmony by all assembled, is none other than the judgment Peter has proclaimed – which is none other than Jesus' own word for all to keep the commandment to live in the Father's love that all our "joy may be complete," that all may be gathered into the Father's kingdom.

Scripture says of the House the Father builds here on earth, of Jerusalem, His Church: "From its ruins I will rebuild it and set it up again, so that all the rest of mankind and all the nations that bear my name may seek out the Lord." What was the house of David now shelters all the nations – the old Jerusalem has become the new City of Peace held in God's own hand, His Holy Spirit breathing upon its members and giving them life. By the favor of Christ has this been accomplished; let no man shorten the arm of the Lord.

Friday
(Acts 15:22-31; Ps.57:8-12; Jn.15:12-17)

"There is no greater love than this:
to lay down one's life for one's friends."

Do not Judas and Silas fulfill the Lord's command to "love one another"; do they not lay down their lives for the Lord when they bring word "to the brothers of Gentile origin in Antioch, Syria, and Cilicia" of the apostles' decision regarding those who have "upset [them] with their discussions and disturbed [their] peace of mind"? Do they not carry the love of the Lord in their persons as well as in the letter in their hands?

And are these Gentiles not made friends of the Lord even as the apostles and elders, even as those who come to them? Jesus says to His disciples in our gospel, "I call you friends, since I have made known to you all that I heard from my Father." And now in the same way these two disciples "go forth and bear fruit" as the Lord has commanded by making known to the children of the nations "the decision of the Holy Spirit," the whole Truth of God's love, thus drawing them into the friendship of Christ.

The apostles and elders, who call themselves "brothers" of those of Gentile origin, "have unanimously resolved to choose representatives and send them" to witness of the Lord's love for them; Paul and Barnabas are called by the apostles, those "who have dedicated themselves to the cause of our Lord Jesus Christ" – there is left no doubt of the strength of the decision that is made and the authority by which it comes. And so "there was great delight at the encouragement [the letter] gave," for it and those who read it hold indeed the love of God, the absolute truth of the Holy Spirit, by whose power they have been freed from the burdens being imposed upon them and brought into the fold and friendship, the love of the Lord Jesus Christ. Alleluia!

"I will give thanks to you among the peoples, O Lord, I will chant your praises among the nations." With David, the Gentile disciples "sing and chant praise" to the living God who is "exalted above the heavens" and "above all the earth." The Spirit of the Lord is upon them now by the love that has been laid down before them, and now they too are called to lay down their lives in the Lord's love, as are we all, that friends of Jesus, sons of the Father, may ever be drawn into His holy fold.

Saturday
(Acts 16:1-10; Ps.100:1-3,5; Jn.15:18-21)

"I chose you out of the world."

What is the world but heartache and sin? From this the Lord would release us.

Jesus tells His disciples: "You do not belong to the world," and yet, as is most evident in the journeys of Paul, to all the world do the apostles go. The Master tells them, "You [will] find that the world hates you"; even so, they preach to a world which has no respect for the name they proclaim, which "know[s] nothing of Him who sent" them. The inevitable persecution they do not fear, the death their work brings they do not flee, but face all in complete readiness.

Indeed, Paul is our example of the commitment we all must have to doing the Lord's will in this world. With great fervor he travels from land to land and, praise God, "through all this, the congregations grew stronger in faith and daily increased in numbers." He transmits the Lord's Gospel message to all waiting ears and perseveres through all trials. For there are those throughout this earth who will listen to the Word that "the Lord is God; He made us, His we are," and that Jesus is His Son – and Paul cannot help but strain forward to find these hearts which long to "come before Him with joyful song." So great is Paul's desire to bring the word of the Lord to those who have never heard it before that he must be restrained by the Holy Spirit. Twice today in our first reading he is prevented from entering and preaching to lands for which it is not time, finally being called in a vision to those who awaited him. Paul and the apostles' readiness to do the Lord's will is related clearly in Luke's statement, "After the vision, we immediately made efforts to get across to Macedonia, concluding that God had summoned us to proclaim the Good News there."

We must go where we are called and move as we are led by the Spirit of Jesus the Christ. Into the world He leads us all to bring His light forth.

Though never of the world, we must encourage all the world to "sing joyfully to the Lord," to "serve the Lord with gladness." By our words and by our lives we must show that we are "His people, the flock He tends," and others will be drawn from the clutches of a world that hates the truth and into the protecting arms of God.

Sixth Week

Sunday (A)
(Acts 8:5-8,14-17; Ps.66:1-7,16,20; 1Pt.3:15-18; Jn.14:15-21)

"Put to death in the flesh, He was brought to life in the Spirit."

It is of this way to life Jesus teaches us when He says, "If you love me, you will keep my commandments," for what is it to keep His commandments but to carry His cross – to lay down our lives, to die to the flesh, to suffer for His sake – and what is love but the life the Spirit brings? And both dying to self and loving God we find the Spirit at work in our lives; He is "the Spirit of truth," yes, but also the Spirit of love, for He is the love of the Father and the Son, and it is by Him we become one in love with Father and Son, and so share in the oneness of the Holy Trinity.

Love and truth are really one and the same; neither exists without the other, for both are of God who is one in Himself. We know the commandment of God, which calls us by the fire of truth to kill all the sin within our souls, is simply a commandment to love, for the whole law is summed up in love. And when Peter calls us to "always be ready to give an explanation to anyone who asks [us] for a reason for [our] hope" (in other words, to speak the truth of the risen Christ), he cannot but immediately add, "Do it with gentleness and reverence, keeping your conscience clear"; for if not spoken in love, it is no truth at all – it is but vain posturing.

Truth and love may also be seen in Philip's work in the city of Samaria. He went and "proclaimed the Christ to them" – thus the sword of truth goes forth to pierce hearts and bleed them of sin – but the new life that is brought about by this death to the flesh is also evident, in the signs of God's love he enacted in casting out evil spirits and in the "many paralyzed or crippled people [who] were cured." And O how the fullness of truth and the perfection of love came upon these converts when Peter and John "laid hands on them and they received the Holy Spirit." Alleluia! If before "there was great joy in that city" upon being "baptized in the name of Jesus," now what joy there is for them to know this blessing would never leave.

Jesus promises to send "another Advocate to be with [us] always"; this is the Holy Spirit who confirms in us that once dead to sin, we shall live forever in Him. For this blessing let us "shout joyfully to God" and "sing praise to the glory of His name." For indeed now by His kindness and His truth, by His grace and by His might, in love and justice He has set us free from the death of sin and brought us to life in Him. Alleluia!

Sunday (B)
(Acts 10:25-26,34-35,44-48; Ps.98:1-4; 1Jn.4:7-10; Jn.15:9-17)

"This I command you: love one another."

And so we hear the Lord's essential instruction: love. If we keep His commandments we will love, and if we love we will keep His commandments. His commandment is to love.

But what is love? John gives us the simple answer, of course: "God is love," but also indicates further the nature of love, corroborated by the Lord Himself. It is "not that we have loved God, but that He loved us." Love comes not from us but from God, because, as we have said, God is love; we are not love. It is God the Father who has sent His Son to reveal His love by dying for our sins; without this sacrifice we would not know love, could not comprehend the love that is God, that is willing to lay down His very life for the sake of His children. Apart from this love we remain in the dark about love – any love separated from this offering is not love at all.

And as it is not we who love but He who gives love, who is love, so it is not we who choose Him but He us. We did not contrive the sacrifice of the Son: we could never have imagined it. We have, in fact, great difficulty in simply accepting it, so beyond our concept of love it is. But there it is. There He is, calling us to His love, to this love, to the sacrifice of our own selves for one another, that we might thoroughly share in the gift of love. We need but respond to know love.

And who may share in this love? Let us come to Peter's realization: "In every nation whoever fears Him and acts uprightly is acceptable to Him." There is none from whom the Spirit can be withheld, for, as John confirms, "Everyone who loves is begotten by God and knows God." So we need but love. We need but put our hope in Him and in His love. We need but keep His command, and His love shall be our own, and we shall find ourselves "speaking in tongues and glorifying God"; whomever we are and wherever we come from, we know "the salvation by our God" by living in the love of the Spirit and being "baptized in the name of Jesus Christ."

Alleluia! There is not much else to say. Alleluia! Praise the Lord! Let us forever live in His love. Let us forever die for one another.

Sunday (C)

(Acts 15:1-2,22-29; Ps.67:2-6,8; Rv.21:10-14,22-23; Jn.14:23-29)

"The wall of the city had twelve courses of stones as its foundation,
on which were inscribed the twelve names
of the twelve apostles of the Lamb."

And so is "the holy city Jerusalem" protected; and so are its boundaries defined. And so we come to the apostles to find the true teaching of Christ.

When "there arose no little dissension and debate" between Paul and Barnabas and certain brothers from Judea who were insisting the Gentile converts must be "circumcised according to the Mosaic practice," what was the recourse needed to settle this most crucial of questions – the first great question of the Church? "It was decided that Paul, Barnabas, and some of the others should go up to Jerusalem to the apostles and elders." There the debate would be settled. There authority is found – in the apostles and those they appoint. There is nowhere else on earth any could turn to secure the truth, to find genuine guidance of the Holy Spirit, whom Jesus has promised "will teach [the disciples] everything," who will be with the Church as its Advocate till the end of time. And so the apostles and elders speak in truth when they write to the waiting souls of the Gentiles: "It is the decision of the Holy Spirit and of us not to place on you any burden," for indeed they speak of the Holy Spirit and for and by the Holy Spirit – indeed they speak the truth.

Brothers and sisters, is not the reason the Church is fractured into hundreds if not thousands or even millions of pieces (each soul following his own way without regard for the teaching of the Church), is not the reason some advocate for abortion, or euthanasia, or female or homosexual priests, or a thousand other indiscretions and blasphemies – is not the cause of the great turmoil within the walls of the temple as well as, inevitably, outside it in the world... is it not fundamentally a lack of obedience to the teachings of Christ, to the teachings of His apostles? And though it is so that upon all His baptized is placed the seal of the Spirit, and so all may know the truth, yet it is just as so that without the confirmation of the apostles – as even Paul realized – one cannot be sure of his thoughts, and certainly has no right to teach! Surely the Jews thought they were right in insisting the Gentiles be circumcised. Let none be presumptuous of the Spirit's word.

In the heavenly city there is "no temple," there is "no need of sun or moon" – "the glory of God [gives] it light, and its lamp [is] the Lamb." But we do not dwell in the fullness of Jerusalem here; this I can assure you. On

671

earth we have unquestionable need for a Church. And that Church is now founded in Rome with the Pope.

Monday
(Acts 16:11-15; Ps.149:1-6,9; Jn.15:26-16:4)

"You must bear witness."

The Spirit will come and call to your hearts to speak of the name of Jesus and His salvation. As He prompts you, you must speak the truth in love, you must go as He calls – you must bear witness. And sometimes the word you speak, and you yourself, will be accepted with the faith and great hospitality as known in Lydia (who is said to be "one who listened," for "the Lord opened her heart to accept what Paul was saying," and who generously invited Paul and his companions, foreigners traveling to distant lands, to "come and stay at [her] house"); and other times those who "know neither the Father nor [the Son]" will "expel you from synagogues," will cast you violently from their midst, and "anyone who puts you to death will claim to be serving God!" It does not matter. The Word must go forth, in season and out.

How few true witnesses there seem to be today, for in the time and place in which I stand certainly the Word of God is out of season. False witnesses with strange gospels abound, but the tongue of the apostles is tied, and what *is* spoken seems to land upon deaf ears. Those who have no conception of the Holy Spirit and so know neither Father nor Son are emboldened to speak as messengers of Jesus, though the Jesus they know is not the Christ and what they speak but serves to lead the sheep astray. And where is His Church? Will no one stand to speak of His love?

Today instead of "sing[ing] for joy upon [our] couches... the high praises of God... in our throats," the houses in which we dwell seem to swallow our souls, and we are left mute in the face of destruction. And it is hard to say that our faith is shaken, for who can find any faith at all? Neither persecution nor glad acceptance do we find, for we speak no word to challenge the world.

Let us pray to the Lord, brothers and sisters, that He will send laborers forth, that even in this time of lethargy upon His Church, new life is beginning to grow. For until the end of time the Word must go forth; before then it shall not have reached its goal. However well the devil may fool us into complacency, we must know that it is always time to preach the Word, for ever will hearts be seeking Him – and ever hands seek to destroy Him. "The Lord loves His people, and He adorns the lowly with victory." This call to the humble must be heard by all.

Tuesday
(Acts 16:22-34; Ps.138:1-3,7-8; Jn.16:5-11)

"Immediately all the doors flew open
and everyone's chains were pulled loose."

"Your right hand saves me," David sings unto the Lord this day in our psalm. Mighty indeed is His power, and so we should "worship at [His] holy temple, and give thanks to [His] name," for He has "built up strength within [us]"; by the power of the Holy Spirit He has set us free from our prisons, from the chains of sin.

"When I called you, you answered me," David sings. And how the Lord answers Paul and Silas as they call unto Him in song of their own. "After receiving many lashes they were thrown into prison, and the jailer... put them in maximum security, going so far as to chain their feet to a stake." Yet what do we find these apostles doing in the deep of the night? – "praying and singing hymns to God as their fellow prisoners listened." And God hears their prayers; they bring "a severe earthquake [which] suddenly shook the place, rocking the prison to its foundations" and setting all those inside free of their chains.

Can we have a clearer sign of the Holy Spirit's presence and power than this? Well, yes, because as wondrous as earthquakes are, the truest sign of the Spirit came this night when the jailer "and his whole household were baptized." The earthquake and the flying open of prison doors may have opened his heart to hearing the word of God, but his wholehearted acceptance of "his newfound faith in God" is the Spirit's greatest work. For what is of greater importance, the stone and steel of a prison cell shaken and cast to the ground, or the salvation of the eternal soul of man?

The Lord Jesus has promised to send the Spirit as Advocate to plead our cause and prove us right about our faith in the One who saves from sin. In justice and in truth He goes to the Father, and from His exalted throne He sends forth the Paraclete to prove His presence with us still; and by the grace and power of the Holy Trinity at work in our midst, "the prince of this world has been condemned" and the prison he built to contain us destroyed.

"I will give thanks to you, O Lord, with all my heart." Let us sing to Him, brothers and sisters. Let us join with David and Silas and Paul, and all the redeemed of the Lord, and "joyfully celebrate with [our] whole family," with all the children of our God, our everlasting faith in the Father, Son, and Spirit. From prison we have been released; with the Savior we are risen. His Spirit is upon us now.

Wednesday
(Acts 17:15,22-18:1; Ps.148:1-2,11-14,Is.6:3; Jn.16:12-15)

"It is He 'who gives' to all life and 'breath' and everything else."

"His majesty is above earth and heaven," brothers and sisters. And so our psalmist today encourages all in the heavens and all on earth to "praise the name of the Lord, for His name alone is exalted." "From one stock He made every nation of mankind to dwell on the face of the earth," and it is "in Him we live and move and have our being." And so should we, "His faithful ones," not offer Him praise?

Brothers, be not ignorant as the men of Athens who thought "the God who made the world and 'all that is in it,' the Lord of heaven and earth," as "something like a statue of gold or silver or stone, a product of man's genius and his art." Could man with all his intelligence make the sun or wind? Then how can it be that he might contrive the Creator of these? Such groping in darkness for the God who is "not really far from any of us" shall not be tolerated forever. For the time has come to turn on the lamp which lights the room and let all shadows flee. He who is going to "judge the world with justice" is among us now; it is He whom God "has endorsed in the sight of all by raising Him from the dead." And it is faith in Him to which we must come.

Jesus promises the disciples that "the Spirit of truth... will guide [them] to all truth." It is He who "will not speak on His own, but will speak only what He hears." He receives from Jesus, who possesses "all that the Father has," all that He announces to us. And Paul is His mouthpiece today, speaking not what he has invented by his erudite learning and fanciful imagining, but rather proclaiming the truth he hears the Spirit inspiring in his soul and burning in his heart.

We shall not get to heaven on stairs we make with our soiled hands; they can but crumble under the pressure of time and the weight of truth. Only by obedience to the Spirit who inspires all, shall all find the presence of the "God Unknown" to hearts of stone and minds as fleeting as a wisp of smoke. "He calls on all men everywhere to reform their lives," for their scoffing at truth shall bring them alone to a dark room, where there shall be no breath of the Spirit. But we who know all wisdom comes from God, living in its light are made His children.

Ascension of the Lord

(Acts 1:1-11; Ps.47:1-3,6-9; Eph.1:17-23 or Eph.4:1-13 or Heb.9:24-28,10:19-23;
Mt.28:16-20 or Mk.16:15-20 or Lk.24:46-53)

"God mounts His throne amid shouts of joy;
the Lord, amid trumpet blasts."

Three events are the subject of today's readings. The key of these is certainly the Lord's ascending into heaven and taking His place at the right hand of the Father. Without this the other two could not follow. And so we celebrate the Lord's Ascension in particular; but we also hear of the coming Pentecost and the apostles' call to go forth to the ends of the world.

"As they were looking on, He was lifted up, and a cloud took Him from their sight." Now He goes to heaven, returning to the Father, as He has said, to enter into glory. And as He has asked, we should be joyful, we should "shout to God with cries of gladness. For the Lord, the Most High, the awesome, is the great King over all the earth," and now Jesus, our Savior and our brother, is with Him, and so brings us to Him. His glory becomes our own, and so His now assuming His throne in heaven should cause us to "sing hymns of praise" to Him who now "reigns over the nations."

And from His place seated "at the right hand of God" "upon His holy throne," the Lord keeps "the promise of the Father about which [we] have heard [Him] speak." For "in a few days [we] will be baptized with the Holy Spirit"; Pentecost will be here, and Jesus' words to His disciples as He prepares to ascend will be our own: "You will receive power when the Holy Spirit comes upon you." It is from this Holy Spirit that the Church takes its strength, through whom we are all made one in "faith and knowledge of the Son of God," and by whom we attain to "the full stature of Christ." He it is who inspires all, and He could not come except that our high priest has entered the sanctuary of heaven – opening for us the way to enter there – and from there delivered unto us the grace which through Him comes.

And what does this inspiration, this absolute strength we take in the Spirit call us to do but to heed the Lord's words and "go into the whole world and proclaim the Gospel to every creature," knowing as He has said, "I am with you always, until the end of the age"? And so, apostles and prophets and evangelists and all His children go forth empowered by His Spirit that "hearts [may] be enlightened," that all might know "the hope that belongs to His call... the riches of glory in His inheritance... and what is the surpassing greatness of His power" – that all might believe in the Father, Son, and Holy Spirit.

Jesus is now seated at the Father's right hand in heaven, "far above every principality, authority, power, and dominion, and every name that is

Easter

named not only in this age but also in the one to come." All things are "beneath His feet," for "King of all the earth is God," and Jesus is God. But though the Son has joined the Father, remember He is with us always, suffering with us still and bringing us to His side by the power of His Spirit. Wait now on His Word.

Friday

(Acts 18:9-18; Ps.47:2-8; Jn.16:20-23)

"Go on speaking and do not be silenced,
for I am with you."

As Paul continues his missionary journey, his fears are calmed by the Lord, who assures him: "No one will attack you or harm you," though he be in Corinth, whose infamous immorality is illustrated in the riotous behavior of the Jews in its court, and to which the court "paid no attention at all." And the Lord is true to His word, protecting Paul throughout his year-and-a-half stay, and keeping him even from having to defend himself from charges in today's first reading.

In our gospel Jesus reassures the disciples at the Last Supper, as He is about to leave them and their hearts begin to be troubled: "You will grieve for a time, but your grief will be turned into joy." And though there remains ever a measure of grief in our hearts as we labor in this world, our bodies apart from the fullness of the grace of heaven, yet we know that Jesus' promise has indeed been kept in His sending His Spirit upon the apostles from His heavenly kingdom. It is, of course, this Holy Spirit who inspires and guides and protects Paul, making his missionary work fruitful, for he does all having been baptized by the fire of Christ. And, of course, the disciples to whom Jesus speaks today will soon have no more fear, for Pentecost is not far from them.

Pentecost is not far from any of us, brothers and sisters. The promised Spirit is come into the world to answer all questions, to calm all our anxieties. As we wait these nine days to celebrate this great feast of the Church, as we prepare again to enter into its birth in the Spirit of God, let us be assured that the Lord's promise remains: "You are sad for a time, but I shall see you again; then your hearts will rejoice with a joy no one can take from you."

No one can take from us the promised joy we now hold in our hearts and which is renewed in this season. As Paul is emboldened even through his most difficult trials, as the apostles rejoice at their persecutions for Jesus' sake, so we should know that the Lord "brings people under us, nations under our feet"; and so, as powerful as the world may seem in all its brazen immorality, yet we are assured that "He chooses for us our inheritance, the glory of Jacob, whom He loves." "There are many of [His] people in this city," here where we dwell on earth, and we must speak to them of the Lord's glory, His love strengthening us for every task. It is He who accomplishes all in us, and so He will guide and guard our way.

Saturday
(Acts 18:23-28; Ps.47:2-3,8-10; Jn.16:23-28)

"He went about establishing from the Scriptures
that Jesus is the Messiah."

In our gospel today, Jesus again assures the disciples, "Whatever you ask the Father, He will give you in my name," He tells them of the time when He will no longer speak to them "in veiled language," but "shall tell [them] about the Father in plain speech." A most fascinating quote is His statement, "I do not say that I will petition the Father for you." So great is our oneness with Jesus because we "have believed that [He] came from God," that now as He returns to the Father, we go there with Him; and since we are thus with the Father through Him, He need not ask for us of the Father, but we ask ourselves. When Jesus declares, "The Father already loves you, because you have loved me," He is telling us that we are indeed one with Him in the Father's love, and so, of course, the Father hears all our prayers.

In our reading from the Acts of the Apostles, we hear of Apollos, who was "a man full of spiritual fervor. He spoke and taught accurately about Jesus." His love for the Lord is most evident in His "express[ing] himself fearlessly in the synagogue," in his "vigorous" preaching of Jesus as the Messiah. He also shows himself to be a humble man, very acquiescent to Priscilla and Aquila, who "took him home and explained to him God's new way in greater detail." As strong as he was, and as much as "he greatly strengthened those who through God's favor had become believers," he was very willing to learn of his weakness. And so he becomes a model of faith and of the oneness with God we find in the Spirit through the love of Christ. And so his words are like prayers which never fall short of the glory of God. And so the Father answers all he has in his heart.

"He is supreme," brothers and sisters. The Lord Jesus now sits on the throne of God in the highest heavens. And we who believe in Him become one with Him, and so, one with the Father of all. And thus do we find all our prayers answered; thus do we find all our work blessed. Thus do we find ourselves moving as one with the will of God by the love the Father shares with all of us through our faith in His Son. As great as Apollos and

Easter

Paul and all the apostles are, we can be, if we but believe that Jesus is God and so share in the Father's love, and so hear the Holy Spirit speaking plainly to our hearts.

Seventh Week

Sunday (A)
(Acts 1:12-14; Ps.27:1,4,7-8,13; 1Pt.4:13-16; Jn.17:1-11a)

"One thing I ask of the Lord; this I seek:
to dwell in the house of the Lord all the days of my life."

Obedient to the instructions of the Lord, the apostles returned to Jerusalem, where they gathered together in "the upper room" and "devoted themselves with one accord to prayer," waiting for the promised gift of the Spirit of God. With David they long to "gaze on the loveliness of the Lord and contemplate His temple," and so, with him they sing, "Of you my heart speaks, you my glance seeks."

The Pentecost is soon to come; the Spirit shall soon fall upon the apostles and fulfill their longing for union with God. But as they wait, they suffer, as do we all, for waiting means to suffer – finding patience is to share in the passion of Christ, in the absolute subjection of our wills to the Father and so the death of our own ways. But Peter's words come as comfort to us as we ourselves wait for the glory of God to come to us: "Beloved: Rejoice to the extent that you share in the sufferings of Christ, so that when His glory is revealed you may also rejoice exultantly." He knows of what he speaks. For his patient waiting, his dying to self, has been rewarded by the gift of the Spirit now with him as he speaks... and each day his continued suffering brings renewed joy. He is able to sing with full voice the words of David's psalm: "The Lord is my life's refuge; of whom should I be afraid?" And to such fullness of the glory of God we all should come.

In our gospel Jesus calls down the glory of the Father upon Himself and so, in turn, upon all who love Him, that He may "give eternal life to all [the Father] gave Him." As the Son has glorified the Father on earth, now He seeks to be glorified by Him in heaven, and not for His own sake, but for the benefit of those who listen as He prays to His Father. In our midst He prays for us that the power of the Holy Spirit might make us one with Him as He is one with the Father, that we might share in the glory of God.

"Now this is eternal life, that they should know you, the only true God, and the one whom you sent, Jesus Christ." "Out of the world" He calls us, away from its darkness He brings us, that "in the world" we may be, sharing

His glory with all... so to find eternal life, so to find ourselves in the hand of God, in His Temple, gazing always upon the light of His face. Alleluia!

Sunday (B)
(Acts1:15-17,20a,20c-26; Ps.103:1-2,11-12,19-20; 1Jn.4:11-16; Jn.17:11b-19)

"As you sent me into the world,
so I sent them into the world."

Jesus sent the apostles forth, and "none of them was lost except the son of destruction"; and Judas was lost only "that the Scripture might be fulfilled," that the betrayal of the Christ might be accomplished. Otherwise, those whom He sent He also protected, He also guarded well from the evil one, that what must be accomplished in them should likewise be brought to fulfillment – that they be one with Jesus in the Father and bring His holy Name to the world, that all might be gathered together as one in God's truth and His love.

To begin the accomplishment of this mission after the departure of the Christ, the principal soul whom Jesus sends stands up in the midst of all his brothers and calls for the replacement of Judas, that Scripture – "*may another take his office*" – continue to be fulfilled. Matthias is chosen by the Lord to become the twelfth "witness to His resurrection," and so "the apostolic ministry" is now in place; and so the army of God can now go forth to reveal that "His kingdom rules over all."

And what is His kingdom, brothers and sisters, but a kingdom of love? Our beloved John ever makes this clear, ever emphasizes this essential word of truth, and we must declare in truth his essential word of God's love: "We have come to know and to believe in the love God has for us." His proclamation must be our own. We must see and know how the Lord guards us, how He protects us from the snares of the world and preserves us in His love by putting "our transgressions [far] from us," that we might praise His name in faith even unto heaven. We must say with John, "We have seen and testify that the Father sent His Son as savior of the world." In genuine recognition of this basic truth we shall find the love of God living in us.

And "if God so loved us" by sending His only Son to us, "we must love one another" by heeding His call to be sent to others. Like Matthias and the apostles, we too have a blessed vocation in Christ to bring His love and His truth to this dying world. To this let us consecrate ourselves as freely as has our Jesus, as freely as the Twelve... "that we might share [the Lord's] joy completely." We "do not belong to the world any more than [He] belong[s] to the world": let us find our place in His kingdom.

Easter

Sunday (C)
(Acts 7:55-60; Ps.97:1-2,6-7,9; Rv.22:12-14,16-17,20; Jn.17:20-26)

"I wish that where I am they also may be with me,
that they may see my glory that you gave me."

The Father gave Jesus His glory. It is Jesus' own glory He owns, for He had it "before the foundation of the world," but now the Father has given it to Him anew in His incarnation as the Son of Man; and in His death and resurrection He shall not only confirm it in Himself, but serve thus to make it our own.

What glory is ours in this Son of God who has come among us to draw us into the Father's immortal, eternal love! It is the same glory the Father and Son know and share in the Spirit who makes them one. We are called to be so one with this Holy Trinity. Our jaws should drop at such a prospect, our hearts reach up, and praise of the Most High God resound upon our tongues; for what does Jesus pray for us but that we be one in glory with the Righteous One?

And this glory is "coming soon." Jesus promises John that soon He shall return, and then absolute glory will be our own, if we have washed clean our robes from sin, if we have prepared our souls to eat from "the tree of life and enter the city through its gates," coming thus to where the glory of God dwells in eternity. But if we are not clean, if we attempt to enter the city by other means than the gate before us, the gate who is Jesus and His teachings – climbing over the wall we shall but fall, and find the taste of the fruit of the tree terribly bitter.

The people and their leaders could not well partake of the blessed word Stephen brought to their ears. Of the glory of God and their own falling short they would not hear... and so could but stone its bearer to death. But Stephen finds himself present there within the City gates, even while upon his knees and crying out; for his eyes are open to see God's glorious One, and these stones he returns to their throwers with but a prayer for peace.

Open your ears, my brothers and sisters. Open your hearts to His call. "The Spirit and the bride say, 'Come,'" and you must echo their glorious song to the Alpha and the Omega. To us soon Jesus the Christ is coming; "all peoples [will] see His glory." Invite Him in and be one with Him, even as the stones are falling. "Amen! Come, Lord Jesus!" Amen and Alleluia!

Monday

(Acts 19:1-8;   Ps.68:2-7,33;   Jn.16:29-33)

"You will suffer in the world.
But take courage! I have overcome the world."

"An hour is coming – has indeed already come – when you will be scattered and each will go his way, leaving me quite alone." Yet the Father is always with Jesus, even as He faces His imminent execution, and Jesus is with us by the power of the Spirit through all the trials *we* face.

"In me you may find peace," the Lord assures us, bearing out the words of David's psalm: "The father of orphans and defender of widows is God in His holy dwelling. God gives a home to the forsaken; He leads forth prisoners to prosperity." Such the Father does for the Son, who is brought from being utterly forsaken and alone upon the cross to the absolute fruitfulness and glory of heaven; and so the Son does for His sons, as from His place in the kingdom He delivers us the same grace of salvation and prosperity in His name.

In the Lord Jesus, Paul finds his peace and his inspiration, fearlessly defending the Gospel in all synagogues "with persuasive arguments"; and this same fire of the Holy Spirit he imparts to the disciples by Baptism "in the name of the Lord Jesus" and by laying his hands on them. In these, as in us all to this day, God's grace and power go forth: "The Holy Spirit came down on them and they began to speak in tongues and utter prophecies." More than just repentance for sins, this Baptism in the Spirit prepares all to do the work of the Lord despite any difficulties in the world. It convinces us of the divinity of Christ and causes us to declare in truth to our Lord, "There is no need for anyone to ask you questions. We do indeed believe you came from God." And it enables us to prove such complete faith and trust in the One the Father has sent.

When the Baptism of the Lord comes upon us, God's "enemies are scattered"; all doubt and fear are driven from us "as smoke is driven away... as wax melts before the fire." And though we need be refined in the crucible that is our earthly life, yet at every moment God is near to preserve the grace and peace He has planted in our souls, to see that our faith does grow.

> Lord, be with us always. Send your Spirit forth.
> Let the ends of the earth be convinced of your loving presence
>   and the salvation it brings to all hearts.

Tuesday

(Acts 20:17-27; Ps.68:10-11,20-21,33; Jn.17:1-11)

"Father, the hour has come!
Give glory to your Son that your Son may give glory to you."

A day of departures. A day of final words and commendations. Paul bids farewell to the leaders of Ephesus, declaring his faithfulness to them; and Jesus prays to the Father in the hearing of the disciples, calling the Lord's blessing upon them.

"The Holy Spirit has been warning me from city to city that chains and hardships await me," Paul confesses as he makes his way to Jerusalem; Jesus now has the cross directly before His eyes, having supped for the last time with His disciples. "Never did I shrink from telling you what was for your own good, or from teaching you in public or in private," Paul reminds his disciples; while Jesus states to His Father: "I have made your name known to those you gave me out of the world." "I have never shrunk from announcing to you God's design in its entirety," Paul declares; "I have given you glory on earth by finishing the work you gave me to do," Jesus says to the Father. And as Paul hopes, "If only I can finish my race and complete the service to which I have been assigned by the Lord Jesus, bearing witness to the Gospel of God's grace" – not caring for his own life or any suffering ahead – Jesus' only concern as He moves toward His own death and His return to the "glory [He] had with [the Father] before the world began" is that the Father will bless His disciples, for, as He says, "It is in them that I have been glorified." These who remain in the world, as has Paul, are those who bring His glory forth, even as Jesus has revealed the glory of the Father.

The hour of death has come but "God, who is our salvation... controls the passageways of death" because He "bears our burdens." The Lord Jesus Christ has borne, and will bear, all the temptations the devil can mount – the greatest of these illusions being death – and has conquered them all. And now His disciples follow in His footsteps, like Paul, who has "served the Lord in humility through the sorrows and trials that came [his] way." By this sacrifice the Lord "restored the land when it languished," and now all are called to "repentance before God and... faith in our Lord Jesus" to know that redemption. This life that comes from His death is the glory of the Lord that goes now forth.

Wednesday

(Acts 20:28-38; Ps.68:29-30,33-36; Jn.17:11-19)

"O Father most holy,
protect them with the name you have given me."

In our gospel today Jesus prays to the Father, "who rides on the heights of the ancient heavens," to "guard [His disciples] from the evil one." And the parallels continue between His and Paul's parting words, as the Apostle warns his own disciples, "When I am gone, savage wolves will come among you who will not spare the flock," and therefore exhorts them to "be on guard."

It is the Lord's earnest desire of the Father that we His disciples "be consecrated in truth." If truth be with us, if the Holy Spirit He promises to send be ours, the "careful watch" Jesus has kept "as long as [He] was with [us]" will continue. In fact, Paul's instruction to the elders of Ephesus to "shepherd the Church of God, which He has acquired at the price of His own blood" – blood the Lord is about to shed in our gospel – will be realized, and His apostles will become themselves those who care for the safety of the people of God. "I consecrate myself for their sakes now," Jesus says, offering Himself, His blood, as sacrifice for the Church; and Paul commends his disciples to this same Lord, "to that gracious word of His which can enlarge [them], and give [them] a share among all who are consecrated to Him." In His name all are saved.

"Awesome in His sanctuary is God, the God of Israel; He gives power and strength to His people." David sings mightily of the majesty of God, whose "voice resounds, the voice of power," and calling all to "confess the power of God!" indicates how we share in that great power. In declaring of the Father, with Jesus and with Scripture, "Your word is truth," that truth in essence becomes our own; we are thereby consecrated to it. And so Paul can exhort those he has placed in positions of power: "Keep watch over yourselves, and over the whole flock the Holy Spirit has given you to guard," for he knows as long as (like Paul) they do not "set [their] hearts on anyone's silver or gold," as long as they work tirelessly to "help the weak," to serve the Church, they shall indeed be sharing in the power and authority of God.

Brothers and sisters, we "do not belong to the world" but to God and to His truth. His Spirit is with us to guide us and protect us here on our journey through death to life. As we humble ourselves in prayer before Him, He hears and answers all our needs. Remain in Him this day.

Thursday

(Acts 22:30,23:6-11; Ps.16:1-2,5,7-11; Jn.17:20-26)

"I set the Lord ever before me;
with Him at my right hand I shall not be disturbed."

Yes, "the Lord appeared at Paul's side" at night, in prison, after his testimony and the near riot it caused in Jerusalem. He comes to encourage him, to strengthen him for further trials; and through all Paul shall remain strong.

"Keep me, O God, for in you, I take refuge," David prays, and sings of the confidence his heart and soul find in the Lord, his "allotted portion and cup... who hold[s] fast [his] lot." He knows deep in his spirit that the Lord "will not abandon [his] soul to the nether world, nor will [He] suffer [His] faithful one to undergo corruption." And certainly, the same faith Paul exhibits; the same trust in the Lord, Paul holds in his own spirit. He, too, is not disturbed, though he finds himself "on trial now because of [his] hope in the resurrection of the dead."

And whence comes such confidence? How can a man so attacked, a man so beaten and cursed, be so without fear? Does not Jesus answer this question in His prayer to the Father, which we are all blessed to hear? Here He prays that we be one in Him even as He is one with the Father. Here He asks that our "unity may be complete." And if our unity is complete with the Father and with the Son, as well as with one another, what, brothers and sisters, have we to fear? If the love of God which the Father "bore [the Son] before the world began" is in our hearts now, what can disturb them? "That your love for me may live in them, and I may live in them" is Jesus' prayer to the Father for us all – and do you think the Father does not listen, does not answer His Son? He would have us in His company where He is, gazing upon His glory – and this is where Paul dwells. And so he cannot be moved.

"You will show me the path to life, fullness of joys in your presence, the delights at your right hand forever." The Spirit brings us now that of which David sings, that which Paul knows, that all might know the glory of God, that all might be one in Him, and so, safe from all harm. As Jesus is resurrected from the dead, so shall we all be. What have we to fear? We must but set Him before us always.

Friday
(Acts 25:13-21; Ps.103:1-2,11-12,19-20; Jn.21:15-19)

"When you are older you will stretch out your hands,
and another will tie you fast and carry you off against your will."

And so the Lord "indicate[s] the sort of death by which Peter was to glorify God." And by his laying down of his life, this leader of the apostles shall indeed feed the Lord's sheep.

After "they had eaten their meal," when there was nothing to distract them – as the apostles gaze at the wonder of the risen Christ before their eyes – the Lord quietly speaks to Peter in the hearing of all. Three times Jesus inquires of His blessed Rock, calling him by his earthly name to assume the name heaven has assigned him. Three times the risen Lord asks, "Simon, son of John, do you love me?" and three times Peter must publicly declare his love for God above all things, three times negating his previous denials. It is a simple scene, but beautiful, and remarkably weighty. Not only does Jesus place the care of the Church into this poor apostle's hands, but He speaks clearly of the sacrifice His Rock must make, teaching him what love of God and care for His people entail... nothing less than death.

And of Paul's death for the Lord we continue to read. Though the Apostle does not himself appear in our first reading, he is spoken of clearly. Two things we learn of him: first, he is a "prisoner" "kept in custody"; second, the reason for his arrest – he differed with the Jewish leaders "about a certain Jesus who had died but who Paul claimed is alive." In his imprisonment is Paul's death and in his profession of the risen Lord he shows his love for God and the people. Here he clearly follows in the steps of Jesus, fulfilling his call from the Lord.

And, brothers and sisters, the call to death, the call to love of the Lord and care for all His children, is all our own. What the Lord speaks to Peter He speaks indeed to all the apostles seated there on the shore in Galilee; and He speaks the same in our hearing today, calling all who would follow Him in the same way. And follow Him we must. It is only by this same sort of death that any of us will come to life; it is only sharing in His cross that we will find the resurrection. We cannot see the risen Lord, nor rise ourselves, if we are not willing to die for Him and with Him.

But do not fear: "The Lord has established His throne in heaven, and His kingdom rules over all." Neither Festus nor Felix nor King Agrippa nor the Jewish elders can judge Paul, for he is only in God's hands. And so, though we be dragged to certain crucifixion, the world holds no sway over our souls – the life the Spirit provides and the strength He instills cannot be

685

destroyed. Let us stretch out our hands freely to embrace our blessed Lord and "all His benefits" receive through our sharing in His sacrifice of love.

Saturday
(Acts 28:16-20,30-31; Ps.11:4-5,7; Jn.21:20-25)

"I wear these chains solely because I share the hope of Israel."

The hope of Israel indeed wears chains. The Son of God, the Messiah, the Savior of the nation, is fixed to a cross. This is the call of all who follow Jesus – to die.

But, Peter is prompted to ask as he walks with Jesus and the Lord explicates his dual call to serve as leader of the Church and to die for his faith, "What about him?" What about John, who follows them? The question pertains not simply to whether or not John also must suffer a martyr's death, but principally – as the principal call of Peter is to feed the Lord's flock – to why Jesus does not call John to serve as His first of priests, standing in His stead, for it is clear to all that John is "the disciple whom Jesus loved." Jesus responds, "Suppose I want him to stay until I come," suppose He does not want John to pour himself out as a libation on His holy altar... that should be of no concern to the Rock of the Church. Jesus calls whom He wills to what He wills for His blessed purpose. And John is not called to die, or to lead.

John is, in fact, the only one of the Twelve who does not suffer a martyrdom of blood. He does remain until a very old age. His martyrdom is white, that of suffering a long life. And in several ways he remains ever with the Church on earth, in a sense, *as* the Christ's beloved Church. It is he to whom the Blessed Mother is entrusted, she who is with us always to nurture us here on our journey. And in our gospel today, the principal call of John is most evident: he is called to "witness to... the things that Jesus did" and to "record them." "It is he who wrote them down," he who is the great Evangelist – he whose words remain with us even today as we read his gospel throughout the most blessed season of Easter. And, of course, it is he who, in his old age, while exiled on the island of Patmos, will receive the great vision that has become the Book of Revelation, thus telling us so thoroughly not only of Jesus' life on earth, but also of His life in heaven.

In our first reading, Paul is "allowed to take a lodging of his own." Though "a soldier was assigned to keep guard over him... with full assurance, and without any hindrance whatever, he preached the reign of God and taught about the Lord Jesus Christ." What Paul does in earthly chains for two years – for soon he, too, shall be martyred for the faith – John does, in a sense, endlessly, or at least until its natural end.

"The Lord is in His holy temple... His searching glance is on mankind." He calls all to the martyrdom He chooses. Let us each wear the chains He provides, each find the place in the kingdom to which He leads us, knowing always that "the upright shall see His face."

Pentecost Sunday (A,B,C)
(Acts 2:1-11; Ps.104:1,24,29-31,34; 1Cor.12:3b-7,12-13; Jn.20:19-23)

"Suddenly there came from the sky a noise like a strong driving wind,
and it filled the entire house in which they were."

What our first reading captures in all its dramatic moment, David's psalm declares in clarity – "When you send forth your spirit, they are created, and you renew the face of the earth" – and our gospel defines in Jesus' word and action with His apostles: "He breathed on them and said, 'Receive the Holy Spirit.'" The Spirit comes from heaven above, through the only Son, to redeem, renew, and strengthen all on the face of the earth.

"And they were all filled with the Holy Spirit," and they all spoke "of the mighty acts of God," and each one of those gathered there "from every nation... heard them speaking in his own language." For the language in which they spoke was the language of the Spirit, the language all understand. "For in one Spirit we were all baptized into one body... and we are all given to drink of one Spirit"; and what does this Spirit say but, "Jesus is Lord," the truth to which all are called, for which every heart yearns?

And though all find life in "the same Spirit," though all declare as one that Jesus is Lord, for each of us "there are different kinds of spiritual gifts." As David exclaims, "How manifold are your works, O Lord!" And is not this call to "different forms of service" revealed in the fact that "there appeared to them tongues as of fire, which parted and came to rest on each of them"? Each is thereby given his own "theme," his own song to sing to please the Lord, and our prayer should therefore always be, "May the Lord be glad in His works!" (And for those who deny that man has been given the gift of forgiving sins, do they not read the Lord's straightforward words to His disciples at this most decisive moment: "Whose sins you forgive are forgiven them, and whose sins you retain are retained"?)

Praise God for the gifts He imparts to all His children. Praise Him for the peace He leaves us and the mission on which He sends us. But praise Him most especially for the breath of the Holy Spirit which animates our very beings, for "if [the Lord] take away [our] breath, [we] perish, and return to [our] dust," but with this Spirit we share in the very power of God.

687

Fill this house, O Lord, with the power of your Spirit.
Let the Church always proclaim your praise.

Pentecost Sunday (B)

(Acts 2:1-11; Ps.104:1,24,29-31,34; Gal.5:16-25; Jn.15:26-27,16:12-15)

"The time for Pentecost was fulfilled."

A driving wind comes from the sky. It fills the house. Tongues of fire come to rest on the disciples, and they speak in tongues of every nation. The gathered crowd of "Jews from every nation under heaven" ask in wonder, "How does each of us hear them in his native language?" How is such perfect communication possible? How could such light fall upon mankind? How can we be made one?

"The Advocate comes." "The Spirit of truth that proceeds from the Father," sent by the Son to "guide [us] to all truth," declares the glory of God in our midst, fulfills the Word among us, making us brothers and sisters in the light of the Lord.

"O Lord, my God, you are great indeed!" What wonders you work before the eyes of man! What glorious speech you bring to our ears! So far are your ways above our ways; so little of the truth can we weak human beings bear. But you strengthen us. You give us your Word. You anoint us with your Spirit to destroy this sinful flesh and prepare our hearts to receive the grace that comes only by your power. We praise you, Lord, for the glory you impart to our souls.

"May the glory of the Lord endure forever," and we endure forever in Him. Let us never be separated from the blessing which comes from the One who never dies, the One who brings life to every creature upon the face of the earth, and in the heavens above. "Brothers and sisters, live by the Spirit" now. Hold closely to the gifts He offers freely and powerfully forth this holy day and every day of your lives. In no other way will you be fulfilled; by no other means will you come to heaven. The Spirit is the source of all truth and only by His guidance you will hear of the glory of God. And only by His power will you keep it.

In the Church now the Spirit dwells, teaching all her children. From the four corners they come to receive the bread of life. Let us be fed well for the time is at hand when all the Lord's words will be fulfilled, when the Son shall return again. Our refuge now is the Spirit. In Him let us place our trust.

Pentecost Sunday (C)
(Acts 2:1-11; Ps.104:1,24,29-31,34; Rom.8:8-17; Jn.14:15-16,23b-26)

"Whoever loves me will keep my word, and my Father will love him,
and we will come to him and make our dwelling with him."

The Spirit of God is with those who keep His commandments; and His Commandment is to love. In such love all become sons of God, all are made one in His Name. (Spirit of Love, anoint us.)

In our first reading the oneness of God's children is emphasized: "They were all in one place together" and "they gathered in a large crowd." The first quote refers to the disciples of Christ waiting for His Holy Spirit, the second to "devout Jews from every nation under heaven" who would be made one with the disciples by the power of the Spirit. We note particularly the word "devout": because they were keepers of the Word of God, the Spirit descended upon them.

Our psalm exalts the renewing power of the Spirit of God; all creatures in the palm of God are given life, and new life, by the power of the Holy Spirit. Alleluia! We rejoice in His grace. In our second reading, Paul contrasts the life-giving Spirit with the death-bringing flesh, speaking, much as Jesus in our gospel, of the Spirit who dwells in those of God. "Whoever does not have the Spirit of Christ does not belong to Him," but belongs to sin and the world. He does not keep the Word of Jesus and so dies in the flesh; his flesh lacking the Spirit that gives life, he becomes as an empty shell. The love of God is not in him.

But for those who keep the Word of God, their hearts cry out in joy to the Father of all as they are made one with Him and one another, and led to the truth of everlasting life in His Spirit. May the Spirit of Jesus be with us.

Further note: expounding on the theme of keeping the Lord's Word, we see in the fact that people of all languages hear this one language of the Spirit that the Word is not beholden to any tongue; it is the tongues of flame, the tongue of the Spirit which speaks the Word of God, we all must keep.

VI. Solemnities and Feasts

Conversion of St. Paul

(Acts 22:3-16 or Acts 9:1-22; Ps.117:1-2,Mk.16:15; Mk.16:15-18)

"Go into the whole world and proclaim the good news to all creation."

One would not have expected these words to be spoken so profoundly to the heart of St. Paul. For he, then known as Saul, had spent such time and with such vigor had persecuted the followers of Christ. Why does the Lord shine His light all about him? Why does He speak to him and reveal Himself to him? Why is it this man who is picked to bring the Name of Jesus to all the nations? Perhaps it was his very vigor in persecuting His followers Jesus admired. Perhaps his sincerity and commitment to this cause in the name of God He knew He could use for the cause of justice and right. Perhaps he is a sign to us all that none is beyond the redemption the Lord offers. We know only that he who was persecuting the Church now works to build it up. We know only the story of this great Apostle to the world.

"Recover your sight," Ananias says to this Saul, and so Paul, once blinded by the light of the Lord, now has his eyes open to see. So he who once went about with scales on his eyes, he whose vision was once so prevented from realizing the truth of the Jesus in his midst... he who was once so like his brother Pharisees, now sees. And what he sees is not simply Ananias standing before him. What he sees standing before him in this faithful disciple of Jesus, is Christ Himself. And he realizes whom he has been persecuting, and repents. And so he is baptized. And so his mission, one wrought in the suffering of Christ, begins.

"Praise the Lord, all you nations; glorify Him, all you peoples!" are the words of our psalmist, but they could as easily be the exhortation of the Apostle Paul. Having himself believed in the Good News proclaimed to all creation and accepted Baptism into its way, he himself now brings so many others to walk along the same path. Great signs accompany him, and his words to our ears are as those of Jesus to him, for now he is such a strong part of the Body of Christ, persecuted by this world and calling it to salvation. On this day all our hearts should turn to the Lord, that we might join Paul and profess our faith in His Name.

Presentation of the Lord

(Mal.3:1-4; Ps.24:7-10; Heb.2:14-18; Lk.2:22-40)

"Suddenly there will come to the temple
the Lord whom you seek."

"And He will purify the sons of Levi, refining them like gold or like silver that they may offer due sacrifice to the Lord." "To expiate the sins of the people" He has come – to bring us light. But to do this "He had to become like His brothers and sisters in every way"; He had to "share in blood and flesh" with us, and so share in our death, to overcome death and make us holy in the sight of God, that our lives might be like His: a true sacrifice to the Lord.

Hear in our gospel how many times is stated that when "Mary and Joseph [take] Jesus up to Jerusalem to present Him to the Lord" this is done "just as it is written in the law of the Lord." Because it says, "Every male that opens the womb shall be consecrated to the Lord," His parents do so "in accordance with the dictate in the law of the Lord." They "brought in the child Jesus to perform the custom of the law in regard to Him"; they "fulfilled all the prescriptions of the law of the Lord" before returning to Galilee to raise Him. Of what significance is this in this day and age when so many place themselves above the need to be obedient to the dictates of the Church and the Holy Spirit which speaks through her. Though the Lord Himself did all according to the way it is written, so many find no necessity for themselves to go to church on Sunday, to confess their sins, to give their tithe… and on. In their minds they need no "religion" to follow. Let them learn from the Lord and His obedience, and His humility, in the place where God is found.

And see what happens when this humble Child allows Himself to be brought into the temple of the Lord: light comes to His people. Simeon the prophet proclaims in joy, "My eyes have seen your salvation, which you prepared in the sight of all the peoples," and declares his readiness for death. Anna the prophetess gives thanks to God and speaks "about the child to all who [are] awaiting the redemption of Jerusalem." It is not to a street corner He comes to bring salvation; it is to the temple. There we await Him. There we find Him, in His Father's house.

Finally, we must relate the pain His coming brings. Though leading to glory, for us as well as for Him, the performance of the Father's will in all things is not easy. As "a sword will pierce" the Mother's heart, so in our purgation, in our persecution as we turn from the darkness of this world to be purified for the next, there shall be suffering. But this suffering does lead to life. But our waiting shall be answered. The light is powerful that comes when we "lift up" the gates of our hearts "that the king of glory may come in," but in Him we find all our hearts need. His is the perfect sacrifice.

Chair of St. Peter
(1Pt.5:1-4; Ps.23:1-6; Mt.16:13-19)

"On this rock I will build my Church."

And Simon's name is changed to "Peter", which means "Rock", to signify that here is the chief shepherd of the Church, upon whom the Church rests. It is he to whom Jesus gives "the keys to the kingdom of heaven." Though all the apostles are given the power to bind and loose, it is Peter who leads – "a fellow elder" among all the elders and yet the one who speaks for all.

It is not by man's decision that Peter is the Rock of the Church, but by the word of the Lord Himself. Just as "no mere man ha[d] revealed" to him that Jesus is "the Messiah... the Son of the living God," so no mere man works through him today as our Pope guides the ship that is the Church by the power of the Holy Spirit. It is led by the Church and its teachings we are guided "in right paths." It is as we dwell in this "house of the Lord" that we are protected from all harm. "The Lord is my shepherd," and the Shepherd of all, and into the hands of Peter and the apostles He places care for His flock.

How well this first among equals instructs his fellow shepherds today in his letter: "God's flock is in your midst; give it a shepherd's care." How well does Peter answer the Lord's call to strengthen his brothers, to see that His sheep are fed. The key pitfalls of "coercion" and "shameful profit" and "lording it over those assigned" to them, he warns them clearly against, and reminds them of "the unfading crown of glory" that awaits them. It is they who must give "courage" to the flock, they who anoint heads with oil to make the cup of the Church overflow, even here on earth... and as they are faithful, they are Christ's own special children.

To those who still doubt the primacy of Peter and its absolute necessity, I invite you to read Scripture again and notice how often and always Peter speaks for the whole and acts for the whole body as he does today. It is to all the apostles Jesus asks, "Who do you say that I am?" and though all may have faith, only one speaks up and answers in no uncertain terms. As he does at the first council at Jerusalem, as he did in coming to the Lord on the water, Peter speaks and leads in the power of the Spirit. The Church is one in Christ, and it has one rock it is set upon.

694

St. Joseph, Husband of Mary
(2Sm.7:4-5,12-14a,16;   Ps.89:2-5,27,29,37;   Rom.4:13,16-18,22;
Mt.1:16,18-21,24a or Lk.2:41-51a)

"I will be a father to him,
and he shall be my son."

It is through Joseph that Jesus is a son of David and so fulfills the promise to the king made by God: "Your house and your kingdom shall endure forever before me; your throne shall stand firm forever," for He is the heir "raise[d] up" after David "who shall build a house for [His] name." "In heaven [the Lord has] confirmed [His] faithfulness," and on earth He has made it known. And so Jesus says of God, "You are my Father, my God, the Rock, my Savior!" and we of faith join His refrain.

As with Abraham, Joseph is made foster father of Jesus not merely by physical descent from David but "through the righteousness that comes from faith."   For as Abraham believed and so became "the father of many nations," so Joseph believed that it was "through the Holy Spirit that [Jesus] ha[d] been conceived" and "did as the angel commanded him and took his wife into his home," thus becoming a father to Him who would "save His people from their sins." Like Abraham "he believed, hoping against hope," and like Abraham he is blessed.

But, of course, Jesus is more than the Son of Joseph; in fact, this is the great sacrifice Joseph makes. For truly he cares for Him who is more Son to the Father in heaven and Son of Man, born for all the human race. Evident this is when He is found by Joseph and Mary in the temple after three days and He asks them (a question much like those He might have been putting to the teachers of the faith): "Did you not know that I must be in my Father's house?" and in the curious fact that His parents waited a day before journeying back to Jerusalem to look for Him, for they were "thinking that He was in the caravan" – so much a part of His people had He become.

Jesus is Son of God and Son of Man, yet "obedient to them" – Joseph and Mary – He ever was. And they were ever obedient to the dictates of the Father, that they should care for His only Son. And so Joseph, husband of Mary, a simple carpenter, fulfills in simple fashion all the Lord had set out for him. May we, too, by faith fulfill all the care we must take for Jesus, His mother, and His people.

695

Annunciation

(Is.7:10-14,8:10;   Ps.40:7-11;   Heb.10:4-10;   Lk.1:26-38)

"Behold, I come to do your will."

Today we celebrate the fact that the Word became flesh, that God became man through Mary and dwells among us to take away our sins. In this is fulfilled the words of the prophet Isaiah, "The Lord Himself will give you this sign: the virgin shall conceive, and bear a son, and shall name Him Emmanuel, which means 'God is with us!'" She is the Virgin; He is the Son – we are they with whom He dwells. Praise God for His grace!

Obediently Jesus takes on the body prepared for Him by the Father for all ages; humbly He bows under the Hand of God. To come among us is His delight. For He shall fulfill the prescriptions of the old law – as it is written, so shall it come to be. And in His blood poured out for our sakes, in the love He shares with us men, indeed shall be fulfilled the will of God. No longer need we wait or search in vain, for all that is written is accomplished in Him.

And Mary is, of course, the perfect reflection of the Lord's obedience; it is she in whom He is formed. As He says, "Behold, I come," she says, "Behold, I am the handmaiden of the Lord." As the Lord says, "In the written scroll it is prescribed for me. To do your will, O God, is my delight," His Lady says, "May it be done to me according to your word." And so by the obedience won from her by the angel, this Blessed Virgin "will conceive in [her] womb and bear a son, and [she] shall name Him Jesus"; and "the child to be born will be called holy, the Son of God." She in her innocence and by the fullness of grace at work in her believes the reply to her question, "How can this be?" She is assured by the miracle spoken of Elizabeth – for which this holy woman must certainly have prayed – and so the words of the angel: "The Holy Spirit will come upon you, and the power of the Most High will overshadow you," are realized; and she who believes becomes the instrument of our salvation.

Brothers and sisters, "we have been consecrated through the offering of the body of Jesus once for all." His coming among us is more than the greatest miracle; it means life for our very souls. For by His incarnation and by the sacrifice of His flesh for our sakes is effected the cleansing of our sins and the drawing up of our lives unto heaven where He eternally dwells. As He has dwelt with us, so may we now dwell with Him who has come for this purpose. Let no fear grip your heart. Consecrate yourself to Him and to His holy sacrifice. And give yourself to His Mother, that she may form you in His image, and you may know the blessed obedience which both hold, and which is itself the means of our salvation.

696

St. Mark

(1Pt.5:5-14; Ps.89:2-3,6-7,16-17; Mk.16:15-20)

"Go into the whole world and proclaim the Good News to all creation."

Such is the call and accomplishment of our evangelist Mark, whose gospel reflects the song of our psalmist today, "The favors of the Lord I will sing forever; through all generations my mouth shall proclaim your faithfulness." For his inspired Word lives forever to declare the faithfulness of God. And "happy the people who know the joyful shout," who exclaim like Peter in our first reading, "Dominion be His throughout the ages!" For they "walk in the light of [the Lord's] countenance," and so "they rejoice all the day."

"The Eleven went forth and preached everywhere," and those who believed in the Good News they proclaimed indeed were saved, as are we today. The promise Peter makes in our first reading is true: "The God of all grace, who called you to His everlasting glory in Christ, will Himself restore, confirm, strengthen, and establish those who have suffered a little while." Though answering the call of the Lord bring suffering in this world, it is but little to endure for the surpassing glory which is ours in the name of our Lord and Savior Jesus Christ. And so to "bow humbly under God's mighty hand, so that in due time He may lift [us] high," is a joy in itself; the suffering we experience for the sake of the Word is itself laced with great joy, for we know in our souls and have seen that it but leads to exaltation at the right hand of God. "Through your justice they are exalted" – so our psalmist praises God for His mercy and His truth. And all souls converted to the Lord will know the Lord's justice in full flower.

And O the signs that "will accompany those who have professed their faith," the strength in the Name and the Spirit of God and the healing graces that are known in them. Every day and in every situation such power is invoked and implemented by those who believe. Be not so forgetful of the wonders Jesus works through those who walk with Him. "The heavens proclaim your wonders, O Lord, and your faithfulness, in the assembly of the holy ones." The verse is true, my friends. And as "the Lord continued to work with [the apostles] throughout and confirm the message [they proclaimed] through the signs which accompanied them," so He will not leave alone this day anyone who takes up His cross and even in the humblest fashion proclaims His holy Name. The news is good and the Lord wishes all to hear. Make His message known to the ends of the world: salvation has come to all.

Sts. Philip and James
(1Cor.15:1-8; Ps.19:2-5; Jn.14:6-14)

"The man who has faith in me will do the works I do."

What is the message the apostles preach "to the ends of the world"? What is "the glory of God" that "the heavens declare" and "the firmament proclaims"? It is none other than Jesus' words to Thomas: "I am the way, and the truth, and the life; no one comes to the Father but through me"; it is His answer to Philip: "I am in the Father and the Father is in me." The Father "lives in [Jesus] accomplishing His works," and Jesus lives in His apostles continuing the great work of God.

Here is the Gospel in short, which Paul preaches to the Corinthians in our first reading: "Christ died for our sins in accord with the Scriptures... He was buried and, in accord with the Scriptures, rose on the third day." He has appeared to all the apostles who preach His Name, who declare His salvation to all men; and He is known to us this day in His Spirit, in His Church, in His Sacraments and in His Word. And indeed it is so that knowing Him we know the Father; filled with His Spirit we cannot but proclaim the majesty of the grace at work in Him through His Church. Standing on the solid foundation the apostles have set, what can shake our faith or keep us from His glorious presence?

Brothers and sisters, on days such as this – and indeed on all days – our hearts should burn intensely with the love of the Lord. Our souls should join with the blessed spirit of these holy apostles and declare aloud the silent Word that "imparts knowledge" to the minds of all. So should our "voice[s] resound" of the glory of God and the grace He has poured forth in our spirits. Let the earth be filled with His light!

St. Matthias
(Acts 1:15-17,20-26; Ps.113:1-8; Jn.15:9-17)

"It was I who chose you to go forth and bear fruit."

Since "the saying in Scripture uttered long ago by the Holy Spirit through the mouth of David was destined to be fulfilled in Judas" and he "went the way he was destined to go," now the word of the Lord must be accomplished: "May another take his office." And though "Peter stood up in the center of the brothers" and declared the need expressed in Scripture, and though the one hundred and twenty brothers gathered together "nominated two," the prayer of the disciples, as well as their actions, makes clear by whom Matthias is chosen: "O Lord, you read the hearts of men.

Make known to us which of these two you choose for this apostolic ministry." As Judas is destined for perdition, so Matthias is chosen by the Lord to take his place, for all is indeed in the hands of God.

And what loving hands these are, brothers and sisters; and what loving hands all His disciples are called to employ. The words of the Lord in today's gospel breathe the very love of God upon His apostles. "Love one another as I have loved you" is His command to them. "Live on in my love." Our "fruit must endure," and it can only endure, we can only bear fruit, sharing in the love of Father and Son. For then the Holy Spirit is upon us, who brings all to life. And the way in which we share in divine love the Lord makes clear as well: "There is no greater love than this: to lay down one's life for one's friends." And it is this laying down of his life to which Matthias is called today; and it is the same service in His name that makes us all friends of Jesus.

"From the rising to the setting of the sun is the name of the Lord to be praised," for indeed "high above all nations is the Lord; above the heavens is His glory." His ways are certainly far above our own, and it is His ways to which we must come, obediently following His command, His command to love. Today He reaches down and "raises the lowly from the dust... to seat [Matthias] with princes, with the princes of His people." Today His choice is made of who will follow the Son. None but He knows the ones He chooses, the way we must walk, for none is "like the Lord, our God, who is enthroned on high and looks upon the heavens and the earth below"; and our joy is made complete only in going forth as He leads, for, simply put, none can compare with His love.

Visitation
(Zeph.3:14-18 or Rom.12:9-16; Is.12:2-6; Lk.1:39-56)

"Sing praise to the Lord for His glorious achievement;
let this be known throughout all the earth."

How can we capture the joy of this day? For here is the sign of our promised salvation; here we find the first apostolic act in Mary's bringing the Word of God, so recently conceived in her womb, to Elizabeth, and to her son John the Baptist.

"Shout for joy, O daughter Zion! Sing joyfully, O Israel!" Zephaniah encourages the holy nation. And for what does Zion, and indeed the whole world, rejoice but that which we celebrate this day? Here in these simple, lowly women we find all of Israel rejoicing as she brings to birth her Savior. Yes, even now "the Lord, [her] God, is in [her] midst," even in her womb; and already He begins to bring salvation forth. Already we find a kind of

699

Pentecost as first, "Elizabeth was filled with the Holy Spirit and cried out in a loud voice: 'Blessed are you among women and blessed is the fruit of your womb'... and then Mary said: 'My being proclaims the greatness of the Lord, my spirit finds joy in God my savior?'" And already the Baptist in the womb of his aged mother has been inspired by the presence of the Son of God; already he has "stirred in [her] womb for joy," just at the sound of Mary's voice touching the ears of his mother, even as Jesus is but days old in Mary's blessed womb.

And how does all this joy come but through humility. "For He has looked upon His servant in her lowliness; all ages to come shall call [her] blessed." Yes, Mary is raised "to high places," is become the Mother of God, because of her great humility before Him. It is this lowliness she proclaims in her canticle today; it is this lowliness Elizabeth exudes when she asks, "Who am I that the mother of my Lord should come to me?" – and it is this same lowliness which is required of all the children of Israel, of all Abraham's descendants, if we are to know that "the Lord has removed the judgment against [us]," if we are to "shout with exultation" for "the Holy One of Israel" in our midst.

Let us heed Paul's instruction to the Romans to "put away ambitious thoughts and associate with those who are lowly" that we might "rejoice with those who rejoice." As our holy women today, these models of faith, let us "look on the needs of the saints as [our] own" and "be generous in offering hospitality." "Be fervent in spirit; He whom you serve is the Lord." For it is He who comes under your roof this day. It is His holy name you should proclaim in all you do and say. And the blessing of salvation shall be upon you.

> Mother of God, bring to us this day our Savior,
> that we might rejoice with you in heaven.

Trinity Sunday (A)
(Ex.34:4b-6,8-9; Dn.3:52-56; 2Cor.13:11-13; Jn.3:16-18)

> "The Lord, the Lord, a merciful and gracious God,
> slow to anger and rich in kindness and fidelity."

"Blessed are you, O Lord, the God of our fathers, praiseworthy and exalted above all forever; and blessed is your holy and glorious Name." Brothers and sisters, let us praise God this holy day; let us rejoice in His love. Let us be as Moses, who upon hearing the NAME of the Lord spoken in his hearing, upon having the Lord's presence revealed to him, "at once bowed down to the ground in worship." He did not fail to bless

God "in the temple of [His] holy glory," but as the LORD "look[ed] into the depths from His throne upon the cherubim" – as He who transcends all made Himself known to His servant upon the earth – cried aloud to God for His protection, for the protection that the three holy men (Shadrach, Meshach, and Abednego) knew by the Hand of God, by His blessed angel, when saved from the flames in the fiery furnace. And though "exalted above all forever," the LORD hears and answers His children.

God is three and God is love. The One God – Father, Son, and Holy Spirit – is made known in His love. Both the unity of God and His gracious and merciful love are evident today in John's famous quote: "God so loved the world that He gave His only Son, so that everyone who believes in Him might not perish but might have eternal life." They are, of course, Jesus' words whispered to Nicodemus in his night of doubt and question, and they should fall deeply into our own ears and speak clearly to our hearts of the intimacy of Father and Son and the love one holds and the other carries, a love which is in essence the working of the Spirit. It is this love and union with these to which we are all called, and which we all find by believing "in the name of the only Son of God."

Brothers and sisters, the presence of God is among us always; the Son has come to save our race, and has thus made all things holy. What Moses knew on Mount Sinai with the "two stone tablets" in his hands, we should know simply by opening our eyes – for His NAME should be written on our hearts. And so, always we should be in prayer and praise of the majesty of God. With the living creatures and the elders in heaven we should continually bow down before Him and stand to shout of His glory. Open your hearts to Him who is all in all.

On this Trinity Sunday I will leave you with Paul's parting words to the Corinthians: "The grace of the Lord Jesus Christ and the love of God and the fellowship of the Holy Spirit be with all of you."

Trinity Sunday (B)
(Dt.4:32-34,39-40; Ps.33:4-6,9,12,18-20,22; Rom.8:14-17; Mt.28:16-20)

"You must know now, and fix in your heart,
that the Lord is God in the heavens above and on earth below,
and that there is no other."

"Did a people ever hear the voice of God speaking from the midst of fire, as you did, and live?" Moses asks the Israelite nation. "Did any god venture to go and take a nation for himself" with the great "signs and wonders" that accompanied Israel's release from Egyptian bondage? No. For the God of Abraham, Isaac, and Jacob is the God of heaven and earth,

701

the one true God. For "by the word of the Lord the heavens were made; by the breath of His mouth all their host." Yes, "He spoke, and it was made, He commanded and it stood forth." None is great as the Father in heaven.

And in the power of the Father, Jesus, the Son, shares: "All power in heaven and on earth has been given to me," He declares in truth. It is He who suffers and dies for us; it is He who thus reveals God's love – it is He whom all nations adore in the holy court. The words of the Father He brings to our ears; His commands, which bring life and "deliver... from death," He speaks in our hearing. Here is the Word by which all comes to be made flesh in our sight.

And we, "we are children of God, and if children, then heirs, heirs of God and joint heirs with Christ" – to this "the Spirit Himself bears witness," speaking in our souls the NAME of God. Yes, "those who are led by the Spirit of God are sons of God," and the Spirit is now with us to lead us, to help us "keep His statutes and commandments," that we might "have long life on the land which the Lord, [our] God, is giving [us] forever." And now so on fire with the Spirit of God, Jesus present with us always in body and soul, and standing as holy children of the Father... we must "make disciples of all nations, baptizing them in the Name of the Father, and of the Son, and of the Holy Spirit, teaching them to observe all that [the Lord has] commanded."

"Our soul waits for the Lord, who is our help and our shield." His presence is upon us always for good, and we long now to know the fullness of the Trinity. He whose "works are trustworthy" we seek to make our own, that we might be one with Him who is One. "Of the kindness of the Lord the earth is full." May He who "loves justice and right" be known in His fullness by all.

Trinity Sunday (C)
(Prv.8:22-31; Ps.8:2,4-9; Rm.5:1-5; Jn.16:12-15)

"Everything that the Father has is mine."

From the beginning Jesus is with the Father, one with the Father, the pure reflection of His being which cannot be separated from the substance of the Father. Through Him all things were made, and indeed He is reflected in all things. And it is by the power of the Holy Spirit, who takes from what is the Father's and Son's, that anything that comes to be comes to be.

And man is the crown of the creation of this Most Holy Triumvirate. It is he who is the purest reflection of the love of Father and Son brought to birth by the Holy Spirit. It is he in whom the wisdom of God takes great delight. And all the wonders of earth and heaven are put in our hands: "You have given him rule over the works of your hands, putting all things under his feet."

But a greater gift than this earth has the Lord in store for us: it is a oneness with the one God which we could not have imagined, and still strive forward to see. "The love of God has been poured into our hearts through the Holy Spirit"; and that same Spirit, left to us by the Father and the Son, remains ever with us to bless and guide us to that magnificent vision of glory we hope one day to be able to bear in its fullness. The Spirit declares unto us the beauty that will be, and calls us to prepare ourselves to receive it.

And our afflictions do not deter us from attaining the promise of all truth; they do but strengthen us in our resolve as we conquer them day by day in the Spirit. "We have gained access by faith to this grace in which we stand," and our suffering shall not shake us – even Jesus' own leaving us does not hinder our journey to God, for we indeed have faith that His Spirit is with us and that His Spirit has all that is of Jesus, who has all that is of the Father... and so we have all things through Him.

The first glory in which we were set is a marvel to behold, for His fingerprints are on all we see. But the second glory to which we are now called is simply beyond words, ineffable as is our God. Alleluia!

The Body and Blood of Christ (A)
(Dt.8:2-3,14b-16a; Ps.147:12-15,19-20; 1Cor.10:16-17; Jn.6:51-58)

"I am the living bread that came down from heaven;
whoever eats this bread will live forever."

"Not by bread alone does one live, but by every word that comes forth from the mouth of the Lord." And here is the Word standing before our eyes. Here is the Bread that gives us life. Here is Jesus Christ, in this Blessed Sacrament, nourishing all our lives.

Yes, His "flesh is true food, and [His] blood is true drink," for it feeds not only our bodies, but our souls as well, anointing us with His presence, joining us to His sacrifice. And so it becomes His flesh we carry in our bodies; so it becomes His blood running in our veins. For, as Paul asks so pointedly, "The cup of blessing that we bless, is it not a participation in the blood of Christ? The bread that we break, is it not a participation in the body of Christ?" And so, do we not become like our God, who comes to us so humbly in this food, who becomes one with our own flesh and blood? Is heaven not here with us and within us as we eat of His presence? Or does He lie about His gift?

703

Solemnities and Feasts

Brothers and sisters, the mind of man could conceive of nothing more wonderful than this blessed gift we receive at the hands of our own Savior. It is a wonder beyond our understanding and yet a wonder truly present with us, as real as our own flesh and blood. As the Lord "fed [the Israelites] in the desert with manna, a food unknown to [their] fathers," so we feed now on this food unknown to all – this bread of the angels. And though our doubting hearts may question, "How can this man give us His flesh to eat?", when we partake of this Sacrament of the altar, we find no question remaining; for in faith we taste His glory.

Over and over Jesus repeats His refrain: "Whoever eats my flesh and drinks my blood has eternal life," knowing how slow we are to hear, so slow of heart to believe – how easily we "forget the Lord, [our] God, who brought [us] out of the land of Egypt, that place of slavery." And falling back to the "waterless ground," we fall away from His table and fail to realize that "with the best of wheat He fills" us. But listen to Him. Come to Him. Eat. Drink. Do not have unbelieving hearts – but believe! Be as children, pure and lowly, and "glorify the Lord, O Jerusalem; praise your God, O Zion," and what is beyond your understanding will become the light of your understanding, and lead you to eternal life. He has given His "flesh for the life of the world." Live in Him, brothers and sisters. Live in Him.

The Body and Blood of Christ (B)
(Ex.24:3-8; Ps.116:12-13,15-18; Heb.9:11-15; Mt.14:12-16,22-26)

"The cup of salvation I will take up,
and I will call upon the name of the Lord."

The blood of sacrifice, the blood that seals all covenants with God, is upon all our readings today. In our first reading, on the altar Moses has "erected at the foot of the mountain" where he received the commandments of the Lord – an altar surrounded by "twelve pillars for the twelve tribes" – "young men of the Israelites... offer holocausts and sacrifice young bulls as peace offerings to the Lord." Half of the blood of the bulls Moses "splashed on the altar"; the other half he "sprinkled... on the people, saying, 'This is the blood of the covenant that the Lord has made with you in accordance with all these words of His.'" And so the people promise to heed the Lord's commands; and so the first covenant is instituted.

Our psalm tells us, "Precious in the eyes of the Lord is the death of His faithful ones." And our second reading informs us just how precious is the death of the Lord's Faithful One. Yes, "Christ came as high priest"; as "mediator of a new covenant" He entered the "perfect tabernacle not made by hands... not belonging to this creation," and offered not "the blood of

704

goats and bulls" but rather "His own blood." His "death has taken place for deliverance from transgressions under the first covenant." And so does "the blood of Christ, who through the eternal Spirit offered Himself unblemished before God, cleanse our consciences from dead works to worship the living God."

And in our gospel, in anticipation of His crucifixion, on the feast of Passover – when the lamb was sacrificed and its blood used to anoint the houses of the Israelites to thus save them from death – Jesus institutes the New Covenant with His disciples. First "He took bread, said the blessing, broke it, gave it to them, and said, 'Take it. This is my body.'" Then with the cup He said, "This is my blood of the covenant, which will be shed for many." It is, of course, this New Covenant we celebrate this day, as we come to the table where all the disciples of the Lord have eaten, where all His faithful have been washed clean in His blood. Here we share not only with our minds – for then why should it be necessary to eat and drink (one does not eat and drink a symbol, but feasts with eyes alone) – but with our very bodies, with the fullness of our beings; and our very human nature is transformed by His sacrificial presence. Brothers and sisters, the Lord gives Himself entirely for us; let us here lay down our lives in His flesh and blood. Let us take up the cup of salvation and each day call upon His Name.

Solemnity, Sun. after Trinity Sun. (C)

The Body and Blood of Christ (C)
(Gn.14:18-20; Ps.110:1-4; 1Cor.11:23-26; Lk.9:11b-17)

"The Lord Jesus, on the night He was handed over,
took bread, and, after He had given thanks, broke it and said,
'This is my body that is for you.'"

There is food for all, and it is ever available. The Lord feeds us with His own Body and Blood, and He is generous in giving His eternal self to us. Both eternal priest and victim "of God Most High," and God Himself, we need never fear that His provision for us will lapse. And so we "proclaim the death of the Lord until He comes"; we share in His holy sacrifice until it is made complete in heaven. For it is His death which gives us life, it is the holy offering of Himself which feeds us on our journey here. Let us come always to the altar of His Sacrament and feast upon the nourishment He provides.

In our gospel we hear that "Jesus spoke to the crowds of the kingdom of God," healing those in need. After the Word was opened to them, the bread was brought forth. "Looking up to heaven, He said the blessing over [the loaves], broke them, and gave them to the disciples to set before the crowd." As He would do the night before He died, so He does here, in answer to the concern of the Twelve for the people. He says to His chosen, "Give them some food yourselves." He thus invites them to share in His sacrifice and in His ministry by laying down their lives for the Church.

Here is the Mass clearly foreshadowed. Here it is present even before the death of Christ. Even before the victim has fully offered Himself, He leads us to the table upon which we ever feed. And that which was begun in this desert place so long ago comes down to us this day. The twelve baskets of food remaining we continue to be fed with today; and this Bread continues to be multiplied – the more we eat of it, the more there is to be eaten. Such is God's love and generosity. Such is the richness of the table He sets before us. Like our priest and victim, it is eternal. There is no end to God's grace and the blessings He holds for us. We cannot consume the depths of His love.

And so we are to contribute to the spreading and the sharing of the holy offering Jesus is for us. We must call all to the altar of the Lord; we must see that His gift is multiplied. He is "a priest forever"; as long as we live, He dies for us – for as long as we breathe upon this earth, His blood is poured forth. Let us pray in words and in deeds that this blood will come to many and cleanse them of their sins. Let us pray that many will come to life by His sacrifice, that many will partake of His Body and His Blood. By each one who comes to the table, we are all strengthened, for the Body is made more whole. Until the time this one Body has reached fulfillment, until His sacrifice is complete, let us continue indeed to "proclaim the death of the Lord," who thereby feeds us with His eternal love.

Solemnity, Fri. after 2nd Sun. after Pentecost (A)

Sacred Heart (A)
(Dt.7:6-11; Ps.103:1-4,8,10,17; 1Jn.4:7-16; Mt.11:25-30)

"He has loved us
and has sent His Son as an offering for our sins."

Who better to hear from on this blessed feast than John, the Lord's beloved disciple, whose words indeed continually breathe the fact that "God is love" and who eternally exhorts us to "love one another." John cannot but speak of the love God has for His children and the love we must offer in return; and all of our Scripture today echoes his understanding and calls us to be washed in the blood of Christ.

In our gospel Jesus calls unto the hearts of all: "Come to me, all you who are weary and find life burdensome, and I will refresh you." He invites His little ones: "Take my yoke upon your shoulders and learn from me, for I am gentle and humble of heart." O so gentle and humble of heart is the Lord our God... so loving, so kind! David sings of Him so well in his psalm

706

of praise and thanksgiving: "Merciful is the Lord, slow to anger and abounding in kindness." Why does God's king "bless the Lord" with "all [his] being" today? Because "not according to our sins does He deal with us." Because of His forgiving grace – this greatest sign of His love, embodied in His only Son. And so, as Moses says to all the people in our hearing on this holy feast, we should "love Him and keep His commandments," for He is "the faithful God who keeps His merciful covenant down to the thousandth generation." Yes, this covenant of love has been fulfilled in Jesus' blood, in Jesus' heart from which His blood does come, and "when anyone acknowledges that Jesus is the Son of God, God dwells in him and he in God"; then we "come to know and believe in the love God has for us."

And to whom does the love of God come so readily? Who finds such faith in the Lamb of God and knows that "He pardons all [our] iniquities" and "crowns [us] with kindness and compassion"? Jesus in His prayer to the Father states, "What you have hidden from the learned and the clever you have revealed to the merest children," and this is confirmed by Moses, who tells the Israelites, "It was not because you are the largest of all nations that the Lord set His heart on you and chose you, for you are really the smallest of all nations." It is not the strong and the wise of the world the Lord showers His love upon, but the humble and the lowly. These know the love the mighty and humble, gentle Lord holds in His Sacred Heart. Alleluia!

Brothers and sisters, "it was because the Lord loved you... that He brought you out with a strong hand from the place of slavery." Let your soul "find rest" in that merciful love this day, and let it share that love with all others.

Solemnity, Fri. after 2nd Sun. after Pentecost (B)

Sacred Heart (B)
(Hos.11:1,3-4,8-9; Is.12:2-6; Eph.3:8-12,14-19; Jn.19:31-37)

"With joy you will draw water
at the fountain of salvation."

"Shout with exultation, O city of Zion, for great in your midst is the Holy One of Israel!" From His pierced heart flow forth the waters of salvation; in Jesus' blood we find our life. O how wonderful to have a God whose "heart is overwhelmed," whose "pity is stirred," who bleeds and dies for us upon the cross to reveal the limitless nature of His love. Here is "God's manifold wisdom" made known, here in "the unfathomable riches of Christ" freely given to all, that all might "grasp fully, with all the holy ones, the breadth and length and height and depth of Christ's love, and experience this love which surpasses all knowledge." Such unsurpassable grace can but leave us breathless in praising His name!

"When Israel was a child I loved him," says the Lord through the prophet Hosea. His love "like one who raises an infant to His cheeks" does not leave His blessed child; it only grows with time. Even though "they did not know that [He] was their healer," yet He did not turn away – He multiplied His love for us in the sacrificial offering of His Son. Now having been redeemed of our sin in the cleansing shower of His blood, we can only claim to be "confident and unafraid." For with Isaiah we fully proclaim: "My strength and my courage is the Lord, and He has been my savior." What the prophet knew in shadow we see now in the fullness of the light that is the Son, and so "in Christ and through faith in Him we can speak freely to God, drawing near Him with confidence" and "attain[ing] to the fullness of God Himself" and to His love.

My dear brothers and sisters, let our prayer for one another be joined on this "solemn feast day" with Paul's desire for the Ephesians: "May Christ dwell in your hearts through faith, and may charity be the root and foundation of your life." Then like this blessed Apostle who went from being "the least of all believers," persecuting the Church of Christ, to being shown "the mysterious design which for all ages was hidden in God" – and indeed "enlighten[ing] all men" of the Father's love revealed in Christ Jesus – we too will be raised from our lowly state in this world of sin to our place with the Son at the right hand of God. The fountain of salvation is open now; come to the water and drink fully of His love, of His blood.

Solemnity, Fri. after 2nd Sun. after Pentecost (C)

Sacred Heart (C)
(Ez.34:11-16; Ps.23:1-6; Rm.5:5-11; Lk.15:3-7)

"I have found my lost sheep."

"We have found reconciliation" through the blood of Jesus Christ. So the Apostle Paul tells us, and so we know to the depths of our hearts, which are united to His Sacred Heart. Once we were sinners, scattered like sheep on the hillside, but the Lamb of God has come and died for us, and so we His scattered sheep are led home. He has brought to fulfillment the promise of the Father to walk among us and rescue us from the darkness that envelops this world. "The lost," "the strayed," "the injured," "the sick," He has come to lead back to the bosom of the Father, where we may take refuge in His Sacred Heart.

"While we were still sinners, Christ died for us"; so let us recognize our sin that His blood might be efficacious. Let us not deny His grace as "people who have no need to repent." For if we say we are righteous, the darkness will continue to surround us and He will not be beside us to guide us to the Father's pasture: we will be left alone and forsaken. No, let us cause heaven to rejoice by repenting of our sin each day and always finding His blood at work within us. To what pasture He leads us! What protection we find even in this life, a blessing known especially in His Sacrament. And what future awaits us in His heavenly kingdom. We taste it and make our boast in it now, but there it shall be known in its fullness when, indeed, nothing shall ever harm us. For, now we rejoice in the refuge He gives as we "walk in the dark valley"; even still He is gathering His scattered sheep. Yes, to this day He moves among us as our Shepherd, and then we shall rest eternally in the Father's arms.

We give thanks to the Lord for the blessings He provides us on our path to His glory. We thank Him for His Church and its sacraments. We come to the altar and receive His sacrifice this day, knowing we are not worthy of such a call. But we confess our sins to Him. We seek His forgiveness through the ministry of the shepherds He has left us, and His mercy finds a place in us.

> Sacred Heart of Jesus, thank you for your grace and mercy.
> Lead us home to the Father's arms.

> O Lord, like sheep we have all gone astray;
>   lead us back today,
>   and on your holy mountain
>   may we take rest.

Solemnity, June 24

Birth of St. John the Baptist
(Is.49:1-6; Ps.139:1-3,13-15; Acts 13:22-26: Lk.1:57-66,80)

> "I will make you a light to the nations,
> that my salvation may reach to the ends of the earth."

The voice of one crying in the wilderness, he who hails the coming of the Lord, is born today. This voice speaks of the Word among us. And from before his birth he is called, in the womb he is formed, to proclaim with the sword of truth God's salvation for His people. "Surely the hand of the Lord was with him," and surely we find the grace of God by walking the path he blazed for us in the desert; for surely that way leads to the glory who is the Son of David.

Yes, "to us this word of salvation has been sent." To us this light has been brought forth. We "distant peoples" hear now the call of the voice which pierces our souls: Make straight the way of the Lord! The tongue now speaks; no longer silenced, no longer hidden, it has risen from "the depths of the earth" to plainly declare the coming of Christ. Yes, in the womb of the Old Testament the Lord wonderfully formed the salvation of Israel, probing and scrutinizing all its ways and preparing it for birth in the light of day. And now what He hid in His quiver He shoots forth to wound with amazement the hearts who have waited to hear the Word of life. "John heralded His coming by proclaiming a baptism of repentance to all the people of Israel"; by his voice a place is made for the Savior, Jesus.

At the turning point of the history of salvation John stands. He has come to direct souls to the Promised Land. For this he was made. To this call he answers – to lead us to the Son of Man. The old is passed away; now all is made new. Fulfillment has come. The womb has brought forth. The time of salvation is here. For He through whom time and the earth and heavens were made is now come to wash even the dirt from our feet. Listen to the voice which hails the Word of God in our midst. His call is for all ears; the light shines for all "who are God-fearing."

Your recompense is upon you now. You, too, make known His light to the world.

Sts. Peter and Paul
(Acts 12:1-11; Ps.34:2-9; 2Tm.4:6-8,17-18; Mt.16:13-19)

"On this rock I will build my Church,
and the jaws of death shall not prevail against it."

We go through death to life, for death has no power over us: the power of Jesus founded firmly on Peter, brought forward by Paul, and present in all the members of the Church and in its faith, has conquered death and leads us all to heaven.

Today we celebrate the solid foundation of the Church in Peter, the man of faith, first of the apostles and rock upon whom we are firmly set; and Paul, the great Apostle, through whom that faith went out to "all the nations." Our readings today clearly manifest the faith we possess, which overcomes even death, in Jesus' commissioning of Peter and in the example shown in the lives of both Peter and Paul.

Our first reading describes Peter's mystical release from prison and reveals in this act our own coming to the heavenly kingdom: the chains of sin fall from us, we are clothed in righteousness, and led through the snares of this world to freedom. And it is he who holds "the keys of the kingdom of heaven" who is led out; and indeed by these keys, by this office and its grace, "the iron gate leading out to the city" opens before us "of itself." And in our second reading we find Paul declaring the faithful life he has led even

710

unto the end, which he now faces, and that his fighting of the good fight has merited the crown which awaits him on the Day of the Lord. He is able to state with confidence, "The Lord will continue to rescue me from all attempts to do me harm and will bring me safe to His heavenly kingdom." Finally, our psalm confirms the protection the Lord grants His faithful ones: "The angel of the Lord encamps around those who fear Him, and delivers them."

We are sharers in this faith with Peter and Paul. This is evident in the Church who "prayed fervently to God" on behalf of Peter, and whose prayers were answered in such astounding fashion, and is made certain in Paul's proclaiming that Jesus gives the reward of a heavenly crown not only to Paul himself "but to all who have looked for His appearing with eager longing." The Church is one in all its members, and though the Lord has chosen certain of us to special places and granted them special blessings and powers, all are blessed by this same God.

So, today as we rejoice in this faith with which we have been gifted by the Lord, as we "together extol His name," let us consider the place we have in His holy Church and the work to which He calls us. And let us resolve to fulfill that call, pouring ourselves out unto death, that we might be assured of our entering through the heavenly gate. Let us walk in faith the narrow path the Lord has set before us, for it leads beyond death to life.

Feast, July 3

St. Thomas
(Eph.2:19-22; Ps.117:1-2,Mk.16:15; Jn.20:24-29)

"Blest are they who have not seen and have believed."

The faith of Thomas. By his faith we find faith. In his desire to know beyond all doubt that the Lord has risen, all our doubt is taken away, and we declare with him, "My Lord and my God!" If Thomas had not doubted so much, we would not believe so much his clear proclamation of the divinity of Jesus. As it is, we no longer have room for doubt. Indeed, Thomas' ardent need to touch the nail marks in the Lord's hands and sides is a cry to believe as firmly as bedrock, and indeed his declaration of faith is the strongest in all Scripture. "My Lord and my God!" In this we take refuge.

And how beautifully Paul speaks today of the faith, of the Church wherein we take refuge and dwell as one with "all the saints and members of the household of God... with Christ Jesus Himself as the cornerstone." It is architectural fact that in the cornerstone "the whole structure is fitted together and takes shape"; first it is laid, and then the rest of the foundation extends from it, giving the foundation its direction, its form. And, of course, the entire building rests on and is supported by this cornerstone and foundation. And so is the Church. Christ is our cornerstone around which we are all formed, and the apostles, those who have seen Him and proclaimed His glory, are the foundation upon which our faith rests. And we are all one structure, all made one in faith by the apostles and, of course, by the Lord, who is present in every stone of the building.

Let us firm up our faith this day, brothers and sisters. Wherever we may be throughout the world and at whatever time, let us feel beneath our feet the solid foundation upon which we are built and the blessed cornerstone which is its very source and so the source of all the life and the faith within us. Let us indeed be "built into this temple" and so become temples ourselves, knowing the surpassing blessing of becoming "a dwelling place for God in the Spirit." *A dwelling place for God in the Spirit.* My brothers and sisters, can there be a more marvelous call? Let us have the faith of Thomas, crying out "My Lord and my God!" each day of our lives and in all we think, say, and do. Let this faith permeate our very beings and we shall find ourselves standing firmly in the presence of the Lord Jesus Christ and in His kingdom, which is beyond all that eye can see.

Feast,   July 22

St. Mary Magdalene
(Sg.3:1-4 or 2Cor.5:14-17; Ps.63:2-6,8-9; Jn.20:1-2,11-18)

"On the first day of the week,
Mary Magdalene came to the tomb early in the morning."

Let us stand with Mary Magdalene at the tomb of our risen Lord. Let us weep a little that our hearts might bleed with her same love and so our eyes be opened to see Jesus standing before us. Let us hear Him call us by name.

O let us search night and day for our God! thirsting for Him "like the earth, parched, lifeless and without water." Let us know that without Him we are lost in darkness, empty as the tomb. May it be "the love of Christ [that] impels us" further outside ourselves and toward the Lord, allowing nothing to impede our progress as we pass every watchman, as we leave even our senses behind to become one with our lover, partaking of "the riches of [His] banquet."

Let us "regard no one according to the flesh anymore," not even the Christ, but release His body from our grasp that He might ascend to Heaven and we follow in His wake. A "new creation" let us be with a heart burning with love, a love that transcends everything and discovers our God within.

"In the shadow of [His] wings [we] shout for joy," declaring His glory to all, for He looks upon our tears, upon every heart longing for His presence, and our desire He does not disappoint.

712

St. James
(2Cor.4:7-15; Ps.126:1-6; Mt.20:20-28)

"Continually we carry about in our bodies the dying of Jesus,
so that in our bodies the life of Jesus may also be revealed."

In His apostles the death and resurrection of Jesus are most clearly shown. It is particularly their place to suffer persecution, to be "afflicted" and "crushed", "constantly being delivered to death for Jesus' sake"; and it is particularly their grace to show forth the glory of the resurrection. In this selfless service of the Lord, what comes through them is the preaching of the Word; "the spirit of faith" prompts them to speak, and though it bring their death, they do not hesitate: "We believe and so we speak, knowing that He who raised up the Lord Jesus will raise us up along with Jesus and place both us and you in His presence." Paul speaks here for all the apostles, and for the grace which comes to us as well through their service.

The Son of Man has come "to give His life as ransom for the many," and James truly moves quickly "to drink of the cup" of which the Lord partakes. As the first apostle martyred for the faith, he leads all the apostles forth to such sacrifice, in which they shall all soon join him. Once the Spirit is upon them, speaking through them, they will have the unquestioned faith necessary to confront without fear, but indeed with holy joy, the death to which each is called. They "possess a treasure in earthen vessels" and the vessels must be broken for the "surpassing power" of God to come to fulfillment in them and through them. Willingly do they lay down their lives once the Spirit inspires them, once their faith has been strengthened – once they have lost entirely any preoccupation with honors and attachments of this life, they come preaching and serving, facing the death the world inflicts therefore without a thought to run and hide, but knowing the joy it shall bring deep inside.

"Those that sow in tears shall reap rejoicing." We are taken as captives from this world, our hands tied behind us. But upon returning from this exile, after this death we suffer, we know our mouth will be "filled with laughter, and our tongue with rejoicing." So surpassing is the peace which awaits us, the troubles of this life of mission in His Name are as nothing. Let us pray to the Lord that we shall always speak freely in His Name. Let us pray to imitate James and all the apostles in their selfless service of Christ. May we have always that Spirit of faith that led them forth, that in the death of our bodies, we, too, may know and reveal the life of Jesus Christ.

713

The Transfiguration

(Dn.7:9-10,13-14; Ps.97:1-2,5-6,9; 2Pt.1:16-19;
Mt.17:1-9 – Mk.9:2-10 – Lk.9:28b-36
Note: since the three gospel accounts vary only in detail,
they are treated as one in this one exposition for the day)

"I saw one like a Son of man coming on the clouds of heaven."

Daniel's vision, as John's vision in the Book of Revelation, is perceived in the flesh by the three apostles on Mount Tabor, and is known by us all as "the morning star" of faith rises in our hearts. It is the coming of Jesus in all His glory that Peter, James, and John glimpse here in the Transfiguration, and it is this same glory to which we are all called.

The Lord wishes that the faith of the apostles and so the faith of the Church be strengthened against the "dark place" in which we find ourselves, so He here provides "a lamp shining" for them and for us, that we might not doubt the overwhelming "dominion, glory, and kingship" that are His and that will one day be ours as we join Him at the throne of God. He is indeed "the Most High over all the earth, exalted far above all gods," and the "flames of fire" which flow out from where He sits, the brightest of lights He is for "all peoples, nations, and languages," we must ever be "attentive to."

So Jesus leads His three principal apostles up the mountain. Apart by themselves and in prayer Himself, Jesus is "transfigured before them": "His face change[s] in appearance and His clothing [becomes] dazzling white." What a fearful, absolutely awesome scene it is for Peter, James, and John. Moses the great lawgiver and Elijah the great prophet appear in glory as well before them, speaking with Jesus of His coming sacrifice. If this is not enough to stir their hearts, and our own, they are overshadowed by a fearsome cloud and the Father's own voice speaks to them: "This is my beloved Son. Listen to Him." Then they see Jesus alone, the Son of God Himself before their wide-open eyes. He tells them not to speak yet of the vision, but their mouths are already shut tight in awe. After the resurrection and the coming of the Spirit they will speak openly of the Lord's glory – as Peter does for us today in our second reading, saying, "We had been eyewitnesses of His Majesty" – but for now they cannot utter the truth of such glory.

"The power and coming of our Lord Jesus Christ" has been well documented for us now; "the prophetic message" reaches to the ends of the earth: Jesus is the Son of God and "all peoples shall see His glory." What the apostles glimpsed on Mount Tabor, what Daniel and the prophets foresaw, what the psalms sing about and the proverbs and parables speak of

714

is come. It dawns now on our human sight, the surpassing glory of the only Son; let us treasure that light with all our hearts. He comes now on the clouds of heaven.

St. Lawrence
(2Cor.9:6-10;   Ps.112:1-2,5-9;   Jn.12:24-26)

"The just man shall be in everlasting remembrance."

The servant of the Lord lays down his life in His name. Today we celebrate St. Lawrence, deacon, servant, and martyr, who gave his life and his death generously to God. His life must be that of every Christian; his witness is one we are called to follow.

"The man who hates his life in this world preserves it to life eternal," the Lord tells His disciples in today's gospel. As "the grain of wheat falls to the earth and dies," so must we if we are to produce "much fruit." We cannot hold on to our lives and our pride but must give them over in service of God, or they will be nothing worth. We must trust in the words of Paul that "God can multiply His favors" among us, that as much as we give generously of ourselves, the more He will provide; and the greater will thus be our reward as we draw ever closer to Him and His sacrifice. "Where I am, there will my servant be." By these words Jesus both calls and assures all who would follow Him that the laying down of their lives will bring them "honor" in the presence of the Father. To be so "exalted in glory," we must be washed in His blood.

The blood of the martyrs is the seed of the Church; it is by their sacrifice, their total giving of themselves, that the Church does grow. They bear witness to God's power working in the world, and we must sow bountifully with them in order to "reap bountifully" the graces of the Lord. He provides the seed we sow and will "multiply the seed" and its yield; as long as we remain "firm, trusting in the Lord," our posterity shall endure unto heaven. So let us plant our prayers and our works and our lives in the fertile earth where the martyrs found their joy, and whether we live or die, we "shall be blessed in His holy presence."

May all the Church ring out their praises to the God who calls and blesses us with the holy example of those who serve Him and give their lives completely to Him. "Lavishly He gives to the poor; His generosity shall endure forever," so let us pray that this blessed yield the Lord provides will be increased in our own time, and that we may join in the grace of such sacrifice. In His Spirit and in His blood may we ever grow away from the earth and the death it holds and unto the life of "everlasting remembrance" in heaven with God.

715

Solemnities and Feasts

Assumption

(Rv.11:19a,12:1-6a,10ab; Ps.45:10-12,16; 1Cor.15:20-26; Lk.1:39-56)

"A great sign appeared in the sky, a woman clothed with the sun,
with the moon beneath her feet, and on her head a crown of twelve stars."

The Queen of Heaven here appears to us in her glory, she who has been taken up by her Son to His heavenly kingdom to stand at His side: "The queen takes her place at your right hand in gold of Ophir." Yes, Lord, the Mother you preserved from sin for all eternity you have preserved from the jaws of death; she who has suffered so intimately with you here on earth now shares your glory in heaven. And as she has said, "All generations will call me blessed," for you have "lifted up the lowly" and she your humblest and most holy of all creatures can be nowhere but with you in your eternal life. May she bless us from her place with you this holy day.

In Mary we find our hope, brothers and sisters; in her we find it fulfilled, made real by the hand of God. We know that "in Christ shall all be brought to life," and "in proper order" she so blessed in life is now so blessed in death, having been preserved from its clutches and preceding us into God's heavenly realm. The devil would have devoured her and her child, but she and He, and we with them, have escaped his gaping mouth and the fire it breathes; this enemy and the death he wrought is destroyed by our Lord and His birth through the Virgin Mary, and so, "now have salvation and power come." "The kingdom of our God and the authority of His Anointed One" now reign supreme, and she who has been His special instrument in bringing such salvation now stands at His side in His paradise.

"How does this happen to me, that the mother of my Lord should come to me?" asks Elizabeth in wonder at the blessed presence of Mary in her midst. She who carries the Lord shares in His divinity in a way beyond our comprehension, for if her own kinswoman could be filled with such awe, recognizing whence Mary comes, how much more should we be filled with veneration for the Virgin daughter of Israel? Indeed, it is her voice which causes the Baptist to leap for joy in the womb; with such joy we should approach this sacred day.

As intimately as she was with Jesus, and is with Jesus now, so intimately is she with His Church here on earth as well as in heaven. From her place at His side she watches over us and cares for our needs as any mother for her son. We are her sons and daughters, united to her through the One Lord, Jesus Christ. She comes to us now at the end of the age granting wisdom and direction to those who seek their place with her Son. Call her blessed, brothers and sisters in Christ, and see her glory shining forth at the right hand of God. In her you will find light greater than sun and moon and stars. You will find the presence of our Lord and our God.

Feast, August 24

St. Bartholomew
(Rv.21:9-14; Ps.145:10-13,17-18; Jn.1:45-51)

"Come, I will show you the woman who is the bride of the Lamb."

Nathanael (who is Bartholomew) is taken by Philip (whose name means "love") to meet the bridegroom of his soul – and immediately he weds himself to the Lord, recognizing Him as the Son of God. As Bartholomew is without guile, so must all the Church be so sincere to find the glory that awaits us "under the fig tree" in the absolute peace and splendor of Jesus' presence. How else will we see Him? How else can we recognize Him? How else will we become one with Him if we don't come to Him even with the faith of this innocent child?

"You shall see the sky opened and the angels of God ascending and descending on the Son Man." He it is who stands in the breach between earth and heaven; He it is who is as the ladder we climb to find God's eternal kingdom: by Him it is heaven comes to us and we fly to heaven – His angels are with us to guide us to the vision of His splendor and lead us to safety within the protective walls of His Church as His bride. As the angel comes to John, leading him to vision of the heavenly kingdom, so by Jesus the angels come to us to carry us home in His arms. May we find the peace that awaits us within His walls and enter through its gates.

And who are the foundation stones of this glorious kingdom but John and Bartholomew and the Lord's blessed apostles? These simple men who walked the earth as you and I have become the radiant gems on which Holy Church is set – they serve now to support the Bride of the Lamb and bring her to His "dominion" which "endures through all generations." These generations include our own, and we simple men are now called and guided by the "discourse" of these "faithful ones" to enter in and take our own place in the city which has "the radiance of a precious jewel that sparkle[s] like a diamond." But to do so we must be like Him who is "just in all His ways and holy in all His works." We must come as Nathanael, without guile, guided only by love, to find our place in the peaceful kingdom.

The Lord sees us all, brothers and sisters. He knows us all. He knows we are but simple men and women, but this is who He seeks. Let us trust utterly in Him, and His angels will take us to the bridal chamber, and we shall enter in and dwell with Him in His "kingdom for all ages" with all His holy ones redeemed in His blood.

717

Birth of Mary

(Mic.5:1-4 or Rm.8:28-30; Ps.13:6,Is.61:9; Mt.1:1-16,18-23
Note: I shall treat of both first readings)

"It is by the Holy Spirit that she has conceived this child."

"God is with us," brothers and sisters, and how has He chosen to come among us but through a woman, but through a virgin found with child? And this Virgin daughter of Israel from "Bethlehem-Ephrathah, too small to be among the clans of Judah" – she the humblest of the chosen people, the meekest servant of our race – has been thus greatly blessed "according to His decree," for she is the first whom God "predestined to share the image of His Son." She is the first of Christians prepared and called by the Lord, and now "in turn glorified" in His presence. It is her birth, it is her role in our salvation we celebrate today, for by her complicity with the will of God "now His greatness shall reach to the ends of the earth; He shall be peace."

The fact that "God makes all things work together for the good of those who have been called" is evident both in the situation of Mary's life as Mother of the Lord and in the very fact of her call itself. First of all, God chooses this woman, this humble creature of the chosen race of His most humble creation to participate with Him in bringing His Son and His salvation into the world. The lengthy genealogy at the start of our gospel also bears witness to the very human nature of Jesus, whose "family record" can indeed be traced so precisely, and among whose ancestors are many who were far less perfect than He – including a prostitute, an adulterer, and evil kings. God chooses to come through man, through a woman, to make quite real His redemptive power over the sins of our race, to put flesh to the eternal Word of the Father.

And in the particular situations of Mary's life, we see how difficulty, how "bitterness," if you will, is turned to sweetness, too, for we note that Joseph was prepared to divorce his betrothed wife found with child, and we know that the prophet tells us a sword shall pierce her heart as well as her Son's; but that notwithstanding, and indeed through that cross she bears with Him, she shall find the glorification promised all children of the Most High. She certainly shares now in the fruits of His redemption.

And we also share in these same fruits, brothers and sisters. We are likewise predestined and called and justified and glorified if we make ourselves as obedient as our Mother in the faith. He "whose origin is from of old" is with us now, too, and so we should "sing of the Lord, 'He has been good to me,'" as we "rejoice in [His] salvation" at work within us, a salvation whose coming was prepared in the birth of the Immaculate Virgin

718

Mary and by the power of the Holy Spirit brought to us through one who shares our own flesh.

Triumph of the Cross
(Nm.21:4b-9; Ps.78:1-2,7,34-38; Phil.2:6-11; Jn.3:13-17)

"God greatly exalted Him, and bestowed on Him
the name which is above every name."

And why is it that "at the name of Jesus every knee should bend"? Why does "every tongue confess that Jesus Christ is Lord"? It is because "He humbled Himself, becoming obedient to the point of death, even death on a cross." It is precisely because "He emptied Himself, taking the form of a slave, coming in human likeness" and dying as a cursed criminal, that this innocent dove who was "in the form of God" became the praise of our race and the source of our salvation.

Yes, He and His cross are now the source of our salvation. By His cross we find the forgiveness of our sins. Now that "the Son of Man has been lifted up... everyone who believes in Him may have eternal life." Now that we have been shown both our sins and the love God has for us sinners in the Lord's being nailed to the cross, we may find the forgiveness of our sins and eternal life. Just as the Israelites looked upon their sin, recognizing their guilt in the serpents God had sent among them – and finding also its conquering in the serpent's being bronzed and "mounted on a pole" – so now we who look upon our crucified Lord cannot help but see how we have injured our God, and at the same moment find cleansing for those sins in His blood upon the cross to which we have nailed Him.

He loves us so, brothers and sisters. "God so loved the world that He gave His only Son, so that He who believes in Him might not perish but might have eternal life." And so the cross becomes a sign of triumph not only for our Lord, but for ourselves; for indeed by it we are saved – without it we would yet be lost in our sin. But as it is He "has come down from heaven." As it is He has been "lifted up" before our eyes. As it is He has sacrificed Himself in absolute love to draw us unto Him and His love. As with the Israelites "He, being merciful, forgave their sin and destroyed them not," so now He forgives our sins and carries us "up to heaven," whence He has come. And so we rejoice in the victory of His holy cross.

Do not be afraid to come to His cross, brothers and sisters. Do not shy away from His love or turn away from the recognition of your guilt. By it alone will you, too, be exalted with the Lord who has humbled Himself and died for you. By it alone will you find glory in God eternally.

St. Matthew

(Eph.4:1-7,11-13; Ps.19:2-5; Mt.9:9-13)

"Through all the earth their voice resounds,
and to the ends of the world, their message."

"Till we become one in faith and in the knowledge of God's Son, and form that perfect man who is Christ come to full stature," the Word of the Lord shall be carried forth by all His "apostles, prophets, evangelists, pastors, and teachers"; indeed, "each of us has received God's favor in the measure in which Christ bestows it," and each of us plays a role in bringing to fulfillment the Gospel of our "one Lord."

"Matthew got up and followed Him." He was called, he was chosen, and he answered the Lord's call without hesitation. And he brought the Lord in immediately to dine with Him, welcoming Him fully at his table. And because of his openness to God and His Word, and because of his generous response, we see that it is Jesus who in fact feeds him, that he in turn might feed others with the true teaching, "the one faith" in the "one God and Father of all, who is over all, and works through all, and is in all," from the least of sinners to the greatest of apostles. We are all thus called to follow Jesus Christ, to find the mercy He so greatly desires to impart to our sinful lives, that we might be whole and able to serve Him well.

One day we shall come to perfection in Him; in Him it is already fulfilled. And now insofar as we share His love, insofar as we "live a life worthy of the calling [we] have received, with perfect humility, meekness, and patience," the Spirit who is indeed the origin of our unity in Him works through us and we, even with the twelve apostles, serve to bring His blessed peace, His divine life of salvation, to the world. Yes, "day pours out the word to day, and night to night imparts knowledge," and soon that Word will reach to the ends of the earth; and soon it will come to fulfillment in our sight.

Brothers and sisters, we are called to a great hope, and to a great mission to bring it to light. Let us keep our hearts set on the Gospel and the promise it contains, and "build up the Body of Christ" until we stand with Him, as Him, in His eternal kingdom which stands in our midst even today through the words of His apostle and evangelist, in the breath of the Spirit upon us and in its message.

Sts. Michael, Gabriel, and Raphael

(Dn7:9-10,13-14 or Rv.12:7-12; Ps.138:1-5; Jn.1:47-51)
I shall treat of both first readings)

"You shall see the sky opened and the angels of God
ascending and descending on the Son of Man."

And who shall see such visions? He whose own vision is pure, he who is as Nathanael – he who has "no guile in him." Such is the case both with Daniel and John the Evangelist, of whose visions we hear in either first reading. The angels are with them, indeed, and they lift them up to look upon the Most High God and His Anointed One.

Both first readings reveal vision of Jesus the Son, whose "dominion is an everlasting dominion" and by whom "salvation and power have come." In Daniel is shown the Ancient One, the Father, from whom all power comes as "surging streams of fire" from His throne; and in Revelation, John presents the defeat of Satan, who would presume to be like God but is "driven out" and "hurled down to earth" by the archangel Michael (whose name tells us that none is like God) before "the reign of our God" comes. In Revelation is included, too, our own participation in "the blood of the Lamb," that the Church, "by the word of their testimony," will share in the Lord's dominion.

And David's psalm sings today: "Great is the glory of the Lord." His voice joins with the "thousands upon thousands… ministering to Him, and myriads upon myriads" attending Him. "In the presence of the angels I will sing your praise," he declares, and finds himself "worship[ing] at [His] holy temple" Him whose name is "great above all things." Is not the vision promised Nathanael and witnessed to by Daniel and John shared here with David, too; does he not glimpse, and share with us who long for the presence of the Lord, the ladder which reaches to heaven made known to Jacob in dream? Is not Jesus, His Lord, with him even in this time before His coming? It is one Jesus the eyes of all the pure of heart see and shall see. And did not the Old Testament prophet see that which was to come? Was not the eternal vision of heaven revealed to his eyes, as well as John's? And how can this be, that they see what we would call the future, except that it has always been?

Brothers and sisters, we must declare with Nathanael, "You are the Son of God; you are the king of Israel," but we must do so as he does – in absolute honesty and utter faith. We must believe without guile and declare without hesitation that Jesus is Lord. To do so and see the angels ascending and descending upon Him, our hearts and eyes must be pure. Let us pray we will come now to vision of heaven, where His angels and His saints reign.

721

St. Luke
(2Tm.4:9-17; Ps.145:10-13,17-18; Lk.10:1-9)

"The Lord stood by my side and gave me strength,
so that through me the preaching task might be completed
and all the nations might hear the Gospel."

As I read of Jesus' instruction to the disciples as He "sent them in pairs before Him to every town and place He intended to visit," and particularly His words to them to "eat what they set before you," I am reminded of the command given Peter in his dream to "take and eat" of the unclean animals (Acts 10:13), this just before the first Gentile converts came to him seeking the Word of God. And, of course, similar terminology is present in Jesus' sending his workers as if into a harvest: in this case, the Lord shall eat of the feast the disciples are sent forth to prepare.

We know our work is our food, that the labor the Lord imparts to us serves as our daily bread. And we know that the wheat that becomes His precious Body and the Word that is cultivated by His apostles, by His preachers and prophets, is the food that sustains us, that strengthens us for our daily tasks. All we do must be blessed by Him and be, as it were, a "discourse of the glory of [His] kingdom," and His kingdom, which is "a kingdom for all ages," and His dominion, which "endures through all generations," shall become known in our midst.

It is not easy to eat of this food, to drink of this cup. We see how alone Paul finds himself in our first reading. "Everyone abandoned me," he declares in reference to his trial before the courts of this world. He pleads with Timothy to join him soon, for many have left his side: "I have no one with me but Luke." Indeed, he has nothing but the Word of God. And most apparent in the Lord's instruction to His disciples is the utter reliance on God we must find. Impoverished He sends them forth, dependent only on their preaching and healing to feed themselves. Yes, He sends them forth "as lambs in the midst of wolves." Not a happy prospect. But they have the Word of the Lord to make them strong and protect them from all evil of this world, and nothing could be more sure than this.

Into so many homes Luke's gospel has come, bringing its peace to all who abide in the Lord. The proclamation by this great evangelist that "the reign of God is at hand" comes to our hearts even this day. Let us make room for this Word within ourselves and it shall feed us on our journey to the kingdom, and by its grace we shall complete our work on this earth. May the word of the Lord go ever forth.

Sts. Simon and Jude
(Eph.2:19-22; Ps.19:2-5; Lk.6:12-16)

"You are fellow citizens with the saints
and members of the household of God."

And whom is this building founded upon but our Lord Jesus Christ; He is the cornerstone by which the apostles and prophets are set in place, and we are built upon this firm foundation, all integrated as one "holy temple in the Lord." This Church is "the dwelling place for God in the Spirit." Alleluia!

O that blessed night Jesus spent "in communion with God"! Praise God for the mountain on which He prayed! For that night, in that place, in these prayers was conceived the foundation stones of His holy temple: in the Spirit that night the essential structure of the Church was given birth in the names of these poor apostles, these simple human beings.

And at daybreak He called them forth by name. Upon them His favor rested. And though one "turned traitor" and had to be replaced, yet here are the pillars on which the Church rests. And to this day their descendants, their blessed successors, remain with us, holding up the Church despite their frailties – yes, the power of the Spirit continues to go forth from their call. "Day pours out the word to day, and night to night imparts knowledge." Nothing can stem the passage of this Word to the ends of the earth, for it is founded in the silent communion with God.

Who can touch this silence? Who can tear down this oneness in the presence of God? No one can hold the wind in his hands and no one can restrain the power of the Spirit. It indeed goes forth. Yes, "the whole structure" continues to be "fitted together" in the Lord's Name, and no persecution can stop its growth, can prevent its inevitable coming to fullness in the eternity of heaven. And so, let us thank God for His blessed apostles and prophets and martyrs today. Let us pray we shall be found worthy to be one with them in the House they build. And let us come to know the Lord even more, who is at the heart of us all.

All Saints

(Rv.7:2-4,9-14; Ps.24:1-6; 1Jn.3:1-3; Mt.5:1-12)

"Everyone who has this hope based on Him
makes himself pure, as He is pure."

All our readings speak of this purity this holy day. In the first reading we hear of the saints who "have washed their robes and made them white in the blood of the Lamb." Our psalm tells us it is "one whose hands are sinless, whose heart is clean," who stands in God's presence. The above quote is from our second reading, and Jesus tells us in our gospel, "Blessed are the clean of heart, for they will see God." Indeed, this purity of heart is the essential characteristic possessed by all the saints in heaven; and so we must strive to attain it.

I note a striking parallel particularly between our first reading from Revelation and David's psalm: the reading begins with the image of the four angels (at the four corners of the universe) being prevented from their call "to damage the land and the sea" until the seal of God is placed upon the foreheads of the "one hundred and forty-four thousand [symbolizing absolute fullness in number] marked from every tribe of Israel"; and our psalm begins by proclaiming, "The Lord's are the earth and its fullness; the world and those who dwell in it." The reading continues with John's "vision of a great multitude" who "stood before the throne and the Lamb" in their white robes; while, as it continues, our psalm tells us that only the pure of heart "can ascend the mountain of the Lord" or "stand in His holy place." Then the reading from Revelation cries out, "Salvation comes from our God" and exclaims of the blessings upon the Lord and so His faithful; and David's psalm concludes that it is he who seeks Him who "shall receive a blessing from the Lord, a reward from God his savior."

What does all this tell us but what John states quite simply in his letter, our second reading: "Beloved, we are God's children now," and that when "what we shall be... is revealed we shall be like Him, for we shall see Him as He is." Yes, we are anointed by Him as His own creation and shall come to stand in His presence with all the angels and saints, proclaiming the blessing He is and the salvation He has provided us.

And in our gospel Jesus climbs the mountain and sits and teaches those who gather around Him. And how blessed are these eyes that see Him! How blessed are these ears that hear Him! And how blessed are we, too, insofar as we hear Him this holy day as He calls to our hearts to have faith in Him and in the kingdom of heaven, to set our hearts on the hope of which He speaks. And blessed are we most when we suffer insult and persecution for the sake of the Lord, for by this we are purified, and through this "our reward will be great in heaven." For we must die in Him before we rise in Him with all the saints in glory.

All Souls
(Wis.3:1-9; Ps.23:1-6; 1Cor.15:51-57; Jn.6:37-40
Note: there are any number of readings possible for this day)

"The souls of the just are in the hand of God,
and no torment shall touch them."

Is this not what it means to be a Christian? To have faith in the resurrection from the dead. To believe that after our time of trial there shall be peace, that we shall be refined by the hand of God to stand in His presence, to share in His kingship. "Grace and mercy are with His holy ones, and His care is with His elect." This is our faith.

"The Lord is my shepherd, I shall not want." And so we have no fear. The Lord watches over us and guides our path, and in His blessing we take refuge, knowing we shall come to be with Him, knowing He is with us even this day, knowing even death we shall conquer in His Name. "I shall dwell in the house of the Lord for years to come." Nothing shall remove us from His presence. "We shall not all fall asleep, but we will all be changed." Indeed, though all die, all shall come to life. None can remain as they are; all must be changed. All that is mortal must take on immortality, and in this immortality, in this incorruptibility we gain, death is swallowed up – it is no more. "Thanks be to God who gives us the victory through our Lord Jesus Christ." It is an eternal victory.

"Everything that the Father gives me will come to me." It cannot be that the Father's will not be done. Jesus awaits us with open arms. He has gone before us, He has prepared a place for us, and we must but come to Him as drawn by the will of the Father. "Everyone who sees the Son and believes in Him may have eternal life, and I shall raise Him up on the last day." Praise to you, Lord Jesus Christ!

Death is not our realm, brothers and sisters. Though it comes to us all, it is but a passageway into Heaven, it is but the Lord's means of preparing us for the kingdom. And so, whether we experience it today or tomorrow or yesterday is of no consequence. It is there. It shall come to us all. But all who believe are preserved from its clutches and drawn into the life the Father offers. Let us pray this day for all holy souls to come by the Son into the hands of the Father.

Dedication of St. John Lateran
(Ez.47:1-2,8-9,12; Ps.46:1-3,5-6,8-9; 1Cor.3:9c-11,16-17; Jn.2:13-22)

"There is a stream whose runlets gladden the city of God,
the holy dwelling of the Most High."

On this the feast set aside to commemorate the cathedral of Peter, the Bishop of Rome, himself the founding stone upon which Christ builds His Church, we hear much of temples. In our first reading Ezekiel sees in his vision, "water flowing out from beneath the threshold of the temple," water which brings life to the great sea and the fruit that grows upon its banks; the water that gladdens the holy dwelling of the Most High is spoken of in our psalm; Paul tells us we are "the temple of God," "God's building"; and zeal for the Father's house consumes the Lord, and so He purges it with whip in hand in our gospel today. But perhaps the most revelatory statement is, "He was speaking of the temple of His body," also from our gospel, and noted as explanation of Jesus' challenge to the Jews to destroy the temple and He would rebuild it in three days. This essential truth of the nature of the temple is substantiated by Paul's teaching of the care needed by those who build within the Church: "No one can lay a foundation other than the one that is there, namely, Jesus Christ." Though he then goes on to say that we are the temple of God wrought in all holiness, and though this is an equal truth, yet neither this truth nor that which holds Peter as the founding "rock" of this Temple in which we dwell have any basis without the essential understanding that Jesus is at the very heart of all our worship, of the Church we are. The Lord has indeed wrought "astounding things... on earth." He has made us as those trees along the banks of His river of life, bearing His fruit each month for the benefit of the world. He has made us His holy dwelling place and placed His Spirit upon us for the building up of His kingdom... But all of this has its source in the water of life itself, our Lord Jesus Christ.

Brothers and sisters, as we celebrate our Church this day and the glorious blessings the Lord has bestowed upon us as His temple, as His children, let us not forget our Savior who has been the cause of and continues to be the cause of our joy. Let us be washed in the water from His side and be built up in His Body and His Blood. May we have His same zeal for the Father's House.

St. Andrew

(Rm.10:9-18; Ps.19:2-5; Mt.4:18-22)

"How beautiful are the feet of those who announce good news!"

Alleluia!

We must have "faith in the heart" and "confess with [our] lips that Jesus is Lord"; but how can we believe in Him and call on Him if we have not heard of Him? "And how can [we] hear unless there is someone to preach? And how can men preach unless they are sent?" Thank the Lord that He has sent the apostles out to the ends of the world, that "their voice has sounded over the whole earth." Where would we be without them?

"Come after me and I will make you fishers of men," Jesus says to His first apostles, two brothers. And two brothers Jesus chooses after them, as if He is looking for brothers to call to emphasize our solidarity with Him and with one another. Indeed, we are family in the Lord. We are His mother and His brothers. David's psalm today speaks of Him who would be called his Son, and illustrates the work of His brothers to come. All are one in Him, through time, through space... for He who is the beginning and end truly becomes our brother.

I thank God today for Andrew and his brother Peter, their brothers James and John, and all brothers and sisters in the Lord. I thank God especially for their answering His call, their readiness to respond. "They immediately abandoned their nets and became His followers." And so strong in the Lord they would become. And so, clearly their words would be spoken of Him who is risen from the dead, of Him in whom our hearts trust – of Him of whom we now speak.

A joy fills me this day, and should fill us all, for the beauty of the apostles and of their call. For now our ears ring with the love of our Jesus, the truth of the ages. Now through these faithful disciples we have heard "the word of Christ" and find it abiding in our souls. Let us open our mouths and proclaim Him Lord of all!

Immaculate Conception

(Gn.3:9-15,20; Ps.98:1-4; Eph.1:3-6,11-12; Lk.1:26-38)

"He chose us in Him, before the foundation of the world,
to be holy and without blemish before Him."

And she is the sign of such preservation from evil.

"Hail, full of grace! The Lord is with you." And so the Virgin Mother is greeted by the power of the Most High. So she is called – "full of grace" is her title. She whom all generations will call blessed is revealed in this simple greeting as having "found favor with God." And so, "the child to be born will be called holy, the Son of God," the Son of her who has been preserved by grace.

"In accord with the favor of His will, for the praise of the glory of His grace," this has been done – she has been immaculately conceived, kept from the stain of sin. Not that she herself might be worshiped is the Virgin kept pure, but indeed she does "exist for the praise of His glory." "My soul magnifies the Lord," she has proclaimed… and it is so. She is but the sign that "His right hand has won victory for Him"; she is the instrument through which "the Lord has made His salvation known."

How wonderfully this is expressed in her own words of consent to His call: "Behold, I am the handmaid of the Lord. May it be done to me according to your word." Here in this blessed obedience she sets in motion the cleansing of our sin of disobedience (which shall be fulfilled by the fruit of her womb), a disobedience painfully recounted for us in our first reading – a disobedience which has caused us to hide from the face of God. But no longer will we be trapped in this hell. No more will we flee from the presence of Him who is our Creator, for by her humble obedience, and our own, in the grace of the Lord Jesus Christ we will have our nakedness covered over and become holy as He.

The Virgin is our Mother. She who has "no relations with a man" has brought about the salvation of all men "in accord with the purpose of the One who accomplishes all things according to the intention of His will." And so the curse is removed from us. And so we might "sing joyfully to the Lord," for "in the sight of the nations He has revealed His justice"; through this simple virgin He has brought us His grace. And now we may be pure as He.

About the Author

At the time of this writing, James Kurt lived much as a hermit in the city – Jersey City, New Jersey – spending about six hours a day in prayer, including Catholic Mass, Liturgy of the Hours, full Rosary, Stations of the Cross, meditation on Scripture and the writings of the saints, and silent prayer before the Blessed Sacrament; while working another five or six hours on his writing and serving as an adjunct ESL instructor at a local university to support his vocation.

Since then he has become a "married hermit." He and his wife Sylvia live most of the year in Sarasota, Florida, with his elderly mom. He continues to spend his days in prayer and writing (now having published 13 books), as well as in volunteer pro-life work.

Author's Website:
www.writingsofjameskurt.org

Podcasting Site
(featuring all the entries of this book):
www.hermitinthecity.libsyn.com

OTHER BOOKS by JAMES KURT

Remembrance of Things Present –
A mystical work seeking the presence of the LORD in the moment, where He dwells at all times. 100 pp. 2018. w/ imprimatur.

Two Books: Paradox and the Christian Faith / Hippie Convert –
The apparent contradictions of the Faith are explained for those who seek wisdom; and a member of the flower generation addresses true love and peace, in poetic form. 238 pp. 2016. w/imprimatur.

Lines of Grace: Meditations on Verses of Holy Scripture, The Stations of the Cross, and The Most Holy Rosary –
A Catholic devotional especially for the encouragement of the practice of plenary indulgence. 195 pp. 2016.

Christian Vision of the Old Testament –
Synopsis and exhortation; faith-filled overview of all books of the Old Testament as prefiguration of Jesus, with a focus on the prophetic nature of God's Word. 273 pp. 2013. w/ imprimatur.

Blessed Guilt: A Universal Conversion Story –
On the life-giving repentance found in Jesus' blood; vaguely autobiographical but without particulars. 119 pp. 2013. w/ imprimatur.

Chapters of the Gospels –
Exposition of the four gospels, chapter by chapter; in the style of *Our Daily Bread*. 114 pp. 2009. w/ imprimatur.

The Most Holy Trinity and the Four Corners of the Universe –
A collection of writings on the Trinity and its reflection in Creation; founded upon the Shema. 300 pp. 2008. w/ imprimatur.

YHWH: Order of the Divine NAME –
On the significance of the contemplative silence that is the NAME of God, and its application to a spiritual life. 260 pp. 2008. w/ imprimatur.

Prayers to the Saints –
A page of prayer to each saint on the General Roman Calendar for the United States. 230 pp. 2007. w/ imprimatur.

Turn of the Jubilee Year: A Conversion Song –
Autobiographical depiction of vocation search through pilgrimage to Medjugorje and stays at a hermitage or two. 230 pp. 2004.

Songs for Children of Light: Ten Albums of Lyrics –
A white on black conceptual work with simple drawings for each song. 150 pp. 2003.

silence in the city –
Short contemplative poems; moments of divine silence in the midst of city life. 148 pp. (74 pieces). 2003.

Printed in the United States
By Bookmasters